Principles of Supply Chain Management:

A Balanced Approach

Joel D. Wisner
University of Nevada, Las Vegas

G. Keong Leong
University of Nevada, Las Vegas

Keah-Choon Tan
University of Nevada, Las Vegas

Australia · Canada · Mexico · Singapore · Spain · United Kingdom · United States

THOMSON

SOUTH-WESTERN

Principles of Supply Chain Management: A Balanced Approach

Joel D. Wisner, G. Keong Leong, Keah-Choon Tan

VP/Editorial Director:
Jack W. Calhoun

VP/Editor-in-Chief:
George Werthman

Senior Acquisitions Editor:
Charles E. McCormick, Jr.

Developmental Editor:
Taney H. Wilkins

Senior Marketing Manager:
Larry Qualls

Production Editor:
Tamborah E. Moore

Manager of Technology Solutions:
Jim Rice

Technology Project Editor:
Chris Wittmer

Media Editor:
Amy Wilson

Manufacturing Coordinator:
Diane Lohman

Printer:
Phoenix Color
Hagerstown, Maryland

Production House:
Shepherd, Inc.

Design Project Manager:
Justin Klefeker

Internal Designer:
Justin Klefeker

Cover Designer:
Justin Klefeker

Cover Images:
© PhotoDisc and Digital Vision.

For permission to use material from this
text or product, submit a request online
at http://www.thomsonrights.com.

For more information
contact South-Western,
5191 Natorp Boulevard,
Mason, Ohio 45040.
Or you can visit our Internet site at:
http://www.swlearning.com

To my loving wife CJ, who has always been there for me, and my wonderful kids Hayley and Blake, who never cease to amaze and delight me. I promise to start mowing the lawn and taking out the garbage more often now.

—Joel D. Wisner

To my wife, Lin Leong, and daughter, Michelle Leong, for their patience and love.

—G. Keong Leong

To my parents for their unconditional love and sacrifice for my education, and to my wife, Shaw Yun, daughter, Wen Hui, and son, Wen Jay, for their patience and love.

—Keah-Choon Tan

Brief Contents

Contents

Case Studies 107

Part 3 Operations Issues in Supply Chain Management 121

Preface

Welcome to *Principles of Supply Chain Management: A Balanced Approach.* The practice of supply chain management is becoming widespread in all industries around the globe today, and firms are quickly realizing the benefits provided by supply chain management. This text is unique in that it uses a novel and logical approach in its discussions of this topic from four perspectives: purchasing, operations, logistics, and the integration among supply chain participants of these three vitally important areas of the firm. This book is somewhat different than other supply chain management texts, since we present a more balanced view of the topic. Many of the texts available today concentrate primarily on just one of the three areas of purchasing, operations, or logistics.

The objective of the book is to make readers think about how supply chain management impacts all areas of the firm, and to show how managers can improve their competitive position by employing the practices we discuss throughout the text. Junior- or senior-level business students and beginning MBA students as well as practicing managers can benefit from reading and using the text.

The textbook utilizes some notable features including opening quotes and three or more boxed features for each chapter that profile companies practicing or utilizing the techniques discussed in the chapters. Additionally, there are a total of fifteen cases spread throughout the text, varying from fairly simple to complex treatments of various supply chain management topics. Some of the companies and cases are real, while others are fictional. In the Chapter 1 appendix, there is a discussion of the Beer Game, with game boards and inventory tracking sheets to allow instructors to actually play the game with their students. Within each chapter we have incorporated up-to-date and interesting examples of organizations utilizing the methods being discussed. Finally, there are quantitative as well as qualitative problems and questions, Internet exercises, and Excel problems spread throughout most of the chapters.

Part 1 is the overview and introduction of the topic of supply chain management. This chapter introduces the basic understanding and concepts of supply chain management, and should help students realize the importance of this topic. Core concepts such as the bullwhip effect, supplier relationships, forecasting and demand management, enterprise resource planning, transportation management, and customer relationship management are discussed.

Part 2 presents purchasing issues in supply chain management. This very important topic is covered in three chapters, building from an introduction to purchasing management to employing strategic concepts aimed at increasing supply chain management success. There are five cases at the end of Part 2, four of which are real cases about Deere & Company, written by professors who were invited to Deere's Moline, Illinois, facility specifically to write cases for and about Deere & Company. We hope you find these cases interesting.

Part 3 includes four chapters regarding operations issues in supply chain management. This section progresses from forecasting to aggregate planning and inventory management and then to enterprise resource planning. A final chapter on just-in-time operations and quality management discusses the importance of process management throughout the firm. At the end of Chapter 8 there are six very interesting cases that will challenge students to apply the topics and practices presented in these four chapters.

Part 4 presents distribution issues in supply chain management for services and manufacturing firms. The section starts off with a review of domestic and international transportation and then moves on to customer relationship management, location analysis, and service response logistics. There are two cases included at the end of this part—one is a service case, the other is a manufacturing case.

Finally, Part 5 discusses integration issues in supply chain management. While cooperation and integration are frequently referred to in the text, this section brings the entire text into focus, tying all of the parts together first by discussing integration in detail followed by performance measurement and then a view towards the future of supply chain management. Two integration-oriented cases are included at the end of Part 5.

We think we have compiled a very interesting set of supply chain management topics that will keep the reader interested and we hope you enjoy it. The disk that comes with the teacher's edition contains sample syllabi, PowerPoint slides, sample tests, answers to end-of-chapter questions and problems, and case notes for each of the 15 cases. We welcome your comments and suggestions for improvement.

Acknowledgments

We greatly appreciate the efforts of a number of people at Thomson/South-Western. Without their feedback and guidance, this text would not have been completed. Charles E. McCormick, Jr., Senior Acquisitions Editor, got us all on the "same page" and helped us to stay motivated and on schedule. Taney Wilkins, Development Editor, dealt with all of our day-to-day problems and questions, and thus deserves a special thank-you for the very hard work she has done on this project. Larry Qualls, Marketing Manager, has been instrumental in helping to get the word out about the text. Thank you to Production Editor Tamborah Moore, and to the great people at Shepherd Inc., especially Mary Grivetti, who put the manuscript into final form.

Additionally, we wish to thank all of the reviewers who graciously gave their time to this effort, greatly improving our final product. These people are:

Abe Feinberg	*California State University, Northridge*
Zhi-Long Chen	*University of Maryland*
Brooke Saladin	*Wake Forest University*
Les Foulds	*University of Waikato, New Zealand*
Gurpreet Dhillon	*Virginia Commonwealth University*
Vijay R. Kannan	*Utah State University*
Bret J. Wagner	*Western Michigan University*
James F. Campbell	*University of Missouri, St. Louis*
Ling Li	*Old Dominion University*
Linda L. Stanley	*Arizona State University West*

Finally, we would like to thank all of the case writers who contributed to this textbook:

Tarek M. Amine	*Bechtel Global Engineering and Construction Co.*
Terry A. Anderson	*Troy State University*
Mauro Caon	*Fundação Getulio Vargas*
Henrique Corrêa	*Fundação Getulio Vargas*
João Mario Csillag	*Fundação Getulio Vargas*
Krishna S. Dhir	*Berry College*
Keith Drumheller	*Elizabethtown, Pennsylvania*
Howard Forman	*Penn State University*
Donald A. Forrer	*Troy State University*

Jeffrey S. Harper	*Indiana State University*
Donald R. Jackson	*Ferris State University*
David H. Klose	*Enola, Pennsylvania*
Helen LaVan	*DePaul University*
Hélcio Lima	*Genexis*
William H. Moates	*Indiana State University*
A. Mukund	*ICMR, India*
Denio Nogueira	*General Motors*
Joshua Perry	*Mt. Baker Products, Inc.*
Manus Rungtusanathem	*Arizona State University*
Fabrizio Salvador	*Arizona State University*
Mark C. Springer	*Western Washington University*
K. Subhadra	*ICMR, India*
Stephen Sucheski	*Harrisburg, Pennsylvania*
John K. Visich	*Bryant College*
Angela M. Wicks	*Bryant College*
Ronald M. Zigli	*The Citadel*

We most likely left some valued contributors out of this acknowledgments section. We apologize for any oversight and wish to thank these people as well.

About the Authors

Joel D. Wisner is Professor of Supply Chain Management at the University of Nevada, Las Vegas. He earned his BS in Mechanical Engineering from New Mexico State University in 1976 and his MBA from West Texas State University in 1986. During that time, Dr. Wisner worked as an engineer for Union Carbide at their Oak Ridge, Tennessee, facility and then worked in the oil industry in various Louisiana Gulf Coast and West Texas areas. In 1991, he earned his PhD in Operations and Logistics Management from Arizona State University. He is certified in transportation and logistics (CTL) and in purchasing management (C.P.M.).

He is currently keeping busy editing the *International Journal of Integrated Supply Management* while teaching undergraduate and graduate courses in operations and supply chain management. His research interests are in quality assessment and improvement strategies along the supply chain. His articles have appeared in numerous journals including *Journal of Business Logistics, Journal of Operations Management, Journal of Supply Chain Management, Journal of Transportation, Production and Operations Management Journal,* and *Quality Management Journal.* More information about Dr. Wisner can be found at his website: www.scsv.nevada.edu/~wisnerj

G. Keong Leong is Professor and Chair of the Management Department in the College of Business at the University of Nevada, Las Vegas. He received an undergraduate degree in Mechanical Engineering from the University of Malaya and an MBA and PhD from the University of South Carolina. He was previously a member of the faculty at The Ohio State University and held a visiting position at Thunderbird, The American Graduate School of International Management.

His articles appear in academic journals such as *Decision Sciences, Journal of Operations Management, Interfaces, Journal of Management, European Journal of Operational Research,* and *International Journal of Production Research,* among others. He has co-authored three books including *Operations Strategy: Focusing Competitive Excellence* and *Cases in International Management: A Focus on Emerging Markets* and received research and teaching awards, including an Educator of the Year award, from the Asian Chamber of Commerce in Las Vegas. He has been actively involved with the Decision Sciences Institute, serving as Editor of *Decision Line,* At-Large Vice President, Chair of the Innovative Education Committee, Chair of the Doctoral Student Affairs Committee, and Manufacturing Management Track chair. In addition, he served as Co-Chair of the Operations Management Doctoral Consortium and Chair of the Professional Development Workshop, Operations Management Division of the Academy of Management. Professor Leong is listed in Marquis *Who's Who in the World, Who's Who in America,* and *Who's Who in American Education.*

Keah-Choon Tan is Associate Professor of Operations Management at the University of Nevada, Las Vegas. He received a BS degree and an MBA from the University of South Alabama, and his PhD in Production and Operations Management from Michigan State University. He is a Certified Purchasing Manager (C.P.M.) of the Institute for Supply Management (ISM), and is certified in production and inventory management (CPIM) by the American Production and Inventory Control Society (APICS). He has published numerous articles in the areas of supply chain management, quality, and operations scheduling in a variety of magazines and journals, including *Decision Sciences, European Journal of Purchasing and Supply Management, International Journal of Operations and Production Management, International Journal of Production Research, Journal of Supply Chain Management, Omega,* and *Quality Management Journal.*

Prior to academia, he was the hospital administrator of a specialist hospital and the account comptroller of a listed manufacturing firm. He has served as the Manufacturing Management co-track chair, and on the Doctoral Student Affairs Committee and Member Services Committee for the Decision Sciences Institute, and as the Management and Operations Research Track chair and facilitator for the 39th Mountain Plains Management Conference. In addition, he served as the Supply Chain Management column editor for APICS Performance Advantage. Dr. Tan has received numerous research awards and was voted Person of the Year by the Western Colorado chapter of the ISM in 1997/98.

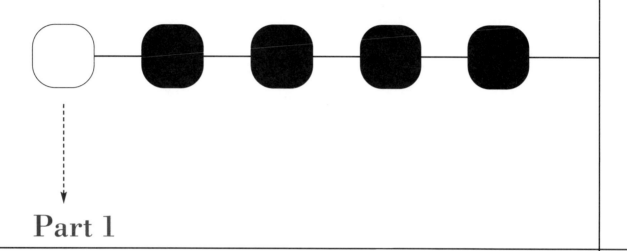

Part 1

Supply Chain Management: An Overview

Chapter 1   Introduction to Supply Chain Management

Chapter 1

INTRODUCTION TO SUPPLY CHAIN MANAGEMENT

. . . [We] draw a definite distinction between supply chains as phenomena that exist in business and the management of those supply chains. The former is simply something that exists . . . , while the latter requires overt management efforts by the organizations within the supply chain.[1]

Improved supply chain management has been helpful in our economy's "soft landing" by keeping inventory in line with the downturn.[2]

Learning Objectives

After completing this chapter, you should be able to
- Describe a supply chain and define supply chain management.
- Describe the objectives and elements of supply chain management.
- Describe local, regional, and global supply chain management activities among services and manufacturing companies.
- Describe a brief history and future trends of supply chain management.

Chapter Outline

Introduction

What Is Supply Chain Management?

Why Is Supply Chain Management Important?

The Origins of Supply Chain Management

Important Elements of Supply Chain Management
  Purchasing Elements
  Operations Elements

Distribution Elements
Integration Elements

Future Trends in Supply Chain Management
  Expanding the Supply Chain
  Increasing Supply Chain Responsiveness
  The Greening of Supply Chains
  Reducing Supply Chain Costs

SUPPLY CHAIN MANAGEMENT IN ACTION   *Dell Inc.*[3]

Excess inventory is like a leech that slowly sucks resources and money out of a business. To kill the creature, Dell Inc. is steadily replacing inventory with information. "Inventory is a security blanket," says Lance Van Hooser, director of e-commerce at Dell. "The only reason companies build up inventory is because they don't know about events that are going to happen. The more you know, the less inventory you will have to carry." Right now, Dell carries about seven days of finished product. The goal is to count that already low figure in minutes. The company is turning to the Internet to collaborate and conduct business with suppliers and customers at unprecedented levels.

Dell recently created customized Web pages for its top thirty suppliers, whose employees can log on to a secure, personalized site to view demand forecasts and other customer-sensitive information—such as who Dell's customers are and how much equipment each is ordering—to help them better gauge demand. As a result, suppliers can more easily match their production schedules to Dell's—making only what is needed when it is needed.

Dell is also passing on data about its defect rates, engineering changes, and product enhancements to these suppliers. Since both Dell and its suppliers are in constant communication, the margin for error is reduced. Also, partners are now able to collaborate in real time on product designs and enhancements. Suppliers are also required to share sensitive information with Dell, such as their own quality problems. Van Hooser says it is easy to get its suppliers to follow Dell's lead because they also reap the benefits of faster cycle times, reduced inventory, and improved forecasts; and ultimately, the customer gets a higher-quality product at a lower price.

Dell is also using the Internet to create a community around its supply chain. The Web sites all have links to bulletin boards where partners from around the world can exchange information about their experiences with Dell and its supply chain. "The Internet is the core of everything we are doing," says Kevin Rollins, vice chairman of Dell. "It provides the capacity to improve the flow of information, eliminate paper-based functions, and link global organizations."

Dell is using the Internet to form tighter links with customers, too. For many of its business users, the company has created Web pages containing approved configurations, prenegotiated prices, and new work-flow capabilities, so when an employee requests a new computer, the order is automatically routed to the appropriate person within the buying organization for approval. Rollins says Ford Motor Company saved about $2 million in initial procurement costs by using its customized Web page. "With information technology, the value of inventory is quickly being replaced by the value of information," he says.

Introduction

Competing successfully in any business environment today requires companies to become much more involved in how their suppliers and customers do business. As global competition increases, making products and services that consumers want to buy means that businesses must pay closer attention to where materials come from, how their suppliers' products and services are designed and assembled, how finished products are transported and stored, and what consumers or end-product users are really asking for (for instance, many companies may not even know how their products are used in the final products bought by consumers or end users!).

Over the past ten years, many large firms or conglomerates have found that effectively managing all of the business units of a **vertically integrated firm**—a firm whose business boundaries extend to include one-time suppliers and/or customers—is quite difficult. What is occurring at many of these firms today is an effort to pare down the organization to focus more on core capabilities while trying to create alliances or strategic partnerships with suppliers, transportation and warehousing companies, distributors, and other customers who are good at what they do. This team approach to making and distributing products and services to customers is becoming the most effective and efficient way for businesses to stay successful—and is central to the practice of supply chain management.

Several factors require today's firms to work together more effectively than ever before. Communication and information exchange through computer networks using enterprise resource planning (ERP) systems (discussed further in Chapter 7) and the Internet has made global teamwork not only possible but also necessary for firms to compete in most markets. Communication technology continues to change rapidly, making global partnerships and teamwork much easier than ever before. Competition is expanding rapidly in all industries and in all markets around the world, bringing new materials, products, people, and resources together, making it much more difficult for the local, individually owned, "mom-and-pop" shops to keep customers. New markets are opening up as governments change and as consumers around the world learn of new products from television, radio, and contact with tourists. It is an exciting time for companies seeking to find new customers, develop new products, and compete more successfully. New jobs and opportunities are opening up in the areas of purchasing, operations, logistics, and supply chain management as firms build a better competitive infrastructure.

As you read this textbook, you will be introduced to the concepts in supply chain management and how to use these concepts to become better managers in today's global economy. We use examples throughout the text to illustrate the topics discussed; and we provide cases in each section of the textbook to enable you to test your problem-solving, decision-making, and writing skills in supply chain management. We hope that by the end of the text you will have gained an appreciation of the value of supply chain management and will be able to apply what you have learned here both in your profession and in future courses in supply chain management.

In this chapter, the term *supply chain management* is defined, including a discussion of its importance, history, and developments to date. The chapter ends with a look at the newest and future trends in supply chain management.

What Is Supply Chain Management?

There are many definitions of supply chain management in the literature today, but we start with a discussion of a **supply chain,** as shown in Figure 1.1. The supply chain shown in the figure starts with firms extracting raw materials from the ground—such as iron ore, oil, wood, and food—and then selling them to raw material manufacturers. These companies, acting on purchase orders and specifications they have received from component manufacturers, turn the raw materials into materials that are usable by these customers (materials like sheet steel, aluminum, copper, lumber, and inspected foodstuffs). The component manufacturers, responding to orders and specifications from their customers (final product manufacturers) make and sell intermediate components (electrical wire, fabrics, plumbing items, nuts and bolts, molded plastic components, processed foods). The final product manufacturers (companies like IBM, General Motors, Coca-cola) assemble finished products and sell them to wholesalers or distributors, who then resell these products to retailers as their product orders are received. Retailers in turn sell these products to us, the end customers. We buy products based on cost, quality, availability, maintainability, and reputation and hope they satisfy our requirements and expectations. Companies and their supply chains that can provide these things will be successful. Later, we may need to return products or need warranty repairs or may just throw products away or recycle them. These **reverse logistics activities** are also included in the supply chain.

Referring again to Figure 1.1, the firm in the middle of the figure is referred to as the *focal firm.* While the focal firm is presented here and in later discussions as an end-product assembly

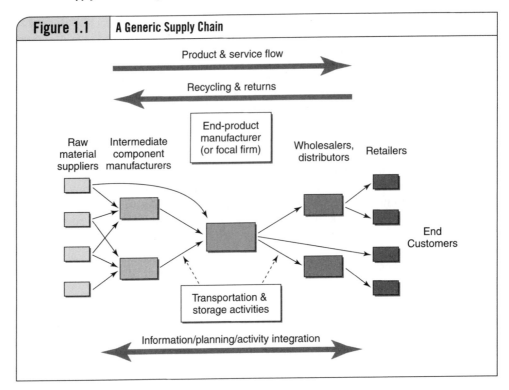

Figure 1.1   A Generic Supply Chain

firm, it can be any of the firms involved in the supply chain, depending on the frame of refer-ence of the manager viewing the diagram.

Thus, the series of companies that eventually make products and services available to con-sumers, including all of the functions enabling the production, delivery, and recycling of ma-terials, components, end products, and services, is called a supply chain. All products reach consumers via some type of supply chain, some much larger and more complicated than others. With this idea of a supply chain in mind then, it is easy to come to the realization that there really is only one true source of income for the entire chain of organizations—the end consumer. When individual firms in the supply chain make business decisions that ignore the interests of other chain members, this suboptimization only transfers costs and addi-tional waiting time along the supply chain, ultimately leading to higher end-product prices, lower supply chain service levels, and consequently lower end-customer demand.

A number of other companies are also indirectly involved in most supply chains, and they play a very important role in the eventual delivery of end products to customers. These are the many service providers, such as trucking and airfreight shipping companies, information sys-tem providers, public warehousing firms, freight forwarders, agents, and consultants. These service providers are extremely useful to the firms in most supply chains, since they can get products where they need to be in a timely fashion, allow buyers and sellers to communicate effectively, allow firms to serve outlying markets, enable firms to save money on domestic and foreign shipments, and in general allow firms to adequately serve their customers for the low-est possible cost. The Global Perspectives profiles Li & Fung, a trading company specializing in bringing suppliers and buyers together and managing the resulting supply chains.

So, now that a general description of a supply chain has been provided, what is supply chain management? A number of similar definitions are available in the literature and among various professional associations. For example:

- The Institute for Supply Management describes supply chain management as
  "*[t]he design and management of seamless, value-added processes across*

Global Perspective

LI & FUNG[4]

Li & Fung, a Hong Kong trading company, manages the inbound supply chains of U.S. and European retailers who purchase Asian-brand clothing, home furnishings, sporting goods, and toys. Their job is to work with their retailer partners in developing products; to find Asian suppliers who can meet the retailers' product and purchase requirements; to ensure that products are manufactured to the retailers' specifications; and then, finally, to prepare the necessary export documentation, clear the products through customs, and deliver the items on time to their clients.

To make this happen, teams of Li & Fung product specialists are assigned to customers from a global network of offices in forty countries, who identify the best suppliers to meet their customers' product and delivery date requirements. Li & Fung does not own any manufacturing facilities; rather, the product specialists bring the buyers and sellers together and then ensure that both parties are satisfied with the particular product and service arrangements.

Founded in 1906, Li & Fung has been a leader in product management and delivery since the 1970s, when Victor and William Fung, both educated in the United States, returned to Hong Kong to help their father restructure the company. In the 1990s, Li & Fung acquired several buying services companies and formed an e-commerce subsidiary to broaden its supply base and expand its service capabilities. Today, it employs 5,000 people worldwide and handles over $4.2 billion in purchases for clients each year. Recently, it has been expanding its supplier base to include suppliers found in Eastern Europe and Central America, to enable faster service to their European and U.S. customers.

To further enhance its supply chain management capabilities, Li & Fung has also recently entered into a collaborative agreement with Microsoft® Hong Kong, who will supply several software products to more effectively and efficiently connect Li & Fung to its geographically dispersed customers and suppliers, numbering in the thousands. This new information sharing technology will also allow Li & Fung to be more flexible to meet its customers' changing demands. Today, it has become a truly global supply chain management and trading company.

organizational boundaries to meet the real needs of the end customer. The development and integration of people and technological resources are critical to successful supply chain integration."[5]

- The Supply-Chain Council's definition of supply chain management is "[m]anaging supply and demand, sourcing raw materials and parts, manufacturing and assembly, warehousing and inventory tracking, order entry and order management, distribution across all channels, and delivery to the customer."[6]

- The Council of Logistics Management defines supply chain management as ". . . the systemic, strategic coordination of the traditional business functions and the tactics across these business functions within a particular company and across businesses within the supply chain for the purposes of improving the long-term performance of the individual companies and the supply chain as a whole."[7]

- Finally, in a research paper authored by a notable expert in supply chain management, Dr. Hau Lee and his coauthor Mr. Corey Billington define supply chain management as "the integration activities taking place among a network of facilities that procure raw materials, transform them into intermediate goods and then final products, and deliver products to customers through a distribution system."[8]

Consistent across these definitions is the idea of coordinating or integrating a number of product-related activities among supply chain participants to improve operating efficiencies, quality, and customer service in order to gain a sustainable competitive advantage for all of the organizations involved in this collaboration. Thus, for supply chain management to be successful, firms must work together by sharing information on things like demand forecasts; production plans; capacity changes; new marketing strategies; new product and service developments; new technology developments; purchasing plans; delivery dates; and anything else impacting the firm's purchasing, production, and distribution plans.

In theory, supply chains work as a cohesive, singularly competitive unit, accomplishing what many large, vertically integrated firms have tried and failed to accomplish. The difference is that firms in a supply chain are relatively free to enter and leave supply chain relationships if these relationships are no longer proving beneficial; it is this free market organization that helps supply chains operate more effectively than vertically integrated conglomerates. For example, when a particular material or product is in short supply accompanied by rising prices, a firm may find it beneficial to align itself with one of these suppliers to ensure continued supply of the scarce item. This alignment may become beneficial to both parties— new markets for the supplier, leading to new, future product opportunities; and long-term continuity of supply and stable prices for the buyer. Later, when new competitors start producing the scarce product or when demand declines, the supplier may no longer be valued by the buying firm; instead, the firm may see more value in negotiating with other potential suppliers for its purchase requirements and may then decide to dissolve the original buyer-supplier alignment. As can be seen from this example, supply chains are often very dynamic or fluid, which can also cause problems in effectively managing them.

While supply chain management may allow organizations to realize the advantages of vertical integration, certain conditions must be present for successful supply chain management to occur. Perhaps the single most important prerequisite is a change in the corporate cultures of all participating members in the supply chain to make them conducive to supply chain management. More traditional organizational cultures that emphasize short-term, company-focused performance are in many ways in conflict with the objectives of supply chain management. Supply chain management focuses on positioning the organizations in such a way that all participants in the supply chain benefit. Thus, effective supply chain management relies on high levels of trust; cooperation; collaboration; and honest, accurate communications.

Purchasing, operations, logistics, and transportation managers not only must be equipped with the necessary expertise in these critical supply chain functions but also must appreciate and understand how these functions interact and affect the entire supply chain. Rebecca Morgan, president of Fulcrum Consulting Works, an Ohio-based supply chain management consulting firm, says too many companies go into agreements they call partnerships, then try to control the relationship from end to end. "A lot of the automotive companies did this in the beginning," she says. "They issued a unilateral ultimatum: you will do this for me if you want to do business with me, no matter what it means for you."[9] This type of supply chain management approach almost never works.

Boundaries of integrated supply chains are also dynamic. It has been often said that supply chain boundaries extend from "a firm's suppliers' suppliers to their customers' customers"; today, most firms' supply chain management coordination efforts do not extend beyond those boundaries. In fact, in many cases, firms find it very difficult to extend coordination efforts beyond a few of the firms' most important direct suppliers and customers (in fact, in one survey, a number of firm representatives stated that most of their supply chain efforts were with the firm's *internal* suppliers and customers only!).[10] However, with time and successful initial results, many firms are extending the boundaries of their supply chains.

Why Is Supply Chain Management Important?

While all firms are part of a chain of organizations bringing products and services to customers (and most firms operate in a number of supply chains), certainly not all supply chains are managed in any truly integrated or coordinated fashion. Firms continue to operate independently in many industries (particularly small firms). It is often easy for managers to be focused solely on their immediate customers and their internal daily operations. With customers complaining, employees to train, late supplier deliveries, creditors to pay, and equipment to repair, who has time for relationship building and other supply chain management efforts?

Many firms, though, have discovered value-enhancing, long-term benefits from their supply chain management efforts. Firms with large system inventories, many suppliers, complex product assemblies, and highly valued customers with large purchasing budgets have the most to gain from the practice of supply chain management. For these firms, even moderate supply chain management success can mean lower purchasing and inventory costs, better product quality, and higher levels of customer service and sales. According to the U.S. Census Bureau's Annual Survey of Manufacturers, the cost of inventories was over $2.2 trillion just among U.S. manufacturers in 2000. Additionally, transportation and inventory carrying costs in the United States totaled $434 billion in 2000.[11] Thus it can be seen that purchasing, inventory, and transportation cost savings can be quite sizable for firms utilizing supply chain management strategies.

Firms must realize that their management efforts can start small—for instance, with just one key supplier—and build through time to include more supply chain participants—such as other important suppliers, key customers, and shippers—and, eventually, **second-tier suppliers and customers** (these are the customers' customers and the suppliers' suppliers). So why is this integration activity important? As alluded to earlier, when a firm, its customers, and its suppliers all know each others' future plans, the planning process is easier and more accurate. A fictitious example is provided in Example 1.1.

EXAMPLE 1.1

ABC Bearings makes roller bearings for Grebson Manufacturing on a fairly regular basis. For the next quarter, they have forecasted Grebson's roller bearing demand to be 25,000 units. Since Grebson's demand for bearings from ABC has been somewhat erratic in the past due to the number of bearing companies competing with ABC and the fluctuation of demand from Grebson's customers, ABC's roller bearing forecast includes 5,000 units of safety stock. The steel used in ABC's bearings is usually purchased from Specialty Steels, Inc. Specialty Steels has, in turn, forecasted ABC's quarterly demand for the high-carbon steel it typically purchases for roller bearings. The forecast also includes safety stock of about 20 percent over what Specialty Steels expects to sell to ABC over the next three months.

This short description has exposed several problems occurring in most supply chains. Because ABC does not know what Grebson's roller bearing demand will be for the coming quarter (it could be zero, or it could be something over 25,000 units), ABC will incur the extra cost of producing 5,000 units of safety stock. Additionally, ABC risks having to carry in inventory any units not sold to Grebson along with lost current and future sales to Grebson if its demand exceeds 25,000 units over the next quarter. Specialty Steels faces the same dilemma—extra materials and labor costs for safety stock production along with the still-present stockout costs of lost present and future sales. Additionally, Grebson's demand for roller bearings from its suppliers includes some safety stock, since it uses roller bearings in one of the products it makes for a primary customer.

Example 1.1 illustrates one of the costs of independent planning and lack of supply chain information sharing and coordination. Grebson's safety stock, which is built in to its roller bearing purchase order, has manifested itself in the form of additional and even greater safety stock levels at the ABC plant. In turn, an even greater percentage of Specialty Steels' production is in the form of safety stock. If the supply chain was larger, this magnification of safety stock, based on forecasts derived from demand already containing safety stock, would continue as orders pass to more distant suppliers up the chain. This supply chain inventory and production problem is known as the **bullwhip effect.** If Grebson Manufacturing knew its customers' purchase plans for the coming quarter, the forecasting methods used, and the way the purchase plans were derived, it would need to add little, if any, safety stock to its production plan for roller bearings. In turn, if Grebson purchased its roller bearings from only ABC and told ABC what Grebson's quarterly purchase plans were, and if ABC did likewise with Specialty Steels, safety stocks throughout the supply chain would be reduced drastically, driving down the cost of roller bearings at each stage of production and distribution.

The result? There would be lower costs and better customer service (remember, there would be few, if any, stockouts if purchase quantities were decided ahead of time and shipping companies delivered on time; additionally, production quantities would be less, reducing purchase costs and production time). Trade estimates suggest that the bullwhip effect results in excess costs on the order of 12 to 25 percent at each firm in the supply chain, which can be a tremendous competitive disadvantage.

Process integration and the other supply chain efforts described in the example can also result in better quality, since potentially higher profit margins may mean more investment into materials research, better production methods, and more reliable transportation and storage facilities. Additionally, as working relationships throughout the supply chain mature, firms will feel more comfortable investing capital in better facilities, better products, and better services for their customers. Additionally, customers will share more information with suppliers and suppliers will be more likely to participate in their key customers' new product design efforts, for instance. These then, become some of the more important benefits of a well-integrated supply chain. In the following chapters of the text, other associated benefits will also become apparent.

The Origins of Supply Chain Management

During the 1950s and 1960s, U.S. manufacturers were employing mass production techniques to reduce costs and improve productivity, while relatively little attention was typically paid to creating supplier partnerships, improving process design and flexibility, or improving product quality (see Table 1.1). New product design and development was slow and relied exclusively on in-house resources, technologies, and capacity. Sharing technology and expertise through strategic buyer-supplier partnerships was essentially unheard of back then. Processes on the factory floor were cushioned with inventory to keep machinery running and maintain balanced material flows, resulting in large investments in work-in-process inventory.

In the 1960s and 1970s, material requirements planning (MRP) systems and manufacturing resource planning (MRPII) systems were developed, and the importance of effective materials management was recognized as manufacturers became aware of the impact of high levels of inventories on manufacturing and storage costs. As computer capabilities grew, the sophistication of inventory tracking software also grew, making it possible to further reduce inventory costs while improving internal communication of the need for purchased parts and supplies.

The 1980s were the breakout years for supply chain management. One of the first widely recorded uses of the term *supply chain management* came about in a paper published in 1982.[12] Intense global competition beginning in the 1980s (and continuing today) provided an incentive for U.S. manufacturers to offer lower-cost, higher-quality products along with

Table 1.1	Historic Supply Chain Management Events in the United States

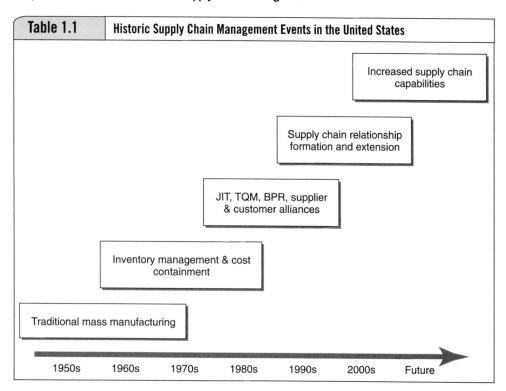

higher levels of customer service. Manufacturers utilized just-in-time (JIT) and total quality management (TQM) strategies to improve quality, manufacturing efficiency, and delivery times. In a JIT manufacturing environment with little inventory to cushion scheduling and/or production problems, firms began to realize the potential benefits and importance of strategic and cooperative supplier-buyer-customer relationships. The concept of these partnerships or alliances emerged as manufacturers experimented with JIT and TQM.

As competition in the United States intensified further in the 1990s accompanied by increasing logistics and inventory costs and the trend toward market globalization, the challenges associated with improving quality, manufacturing efficiency, customer service, and new product design and development also increased. To deal with these challenges, manufacturers began purchasing from a select number of certified, high-quality suppliers with excellent service reputations and involved these suppliers in their new product design and development activities as well as in cost, quality, and service improvement initiatives. In other words, companies realized that if they started giving only their best suppliers most of their business, then, in return, they could expect these suppliers to help generate more sales through improvements in delivery, quality, and product design and to generate cost savings through closer attention to the processes, materials, and components they used in manufacturing their products. Many of these buyer-supplier alliances have proven to be very successful.

Business process reengineering (BPR), (radically rethinking and redesigning business processes to reduce waste and increase performance was introduced in the early 1990s and was the result of a growing interest during this time in the need for cost reductions and a return to an emphasis on the key competencies of the firm to enhance long-term competitive advantage. As this "fad" died down in the mid- to late 1990s (the term became synonymous with downsizing), supply chain management rapidly increased in popularity as a source of competitive advantage for firms.

Also during this time, managers, consultants, and academics began developing an understanding of the differences between logistics and supply chain management. Up until then, supply chain management was simply viewed as logistics outside the firm. As companies began implementing supply chain management initiatives, they began to understand the necessity of integrating all key business processes among the supply chain participants, enabling the supply chain to act and react as one entity. Today, logistics is viewed as one important element of the much broader supply chain management concept.

At the same time, companies also saw benefits in the creation of alliances or partnerships with their customers. The focal firm became the highly valued and heavily used supplier to its customers. Developing these long-term, close relationships with customers meant holding less finished product safety stock (as discussed earlier in the bullwhip effect example) and allowed firms to focus their resources on providing better products and services to these customers. In time, when market share improved for its customers' products, the result was more business for the firm.

Thus, supply chain management has evolved along two parallel paths: (1) the purchasing and supply management emphasis from industrial buyers and (2) the transportation and logistics emphasis from wholesalers and retailers. The increasing popularity of these alliances with suppliers and customers (and suppliers' suppliers and customers' customers) in the later part of the 1990s and continuing today has also meant a greater reliance on the shipping, warehousing, and logistics services that provide transportation, storage, documentation, and customs clearing services to many firms within a typical supply chain. Relationship building has also occurred increasingly with many of these **third-party service providers** and the firms that use them to ensure a continuous, uninterrupted supply of goods. The need to assess the performance of these relationships periodically has also accompanied the growth of supply chain management. One of the challenges faced today by many firms involved in supply chain management is how to adequately assess overall performance in often extremely complex, global supply chains.

For the wholesaling and retailing industries, the supply chain management focus is on location and logistics issues more often than on manufacturing. Supply chain management in these industries has often been referred to as **quick response, service response logistics,** or **integrated logistics.** The advancement of electronic data interchange (EDI) systems, bar coding, Internet systems, and radio frequency scanning technologies over the past two decades has greatly aided the evolution of the integrated supply chain concept. Organizations in the retail industry have utilized supply chain management to meet the ever-increasing uncertainty and complexity of the marketplace and to reduce inventory throughout the supply chain.

Most recently, the rapid development of client/server supply chain management software that typically includes integrated supply chain management and electronic commerce components has aided in the evolution and adoption of supply chain management. Sharing information with supply chain partners through EDI and the Internet has enabled firms to integrate stocking, logistics, materials acquisition, shipping, and other functions to create a more proactive and effective style of business management and customer responsiveness.

In the future, it is expected that supply chain management emphasis will concentrate on supply chain expansion, increasing supply chain responsiveness, increasing the emphasis on "green" supply chains, and further reducing supply chain costs. These topics are discussed in more detail in a later section of this chapter.

Important Elements of Supply Chain Management

A number of important elements within the topic of supply chain management are introduced here. These elements essentially make up the table of contents for this textbook and are shown in Table 1.2 along with the chapters where they are discussed.

Table 1.2	Important Elements of Supply Chain Management	
Supply Chain Elements	**Important Issues**	**Chapters**
Purchasing	Supplier alliances, supplier management, strategic sourcing	2, 3, 4
Operations	Demand management, MRP, ERP, JIT, TQM	5, 6, 7, 8
Distribution	Transportation management, customer relationship management, network design, service response logistics	9, 10, 11, 12
Integration	Coordination/integration activities, global integration problems, performance measurement	13, 14, 15

Purchasing Elements

Traditional buyer-supplier relationships emphasize multiple sourcing, competitive bidding, and use of short-term contracts; these often-adversarial relationships pit the buyer against the supplier and focus primarily on the purchase price of the product instead of the capabilities of the suppliers and how they can contribute to the long-term competitiveness of the buying organization. Recently, there has been a shift toward developing more long-term supplier relationships for the competitive benefits described earlier. Purchasing is an extremely important element in supply chain management, since incoming material quality, delivery timing, and purchase price are dependent on the buyer-supplier relationship and the capabilities of the supplier. Problems with suppliers will ultimately cause end-product customers to get less and pay more. For instance, TaylorMade Golf, maker of the number one clubs on the PGA Tour, began instituting strict rules for its supplier partnerships a few years back when its customers began complaining that their orders were often late. "We are big enough to drive what our supply chain looks like and how it performs," says Mark Leposky, vice president of global operations for TaylorMade. "But we try to establish partnerships with our suppliers that work to our mutual benefit."[13]

One of the most crucial issues in purchasing is **supplier management.** Simply put, this means getting your firm's suppliers to do what you want, and there are a number of ways to do this. This involves assessing your suppliers' current capabilities and then figuring out how to improve them. Thus, one of the key activities in supplier management is **supplier evaluation,** or determining the capabilities of suppliers. This occurs both when potential suppliers are being evaluated for a future purchase and when existing suppliers are periodically evaluated for performance purposes. A closely related activity is **supplier certification.** Certification programs can either be company-designed and administered, or they can be internationally recognized and standardized programs like the ISO 9000 series of certifications. Supplier certification allows buyers to assume the supplier will meet product quality and service requirements, thus reducing duplicate testing and inspections and the need for extensive supplier evaluations.

Over time, careful and effective supplier management efforts allow firms to selectively screen out poor-performing suppliers and build successful, trusting relationships with the remaining top-performing suppliers. These suppliers can provide tremendous benefits to the buying firm and the entire supply chain. As discussed in greater detail in the next chapter, higher purchase volumes per supplier typically mean lower costs (causing a much greater impact on profits than a corresponding increase in sales), higher quality, and better delivery service. These characteristics are viewed as strategically important to the firm because of their impact on the firm's competitiveness. Suppliers also see significant benefits from these relationships in terms of long-term, high-volume sales. These trading-partner relationships have come to be termed **strategic partnerships** and are emphasized throughout this text as one of the foundations of supply chain management.

Operations Elements

Once materials, components, and other purchased products are delivered to the buying organization, a number of internal operations elements become important in assembling or processing the items into finished products, ensuring that the right amount of product is produced and that finished products meet specific quality, cost, and customer service requirements.

During a calendar year, seasonal demand variations commonly occur. Firms can predict when these variations occur, based on historic demand patterns, and use forecasting techniques to guide weekly or monthly production plans. If demand does not materialize as forecasted, then the firm is left with either too much inventory (or service capacity) or not enough. Both situations cost the firm money and can even cause permanent lost future business if a stock-out has occurred. To minimize these costs, firms rely on **demand management** strategies and systems, with the objective of matching demand to available capacity, either by improving production scheduling, curtailing demand, using a back-order system, or increasing capacity. Rapid-Line of Grand Rapids, Michigan, uses a package called SyteLine APS from Frontstep to schedule production of the metal parts it supplies for customers in the office furniture, appliance, and automotive industries. Rapid-Line typically has two weeks to turn around its customers' orders, and some want as little as seven-day or less turnaround. Their scheduling system works like an airlines reservation system. They get preliminary order information and use this information to reserve capacity for their bigger customers. "We want to be able to reserve capacity for our customers' orders, then hold off on the actual production of those orders until the last possible minute, while still ensuring that all orders will reach their destinations at the right time," says Mark Lindquist, Rapid-Line's president.[14]

Controlling or managing inventory is one of the most important aspects of operations and certainly valuable to the firm. Firms can and typically do have some sort of **material requirements planning (MRP)** software system for managing their inventory. These systems can be linked throughout the organization and its supply chain partners using **enterprise resource planning (ERP)** systems, providing real-time sales data, inventory, and production information to supply chain participants. These system configurations vary considerably, based on the number and complexity of products and the design of the supply chain. Retailers (Wal-Mart, for example) scan the bar codes of the products purchased, causing the local MRP system to deduct units from inventory until a preset reorder point is reached. When this occurs, the local computer system automatically contacts the supplying distribution center's MRP system and generates an order. At the distribution center, the order is filled and sent along with other orders to the particular Wal-Mart. Eventually, the inventory at the distribution center needs replenishing; and, at that time, the distribution center's MRP system automatically generates an order with the manufacturer who sells the product to Wal-Mart. This order communication and **inventory visibility** may extend farther back up the supply chain, reducing the likelihood of stock-outs or excess inventories.

Another common form of inventory management is through use of a **just-in-time (JIT) production system.** Also called a **pull-type production system,** as opposed to MRP's **push-type production system,** the objectives are to create a fast, flexible system capable of delaying final assembly until a downstream (customer) order occurs. Implementing this type of system usually results in faster delivery times, lower inventory levels, and better quality. An example here would be Dell Inc. A customer calls or contacts Dell through its Web site and custom-configures his computer. Once the computer is ordered, Dell assembles the computer from in-stock, mass-produced components and delivers the computer in just a few days. Thus, Dell can mass-manufacture computer components and still be able to offer customized products to its customers.

An important aspect of JIT is the quality of the incoming purchased items and the quality of the various assemblies as they move through the various production processes. This is due to the characteristically low inventory levels of purchased goods and work in process in JIT-oriented facilities. Thus, firms and supply chains employing JIT usually have a **total quality management (TQM)** strategy in place to ensure continued quality compliance among suppliers and with internal production facilities. The type of inventory control system used (MRP versus JIT) is especially important when considering the design of the supply chain (for instance, where to construct distribution centers, what transportation services to use, and how big to make the various production facilities and warehouses).

Distribution Elements

When products are completed, they are delivered to customers through a number of different modes of transportation. Delivering products to customers at the right time, quality, and volume requires a high level of planning and cooperation between the firm, its customers, and the various distribution elements or services employed (such as transportation, warehousing, and break-bulk or repackaging services). For services, products are produced and delivered to the customer simultaneously in most cases, so services are extremely dependent upon server capacity and successful service delivery to meet customer requirements.

Transportation management decisions typically involve a trade-off between cost and delivery timing or customer service. Motor carriers (trucks) are typically more expensive than rail carriers but offer more flexibility and speed, particularly for short routes. Air carriers are yet more expensive but much faster than any other transportation mode. Water carriers are the slowest but are also the least expensive. Finally, pipeline transportation is used to transport oil, water, natural gas, and coal slurry. Many transportation services offer various modal combinations, as well as warehousing and customs-clearing services. In a typical integrated supply chain environment where JIT deliveries are the norm, transportation services are critical to the overall success of the supply chain. In many cases, these services are considered supply chain partners and are viewed as a key value enhancers for the supply chain.

The desired outcome of distribution is customer service. In order to provide the desired level of customer service, firms must identify customer requirements and then provide the right combination of transportation, storage, packaging, and information services to successfully satisfy those requirements. Through frequent contact with customers, firms develop **customer relationship management** strategies regarding how to meet delivery due dates, how to successfully resolve customer complaints, how to communicate with customers, and how to determine the distribution services required. From a supply chain management perspective, these customer activities take on added importance, since second-tier, third-tier, and final-product customers are ultimately dependent on the distribution outcomes at each stage within the supply chain.

Designing and building a **distribution network** is one method of ensuring successful product delivery. Again, there is typically a trade-off between the cost of the distribution system's design and customer service. For example, a firm may utilize a large number of regional or local warehouses in order to deliver products quickly to customers. The transportation cost from factory to warehouse, the inventory holding cost, and the cost to build and operate warehouses would be quite high, but the payoff would be better customer service flexibility. On the other hand, a firm may choose to operate only a few highly dispersed warehouses, saving money on the inbound transportation cost, the inventory holding cost, and the warehouse construction and operating cost but then having to be content with limited customer service capabilities. Customer desires and competition levels play important roles in this network design decision.

For service products, the physical distribution issue is typically much less complex. Making sure services are delivered in a timely fashion is the topic of service response logistics. Services are, for the most part, delivered by a server when customers request service. For instance, consider an example in which a customer walks into a bank in search of a loan for a used automobile. He may contact three separate bank employees during this transaction but eventually will complete a loan application, wait for loan approval, and then receive funds, assuming his loan is approved. He will leave, satisfied with the service products he received provided that a number of things occurred: he got what he came for (the loan); he got the type of service he expected to get (reasonable amount of waiting, knowledgeable servers); and he got his product at a reasonable price (a good interest rate for the right period of time).

Thus, successful service delivery depends on service location (service providers must be close to the customers they are trying to serve), service capacity (customers will leave if the wait is too long), and service capability (customers must be able to trust what servers are telling them or doing for them). Hard goods producers must also be concerned with the delivery of service products for their customers, such as providing warranty repairs and information, financing, insurance, and equipment troubleshooting and operating information. Thus, all firms must be cognizant of the impact of service location, capacity, and capability on customer satisfaction.

Integration Elements

Up until now, the basic elements of supply chain management have been discussed: purchasing, operations, and logistics or distribution process activities occurring among the firm and its (potentially several) tiers of customers and suppliers. The final step—and certainly the most difficult one—is to coordinate and hopefully seamlessly integrate these practices among the supply chain's participants.

Activities in a supply chain are said to be coordinated when members of the supply chain work together when making delivery, inventory, production, and purchasing decisions that impact the profits of the supply chain. If one activity fails or is performed poorly, then supply along the chain is disrupted, which jeopardizes the effectiveness of the entire supply chain. Successful **supply chain integration** occurs when the participants realize that supply chain management must become part of all of the firms' strategic planning processes, in which objectives and policies are jointly determined based on the final customers' needs and what the supply chain as a whole does well. Ultimately, firms act together to maximize total supply chain profits by determining optimal purchase quantities, product availabilities, service levels, lead times, production quantities, and technical and product support at each tier within the supply chain.

This integration process also requires better internal functional integration of activities within each of the participating firms, such that the supply chain acts as one entity. This idea of supply chain integration can run contrary to the notion among many potential supply chain participants of their firm's independent profit-maximization objectives, making supply chain integration a very tough sell in many supplier-buyer-customer situations. Thus, continued efforts are required to break down obstacles, change attitudes, change adversarial relationships, reduce conflict, and bridge various functional barriers within and between companies if supply chain integration is to become a reality.

Business periodicals have many examples of companies that could have benefited from successful supply chain management. The Kmart Corporation is one possible example. Kmart operates approximately 1,500 stores and supercenters around the world and competes as a low-price retailer with primary rivals Wal-Mart and Target. Like its competitors, Kmart's strategy has been to provide a wide range of common consumer products at reasonable quality levels for a low price. To succeed, Kmart must have very efficient global, regional, and local distribution systems; capable low-cost suppliers; and lots of easy-to-find product varieties at every location.

In January 2002, Kmart filed for Chapter 11 bankruptcy protection, at the time the largest in U.S. history for retailers. This problem could potentially have been avoided through use of the supply chain management techniques introduced in this chapter. As a matter of fact, many in the mass-retailing industry blame the bankruptcy of Kmart on the company's fail-ure to match the supply chain management standards set by Wal-Mart and Target.[15] Increas-ing supplier and distributor alliances, for instance, should result in fewer stock-out situations at the stores, lower prices, and greater levels of customer service. Taking a look at where Kmart is now, relative to January 2002, would be a good indicator of the success or failure of their most recent supply chain management efforts.

When firms operate globally, their supply chains are much more complex, making supply chain integration much more difficult. The increasing demand for products in foreign and emerging markets and growing foreign competition in domestic markets, along with low production costs in some foreign locations, have made overseas business commonplace for many companies. Firms must understand both the risks and advantages of operating on a global scale and the impact this may have on their **global supply chains.** Some of the advan-tages include a larger market for products, allowing for economies of scale in purchasing and production, which reduces costs; lower labor costs; access to a foreign supply base of poten-tially cheaper, higher-quality suppliers; access to foreign employees; and the generation of new product ideas from these foreign suppliers and employees. Some of the risks include fluctuating exchange rates affecting production, warehousing, and purchasing and selling prices—**operating exposure;** government intervention or political instabilities, causing changes in subsidies, tariffs, taxes, or corporate operating laws; and, finally, failure to identify particular foreign customer needs and local reactions to products.

Firms can successfully react to these problems by building flexibility into their global supply chains. This is accomplished by using a number of suppliers, manufacturing, and storage facili-ties in various foreign locations. As product demand and economic conditions change, the sup-ply chain can react to take advantage of opportunities or cost changes to maximize profits.

One additional integration topic is the use of a **supply chain performance measurement** system. Performance measurements must be utilized across the supply chain to help firms keep track of their supply chain management efforts. It is crucial for firms to know whether certain strategies are working as expected—or not—before they become financial drains on the organizations. Firms work together to develop long-term supply chain management strategies and then devise short-term tactics to implement these strategies. Performance measurements help the firms decide the value of these tactics and should be developed to highlight performance within the areas of purchasing, operations, distribution, and integra-tion. Performance measures should be designed around the tactics themselves and should be detailed pieces of information instead of merely sales figures or inventory levels.

High levels of supply chain performance occur when the strategies at each of the firms fit well with overall supply chain strategies. Thus, each firm must understand its role in the sup-ply chain, the needs of the ultimate customer, the needs of its immediate customers, and how these needs translate into internal operations requirements and the requirements being placed on suppliers. Once these needs and the products and services themselves can be com-municated and transported through the supply chain effectively, successful supply chain management and its associated benefits will be realized.

Future Trends in Supply Chain Management

The practice of supply chain management is a very recent phenomenon, as many organiza-tions are just now beginning to realize the benefits and problems that accompany an integrated supply chain. Supply chain management is an incredibly complex undertaking involving cultural change among most or all of the participants, investment and training in new software and com-munication systems, and a change or realignment of the competitive strategies employed among the participating firms. As competitive situations, products, technology, and customers change, the priorities for the supply chain also must change, requiring supply chains to be ever more flexible to respond quickly to these changes. As we look at the most recent practices and the future trends of supply chain management, a number of issues present themselves as areas that need to be addressed including the expansion of the supply chain, increasing supply chain responsiveness, creating an environmentally friendly supply chain, and reducing total supply chain costs.

Expanding the Supply Chain

As markets for the supply chain grow, so too must the supply chain. Today, U.S. firms are increasing their partnerships with foreign firms and building foreign production facilities to accommodate their market expansion plans and increase their responsiveness to global economic conditions and demand. The supply chain dynamic today is changing, and companies are now working with firms located all over the globe to coordinate purchasing, manufacturing, shipping, and distribution activities. While this global expansion of the supply chain is occurring, firms are also trying to expand their control of the supply chain to include second- and third-tier suppliers and customers. Thus supply chain expansion is occurring on two fronts: increasing the breadth of the supply chain to include foreign manufacturing, office, and retail sites, along with foreign suppliers and customers; and increasing the depth of the supply chain to include second- and third-tier suppliers and customers.

With advances and improvements in communication technology, manufacturing, and transportation, more and more companies around the globe have the capability to produce and sell high-tech parts and products and move these quickly to world markets as demand develops. Trade agreements such as the European Union, the World Trade Organization, and the North American Free Trade Agreement have also facilitated the production and movement of goods between countries; and this has enabled firms to easily expand their supply bases and their markets. New software tools and "market makers" such as Perfect Commerce and FreeMarkets Online, who bring buyers and suppliers together in e-marketplace reverse auctions, have also helped to expand supply chains considerably and easily, using the Internet. Over the past few years, a rapid expansion of the global marketplace has occurred; and this pace should continue as new market enablers, producers, customers, and transportation infrastructures come into the global picture.

e-BUSINESS CONNECTION
PERFECT COMMERCE[16]

Perfect Commerce, Inc., headquartered in Palo Alto, California, provides a holistic approach to supply management for its customers, which includes supply planning and collaboration, sourcing event execution, and supplier performance management. The front-end planning and collaboration work captures critical stakeholder input, while the supplier performance management activities ensure that suppliers meet commitments and deliver ongoing value for their customers. Through these sourcing arrangements, customers can save from 10 to 40 percent in purchase costs and achieve cycle time reductions of 25 to 50 percent.

Perfect Commerce has a number of purchasing-oriented software products available for users, such as Perfect Supply Manager™, which includes supplier selection, request for quote creation and distribution, and supplier performance measurement capabilities; and Perfect Bid Manager™, a self-serve, Web-based reverse auction, which is capable of providing multiple-product bidding, multicurrency bidding, and value-adjusted pricing, along with multisource award assessments.

Additionally, as firms become more comfortable and experienced with their supply chain relationships with immediate suppliers and customers, there is a tendency to expand the depth or span of the supply chain by creating relationships with second- and third-tier suppliers and customers. This span expansion phenomenon is just now taking place in most industries and should continue to increase as the practice of supply chain management matures. In a survey of firms already practicing supply chain management, about one-third of the respondents stated that they practiced supply chain management with second-tier suppliers, while somewhat fewer practiced supply chain management with second-tier customers.[17]

Increasing Supply Chain Responsiveness

Agile manufacturing, JIT, mass customization, efficient consumer response, and *quick response* are all terms referring to concepts that are intended to make the firm more flexible and responsive to customer requirements and changes. Particularly with the tremendous levels of competition in almost all avenues of business, firms (and their supply chains) are looking today at ways to become more responsive to their customers. To achieve greater levels of customer responsiveness, supply chains must identify the end customers' needs, look at what the competition is doing and position the supply chain's products and services to successfully compete, and then consider the impact of these requirements on the supply chain participants and the intermediate products and services they provide. Once these issues have been adequately addressed among the firms in the supply chain, additional improvement in responsiveness comes from designing more effective and faster product and service delivery systems as products are passed through the supply chain and by continuously monitoring changes occurring the marketplace and using this information to reposition the supply chain to stay competitive.

Saying these things is easy, but improving customer responsiveness requires firms to reevaluate their supply chain relationships, to utilize business process reengineering, to reposition warehouses, design new products and services, reduce new product design cycles, standardize processes and products, empower and train workers in multiple skills, build customer feedback into daily operations, and, finally, link together all of the supply chain participants' information and communication systems. So, very quickly, you can see that achieving high levels of customer satisfaction through responsiveness requires potentially significant changes not only in firm culture but also in the technical aspects of providing products, services, and information throughout the supply chain. This remains a significant and ongoing challenge for supply chain effectiveness. Today, Web-based systems are proving to be ideal for connecting supply chain members efficiently. One such tool is Formation Systems' Optiva 4.0, a Web-based product life cycle management platform that provides business intelligence and collaboration from product concept through introduction to improvement. It can be integrated within a supply chain to help products get to market faster.[18]

The Greening of Supply Chains

Producing, packaging, moving, storing, repackaging, and delivering products to their final destinations can pose a significant threat to the environment in terms of discarded packaging materials, carbon monoxide emissions, noise, traffic congestion, and other forms of industrial pollution. As the practice of supply chain management becomes more widespread, firms and their supply chain partners will be working harder to reduce these environmental problems. In fact, relationships between companies in an integrated supply chain are much more conducive to taking a more proactive approach to reducing the negative environmental consequences of producing, moving, and storing products as they move through the supply chain.

Over time, consumer sentiment toward environmentally friendly processes has tended to increase, making this topic one of concern for companies managing their supply chains. As mentioned in one study, 75 percent of U.S. consumers say their purchasing decisions are impacted by a firm's environmental reputation.[19] Additionally, companies are finding that pollution control activities and waste reduction can reduce cost.

Added to this increasing concern and awareness among the general public for environmentally friendly business processes is the growing cost of natural resources such as wood products, oil, and natural gas. Strategies to successfully compete under these conditions include using recyclable materials in products; using returnable and reusable containers and pallets; using recyclable and reusable packaging materials; managing returns along the supply chain efficiently; designing effective transportation, warehousing, and break-bulk/repackaging strategies; and using environmental management systems from initial producer to final consumer in the supply chain. The benefits of these activities will include lower systemwide costs, fewer duplicate activities, marketing advantages, less waste, and, ultimately, better customer satisfaction.

Reducing Supply Chain Costs

Considering again the objectives of supply chain management, cost reduction is clearly high on this list of priorities. Cost reduction can be achieved throughout the supply chain by reducing waste as already described, by reducing purchasing costs, and by reducing excess inventories and non-value-adding activities among the supply chain participants. As supply chains become more mature, they tend to improve their performance in terms of these cost reduction activities through use of continuous improvement efforts, better supply chain communication, and a further integration of processes.

As time passes, supply chain costs continue to decrease due to trial and error, increased knowledge of the supply chain processes, use of technology to improve information flow and communication, **benchmarking** other successful supply chains to copy what they are doing well, and continued performance measurement and improvement efforts. The purchasing function among supply chain participants will continue to be viewed as a major strategic contributor to cost reduction through better supplier evaluation techniques, value engineering and analysis in product design and production, standardization and reduction of parts and materials, and through make-or-buy decisions. Finally, the transportation and logistics function will also play a major role in cost reduction along the supply chain through better design of the distribution networks and more efficient use of third-party logistics service providers.

Summary

Supply chain management is the integration of key business processes from initial raw material extraction to the final or end customer, including intermediate processing, transportation, and storage activities and final sale to the end customer. Today, the practice of supply chain management is becoming extremely important to achieve and maintain competitiveness. Many firms are just now beginning to realize the advantages of supply chain integration. Supply chain management is an outgrowth and expansion of logistics and purchasing activities and has grown in popularity and use since the 1980s. Important elements in supply chain management are in the areas of purchasing, operations and production, and distribution. Finally, as markets, political forces, technology, and competition change around the world, the practice of supply chain management must also change.

Key Terms

benchmarking, 20
bullwhip effect, 10
business process reengineering (BPR), 11
customer relationship management, 15
demand management, 14
distribution network, 15
enterprise resource planning (ERP), 14
global supply chains, 17
integrated logistics, 12
inventory visibility, 14
just-in-time production system, 14
material requirements planning (MRP), 14

operating exposure, 17
process integration, 10
pull-type production system, 14
push-type production system, 14
quick response, 12
reverse logistics activities, 5
second-tier suppliers and customers, 9
service response logistics, 12
strategic partnerships, 13
supplier certification, 13
supplier evaluation, 13

supplier management, 13
supply chain, 5
supply chain integration, 16
supply chain performance measurement, 17
third-party service providers, 12
total quality management (TQM), 15
transportation management, 15
vertically integrated firm, 4

Discussion Questions

1. Why is supply chain management more popular today than, say, twenty years ago?
2. How can a small business like a local sandwich or bicycle shop benefit from supply chain management?
3. Do you think larger firms can succeed more easily than smaller firms in supply chain management? Why or why not?
4. What role do you think "trust" plays in the practice of supply chain management?
5. Is supply chain management just another passing business "fad" or is it here to stay? Why?
6. What are the differences between the terms *purchasing, logistics, inventory management,* and *supply chain management?*

7. Can nonprofit, educational, or government organizations benefit from supply chain management? How?

8. How do the firm's customers benefit from supply chain management? What about the final or end customers?

9. Could a firm have more than one supply chain?

 ## Internet Questions

1. Visit the Web sites that are posted to the textbook's Web site for this chapter and describe five different supply chain management applications or activities that are highlighted in the Web sites.

2. Go to a good Internet search engine like Google™ and search on the term *supply chain management.* How many hits did you get? Write a report discussing five of the various Web sites shown in the search.

3. Go to http://www.aginnovationcenter.org and discuss the current state of supply chain management in New Zealand.

References

Burgess, R. "Avoiding Supply Chain Management Failure: Lessons from Business Process Reengineering." *The International Journal of Logistics Management* 9, no. 1 (1998): 15–24.

Chopra, S., and P. Meindl. *Supply Chain Management: Strategy, Planning, and Operation.* N.J.: Prentice-Hall, 2001.

Frazelle, E. *Supply Chain Strategy: The Logistics of Supply Chain Management.* New York: McGraw-Hill, 2002.

Hammer, M., and J. Champy. *Reengineering the Corporation.* London: Nicholas Brealey, 1993.

Handfield, R. B., and E. L. Nichols. *Introduction to Supply Chain Management.* N.J.: Prentice-Hall, 1999.

Lambert, D. M., M. C. Cooper, and J. D. Pagh. "Supply Chain Management: Implementation Issues and Research Opportunities." *The International Journal of Logistics Management* 9, no. 2 (1998): 1–19.

Lee, H. L., V. Padmanabhan, and S. Whang. "Information Distortion in a Supply Chain: The Bullwhip Effect." *Management Science* 43, no. 4 (1997): 546–58.

Simchi-Levi, D., P. Kaminsky, and E. Simchi-Levi. *Designing and Managing the Supply Chain.* New York: McGraw-Hill, 2000.

Stevens, G. C. "Integrating the Supply Chain." *International Journal of Physical Distribution and Logistics Management* 19, no. 8 (1989): 3–8.

Tan, K. C. "A Framework of Supply Chain Management Literature." *European Journal of Purchasing and Supply Management* 7, no. 1: 39–48.

Notes

1. J. T. Mentzer, W. DeWitt, J. S. Keebler, S. Min, N. W. Nix, C. D. Smith, and Z. G. Zacharia, "Defining Supply Chain Management," *Journal of Business Logistics* 22, no. 2 (2001): 1–25.

2. Dr. W. L. (Skip) Grenoble, Executive Director of the Center for Supply Chain Research, in an interview in S. Mason, "Innovation, Economy & Supply Chain," *Global Cosmetic Industry* 171, no. 3 (2003): 22–25.

3. T. Stein and J. Sweat, "Killer Supply Chains," *Informationweek* (9 November 1998): 36–46. Used with permission.

4. Printed with the permission of Li & Fung.

5. Reprinted with permission of the publisher, the Institute for Supply Management™, "Glossary of Key Purchasing and Supply Terms" (2000).

6. Courtesy of the Supply-Chain Council, Inc.

7. Courtesy of the Council of Logistics Management.

8. H. L. Lee and C. Billington, "The Evolution of Supply-Chain Management Models and Practice at Hewlett-Packard," *Interfaces* 25, no. 5 (1995): 42–63.

9. A. Zieger, "Don't Choose the Wrong Supply Chain Partner," *Frontline Solutions* 4, no. 6 (2003): 10–14.

10. K. C. Tan, S. B. Lyman, and J. D. Wisner, "Supply Chain Management: A Strategic Perspective," *International Journal of Operations and Production Management* 2, no. 6 (2002): 614–31.

11. Robert V. Delany, Twelfth Annual "State of Logistics Report," presented to the National Press Club, Washington, D.C., (4 June 2001).

12. O. R. Keith and M. D. Webber, "Supply-Chain Management: Logistics Catches Up with Strategy," *Outlook* (1982), cit. M. G. Christopher, *Logistics, The Strategic Issue* (London: Chapman and Hall, 1992).

13. S. Hill, "Taming the Beast," *MSI* 20, no. 5 (2002): 38–44.

14. S. Hill, "Taming the Beast," *MSI* 20, no. 5 (2002): 38–44.

15. S. Konicki, "Shopping for Savings," *Information Week* (1 July 2002): 36–45.

16. Information obtained from the Perfect Commerce Web page: http://www.perfect.com

17. M. C. Mejza and J. D. Wisner, "The Scope and Span of Supply Chain Management," *The International Journal of Logistics Management* 12, no. 2 (2001): 37–55.

18. S. Mason, "Innovation, Economy & Supply Chain," *Global Cosmetic Industry* 171, no. 3 (2003): 22–25.

19. R. Lamming and J. Hampson, "The Environment As a Supply Chain Management Issue," *British Journal of Management* 7 (Special Issue, 1996): S45–62.

20. Copyright © 1994 President and Fellows of Harvard College (the Beer Game board version) and © 2002 The MIT Forum for Supply Chain Innovation (the Beer Game computerized version). Interested students can visit http://beergame.mit.edu to learn more about the Beer Game and to play the computerized version of the game. Students can also read J. H. Hammond, "The Beer Game: Board Version," Harvard Business School case #9-694-104, rev. 27 October 1999 for more information.

Appendix 1.1

The Beer Game[20]

The Beer Game has become a very popular game played in operations management and supply chain management courses, since it was developed by MIT in the 1960s. The game simulates the flow of product and information in a simple supply chain consisting of a retailer, a wholesaler, a distributor, and a manufacturer. One person plays each supply chain partner. The game is used to illustrate the importance of supply chain communication and information with respect to inventories along the supply chain.

Each supply chain participant follows the same set of activities:

1. The participant forecasts customer demand for the upcoming weeks and then orders beer from his supplier (or schedules beer production if he is the manufacturer), which then takes several weeks to materialize.

2. The participant manages inventories as best he can to minimize back-order and inventory carrying costs.

3. The participant fills his customer orders each week and creates back orders if demand cannot be met.

Figure A1.1 illustrates the supply chain, showing the transportation and information delays. There is no transportation delay from the retailer to the end customer. For the other supply chain members, there is a two-week transportation delay from customer's order to the shipment receipt. It also takes two weeks to complete a production lot at the factory, which would then be ready to fill customer orders.

Figures A1.2 through A1.5 show the game boards for the four players and Table A1.1 shows the inventory record sheet for each player. Here is how the game progresses:

Starting conditions. To start the game, we assume that each member (except the manufacturer) has twelve cases of beer in current inventory (or ending inventory if using Table A1.2), four cases in the second week's delay of incoming shipments, and four cases in the first week's delay of incoming shipments. The manufacturer has twelve cases of beer in current or ending inventory, four cases of beer in the second week's production delay, and four cases in the first week's production delay. Each prayer also

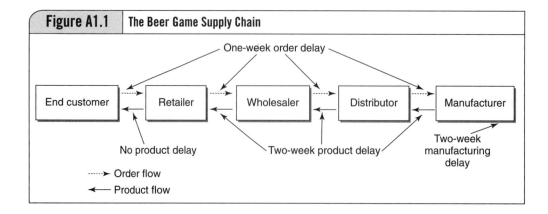

Figure A1.1 | **The Beer Game Supply Chain**

One-week order delay

End customer — Retailer — Wholesaler — Distributor — Manufacturer

No product delay

Two-week product delay

Two-week manufacturing delay

·····▶ Order flow
◀——— Product flow

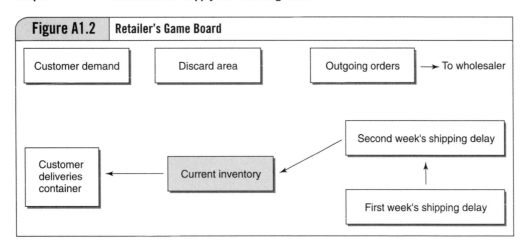

Figure A1.2 | **Retailer's Game Board**

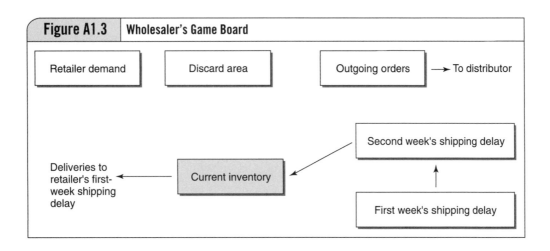

Figure A1.3 | **Wholesaler's Game Board**

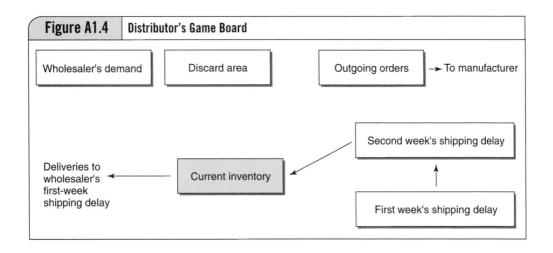

Figure A1.4 | **Distributor's Game Board**

Figure A1.5 | Manufacturer's Game Board

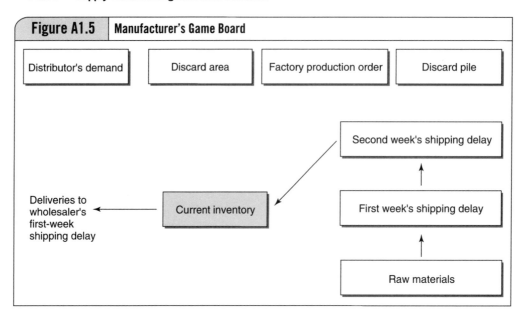

Table A1.1 | Inventory Record Sheet

Your Supply Chain Company:

Your Name: Team Name:

Week	Ending Inventory	Back Orders
1		
2		
3		
4		
5		
6		
7		
8		
9		
10		
11		
12		
13		
14		
15		
16		
17		
18		
19		
20		
Totals		

Note: Ending inventories must be zero when you have a back order. If ending inventory is greater than zero, back orders must equal zero. Back orders equal previous period back orders plus incoming order minus current inventory.

At end of game: Sum inventories and back orders and determine total cost as Total inventory ($1) + total back orders ($2) = $_____.

has an *outgoing order* of four cases sitting in his outgoing order box (or production order box). The retailer must start with twenty weeks of end-customer demand (or longer), provided by the game coordinator or instructor.

1. Each member *ships his beer.* He moves the cases of beer from the second week's delay to current (or beginning) inventory and from the first week's delay to the second week's delay. For the manufacturer, move beer from the second week's production delay to current (or beginning) inventory and from the first week's production delay to the second week's production delay.

2. Each member *gets his customer orders.* The retailer reads his customer demand, then places the card face down in the discard area; the retailer then *fills the order (plus any back orders)* by moving beer cases from current (or beginning) inventory to the customer delivery container (an area off the board). The retailer then records the ending inventory amount and any current back orders in the columns provided on the Inventory Record Sheet (and Table A1.2 if it is being used). Next, the retailer *sends last week's outgoing order* to the wholesaler's incoming order box. Finally, the retailer *decides how much to order* by writing an order on the order sheet provided and placing it face down in the outgoing order box.

   When the wholesaler gets the retailer's order, the firm follows the same steps as above: it *fills the order and any back orders* from current (or beginning) inventory (note that this increases the number of cases in the retailer's first week's shipping delay), it *records the ending inventory and back orders,* it *sends last week's outgoing order* to the distributor, and then it *decides how much to order* and places the order sheet face down in the outgoing order box.

   The distributor goes through the same steps when it gets the order from the wholesaler. The manufacturer follows the same steps also, except instead of sending last week's outgoing order somewhere, it reads the outgoing order and fills the production request by transferring that number of cases from its raw materials storage area to the first week's production delay (it simply creates the cases needed for the order).

3. Repeat Steps 1 and 2 until the game limit is reached.

A typical game progresses in this fashion for twenty weeks. The game can be played with pennies to denote beer cases and sticky note pads for beer orders. Players can alternatively use only the second Inventory Record Sheet (Table A1.2) to track the game instead of the game board for convenience purposes. Players must take care not to talk to the other players during the game or to show what orders they are planning for the next week. The retailer must not peek at future end-customer demand data, provided by the instructor. Remember, this game illustrates what happens when no communication about future orders or order strategies occurs between supply chain members.

At the end of twenty weeks (or shorter if time does not permit), players determine the total cost of their inventories and back orders on the inventory record sheet (back orders cost $2 per unit per week, and inventories cost $1 per unit per week). Given these costs, the basic strategy should be to attempt to minimize total inventory and back-order costs, while forecasting the next period's demand accurately (as time progresses, firms can use their inventory record sheet demand information for forecasting purposes). The winning team is the team with the lowest total supply chain costs (inventory + back order).

Table A1.2	Alternate Inventory Management Sheet

[To be used when no game board is used]

Your Supply Chain Company:

Your Name: **Team Name:**

Incoming demand	Discard area					Outgoing orders

Week	Ending Inventory	Beginning Inventory	Back Orders	Second Week's Delay	First Week's Delay Updated	First Week's Delay Beginning
0	12		0	4	4	
1						
2						
3						
4						
5						
6						
7						
8						
9						
10						
11						
12						
13						
14						
15						
16						
17						
18						
19						
20						
Totals						

Note: Ending inventories must be zero when you have a back order. If ending inventory is greater than zero, back orders must equal zero. Back orders equal previous period back orders plus incoming order minus current inventory.

At end of game: Sum inventories and back orders and determine total cost as Total inventory ($1) + total back orders ($2) = $_____.

Beer Game Questions and Exercises

1. All players but the retailer should answer this question. What do you think the retailer's customer demand pattern looked like? How did your customer's orders vary throughout the game?

2. What happens to the current inventory levels as we move backward, up the supply chain from retailer to manufacturer? Why?

3. How could the supply chain members reduce total inventory and back-order costs in the future?

4. Go to http://beergame.mit.edu and play the Internet version of the game. Report on your experiences playing the game.

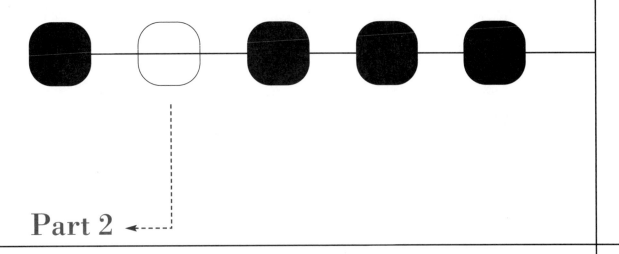

Part 2

Purchasing Issues in Supply Chain Management

Case Studies

Chapter 2:

PURCHASING MANAGEMENT

Purchasing is by far the largest single function at AT&T. Nothing we do is more important.[1]

It's no secret that electronics OEMs are increasingly turning to purchasing to reduce cost. After all, about 60–70 percent of a typical electronics company's revenue is spent with the production suppliers that purchasing manages.[2]

Learning Objectives

After completing this chapter, you should be able to

- Describe the role of purchasing and understand its impact on an organization's competitive advantage.
- Have a basic knowledge of the manual purchasing process and e-procurement.
- Understand and know how to handle small value purchase orders.
- Understand sourcing decisions and the factors impacting supplier selection.
- Understand the pros and cons of single versus multiple sourcing.
- Describe centralized, decentralized, and hybrid purchasing organizations and their advantages.
- Describe and understand how globalization impacts purchasing, and describe and understand the opportunities and challenges of global sourcing.
- Understand total cost of ownership and be able to select suppliers using more than unit price alone.

Chapter Outline

Introduction

The Role of Purchasing in an Organization

The Purchasing Process
  The Manual Purchasing System
  Electronic Procurement Systems (e-Procurement)
  Small Value Purchase Orders

Sourcing Decisions: The Make-or-Buy Decision
  Reasons for Buying or Outsourcing
  Reasons for Making
  The Make-or-Buy Break-Even Analysis

Roles of Supply Base

Supplier Selection

How Many Suppliers to Use
  Reasons Favoring a Single Supplier
  Reasons Favoring More than One Supplier

Purchasing Organization: Centralized versus Decentralized Purchasing
  Advantages of Centralization
  Advantages of Decentralization

International Purchasing/Global Sourcing
  Reasons for Global Sourcing
  Potential Challenges for Global Sourcing
  Countertrade

Stategic Purchasing at Medical Solutions

Siemens, founded in 1847 and headquartered in the Federal Republic of Germany, is an electronics and electrical engineering company employing more than 450,000 people in 190 countries. Their annual sales for fiscal year 2001 were €87 billion (€ is the symbol for euro). Approximately 22 percent of the sales were from Germany, whereas 30 percent each came from the United States and other parts of Europe. Siemens spent about €41 billion, or 47 percent of sales for the year on purchases of production materials, systems components, software, and services. Its diverse business portfolio is segmented into the following areas: information and communications, automation and control, power, transportation, medical, lighting, and financial and real estate. The medical segment, Medical Solutions (Med), provides a broad spectrum of products, solutions, and services for the health-care industry.[3]

Prior to 1997, buyers at Medical Solutions' decentralized purchasing system bought components and materials for their individual plants without communicating and considering the needs of other segments or divisions within the same segment. Purchasers and suppliers were rarely involved in new product design and development. Purchasing was considered strictly a tactical supporting function, and there were no synergies with the design and manufacturing facilities. Purchasing's responsibility was simply to ensure that the right material was available in the right place, at the right time, and at the right price. The decentralized purchasing system missed out on opportunities to leverage purchases of common items among the various business units. It had no long-term contracts with strategic suppliers or control over prices.

When Dietmar Dresp, vice president of strategic purchasing, was hired in 1997, he transformed Medical Solutions' purchasing function into a strategic purchasing organization. The goals of the organization were to leverage Medical Solutions' material purchases with suppliers, exploit the technical expertise of suppliers, and form long-term mutually beneficial relationships with strategic suppliers. Purchasing engineers were hired to work with design engineers and suppliers in product design and development. Eight material groups, each headed by a manager, were formed to handle strategic sourcing of production materials.

The new centralized strategic purchasing structure reduced Medical Solutions' material costs by 25 percent and cut its supplier base by 50 percent to 2,500 over a three-year period. Keys to the strategic efforts included outsourcing, supplier base reduction, strategic alliances, supplier performance evaluation, and supplier involvement in new product design and development. With its new strategic purchasing organization, Medical Solutions drastically reduced its product development and manufacturing cycle times. For example, Medical Solutions' newest ultrasound product, the SONOLINE Antares, is built in hours, whereas previous generations of the equipment took days to manufacture.[4]

Introduction

In the context of supply chain management (SCM), purchasing can be defined as the act of obtaining merchandise; capital equipment; raw materials; services; or maintenance, repair, and operating (MRO) supplies in exchange for money or its equivalent. Purchasing can be broadly classified into two categories—**merchants** and **industrial buyers.** The first category, merchants, includes the wholesalers and retailers, who primarily purchase for resale purposes. Generally, merchants purchase their merchandise in volume to take advantage of quantity discounts and other incentives such as transportation economy and storage efficiency. They create value by consolidating merchandise, breaking bulk, and providing the essential logistical services. The second category is the industrial buyers, whose primary task is to purchase raw materials for conversion purposes. Industrial buyers also purchase services;

capital equipment; and maintenance, repair, and operating supplies. The typical industrial buyers are the manufacturers, although some service firms such as restaurants, landscape gardeners, and florists also purchase raw materials for conversion purposes. Indeed, the Annual Survey of Manufactures[5] shows that the cost of materials exceeded value added through manufacturing. Therefore, it is not surprising that purchasing concepts and theories that evolved over the last two decades focused on the efficiency and effectiveness of industrial buyers' purchases of raw materials.

The primary focus of this chapter is the industrial buyer. This chapter describes the role of purchasing in an organization, the processes of a traditional manual purchasing system and the common documents used, how an electronic purchasing system works, various strategies for handling small order problems, the advantages and disadvantages of centralized versus decentralized purchasing systems, sourcing issues including supplier selection, and other important topics affecting the role of purchasing in supply chain management.

The Role of Purchasing in an Organization

Traditionally, purchasing was regarded as being a service to production, and corporate executives paid limited attention to issues concerned with purchasing. However, as global competition intensified in the 1980s, executives realized the impact of large quantities of purchased material and work-in-process inventories on manufacturing cost, quality, new product development, and delivery lead time. Savvy managers adopted new supply chain management concepts that emphasized purchasing as a key strategic business process rather than a narrow specialized supporting function to overall business strategy.

The *Annual Survey of Manufactures* (Table 2.1), conducted by the U.S. Census Bureau, shows that manufacturers spent more than 50 percent of each sales dollar (shown as "value of shipments") on raw materials from 1977 to 2000. Purchases of raw materials actually exceeded value added through manufacturing (shown as "manufacture"), which accounted for slightly less than 50 percent of sales. Purchases as a percent of sales dollars for merchants are expected to be much higher since merchandise is primarily bought for resale purposes. Unfortunately, aggregate statistics for merchants are not readily available.

However, individual information can easily be obtained from the annual reports of publicly traded companies, either directly or from the U.S. Securities and Exchange Commission (SEC). For example, Wal-Mart Stores, Inc., reported that its cost of sales was more than 78 percent of its net sales for both fiscal years ended January 31, 2002 and 2001. This ratio shows the potential impact of purchasing on a company's profits. Therefore, it is obvious that many successful businesses are treating purchasing as a key strategic process.

The primary goals of purchasing are to ensure uninterrupted flows of raw materials at the lowest total cost, to improve quality of the finished goods produced, and to optimize customer satisfaction. Purchasing can contribute to these objectives by actively seeking better materials and reliable suppliers, working closely with and exploiting the expertise of strategic suppliers to improve the quality of raw materials, and involving suppliers and purchasing personnel in new product design and development efforts. Purchasing is the crucial link between the sources of supply and the organization itself, with support coming from overlapping activities to enhance manufacturability for both the customer and the supplier. The involvement of purchasing and strategic suppliers in concurrent engineering activities is essential for selecting components and raw materials that ensure that requisite quality is designed into the product and to aid in collapsing design-to-production cycle time.

Table 2.1	Cost of Materials as a Percentage of the Value of Shipments						
Year	Value of Shipments $ Millions	Cost of Materials $ Millions	%	Manufacture $ Millions	%	Capital Expenditures $ Millions	%
2000	$4,217,852	$2,231,622	52.9%	$2,002,649	47.5%	$154,914	3.7%
1999	4,031,885	2,084,316	51.7	1,954,498	48.5	150,325	3.7
1998	3,899,810	2,018,055	51.7	1,891,266	48.5	152,708	3.9
1997	3,834,701	2,015,425	52.6	1,825,688	47.6	151,510	4.0
1996	3,715,428	1,975,362	53.2	1,749,662	47.1	146,468	3.9
1995	3,594,360	1,897,571	52.8	1,711,442	47.6	134,318	3.7
1994	3,348,019	1,752,735	52.4	1,605,980	48.0	118,665	3.5
1993	3,127,620	1,647,493	52.7	1,483,054	47.4	108,629	3.5
1992	3,004,723	1,571,774	52.3	1,424,700	47.4	110,644	3.7
1991	2,878,165	1,531,221	53.2	1,341,386	46.6	103,153	3.6
1990	2,912,227	1,574,617	54.1	1,348,970	46.3	106,463	3.7
1989	2,840,376	1,532,330	53.9	1,325,431	46.7	101,894	3.6
1988	2,695,432	1,444,501	53.6	1,269,313	47.1	84,706	3.1
1987	2,475,939	1,319,845	53.3	1,165,741	47.1	85,662	3.5
1986	2,260,315	1,217,609	53.9	1,035,437	45.8	80,795	3.6
1985	2,280,184	1,276,010	56.0	1,000,142	43.9	91,245	4.0
1984	2,253,429	1,288,414	57.2	983,228	43.6	80,660	3.6
1983	2,045,853	1,170,238	57.2	882,015	43.1	67,480	3.3
1982	1,960,206	1,130,143	57.7	824,118	42.0	77,046	3.9
1981	2,017,543	1,193,970	59.2	837,507	41.5	83,767	4.2
1980	1,852,668	1,093,568	59.0	773,831	41.8	74,625	4.0
1979	1,727,215	999,158	57.8	747,481	43.3	65,797	3.8
1978	1,522,937	877,425	57.6	657,412	43.2	58,346	3.8
1977	1,358,526	782,418	57.6	585,166	43.1	51,907	3.8

Source: "Statistics for Industry Groups and Industries: 2000," *Annual Survey of Manufactures* U.S. Census Bureau, (11 February 2002):1.

The Purchasing Process

The traditional purchasing process is a manual, paper-based system. However, with the advent of information technology, personal computers, local area networks, and the Internet, many companies are moving toward a more automated, electronic-based system. The goal of a proper purchasing system is to ensure the efficient transition of information from the users to the purchasing personnel and, ultimately, to the suppliers. Once the information is transmitted to the appropriate suppliers, the system must also ensure the efficient flows of the purchased materials from the suppliers to the users, and the flow of invoices from the suppliers to the accounting department. Finally, the system must have an internal control mechanism to prevent abuse of the system. For example, purchase orders (POs) should be prenumbered and issued in duplicate, and buyers should not be authorized to pay invoices. Prenumbered purchase orders make it easier to trace any missing or unaccounted-for purchase order. A duplicate purchase order should be issued to the accounting department for internal control purposes and to inform the department of a future payment or commitment of resources.

The Manual Purchasing System

Figure 2.1 shows a simplified traditional manual purchasing system. While some manual systems may look slightly different than what is shown in Figure 2.1, it captures the essential elements of a good purchasing system. The manual purchasing system is slow and prone to errors due to duplications of data entries during various stages of the purchasing process. For

Figure 2.1	Traditional Manual Purchasing System

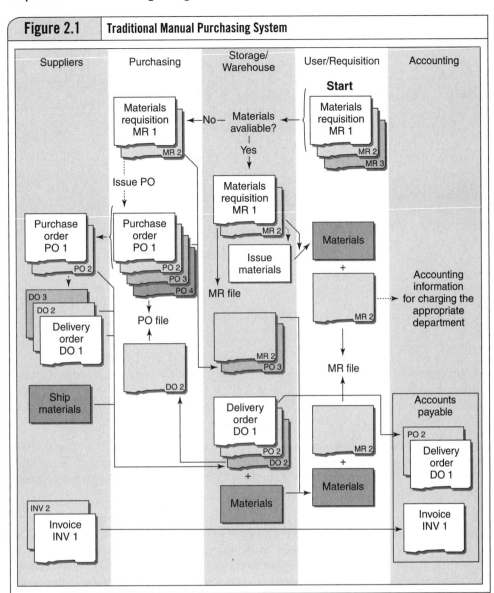

example, similar information on the material requisition, such as the product description, is reproduced on the purchase order.

The Material Requisition

The purchasing process starts when the material user initiates a request for a material by issuing a **material requisition (MR)** in duplicates. A **purchase requisition,** instead of a material requisition, is used in some firms. The product, quantity, and delivery due date are clearly described on the material requisition. The number of duplicates issued depends on the internal accounting control system of the organization. Generally, the issuer retains a copy and the warehouse receives the original plus a duplicate. The duplicate accompanies the material as it moves from the warehouse to the user. This copy also provides the essential information for the accounting department to charge the appropriate user for the material.

While most requisitions are transmitted through the generic material requisition, a **traveling requisition** is used for materials and standard parts that are requested on a recurring basis. Instead of describing the product on the generic material requisition, the product description

"We need 100,000 pencils. Or does
this say 100? Go ahead and order
and I'll let you know later."

and other pertinent information, such as delivery lead time and lot size, are preprinted on the traveling requisition. When a resupply is needed, the user simply enters the quantity and date needed and submits it to the warehouse. Once the resupply information is recorded, the traveling requisition is returned to the user for future requests.

Planned order releases from the material requirements planning (MRP) and/or a **bill of materials (BOM)** can also be used to release requisitions or to place orders directly with the suppliers. This approach is appropriate for firms that use the same components to make standard goods over a relatively long period of time.

If the requested material is available in the warehouse, the material is issued to the user without going through the purchasing department. Otherwise, the requisition is assigned to the appropriate buyer who is responsible for the material. If there is a better substitute for the material, purchasing recommends to and works with the user to see if it is a viable substitute. However, purchasing personnel cannot change the specifications of the materials or parts without the user's knowledge and agreement. While it is the right and responsibility of purchasing personnel to select the appropriate supplier, the user in many cases suggests a list of potential suppliers. A sample material requisition is shown in Figure 2.2.

The Request for Quotation and the Request for Proposal

If the material is not available in the warehouse, the material requisition is channeled to the purchasing department. If there is no current supplier for the item, the buyer must identify a pool of qualified suppliers and issue a **request for quotation (RFQ)**. A **request for proposal (RFP)** may be issued instead for a complicated and highly technical component part, especially if the complete specification of the part is unknown. A request for proposal allows suppliers to propose new material and technology, thus enabling the firm to exploit the expertise of suppliers.

Figure 2.2	Sample Material Requisition

ABC Company
City, State ZIP

Purchase Requisition

RX #: 885967

Requestor: _____   Department: _____

Phone # : _____   Account #: _____   Date: _____

Suggested Vendor: _____

Address: _____ Phone: _____

No.	Description	Price	Quantity

Special instructions: _____

_____

_____

Approval Authority: _____ Date: _____

Distribution: White-Purchasing/Yellow-Purchasing(return to requestor)/Pink-Department

A growing trend among firms that practice supply chain management is **supplier development.** When there is a lack of suitable suppliers, firms may assist existing or new suppliers to improve their processing capabilities, quality, delivery, and cost performance by providing the needed technical and financial assistance. Developing suppliers in this manner allows firms to focus more on core competencies, while **outsourcing** noncore activities to suppliers.

The Purchase Order

When a suitable supplier is identified, or a qualified supplier is on file, the buyer issues a **purchase order** (**PO**) in duplicates to the selected supplier. Generally, the original purchase order and at least a duplicate are sent to the supplier. An important feature of the purchase order is the terms and conditions of the purchase, which is typically preprinted on the back. The purchase order is the buyer's offer and becomes a legally binding contract when accepted by the supplier. Therefore, firms should require the supplier to acknowledge and return a copy of the purchase order to indicate acceptance of the order. A sample purchase order is shown in Figure 2.3.

Figure 2.3	Sample Purchase Order

ABC Company
City, State ZIP

Purchase Order

PO #: 885729

Date: _____

Vendor:

Required Delivery Date: _____
Payment Terms: _____
FOB Terms: _____
Price Agreement No.: _____

Ship To:

Include PO # in all packages, invoice, shipping papers & correspondence. Mail original and one copy of invoice attached to second copy of Purchase Order for payment.

No.	Description	Unit Price	Quantity	Total Price
		Total $ of Order		

Buyer: _____   Phone: _____   Fax: _____

Buyer Signature: _____   Requisition No.: _____

SEE REVERSE FOR TERMS & CONDITIONS

Distribution: White-Vendor/Yellow-Vendor(return with invoice)/Pink & Blue-Purchasing/Green-Fixed Assets

The supplier may offer the goods at the supplier's own terms and conditions, especially if it is the sole producer or holds the patent to the product. Then, a supplier's **sales order** will be used. The sales order is the supplier's offer and becomes a legally binding contract when accepted by the buyer.

Once an order is accepted, purchasing personnel need to ensure on-time delivery of the purchased material by using a **follow-up** or by **expediting** the order. A follow-up is considered a proactive approach to prevent late delivery, whereas expediting is considered a reactive approach that is used to speed up an overdue shipment.

The Uniform Commercial Code (UCC) governs the purchase and sale of goods. The UCC applies only to legal situations arising in the United States, except in the state of Louisiana, which has a legal system based on the Napoleonic Code.

Electronic Procurement Systems (e-Procurement)

Electronic data interchange (EDI) was developed in the 1970s to improve the purchasing process. However, its proprietary nature required significant up-front investments. The rapid advent of Internet technology in the 1990s spurred the growth of nonproprietary and more flexible Internet-based e-procurement systems. Proponents of e-commerce argued that Internet-based systems would quickly replace the manual system, as we saw many e-commerce service providers rise rapidly in the late 1990s. Since then, there has been a shake-up among these companies as they have struggled to find a sustainable market. A large number of e-commerce firms saw their share values plummet in the early 2000s, and many are no longer in business. Critics argued that growth in e-commerce had been over-inflated, and the savings for users were inadequate to justify their time and investments. Today though, many well-managed e-commerce firms are beginning to thrive as users realize the benefits of their services.

Figure 2.4 describes an actual Internet-based business-to-business (B2B) electronic purchasing system used by some prominent resorts in Las Vegas, Nevada, to handle their purchases, ranging from low-cost office supplies to perishable foods and beverages and high-cost engineering items.[6] An e-commerce service provider provided the software and technology for the B2B purchases.

The material user initiates the e-procurement process by entering a materials request and other relevant information, such as quantity and date needed, into the material requisition module. Next, the materials requisition is printed out and submitted to a buyer at the purchasing department (or submitted electronically). The buyer reviews the materials requisition for accuracy and appropriate approval level. Upon satisfactory verification of the requisition, the buyer transfers the materials requisition data to the Internet-based e-procurement system and assigns qualified suppliers to bid on the requisition. The product description, closing dates, and bid conditions are specified on the requisition. Suppliers connected to the e-commerce system receive the bid instantaneously, while others can receive a faxed bid from the service provider. The purchasing department maintains a list of preferred suppliers for each category of material. The list can be edited and shared with other buyers. Thus, the buyer is capable of submitting bid requests to numerous suppliers within seconds.

Upon closing of the bids, the buyer reviews all the bids tendered through the Internet-based e-procurement system or fax and selects a supplier based on quality, cost, and delivery performance. Next, a purchase order is submitted electronically to the selected supplier if it is connected to the e-procurement system. Otherwise, a purchase order is printed and mailed to the supplier.

Advantages of the e-Procurement System

The traditional manual purchasing system is a tedious and labor-intensive task of issuing material requisitions and purchase orders. Although EDI solved some of these problems, its

Figure 2.4	**Internet-Based Electronic Purchasing System**

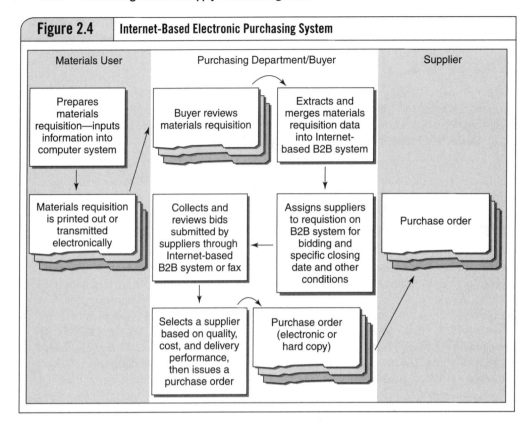

proprietary nature requires a high start-up cost, making it inaccessible to small firms with limited budgets. E-procurement systems have changed the infrastructure requirement, making it readily affordable to most firms. Benefits derived from implementing an e-procurement system include:

1. *Time savings:* E-procurement is more efficient when (1) selecting and maintaining a list of potential suppliers, (2) processing requests for quotation and purchase orders, and (3) making repeat purchases. Individual buyers can create preferred supplier lists for each category of products and services. For example, a small tools supplier group may consist of fifteen suppliers of small tools. The buyer uses this group to purchase small tools. The list can be edited and shared with all buyers in the firm. Supplier performance data can be updated quickly and made available on-line in real time. Collecting, sorting, reviewing, and comparing requests for quotation are labor-intensive and time-consuming processes. A typical firm may have to sort and match hundreds of bids on a daily basis. E-procurement eliminates these non-value-adding collection and sorting activities. Duplicate data entry on the purchase order is eliminated since the information is extracted from the request for quotation, originally entered by the user.

    The system can be programmed to handle automatic bidding of frequently ordered items on a fixed interval, such as daily or weekly. The ability to submit automatic bidding is invaluable for handling perishable goods, which must be ordered in small lot sizes, and other frequently purchased items where the specifications are known.

2. *Cost savings:* Buyers can generate more purchases, and the manual task of matching bids to materials requisitions is eliminated. Other cost savings include lower prices of goods and services since more suppliers can be contacted, reduced inventory costs due to the ability to purchase on a more frequent basis, fewer purchasing staff, lower administrative costs, and faster order fulfillment.

3. *Accuracy:* The system eliminates double-key inputs—once by the materials users and then once again by the buyers. The system also enhances the accuracy of communications between buyers and suppliers. More information on goods and services are readily available on-line.

4. *Real time:* The system enables buyers to initiate bids and suppliers to respond in real time on a 24-hour, 7-days-per-week basis. Once the material requisition is processed, the buyer can post the bid immediately, instead of waiting to contact all the suppliers individually to alert them of the bids.

5. *Mobility:* The buyer can submit, process, and check the status of bids, as well as communicate with suppliers regardless of the buyer's geographical location and time of day. Thus, the e-procurement system is highly flexible.

6. *Trackability:* Audit trails can be maintained for all transactions in electronic form. Tracing an electronic bid and transaction is much easier and faster than tracking paper trails. Buyers and suppliers can ask for additional information on-line, leave comments, or indicate whether they are interested in bidding.

7. *Management:* The system can be designed to store important supplier information, including whether suppliers are minority or locally owned, thus allowing the buyers to support such businesses. Summary statistics and supplier performance reports can be generated for management to review and utilize for future planning.

8. *Benefits to the suppliers:* Benefits include lower barriers to entry and transaction costs, access to more buyers, and the ability to instantly adjust to market conditions, thus making e-procurement attractive to most suppliers.

The e-Business Connection box features an e-procurement benchmarking tool provided by the Center for Advanced Purchasing Studies.

E-BUSINESS CONNECTION
THE EC[3] BENCHMARKING PROCESS

The Center for Advanced Purchasing Studies (CAPS)[7] and e-procurement solutions provider Ariba, Inc., jointly developed an e-procurement benchmarking process known as the eC[3] for tracking e-purchasing activities. The benchmarking process collects, compares, and captures a list of key performance indicators from companies that have implemented e-procurement applications. Results of the benchmarking studies are available at *http://www.ecaps.org*. eC[3] tracks e-procurement of both direct and indirect materials on a monthly basis, and the results are consolidated into a quarterly report. The data are collected automatically by embedding a code into a participating company's ERP or procurement software. The captured data are automatically transmitted to CAPS Research.

The latest survey[8] showed that more than 3.37 million e-procurement transactions were recorded, totaling more than $16.5 billion in 2002. The benchmarking study provides a means for companies to better understand how their e-procurement systems are working and how their system compares with others. This information is very useful for companies that are considering implementing an e-procurement system, particularly after the bursting of the dot-com bubble and the collapse of many Internet firms in 2001. In a recent poll of 350 firms by Forrester Research and the Institute for Supply Management,[9] businesses reported that they purchased 8.3 percent of indirect materials over the Internet during the first quarter of 2002, compared to 9.5 percent in the previous quarter.

Small Value Purchase Orders

The administrative costs to process an order can be quite substantial. It has been estimated that the cost of placing an order using the manual purchasing system could be as high as $175.[10] The figure could be higher when we consider the salary of senior purchasing personnel and other indirect costs incurred by purchasing personnel. It is not uncommon to find that the cost to process a purchase order exceeds the total dollar value of the order itself. While small dollar value is a relative term depending on the size of the firm, $500 to $1,000 can be considered a reasonable cutoff point.

Small value purchases, particularly in a manual system, should be minimized to ensure that buyers are not overloaded with unnecessary purchases that may compromise the firm's competitive position. Due to the efficiency of the e-procurement system, buyers are less likely to be overburdened by small value purchases. To control unnecessary administrative costs and reduce order cycle time, purchasing managers have various alternatives to deal with small value purchases. Generally, the alternatives are used for purchase of office supplies and other indirect materials. Let us review the alternatives.

Procurement Credit Card/Corporate Purchasing Card

Procurement credit cards or **corporate purchasing cards** are credit cards with a predetermined credit limit, usually not more than $1,000 depending on the organization, issued to authorized personnel of the buying organization. American Express and Diners Club cards are commonly used for this purpose. The card allows the material user to purchase the material directly from the supplier, without going through purchasing. Usually, the user must purchase the needed materials from a list of authorized suppliers where prices have been set.

When authorized, the card can also be used to pay for meals, lodging, and other traveling expenses, thus eliminating the need to process travel expenses in advance for the user. At the end of the month, an itemized statement is sent either to purchasing or directly to the accounting department.

Blank Check Purchase Orders

A **blank check purchase order** is a special purchase order with a signed blank check attached, usually at the bottom of the purchase order. It is clearly printed on the check that it is not valid for over a certain amount, usually $500 or $1,000. When the material is shipped, the supplier enters the amount due on the check and cashes it. When the exact amount of the purchase is known, the user or buyer usually enters the amount on the check before passing it to the supplier.

Blanket or Open-End Purchase Orders

A **blanket purchase order** covers a variety of items and is negotiated for repeated supply over a fixed time period, such as quarterly or yearly. The subtle difference of an **open-end purchase order** is that additional items and expiration dates can be renegotiated. Price and estimated quantity for each item, as well as other conditions, are usually negotiated and incorporated in the order. A variety of mechanisms, such as a **blanket order release** or production schedule, may be used to release a specific quantity against the order. Blanket or open-end purchase orders are suitable for buying maintenance, repair, and operating (MRO) supplies and office supplies. At a fixed interval, usually monthly, the supplier sends a detailed statement of all releases against the order to the buying firm for payment.

Stockless Buying or System Contracting

Stockless buying or **system contracting** is an extension of the blanket purchase order. It requires the supplier to maintain a minimum inventory level to ensure that the required items are readily available for the buyer. It is considered stockless to the buyer because the burden of keeping the inventory is on the supplier. Some firms require suppliers to keep inventory at the buyer's facilities to minimize order cycle time.

Petty Cash

Petty cash is a small cash reserve maintained by a clerk or midlevel manager. Material users generally purchase needed materials and then claim the purchase against the petty cash by submitting the receipt to the petty cashier. A benefit of this system is that the exact reimbursement is supported by receipts.

Standardization and Simplification of Materials and Components

Where appropriate, purchasing should work with design, engineering, and operations to seek opportunities to standardize materials, components, and supplies to increase the usage of standardized items. For example, a car manufacturer could design different models of automobiles to use the same starter mechanism, thus increasing its usage and reducing the need for multiple item storage space, while allowing for large quantity price discounts. This will also reduce the number of small value purchases for less frequently used items.

Simplification refers to reduction of the number of components, supplies, or standard materials used in the product or process during product design. For example, an engine starter manufacturer could design all of its starter models to use a single type of housing or solenoid. Thus, simplification can further reduce the number of small value purchases while reducing storage space requirements, as well as allowing for quantity purchase discounts.

Accumulating Small Orders to Create a Large Order

Numerous small orders can be accumulated and mixed into a large order, especially if the material request is not urgent. Otherwise, purchasing can simply increase the order quantity if the ordering cost exceeds the inventory holding cost. Larger orders also frequently reduce the purchase price and unit transportation cost.

Using a Fixed Order Interval for Specific Categories of Materials/Supplies

Another effective way to control small orders is to group materials and supplies into categories and then set fixed order intervals for each category. Order intervals can be set to biweekly or monthly depending on usage. Instead of requesting individual materials or supplies, users request the appropriate quantity of each item in the category on a single requisition to be purchased from a supplier. This increases the dollar value and decreases the number of small orders.

Sourcing Decisions: The Make-or-Buy Decision

While the term *outsourcing* popularly refers to buying materials and components from suppliers instead of making them in-house, it also refers to buying materials or components that were previously made in-house. In recent years, the trend has been moving toward outsourcing combined with the creation of supply chain relationships, although traditionally firms preferred the *make* option by using backward integration and forward integration. **Backward integration** refers to acquiring sources of supply, whereas **forward integration** refers to acquiring customers' operations. For example, an end-product manufacturer acquiring a supplier's operations that supplied component parts is an example of backward integration. Acquiring a distributor or other outbound logistics providers would be an example of forward integration.

Whether to **make or buy** materials or components is a strategic decision that can impact an organization's competitive position. It is obvious that most organizations buy their MRO and office supplies rather than make the items themselves. Similarly, seafood restaurants usually buy their fresh seafood from fish markets. However, the decision on how to acquire highly complex engineering parts that impact the firm's competitive position is a complicated one.

Traditionally, cost has been the major driver when making sourcing decisions. However, organizations today focus more on the strategic impact of the sourcing decision on the firm's competitive advantage. For example, Honda would not outsource the making of its engines because it considers engines to be a vital part of its automobiles' performance and reputation. However, Honda may outsource the production of brake drums to a high-quality, low-cost supplier that specializes in brake drums. Generally, organizations outsource noncore activities while focusing on core competencies. Finally, the make-or-buy decision is not an exclusive either-or option. Firms can always choose to make some components or services in-house and buy the rest from suppliers.

Reasons for Buying or Outsourcing

Organizations buy or outsource materials, components, and/or services from suppliers for many reasons. Let us review these now:

1. *Cost advantage:* For many firms, cost is an important reason for buying or outsourcing, especially for supplies and components that are nonvital to the organization's operations and competitive advantage. This is usually true for standardized or generic supplies and materials for which suppliers may have the advantage of economy of scale because they supply the same item to multiple users. In most outsourcing cases, the quantity needed is so small that it does not justify the investment in capital equipment to make the item. Some foreign suppliers may also offer a cost advantage because of lower labor and/or materials costs.

2. *Insufficient capacity:* A firm may be running at or near capacity, making it unable to produce the components in-house. This can happen when demand grows faster than anticipated or when expansion strategies fail to meet demand. The firm buys parts or components to free up capacity in the short term to focus on vital operations. Firms may even subcontract vital components and/or operations under very strict terms and conditions in order to meet demand. When managed properly, subcontracting is an effective means to expand short-term capacity.

3. *Lack of expertise:* The firm may not have the necessary technology and expertise to manufacture the item. Maintaining long-term technological and economical viability for noncore activities may be affecting the firm's ability to focus on core competencies. Suppliers may hold the patent to the process or product in question, thus precluding the make option, or the firm may not be able to meet environmental and safety standards to manufacture the item.

4. *Quality:* Purchased components may be superior in quality because suppliers have better technology, process, skilled labor, and the advantage of economy of scale. Suppliers may be investing more in research and development. Suppliers' superior quality may help firms stay on top of product and process technology, especially in high-technology industries with rapid innovation.

Reasons for Making

An organization also makes its own materials, components, services, and/or equipment in-house for many reasons. Let us briefly review these reasons:

1. *Protect proprietary technology:* A major reason for the make option is to protect proprietary technology. A firm may have developed an equipment, product, or process that needs to be protected for the sake of competitive advantage. Firms may choose not to reveal the technology by asking suppliers to make it, even if it is patented. An advantage of not revealing the technology is to be able to surprise competitors and bring new products to market ahead of competition, allowing the firm to charge a price premium. For example, Intel or Advanced Micro Devices are not likely to ask suppliers to manufacture their new central processing units.

2. *No competent supplier:* If the component does not exist, or suppliers do not have the technology or capability to produce it, the firm may have no choice but to make an item in-house, at least for the short term. The firm may use supplier development strategies to work with a new or existing supplier to produce the component in the future as a long-term strategy.

3. *Better quality control:* If the firm is capable, the make option allows for the most direct control over the design, manufacturing process, labor, and other inputs to ensure that high-quality components are built. The firm may be so experienced and efficient in manufacturing the component that suppliers are unable to meet its exact specifications and requirements. On the other hand, suppliers may have better technology and processes to produce better-quality components. Thus, the sourcing option ensuring a higher quality level is a debatable question and must be investigated thoroughly.

4. *Use existing idle capacity:* A short-term solution for a firm with excess idle capacity is to use the excess capacity to make some of its components. This strategy is valuable for firms that produce seasonal products. It avoids laying off skilled workers and, when business picks up, the capacity is readily available to meet demand.

5. *Control of lead-time, transportation, and warehousing cost:* The make option provides easier control of lead-time and logistical costs since management controls all phases of the design, manufacturing, and delivery processes. Although raw materials may have to be transported, finished goods can be produced near the point of use, for instance, to minimize holding cost.

6. *Lower cost:* If technology, capacity, and managerial and labor skills are available, the make option may be more economical if large quantities of the component are needed on a continuing basis. Although the make option has a higher fixed cost due to capital investment, it has a lower variable cost because it precludes suppliers' profits.

The Make-or-Buy Break-Even Analysis

The current sourcing trend is to buy equipment, materials, and services unless self-manufacture provides a major benefit such as protecting proprietary technologies, achieving superior characteristics, or ensuring adequate supplies. However, buying or outsourcing has its own shortcomings, such as loss of control and exposure to supplier risks. While cost is rarely the sole criterion in strategic sourcing decisions, **break-even analysis** is a handy tool for computing the cost-effectiveness of sourcing decisions, when cost is the most important criterion. Several assumptions underlie the analysis: (1) all costs involved can be classified under either fixed or variable cost, (2) fixed cost remains the same within the range of analysis, (3) a linear variable cost relationship exists, (4) fixed cost of the make option is higher because of capital investment in equipment, and (5) variable cost of the buy option is higher because of supplier profits.

Consider a hypothetical situation in which a company has the option to make or buy a component part. Its annual requirement is 15,000 units. A supplier is able to supply the part at $7 per unit. The firm estimates that it costs $500 to prepare the contract with the supplier. To make the part, the firm must invest $25,000 in equipment and the firm estimates that it costs $5 per unit to make the part.

Costs	Make Option	Buy Option
Fixed cost	$25,000	$500
Variable cost	5	7

Annual requirements = 15,000

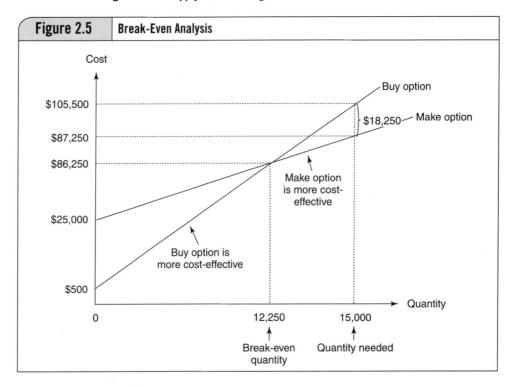

| Figure 2.5 | Break-Even Analysis |

The break-even point Q is found by setting the two options equal to one another and solving for Q (see Figure 2.5):

$$
\begin{aligned}
\text{Total cost to make} &= \text{Total cost to buy} \\
\$25,000 + \$5Q &= \$500 + \$7Q \\
7Q - 5Q &= 25,000 - 500 \\
2Q &= 24,500 \text{ units} \\
\text{Break-even point } Q &= 12,250 \text{ units}
\end{aligned}
$$

1. Total cost at break-even point, TC_{BE} = $\$25,000 + \$5 \times 12,250$
   = $\$86,250$
2. Total cost for make option, TC_M = $\$25,000 + \$5 \times 15,000$
   = $\$87,250$
3. Total cost for buy option, TC_B = $\$500 + \$7 \times 15,000$
   = $\$105,500$

The analysis shows that the break-even point is 12,250 units. Total cost at the break-even point is $86,250. If the requirement is less than 12,250 units, it is cheaper to buy. It is cheaper to make the parts if the firm needs more than 12,250 units. With small purchase requirements (less than 12,250 units), the low fixed cost of the buy option makes this option attractive. With higher purchase requirements (greater than 12,250 units), the low variable cost of the make option makes this option more attractive. The analysis shows that the firm should make the item since the quantity is large enough to warrant the capital investment.

Roles of Supply Base

The **supply base** or **supplier base** refers to the list of suppliers that a firm uses to acquire its materials, services, supplies, and equipment. Firms engaging in supply chain management emphasize long-term strategic supplier alliances by reducing the variety of purchased items and consolidating volume into one or fewer suppliers, resulting in a smaller supply base. For example, both Xerox and Chrysler reduced their supply bases by about 90 percent in the 1980s. An effective supply base that complements and contributes to a firm's competitive advantage is critical to its success. Savvy purchasing managers develop a sound supply base to support the firm's overall business and supply chain strategies, based on an expanded role for the supplier. It is thus vital to understand the strategic role of suppliers.

Besides supplying the obvious purchased items, preferred or top-performing suppliers also supply

1. product and process technology and knowledge to support the buyer's operations, particularly in product design—termed **early supplier involvement;**
2. information on the latest trends in materials, processes, or designs;
3. information on the supply market, such as shortages, price increases, or political situations that may threaten supplies of vital materials;
4. capacity for meeting unexpected demand; and
5. cost efficiency due to economies of scale, since the supplier is likely to produce the same item for multiple buyers.

When developing and managing the supply chain, high-performance suppliers are found or developed to provide these services and play a very important role in the success of the supply chain.

Supplier Selection

The decision of which supplier to use for office supplies or other noncritical materials is likely to be an easy one. However, the process of selecting a group of competent suppliers for important materials, which can potentially impact the firm's competitive advantage, is a complex one and should be based on multiple criteria. In addition to cost and delivery performance, firms should also consider how suppliers can contribute to product and process technology. Factors that firms should consider while selecting suppliers include:

1. *Product and process technologies:* Suppliers should have up-to-date and capable products, as well as process technologies to produce the material needed.
2. *Willingness to share technologies and information:* With the current trend that favors outsourcing to exploit suppliers' capabilities and to focus on core competencies, it is vital that firms seek suppliers that are willing to share their technologies and information. Suppliers can assist in new product design and development through early supplier involvement to ensure cost-effective design choices, develop alternative conceptual solutions, select the best components and technologies, and help in design assessment. By increasing the involvement of the supplier in the design process, the buyer is free to focus more attention on core competencies.
3. *Quality:* Quality levels of the purchased item should be a very important factor in supplier selection. Product quality should be high and consistent since it can directly affect the quality of the finished goods.
4. *Cost:* While unit price of the material is not typically the sole criterion in supplier selection, total cost of ownership is an important factor. Total cost of ownership includes the unit price of the material, payment terms, cash discount, ordering cost, carrying cost, logistical costs, maintenance costs, and other more qualitative costs that may not be easy to assess. An example of total cost analysis is provided at the end of the chapter. Total cost analysis demonstrates how other costs beside unit price can affect purchase decision.
5. *Reliability:* Besides reliable quality levels, reliability refers to other supplier characteristics. For example, is the supplier financially stable? Otherwise, it may not

be able to invest in research and development or stay in business. Is the supplier's delivery lead time reliable? Otherwise, production may have to be interrupted due to shortage of material.

6. *Order system and cycle time:* How easy to use is a supplier's ordering system, and what is the normal order cycle time? Placing orders with a supplier should be easy, quick, and effective. Delivery lead time should be short, so that small lot sizes can be ordered on a more frequent basis to reduce inventory holding costs.

7. *Capacity:* The firm should also consider whether the supplier has the capacity to fill orders to meet requirements and the ability to fill large orders if needed.

8. *Communication capability:* Suppliers should also possess a communication capability that facilitates communication between the parties.

9. *Location:* Geographical location is another important factor in supplier selection, as it impacts delivery lead-time, transportation, and logistical costs. Some organizations require their suppliers to be located within a certain distance from their facilities.

10. *Service:* Suppliers must be able to back up their products by providing good services when needed. For example, when product information or warranty service is needed, suppliers must respond on a timely basis.

There are numerous other factors, some strategic while others tactical, that a firm must consider when choosing suppliers. The days of using competitive bidding to identify the cheapest supplier for strategic items are long gone. The ability to select competent strategic suppliers directly impacts a firm's competitive success. Strategic suppliers are trusted partners and become an integral part of the firm's design and production efforts.

How Many Suppliers to Use

The issue of how many suppliers to use for each purchased item is a complex one. While numerous references propose the use of a single source for core materials and supplies to facilitate buyer-supplier partnerships, **single-sourcing** can be a very risky proposition. Although Xerox and Chrysler had substantially reduced their supply base in the 1980s, it was not documented that the firms resorted to single-sourcing for their vital materials and components. Current trends in sourcing favor using fewer sources, although not necessarily a single source. Theoretically, firms should use single or a few sources whenever possible to enable the development of close relationships with the best suppliers. However, by increasing reliance on one supplier, the firm increases its risk that poor supplier performance will result in plant shutdowns or poor quality finished products. A comparison follows of some of the reasons favoring the use of a single supplier versus using two or more suppliers for a purchased item.

Reasons Favoring a Single Supplier

1. *To establish a good relationship:* Using a single supplier enables the firm to establish a good, trusting, and mutually beneficial relationship, especially when the firm can benefit from the supplier's technology and capabilities. Sometimes, firms reduce their supply base for a particular material to a single source, making it easier to establish a strategic alliance relationship.

2. *Less quality variability:* Since the same technology and processes are used to produce the parts when using a single source, variability in the quality levels is less than if the parts are purchased from multiple suppliers.

3. *Lower cost:* Buying from a single source concentrates purchase volume with the supplier, typically lowering the purchase cost per unit. Single-sourcing also avoids duplicate fixed costs, especially if the component requires special tooling or expensive setups.

4. *Transportation economies:* Because single-sourcing concentrates volume, the firm can take advantage of full-truckload shipments, which are cheaper per unit than the less-than-truckload rate. By moving up to full truckloads, the firm has the option of using both rail and motor carriers. Rail carriers are more efficient for hauling heavy loads over long distances.

5. *Proprietary product or process purchases:* If it is a proprietary product or process, or if the supplier holds the patents to the product or process, the firm has no choice but to buy from the sole or single source.

6. *Volume too small to split:* If the requirement is too small in terms of quantity or dollar value, it is not worthwhile to split the order among different suppliers. Single-sourcing is also a good approach for acquiring nonvital supplies and services.

Reasons Favoring More than One Supplier

1. *Need capacity:* When demand exceeds the capacity of a single supplier, the firm has no choice but to use multiple sources.

2. *Spread the risk of supply interruption:* Multiple sources allow the firm to spread the risk of supply interruptions due to a strike, quality problem, political instability, or other supplier problems.

3. *Create competition:* Using multiple sources encourages competition among suppliers in terms of price and quality. While modern supplier management philosophy discourages the use of multiple sources simply to create competition, this may still be the preferred approach for sourcing nonvital items that do not impact the firm's competitive advantage. Using a single source to develop alliances for these types of purchases may not be cost effective.

4. *Information:* Multiple suppliers usually have more information about market conditions, new product developments, and new process technologies. This is particularly important if the product has a short product life cycle.

5. *Dealing with special kinds of businesses:* The firms, particularly government contractors, may need to give portions of their purchases to small, local, or women- or minority-owned businesses, either voluntarily or as required by law.

The number of suppliers to use for one type of purchase has changed from the traditional multiple suppliers to the more modern use of fewer, reliable suppliers and even to the extent of using sole or single suppliers. Relationships between buyers and suppliers traditionally were short-term, adversarial, and based primarily on cost, resulting in mutual lack of trust. Buyer-supplier relationships, particularly in integrated supply chain settings, have evolved today into trusting, cooperative, and mutually beneficial long-term relationships. Firms today reduce their supply base to only the best suppliers, while further developing suppliers who are continuously improving on the variability of their quality, delivery, service, price, and information performance.

Purchasing Organization: Centralized versus Decentralized Purchasing

Purchasing organization within the firm has evolved over the years as the responsibilities of the purchasing component of firms changed from a clerical, supporting role to playing an integral role in business strategy development. In addition to the actual buying process, purchasing is now involved in product design, production decisions, and other aspects of a firm's operations. The decision of how to organize purchasing to best serve its purpose is firm, industry-specific, and dependent on many factors, such as market conditions and the types of materials required. Purchasing structure can be viewed as a continuum, with centralization at one extreme and decentralization at the other. While there are few firms that adopt a pure centralized or decentralized structure, the benefits of each are worth a closer examination. The current trend is toward purchasing centralization for the vital materials where firms can take advantage of economies of scale and other benefits.

Centralized purchasing is where a purchasing department located at the firm's corporate office makes all the purchasing decisions, including order quantity, pricing policy, contracting, negotiations, and supplier selection and evaluation. **Decentralized purchasing** is where individual, local purchasing departments, such as at the plant level, make their own purchasing decisions. A discussion of advantages and disadvantages to each of these purchasing structures follows.

Advantages of Centralization

1. *Concentrated volume:* An obvious benefit is the concentration of purchase volume to create quantity discounts, less-costly volume shipments, and other more favorable purchase terms. This is often referred to as **leveraging purchase volume.** A centralized system also provides the purchasing organization more clout and bargaining power. Suppliers generally are more willing to negotiate, give better terms, and share technology due to the higher volume.

2. *Avoid duplication:* Centralized purchasing eliminates the possibility of duplication of job functions, since the purchasing personnel are situated in a centralized location. A corporate buyer can research and issue a large purchase order to cover the same material requested by numerous units, thus eliminating duplication of activities. This also results in fewer buyers, reducing labor costs.

3. *Specialization:* Centralization allows buyers to specialize in a particular group of items instead of being responsible for all purchased materials and services. It allows buyers to spend more time and resources to research materials for which they are responsible, thus becoming specialized buyers.

4. *Lower transportation costs:* Centralization allows larger shipments to be made to take advantage of truckload shipments, and yet smaller shipments still can be arranged for delivery directly from suppliers to the points of use.

5. *No competition within units:* Under the decentralized system, when different units purchase the same material, a situation may be created in which units are competing among themselves, especially when scarce materials are purchased from the same supplier. Centralization minimizes this problem.

6. *Common supply base:* A common supply base is used, thus making it easier to manage and to negotiate contracts.

The Global Perspectives box highlights Whirlpool's strategy of centralized purchasing of maintenance, repair, and operating supplies.

Advantages of Decentralization

1. *Closer knowledge of requirements:* A buyer at the individual unit is more likely to know its exact needs better than a central buyer at the home office.

2. *Local sourcing:* If the firm desires to support local businesses, it is more likely that a local buyer will know more about local suppliers. Use of local suppliers can also result in faster delivery and more frequent times and is conducive to the creation of closer supplier relationships.

3. *Less bureaucracy:* Decentralization allows quicker response, due to less bureaucracy, and closer contact between the user and the buyer. Coordination and communication with operations and other divisions are more efficient.

Global Perspective

CENTRALIZED PURCHASING AT WHIRLPOOL[11]

In the mid-1990s, Whirlpool Corp. utilized a decentralized purchasing organization for its maintenance, repair, and operating (MRO) supplies. Each manufacturing division was responsible for buying its own MRO supplies, although commonality existed among items purchased by the various manufacturing divisions. However, in 1997, a centralized procurement organization was formed for indirect materials under the leadership of Roy Armes, corporate vice president for global procurement. Whirlpool spent from $750 million to $1 billion annually on indirect materials and services.

Whirlpool estimated that the centralized purchasing organization helped to reduce costs by 11 percent annually. The centralized purchasing strategy for MRO focused on identifying strategic suppliers and consolidating the company's supplier base. The company also monitored supplier performances in several key areas, including cost reduction, product and service quality, contract compliance, and supplier leadership. The success of the reorganization has prompted Whirlpool to expand the centralized purchasing organization toward partnering with a more global and diverse supplier base in 2002.

Thus, while centralized purchasing may result in lower costs and better negotiating power, the centralized system may also be too rigid and even infeasible for large, multiunit organizations consisting of several unrelated business operations. For these reasons, a **hybrid purchasing organization** that is both decentralized at the corporate level and centralized at the business unit level may be warranted. The hybrid purchasing organization allows the firm to exploit the advantages of both the centralized and decentralized systems. For example, Siemens, featured at the beginning of this chapter, could decentralize its purchasing at the corporate level and utilize centralized purchasing at each of its seven segments.

International Purchasing/Global Sourcing

International agreements aimed at relaxing trade barriers and promoting free trade have provided opportunities for firms to expand their supply bases to participate in **global sourcing.** Indeed, world merchandise trade and commercial services trade reached $6.186 trillion and $1.435 trillion, respectively in 2000.[12] That year, the United States was the world's largest importer and exporter for both merchandise trade (exports were $781.1 billion; imports were $1.26 trillion) and commercial services (exports were $274.5 billion; imports were $198.9 billion). While global sourcing provides opportunities to improve quality, cost, and delivery performance, it also poses unique challenges for purchasing personnel. Engaging in global sourcing requires additional skills and knowledge to deal with international suppliers, logistics, communication, political, and other issues not usually encountered in domestic sourcing.

Various methods are employed for global sourcing. It is not limited to setting up an international purchasing office or using the existing purchasing personnel to handle the transactions in-house. An **import broker or sales agent,** who will perform transactions for a fee, can be used. Import brokers do not take title to the goods. Instead, title passes directly from the seller to the buyer. International purchasers can also buy foreign goods from an **import merchant,** who will buy and take title to the goods, and then resell them to the buyer. Purchasing from a **trading company,** which carries a wide variety of goods, is another option.

Total Cost of Ownership Concept

Total cost of ownership is more than just the purchase price; other qualitative and quantitative factors, including freight and inventory costs, tooling, tariffs and duties, currency exchange fees and fluctuations, payment terms, maintenance, and nonperformance costs must be considered. Firms can use total cost analysis as a negotiation tool to inform suppliers regarding areas where they need to improve.

An Example

Kuantan ATV, Inc., assembles five different models of all terrain vehicles (ATVs) from various ready-made components to serve the Las Vegas, Nevada, market. The company uses the same engine for all its ATVs. The purchasing manager, Ms. Henderson, needs to choose a supplier for engines for the coming year. Due to the size of the warehouse and other administrative restrictions, she must order the engines in lot sizes of 1,000 each. The unique characteristics of the standardized engine require special tooling to be used during the manufacturing process. Kuantan ATV agrees to reimburse the supplier for the tooling. This is a critical purchase, since late delivery of engines would disrupt production and cause 50 percent lost sales and 50 percent back orders of the ATVs. Ms. Henderson has obtained quotes from two reliable suppliers but needs to know which supplier is more cost-effective. She has the following information:

Requirements (annual forecast)	12,000 units
Weight per engine	22 pounds
Order processing cost	$125/order
Inventory carrying rate	20 percent per year
Cost of working capital	10 percent per year
Profit margin	18 percent
Price of finished ATV	$4,500
Back-order cost	$15 per unit

Two qualified suppliers have submitted the following quotations:

Unit Price	Supplier 1	Supplier 2
1 to 999 units/order	$510.00	$505.00
1,000 to 2,999 units/order	500.00	498.00
3,000 + units/order	490.00	488.00
Tooling cost	$22,000	$20,000
Terms	2/10, net 30	1/10, net 30
Distance	125 miles	100 miles
Supplier quality rating	2%	3%
Supplier delivery rating	1%	2%

Ms. Henderson also obtained the following freight rates from her carrier:

Truckload (TL = 40,000 lbs):	$0.80 per ton-mile
Less-than-truckload (LTL):	$1.20 per ton-mile

Note: Per ton-mile = 2,000 lbs per mile

Various international trade organizations are aimed at reducing tariff and nontariff barriers among member countries. A **tariff** is an official list or schedule showing the duties, taxes, or customs imposed by the host country on imports or exports. **Nontariffs** are import quotas, licensing agreements, embargoes, laws, and other regulations imposed on imports and exports. A discussion of three international trade organizations follows.

1. The *World Trade Organization (WTO)* is the largest and most visible international organization dealing with the global rules of trade between nations. It replaced the General Agreement on Tariffs and Trade (GATT) on January 1, 1995. Its primary goal is to ensure that international trade flows smoothly, predictably, and freely among member countries. The WTO Secretariat is based in Geneva, Switzerland. It has 144 member countries as of January 1, 2002.

The total cost analysis (see Figure 2.6) shows that Supplier 1 is more cost-effective, although its unit price and tooling costs are slightly higher than those of Supplier 2. The cash discount, quality cost, and delivery performance set Sup- plier 1 apart from Supplier 2. Using unit cost as the sole criterion to select a supplier would have cost Kuantan ATV $138,926.67 ($6,265,060.00 – $6,126,133.33).

Figure 2.6	Total Cost Analysis			
Description	**Supplier 1**		**Supplier 2**	
1. Total engine cost	12,000 units × $500	$ 6,000,000.00	12,000 units × $498	$5,976,000.00
2. Cash discount				
n/30	$6,000,000 × 10% × 30/360	$ 50,000.00	$5,976,000 × 10% × 30/360	$ 49,800.00
1/10	N/A		$5,976,000(10% × 10/360 + 1%)	$ 76,360.00
2/10	$6,000,000(10% × 10/360 + 2%)	$136,666.67	N/A	
Largest discount		$ (136,666.67)		$ (76,360.00)
3. Tooling cost		$ 22,000.00		$ 20,000.00
4. Transportation cost (22,000 lb LTL)	125 miles × 12,000 units × 22 lbs × $1.20/2000	$ 19,800.00	100 miles × 12,000 units × 22 lbs × $1.20/2000	$ 15,840.00
5. Ordering cost	12,000 / 1,000 × $125	$ 1,500.00	12,000 / 1,000 × $125	$ 1,500.00
6. Carrying cost	1,000 / 2 × $500 × 20%	$ 50,000.00	1,000 / 2 × $498 × 20%	$ 49,800.00
7. Quality cost	$6,000,000 × 2%	$ 120,000.00	$5,976,000 × 3%	$ 179,280.00
8. Delivery rating				
Back order (50%)	12,000 × 1% × 50% × $15	$ 900.00	12,000 × 2% × 50% × $15	$ 1,800.00
Lost sales (50%)	12,000 × 1% × 50% × $4,500 × 18%	$ 48,600.00	12,000 × 2% × 50% × $4,500 × 18%	$ 97,200.00
Total Cost		$6,126,133.33		$ 6,265,060.00

2. The *North American Free Trade Agreement (NAFTA)* was implemented on January 1, 1994. Its goal was to remove trade and investment barriers among the United States, Canada, and Mexico. Under NAFTA, all nontariff agricultural trade barriers between the United States and Mexico were eliminated and many tariffs were either eliminated or to be phased out in fifteen years. All tariffs affecting agricultural trade between the United States and Canada (with the exception of items covered by tariff-rate quotas) were removed by January 1, 1998.

3. *The European Union (EU)* was set up on May 9, 1950, and was comprised of Belgium, Germany, France, Italy, Luxembourg, and The Netherlands. Nine other nations (Denmark, Ireland, United Kingdom, Greece, Spain, Portugal, Austria, Finland, and Sweden) subsequently joined the EU. One of its primary goals is to

create a single market without internal borders for goods and services, allowing member countries to better compete with markets like the United States.

Reasons for Global Sourcing

Firms expand their supply base to include foreign suppliers for many reasons. These can include lower price, better quality, an overseas supplier holding the patent to the product, faster delivery to foreign units, better services, and better process or product technology.

A primary reason that many firms purchase from foreign suppliers is to lower the price of materials. As stated earlier, price generally is an important factor when purchasing standard materials and supplies that do not impact the competitive position of the firm. Many reasons can contribute to cheaper materials from overseas suppliers—for example, cheaper labor costs and raw materials, favorable exchange rates, more efficient processes, or intentional dumping of products by foreign suppliers in overseas markets.

Additionally, the quality of overseas products may be better due to newer and better product and process technologies. Further, while foreign suppliers may be located farther away, they may be able to deliver goods faster than domestic suppliers due to a more efficient transportation and logistical system. Foreign suppliers may even maintain inventory and set up support offices in the host country to compete with domestic sources and to provide better services.

Firms may buy from foreign suppliers to support the local economy where they have subsidiaries, or they may be involved in **countertrade,** in which the contract calls for the exchange of goods for raw materials from local suppliers (discussed later in more detail). While foreign purchasing may provide a number of benefits to the buyer, some problems may also be encountered when buying from foreign firms.

Potential Challenges for Global Sourcing

Over the last few decades, global sourcing has surged due to many factors, such as the improvement of communication and transportation technologies, the reduction of international trade barriers, and deregulation of the transportation industry. However, global sourcing poses additional challenges that purchasing must know how to handle effectively. For example, the complexity and costs involved in selecting foreign suppliers and dealing with duties; tariffs; custom clearance; currency exchange; and political, labor, and legal problems present sizable problems for the international buyer.

Unlike dealing with domestic suppliers, the costs involved in identifying, selecting, and evaluating foreign suppliers can be prohibitive. If the foreign supplier is located at a distant location, custom clearance, transportation, and other logistical issues may render delivery lead time unacceptable, especially for perishable goods.

In addition to the **Uniform Commercial Code (UCC),** which governs the purchase and sale of goods in the United States (except the state of Louisiana), global purchasers must also know the United Nations' **Contracts for the International Sale of Goods (CISG).** The CISG applies to international purchases and sales of goods, unless both parties elect to opt out. The UCC allows either party to modify the terms of acceptance for the purchase contract, but the terms of acceptance cannot be modified under the CISG.

Global purchasers must also deal with more complex shipping terms than domestic buyers. The International Chamber of Commerce created a uniform set of rules to simplify international transactions of goods with respect to shipping costs, risks, and responsibilities of buyer, seller, and shipper. The set of rules is called **incoterms** (International Commercial Terms). There are thirteen incoterms, grouped into four categories.

Countertrade

Global sourcing may involve countertrade, in which goods and/or services of domestic firms are exchanged for goods and/or services of equal value or in combination with currency from foreign firms. This type of arrangement is sometimes used by countries where there is a shortage of hard currency or as a means to acquire technologies. Countertrade transactions are more complicated than currency transactions because goods are exchanged for goods. The American Countertrade Association (ACA) was set up to assist the exchange of goods by bringing buyers and sellers together. The association provides a good definition of the various types of countertrade.[13]

The various forms of countertrade include barter, offset, and counterpurchase. **Barter** is the complete exchange of goods and/or services of equal value without the exchange of currency. The seller can either consume the goods and/or services or resell the items. **Offset** is an exchange agreement for industrial goods and/or services as a condition of military-related export. It is also commonly used in the aerospace and defense sectors. Offset can be divided into direct and indirect offsets. **Direct offset** usually involves coproduction, or a joint venture, and exchange of related goods and/or services; whereas **indirect offset** involves exchange of goods and/or services unrelated to the aerospace or defense sector. **Counterpurchase** is an arrangement whereby the original exporter either buys or finds a buyer to purchase a specified amount of unrelated goods and/or services from the original importer. Many developing countries mandate the transfer of technology as part of a countertrade or offset arrangement.

Summary

Over the last decade, the traditional purchasing function has evolved into an integral part of supply chain management. Purchasing is an important strategic contributor to overall business strategy. It is the largest single function in most organizations, controlling activities and transactions valued at more than 50 percent of sales. Every single dollar saved due to better purchasing impacts business operations and profits directly. Purchasing personnel talk to customers; users; suppliers; and internal design, finance, marketing, and operations personnel, in addition to top management. The information they gain from all this exposure can be used to help the firm to provide better, cheaper, and more timely products and services to both internal and external customers. Savvy business executives are thus turning to purchasing to improve business and supply chain performance.

Key Terms

backward integration, 43
barter, 55
bill of materials, 36
blank check purchase
  order, 42
blanket order release, 42
blanket purchase order, 42
break-even analysis, 45
centralized purchasing, 50
Contracts for the
  International Sale of
  Goods (CISG), 54
corporate purchasing
  cards, 42
counterpurchase, 55
countertrade, 54
decentralized purchasing,
  50
direct offset, 55
early supplier involvement,
  47
expediting, 39

follow-up, 39
forward integration, 43
global sourcing, 51
hybrid purchasing
  organization, 51
import broker or sales
  agent, 51
import merchant, 51
incoterms, 54
indirect offset, 55
industrial buyers, 32
leveraging purchase
  volume, 50
make or buy, 43
material requisition (MR),
  35
merchants, 32
nontariff, 52
offset, 55
open-end purchase order,
  42
outsourcing, 37

petty cash, 43
planned order release, 36
procurement credit cards,
  42
purchase order (PO), 38
purchase requisition, 35
request for proposal, 36
request for quotation, 36
sales order, 39
simplification, 43
single-sourcing, 48
stockless buying, 42
supplier base, 46
supplier development, 37
supply base, 46
system contracting, 42
tariff, 52
trading company, 51
traveling requisition, 35
Uniform Commercial Code,
  54

Discussion Questions

1. Describe the steps in a traditional manual purchasing system.
2. Describe the e-procurement system and its advantages over the manual system. Are there any disadvantages to the electronic system? Do you think the e-procurement system will ultimately replace the manual system? Why or why not?

3. Describe the purpose of a material requisition, a purchase order, a request for quotation, and a request for proposal. Is the material requisition serving the same purpose as the purchase order?

4. Why are small value purchase orders problematic? How can purchasing more effectively deal with this problem?

5. Should unit price be used as the sole criterion for selecting suppliers? Why or why not?

6. Explain backward vertical integration. What are the advantages of outsourcing compared to backward vertical integration?

7. When should a firm outsource instead of making the items in-house?

8. What factors should be considered while choosing suppliers?

9. What are the reasons to use a single supplier? Is this the most efficient way to purchase materials in general?

10. Describe centralized and decentralized purchasing and their advantages.

11. Why do firms purchase from foreign suppliers? What are the risks involved in global sourcing?

12. What is countertrade? Describe the various types of countertrade.

Internet Questions

1. Go to the World Trade Organization's Web site, and use the information to write a report that includes (a) the functions of the WTO, (b) the latest number of membership countries, (c) its relationship with GATT, (d) the number of countries that had originally signed the GATT by 1994, and (e) the last five countries that became members of the WTO.

2. Go to the NAFTA's Web site, and use the information to write a report that includes its brief history, objectives, and membership countries.

3. Go to the European Union's Web site, and use the information to write a report that includes its brief history, membership countries, and the euro.

4. Utilize the Internet to search for the thirteen incoterms. Write a report to explain the primary purpose of the terms in general, and then describe each of the thirteen terms individually.

Spreadsheet Problems

1. You are given the following information:

Costs	Make Option	Buy Option
Fixed cost	$125,000	$5,000
Variable cost	15	17

   a. Find the break-even quantity and the total cost at the break-even point.

   b. If the requirement is 150,000 units, is it more cost-effective for the firm to buy or make the components? What is the cost savings for choosing the cheaper option?

2. A Las Vegas, Nevada, manufacturer has the option to make or buy one of its component parts. The annual requirement is 20,000 units. A supplier is able to supply the parts for $10 per piece. The firm estimates that it costs $600 to prepare the contract with the supplier. To make the parts in-house, the firm must invest $50,000 in capital equipment, and the firm estimates that it costs $8 per piece to make the parts in-house.

   a. Assuming that cost is the only criterion, use break-even analysis to determine whether the firm should make or buy the item. What is the break-even quantity, and what is the total cost at the break-even point?

b. Calculate the total costs for both options at 20,000 units. What is the cost savings for choosing the cheaper option?

3. Given the following information, use total cost analysis to determine which supplier is more cost-effective. Late delivery of raw material results in 60 percent lost sales and 40 percent back orders of finished goods.

Order lot size	1,000
Requirements (annual forecast)	120,000 units
Weight per engine	22 pounds
Order processing cost	$125/order
Inventory carrying rate	20% per year
Cost of working capital	10% per year
Profit margin	15%
Price of finished goods	$4,500
Back-order cost	$15 per unit

Unit Price	Supplier 1	Supplier 2
1 to 999 units/order	$50.00	$49.50
1,000 to 2999 units/order	49.00	48.50
3,000 + units/order	48.00	48.00
Tooling cost	$12,000	$10,000
Terms	2/10, net 30	1/10, net 30
Distance	125 miles	100 miles
Supplier quality rating	2%	2%
Supplier delivery rating	1%	2%

Truckload (TL = 40,000 lbs): $0.85 per ton-mile

Less-than-truckload (LTL): $1.10 per ton-mile

Note: Per ton-mile = 2,000 lbs per mile

4. A buyer received bids and other relevant information from three suppliers for a vital component part for its latest product. Given the following information, use total cost analysis to determine which supplier should be chosen. Late delivery of the component results in 70 percent lost sales and 30 percent back orders of finished goods.

Order lot size	2,000
Requirements (annual forecast)	240,000 units
Weight per engine	40 pounds
Order processing cost	$200/order
Inventory carrying rate	20% per year
Cost of working capital	10% per year
Profit margin	15%
Price of finished goods	$10,500
Back-order cost	$120 per unit

Unit Price	Supplier 1	Supplier 2	Supplier 3
1 to 999 units/order	$200.00	$205.00	$198.00
1,000 to 2999 units/order	195.00	190.00	192.00
3,000 + units/order	190.00	185.00	190.00
Tooling cost	$12,000	$10,000	$15,000
Terms	2/10, net 30	1/15, net 30	1/10, net 20
Distance	120 miles	100 miles	150 miles
Supplier quality rating	2%	1%	2%
Supplier delivery rating	1%	1%	2%

Truckload (TL = 40,000 lbs): $0.95 per ton-mile

Less-than-truckload (LTL): $1.20 per ton-mile

Note: Per ton-mile = 2,000 lbs per mile

References

Burt, D. N., D. W. Dobler, and S. L. Starling. *World Class Supply Management: The Key to Supply Chain Management.* 7th ed. New York: McGraw-Hill Irwin, 2003.

Leenders, M. R., H. E. Fearon, A. E. Flynn, and P. F. Johnson. *Purchasing & Supply Management.* 12th ed. New York: McGraw-Hill Irwin, 2002.

Monczka, R., R. Trent, and R. Handfield. *Purchasing and Supply Chain Management.* 2nd ed. Cincinnati: South-Western, 2002.

Prahalad, C. K., and G. Hamel. "The Core Competence of the Corporation." *Harvard Business Review* 68, no. 3 (1990): 79–91.

Wisner, J. D., and K. C. Tan. "Supply Chain Management and Its Impact on Purchasing." *Journal of Supply Chain Management* 36, no. 4 (2000): 33–42.

Notes

1. S. Tully, "Purchasing's New Muscle," *Fortune* 131, no. 3 (20 February 1995): 75.
2. J. Carbone, "Electronics Design: Involve Buyers!" *Purchasing* 131, no. 5 (21 March 2002): 27.
3. *Annual Report 2001,* Siemens AG; available from http://www.siemens.com
4. J. Carbone, "Strategic Purchasing: Strategic Purchasing Cuts Costs 25% at Siemens," *Purchasing* 130, no. 18 (20 September 2001): 29, 32.
5. "Statistics for Industry Groups and Industries: 2000," *Annual Survey of Manufactures,* U.S. Census Bureau (11 February 2002): 1.
6. K. C. Tan and R. Dajalos, "Purchasing Strategy in the 21st Century: E-Procurement," *PRACTIX : Best Practices in Purchasing & Supply Chain Management* 4, no. 3 (2001): 7–12.
7. J. B. Shah, "CAPS Research Tracking Impact of e-Procurement," *EBN* 1311 (6 May 2002): 42.
8. eC^3 (accessed 11 April 2003); available from http://www.ecaps.org/2002cs.htm
9. A. Williams, "Why e-Procurement Makes Sense," *Financial Executive* 18, no. 7 (October 2002): 45–46.
10. Tan and Dajalos, "Purchasing Strategy."
11. S. Avery, "E-Procurement Helps Set Strategy That Cuts Costs," *Purchasing* 131, no. 4 (7 March 2002): 25–28.
12. World Trade Organization (September 2002); available from http://www.wto.org
13. American Countertrade Association (September 2002); available from http://www.countertrade.org

Chapter 3:

CREATING AND MANAGING SUPPLIER RELATIONSHIPS

If an airplane may be defined as "millions of parts flying together in close formation," then in my book, an aerospace company may be defined as one company and a few hundred of its best suppliers thinking and working in close harmony.[1]

In my mind, real partnerships require participation of a multifunctional group, as a formal team or as a process, where engineering, manufacturing, research, and even marketing get together with purchasing and become part of setting the expectations.[2]

Learning Objectives

After completing this chapter, you should be able to
- Explain the importance of supplier partnerships and strategic alliances.
- Understand the key factors for developing successful partnerships.
- Develop a supplier evaluation and certification program.
- Explain the importance of a supplier awards program.
- Understand the capabilities of supplier relationship management technology.
- Explain the benefits of using SRM software to manage suppliers.

Chapter Outline

Introduction

Developing Successful Partnerships
  Building Trust
  Shared Vision and Objectives
  Personal Relationships
  Mutual Benefits and Needs
  Commitment and Top Management Support
  Change Management
  Information Sharing and Lines of Communication
  Capabilities

  Performance Metrics
  Continuous Improvement

Supplier Evaluation and Certification
  The Weighted-Criteria Evaluation System
  ISO 9000
  ISO 14000

Supplier Development

Supplier Awards

Supplier Relationship Management Software

SUPPLY CHAIN MANAGEMENT IN ACTION   *The Dial Corporation*

The Dial Corporation, a $1.7 billion consumer products company based in Scottsdale, Arizona, employs more than 3,700 people and has manufacturing facilities in the United States and Latin America.[3] Dial's brands include Dial® soaps, Purex® laundry detergent, Renuzit® air fresheners, and Armour Star® canned meats. Dial's products are sold through supermarkets, mass merchandisers, drugstores, and club stores, with Wal-Mart as one of its biggest customers. The company's manufacturing locations are Fort Madison, Iowa; Los Angeles, California; Montgomery, Illinois; St. Louis, Missouri; and West Hazleton, Pennsylvania.

In 1996, the Dial Corporation split from Viad Corporation, its parent company, to focus on the consumer products business. A strategic plan was developed to guide Dial's growth into the twenty-first century. In a fast-paced and competitive environment, there is tremendous pressure to develop new products and introduce them to market ahead of the competition. With savvy consumers looking for value, Dial has to find and trim costs from the production systems. In this dynamic environment, it is imperative that purchasing has access to the best suppliers and be an integral part of the new product development process. As a result, Dial overhauled the purchasing function and moved toward a central sourcing strategy. Today, purchasing has taken a leadership role within the company's cross-functional strategy development process. Dial's overall purchasing goal is "to obtain the highest quality products and services, at the best value" for the company.[4]

According to Michael H. Hillman, CPO and senior vice president, "Dial has many suppliers that it works with strategically to tap the best of both corporations. Whether we're [single] sourcing a commodity product, or the supplier is large enough to our business that they may fine-tune or tailor their supply to our operations, purchasing meets with the suppliers' representatives to identify and review business opportunities. And we ask a lot of questions to ensure that we're not adding non-value-added cost to the system. It's as important to us that our suppliers make a healthy profit as it is that we make a profit."[5] Working closely with several of its strategic suppliers, Dial has implemented vendor-managed inventory programs at its sites. The inventory is kept at Dial's facilities but managed solely by its suppliers.

Dial was successful in its cost-savings effort by getting all employees involved in the process. The cost-savings program is entitled "Slay the dragon." Since employees receive bonuses depending on company profitability, it was relatively easy to get employees to buy into the program. All cost-savings ideas are submitted to purchasing for review. Then the ideas are prioritized based on how well they are aligned with the company's strategic goals.

As part of the restructuring effort, Dial reduced its supplier base, established close relationships with its key suppliers, increased its buying power by consolidating across different business units, and implemented innovative company-wide cost-reduction plans. Dial relies on single-sourcing for some of its products. For example, Dial uses a single contract manufacturer for its Renuzit Adjustable products and a single supplier for its Purex liquid laundry detergent containers.[6] Overall, the focus on purchasing has enabled Dial to reduce $100 million in total system costs over a five-year period, including $10 million in savings in 2001.[7]

Raw material costs have a significant impact on profitability. Since competition levels are high in most of Dial's markets, the company may not be able to raise prices of its products to compensate for increases in raw material prices. As such, managing raw material cost is critical for Dial. During the recent economic downturn, Dial was successful in controlling material costs due to its supplier consolidation efforts. According to Steven Tooker, vice president and general manager of laundry products, Dial had not raised prices yet in 2003 and did not plan to raise prices for the remainder of the year.[8]

Introduction

In today's competitive environment, as companies focus on their core competencies, the level of outsourcing will continue to rise. Increasingly, companies are requiring their suppliers to deliver innovative and quality products not only in just-in-time fashion but also at a competitive price. In the last two decades we have learned from the Japanese that good supplier relations can provide many benefits such as flexibility in terms of delivery, better quality, better information, and better material flows between buyers and suppliers. As part of its "Procurement Innovation 21" strategy, for instance, Fujitsu signed long-term agreements with suppliers to optimize price and delivery and guarantee increasing future orders and information exchange. As a result, Fujitsu reduced its supply base from 1,500 to 700 suppliers within a two-year period and expects to halve its inventory investment to $3.85 billion and increase its return on equity by 10 percent.[9]

A reader poll by *Purchasing Magazine* reports that "supply, sourcing, and purchasing professionals in companies nationwide believe strongly that more and stronger supplier partnerships are critical to achieving competitive corporate performance."[10] As such, companies are realizing the importance of developing win-win, long-term relationships with suppliers. It is critical that customers and suppliers develop stronger relationships and partnerships based on a strategic rather than a tactical perspective and then manage these relationships to create value for all participants. Successful partnerships with key suppliers can contribute to innovations and have the potential to create competitive advantage for the firm. Selecting the right supply partners and successfully managing these relationships over time is thus strategically important, and it is often stated that "a firm is only as good as its suppliers."

According to the Institute for Supply Management's glossary of terms, a supplier partnership "involves a mutual commitment over an extended time to work together to the mutual benefit of both parties, sharing relevant information and the risks and rewards of the relationship. These relationships require a clear understanding of expectations, open communication and information exchange, mutual trust, and a common direction for the future."[11] Good supplier relationships are just one ingredient necessary for developing an end-to-end integrated supply chain.

Developing Successful Partnerships

According to Kenichi Ohmae, founder and managing director of Ohmae & Associates, "Companies are just beginning to learn what nations have always known: in a complex, uncertain world filled with dangerous opponents, it is best not to go it alone."[12] **Strategic alliance** or partnership failure rates have often been reported to be as high as 60 percent. A survey of 455 CEOs by the Conference Board[13] identified the top eight reasons for failure of alliances: They were (1) overly optimistic and (2) characterized by poor communications; there was a (3) lack of shared benefits, (4) slow payback results, (5) lack of financial commitment, and (6) misunderstood operating principles; and there were (7) cultural mismatches along with (8) a lack of alliance experience. Building strong supplier partnerships requires a lot of hard work and commitment by both buyers and sellers. A new reader poll carried out by *Purchasing Magazine* reported that while purchasing managers agreed on the importance of supplier partnerships, "many are not enthusiastic about the merits of their own supplier partnering programs."[14] This indicates that true partnerships are not easily created and much has to be done to get the most out of any partnership. Several key ingredients for developing successful partnerships follow.

Building Trust

Trust is critical for any partnership or alliance to work. Trust enables organizations to share valuable information, devote time and resources to understand each other's business, and achieve results beyond what could have been done individually. Jordan Lewis, in his book *Trusted Partners*, points out that "Trust does not imply easy harmony. Obviously, business is too complex to expect ready agreement on all issues. However, in a trusting relationship, conflicts motivate you to probe for deeper understandings and search for constructive solutions. Trust creates goodwill, which sustains the relationship when one firm does something the other dislikes."[15] With trust, partners are more willing to work together, find compromise solutions to problems, work toward achieving long-term benefits for both parties, and, in short, go the extra mile.

Shared Vision and Objectives

All partnerships should state the expectations of the buyer and supplier, reasons and objectives of the partnership, and plans for the dissolution of the relationship. According to Lenwood Grant, sourcing expert with Bristol-Myers Squibb, "You don't want a partnership that is based on necessity. If you don't think that the partnership is a good mix, but you do it because you have to—possibly because that supplier is the only provider of that material in the market, because you've signed an exclusive contract in the past, or for some other reason—it's not a true partnership and is likely to fail."[16] Both partners must share the same vision and have objectives that are not only clear but mutually agreeable. Many alliances and partnerships have failed because objectives were not well aligned or were overly optimistic. The focus must move beyond tactical issues and toward a more strategic path to corporate success. When partners have equal decision-making control, the partnership has a higher chance of success.

Personal Relationships

Interpersonal relationships in buyer-supplier partnerships are important since it is people who communicate and make things happen. According to Leonard Greenhalgh, author of *Managing Strategic Relationships*, "An alliance or partnership isn't really a relationship between companies, it's a relationship between specific individuals. When you are considering strategic alliances of any kind, the only time the company matters is in the status associated with it [strategic alliance]. Whoever is interfacing with the other company, they are the company."[17]

Mutual Benefits and Needs

Partnering should result in a win-win situation, which can only be achieved if both companies have compatible needs. Mutual needs create not only an environment conducive for collaboration but opportunities for increased innovation. When both parties share in the benefits of the partnership, the relationship will be productive and long lasting. An alliance is much like a marriage, and if only one party is happy, then the marriage is not likely to last. As noted earlier in the Supply Chain Management in Action profile, Dial's relationship with its suppliers is based on the recognition that it is just as important that Dial's suppliers make a profit as it is for Dial to be profitable.

Commitment and Top Management Support

First, it takes a lot of time and hard work to find the right partner. Having done so, both parties must dedicate their time, best people, and resources to make the partnership succeed. According to author Stephen R. Covey, "Without involvement, there is no commitment. Mark it down, asterisk it, circle it, underline it. No involvement, no commitment."[18] Commitment must start at the highest management level. Partnerships tend to be successful when top executives are actively supporting the partnership. The level of cooperation and involvement shown by the organization's top leaders is likely to set the tone for joint problem solving farther down the line.

Successful partners are committed to continuously looking for opportunities to grow their businesses together. Management must create the right kind of internal attitude needed for alliances to flourish. Since partnerships are likely to encounter bumps along the way, it is critical that management adopt a collaborative approach to conflict resolution instead of assigning blame.

Change Management

With change comes stress, which can lead to a loss of focus. As such, companies must avoid distractions from their core businesses as a result of the changes brought about by the partnership. Companies must be prepared to manage change that comes with the formation of new partnerships. According to Stephen Covey, "The key to successful change management is remaining focused on a set of core principles that do not change, regardless of the circumstances."[19]

Information Sharing and Lines of Communication

Both formal and informal lines of communication should be set up to facilitate free flows of information. When there is a high degree of trust, information systems can be customized to serve each other more effectively. Confidentiality of sensitive financial, product, and process information must be maintained. Any conflict that occurs can be resolved if the channels of communication are open. For instance, early communication to suppliers of specification changes and new product introductions are contributing factors to the success of purchasing partnerships. Buyers and sellers should meet regularly to discuss any change of plans, evaluate results, and address issues critical to the success of the partnerships. Since there is free exchange of information, nondisclosure agreements are often used to protect proprietary information and other sensitive data from leaking out. It is not the quantity but rather the quality and accuracy of the information exchanged that indicate the success of information sharing.

Capabilities

Organizations that have a long history of using cross-functional teams to solve problems and who have shown that their employees can collaborate successfully internally have the skills to do so externally. We all know that things do not always turn out as planned. Thus, companies must be willing to accept responsibility and have the capability to correct errors effectively when they are detected. Key suppliers must have the right technology and capabilities to meet cost, quality, and delivery requirements. In addition, suppliers must have the flexibility to respond quickly to changing customer requirements. Before entering into any partnership, an organization must conduct a thorough investigation of the supplier's capabilities and core competencies. Organizations prefer working with suppliers who have the technology and technical expertise to assist in the development of new products or services that would lead to a competitive advantage in the marketplace.

Performance Metrics

The old adage "You can't improve what you can't measure" is particularly true for buyer-supplier alliances. Measures related to quality, cost, delivery, and flexibility have traditionally been used to evaluate how well suppliers are doing. Information provided by supplier performance will be used to improve efficiency in the entire supply chain. Thus, the goal of any good performance evaluation system is to provide metrics that are understandable, easy to measure, and focused on real value-added results for both the buyer and supplier.

By evaluating supplier performance, organizations hope to identify suppliers with exceptional performance or developmental needs, improve supplier communication, reduce risk, and manage the partnership based on an analysis of reported data. FedEx not only has performance scorecards for its suppliers but also has developed a Web-based "reverse scorecard" that allows suppliers to provide constructive performance feedback to the company to enhance the customer/supplier relationship.[20] After all, it is not unusual that the best customers want to work with the best suppliers. Additionally, the best suppliers are commonly rewarded and recognized for their achievements. Supplier awards are discussed later in this chapter.

In a survey of buyers carried out by *Purchasing Magazine,* although price/cost was rated the most important factor when selecting suppliers, other criteria such as technical expertise, lead times, environmental awareness, and market knowledge were also rated highly by the respondents.[21] An earlier study on the electronics industry by Dr. Pearson and Dr. Ellram[22] showed that quality was the most important criterion for selection, followed by cost, current technology, and design capabilities. It would appear that in the electronics industry, which pioneered the six-sigma revolution, quality is the prime selection criteria due to its strategic importance. Thus it is seen that a multicriteria approach is needed to measure performance. Examples of broad performance metrics are shown in Table 3.1.

Over the past several years, **total cost of ownership (TCO),** a broad-based performance metric, has been widely discussed in the supply chain literature. TCO is defined as "all costs associated with the acquisition, use, and maintenance of a good or service" and is comprised of pre-transaction, transaction, and post-transaction costs.[27] Explanations of these three major cost categories follow:

- **Pre-transaction costs:** These costs are incurred prior to order and receipt of the purchased goods. Examples are cost of certifying and training suppliers, investigating alternative sources of supply, and delivery options for new suppliers.

- **Transaction costs:** These costs include the cost of the goods/services and cost associated with placing and receiving the order. Examples are purchase price, preparation of orders, and delivery costs.

- **Post-transaction costs:** These costs are incurred after the goods are in the possession of the company, agents, or customers. Examples are field failures, company's goodwill/reputation, maintenance costs, and warranty costs.

TCO provides a proactive approach for understanding costs and supplier performance leading to reduced costs. However, the challenge is to effectively identify the key cost drivers needed to determine the total cost of ownership. A recent exploratory study of total cost of ownership models indicates that leading-edge companies actually use such models.[28]

Continuous Improvement

The process of evaluating suppliers based on a set of mutually agreed-upon performance measures provides opportunities for **continuous improvement.** The Japanese have demonstrated through the just-in-time philosophy that continuously making a series of small improvements over time results in the elimination of waste in a system. Both buyers and suppliers must be willing to continuously improve their capabilities in meeting customer requirements of cost, quality, delivery, and technology. Partners should focus not on merely correcting mistakes but should work proactively toward eliminating them completely. For example, the Chrysler Corporation first introduced its Supplier Cost Reduction Effort (SCORE) program in 1989 and solicited improvements from its suppliers to reduce cost from the supply chain on a continuous basis. Chrysler shared its cost savings with its suppliers. Typically, the suppliers in the SCORE program enjoyed long-term contracts with Chrysler. In 1998, Chrysler implemented SCORE2, an improved Lotus Notes-based on-line program to speed up the submission of supplier cost savings proposals and the approval process. Using this program the cost reduction is expected to reach $ 2 billion.[29]

Table 3.1	Examples of Performance Metrics[23, 24, 25, 26]

1. Cost/Price
- Competitive price
- Availability of cost breakdowns
- Productivity improvement/cost-reduction programs
- Willingness to negotiate price
- Inventory cost
- Information cost
- Transportation cost
- Actual cost compared to: historical (standard) cost, target cost, cost-reduction goal, benchmark cost
- Extent of cooperation leading to improved cost

2. Quality
- Zero defects
- Statistical process controls
- Continuous process improvement
- Fit for use
- Corrective action program
- Documented quality program such as ISO 9000
- Warranty
- Actual quality compared to: historical quality, specification quality, target quality
- Quality improvement compared to: historical quality, quality-improvement goal
- Extent of cooperation leading to improved quality

3. Delivery
- Fast
- Reliable/on time
- Defect-free deliveries
- Actual delivery compared to: promised delivery, window (i.e., two days early to zero days late)
- Extent of cooperation leading to improved delivery

4. Responsiveness and Flexibility
- Responsiveness to customers
- Accuracy of record keeping
- Ability to work effectively with teams
- Responsiveness to changing situations
- Participation/success of supplier certification program
- Short-cycle changes in demand/flexible capacity
- Changes in delivery schedules
- Participation in new product development
- Solving problems
- Willingness of supplier to seek inputs regarding product/service changes
- Advance notification given by supplier as a result of product/service changes
- Receptiveness to partnering or teaming

5. Environment
- Environmentally responsible
- Environmental management system such as ISO 14000
- Extent of cooperation leading to improved environmental issues

6. Technology
- Proactive improvement using proven manufacturing/service technology
- Superior product/service design
- Extent of cooperation leading to improved technology

7. Business Metrics
- Reputation of supplier/leadership in the field
- Long-term relationship
- Quality of information sharing
- Financial strength such as Dunn & Bradstreet's credit rating
- Strong customer support group
- Total cash flow
- Rate of return on investment
- Extent of cooperation leading to improved business processes and performance

8. Total Cost of Ownership
- Purchased products shipped cost-effectively
- Cost of special handling
- Additional supplier costs as the result of the buyer's scheduling and shipment needs
- Cost of defects, rework, and problem solving associated with purchases

Supplier Evaluation and Certification

Only the best suppliers are targeted as partners. Companies want to develop partnerships with the best suppliers to leverage suppliers' expertise and technologies to create a competitive advantage. Learning more about how an organization's key suppliers are performing can lead to greater visibility, which can provide opportunities for further collaborative involvement in value-added activities. A supplier evaluation and certification process must be in place so that organizations can identify their best and most reliable suppliers. In addition, sourcing decisions are made based on facts and not merely on perception of a supplier's capabilities. Providing frequent feedback on supplier performance can help organizations avoid major surprises and maintain good relationships. For example, Honeywell has a Web-based monthly reporting system for evaluating supplier performance.[30] Suppliers can access their ratings on-line and see how they are performing with respect to the other suppliers. While it is important to evaluate the suppliers, it is equally important that suppliers be allowed to provide constructive feedback to the customer to enhance long-term partnerships. In the Global Perspectives box, Whirlpool's supplier evaluation criteria and expectations are discussed.

One of the goals of evaluating suppliers is to determine if the supplier is performing according to the buyer's requirements. An extension of supplier evaluation is *supplier certification,* defined by the Institute for Supply Management as "an organization's process for evaluating the quality systems of key suppliers in an effort to eliminate incoming inspections."[37] The certification process implies a willingness on the part of customers and suppliers to share goals, commitments, and risks to improve their relationship. A supplier certification program also indicates long-term mutual commitment. For example, a certification program might provide incentives for suppliers to deliver parts directly to the point of use in the buyer firm, thus reducing costs associated with incoming inspection and storage of inventory.

Implementing an effective supplier certification is critical to reducing the supplier base, building long-term relationships, reducing time spent on incoming inspections, improving delivery and responsiveness, recognizing excellence, developing a commitment to continuous improvement, and improving overall performance. Supplier certification allows organizations to identify the suppliers who are most committed to creating and maintaining a partnership and who have the best capabilities. Table 3.2 presents criteria generally found in many certification programs.

Table 3.2	Criteria Used in Certification Programs[38]
• No incoming product lot rejections (e.g., less than 0.5 percent defective) for a specified time period	
• No incoming nonproduct rejections (e.g., late delivery) for a specified time period	
• No significant supplier production-related negative incidents for a specified time period	
• ISO 9000/Q9000 certified or successfully passing a recent, on-site quality system evaluation	
• Mutually agreed-upon set of clearly specified quality performance measures	
• Fully documented process and quality system with cost controls and continuous improvement capabilities	
• Supplier's processes stable and in control	

Global Perspective

PURCHASING AT WHIRLPOOL

The appliance industry is highly competitive with many brands in the market such as GE, Whirlpool, Frigidaire, Maytag, and Kenmore. While many appliance manufacturers have been struggling financially, Whirlpool has remained profitable. One of the keys to success has been Whirlpool's ability to improve its purchasing and supplier management processes. Whirlpool set a target of 3 to 5 percent cost reduction per year for 2002 through productivity improvements and elimination of waste in technology, manufacturing, and purchasing operations. Whirlpool purchases $7 billion per year in production materials; components; and maintenance, repair, and operating materials. As such, the potential for cost reductions from purchased materials can be substantial.

Although Whirlpool has been purchasing globally for many years, one of its latest initiatives is to "integrate design and product development, procurement and manufacturing into a low-cost, high-productivity organization embracing production plants in North America, South America, Europe, and Asia."[31] The goal of global procurement is to develop and manage a supplier base that provides Whirlpool with a competitive advantage in every part of the world. On their Global Procurement Web site, Whirlpool provides a list of requirements for potential companies wanting to become a Whirlpool supplier:[32]

1. *Quality and reliability:* All Whirlpool suppliers are required to pass a Supplier Quality Audit. Whirlpool's Quality System requirements are based on international standards ANSI/ASQC Q90-94, ISO 9000, QS9000, and Whirlpool-specific requirements.

2. *Technology and engineering support:* Requirements such as best cost, quality and manufacturing efficiency, and continuous innovation in design and manufacturing for best-in-class quality and technology must be met.

3. *Integrated supply management (ISM):* ISM provides a common process for doing business with all Whirlpool suppliers through electronic communication. The primary goals of ISM are to have common processes and systems with all suppliers and plants worldwide. This will enable Whirlpool to increase product availability and reduce working capital.

4. *Supplier diversity:* Whirlpool is committed to establishing and maintaining a capable, qualified, competitive, and diverse corporate supply base by providing minority-owned, women-owned, disadvantaged, and small businesses the opportunity to compete and participate on an equal basis as partners and suppliers of goods and services.

5. *Cost management:* Whirlpool will provide each supplier with the plan year's forecast/profit plan volume and cost. This will be used in the calculations for the Total Cost Productivity targets.

Whirlpool has implemented SAP's e-procurement tool to provide a more strategic focus and to put the onus on the ordering back to the requisitioner. "E-procurement has helped us consolidate the supplier base and really understand what is going on in our business. It has also helped to reduce our working capital through improvements in process efficiencies," says Jay Hardman, manager, indirect materials/goods and services.[33]

Whirlpool has formulated a global supplier development strategy that maintains a manageable number of global suppliers, encourages supplier continuous improvement, involves suppliers in the company's six-sigma program, and uses cross-functional teams. For example, Whirlpool has long-term contracts with five domestic and foreign mills, which represent 75 to 80 percent of the company's steel requirements.[34] *Purchasing Machine* ranked Whirlpool's purchasing group as one of the top ten in managing its supply base in North America.[35] According to David R. Whitwam, chairman and chief executive officer at Whirlpool, "Our procurement organization is playing a big role as it is leveraging our supply base on materials and components, helping reduce our design costs, and migrating innovation around the world."[36]

The Weighted-Criteria Evaluation System

One approach of evaluating and certifying suppliers is to use the following weighted-criteria evaluation system:

1. Select the key dimensions of performance mutually acceptable to both customer and supplier.
2. Monitor and collect performance data.
3. Assign weights to each of the dimensions of performance based on their relative importance to the company's objectives. The weights for all dimensions must sum to 1.
4. Evaluate each of the performance measures on a rating between zero (fails to meet any intended purpose or performance) and 100 (exceptional in meeting intended purpose or performance).
5. Multiply the dimension rating by the importance weight and sum to get an overall score.
6. Classify vendors based on their overall score:
    - *Unacceptable (less than 50):* Supplier is dropped from further business.
    - *Conditional (between 50 and 70):* Supplier needs development work to improve performance but may be dropped if performance continues to lag.
    - *Certified (between 70 and 90):* Supplier meets intended purpose or performance.
    - *Preferred (greater than 90):* Supplier will be considered for involvement in new product development and opportunities for more business.
7. Audit and perform ongoing certification review.

An example of the preceding evaluation and certification process is shown in Table 3.3.

Systems in use can vary somewhat from what we have described, although most are quite similar. Roche Diagnostics Corporation (RDC) regularly measures, reviews, and improves its

Table 3.3	Supplier Scorecard Used for the XYZ Company			
Performance Measure	Rating ×	Weight =		Final Value
Technology	80	0.10		8.00
Quality	90	0.25		22.50
Responsiveness	95	0.15		14.25
Delivery	90	0.15		13.50
Cost	80	0.15		12.00
Environmental	90	0.05		4.50
Business	90	0.15		13.50
	Total score	1.00		88.25

Note: Based on the total score of 88.25, the XYZ Company is considered a certified supplier.

Figure 3.1	Roche Diagnostics Corporation Source Development: Supplier Trend Scorecard—2Q2003

July 1, 2003

Greetings:

Enclosed is Roche's Supplier Trend Scorecard, which highlights your company's performance during the period of April 1, 2003, to June 30, 2003. The trending categories are as follows:

Category	Description	Target
Quantity Reliability	The percent of receipts that were received as per PO for quantity Tolerance: 5% short to 5% over	≥ 95%
On-Time Performance	The percent of receipts that were received by Roche on time Tolerance: + 0/–5 days from the agreed-upon delivery date per PO	≥ 95%
Supplier Corrective Action Request (SCAR) and Material Review Notice (MRN)	Documents used to document nonconformances during incoming inspection, production, or after product release	0
SCAR Response Time	Average number of days to respond to corrective action requests	≤ 15 days
Supplier Rating	Ratio of actual score versus the total score possible	≥ 0.90

Please carefully review your performance in each category. For suppliers with on-time performance or quantity reliability below 80% an Action Plan with due dates and deliverables is requested by July 30, 2003, to improve supplier performance.

Please remember to request approval from Roche (Planner/Buyer) for changes to the delivery due date and/or item quantity, prior to release of the material and to obtain a copy of the updated PO, if applicable.

We are adding a customer service metric to the current supplier scorecard that is distributed quarterly to our top 40 suppliers. **We will incorporate this metric into the 3d quarter scorecards.** The customer service metric will encompass feedback from planner/buyers on (1) timely order confirmation and (2) back-ordered product occurrences. For the print commodity, we will also include (3) consistent status reports, (4) confirmation of shipment of finished products and (5) turnaround time on quotations in which the Print Analysts will participate in the scoring. The scoring will be 0—poor, 2—marginal, and 4—good. This average will be included in the calculation of your supplier rating.

We'll be issuing quarterly updates to this report. If you require additional details, please do not hesitate to contact me.

Kind regards,

Source Development Engineer
Roche Diagnostics Corporation
317-521-XXXX

Source: Used with permission of Roche Diagnostic Corporation.

suppliers' performance using the RDC supplier trend scorecard process shown in Figure 3.1 to Figure 3.3. The closed-loop system evaluates the suppliers' actual performance against targeted key measures. Points ranging from 0 to 4 are awarded in each of five categories: on-time delivery, quantity reliability, material review notice (MRN), supplier corrective action request (SCAR), and SCAR response time (see Figure 3.2). A score of 4 indicates that the supplier's performance is meeting Roche's target score. In Figure 3.3, the supplier rating is calculated based on scores in the following areas: on-time delivery, quantity reliability, MRN+SCAR (scores for MRN and SCAR are added together), and SCAR response time. The supplier rating can range from 0 to 1, with 1 representing the highest performance.

In another example, Federal-Mogul rates suppliers on three equally weighted categories of quality, delivery, and tangible value added (TVA). The quality score is based on parts per million defective to meet specifications. The delivery score is calculated by dividing the number of items delivered to the items due from the supplier. The TVA score is based on the suggestions from suppliers for reducing costs. The total score ranges from 0 to 100. Suppliers are considered "preferred" if they score between 90 and 100. Preferred suppliers are those that Federal-Mogul will work with on new product development, approve for new business, and assist in maintaining their market competitiveness.[39]

Figure 3.2	2003 Scorecard Determination Table			
		Scoring system		
Category	**Description**	**% of Receipts Received On Time**	**Points**	**Target Score**
On-Time Delivery	The percent of receipts that were received by Roche on time (+0/–5 days from the agreed-upon delivery date)	100 to 95.00	4	>95.00%
		94.99 to 90.00	3	
		89.99 to 85.00	2	
		84.99 to 80.00	1	
		<80	0	
		% of Receipts Received On Qty	**Points**	
Quantity Reliability	The percent of PO Line Items that were received by Roche within the specified PO quantity (+/–5% of quantity ordered)	100 to 95.00	4	>95.00%
		94.99 to 90.00	3	
		89.99 to 85.00	2	
		84.99 to 80.00	1	
		<80	0	
		# of MRNs or SCARs	**Points**	
MRN/SCAR Quota	Number of MRNs/ SCARs issued	0	4	0
		1	3	
		2	2	
		3	1	
		≥4	0	
		Ave. Response Time (Days)	**Points**	
SCAR Response Time	Average number of days to respond to corrective action requests	0–15	4	<15 days
		16–30	2	
		>30	0	

Source: Used with permission of Roche Diagnostic Corporation.

Finally, Ford Motor Company's Q1 program assesses a supplier's excellence in the important areas of systems capability, performance, manufacturing process, and customer satisfaction. After suppliers are Q1 certified, they must validate their status every six months. Q1-certified suppliers are considered to be preferred suppliers to Ford, provided technical assistance, and recognized worldwide as having exceptional quality.[40]

Today, external certifications such as ISO 9000 and ISO 14000 have gained popularity globally as a natural extension of an organization's internal supplier evaluation and certification program.

ISO 9000

In 1987 the International Organization for Standardization (ISO) developed **ISO 9000,** a series of management and quality assurance standards in design, development, production, installation, and service. The European Union in 1992 adopted a plan that recognized ISO 9000 as a third-party certification; the result is that many European companies prefer suppliers with ISO 9000 certification. Thus, U.S. companies wanting to sell in the global marketplace are compelled to seek ISO 9000 certification. ISO's eleventh international survey[41] showed that 510,616 ISO 9000 certificates had been awarded in 161 countries up to the end of December 2001. This represents an increase of nearly 25 percent over the same period in 2000. In the United States, 37,026 certificates had been issued up to the end of 2001, representing 7.25 percent of the worldwide numbers. The ANSI (American National Standards

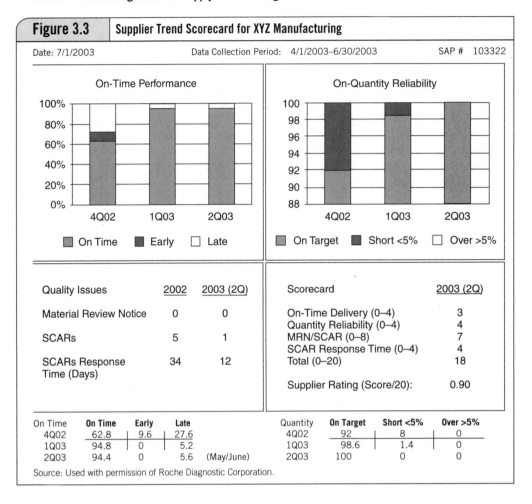

Figure 3.3 | Supplier Trend Scorecard for XYZ Manufacturing

Date: 7/1/2003   Data Collection Period: 4/1/2003–6/30/2003   SAP # 103322

Quality Issues: Material Review Notice 2002: 0, 2003 (2Q): 0; SCARs 2002: 5, 2003 (2Q): 1; SCARs Response Time (Days) 2002: 34, 2003 (2Q): 12

Scorecard 2003 (2Q): On-Time Delivery (0–4): 3; Quantity Reliability (0–4): 4; MRN/SCAR (0–8): 7; SCAR Response Time (0–4): 4; Total (0–20): 18; Supplier Rating (Score/20): 0.90

On Time	On Time	Early	Late		Quantity	On Target	Short <5%	Over >5%
4Q02	62.8	9.6	27.6		4Q02	92	8	0
1Q03	94.8	0	5.2		1Q03	98.6	1.4	0
2Q03	94.4	0	5.6	(May/June)	2Q03	100	0	0

Source: Used with permission of Roche Diagnostic Corporation.

Institute)/ISO/ASQC (American Society for Quality Control) Q9000 standards are the U.S. equivalent of ISO 9000. Obtaining the ISO 9000 certification provides further verification that the supplier has an established quality management system in place. For example, Ford's Q1 process requires suppliers to be ISO 9000 certified.

ISO 14000

In 1996, **ISO 14000,** a family of international standards for environmental management, was first introduced. Interestingly, by the end of 2001, there were 1,645 ISO 14000 certificates in the United States, representing only 4.5 percent of the 36,765 certificates issued globally in 112 countries.[42] The ISO 14000 certification numbers pale in comparison with those for ISO 9000. The benefits of investing in an environmental management system based on ISO 14000 standards include reduced energy and other resource consumption, decreased environmental liability and risk, reduced waste and pollution, and improved community goodwill. As such, investment in environmental management systems is likely to increase in the future. A survey carried out by the ISO 14000 Information Center indicates that 32 percent of respondents will require their suppliers to have ISO 14001 certification within the next two years and 15 percent will require it within two to five years.[43] Additionally, as more organizations are certified in ISO 14000, they are likely to pass this requirement on to their suppliers in the future. For example, Ford is one of the first automakers to certify its global manufacturing facilities (106 facilities in 25 countries) under ISO 14001, including 43 European production facilities. Ford currently requires its suppliers to have at least one manufacturing site certified to ISO 14001. Ford of Europe offers ISO 14001 Awareness Training programs to assist suppliers in meeting this objective.[44]

Supplier Development

Supplier development is defined as "any activity that a buyer undertakes to improve a supplier's performance and/or capabilities to meet the buyer's short- and/or long-term supply needs."[45] Supplier development requires financial and human resource investments by both partners and includes a wide range of activities such as training of the supplier's personnel, investing in the supplier's operations, and ongoing performance assessment. A survey by *Purchasing Magazine* showed that nearly 44 percent of the companies surveyed had supplier evaluation systems, but what is surprising is that 47 percent did not have programs to assist suppliers in improving their performance.[46] This indicates that there are still many companies that do not practice supplier development. As companies outsource more and more parts, a larger portion of costs lie outside the company in a supply chain and it becomes increasingly difficult to achieve further cost savings internally. One way out of this dilemma is for companies to work with their suppliers to lower the total cost of materials purchased. Companies that are able to leverage their supply base to impact their total cost structure will have a competitive advantage in their markets.

A seven-step approach to supplier development follows:[47]

1. *Identify critical products and services:* Assess the relative importance of the products and services from a strategic perspective. Products and services that are purchased in high volume, do not have good substitutes, or have limited sources of supply are considered strategic supplies.

2. *Identify critical suppliers:* Suppliers of strategic supplies who do not meet minimum performance in quality, on-time delivery, cost, technology, or cycle time are targets for development

3. *Form a cross-functional team:* Next, the buyer must develop an internal cross-functional team with a clear agreement for the development initiative.

4. *Meet with top management of supplier:* The buyer's cross-functional team meets with the supplier's top management team to discuss details of strategic alignment, supplier performance measurement, improvement, and professionalism.

5. *Identify key projects:* After the promising opportunities have been identified, they are evaluated in terms of feasibility, resource and time commitment, and expected return on investment. The most promising projects are selected.

6. *Define details of agreement:* After agreement has been reached on the development projects, the partners must jointly decide on the metrics to be monitored such as percent improvement in quality, delivery, and cycle time.

7. *Monitor status and modify strategies:* To ensure continued success, management must actively monitor progress, promote exchange of information, and revise the strategy as business conditions warrant.

By tracking supplier performance over time, Honeywell is able to observe trends and to catch problems early. Honeywell has implemented their six-sigma-plus program aimed at eliminating variations in processes to meet required specifications with no more than 3.4 parts per million (ppm) defective and to apply lean manufacturing techniques to eliminate waste and to synchronize suppliers' activities. Recently, Honeywell implemented the six-sigma-plus initiatives with their suppliers. For example, Wong's-CMAC, a supplier of Honeywell, based in Mexicali, Mexico, was experiencing chronic quality and lead-time problems. With Honeywell's assistance, the supplier was able to improve its quality from 3.2 sigma (44,565 ppm defective) to six sigma. This increase in performance resulted in Wong's-CMAC being considered for a new line of business, assembling printed circuit boards, currently done by its parent company, Wong's Electronics of China.[48]

Siemens Medical Solutions (SMS) established a supplier development program to help suppliers enhance their quality performance. This is important because SMS's products require

FDA approval and their suppliers must have very high quality. It is not unusual to see SMS's quality experts examining a supplier's quality system when there is a quality problem and then providing suggestions for improvement. SMS also conducts various seminars for their suppliers. A survey carried out by SMS's purchasing departments at a variety of locations provided useful information on the problem areas as well as things that were done well in some departments. When a best practice—such as purchasers working with engineers—was found in a department, this information was conveyed to the other business units. Other results from the survey indicated limited communication among the medical groups and a lack of supplier involvement in new product development. Addressing these problem areas and working closely with their suppliers have been rewarding for SMS. Over a three-year period, SMS reduced its supplier base by 50 percent to 2,500, introduced new products to market quicker, and cut manufacturing lead times significantly. SMS is now able to manufacture SONOLINE ANTARES, their newest ultrasound product, in hours compared to days for previous generations of this equipment.[49, 50]

As discussed earlier, Roche Diagnostics Corporation (RDC) has a vendor evaluation system and a supplier development program. For suppliers with on-time performance or quantity reliability below the 80 percent level, an action plan with due dates and deliverables is requested to improve supplier performance. An example of RDC's supplier corrective action request is shown in Figure 3.4. Roche's suppliers work to close the performance gaps by analyzing the root causes of the problem, preparing a corrective action plan, and verifying the outcome of the plan as part of the supplier's continuous improvement effort.

John Deere has numerous supplier development success stories. For example, the Construction and Forestry Division worked closely with a supplier of sheet metal and plastic products to reduce cost and improve quality and delivery performance simultaneously. The outcome is the application of cellular manufacturing techniques that resulted in a 40 percent reduction in cycle time, 40 percent reduction in inventory, 75 percent reduction in rework costs, 50 percent reduction in scrap, 40 percent reduction in indirect labor, and 9 percent reduction in direct labor.[51]

Supplier Awards

It is not sufficient to evaluate and assess suppliers on how well they perform with respect to the metrics jointly agreed upon. Companies should recognize and celebrate the achievements of their best suppliers. Award winners exemplify true partnerships with respect to continuous improvement, organizational commitment, and excellence. As award-winning suppliers, they serve as role models for other suppliers. For example, Ford Motor Company's World Excellence Award is a comprehensive global supplier awards program that annually recognizes Ford's global suppliers based on three performance metrics: quality, cost, and delivery. These metrics are jointly developed with Ford's suppliers. The Gold Award is for suppliers such as A. K. Steel Corporation (United States), Denso Corporation (Thailand), Doktas Dokumculuk Ticaret Ve Sanayi A. S. (Turkey), and Kawasaki Steel Corporation (Japan), who meet the excellence requirements in all three areas of quality, cost, and delivery. The Silver Award is given to suppliers that meet the quality excellence requirement and either the cost or delivery excellence requirement. Past winners in the quality and cost category include Getrag S. P. A. (Germany) and J. Walter Thompson Publicidade Ltda. (Brazil); and winners in the quality and delivery category include Acumuladores Titan, C. A. (Venezuela), SDS Shanghai GKN Driveshaft Co., Ltd. (China), Dupont Automotive (United States), and Johnson Controls, Inc., S. A. (Argentina). The Recognition of Achievement Awards are given to suppliers who have made a significant contribution in Ford's key initiatives of *High Mileage Improvement, Environmental Leadership, Warranty Reduction Program, New Consumer-Focused Technology,* and *Customer Driven Six-Sigma Supplier Achievement.* Overall, for 2001, Ford handed out nine Gold, twenty-one Silver, and twelve Recognition of Achievement awards to suppliers in fifteen countries.[52]

Figure 3.4	Roche Diagnostics Corporation's Supplier Corrective Action Request

Roche Diagnostics Corporation
Supplier Corrective Action Request

SCAR Number:
Date Issued:
Response Due Date:

Supplier Information
Supplier Number: *Quantity:*
Supplier Name: *Part Number:*
Supplier Address: *Lot Number:*
                                                      Description:

Description of Nonconformance:

What has been done to isolate or contain the issue?

Our Quality Improvement Program necessitates the determination of the Root Cause for the Discrepancy, an appropriate Plan for the Corrective Action you intended to take, and a Plan to verify that the CA implemented was effective. Please complete and return the following:

Root Cause Analysis:

In order to be considered an acceptable response, the following questions regarding the Root Cause must be answered:
(1) What specifically caused the nonconformance? (2) How was the root cause determined? (3) Is the nonconformance system related or is it an isolated incident? (4) Has this same issue been seen on this product or similar products in the past?

Corrective Action Plan: *Effective Check Plan:* _____

In order to be considered an acceptable response, the following questions regarding the CA Plan must be answered:
(1) Does the corrective action address the root cause? (2) What are the immediate correction or containment actions versus the long-term fix to the issue? (3) Will the CA require a revalidation of the process being affected? If not, justify why not. (4) Does the CA Plan impact design verification of the material or have clinical implications? If not, justify why not. (5) What is the date that the CA is to be implemented? (6) Is this corrective action applicable to other products?

Note: In general, retraining by itself will not be considered an appropriate response.

Direct Questions/Report: *Quality Principal:*

Phone (317) 521-XXXX,   Phone (317) 521-XXXX
Fax (317) 521-3080

SMT 02-FM01 Rev. 09   **CN 33672 06/05/02**   **Page 1 of 2**

(continued)

Figure 3.4	Roche Diagnostics Corporation's Supplier Corrective Action Request (*continued*)

Roche Diagnostics Corporation
Supplier Corrective Action Request

SCAR Number:
Date Issued:
Response Due Date:

Verification Plan: *Verification Date:* _____

> **In order to be considered an acceptable response, the following questions regarding the Ver. Plan must be answered:** (1) What are the parameters to be monitored? If none, justify why this is acceptable. (2) What methods will be utilized to analyze the data? (3) What is the date of the proposed CA verification?
>
> **When the verification has been completed, an executive summary of the data generated must be forwarded to the Source Development Engineer listed below.**

Supplier Approval

Signature: _____   Date: _____

Printed Name: _____

Title: _____

Source Development Approval

SDE Signature: _____   Date: _____

Printed Name: _____

Quality Approval (if applicable)

QA Signature: _____   Date: _____

Printed Name: _____

Direct Questions/Report: *Quality Principal:*

Phone (317) 521-XXXX   Phone (317) 521-XXXX
Fax (317) 521-3080

SMT 02-FM01 Rev. 09   **CN 33672 06/05/02**   **Page 2 of 2**

Source: Used with permission of Roche Diagnostic Corporation.

Supplier Relationship Management Software

In today's business environment, external purchases represent 45 to 60 cents for every dollar earned in revenues and as such, companies today must consider investing in supplier relationship management (SRM) software as a key to improving profits and reducing costs.[53] Definitions of what is included in these SRM modules vary widely, with i2 Technologies claiming to have coined the SRM term in collaboration with AMR Research. **Supplier relationship management** is an umbrella term that includes "extended procurement processes such as sourcing analytics (e.g., spend analysis), sourcing execution, procurement execution, payment and settlement, and—closing the feedback loop—supplier scorecarding and performance monitoring."[54] The success of e-procurement, which has a predominantly internal focus, created the need for SRM solutions for managing the supply side of an organization's supply chain. According to Nick Ford, European vice president of e-procurement with i2, "The automation that SRM brings creates efficiencies which are clearly a source of sustainable competitive advantage. With shrinking product life cycles, it becomes critical to design, source, plan, and manufacture materials right the first time to take advantage of market trends. By making the scope of supplier relationships broader, more flexible, and more responsive, enterprises can achieve new areas of growth and build profitable new business models."[55] SRM software automates the exchange of information among several layers of relationships that are complex and too time-consuming to manage manually and results in improved procurement efficiency, lower business costs, real-time visibility, faster communication between buyer and seller, and enhanced supply chain collaboration.

Many organizations are investing in SRM software modules due to the wealth of information that can be derived from these systems. SRM software can organize supplier information and provide answers to questions such as:

- Who are our vendors? Are they the right set of suppliers?
- Who are our best suppliers and what are their competitive rankings?
- What is our suppliers' performance with respect to on-time delivery, quality, and costs?
- Can we consolidate our buying to achieve greater scale economies?
- Do we have consistency in suppliers and performance across different locations and facilities?
- What products/services do we purchase?
- What parts can be reused in new designs?

In general, SRM software varies by vendors in terms of capabilities offered. AMR Research has identified five key tenets of an SRM system:[56]

- *Automation* of transactional processes between an organization and its suppliers.
- *Integration* that provides a view of the supply chain that spans multiple departments, processes, and software applications for internal users and external partners.
- *Visibility* of information and process flows in and between organizations. Views are customized by role and aggregated via a single portal.
- *Collaboration* through information sharing and suppliers' ability to input information directly into an organization's supply chain information system.
- *Optimization* of processes and decision making through enhanced analytical tools such as data warehouse and Online Analytical Processing (OLAP) tools with the migration toward more dynamic optimization tools in the future.

According to A. Mizan Rahman, CEO and Chief Software Architect, M2SYS Technology, the key benefits of SRM include the following: (1) Better internal and external communications providing visibility into various cost components; (2) Automated creation, negotiation, execution, and compliance leading to more strategic, long-term relationships; (3) Common and consistent measurements that help focus resources, identify performance glitches, and develop strategies for supply chain improvements; and (4) The elimination of time-intensive, costly processes of performing paper-based business transactions.[57] M2SYS Technology's SRM solution is shown in Figure 3.5. Several SRM software suppliers with a sample of their users are shown in Table 3.4.

SRM software modules can take from three to five months to implement and train users and can cost from $250,000 to $750,000.[59] The challenge is assembling all the data needed for an SRM application to work. For example, analysis of supplier information requires access to

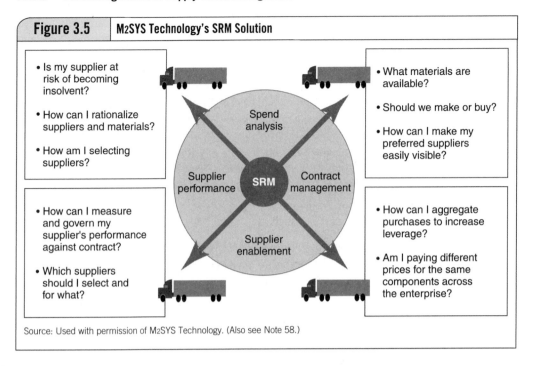

Figure 3.5 | **M2SYS Technology's SRM Solution**

- Is my supplier at risk of becoming insolvent?
- How can I rationalize suppliers and materials?
- How am I selecting suppliers?

- What materials are available?
- Should we make or buy?
- How can I make my preferred suppliers easily visible?

Spend analysis

Supplier performance   **SRM**   Contract management

Supplier enablement

- How can I measure and govern my supplier's performance against contract?
- Which suppliers should I select and for what?

- How can I aggregate purchases to increase leverage?
- Am I paying different prices for the same components across the enterprise?

Source: Used with permission of M2SYS Technology. (Also see Note 58.)

Table 3.4 | **SRM Software Suppliers and Some of Their Customers**

EcVision
Customers: J. C. Penney Company, Inc., MAST Industries, Inc. (buying arm for The Limited family of stores including Express, Lerner New York, Lane Bryant, Limited Stores, Structure, and Henri Bendel)

i2 Technologies, Inc.
Customers: eLSG.SkyChefs, Airbus, PEMSTAR Inc., Nippon Steel Corporation, Hitachi, Toshiba Corporation's Semiconductor Company, Honeywell

Manugistics
Customers: Harley-Davidson, Inc., Cisco

MatrixOne
Customers: 3M, NCR Corp., Texas Instruments

PeopleSoft
Customers: Dartmouth-Hitchcock Medical Center, Aquila Inc., Boise, Beth Israel Deaconess Medical Center

Note: PeopleSoft SRM solution was chosen as Datamation's (INT Media Group) Product of the Year for 2001.

SAP
Customers: Lockheed Martin, Mercedes-Benz Espana (Spain), Deutsche Bank, Kimberly Clark, Proctor and Gamble, Royal Dutch/Shell

SAS Institute
Customers: Bayer CropScience, Schneider Electric

SupplyWorks
Customers: BorgWarner Morse TEC, Barnes & Noble, Ingersoll-Rand, Plasti-Line, Inc.

applications containing data about suppliers, as well as enterprise resource planning (ERP), material requirements planning (MRP), accounting, and existing supplier information databases. Today, buyers (before SRM implementation) typically spend 10 percent of their time on supplier relationship development, 40 percent on expediting, and 50 percent on order processing/tracking. After SRM implementation, the buyer's time allocation is estimated to be 50 percent on collaborative planning, 30 percent on supplier relationship development, 10 percent on expediting, and 10 percent on exception management.[60]

Until recent years, purchasing professionals did not have the right technologies to help them accomplish their jobs effectively. Automating the procurement activities can lead to significant cost savings as buyers move toward managing processes by exception. This effectively frees buyers to focus on more strategic and value-added activities such as collaborative planning. In addition, purchasing professionals can work effectively on maximizing the return on their relationships with suppliers. The greater procurement visibility from using SRM software also translates into smoother processes, faster cycle times, reduced new product development, improved time to market, streamlined purchasing, and reduced inventory costs.

Bayer CropScience recently implemented SAS's analytical SRM technology to maximize its profitable relationships with 16,000 suppliers worldwide and move from tactical to strategic procurement. Bayer must ensure that the purchased materials are delivered at the right time and in the right quality and quantity while reducing cost and supplier delivery risk. The SRM system is used to collect and analyze supplier and historical purchasing data to evaluate supplier performance, rank its supplier base, find cost improvement areas, and match business objectives with individual supplier performance. Bayer expects to save between $10 million and $15 million annually using the SRM software.[61]

e-BUSINESS CONNECTION
M2SYS'S SYNDÉO SERVER AND SRM SOFTWARE

Limitations on visibility into corporate spend data throughout the extended enterprise greatly hinder the ability for a global enterprise to optimize sourcing activities with distributed partners. Discrepancies in product classification schemas across different business units, dispersed contractual commitments, and inefficient methods to rationalize supplier spending and performance create indirect strains on business operations and the effective management of core profitability factors.

With M2SYS's SRM (supplier relationship management) enterprise application, companies can have greater visibility into the critical success factors that govern purchases made among the global network of manufacturing facilities. Enterprise purchasing professionals can utilize the application to streamline and automate supplier relationship processes, im-

proving efficiencies gaining access to real-time information that enhances decision making.

With an investment in SRM, customers can gain features such as

- Consolidated representation of corporate spend activities across the enterprise
- Real-time access to spend data providing rapid response cycles
- Robust analytics depicting commodity, supplier, and contract breakdowns
- Rapid identification of product cost savings opportunities
- Real-time monitoring of supplier price performance
- Develop n-dimensional, complex eRFQs and negotiate with strategic supply base through Internet-based Bid/Ask format

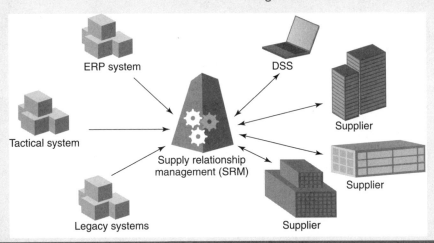

(*continued*)

- Enable the exchange of electronic business documents with entire supply base
- Centralized view of enterprise-wide common naming conventions
- Centralized access to corporate and divisional product and service contracts
- Notification of supplier contractual compliance
- Enhanced capabilities to track supplier performance over time

The features available in M2SYS's SRM application provide global enterprises greater visibility into critical spend and supply data that can be leveraged to create opportunities for cost, consolidation, and compliance improvements. Customers gain benefits such as

- Higher gross margins from reductions in costs of goods sold
- Improved internal process efficiencies

- Optimized sourcing cycle times with improved access to decision criteria
- Better relationships with key suppliers through rationalization
- Enhanced risk management through real-time supplier performance access
- Identification of supply consolidation and savings opportunities

M2SYS's Syndéo Server provides real-time integration of supplier/partners into the SRM application via the Internet. This technology also works as a stand-alone solution to connect multiple, disparate systems within the enterprise. Syndéo Server is the answer to the search for affordable, scalable, automated data connectivity with multiple trading affiliates. Using innovative T^3 technology, customers can rapidly Transport, Transform, and Track electronic data with any other business, regardless of disparate data formats, security standards, and technologies.

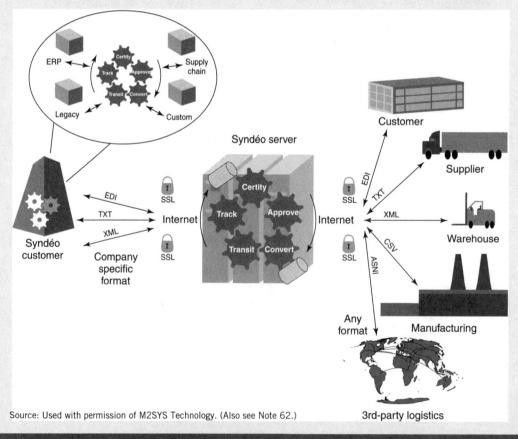

Source: Used with permission of M2SYS Technology. (Also see Note 62.)

Summary

Over the past two decades we have seen the buyer-supplier relationship evolve from an arm's-length/adversarial approach to one favoring developing long-term partnerships. Significant competitive advantage can be achieved by organizations working closely with their suppliers. Without a shared vision, mutual benefits, and top management commitment, partnerships are likely to be short-lived. Other ingredients necessary for developing and managing lasting supplier relationships are trust, creating personal relationships, effective change management, information sharing, and using performance metrics to create superior capabilities. Mutually agreeable measures to monitor supplier performance provide the basis for continuous improvement to enhance supplier quality, cost, and delivery. Supplier certification ensures that buyers continue to work with their best suppliers to improve cost, quality, delivery, and new product development to gain a competitive advantage. Finally, supplier relationship management software automates the exchange of information and allows for improved efficiency and effectiveness in managing supplier relationships and improving performance.

Key Terms

continuous improvement, 65

ISO 9000, 71

ISO 14000, 72

post-transaction costs, 65

pre-transaction costs, 65

strategic alliance, 62

supplier relationship management (SRM), 76

total cost of ownership (TCO), 65

transaction costs, 65

Discussion Questions

1. Why should an organization be concerned with supplier relationships?
2. Compare and contrast the arm's-length/adversarial and partnership approaches to customer-supplier relationship.
3. How can an organization manage its suppliers effectively?
4. What are the key factors that contribute to a lasting supplier partnership?
5. It has often been pointed out that 60 percent of strategic alliances fail? What are the reasons for this?
6. What are the criteria used in evaluating a supplier?
7. Discuss how an organization develops a supplier evaluation and certification program.
8. Why should an organization invest in supplier development programs? What are the challenges of supplier development activities?
9. What are the benefits of ISO 9000 certification?
10. Are environmental concerns impacting purchasing decisions? What are the benefits of ISO 14000 certification?

11. What are the key capabilities of supplier relationship management software?
12. Why do organizations have supplier awards program?
13. Why do organizations use supplier certification? What are the benefits of supplier certification?
14. What are the advantages of using SRM solutions to manage suppliers?
15. **Discussion Problem:** The Margo Manufacturing Company is performing an annual evaluation of one of its suppliers, the Mimi Company. Bo, purchasing manager of the Margo Manufacturing Company, has collected the following information:

Performance Criteria	Score	Weight
Technology	85	0.10
Quality	95	0.25
Responsive	90	0.15
Delivery	80	0.15
Cost	90	0.20
Environment	75	0.05
Business	95	0.10
	Total score	1.00

A score based on a scale of 0 (unsatisfactory) to 100 (excellent) has been assigned for each of the performance category considered critical in assessing the supplier. Different weights are assigned to each of the performance criteria based on its relative importance. How would you evaluate the Mimi Company's performance as a supplier?

Internet Questions

1. Research ISO's Web site (http://www.iso.ch) and discuss the growth of ISO 9000 and 14000 certification by regions of the world such as Africa/West Asia, Central and South America, North America, Europe, Far East, and Australia/New Zealand.
2. What are the similarities and differences in capabilities of SRM software offered by i2, PeopleSoft, and SAP?

References

Austin, J. E. *The Collaboration Challenge: How Nonprofits and Businesses Succeed through Strategic Alliances*. San Francisco: Jossey-Bass, 2000.

Greenhalgh, L. *Managing Strategic Relationships: The Key to Business Success*. New York: The Free Press, 2001.

Grieco, P. L., Jr., M. W. Gozzo, and J. W. Claunch. *Supplier Certification: Achieving Excellence*. Plantsville, CT: PT Publications, Inc., 1988.

Gunasekaran, A., C. Patel, and E. Tirtiroglu. "Performance Measures and Metrics in a Supply Chain Environment." *International Journal of Operations & Production Management* 21, no. 1/2 (2001): 71–87.

Maass, R. A., J. O. Brown, and J. L. Bossert. *Supplier Certification: A Continuous Improvement Strategy*. Milwaukee, WI: ASQ Quality Press, 1990.

McIvor, R., and M. McHugh. "Partnership Sourcing: An Organization Change Management Perspective." *Journal of Supply Chain Management* (summer 2000): 12–20.

Mieghem, V. *Implementing Supplier Partnerships: How to Lower Costs and Improve Service*. Englewood Cliffs, NJ: Prentice-Hall, 1995.

Morgan, J. "New Survey Finds Big Gap between Rhetoric and Reality." *Purchasing* (15 November 2001). Available from http://www.manufacturing.net/pur

Morgan, J. "Performance Measurement: New Competitive Importance!" *Purchasing* (8 February 2002). Available from http://www.manufacturing.net/pur

Parsons, A. L. "What Determines Buyer-Seller Relationship Quality? An Investigation from the Buyer's Perspective." *Journal of Supply Chain Management* (spring 2002): 4–12.

Sarkis, J., and S. Talluri. "A Model for Strategic Supplier Selection." *Journal of Supply Chain Management* 38, no. 1 (winter 2002): 18–28.

Speckman, R. E., L. A. Isabella, and T. C. MacAvoy. *Alliance Competence: Maximizing the Value of Your Partnerships.* New York: John Wiley & Sons, 2000.

Spina, G., and G. Zotteri. "The Implementation Process of Customer-Supplier Partnership: Lessons from a Clinical Perspective." *International Journal of Operations & Production Management* 20, no. 10 (2000): 1164–82.

Underhill, T. *Strategic Alliances: Managing the Supply Chain.* Tulsa, Okla.: Pennwell, 1996.

Whipple, J. M., and R. Frankel. "Strategic Alliance Success Factors." *Journal of Supply Chain Management* (summer 2000). Available from http://www.ism.ws/ResourceArticles/2000/jsummer00p21.efm

Notes

1. H. C. Stonecipher, president and CEO, The Boeing Company, in "Part Flows and Dinosaur Toes: A New Approach to Supplier Relations," *Executive Speeches* (June/July 1999).

2. L. Hoffman, president, Global Sourcing Solutions, in "Buyers Target Strategic Partners," *Purchasing* (5 April 2001); available from http://www.manufacturing.net/pur

3. Dial Corporation's Web site; available from http://www.dialcorp.com

4. The Dial Corporation, WMBE Brochure, Supplier Diversity Program; available from http://www.dialcorp.com/index.cfm?page_id=273

5. C. Reilly, "Central Sourcing Strategy Saves Dial $100 Million," *Purchasing,* no. 1 (17 January 2002); available from http://www.manufacturing.net/pur

6. The Dial Corporation, *2002 Annual Report.*

7. C. Reilly, "Central Sourcing Strategy Saves Dial $100 Million."

8. C. Reilly, "Central Sourcing Strategy Saves Dial $100 Million"; The Dial Corporation Web site; The Dial Corporation, WMBE Brochure, Supplier Diversity Program (Dial Web site); The Dial Corporation, *2002 Annual Report;* K. Walsh, "Soapers Protect Themselves During the Downturn," *Chemical Week* 165, no. 4 (29 January 2003): 24–25.

9. "Fujitsu Cuts Procurement Costs and Suppliers," *Purchasing* (21 February 2002); available from http://www.manufacturing.net/pur

10. J. Morgan, "New Survey Finds Big Gap between Rhetoric and Reality," *Purchasing* (15 November 2001); available from http://www.manufacturing/net/pur

11. "Glossary of Key Purchasing and Supply Terms: Supplier Partnership," Institute for Supply Management.

12. K. Ohmae, "The Global Logic of Strategic Alliances," *Harvard Business Review* (March–April 1989): 143–152.

13. R. E. Speckman, L. A. Isabella, and T. C. MacAvoy, *Alliance Competence: Maximizing the Value of Your Partnerships* (New York: John Wiley & Sons, 2000).

14. J. Morgan, "New Survey Finds Big Gap."

15. J. D. Lewis, *Trusted Partners: How Companies Build Mutual Trust and Win Together* (New York: The Free Press, 1999), 7.

16. "Buyers Target Strategic Partners," *Purchasing* (5 April 2001); available from http://www.manufacturing.net/pur

17. "Supplier Selection & Management Report," Institute of Management and Administration (IOMA) (March 2002).

18. S. R. Covey, Stephen R. Covey Quotations, Stephen R. Covey Sayings, Famous Quotes and Famous Sayings Network Web site.

19. M. MacDonald, "Managing Change: A Matter of Principle," *Supply Chain Management Review* (January/February 2002); available from http://www.manufacturing.net/scm

20. F. M. Babineaux, "Measuring Supplier Performance (How to Get What You Measure and Other Intentional Consequences)," 87th Annual International Supply Management Conference, 2002 International Conference Proceedings (May 2002); available from Institute for Supply Management Web site.

21. S. Avery, "Supplier Performance Is More Important Than Ever," *Purchasing* (7 February 2002); available from http://www.manufacturing.net/pur

22. J. Pearson and L. Ellram, "Supplier Selection and Evaluation in Small versus Large Electronics Firms," *Journal of Small Business Management* 33, no. 4 (October 1995): 53–65.

23. M. A. McGinnis, "Building Better Performance Measures," *NAPM Insights* (1 May 1995): 50–53.

24. P. G. Russell and W. C. Kropf, "Hewlett-Packard's Packaging Supplier Evaluation Process and Criteria", IOPP 16th Educational Symposium on Transport Packaging Proceedings, February 1999.

25. A. Gunasekaran, C. Pate, and E. Tirtiroglu, "Performance Measures and Metrics in a Supply Chain Environment," *International Journal of Operations & Production Management* 21, no. 1/2 (2001): 71–87.

26. L. M. Ellram, "A Structured Method for Applying Purchasing Cost Management Tools"; available from http://www.ism.ws/ResourceArticles/1996/jwinter962.cfm

27. L. Ellram, "Total Cost of Ownership: Elements and Implementation," *International Journal of Purchasing and Materials Management* 29, no. 4 (October 1993): 3–11.

28. B. Ferrin and R. Plank, "Total Cost of Ownership Models: An Exploratory Study," *Journal of Supply Chain Management* 38, no. 3 (summer 2002): 18–29.

29. John Fontana, "Chrysler SCORE's $2 Billion Cost Savings," Internetweek, March 9, 1998; http://www.techweb.com/wire/story/TWB19980309S0005.

30. A. M. Porter, "Just the Facts," *Purchasing* (18 April 2002); available from http://www.manufacturing.net/pur

31. T. Stundza, "Whirlpool Aims to Cut Costs 5% Annually," *Purchasing* (9 August 2001): 17–24; available from http://www.manufacturing.net/pur

32. Available from Whirlpool Web site: http://www.whirlpoolwebworld.com

33. "Whirlpool Transforms Its MRO Buy to Strategic," *Purchasing* (7 March 2002); available from http://www.manufacturing.net/pur

34. T. Stundza, "How Whirlpool Buys Steel," *Purchasing* (9 August 2001); available from http://www.manufacturing.net/pur

35. D. Nelson, P. E. Moody, and J. Stegner, *The Purchasing Machine: How the Top Ten Companies Use Best Practices to Manage Their Supply Chains* (New York: The Free Press/Simon & Schuster, Inc., 2001).

36. T. Stundza, "Whirlpool Aims to Cut Costs 5% Annually": 17–24.

37. "Glossary of Key Purchasing and Supply Terms: Supplier Certification," Institute for Supply Management Web site.

38. "Supplier Certification: A Continuous Improvement Strategy," Tompkins Associates, M-49; available from http://www.tompkinsinc.com

39. J. Ericson, "Measuring Supplier Performance," Line 56, *E-Business Ecosystem* (27 September 2001); available from http://www.Line56.com

40. "Doing Business with Ford" Web site; available from https://fsn.ford.com/dbwf/dbwf_quality.html

41. The ISO Survey of ISO 9000 and ISO 14000 Certificates, Eleventh Cycle (up to and including 31 December 2001); available from http://www.iso.ch/iso/en/ISOOnline.frontpage

42. Ibid.

43. "Will ISO 14001 Become a Requirement?" Capaccio Environmental Engineering, Inc.; available from http://www.capaccio.com/ISOCorner/Article4.htm

44. "Environmental Guide," Ford Motor Company; available from https://fsn.ford.com/dbwf/docs/intro.pdf

45. R. B. Handfield, D. R. Krause, T. V. Scannell, and R. M. Monzka, "Avoid the Pitfalls in Supplier Development," *Sloan Management Review* (winter 2000): 37–49.

46. J. Morgan, "New Survey Finds Big Gap."

47. Handfield, Krause, Scannell, and Monzka, "Avoid the Pitfalls": 37–49.

48. A. M. Porter, "Just the Facts."

49. J. Carbone, "Strategic Purchasing Cuts Costs 25% at Siemens," *Purchasing* (20 September 2001); available from http://www.manufacturing.net/pur

50. J. Carbone, "Siemens Medical Systems: It Takes a Lot of Hard Work to Reach Top Plus Quality," *Purchasing* (15 November 2001); available from http://www.manufacturing.net/pur

51. J. R. Stegner, B. Butterfield, and C. T. Evers, "John Deere Supplier Development Program," 87th Annual International Supply Management Conference, 2002 International Conference Proceedings (May 2002); available from Institute for Supply Management Web site.

52. 2001 World Excellence Award Winners, The Ford Motor Company; available from https://fsn.ford.com/dbwf/FORDUSAToday2001.pdf

53. "Manugistics Supplier Relationship Management Solutions"; available from Manugistics Web site.

54. B. Barling, "The Five Tenets of SRM," *AMR Research* (10 June 2002); available from http://www.amrresearch.com

55. "Survey—Supply Chain Management," *Financial Times,* London (20 June 2001): 6.

56. B. Barling, "The Five Tenets of SRM."

57. "SRM (Supplier Relationship Management): M2SYS Innovate. Implement. Excel," 2002 M2SYS Technology PowerPoint presentation slides.

58. Ibid.

59. T. Wilson, "SRM Offers New Look at Supply Chains" (24 September 2001); available from http://www.internetwk.com/story/INW20010924S0005

60. "Supplier Relationship Management (SRM): The Supply Works Answer to Accelerating Competitive Advantage," *Business Matters #2,* a series of manufacturing SRM business briefs from Supply Works, Inc. (May 2001).

61. "Bayer CropScience in U.S. Harvests Millions in Savings with SAS SRM"; available from SAS Web site.

62. Available from M2SYS Technology Web sites: http://www.m2sys.com/srm.htm and http://www.m2sys.com/syndeo.htm

Chapter 4:

STRATEGIC SOURCING FOR SUCCESSFUL SUPPLY CHAIN MANAGEMENT

"In organizations of the future, world-class operations will require world-class supply management and suppliers. Developing sustainable competitive advantage depends on developing competencies that are not easily duplicated by competitors. Supply management in world-class organizations will evolve into such a competency."[1]

Learning Objectives

After completing this chapter, you should be able to
- Describe how strategic sourcing plans are developed and implemented.
- Describe the various strategic sourcing activities.
- Describe purchasing's role in managing key supplier relationships.
- Describe the performance criteria used in assessing suppliers.
- Describe how strategic supplier relationships can impact the firm.
- Describe how a reverse auction works.
- Understand the importance of sharing the benefits of strategic partnerships.
- Understand the strategic role played by the purchasing function in developing and improving the supply chain.

Chapter Outline

Introduction

Developing Successful Sourcing Strategies

Supply Base Reduction Programs

Evaluating and Selecting Key Suppliers

Strategic Alliance and Supplier Certification Programs

Outsourcing Programs

Early Supplier Involvement

Supplier Management and Alliance Development

Managing and Developing Second-Tier Supplier Relationships

Use of e-Procurement Systems

Rewarding Supplier Performance

Benchmarking Successful Sourcing Practices

Using Third-Party Supply Chain Management Services

Assessing and Improving the Firm's Purchasing Function

SUPPLY CHAIN MANAGEMENT IN ACTION *Cessna Aircraft*

When Michael R. Katzorke, vice president of Supply Management at Cessna Aircraft in Wichita, Kansas, began working on the company's supply chain management system in 1998, Cessna was still a traditional aerospace firm. It had a functional orientation, was vertically integrated, and had traditional processes and practices. Soon, it became clear to Katzorke that making real improvements in Cessna's supply chain would require actions by the entire enterprise. So, Katzorke and his Cessna colleagues developed and deployed a number of practices aimed at improving supplier performance and integrating key suppliers with Cessna's manufacturing and design processes. Discussion of several of these practices follows:

- *Business process model:* A new business process model was developed that was based around five core processes—customer management, product development, order acquisition, order fulfillment, and post-delivery support. The model provided an important step in driving supply chain management into Cessna's corporate culture. Because the number of suppliers in its industry was limited, Cessna needed to share many suppliers with its competitors. This raised the urgency for Cessna to integrate its supply chain better than its competitors.

- *Rationalization plans:* More had to be accomplished to remove nonperforming suppliers from Cessna's supply chain. If buyers were allowed to keep giving work to nonperforming suppliers, the problem would never be solved. What was really needed was a plan—specifically one with names, faces, phase-out dates, and problem areas.

- *Full-time commodity teams:* Full-time commodity teams were created to rationalize the supply base, align business processes with suppliers, help suppliers improve, and integrate suppliers into Cessna's manufacturing processes. The very first thing the commodity teams did was to create strategic plans. These plans dealt with decision making in such areas as make versus buy, sourcing strategies, plant improvement, trading, quality, and supplier mentoring.

- *STARS:* To support its supply base rationalization efforts, Cessna created STARS—Suppliers Tracking and Rating System, a database of historical and current supplier behavior relative to quality, cost, delivery, service, inventory, and technology, using a 1–5 rating scale (1 being good, 5 being unacceptable). The data is shared monthly with the CEO of each major supplier.

- *Sorting process:* Using the same type of 1–5 scoring used in STARS, Cessna commodity teams developed a rating system to compare suppliers based on evaluations by cross-functional teams. Supplier rationalization at Cessna involves a sorting process that ranks suppliers into one of three categories: (1) growth: suppliers whose share of Cessna business will grow; (2) provisional: suppliers whose future prospects as Cessna suppliers are cloudy based on past performance; and (3) phase-out: suppliers whose business with Cessna is about to end.

- *Electronic reverse auctions:* Cessna uses an electronic reverse auction tool to accelerate purchases from growth suppliers. Only growth suppliers are allowed to bid in Cessna auctions. Growth suppliers also are given opportunities to bid on business that was formerly with phase-out suppliers. A decision process that once consumed six months or more is completed at the end of an hour or so.

- *Supplier advisory board:* The idea of the board is to improve communication between critical suppliers, Cessna's senior leadership team, and customers. A major role played by the ten-member supplier advisory board is preparation of a blind survey on supplier satisfaction. The main goals of the board are both to unearth gaps in Cessna's strategies and to solicit suggestions on how to improve.

- *Maturity path development process (MPD):* This is a "sit-down" held with each supplier. Cessna says, "Here, Mr. Supplier, is where you stand in terms of quality, cost, delivery, service, inventory, and so on. Based on that, we want to make a very specific plan that you're willing to commit to for this year," according to Katzorke. MPD teams operate in each of Cessna's commodity areas. The team's job is to poll members of the organization on all the things they feel are important for suppliers to improve for the year. Suppliers do the same. Then the two negotiate a commitment on what they feel can realistically be accomplished.

- *Alignment of measurement systems:* Cessna decided to use Baldrige Quality Award criteria for assessing all its internal processes. At the same time it announced its intention to apply the Baldrige criteria to all its growth suppliers. Cessna and its growth suppliers would thus be judged against the same Baldrige criteria. Only growth suppliers and provisional suppliers that are doing well on their improvement efforts are invited to participate in the improvement plan.

Katzorke also spent a lot of time linking performance objectives with development reviews so that managers understood that something more was expected of them. Katzorke noted, "We had to give them the skills to perform at the higher level. For instance, rather than telling them they needed to improve negotiation skills, we showed them what better is, how to get better, and then equipped them." Katzorke turned to certification programs as sources of fundamental training, and developed relationships with local universities in an effort to raise internal competencies at all levels. Cessna is beginning to chalk up some encouraging performance improvements. But, Katzorke is both optimistic and wary of the future. A challenge, he suggests, will be to keep corporate leaders focused on reducing the company's cost of goods sold (through better purchasing) rather than on reducing direct labor costs. "The profit on a dollar's worth of sales is lucky to net a dime whereas the net on a dollar's worth of savings is still a dollar," he says.[2]

Introduction

As you have read in Chapter 2 and Chapter 3 of this text, purchasing departments are increasingly seen as valuable, strategic contributors to the organization because of their ability to impact product design and quality, cost of goods sold, cycle time, and, hence, profitability and competitive position. Purchasing's ability to span the organization and its boundaries is quite unique, in that it interacts with internal and external customers, suppliers, design, production, finance, marketing, and accounting personnel, as well as the firm's executive managers. As companies move toward taking a more proactive role in managing their supply chains, purchasing is then seen as one of the primary designers and facilitators of these efforts.

A number of recent worldwide economic factors have acted to hasten many organizations' plans to institute supply chain management strategies to reduce costs and delivery cycle times while improving quality, leading to improvements in long-term financial performance. Additionally, the increasing number of global competitors, attempts by firms to become more customer focused, the high costs of globalization and materials, and the need to deliver more innovative products more frequently and cheaply than competitors have also combined to place added pressures on firms to achieve breakthrough performance in supply chain management. Today, these trends have become the drivers of **strategic sourcing** and supply chain initiatives.

As shown in the Supply Chain Management in Action profile, purchasing managers are finding that they must be much more adept at locating and developing good suppliers, integrating them into the firm's business processes and strategies, achieving greater levels of purchased item quality, developing cost-saving action plans, and achieving acceptable supplier delivery performance, as well as ensuring that purchased materials and products are consistent with customer requirements. Furthermore, because of corporate downsizing, purchasing departments often must do these sourcing activities with fewer people. These are some tall expectations for today's purchasing manager. A recent survey of purchasing managers highlighted a number of trends in purchasing, when compared to earlier surveys that had been performed:[3]

1. Purchasing managers supervised almost 50 percent fewer employees compared to 1987.

2. Half of the respondents served on product development teams.

3. Twenty-one percent of the respondents held professional certifications in purchasing, compared to 14 percent in 1987.

4. Eighty percent were consolidating their purchases with fewer suppliers.

5. Sixty-eight percent were using foreign suppliers.

6. Sixty-nine percent were monitoring supplier performance.

7. Sixty percent said they meet with top management at least weekly.

Developing effective sourcing strategies that create sustainable competitive advantage is no easy task. Building, maintaining, and improving supplier alliances pose many benefits for the firms involved; but many of these relationships end in failure because of misaligned strategies, lack of commitment, unrealized goals, and loss of trust in the relationships. Managers proactively managing their supply chains must also come to understand that some sourcing strategies are better suited to some supply chains than others. Firms may have dozens of supply chains among their most important inbound purchased items and outbound finished products. Some of these supply chains may be driven by a low-cost overall strategy, while others may have quality or service as the overriding objective. Even parts and components used in one product may have diverging supply chain strategies. In this chapter, we discuss the development of successful supply chain and sourcing strategies and the specific elements that constitute these strategies.

Developing Successful Sourcing Strategies

To achieve some or all of the supply chain management objectives we have described thus far in this and previous chapters, a number of sourcing or supply-oriented strategies must be considered and implemented. Care must be taken when developing these purchasing plans. Without aligning sourcing strategies with supply chain objectives, organizations may invest considerable resources into designing a particular set of sourcing activities, only to find that the resulting performance is much less than originally predicted.

In one of the more important papers written on this topic, Dr. Martin Fisher describes two types of supply chains: those for **functional products,** and those for **innovative products.**[4] Examples of functional products are MRO items and other commonly purchased items and supplies. These items are characterized by low profit margins, relatively stable demands, and high levels of competition. Thus, companies with functional product purchases most likely concentrate on using sourcing strategies based on securing a stable supply at the lowest cost. Many of Wal-Mart's supply chains, for example, would fall into this category. Examples of innovative consumer goods in the past have been the IBM Thinkpad and HDTV for retailers; in industrial settings, these might be new types of control mechanisms, innovative office software products, or a new piece of communications equipment. These products are characterized by short product life cycles, volatile demand, high profit margins, and relatively less competition. Consequently, the sourcing strategy for these products may rely much more heavily on supplier quality, speed, flexibility, and communication capabilities. Many of Motorola's supply chains for example, would fall into the innovative product category.

Many of the commonly used purchasing strategies of thirty years ago will not work well today. For instance, simply "squeezing" suppliers to generate a lower cost of goods sold may ultimately prove harmful to buyer-supplier relationships and may in fact cause quality to deteriorate, as suppliers seek ways to cut corners in order to keep their profit margins at desired levels. If long-term sourcing plans are to be successful, they must support the long-term supply chain and business strategies; and suppliers must also see some benefit from the initiatives implemented. A six-step framework for supply chain strategy development is shown in Figure 4.1.

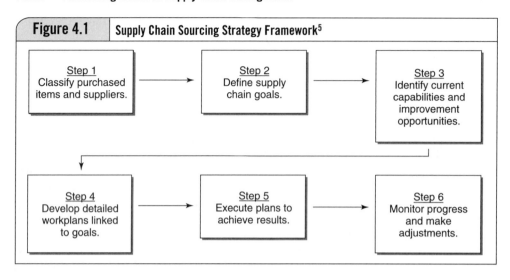

Figure 4.1 | **Supply Chain Sourcing Strategy Framework[5]**

In Step 1, the firm's suppliers and the items they supply are classified as belonging either to the innovative or functional category. In Step 2, the goals and strategies of the inbound portion of the supply chain are developed, assuring that these strategies, and the sourcing strategies derived from them, are consistent with the type of products purchased and also support the overall strategies of the firm. For example, if the firm's overall reputation and strategy are to be the quality leaders in the firm's markets, then sourcing strategies for most of the innovative products, components, and parts that make up the finished products must concentrate on assuring high levels of quality, flexibility, and service as well. In Step 3, supply chain capabilities are evaluated and compared to the performances necessary to achieve the sourcing strategies from Step 2, thus identifying areas for improvement. For a company geared toward quality leadership, key suppliers will be evaluated based on their quality and service capabilities and commitment toward contributing to the firm's long-term sourcing strategies. Step 4 takes the areas for improvement identified in Step 3 and sets goals for improving capabilities and closing these gaps. The goals must be specific and measurable, and may be the result of industry benchmarking. Measurement or performance targets are then determined to identify success in achieving these goals. The second objective of Step 4 is to develop specific work plans to meet these goals. The work plans are broken down into smaller project tasks, with target implementation dates for each of the tasks. For example, if we extend the quality thread through these last few steps, the firm may institute a goal to develop a quality certification program and then require certification of all key suppliers. Thus, the certification process must be designed and communicated to all key suppliers, and then a time-phased certification implementation plan would be developed. Step 5 involves implementing the work plan successfully. This may involve an initial pilot study at one plant, for instance, to gauge the ability of the certification program to improve incoming supply quality. Finally, Step 6 is to monitor the progress and outcomes and adjust the work plans to more adequately meet the original supply chain goals. In this example, it may be that certain elements in the certification program need to be revised to more adequately meet desired quality goals.

Let us now discuss a number of strategic sourcing initiatives, some of which have already been introduced in earlier chapters, that may be used separately or in some combination to support the organization's long-term goals while providing financial benefits to the organization. These proactive sourcing initiatives, when combined with internal operations and customer relationship initiatives, form the foundation of a successful supply chain management strategy and, ultimately, competitive advantage for the firm.

Supply Base Reduction Programs

As we saw in this chapter's Supply Chain Management in Action and in Chapter 3, firms taking an active role in supply chain management seek to reduce purchases from marginal or poor-performing suppliers while increasing and concentrating purchases among their top-performing key suppliers. Firms have thus been *optimizing* or *rationalizing* the size of their supply bases, and this has been a common occurrence since the late 1980s. Indeed, activities aimed at fostering buyer-supplier partnerships and increasing the performance and value of suppliers are simply easier when fewer suppliers are involved. Thus, supply base reduction programs have the benefits of reduced purchase prices, fewer supplier management problems, closer and more frequent interaction between buyer and supplier, and greater overall levels of quality and delivery reliability, since only the best suppliers remain in the supply base. Even if the goal in a supply chain is predominantly cost minimization, there are still typically enough competing suppliers such that only the best-performing, highest-quality, low-cost suppliers can constitute an organization's supply base. Supply base reduction is most often the initial supply chain management effort and usually precedes the formation of buyer-supplier strategic relationships.

In some cases, firms must restructure their supply bases while optimizing their size, by identifying new and better suppliers external to the original supply base. This can result in even greater levels of supply base performance and possibly even increase the size of the firms' supply bases. Supply bases should also be viewed as dynamic or evolving entities. Suppliers come and go, and they develop new and better capabilities; thus, revisiting supply bases annually or as contracts are about to expire makes good economic sense. Obviously, monitoring the performance of existing suppliers also helps in assuring that the supply base is meeting quality, cost, and service standards.

Evaluating and Selecting Key Suppliers

Supplier evaluation and selection as discussed in general in Chapter 2 and more specifically in Chapter 3 involve the careful use of multiple criteria for screening and evaluation purposes. Optimizing supply bases, as discussed in the previous section, requires use of performance criteria that relate to the strategies of the firm and the particular supply chain. When evaluating suppliers to be used in a strategic partnering or collaborative relationship, these criteria take on added importance. In these cases, purchase cost becomes relatively less important, although it is likely that, over time, long-term agreements allow suppliers to concentrate more resources on reducing their costs, resulting in lower selling prices. As the reliance on these key suppliers increases, firms must manage their supply base as an extension of their internal operations.

Supplier evaluation and selection criteria, described in detail in Chapter 3, can initially allow firms to screen out undesirable suppliers but are also used to build better ongoing supplier relationships, improve the overall performance of the supply base, and, ultimately, provide competitive advantage to the organization and its supply chain. Studies indicate that only about half of the firms in the United States formally evaluate suppliers using evaluation forms that have been created for this purpose.[6] Providing these supplier evaluation criteria and minimum performance expectations to existing and potential suppliers communicates the firm's expectations and creates performance standards that, in turn, become strategic goals for the suppliers. Incremental improvements can also be achieved by increasing the performance expectations over time. These criteria, then, act to further integrate key suppliers with the organization.

Once the buyer-supplier relationship is established, firms periodically monitor supplier performance using essentially the same criteria. Contracts with strategic suppliers are increasingly becoming long term, resulting in even closer relationships, more effective two-way communication, a greater willingness to share information, and even better supplier performance. These important channel partnerships provide continuous and increasing value for all of the participants, and this is termed **channel equity.**[7] Many firms are requiring that their supply bases must pursue the same continuous improvement strategies they have created for themselves. Motorola does this by requiring suppliers to satisfy improvement goals in four areas: progressing toward attaining perfect product quality, remaining on the leading edge of product and process technology, practicing just-in-time manufacturing and delivery, and offering cost-competitive service. To these ends, Motorola uses a comprehensive performance evaluation system to keep track of suppliers' progress.[8]

When selecting key suppliers to use for important purchased items or services, a cross-functional team selection approach is used, wherein purchasing staff, primary users, product designers, and manufacturing personnel are involved in designing the supplier evaluation instrument and its distribution to various suppliers. Once evaluations are completed, suppliers are selected and agreements are discussed and finalized between this group and the suppliers. Ongoing evaluations are also frequently administered using the same or a similar group.

Strategic Alliance and Supplier Certification Programs

Proactively seeking and creating strategic alliances have become important objectives of firms seeking to manage their supply chains, as we read in Chapter 3. Strategic alliances are a more formalized type of collaborative relationship, involving commitments to long-term cooperation, shared benefits and costs, joint problem solving, continuous improvement, and information sharing. Because of these relationships, suppliers are able to invest more of their resources toward becoming specialized in areas required by the buyer-partner, to establish production and/or storage facilities close to the buyer's facilities, to purchase compatible communication and information systems, and to invest in better technology that will ultimately improve product quality and delivery time.

Supplier certification programs are one way to identify strategic alliance candidates. In many cases, certification programs are simply based on internationally recognized certifications like the International Organization for Standardization's ISO 9000 series of quality certifications. Unfortunately, as these industry certifications become more commonplace and are required by more buyers, the organization is left with a reduced ability to compare suppliers. For the organization actively managing its supply chain, this type of certification requirement is simply not enough. These firms have developed their own formal certification programs, most of which require ISO 9000 or similar quality certifications as one element of the certification process.

An extensive site audit may be performed using a cross-functional team to identify a supplier's process capabilities, materials and methods used, and to assure that a certain level of management control exists. Buyers can monitor the quality assurance methods, for instance, and identify the type of **acceptance sampling** and **statistical process control** methods used. Teams can also detect potential weaknesses and areas in need of improvement during these site audits, which can mean the difference between a successful and an unsuccessful supplier relationship. Formal certification programs contain this type of physical contact, as well as visits of supplier representatives to the buyer facility to discuss buyer requirements, production characteristics, and other typical buyer-supplier interactions or sourcing elements. Additionally, certification programs typically include surveys given to the supplier and meetings with existing customers of the supplier to obtain feedback on supplier performance.

For existing suppliers, certification procedures can be somewhat different, since much of the information is already known to the buyer. Still, certifications and recertifications of existing suppliers most likely contain periodic surveys, site visits, and reviews of performance. Formal certification programs thus assure a level of capability among suppliers and act as a way to communicate performance requirements and areas in need of improvement to the supplier or supply base. Taken in a positive way, strategic partners can see this feedback as an extremely important tool for improving their performance and competitiveness. In this environment, certification programs are viewed as win-win exercises.

Outsourcing Programs

Purchasing costs as a percentage of sales have been growing over the years, as firms have opted to outsource materials, parts, services, and assembled components to concentrate more resources and energy on core business activities. Simply put, firms are buying more and making less these days. In the recent Center for Advanced Purchasing Studies (CAPS) Cross-Industry Benchmarking Report combining both service and manufacturing firms, annual purchase dollars as a percentage of sales in the United States grew to approximately 42 percent as of August 2002.[9] Firms are outsourcing noncore products and service functions (i.e., maintenance, janitorial, or other support services) and, in some cases, more important items or services that can impact the competitiveness of the firm. Notably, outsourcing gives firms the potential to leverage larger purchase volumes to gain quantity discounts, particularly if purchases are concentrated among fewer suppliers. Additionally, industrial buyers can typically negotiate better associated supply services as well, when purchasing in larger quantities.

Aside from allowing firms to concentrate more on core capabilities while potentially reducing cost, outsourcing can also result in reduced staffing levels, accelerated reengineering efforts, reduced management problems, and gains in manufacturing flexibility. These benefits must be weighed against the risks associated with outsourcing, including loss of control, increased need for supplier management, and an increased reliance on the supplier. When outsourcing strategically important products or services, these risks can be very significant. Thus, supplier selection can be extremely important when outsourcing. Outsourcing typically occurs as the result of a make-or-buy analysis, as addressed in Chapter 2. At this point, an outsourcing team is created with representation from all stakeholder areas in the firm. The team leader is most often a staff member from purchasing. The team's objective is to identify the organization's long-term needs for the outsourcing project, identify and select the supplier, negotiate and finalize the outsourcing agreement with the supplier based on the identified long-term needs, and then plan the transition and execution of the outsourcing project.

In cases where firms are actively managing their supply chains, firms often outsource key products and services to suppliers who are already or are on the verge of becoming strategic partners or key suppliers. These outsourcing arrangements can be used to further solidify a trading relationship, to gain additional negotiating leverage, and to minimize the outsourcing risks mentioned in the preceding paragraph. In these cases, outsourcing to highly capable and reliable suppliers can lead to improved quality in addition to lower prices, particularly when the outsourced product or service is a core product of the supplier. In some trading relationships, outsourcing is done in both directions if the supplier and buyer both have core competencies in product areas desired by the other.

Early Supplier Involvement

As the adoption of **concurrent engineering** and **design for manufacturability** techniques become more commonplace and relationships with suppliers become more trusted, reliable, and long-term in nature, key suppliers become more heavily involved in the internal operations of the firm, particularly with respect to new product and process design. Key suppliers become contributors to these efforts by serving in a decision-making capacity on new product and process design teams within the firm. They become involved in the buyer firm's product part and assembly design, new product materials usage, and even the design of the processes to be used in producing new products. Thus, strategic suppliers begin to play a greater role in the organization's decision-making processes as these relationships grow, further solidifying the supply chain relationship.

These **value engineering** activities help the firm to reduce cost, improve quality, and reduce new product development time. Cost reductions come about through use of more standardized parts, fewer parts, and less-expensive materials. Cost, quality, and timing improvements all come about when suppliers use the information gained through early supplier involvement to design parts and processes at their own facilities to match the buyer's specifications. Also, since they have been involved early in the buyer's new product design process, these part and process changes can be timed to be in place and available when needed by the buyer. These activities contribute to an organization's continuous improvement efforts, as process and product design changes result in better quality, cost, and turnaround time. Use of value engineering allows firms to design better quality and cost savings into the products from the start of a product's useful life. Over the life of a product, this can generate significant savings and revenues, while reducing the need for cost-savings initiatives in the future.

Early supplier involvement is perhaps one of the most effective supply chain integrative techniques. Working together—sharing proprietary design and manufacturing information that both the supplier's and buyer's competitors would love to see—establishes a level of trust and cooperation that results in many future collaborative and potentially successful projects.

Supplier Management and Alliance Development

As the growth of supply chain management continues, firms must also become more adept at managing their suppliers and more willing to help their supply bases improve their production and service capabilities. Simply put, supplier management is concerned with getting suppliers to do what firms need them to do, while **alliance development,** an extension of *supplier development* (covered in Chapter 3), refers to increasing a *key or strategic supplier's* capabilities. A number of activities we have already discussed such as supply base reduction, supplier evaluation, and certification programs constitute forms of supplier management. As supply bases become smaller, they also become more manageable. Supplier management activities tend to become somewhat less time-consuming as supplier alliances begin to constitute more and more of the supply base, while alliance development begins to occupy more of the purchasing function's time and resources.

Firms are beginning to realize that supplier alliances result in better market penetration, access to new technologies and knowledge, and higher return on investment than competitors with no such strategic alliances. Alliances can also become very expensive failures, perhaps as much as 60 to 70 percent of the time[10] and thus require a significant effort on both sides to see to it that these relationships stay beneficial to both parties.

As discussed in Chapter 3, a number of supplier or alliance development activities exist and become more vital to the firm as outsourcing continues and as the firm comes to depend more on a smaller group of vital suppliers. Alliance development will eventually even extend to a firm's second-tier suppliers, as the firm's key suppliers begin to form their own alliance development activities. Alliance development among the firm and its key suppliers tends to be much more of a shared, proactive activity, requiring both sides to commit time, people, communication, and monetary resources to achieving goals that will benefit both parties. Instead of simply providing help to solve a particular problem or offering a short seminar that will soon be forgotten, alliance development results in long-term retained learning because of the full-time commitment of relationship management personnel from both sides to this idea of collaborative development. The focal firm and its key suppliers jointly decide on improvement activities, resources required, and the means to measure progress. As the improvements and learning take place, suppliers eventually become capable of passing these same capabilities on to their suppliers, thus extending these learned capabilities up the supply chain, resulting in improved overall supply chain performance and competitiveness.

Alliance development requires companies to actively develop and improve relationship value systems within their organization's culture, learn from their mistakes and from the success stories of other alliances within and from outside the firm, and to invest in communication tools that enable collaborative problem solving. Many firms are hiring strategic relationship managers, whose sole job is to build trust, commitment, and mutual value within the alliance. These relationship managers work on institutionalizing the idea of collaboration and mutual benefit, so that alliances become the norm among the various business units in the organization. Alliances, like products, have their own life cycles, requiring ongoing management and development activities to monitor success, manage conflict, evaluate the current fit with partners, revisit the ground rules for working together, and make adjustments through mutual problem solving and information sharing.

Some of the more successful alliance-generating companies like Hewlett-Packard, Oracle, and Eli Lilly & Co. have directors of strategic alliances with their own staff.[11] They function as the centers in their organizations for coordinating alliance programs and other alliance-related activities, like providing educational programs, developing guidelines for alliance management, finding alliance partners, and creating alliance teams. These alliances also create external visibility for the firm, affect the firm's reputation, and create significant value for the firm. In fact, in their study on strategic alliances, Dyer, Kale, and Singh found that a firm's stock price jumped 1 percent for each announcement of a new alliance.[12] Numerous alliance-seeking Web sites can now be found on the World Wide Web of companies of all types, seeking to attract new alliance partners. Organizing a successful alliance program is thus very important to the firm's competitiveness and can be quite challenging. Table 4.1 describes the organization process.

To make strategic alliance programs successful, firms must determine how to organize a program that can cut across firm functions; disseminate information quickly and effectively throughout the organization; acquire the necessary resources; be accepted by the line managers and their employees; and achieve concrete, measurable success. Some firms have chosen to organize around their key alliance partners by assigning alliance managers to each of these partners. Others have decided to create an alliance board to oversee alliances and coordinate alliance managers in various divisions within the organization or in different geographic regions of the world. An extremely important responsibility of the alliance managers is to facilitate the distribution of alliance development information throughout the organization. The alliance function can act as a clearinghouse for information regarding all types of alliance needs, from negotiation strategies to problem-solving assistance to outreach programs and workshops. To give the alliance function credibility, the program director should report to the organization's top management. This facilitates the use of company resources as well as provides internal visibility to the function. Alliance strategies, goals, policies, and procedures can then be generated and communicated across the entire organization. Finally, since alliances change over time, they must be evaluated periodically. Some alliances may need to be discontinued. Performance evaluation metrics must be established; and, as alliances show signs of success, strategies can be shared across the various alliance boundaries. Alliance directors can thus use success stories to increase visibility both within and outside the firm and to support the request for additional resources.

Table 4.1	Maintaining a Successful Strategic Alliance Program[13]
1. Determine the key strategic parameters, and organize around them.	Parameters are based on business units, geographic areas, industries, key alliance partners, or combinations of these.
2. Facilitate the dissemination of information.	Alliance generating and management and development information should be centrally controlled and available through internal Web sites, pamphlets, internal experts, and workshops.
3. Elevate the importance of the alliance function.	Assign a director or vice president of alliance programs who reports to top management. Establish consistent procedures for alliance programs throughout the organization.
4. Provide continuous evaluation of alliance performance, visibility, and support.	Management can increase the value and acceptance of alliance programs when successes are made visible to the firm's lower-level managers and employees. Alliance management requires resources and ongoing reevaluation.

Managing and Developing Second-Tier Supplier Relationships

As we have alluded to, developing effective alliances with key suppliers tends to create effective second-tier relationships as suppliers embark on alliance development programs of their own. A recent study by Dr. Park and Dr. Hartley confirms this. They showed that supplier management practices adopted by first-tier suppliers impacted second-tier supplier performance, which then, in turn, impacted the first-tier suppliers' quality and delivery performance to the focal firm.[14]

Thus, successful alliance development can indirectly create successful, high-performing second-tier and, eventually, even third-tier relationships as well, as supplier management and development practices are implemented and sequentially passed up the supply chain from tier to tier. This becomes yet another benefit of long-term supplier alliance building efforts. Organizations can also take a more direct approach to second-tier supplier management and development by requiring direct suppliers to acquire goods and services from specific suppliers and under specific conditions. They can also work directly with supplier alliance partners in solving second-tier supplier problems, designing supplier selection and certification programs, and implementing alliance development strategies. Doing the math, though, shows that a firm's influence is substantially reduced among second-tier and third-tier suppliers (e.g., if each firm in the supply chain has twenty suppliers, the focal firm will have 400 suppliers in its second-tier network and 8,000 suppliers in its third-tier network). However daunting these numbers may seem, managing these more distant supplier networks will significantly impact the overall cycle time, cost, and quality of the firm's supply chains, creating even greater competitive advantage.

Use of e-Procurement Systems

As discussed in Chapter 2, using the Internet in procurement can create enormous benefits to organizations with mostly paper-based procurement systems and a large volume of standard; functional item; or maintenance, repair, and operating (MRO) supplies purchases. The primary strategic benefits of e-procurement include significant cost savings and the freeing-up of time for purchasing staff to concentrate on more of the core business activities. This comes about because e-procurement systems enable the concentration of a large volume of small purchases with a few suppliers in electronic catalogues, which are made available to the organization's users. The users then select items directly from the catalogues and buy on contracts that allow repeat purchases. The firm's computer system automatically routes transactions for approvals, sends the information along to the accounting system, and routes the purchase order directly to the supplier.

Another form of e-procurement is the use of the Internet to conduct **reverse auctions.** Reverse auctions utilize the Internet to allow suppliers to enter a reverse auction Web site supported by one of many application service providers (ASPs). At a predesignated time and date, qualified suppliers try to underbid their competitors and can monitor the bid prices until the session is over (company identities are known only by the buyer). These third-party reverse auction services charge a fee in many cases to both the buyer and the suppliers to participate. Many ASPs sell reverse auction software to companies and offer technical support for a monthly fee; the costs vary tremendously based on security required, the number of sellers, reporting features, buyer-supplier communication capabilities, and other desired customized services. Self-serve reverse auction sites are also very easy to find on the Internet and are extremely low cost. A quick Web search on the term "reverse auction software providers" resulted in hundreds of company sites, most offering similar services. A few examples of these ASPs were: LookTrade, FreeMarkets.com, and GreatShop.com. As we can see here, the Internet is an extremely useful sourcing tool, in that it allows firms to efficiently screen and select suppliers and then automate the buying activity, greatly reducing the time required to manage these activities while creating significant opportunities for cost savings.

e-BUSINESS CONNECTION

FREEMARKETS INC.

FreeMarkets Inc., a Pittsburgh provider of Internet sourcing services, says reverse auctions are a safe and transparent method to help owners make effective real-time buying decisions. "We started doing reverse auctions in 1995 and have completed over 20,000 in all industry sectors," says Greg Anderson, the firm's director of global market operations. "We have helped source $45 billion in goods and services." Karen J. Kovatch, a FreeMarkets spokeswoman, says customers save 17% on average. "That translates into about $9 billion to date," she says.

FreeMarkets is one of dozens of consulting firms, software providers, or industry-sponsored exchanges that now provide reverse auction services. It offers "selfserve" software, or full-service support where FreeMarkets manages all reverse auction operations and promotion. The latter requires a client to sign a long-term contract. According to Anderson, bidders and buyers sign agreements that vouch for the validity of their bids and/or contract awards. If a party reneges, it is suspended from further network participation.

FreeMarkets also helps full-service clients develop requests for qualifications (RFQs) and pre-qualified supplier lists. The firm also monitors log-ons to see if all bidders are participating. "We are a no-cost sales channel to buyers, and we are passionate about integrity, neutrality, and trust," says Anderson. "We're not out to crack relationships, just give assurances that owners are getting true market pricing."

FreeMarkets has used the system for industrial, infrastructure, and commercial construction projects. A recent reverse auction for a line-item, lump-sum powerplant project look four months to develop and drew four bidders. Preparation also included a site walk. "Anything traditionally done with sealed bids still happens before an online auction," says Krish Y. Pandya, engineering and construction market development manager for FreeMarkets. "Plus, we also encourage buyers not to short-list."[20]

Rewarding Supplier Performance

Rewarding suppliers for improving or maintaining high levels of performance accomplishes several objectives: it provides a continuous incentive to all key suppliers to meet and surpass specific performance goals; it provides an incentive for marginal (unrewarded) suppliers to achieve a level of performance that will allow their supplier status to be upgraded and potentially result in rewards; and, finally, it gives suppliers an incentive to create and share rewards, in turn, with *their* suppliers. Sharing the benefits of performance in this way is one of the central foundations to building effective supply chains. As we mentioned at the start of the chapter, suppliers, in addition to buyers, must be able to realize benefits from supply chain relationships. Without this incentive, suppliers may keep any improvements realized within their operations quiet, while keeping the benefits as well. With time, this lack of information and benefit sharing stunts the growth of relationships within the supply chain and results in lower overall supply chain performance.

As many of us may remember from growing up or from raising our own children, performance motivation can come in two forms—punishment and rewards. With suppliers, these same motivational tools can be used as an integral part of supplier management and supplier development programs. Punishment may take the form of reduced future business with the focal firm; a downgrade of the supplier's status from key to marginal, for instance; or a **billback** amount equal to the incremental cost resulting from a late delivery or poor material quality. On the other hand, when performance meets or exceeds expectations, suppliers can be rewarded in some way. Many formal strategic supplier agreements allow suppliers to benefit in the following ways:

- A share of the cost reductions resulting from supplier improvements
- A share of the cost savings resulting from suggestions made during early supplier involvement in the firm's product and process design efforts
- More business and/or longer contracts
- Access to in-house training seminars and other resources
- Company and public recognition in the form of awards

These benefits tend to stimulate further capital investment among suppliers to improve their operating capabilities, leading to even greater levels of quality, cost, and service performance.

Benchmarking Successful Sourcing Practices

Benchmarking, or the practice of copying what other businesses do best, is a very effective way to quickly improve sourcing practices and supply chain performance. Without benchmarking, firms must learn through experience the methods and tools that work the best. Successful benchmarking allows firms to leapfrog the experience-gaining stage and try things that have worked well for other companies. Meaningful benchmarking data regarding sourcing practices can be obtained in any number of ways, both formal and informal, from using evaluation surveys distributed to a firm's customers and suppliers regarding *their* supplier management and development practices, to discussing sourcing strategies with colleagues at business association meetings or conferences, to collecting published trade information on benchmarking studies.

A large number of resources are available for firms seeking to learn about and implement successful sourcing practices. The Center for Advanced Purchasing Studies (CAPS), a nonprofit independent research organization, helps organizations achieve competitive advantage by providing leading-edge research information regarding strategic purchasing. For instance, CAPS provides research studies, benchmarking reports, and best practices case studies, along with annual purchasing symposiums and roundtable discussions for purchasing professionals and academics. Another organization, the Supply-Chain Council, which exists to help practitioners reduce supply chain costs and improve customer service, provides the Supply-Chain Operations Reference (SCORE) model as a framework for supply chain improvement, provides case studies, and brings together practitioners to discuss best practices in periodic business conferences around the world. The Institute for Supply Management (ISM), established in 1915, provides a wide variety of resources to supply management professionals worldwide, including a monthly publication featuring the latest supply management trends and information and the globally recognized Certified Purchasing Manager (C.P.M.) and Accredited Purchasing Practitioner (A.P.P.) programs.

The issue of best purchasing practices has been the subject of a number of research studies recently, and the findings have proven very beneficial for firms seeking to benchmark best sourcing practices.[15] Some of the research has found a positive relationship between purchasing benchmarking and firm performance. Some of the sourcing practices found to be common among the companies studied were

- use of a central database to access information on parts, suppliers, lead times, and other purchasing information;
- software tools for sharing information with suppliers;
- use of the Internet for supplier searches;
- long-term contracts or alliances with key suppliers for specific components;
- supplier certification and the elimination of incoming quality checks for key supplier deliveries;
- involving suppliers in the research and development processes of new products;
- the development and use of articulated and coordinated purchasing and supply management strategies;
- optimizing the firm's supply base;
- continuous measurement of supplier performance, and establishing supplier improvement targets; and
- a continuous effort to drive down purchasing costs.

Finally, Dr. Trent and Dr. Monczka identify from their research (Note 15) three sourcing trends that continue to impact companies today:

1. a focus on core competencies and technologies with outsourcing of noncore requirements;
2. pressure to innovate and improve continuously in critical performance areas, including quality, delivery, cycle time, and product/process technology; and
3. the presence of intense, worldwide competition with constant cost reduction pressure.

Using Third-Party Supply Chain Management Services

The use of **third-party logistics (3PL)** and supply chain management providers is a growing trend, as firms seek to gain quick competitive advantage from the development of effective supply chain strategies. Use of these consulting firms is growing at about a 20 percent per year rate, and today the market is estimated at greater that $61 billion.[16] These services assume some or all of a firm's sourcing, materials management, and product distribution responsibilities; charging a fee for their services while saving costs (estimated at 10 to 20 percent of total logistics costs); and improving service, quality, and profits for their clients. For firms with limited resources and supply chain management experience, these services can be a worthwhile investment. Even large firms use these services, since supply chain cost savings can amount to tens of millions of dollars annually. For instance, Ford Motor Company uses one international logistics provider to move

Global Perspective

RYDER SYSTEM, INC.

Ryder System, Inc., is one of the global leaders in supply chain and transportation management, with annual revenues exceeding $5 billion. Starting as a truck leasing contract carrier company nearly seventy years ago, Ryder today has expanded to include over 800 management offices in North America, Latin America, Europe, and the Asia/Pacific regions with services that include total supply chain management, distribution and transportation management, e-business system design, vehicle maintenance, and parts procurement. Additionally, they have been named the top 3PL provider three times by *Inbound Logistics* magazine and have won numerous service and quality awards from companies like Chrysler, Domino's Pizza, GM, Nissan, Pier 1, Target, and Xerox.

Ryder offers comprehensive solutions for the entire supply chain management process as well as design solutions for smaller parts of the supply chain like distribution networks, lo-gistics management, and e-fulfillment. Ryder comes to an organization and evaluates all processes and information flows beginning with purchase order and supplier management through production and final delivery of finished products to end users. Using this assessment, Ryder can offer optimal solutions to achieve required customer service levels at the lowest cost and aid customers in implementing integrated purchasing, production, and distribution processes within their supply chains.

Some of their e-business services include e-Channel Solutions, for Internet-based fulfillment from order to delivery; and p-Freight, an e-marketplace for the trucking industry. Finally, their procurement services allow firms to use Ryder's leverage for buying spare parts, shop supplies, safety products, and fleet products for company vehicles.

Source: Ryder System, Inc. Web page. Printed with permission.

products between continents, while using another 3PL provider to coordinate shipments from its North American assembly plants to its North American dealer network. In the first year of this arrangement, Ford saved $125 million in inventory carrying costs while decreasing delivery time to dealers by four days.[17] The term *3PL* today has come to mean both logistics and the more inclusive term of supply chain management; thus, we will use *3PL* here to mean all potentially outsourced supply chain management activities.

As with benchmarking, use of **3PL providers** allows firms to quickly gain competitive advantage without gaining the experience beforehand. It also allows firms not specializing in supply chain management to focus more resources on core capabilities while conserving valuable resources. Investments in technology, buildings, people, and equipment for supply chain management purposes can be quite high and subject to change as customers, competition, products, and other requirements change, making the use of these services seem even more appealing. Supply chain management services also provide geographical flexibility. Firms can enter new regional and global markets quickly with less capital investment and then leave quickly with smaller losses if sales or long-term contracts do not materialize. Some key disadvantages when using 3PL providers include loss of control, loss of communication with customers and suppliers, the potential spread of confidential information to customers and suppliers, and the potential damage to the firm's reputation if mistakes are made by the 3PL providers. Companies must realize that these service providers are not internal employees and may not be intimately aware of company policies and practices.

Also, companies providing logistics and supply chain management services must be evaluated the same way as other suppliers. Care must be taken to identify, screen, and select the appropriate 3PL service provider, and their performance should be periodically monitored. Flexibility may be one of the primary criteria for selection; for instance, can they adjust to new product requirements, can they tailor services to exactly fit the firm's needs, and can they handle last-minute requests? Alliances can be undertaken with these services as well, providing long-term benefits to both parties.

Firms may use a number of specialized supply chain management service companies for transportation management, repair services, inventory management, Web-enabled communications, public warehousing, reverse auction services, or small package delivery services; or they may contract out a wide range of supply chain management services to one company, such as Ryder, UPS, or Federal Express.

Providing **vendor-managed inventory (VMI) services** is one of the more popular roles of 3PL firms today. In many cases, suppliers are better able to manage their customers' inventories if they can have real-time visibility of inventory in the customers' storage areas. This allows the supplier to profile demand and determine an accurate forecast, reserve capacity to meet the demand forecast, and then ship a predetermined order quantity when the inventory levels become low enough—the **reorder point.** For example, Lake Erie Screw, a fastener and bolt manufacturer, uses a local supplier to manage its inventory of stock-keeping unit (SKU) bar code labels. Once a week, bar code inventory data is automatically transmitted to the supplier's inventory tracking system, where it is compared to the minimum inventory level, and reorder quantities are shipped when the minimum level is reached.[18]

Finally, as an extension of VMI, some firms today are experimenting with outsourcing some or all of the purchasing function itself to 3PL services. Arguments in favor of this are that overhead costs are reduced, knowledgeable buyers can be utilized, and purchase costs can be lowered since the centralized buying firm gains huge purchase volume leverage by combining the demand from all of its customers, resulting in quantity pricing discounts. The downside, particularly for firms engaged in proactive supply chain management, should be fairly obvious. Purchasing does much more than just purchasing. As more of the purchasing function is performed by outside services, purchasing ceases to be viewed as a strategic component of the firm. Additionally, the firm risks the loss of important supplier alliances. However, firms have successfully outsourced the purchasing of items with less strategic importance, such as MRO items. Using a 3PL provider for purchasing may also make sense for small firms with limited purchasing staff and knowledge.

Assessing and Improving the Firm's Purchasing Function

As has been stated throughout this segment of the textbook, the purchasing function is one of the most value-enhancing functions in any organization, including services. Today, as purchasing staff members are expected more often to generate cost savings and service and quality enhancements for the organization, they must be viewed as strategic internal suppliers of the organization. Bearing this in mind, it may then be preferable to periodically monitor the purchasing function's performance against set standards, goals, and/or industry benchmarks, if possible. Thus, as the firm strives to continuously improve its products and processes, purchasing can also gauge its success in improving its value-enhancing contributions to the firm and its varied supply chains.

As was stated earlier in this chapter and in Chapter 3 when discussing supplier assessment, criteria can also be utilized here to provide feedback to the purchasing staff regarding their contributions to the strategic goals of the firm. Surveys or audits of this nature can be

"We're a little behind in purchasing, so would you mind using this handheld computer until we can order your workstation?"

administered as self-assessments among purchasing staff as part of the annual evaluation process, and assessments can also include feedback from internal customers of the purchasing function, such as engineers and sales or marketing and finance personnel. Feedback may even be included from supplier representatives. Assessment criteria to evaluate purchasing's performance should include some or all of the following:

- participating in and leading of multifunctional teams;
- participating in value engineering/value analysis efforts;
- finding and evaluating suppliers, and optimizing the supply base;
- managing and developing local, regional, and global suppliers;
- creating early supplier involvement initiatives;
- entering into strategic supplier alliances;
- furthering the integration and development of existing key suppliers;
- contributing to new product development efforts;
- utilizing e-procurement systems;
- initiating supplier cost reduction programs;
- contributing to the improvement of purchased product and service quality;
- improving time to market; and
- maintaining and improving intrafirm cooperative relationships.

Since these criteria require both qualitative and quantitative assessments, the decision tool recommended here would be the weighted-factor rating method, covered in Chapter 3. Because of the tremendous potential value of these many activities, the purchasing staff members should be continuously auditing their capabilities and successes in these areas.

Thus, the skill set requirements of purchasing professionals have been changing as purchasing has evolved from the tactical, clerical function it was about thirty years ago to the highly demanding strategic function it is today. To achieve the type of world-class performance suggested by the preceding assessment criteria, purchasing personnel must today exhibit world-class skills. While quite a bit of research has been conducted on this topic over the years, a recent study has identified just such a world-class skill set for purchasing.[19] The ten skills identified by 136 experienced purchasing professionals were

1. interpersonal communication,
2. ability to make decisions,
3. ability to work in teams,
4. analytical skills,
5. negotiation skills,
6. ability to manage change,
7. customer focus,
8. influencing and persuasion skills,
9. strategic skills, and
10. understanding business conditions.

We can see that purchasing personnel today must develop an impressive set of skills to achieve the type of influence within the organization that leads to long-term success for the department, the firm, and its supply chains.

Summary

Achieving supply chain management success starts with the sourcing activity. We hope we have provided in this chapter, and the previous two, evidence of the strategic role played within the firm by the purchasing function and the impact of purchasing on the management of the supply chain. Firms that fail to recognize this importance will simply not experience the same level of success in the long run. The sourcing activity is comprised of a number of related activities that, when taken together, provide sustainable competitive advantage for the firm. Firms can maximize this advantage by developing effective supply chain strategies and then assessing and revising these strategies periodically as markets, competitors, and technologies change. As we head into the internal operations segment of this text, we hope you will continue to consider the purchasing issues discussed in Part 1 and how they interact with other processes as materials, services, and information move down the supply chain toward the immediate customers and, eventually, the end users.

Key Terms

acceptance sampling, 92
alliance development, 94
bill-back, 98
channel equity, 92
concurrent engineering, 93
design for manufacturability, 93

functional products, 89
innovative products, 89
reorder point, 101
reverse auctions, 97
statistical process control, 92
strategic sourcing, 88

third-party logistics (3PL), 99
3PL providers, 100
value engineering, 94
vendor-managed inventory (VMI) services, 101

Discussion Questions

1. Describe the differences between functional and innovative products, and provide some examples of each of these from your household possessions.
2. Using the strategy development framework shown in Figure 4.1, show how an electronics retail store might benefit from its use.
3. What are the advantages of reducing the size of the supply base? Could there be any disadvantages?
4. What do you think the most important evaluation criteria would be for Wal-Mart's suppliers? McDonald's suppliers? Harley-Davidson's suppliers?
5. Define *channel equity* and discuss what it has to do with supply chain management.
6. What advantages do company-designed supplier certification programs have over industry certifications like ISO 9000?
7. What is purchasing's role in value engineering, and what benefits does this give to the firm?
8. What is the difference between supplier management and alliance development?
9. What makes supplier alliances fail? How can firms reduce the failure rate?
10. Why are second- and third-tier suppliers important to the focal firm?

11. What is a common method for developing second-tier suppliers?

12. **Discussion Problem:** If your firm had 500 suppliers and they each had 100 suppliers, how many second-tier suppliers would your firm have? What if your firm reduced its supply base to twenty?

13. If you work for a company, describe how it rewards and punishes its suppliers. Do you think appropriate methods are used? Why or why not?

14. What are some different ways you could use benchmarking to improve your performance at school?

15. What is a 3PL provider? What advantages could a 3PL provider give to a small firm? A large firm?

16. Define vendor-managed inventory services and describe why a firm might want to use them. Are there any disadvantages to the use of VMI?

17. Go to the secretary in the department office where this course is taught or to a secretary where you work, and ask that person how easy it is to order more printer paper or typing paper. Does it sound like the purchasing department has made these purchases easy? How long does it take?

18. How would you rate your skill-level on the world-class skill set listed at the end of the chapter?

Internet Questions

1. Go to the International Organization for Standardization Web site (http://www.iso.ch) and write a short description and history of the organization, including the various certifications that can be obtained.

2. Go to the CAPS Web site (http://www.capsresearch.org) and find the latest cross-industry benchmarking report and determine the overall purchase dollars as a percent of sales in the United States. What benchmarking research are they doing now?

3. How is a reverse auction different from an auction like you might find at eBay? How is it different from a competitive bid process?

4. What is an ASP? Find some on the Internet that are not listed in the chapter, and describe what they do.

References

Anderson, M. G., and P. B. Katz. "Strategic Sourcing." *International Journal of Logistics Management* 9, no. 1 (1998): 1–13.

Burt, D. N., D. W. Dobler, and S. L. Starling. *World Class Supply Management[SN]: The Key to Supply Chain Management.* 7th ed. New York: McGraw-Hill/Irwin, 2003.

Kaplan, N. J., and J. Hurd. "Realizing the Promise of Partnerships." *Journal of Business Strategy* 23, no. 3 (2002): 38–42.

Lummus, R. R., R. J. Vokurka, and K. L. Alber. "Strategic Supply Chain Planning." *Production and Inventory Management Journal* 39, no. 3 (1998): 49–58.

Simchi-Levi, D., P. Kaminsky, and E. Simchi-Levi. *Designing and Managing the Supply Chain: Concepts, Strategies, and Case Studies.* 2d ed. New York: McGraw-Hill/Irwin, 2003.

Vonderembse, M. "The Impact of Supplier Selection Criteria and Supplier Involvement on Manufacturing." *Journal of Supply Chain Management* 35, no. 3 (1999): 33–39.

Notes

1. P. Carter, J. Carter, R. Monczka, T. Slaight, and A. Swan, "The Future of Purchasing and Supply: A Ten-Year Forecast," *Journal of Supply Chain Management* 36, no. 1 (2000): 14–26.

2. Adapted from J. P. Morgan, "Cessna Aims to Drive SCM to Its Very Core," *Purchasing Magazine* 131, no. 10 (2002): 31–35 (www.purchasing.com). Printed with permission.

3. K. R. Fitzgerald, "Profile of the Purchasing Professional," *Purchasing* 127, no. 1 (1999): 74–84.

4. M. L. Fisher, "What Is the Right Supply Chain for Your Product?," *Harvard Business Review* 75, no. 2 (1997): 105–116.

5. Adapted from R. H. Lummus, R. J. Vokurka, and K. L. Alber, "Strategic Supply Chain Planning," *Production and Inventory Management Journal* 39, no. 3 (1998): 49–58.

6. P. M. Simpson, J. A. Siguaw, and S. C. White, "Measuring the Performance of Suppliers: An Analysis of Evaluation Processes," *Journal of Supply Chain Management* 38, no. 1 (2002): 29–41; and J. D. Wisner and K. C. Tan, "Supply Chain Management and Its Impact on Purchasing," *Journal of Supply Chain Management* 36, no. 4 (2000): 33–42.

7. Simpson, Siguaw, and White, "Measuring the Performance of Suppliers": 29–41.

8. R. J. Trent and R. M. Monczka, "Achieving World-Class Supplier Quality," *Total Quality Management* 10, no. 6 (1999): 927–38.

9. *Cross-Industry Benchmarking Report, August 2001–August 2002*, Center for Advanced Purchasing Studies (Copyright 2002).

10. D. Ertel, "Alliance Management: A Blueprint for Success," *Financial Executive* 17, no. 9 (2001): 36–41.

11. J. H. Dyer, P. Kale, and H. Singh, "How to Make Strategic Alliances Work," *Sloan Management Review* 42, no. 4 (2001): 37–43.

12. Ibid.

13. Ibid., adapted.

14. S. Park and J. L. Hartley, "Exploring the Effect of Supplier Management on Performance in the Korean Automotive Supply Chain," *Journal of Supply Chain Management* 38, no. 2 (2002): 46–52.

15. See, for instance, B. Andersen, T. Fagerhaug, S. Randmael, J. Schuldmaier, and J. Prenninger, "Benchmarking Supply Chain Management: Finding Best Practices," *Journal of Business and Industrial Marketing* 14, no. 5/6 (1999): 378–89; A. S. Carr and L. R. Smeltzer, "The Relationship among Purchasing Benchmarking, Strategic Purchasing, Firm Performance, and Firm Size," *Journal of Supply Chain Management* 35, no. 4 (1999): 51–60; Trent and Monczka, "Achieving World-Class Supplier Quality": 927–38; and L. M. Ellram, G. A. Zsidisin, S. P. Siferd, and M. J. Stanly, "The Impact of Purchasing and Supply Management on Corporate Success," *Journal of Supply Chain Management* 38, no. 1 (2002): 4–17.

16. M. Verespej, "Logistics' New Look? It's Now Service," *Frontline Solutions* 3, no. 6 (2002): 24–33.

17. Ibid.

18. B. Albright, "No More Label Worries," *Frontline Solutions* 3, no. 9 (2002): 54.

19. L. C. Giunipero and D. H. Pearcy, "World-Class Purchasing Skills: An Empirical Investigation," *Journal of Supply Chain Management* 36, no. 4 (2000): 4–13.

20. Adapted from N. Angelo, "Reverse Auctions Raise New Specter of Bid Shopping on Industry Projects," *Engineering News-Record* 249, no. 19 (2002): 34. Printed with permission. Copyright The McGraw-Hill Companies Inc. All rights reserved.

Case Study 1
John Deere and Complex Parts, Inc.

On Friday, November 22, 2000, Blake Roberts, Hayley Marie, Stan Eakins, and John Pearson, members of one of John Deere's supplier evaluation teams, were discussing the performance of Complex Parts. It had provided questionable service to John Deere's Moline unit over the past year, and they were wondering if this merited giving Complex Parts' business to a different supplier. They needed to recommend a course of action to their project manager next week.

Company Backgrounds

Deere & Company, headquartered in Moline, Illinois, was founded in 1837, and in 2000 conducted business in over 160 countries and employed 43,000 people worldwide. It produced agricultural, construction, commercial, and consumer equipment. Other products and services produced by Deere included equipment financing, power systems, special technologies, and health care. Net sales in 2000 were over $11 billion with total assets of almost $12 billion. Purchases in 2000 were approximately $6 billion.

Complex Parts, Inc., had been a supplier of John Deere for the past ten years with annual sales to its Moline unit of approximately $3.5 million. Complex Parts supplied Deere with a key manufactured part requiring significant engineering input and testing. Two other Deere suppliers were capable of supplying this part; however, Complex Parts was providing all of Deere's needs at the time. The supplier had always taken a proactive approach to its dealings with John Deere, with sales engineers visiting weekly, participating in Deere's cost reduction strategies, staying up with Deere's design changes, and internalizing the Deere Product Quality Plan. Complex Parts was interested in increasing its sales to Deere.

John Deere's Achieving Excellence Program

The Achieving Excellence Program (AEP) was a dynamic supply management strategy aimed at giving Deere and its suppliers the competitive advantage necessary to deliver world-class equipment to customers. The AEP strived to develop long-lasting supplier relationships through use of a supplier evaluation process that promoted communication, trust, cooperation, and continuous improvement. Suppliers were evaluated in five key areas by teams of Deere personnel from supply management, operations, quality engineering, and product development. These evaluation areas were quality, delivery, cost management, wavelength, and technical support.

The quality rating was a quantitative measure calculated as

$$(\# \text{ rejects/units of supplied product}) \times 1{,}000{,}000.$$

Thus, a quality rating of 1,000 would be equivalent to one reject per 1,000 units delivered. The delivery rating provided a measure of how well a supplier met Deere's specified delivery dates and purchase quantities. The delivery rating was calculated as

$$[(\# \text{ early} + \text{late} + \text{over deliveries)/delivery instances}] \times 1{,}000{,}000.$$

Thus, a delivery rating of 75,000 would be equivalent to seventy-five delivery "defects" per 1,000 deliveries. The cost management rating was a composite rating derived by the evaluation

Source: Reprinted with permission from the publisher, the Institute for Supply Management™, "John Deere and Complex Parts, Inc." by Joel Wisner, PhD, C.P.M., University of Nevada, Las Vegas, *2001 Case Writing Workshop*.

Table C.1	Supplier Classification Criteria				
	Quality	**Delivery**	**Wavelength**	**Technical**	**Cost Mgt.**
Partner	<1,000	<30,000	>4.6	>4.6	>4.6
Key	<2,500	<80,000	>4.0	>4.0	>4.0
Approved	<5,000	<150,000	>3.0	>3.0	>3.0
Conditional	5,000+	150,000+	<3.0	<3.0	<3.0

team, based on performance in five areas: cost management initiative, cost reduction activity, cost index performance, performance during new programs, and global market competitiveness. A consensus cost management rating of 1 to 5 was eventually reached by the evaluation team. The wavelength rating was a composite analysis of the supplier's initiative, attitude, responsiveness, attention to detail, and communication performance. In general, good performance in this area meant the supplier was customer-focused with a continuous commitment to improvement in quality, technical support, delivery, cost, lead time, inventory turnover, and EDI capability. The technical support rating was also a five-point consensus composite rating comprised of the group's assessment of the supplier's performance in the areas of assembly line support, design and process change information, manufacturing and design improvements, field problem resolution, test support, environmental responsibility, and supply management support.

Recognition of supplier performance was an integral part of Deere's AEP. Suppliers were classified as Conditional, Approved, Key, or Partner, based on their overall performance in the five rating categories (although the weakest category tended to heavily influence the overall evaluation). These classifications, with their required performance levels for each rating category are shown in Table C.1. Performance level cutoffs were revised annually by Deere. Suppliers were given a Supplier Performance Summary each quarter, providing suppliers with their performance information as well as the cutoff information. Conditional suppliers did not receive any formal recognition or training from Deere and were in danger of losing future Deere business. Approved suppliers were eligible to participate in Deere training programs. Key suppliers received a special Deere plaque and training benefits, while Partners received the training benefits and were also honored at a Deere awards banquet.

Complex Parts' Performance Information

Complex Parts had achieved a Quality rating of 666 for the past year and a Delivery rating of 8,650. Blake Roberts, the strategic member of the evaluation team with eight years experience as a Deere buyer, thought some of Complex Parts' subjective category performances were showing signs of weakness. For instance, he thought Complex Parts should be making more suggestions for cost reductions and eliminating more of the problems that had resulted in a number of late deliveries over the past year. Some requested price quotes had also not reached Deere on time. The company had been doing a good job, though, of following through on suggestions for quality improvement offered by Deere. Roberts considered its business approach with Deere to be very proactive.

Hayley Marie, a manufacturing planner for twenty-three years with Deere, was in charge of the team's technical evaluation. Hayley noted that Complex Parts had taken an active role in keeping up with Deere's required specification changes, but she was very concerned with Deere's frequent inability to return phone calls to Complex Parts' customer service group. An increasing number of deliveries had to be expedited over the past year, costing Deere in the process. It seemed as though expediting had recently become a weekly requirement. Over the past quarter, Complex Parts' Delivery rating was a dismal 155,000.

Stan Eakins, the team's quality advisor, had been a quality engineer for Deere for over twenty years. He thought Complex Parts had done an excellent job internalizing the Deere

Quality Plan elements, and he took a lead role in getting the elements implemented. Complex Parts' quality performance had improved significantly over the past year. Recently, it had also become ISO certified. The one area of concern noted by Greg was that Complex Parts had fallen behind in implementing the Deere Quality Plan at its new facility, which had been operational since June. This was beginning to concern him.

John Pearson was the assessment team's design/engineering advisor and had been an engineer at Deere for twelve years. He was impressed with Complex Parts' R&D department, noting that several suggestions from the department had resulted in successful Deere new product programs. Unfortunately though, a number of the items supplied by Complex Parts for these products had not met Deere's cost targets, effectively reducing Deere's projected profits on these products. Also a troubling problem over this past quarter was getting quotes for some of these new parts in a timely fashion.

Conclusion

The team was faced with evaluating a long-term supplier for Deere who was performing impressively in several areas. Unfortunately, there were also some areas of concern in the minds of all four members of the evaluation team. Reaching a consensus was going to require all of the team members to be very thorough in their evaluations of Complex Parts. The evaluation group had to reach a consensus quickly to meet the required deadline of their project manager.

Questions for Discussion

1. Discuss the strengths and weaknesses of John Deere's Achieving Excellence Program. Consider and discuss other criteria to include in the analysis.

2. Do you think Complex Parts has performed adequately over the past year? Why or why not? Which of the Deere supplier assessment classifications should be assigned to Complex Parts?

3. If you were a member of the supplier evaluation team, what alternative courses of action would you consider for Complex Parts? What recommendation should the team make to the project manager?

4. What are the short-term and long-term implications of your recommendation?

Case Study 2
CJ Industries

In October of 2002, CJ Industries had just been awarded a five-year contract, amounting to $10 million per year, commencing on July 2003 to supply Great Lakes Pleasure Boats a number of key engine components for its luxury line of pleasure boats. The award marked an important milestone for CJI, in that it was the culmination of several years of hard work and dedicated service, supplying Great Lakes parts for its boats on an as-needed basis. The contract had significant long-term follow-on potential as well, if CJI could continue to show Great Lakes it had the capabilities to be one of its valued alliance partners. Additionally, with this contract, Great Lakes would represent about 30 percent of CJI's annual sales, so performing adequately on this contract had a significant long-term financial impact on CJI.

One of the parts, a bilge pump, was an item that CJI had been purchasing from one of its suppliers—Caolinn Pumps, a small local specialty pump manufacturer—on an informal, noncontract basis. The remaining items were all built in-house by CJI and supplied to Great Lakes from one of its two finished-goods warehouses located near the Great Lakes production facilities. Caolinn Pumps was producing and delivering fifty bilge pumps at a time—at a cost of $1,500 per unit and built to Great Lakes' specifications—to one of the CJI warehouses whenever an order was telephoned in by CJI. The delivery costs (about $500, depending on the carrier used) were included in the $1,500 per unit price. This scenario typically occurred about every four to six months. Normally, CJI would order another batch of fifty about eight to ten weeks ahead of time, and Caolinn had always been able to supply the pumps before CJI's stock was depleted.

While CJI had sufficient excess capacity to ramp up production on the parts to be supplied in the Great Lakes contract, it was not sure about the ability or willingness of Caolinn to increase its production of the bilge pumps. The new demand for bilge pumps starting in July would be fifty pumps per month, and potentially more, depending on Great Lakes' demand and the ability of CJI to perform on the contract.

There were a number of issues that Chris Heavey, the purchasing manager who put the contract together with Great Lakes, needed to work out with both Caolinn and the production manager at CJI for this contract to be met with as few problems as possible. The issues with Caolinn Pumps were whether or not it could guarantee delivery of fifty pumps per month to one of the CJI warehouses. This had been the one item that had "slipped through the cracks" on the contract with Great Lakes, and it now loomed as something that could conceivably put the contract in jeopardy. There were potentially additional equipment, labor, and other production costs for Caolinn associated with the extra demand for bilge pumps, not to mention extra delivery costs as well. Caolinn had been a reliable supplier for CJI for a number of years, but nothing else had ever been purchased from Caolinn. Additionally, because the demand for these pumps was rather low and the deliveries were sporadic, no performance records had ever been kept for Caolinn. Mr. Heavey had also not known specifically about the quality history of the Caolinn bilge pump, although he could not remember ever getting one returned by Great Lakes for any reason. Up until now, the pump issue did not seem like anything to worry about.

Another possibility for CJI would be to make these pumps in-house. Chris Heavey knew that CJI had the capability to make this pump, but it would require an initial capital investment of about $500,000, according to the CJI production manager, along with the clearing out of some space and the hiring of three additional employees. With only about nine months remaining until the contract start date, it would be tight, but the production manager had assured Chris that CJI could do this, if needed. While Mr. Heavey did not doubt the production manager's assurances that the production line could be ready, he was not sure that going to this added expense was a good investment for CJI, given its lack of pump manufacturing experience. There were also at least two other bilge pump manufacturers that Mr. Heavey knew of, but both of them were about 500 miles farther away from the CJI warehouses, and he had never used either of these firms in the past.

This whole thing seemed to Chris like an ideal job for his special project buyer, Linda Stanley. He figured he had a week or two to hammer out a plan to assure contract compliance with Great Lakes, and Linda was known for her ability to put things together quickly. So, he called her.

Questions for Discussion

1. What are all the issues here, from both CJI's and Caolinn's perspectives, that need to be researched by Ms. Stanley?

2. Should CJI continue to use Caolinn to supply pumps, should it make them in-house, should it contact one of the other suppliers, or should it do some combination of these alternatives? Discuss the advantages, disadvantages, and risks of each of these alternatives.

3. How can CJI assure continued contract compliance and additional contract business from Great Lakes in the future?

Case Study 3
Don't Shoot the Messenger

On July 5, 2000, the unit general manager of Billings Equipment, Inc., instructed the supply management team to renegotiate existing agreements for a 10 percent reduction with major suppliers due to target costs exceeding expectations. Jeff Martin, a supply management engineer, was instructed along with the entire purchasing staff to contact his suppliers immediately with what they would view as very bad news. Jeff had to face his suppliers with this demand.

Company Background

In June 1998 Billings Equipment, Inc., formed a new business unit and opened a plant in Seattle to produce a new line of earth-moving machines for the construction industry. The organization had a history of impeccable ethical treatment of suppliers and was considered to be a leader in the industry. For two years, Jeff was actively involved in reducing costs and cycle times of his suppliers. Everyone involved would agree that the process was emotionally heated on occasion, with shedding of cooperative blood, sweat, and tears. Jeff's suppliers had invested many personal hours and sizable expense to reach this point in time. It had evolved into a strained but working relationship.

Relationship with Suppliers

During the start-up period of the program, a very aggressive time line and target cost drove emotions to a frenzied pace. Early supplier involvement in prototype and testing activity was cultivated to encourage active participation in the development of this new product line by all that had equity in its future. Suppliers were pushed to the limit on material and tooling lead times, exhausting goodwill and testing commitments. Everyone involved, including suppliers, invested personal time and effort toward meeting the market time lines. Purchase agreements were negotiated, and parts now were being received to support production ramped up toward market introduction.

The Problem

The push to production forced acceptance of early design of many components, which inhibited additional cost reduction. Customarily, 80 percent of cost reduction occurs during the design phase. Tooling was developed during early design configurations to meet the production schedule. As designs became frozen and cost information became more complete, the projected total costs were going to exceed target levels by as much as 20 percent. As the costs for the bill of materials (BOM) continued to rise above target levels, it became clear that this increase was not simply due to procedural or accounting errors but, rather, represented true costs. The general manager realized the rising cost situation was beyond recovery and would impact the market pricing and success of the entire product line. At this time Billings Equipment, Inc., had invested $20 million to $30 million in sunk costs for the plant and pre-production efforts. Something drastic would have to be done.

The Ethical Issue

In an effort to at least "stop the bleeding," a letter was sent to suppliers on July 5 declaring the regrettable necessity to reduce prices by 10 percent within thirty days. Buyers were to fol-

Source: Reprinted with permission from the publisher, the Institute for Supply Management™, "Don't Shoot the Messenger," by Donald R. Jackson, PhD, C.P.M., Ferris State University, *2001 Case Writing Workshop.*

low up immediately by contacting their top thirty suppliers. The veiled threat for noncompliance to re-open previously negotiated agreements indicated a possible cancellation of the product line altogether, or at least a consideration of other sources of supply. Jeff believed he would be violating a trusted relationship based on the heroic collaborative effort to meet demands over the past year. How could he carry this message to the suppliers?

Even with some additional eroding of supplier tolerance for concessions, Jeff succeeded within the thirty days to get agreement from four of his five major suppliers, which represented 80 percent of the cost of materials he purchased. About 20 percent of the suppliers complied promptly, within thirty days. Other buyers had mixed results. Everyone was uncomfortable moving the supplier relationships from a cost-based approach to a simple request for price reduction.

Now the Other Shoe Drops

Shortly after the most faithful of the major suppliers reluctantly committed to cutting prices, the general manager made an announcement during a strategy meeting with buyers. "Because some suppliers complied readily with the 10 percent price reduction," he said, "we are now going to push for an additional 5 percent." This implied that suppliers had padded prices and further reductions could have been done all along. In effect, the suppliers who had complied with the first request were to be penalized.

Jeff was now faced with an ethical situation pitting his responsibilities to the general manager against carefully developed supplier relationships.

Questions for Discussion

1. If you were in Jeff's position, what would you have done to preserve relationships?

2. Describe the ethical issues involved.

3. What is your assessment of the general manager's approach to meeting target cost objectives?

Case Study 4
Early Supplier Integration in the Design of the Skid-Steer Loader

"Congratulations, Scott. You are the new supply management manager of our new Deere & Company Commercial Worksite Products manufacturing facility in Knoxville, Tennessee. As you know, we really need your help to make this new facility fully operational in twenty-four months. I am sure you realize that a critical responsibility of your new job is to integrate suppliers into the product development process for our own Deere manufactured skid-steer loader as quickly as needed. You will be reporting directly to me, and I need a proposal from you by the time we meet next week on June 15, 1996."

As Scott hung up the telephone with James Field, plant manager and his immediate boss, he realized that this was not a simple request. In his proposal, he knew he would need to (a) identify and justify which suppliers to integrate in the product development phase and (b) specify how to structure the interactions with these chosen suppliers. The recommendations in his proposal had to ensure that this new plant would be up and running smoothly by the target date in July 1998.

Deere & Company

Deere & Company, headquartered in Moline, Illinois, had more than 150 years of history, making it one of the world's oldest business enterprises. A well-respected company, Deere & Company had a core business portfolio in 1996 comprised of the manufacturing, distributing, financing, and servicing of agricultural equipment (e.g., combines and tractors), construction and forestry equipment (e.g., log skidders and forklifts), and commercial and consumer lawn care equipment (e.g., lawn and garden tractors and mowers), as well as other technological products and services. With more than 38,000 employees worldwide, Deere & Company conducted business in more than 160 countries.

The Skid-Steer Loader
The Product

The skid-steer loader, a small loader with a 1,000- to 3,000-pound load capacity, was targeted for construction and ground care sites in need of light, versatile, and easy handling land-moving equipment. Deere & Company pioneered the skid-steer loader market more than twenty-five years ago; but, subsequently, the company had contracted the engineering and manufacturing to New Holland, an independent contractor. Although New Holland produced its own line of skid-steer loaders that competed directly with the Deere brand, it agreed to sell its excess capacity to manufacture essentially the same product for Deere & Company, allowing aesthetic changes for brand differentiation only.

The Market

In 1995–1996, Deere's average market share for the skid-steer loader varied between 1 to 3 percent. Market data indicated that this market niche was growing at 15 to 20 percent per year and was projected to reach overall sales of $1.2 billion or approximately 60,000 units by

Source: Reprinted with permission from the publisher, the Institute for Supply Management™, "Early Supplier Involvement in the Design of the Skid-Steer Loader," by Manus Rungtusanathem, PhD, and Fabrizio Salvador, PhD, Arizona State University, *2001 Case Writing Workshop.*

year 2000–2001. Given these numbers, corporate headquarters became increasingly interested in establishing the Deere skid-steer loader as one of the leading worldwide competitors in this market niche with a goal of more than tripling its market share.

In order to reach such an aggressive goal, Deere realized its market penetration strategy needed to focus on fundamental order-winning criteria in such areas as:

- *Product features:* Because the skid-steer loader is a fixed investment asset, product features that improve ease of use (e.g., versatility of load placement), reduce operational costs (e.g., fuel efficiency), and reduce maintenance requirements (e.g., self-lubricating parts) would make the difference between the Deere brand and competing products.

- *Product range:* To better serve the customers, Deere knew that it needed to offer some product variety, as typically required for industrial equipment, given different usage requirements. Therefore, a range of models, perhaps differentiated on load capacity and available options (e.g., hand or foot controls) was needed.

- *Product delivery:* Deere knew that demonstrating its skid-steer loader's versatile functionality, and being able to demonstrate and deliver the product to the actual work site was an important sales incentive.

- *Price:* Last but not least, the demand for skid-steer loaders was highly price sensitive. As a result, minimizing cost of goods sold without sacrificing timely delivery of a high-quality Deere skid-steer loader was imperative.

The situation before 1996 was, therefore, pretty clear. As long as engineering and production of Deere brand skid-steer loaders were in the hands of a third party—one that, in fact, competed in the same market niche—there would be little opportunity to gain significant benefits over competing products and product features. The same argument held for cost considerations, making better delivery and service the only competitive advantages. Furthermore, expecting market demand for skid-steer loaders would increase; New Holland had refused to sell additional production capacity to Deere & Company. As a result, Deere & Company decided that it needed to regain direct control of the design and manufacturing of this potentially lucrative product.

The "Greenfield" Knoxville Decision

In April 1996 corporate headquarters approved a capital investment project of $35 million dedicated to regaining control of the design and manufacturing of the skid-steer loader. This capital investment decision also approved the placement of the design, manufacturing, and marketing functions in a new facility to be built near Knoxville, Tennessee. The mandate was clear: engineer and manufacture a high-quality skid-steer loader that would be 20 percent lower in costs than that of the best competitor by August 1998, consistent with other identified order-winning criteria.

Scott Nolan, CQE, PE, and New Supply Management Manager

Nolan joined Deere & Company as a manufacturing engineer, after graduating from Iowa State University with a mechanical engineering degree in 1979. Along the way, he has received an MBA (in 1989) from the University of Iowa, as well as professional certification as a Certified Quality Engineer and as a Professional Engineer. In 1989 Nolan began working in supply management for the Horicon, Wisconsin, lawn and garden equipment manufacturing facility. The opportunity to join a new Deere manufacturing facility in the role of supply management manager was a welcomed promotion and challenge.

Supplier Integration in Skid-Steer Loader Design

Having worked in supply management for the seven past years, Nolan was well aware of the general principle of involving suppliers in product development and manufacturing decisions and the frequently touted benefits of lower costs structures, faster product development cycle, and reduced operational inefficiencies. He believed, however, that not all suppliers needed to be or should be involved, especially in the early stages of the new product development process. Furthermore, involving suppliers should not be "lip service"; the selected suppliers should be well integrated into the various product development activities.

Student Assignment

Imagine you are in the position of Scott Nolan. Write a two-page memorandum that (a) identifies, defines, and justifies the criteria (limit four) for screening suppliers to integrate into the early phases of the Deere skid-steer loader development process; and (b) recommends guiding principles, practices, and/or specific techniques to provide for effective integration of early supplier integration in the Deere skid-steer loader development process.

Questions for Discussion

1. Suppose there are 100 potential suppliers, how many suppliers do you think should ideally be integrated in the early skid-steer development process? Why that many or that few?

2. Are there trade-offs in terms of the number of suppliers to integrate? If so, what are the trade-offs?

3. Are there trade-offs among the identified criteria? Can you tell? What do you need to know to better answer this question?

4. Would you mandate weekly meetings as an interorganizational policy to structure the interactions? If not, how can you facilitate communication?

5. What role can information technology (IT) play or should it play in structuring these interactions? What concerns do you have with the suggested IT role?

6. If the criteria you developed suggest that you integrate Supplier X into the product development process for the skid-steer loader, what reasons might lead you to choose to not do so or to reduce the convenience of doing so?

7. What do you think might be hurdles to overcome at Deere to integrate suppliers into the early phases of the product development process?

Case Study 5
Supplier Development at Deere & Company

On May 30, 2001, at one o'clock, an in-house meeting of the supplier development team for Excelsior Equipment Corporation and Deere & Company had just adjourned. Benjamin Aldrin, the project manager for the Deere group was gathering up his materials. With the supply of crucial equipment and the long-term competitiveness of an established supplier in jeopardy, he was concerned about the effectiveness of the group's decision to force Excelsior to improve its antiquated manufacturing processes by lowering its prices.

Company Background

Deere & Company was one of the world's major providers of agricultural equipment with offices, manufacturing facilities, and suppliers located in 160 countries. In order to maintain its position as the one of the world's leaders, Deere relied on its global supply chain as a source of competitive advantage. Deere was committed to the concept of maintaining its supply chain by actively partnering with its suppliers. Many of these partnering activities focused on reducing suppliers' manufacturing cycle time—the typical amount of time from when a manufacturing order is created until the first, single piece of that order is delivered to the customer—to lower manufacturing costs and improve deliveries of finished products. At Deere, working closely with suppliers meant, among other things, designing or redesigning manufacturing facilities and operations to eliminate waste, providing and facilitating the use of software packages, training supplier personnel, and providing on-site personnel for specific projects. The individuals responsible for helping suppliers improve their operations were in the supplier development group.

Supplier Development Groups

The supplier development groups (SDGs) consisted mostly of process engineers. However, members of project teams, such as the team assembled for the Excelsior Equipment project, included professionals from other areas. Each Deere division had an SDG. Company-wide, Deere had about 100 individuals assigned to SDGs.

The Charter

Deere and Company entered into an agreement (charter) with Excelsior in March 1999 delineating all of the terms and conditions and responsibilities of each party, the statement of work of the project, and how the resulting savings would be divided between the parties. A copy of the charter is shown in Figure C.1.

Excelsior Equipment

For more than thirty years, Excelsior, a 150-employee company located in Cedar Rapids, Iowa, supplied a major tractor attachment to Deere. Excelsior was a vertically integrated company with very little flexibility. As time progressed and Deere purchased more from Excelsior, it became more and more dependent on Deere as a customer. For instance, in 2000, Deere's purchases accounted for over 95 percent of Excelsior's revenue. Similarly, Deere found itself growing dependent on Excelsior. For example, there are very few manufacturers of tractor attachments that Deere buys and Excelsior owned the design of those attachments

Source: Reprinted with permission from the publisher, the Institute for Supply Management™, "Supplier Development at Deere & Company," by Howard Forman, PhD, Penn State University, *2001 Case Writing Workshop.*

1. Business

Excelsior Equipment Corporation of Cedar Rapids, Iowa, is a major supplier to John Deere. In terms of annual sales, Excelsior is currently in the top five suppliers to John Deere's Commercial and Consumer Equipment Division.

2. Situation and Goal Statement

For fiscal years 1999 and 2000, John Deere has limited Excelsior to price adjustments on material costs only. John Deere has declined to allow price adjustments on material costs for fiscal 2001. Excelsior has been unable to fully offset increases in value-added costs, resulting in a reduction of Excelsior's margins. John Deere's C&CE Division has a 5 percent price reduction goal for fiscal 2001. The goal of this project is to reduce Excelsior's cost so that current Deere prices on affected product lines can be reduced at least 5 percent and Excelsior's margins can be increased.

3. Mission and Vision

A closer, mutually beneficial business relationship.

4. Project Scope

Primarily, Excelsior's commercial tractor attachment product lines sold to John Deere, although all similar Excelsior commercial tractor attachment products will be included in the project.

5. Schedule and Deliverables

Reduce Commercial tractor attachment Manufacturing Cycle Time—from 8 to 9 months to 20–40 days. Streamline Deere-Excelsior order fulfillment process—from 8 to 9 months to 20–40 days.

6. Assignments and Roles

Project sponsors:

- Samuel Montgomery, Deere, Purchasing Agent, Outside Purchased Product
- James Franks, Excelsior, Vice President, Sales & Marketing

Process owner:
- Edward Smith, John Deere, Manager, Supplier Development, C&CE Division

Project managers:
- Benjamin Aldrin, John Deere, Supplier Development Engineer, Horicon
- Bill Sanderson, Excelsior, Director of Quality Assurance

7. Implementation

a. Manufacturing Cycle Time will be the primary focus of the project, but all opportunities for cost reduction will be explored. Specification changes resulting in lower material and/or processing costs will become part of the project.
b. John Deere services will be provided at no cost.

8. Savings

a. Capital expense required to implement this project will be offset by withholding all cost reduction benefit until that portion of those capital expenses applicable to the production of product for John Deere has been absorbed.
b. If savings are realized, they go toward both increasing Excelsior margin and reducing prices to John Deere. John Deere will receive 50 percent of the savings in the form of price reductions.
c. Current commercial tractor attachment pricing is the basis against which savings will be applied, and such savings will be measured utilizing agreed-upon metrics taken before and after the project.
d. No price reductions will be implemented until improvements are implemented and savings are confirmed.
e. Windfall raw material cost savings resulting from the project will be passed on to John Deere after normal markups.

9. Change Management Plan

a. Excelsior will assign a Project Manager from its Manufacturing Group who will have overall project responsibility. This person, in conjunction with a John Deere Project Manager, will call in additional Excelsior and John Deere resources as needed.
b. After analysis, a project plan will be developed and submitted to Excelsior management for approval.
c. Only after the project plan has been approved may execution of it proceed.

10. Communication Plan

a. Weekly progress meetings will be held with Excelsior management. Excelsior's Project Manager will chair them. Minutes will be published. The John Deere Project Manager will be a part of these meetings.
b. Monthly progress reports will be generated and distributed to a commonly agreed-upon distribution list.
c. Joint Excelsior-Deere meetings may be called at the discretion of project sponsors to review project status. These may be by phone or face to face.

11. Confidentiality

The project and the results are the property of Excelsior. Requests for project information from other parties are to be referred to the Process Owner.

_____   _____
(Sponsor, John Deere)   (Sponsor, Excelsior)

_____   _____
Date   Date

_____
(Process owner, John Deere)

_____
Date

that Deere purchased. At the time of the signing of the charter, James Franks, vice president of sales and marketing, and Bill Sanderson, director of quality assurance, were the key contacts at Excelsior working with the SDG project team. These individuals authorized the charter with Deere. It was their responsibility to accept/reject, implement/not implement the changes recommended by the SDG.

The Problem

Each party considered the business relationship important. Excelsior relied on Deere for most of its sales. Deere wanted to keep Excelsior as a supplier because it would be cost-prohibitive for Deere to produce these tractor attachments in-house. Deere also believed that if it had to find another supplier for all the equipment purchased from Excelsior, Deere would have to make a significant human resource effort and incur significant risk.

The manufacturing cycle time for Excelsior's antiquated processes was 250 days. This created problems for Deere and its customers in terms of delivery and price. In an effort to reduce cycle time from about 250 days to 20–40 days and cut costs by an estimated 10 percent, the SDG created a team to work on the project. The Excelsior Equipment project team was assembled in March 1999 and consisted of four key individuals: Benjamin Aldrin, supplier development engineer and project manager; Samuel Montgomery, in charge of purchasing; Joshua Wilson, in charge of strategic sourcing; and Edward Smith, the manager of the SDG. Though Smith was a member of the team in March 1999, he was replaced by Robert Jammone in mid-May 2000. The team's task was to work with Excelsior to redesign its manufacturing process to meet the cycle time and cost goals.

The team worked for twenty-three months, investing hundreds of man-days, and prepared and presented a report on February 24, 2001, to Franks and Sanderson. The report showed that cycle time and cost reduction targets could be met. The basic parameters of the plan had been available much earlier, but the planning phase continued extending out due to Excelsior's reluctance to make changes, in general, and its specific reluctance to adopt a plan advocating such a fundamental change to its manufacturing process. Consequently, the bulk of the twenty-three months involved gathering more information in an effort to justify the benefits of making the change to Excelsior management.

Excelsior personnel studied the report, and Franks and Sanderson contacted Deere on April 28, 2001. Excelsior's unwillingness to change its manufacturing process was the biggest obstacle faced by Deere in May 2001. Franks and Sanderson did not want to invest in the equipment and facilities recommended by Deere. According to their assessments, the maximum amount of savings that could be realized by restructuring their manufacturing process would be, at most, less than 1 percent. In addition, based on Deere's accounting system, and contrary to its own estimation, Excelsior believed that its quality was better than IBM's and it had world-class levels of work in process. Armed with these beliefs, Franks and Sanderson were reluctant to invest the $5 million necessary to implement the changes recommended by the SDG. In their minds, the manufacturing process at Excelsior was about as efficient as it could be. Deere was getting pressure from its customers for quicker and more reliable delivery of the tractor attachments. Deere also wanted improved profitability on the attachments. This situation was important and of the highest priority to Deere, and the team needed to devise a tactic to get Excelsior to buy into the proposed manufacturing redesign. Deere management was also interested in getting a payback on the extensive level of support that it had invested in Excelsior.

The Meeting

Benjamin called today's meeting with the objective of determining the best way to solve Excelsior's objections. In this meeting, he reviewed the case for the redesign of the manufacturing process with the members of the project team. After considerable discussion, the team decided to utilize Deere's position and demand that Excelsior lower its prices at least 5 percent or half the amount Deere thought was obtainable by implementing the project. The team believed that Excelsior was interested in the stability of a new long-term agreement; and they knew that, without the changes, Deere was not interested in extending its long-term commitment to Excelsior. The team thought this process would force Excelsior to make the appropriate changes to its manufacturing process. On the other hand, if Excelsior did give the price reduction and still refused to implement the necessary manufacturing flow improvements, Deere would have an indication that Excelsior was not a supplier that would remain viable in the long run. Deere would be forced to initiate activity to resource the business at the end of the contract. It would take a significant amount of time and planning to find and develop a new supplier.

Benjamin knew that he and Joshua Wilson were in agreement with the plan. Samuel Montgomery, not wanting to anger his supplier, did not like the proposed tactics, but he agreed to go along with the plan. Robert Jammone expressed no opposition and agreed to go along and remain quiet. Even though the team agreed to the approach, Benjamin privately wondered whether it would work and whether it would be an effective way of getting Excelsior to improve its antiquated manufacturing processes.

Questions for Discussion

1. Is Deere's tactic an appropriate one?

2. What are the implications of this tactic and the possible consequences, positive or negative?

3. If it is not an appropriate tactic, what are some other alternatives?

4. Is this an ethical approach?

5. What are some of the implications as far as human resource management is concerned? How can the group members better manage the consensus building to present an undivided front to Excelsior?

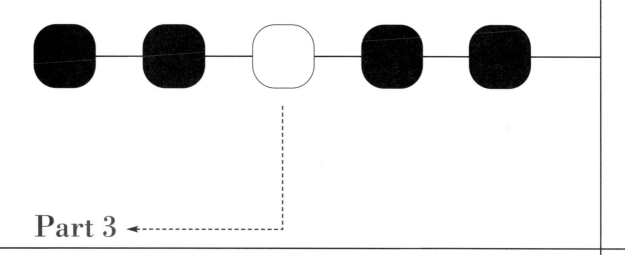

Part 3

Operations Issues in Supply Chain Management

Case Studies

Chapter 5:

DEMAND FORECASTING AND COLLABORATIVE PLANNING, FORECASTING, AND REPLENISHMENT

An organization's ability to control variability in areas such as forecasts and customer demand will be key to effective responsiveness. Massachusetts Institute of Technology (MIT) research of corporate supply chain practices reveals that variability at the end of the supply chain is magnified and distorted as it proceeds up the chain. In the business world, such distortions and miscommunications of supply and demand information can have a negative impact across the supply chain, raising inventory levels, increasing manufacturing and transportation costs, and limiting the optimization of available resources.[1]

Learning Objectives

After completing this chapter, you should be able to

- Explain the role of demand forecasting in a supply chain.
- Identify the components of a forecast.
- Compare and contrast qualitative and quantitative forecasting techniques.
- Assess the accuracy of forecasts.
- Explain collaborative planning, forecasting, and replenishment.

Chapter Outline

Introduction

Matching Supply and Demand

Forecasting Techniques
  Qualitative Methods
  Quantitative Methods
  Components of Time Series Data
  Time Series Forecasting Methods

Forecast Accuracy

Collaborative Planning, Forecasting, and Replenishment

Software Solutions

SUPPLY CHAIN MANAGEMENT IN ACTION   *Demand Forecasting and CPFR at Wal-Mart*

Sam Walton opened the first Wal-Mart in 1962 in Rogers, Arkansas. Today, the company offers four different retail concepts: Wal-Mart discount stores, Supercenters, Neighborhood Markets, and SAM'S Club warehouses. The emphasis on customer satisfaction and "Always Low Prices" for their products has resulted in Wal-Mart becoming the world's largest retailer with annual revenues exceeding $218 billion. Years ago, Sam Walton said, "Let's be the most friendly—offer a smile of welcome and assistance to all who do us a favor by entering our stores. Give better service—over and beyond what our customers expect. Why not? You wonderful, caring associates can do it and do it better than any other retailing company in the world . . . exceed your customers' expectations. If you do, they'll come back over and over again."[2] The company with 1.3 million employees worldwide has more than 3,200 facilities in the United States and more than 1,200 units in Mexico, Puerto Rico, Canada, Argentina, Brazil, China, Korea, Germany, and the United Kingdom. Wal-Mart is considered one of the world's best supply chain operators, with cost of goods 5 percent to 10 percent less than its major competitors, thus providing the company with a competitive advantage.

Wal-Mart is one of the early adopters of collaborative planning, forecasting, and replenishment (CPFR), a holistic approach to managing a network of trading partners in the supply chain. CPFR enabled Wal-Mart to develop a single, short-term forecast for each item sold, which is then frozen. This mutually agreed-upon single forecast becomes the driver of improved demand management, resulting in better control over replenishment and inventory levels. The CPFR program implementation enabled Wal-Mart to move to a just-in-time system that resulted in significant savings in inventory carrying costs for Wal-Mart, as well as its suppliers

According to Joseph Eckroth Jr., Chief Information Officer at Mattel, Inc., "My ability to get information about the sales pace of a toy and either ramping up or shutting down manufacturing depends on my having data. Having sales data on a daily or hourly basis is necessary to figure out on a micro level what is selling best where and tailoring manufacturing accordingly. The greatest efficiencies will appear when the kind of trusting, mutually beneficial relationship Mattel has with Wal-Mart is duplicated with the rest of the manufacturer's retail outlets. . . . Having that data on a global basis from every one of my customers allows me to optimize the sales of my products and the fill rates of my customers."[3]

Wal-Mart initiated a data warehouse program to enable it to accumulate historical data in a central computer, analyze the data, have a better understanding of the business environment, and consequently make better decisions. Initially only point of sales and shipment data were collected. Subsequently, the data warehouse was expanded to include sixty-five weeks of data on inventory, forecasts, demographics, markdowns, returns, and market baskets by item, by store, and by day. The warehouse contains data on Wal-Mart's operations as well as its competitors. These data are not only accessible to Wal-Mart's buyers, merchandisers, and logistics and forecasting associates but also to Wal-Mart's 3,500 partners. For example, when a competitor expands its grocery department, Wal-Mart is interested in finding out the effect of this

Sources: C. Stedman, "Wal-Mart Mines for Forecasts," *Computerworld* (26 May 1997); P. S. Foote and M. Krishnamurthi, "Forecasting Using a Data Warehousing Model: Wal-Mart's Experience," *The Journal of Business Forecasting Methods & Systems* 20, no. 3 (fall 2001): 13–17; Wal-Mart Web site, http://www.walmart.com

action on its sales performance. The forecasting process begins with the data warehouse. Wal-Mart uses data mining software developed by NeoVista Software (acquired by J&A Software Group, Inc.) to analyze a year's point-of-sale data in Wal-Mart's data warehouse and generates buying patterns and other results for each of its U.S. stores. The objective is to save millions of dollars of inventory by having a better understanding of seasonal and week-to-week variations in sales and alignment of marketing and business plans with customer demand.

The forecasting process works this way: Wal-Mart's buyers generate a preliminary forecast, which appears on the Warner-Lambert's CPFR server. (In 2000, Warner-Lambert, a global pharmaceutical company, merged with Pfizer.) The comments and revisions suggested by Warner-Lambert's planning staff are shared with Wal-Mart's planners. A final consensus forecast is generated for each product and used for inventory management at Wal-Mart and production planning at Warner-Lambert. Wal-Mart uses the same system with its other suppliers.

The data mining software has found some interesting surprises. For example, the buying patterns vary significantly from store to store and throughout the year for high-inventory consumer products such as mouthwash and pet food. The findings are used to continuously improve Wal-Mart's automated product ordering and replenishment system. The application allows Wal-Mart to analyze up to 700 million store-item combinations and deliver the right item, at the right store, at the right time, and at the right price to the customers. As a result, Wal-Mart has achieved increased accuracy in its forecasting process and a competitive advantage in the retail industry.

Introduction

Forecasting provides an estimate of future demand and the basis for planning and sound business decisions. Since all organizations deal with an unknown future, some error between a forecast and actual demand is to be expected. Thus, the goal of a good forecasting technique is to minimize the deviation between actual demand and the forecast. Since a forecast is a prediction of the future, factors that influence demand, the impact of these factors, and whether these factors will continue to influence future demand must be considered in developing an accurate forecast. In addition, buyers and sellers should share all relevant information to generate a single consensus forecast so that the correct decisions on supply and demand can be made. Improved forecasts benefit not only the focal company but also the trading partners in the supply chain. In today's competitive business environment, collaboration (or cooperation and information sharing) between buyers and sellers is the rule rather than the exception. The benefits of better forecasts are lower inventories, reduced stock-outs, smoother production plans, reduced costs, and improved customer service.

For more than sixty years, the Institute of Supply Management (ISM) has been publishing monthly indices for the manufacturing sector such as Customers' Inventories, New Orders, Production, Manufacturing Employment, Supplier Deliveries, Inventories, Price, Backlog of Orders, New Export Orders, and Imports. Many business executives use these indices to forecast the overall direction of the economy and the health of the manufacturing sector. For example, purchasing and supply managers utilize the Customers' Inventories Index to help forecast future new orders and make production decisions and to measure changes in supply chain activity. The ISM's Report on Business is profiled in the following Supply Chain Management in Action box.

SUPPLY CHAIN MANAGEMENT IN ACTION *The ISM Report on Business*

The Institute of Supply Management (ISM), formerly known as the National Association of Purchasing Management (NAPM), surveys more than 400 purchasing and supply executives in the United States using a questionnaire seeking information on monthly changes in production, new orders (from customers), new export orders, imports, employment, inventories, prices, lead times, and the timeliness of supplier deliveries. The Manufacturing Report on Business, available the first business day of each month, is considered to be an accurate indicator of the overall direction of the economy and the health of the manufacturing sector. Three quotes regarding the value of the report follow:

I find the surveys conducted by the purchasing and supply managers to be an excellent supplement to the data supplied by various departments and agencies of the government.

Alan Greenspan, Chairman of the Federal Reserve Board

The ISM Manufacturing Report on Business has one of the shortest reporting lags of any macro-economic series and gives an important early look at the economy. It also measures some concepts (such as lead times and delivery lags) that can be found nowhere else. It makes an important contribution to the American statistical system and to economic policy.

Joseph E. Stiglitz, former Chairman of President Clinton's Council of Economic Advisors

The ISM Manufacturing Report on Business is extremely useful. The PMI, the Report's composite index, gives the earliest indication each month of the health of the manufacturing sector. It is an essential component for assessing the state of the economy.

Michael J. Boskin, Hoover Institute Senior Fellow

The ISM report provides several indices for the manufacturing sector: Customers' Inventories, New Orders, Production, Manufacturing Employment, Supplier Deliveries, Inventories, Price, Backlog of Orders, New Export Orders, and Imports. The most important index is the Purchasing Managers Index (PMI) developed by Theodore Torda, Senior Economist of the U.S. Department of Commerce, and introduced in 1982. The PMI is a composite of five weighted seasonally adjusted indices (weights are shown in parentheses): New Orders (0.30), Production (0.25), Employment (0.20), Deliveries (0.15), and Inventories (0.10). The purchasing surveys provide comprehensive information for tracking the economy and developing business forecasts. The ISM Report on Business has been tested and found to accurately forecast the major shifts in the business cycle for sixty years, with the exception of four years during World War II.[4]

Purchasing and supply executives use the report in a variety of ways. For example, the Customers' Inventories Index is a strong indicator of future new orders and production, and used to measure changes in supply chain activity. According to Steve Daniels, Dresser Equipment Group of Halliburton and Co., "The data indicated in the monthly ISM Report on Business is an integral part of our own forecasting efforts, project planning, and ongoing communication with both suppliers and customers. Sharing this information with suppliers and customers provides an opportunity to work together to achieve more effective cost management in our supply chain network."

Sources: R. G. Kauffman and J. H. Hoagland, "Developing Purchasing Strategies with NAPM Business Survey Data: What's Available and How to Use It," NAPM's 81st Annual International Conference Proceedings (28 April 1996); "The Institute for Supply Management Manufacturing Report on Business," The Institute for Supply Management (September 2002).

Many have argued that demand forecasting is both an art and a science. Since there are no accurate crystal balls available, it is therefore impossible to expect 100 percent forecast accuracy at all times. For instance, a Sony Web site crashed after receiving an unexpected 500,000 hits in just a few minutes after it began accepting advanced sales of PlayStation2 (PS2) in late February 2000.[5] Initial sales for Sony's PS2 in March 2000 were more than ten times that of the original PlayStation's introduction five years earlier.[6] Even though Sony had prior experience with the launch of the original PlayStation, the company was yet unable to accurately predict the tremendous response from consumers for PS2. Sony, the dominant player in the video game market, had to double its production in a short time period before new competitor products such as Nintendo's Gamecube and Microsoft's X-box were introduced. This exemplifies the challenges faced by companies in forecasting sales and ramping up production quickly to meet the unexpectedly high demand for their products and to defend their market position.[7] Procter & Gamble found that retailers lose sales 41 percent of the time when they run out of stock. A similar study by the Grocery Manufacturers of America showed that grocery stores could lose as much as $6 billion in sales from products being out of stock.[8]

The impact of poor communication and inaccurate forecasts resonates all along the supply chain and results in the *bullwhip effect* (described in Chapter 1) causing stock-outs, lost sales, high costs of inventory and obsolescence, material shortages, poor responsiveness to market dynamics, and poor profitability. For example, Nike's earnings were 33 percent below initial estimates in March 2001 because of inventory problems caused by inaccurate demand forecasts.[9] As a result, Nike had to scramble to get rid of excess inventory created by the forecasting problem from the previous year. As another example, the telecommunications industry today faces a glut of fiber-optic cables installed in the late 1990s. Millions of miles of fiber-optic cables were installed in the United States, but as of the end of 2002 only 2.7 percent of capacity is actually being used. Level 3 Communications, Inc.'s plan to build the largest and most advanced fiber-optic network stalled in the face of this largest surplus in history. While today the company has survived the crisis, its stock lost more than 95 percent of its value. Clearly this is an example of a mismatch among supply and demand brought about by the optimistic forecasts of extreme growth in Internet traffic continuing into the future. Unfortunately, growth slowed dramatically in the late 1990s leading to an oversupply of fiber-optic lines.[10]

Matching Supply and Demand

The business environment today is such that we have consumers who are more demanding and discriminating. The market has evolved into a "pull" environment with customers dictating to the supplier what products they desire and when they need them delivered. If a retailer cannot get the product it wants at the right quantity, price, and time from one supplier, the retailer will look for another company that can meet its demands. Any temporary stock-out has a tremendous downside on sales, profitability, and customer relationships. Managing demand is challenging because of the difficulty in always forecasting future consumer requirements accurately.

In order for supply chain integration to be successful, suppliers must be able to accurately forecast demand so they can produce and deliver the right quantities demanded by their customers in a timely and cost-effective fashion. There are several ways to closely match supply and demand. One way is for a supplier to hold plenty of stock available for delivery at any time. While this approach maximizes sales revenues, it is also expensive because of the cost of carrying inventory and the possibility of write-downs at the end of the selling season. Use of flexible pricing is another approach. During heavy demand periods, prices can be raised to reduce peak demand. Price discounts can then be used to increase sales during periods with excess inventory or slow demand. This strategy can still result in lost sales, though, as well as stock-outs and thus cannot be considered an ideal or partnership-friendly approach to satisfying demand. In the short term, companies can also use overtime, subcontracting, or temporary workers to increase capacity to meet demand for their products and services. In the interim, though, firms will lose sales as they train workers and quality may also tend to suffer.

Thus, it is imperative that suppliers along the supply chain find ways to better match supply and demand to achieve optimal levels of cost, quality, and customer service to enable them to compete with other supply chains. Any problems that adversely affect the timely delivery of products demanded by consumers will have ramifications throughout the entire chain. Sport Obermeyer, a high-end fashion skiwear design and merchandising company headquartered in Aspen, Colorado, sells its products through department stores and ski shops. Sport Obermeyer's selling season is from September to January, with peak sales in December and January. Since the selling season is short and sales of high-end fashion apparel are more profitable than those of traditional apparel, it is critical that Sport Obermeyer supply the demand for high-end fashion apparel without getting stuck with excessive inventories at the end of the season. With improved forecasting capabilities and implementation of a quick response program that keeps its suppliers notified of forecasts, sales patterns, and marketing campaigns, Sport Obermeyer is able to mitigate the supply-demand mismatch problem thus reducing stock-outs during the season and heavy markdowns at the end of the season.[11] Sport Obermeyer thus represents an effective approach to matching supply and demand while minimizing risk and cost.

Forecasting Techniques

Understanding that a forecast is very often inaccurate does not mean that nothing can be done to improve the forecast. Both quantitative and qualitative forecasts can be improved by seeking inputs from trading partners. **Qualitative forecasting methods** are based on opinions and intuition, whereas **quantitative forecasting methods** use mathematical models and relevant historical data to generate forecasts. The quantitative methods can be divided into two groups: time series and associative models.

A recent study[12] on forecasting in the United States finds that time series models are the most frequently used among all the forecasting models with nearly 60 percent of the respondents using such models. Other popular methods used were the moving average and simple trend forecasts. Twenty-four percent of the companies in the survey used associative forecasting models, with simple regression analysis rated as the most popular method. The qualitative or judgmental models such as the Delphi method and market surveys were used by only 8 percent of the companies when little or no data existed. The Global Perspective box features a discussion of forecasting at Wells Lamont.

Qualitative Methods

Qualitative forecasting methods are approaches to forecasting based on intuition or judgmental evaluation and are generally used when data are limited, unavailable, or not currently relevant. While this approach can be very low cost, the effectiveness depends to a large extent on the skill and experience of the forecaster(s) and the amount of relevant information available. The qualitative techniques are often used to develop long-range projections when current data is no longer very useful, and for new product introductions when current data does not exist. Discussions of four common qualitative forecasting models follow:

- **Jury of executive opinion:** A group of senior management executives who are knowledgeable about the market, competitors, and the business environment collectively develop the forecast. This technique has the advantage of several individuals with considerable experience working together, but if one member's views dominate the discussion, then the value and reliability of the

Global Perspective

FORECASTING AT WELLS LAMONT

In 1907, W. O. Wells started the Wells Lamont Company, a manufacturer of work gloves in Aberdeen, South Dakota. The company moved first to Minneapolis and then finally to Chicago. Today, Wells Lamont belongs to The Marmon Group, which has more than 100 autonomous manufacturing and service companies operating more than 300 facilities in forty countries. As the largest manufacturer of gloves in the world, Wells Lamont has manufacturing facilities in the United States, Canada, Asia, Europe, and the Far East.[13] The vision that W. O. Wells had instituted earlier of, "delivering a top quality product to our customers, made from top quality materials with top quality methods," is still the driving force behind the company's success and leadership position in the glove industry.[14]

Wells Lamont's product lines include hand coverings, work gloves, garden gloves, hunting gloves, skiing gloves, mittens, and oven mitts. The objective is to provide a wide range of gloves for different jobs in a variety of sizes for all types of hands. To help better manage its inventory and production capacity across its global network of production facilities, Wells Lamont implemented the Demand Solutions Forecast Management (DSFM) software supplied by Demand Management, Inc. Maria Raimondi, forecast manager for Wells Lamont, says, "The planning tool makes it much easier to control monthly production. Our models are consistently much closer to what we are really producing. It's a very comfortable feeling. We have better control of demand."[15]

The DSFM software generates reports at differing levels for use by various groups within the company. For example, month-to-month reports showing any item or aggregated inventory changes are used for master planning purposes. At the company level, sales by account or by trade class can be aggregated giving an overview of the market. The software does the hard data crunching, allowing managers to devote less time to developing forecasting models and more time on planning, analyzing, and responding to exception reports. A feature in the program provides access to the customer forecast for the next twelve months. Wells Lamont can make adjustments to its own forecast if a customer has information about demand previously unknown to Wells Lamont, to avoid any surprises.

outcome can be diminished. This technique is applicable for long-range planning and new product introductions.

Forecasting high fashion, for instance, is risky business since there is often no historical basis to generate the forecast. Sport Obermeyer's buying committee estimates its demand based on a general consensus reached by committee members. Because a dominant member of the group might carry more weight in the discussion, the resulting forecast could potentially be biased and inaccurate. Consequently, Sport Obermeyer averages the individual forecast of each committee member to provide an overall demand forecast.[16]

- **Delphi method:** A group of internal and external experts are surveyed during several rounds in terms of future events and long-term forecasts of demand. Group members do not physically meet and thus avoid the scenario where one or a few experts could dominate a discussion. The answers from the experts are accumulated after each round of the survey and summarized. The summary of responses is then sent out to all the experts in the next round, wherein individual experts can modify their responses based on the group's response summary. The iterative process goes on until a consensus is reached.

The process can be both time-consuming and very expensive. This approach is applicable for high-risk technology forecasting; large, expensive projects; or major, new product introductions. The quality of the forecast depends largely on the knowledge of the experts.

- **Sales force composite:** The sales force represents a good source of market information. This type of forecast is generated based on the sales force's knowledge of the market and estimates of customer needs. Due to the proximity of the sales personnel to the consumers, the forecast tends to be reliable but individual biases could negatively impact the effectiveness of this approach. For example, if bonuses are paid when actual sales exceed the forecast there is a tendency for the sales force to underforecast.

- **Consumer survey:** A questionnaire is developed that seeks input from customers on important issues such as future buying habits, new product ideas, and opinions about existing products. The survey is administered through telephone, mail, Internet, or personal interviews. Data collected from the survey are analyzed using statistical tools and judgment to derive a set of meaningful results. For example, Wyeth-Ayerst, the ninth-largest pharmaceutical company in the world, uses this type of market research to create forecasts for new products.[17] The challenge is to identify a sample of respondents who are representative of the larger population and to get an acceptable response rate.

Quantitative Methods

Quantitative forecasting models use mathematical techniques that are based on historical data and can include causal variables to forecast demand. **Time series forecasting** is based on the assumption that the future is an extension of the past, thus, historical data can be used to predict future demand. **Associative forecasting** assumes that one or more factors (independent variables) are related to demand and, therefore, can be used to predict future demand. Since these forecasts rely solely on past demand data, all quantitative methods become less accurate as the forecast's time horizon increases. Thus, for long time horizon forecasts, it is generally recommended to utilize a combination of both quantitative and qualitative techniques.

Components of Time Series Data

Time series data typically have four components: trend, cyclical, seasonal, and random variations:

- **Trend variations:** Trends represent either increasing or decreasing movements over many years and are due to factors such as population growth, population shifts, cultural changes, and income shifts. Common trend lines are linear, S-curve, exponential, or asymptotic.

- **Cyclical variations:** Cyclical variations are wavelike movements that are longer than a year and influenced by macroeconomic and political factors. One example is the **business cycle** (recession or expansion). Dating to the nineteenth century in the United States, there are thirty-two complete business cycles, with an overall average length of 4.5 years per cycle. More recent business cycles have been affected by world events such as the 1973 oil embargo, the 1991 Mexican financial crisis, the 1997 Asian economic crisis, and the September 11, 2001, terrorist attacks in the United States.[18]

- **Seasonal variations:** Seasonal variations show peaks and valleys that repeat over a consistent interval such as hours, days, weeks, months, years, or seasons. Due to seasonality, many companies do well in certain months and not so well in other months. For example, snow blower sales tend to be higher in the fall and winter, then taper off in spring and summer. A fast-food restaurant will see higher sales during the day around breakfast, lunch, and dinner. U.S. hotels experience large crowds during traditional holidays such as July 4, Labor Day, Thanksgiving, Christmas, and New Year.

- **Random variations:** Random variations are due to unexpected or unpredictable events such as natural disasters (hurricanes, tornadoes, fire), strikes, and wars. For example, in October 2002, the Pacific Maritime Association, representing shipping companies and terminal operators, locked out more than 10,000 dock workers at twenty-nine West Coast ports in California, Oregon, and Washington. The unexpected shutdown of West Coast ports caused shipment delays of parts that forced several automakers— such as Honda's manufacturing plants in the United States and Canada, NUMMI's (joint venture between Toyota Motor Corp. and General Motors Corp.) plant in Freemont, and Mitsubishi Motors Corp.'s Illinois plant—to stop production briefly.[19]

Time Series Forecasting Models

As discussed earlier, time series forecasts are dependent on the availability of historical data. Forecasts are estimated by extrapolating the past data into the future. Time series forecasting is one of the most widely used techniques. A survey of purchasing professionals indicates that the top three quantitative forecasting techniques used are simple moving average, weighted moving average, and exponential smoothing.[20] Ocean Spray uses primarily time series models in its forecasting system and three years of historical data to generate forecasts, which can be revised based on event-based inputs such as promotions and advertising.[21] At Ocean Spray, the forecasts are used in planning for procurement, supply, replenishment, and corporate revenue.

Some of the more common time series approaches such as simple moving average, weighted moving average, exponential smoothing, and trend-adjusted exponential smoothing are discussed next.

Simple Moving Average Forecasting Model. The **simple moving average forecasting** method uses historical data to generate a forecast and works well when the demand is fairly stable over time. The *n*-period moving average forecast is

$$F_{t+1} = \frac{\sum_{i=t-n+1}^{t} A_i}{n}$$

where

F_{t+1} = forecast for Period $t + 1$,
  n = number of periods used to calculate moving average, and
  A_i = actual demand in Period i.

The average tends to be more responsive if fewer data points are used to compute the average. However, random events can also impact the average adversely. Thus the decision maker must balance the cost of responding slowly to changes versus the cost of responding to random variations. The advantage of this technique is that it is simple to use and easy to understand. A weakness of the simple moving average forecast is its inability to respond to trend changes quickly. Example 5.1 illustrates the simple moving average technique.

EXAMPLE 5.1   Simple Moving Average Forecasting

Using the following data, calculate the forecast for Period 5 using a four-period moving average.

Period	Demand
1	1,600
2	2,200
3	2,000
4	1,600
5	2,500
6	3,500
7	3,300
8	3,200
9	3,900
10	4,700
11	4,300
12	4,400

Solution

$$F_5 = \text{forecast for Period 5} = \frac{1,600 + 2,200 + 2,000 + 1,600}{4} = 1,850$$

The solution using a Microsoft Excel spreadsheet is shown in Figure 5.1.

Figure 5.1 | **Forecasting Using Moving Averages and the Microsoft Excel Spreadsheet**

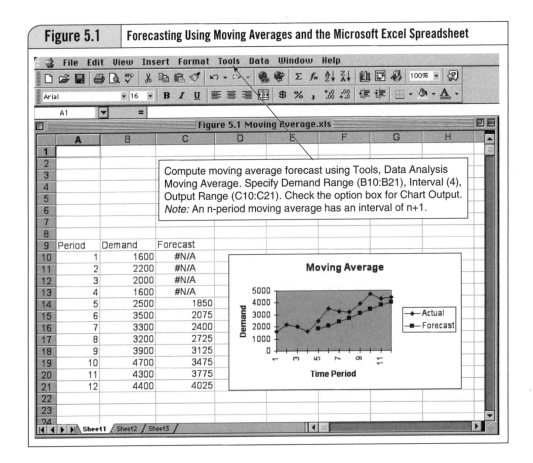

Weighted Moving Average Forecasting Model. Weighted moving average forecasting, which is based on an n-period weighted moving average, follows:

$$F_{t=1} = \sum_{i=t-n+1}^{t} w_i A_i$$

where

F_{t+1} = forecast for Period $t + 1$,
  n = number of periods used in determining the moving average,
  A_i = actual demand in Period i, and
  w_i = weight assigned to Period i (with $\Sigma w_i = 1$).

The weighted moving average allows greater emphasis to be placed on more recent data to reflect changes in demand patterns. Weights used also tend to be based on experience of the forecaster. Although the forecast is more responsive to underlying changes in demand, the forecast still lags demand because of the averaging effect. As such, the weighted moving average method does not do a good job of tracking trend changes in the data. Example 5.2 illustrates the weighted moving average forecast.

EXAMPLE 5.2   **Weighted Moving Average Forecasting**

Using the data provided in Example 5.1, calculate the forecast for Period 5 using a four-period weighted moving average. The weights of 0.4, 0.3, 0.2, and 0.1 are assigned to the most recent, second most recent, third most recent, and the fourth most recent periods, respectively.

Solution

$$F_5 = 0.1(1,600) + 0.2(2,200) + 0.3(2,000) + 0.4(1,600) = 1,840$$

The solution using Microsoft Excel spreadsheet is shown in Figure 5.2.

Exponential Smoothing Forecasting Model. Exponential smoothing forecasting is a sophisticated weighted moving average forecasting in which the forecast for the next period's demand is the current period's forecast adjusted by a fraction of the difference between the current period's actual demand and its forecast. This approach requires less data to be kept than the weighted moving average method because only two data points are needed. Due to its simplicity and minimal data requirement, exponential smoothing forecasting is one of the more popular techniques. This model, like the other time series models, is suitable for data that show little trend or seasonal patterns. Other higher order exponential smoothing models described in the following sections can be used for data exhibiting trend or seasonality characteristics. The exponential smoothing formula is

$$F_{t+1} = F_t + \alpha(A_t - F_t) \text{ or } F_{t+1} = \alpha A_t + (1 - \alpha)F_t$$

where

F_{t+1} = forecast for Period $t + 1$,
  F_t = forecast for Period t,
  A_t = actual demand for Period t, and
  α = a smoothing constant $(0 \leq \alpha \leq 1)$.

With an α value closer to 1, there is a greater emphasis on recent data, making the model more responsive to changes in the recent demand. When α has a low value, more weight is placed on past demand (which is contained in the previous period's forecast value) and the

Figure 5.2	Forecasting Using Weighted Moving Averages and the Microsoft Excel Spreadsheet

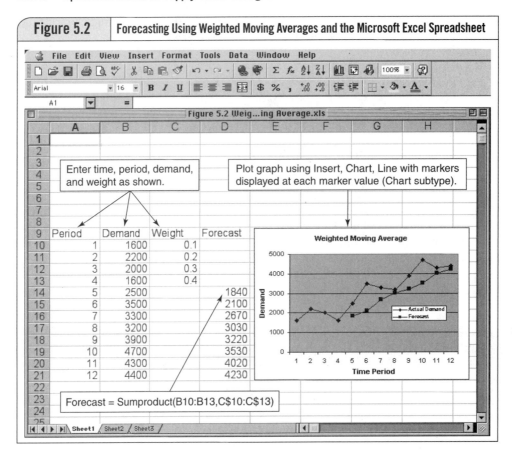

model responds more slowly to changes in demand. The impact of using a small or large value of α is similar to the effect of using a large or small number of observations in calculating the moving average. In general, the forecast will lag any trend in the actual data because only partial adjustment to the most recent forecast error can be made. The initial forecast value can be estimated using one of the qualitative methods, such as the Delphi forecast, or by simply setting the initial forecast equal to the demand for that period. Example 5.3 illustrates exponential smoothing forecasting.

EXAMPLE 5.3   Exponential Smoothing Forecasting

Based on data provided in Example 5.1, calculate the forecast for Period 3 using the exponential smoothing method. Assume the forecast for Period 2 is 1,600. Use a smoothing constant of $\alpha = 0.3$.

Solution

Given:

$F_2 = 1,600$, $\alpha = 0.3$

$F_{t+1} = F_t + \alpha (A_t - F_t)$

$F_3 = F_2 + \alpha(A_2 - F_2) = 1,600 + 0.3(2,200 - 1,600) = 1,780$

Thus the forecast for Week 3 is 1,780.

The solution using Microsoft Excel spreadsheet is shown in Figure 5.3.

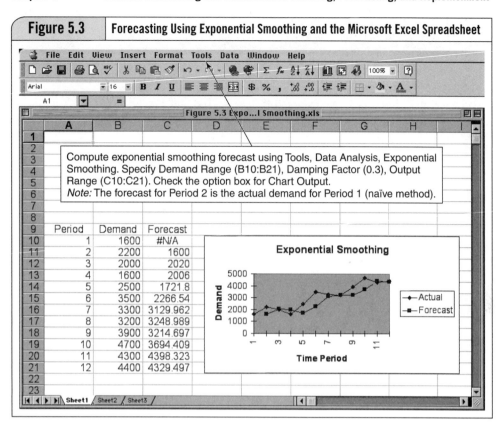

Figure 5.3 | **Forecasting Using Exponential Smoothing and the Microsoft Excel Spreadsheet**

Trend-Adjusted Exponential Smoothing Forecasting Model. The exponential smoothing method can be modified to include a trend component when the time series show a systematic upward or downward trend in the data over time. This method requires two smoothing constants, one for the smoothed forecast (α) and the other for the trend (β). The equations for this model are

$$F_t = \alpha A_t + (1 - \alpha)(F_{t-1} + T_{t-1}),$$
$$T_t = \beta(F_t - F_{t-1}) + (1 - \beta)T_{t-1},$$

and the trend-adjusted forecast,

$$TAF_{t+m} = F_t + mT_t$$

where

F_t = exponentially smoothed average in Period t,
A_t = actual demand in Period t,
T_t = exponentially smoothed trend in Period t,
α = smoothing constant ($0 \leq \alpha \leq 1$), and
β = smoothing constant for trend ($0 \leq \beta \leq 1$).

A higher value of β indicates greater emphasis on recent trend changes, while a small β places less weight on recent changes and has the effect of smoothing out the current trend. The smoothing constants, α and β, are estimated using a trial and error approach, matching actual historical demand data to the forecasted demand in search of the smoothing constants that minimize the forecast errors. Example 5.4 illustrates **trend-adjusted exponential smoothing forecasting.**

EXAMPLE 5.4   Trend-adjusted Exponential Smoothing Forecasting

Using the data provided in Example 5.1, calculate the forecast for Period 4 using the trend-adjusted exponential smoothing method. Assume the smoothed average for the series in Period 2 is 1,600 and smoothed trend is 300. Use $\alpha = 0.3$ and $\beta = 0.4$.

Solution

Given:

$F_2 = 1{,}600$, $T_2 = 300$, $\alpha = 0.3$, $\beta = 0.4$, $A_3 = 2{,}000$

$F_3 = \alpha A_3 + (1 - \alpha)(F_2 + T_2)$

$\quad = 0.3(2{,}000) + (1 - 0.3)(1{,}600 + 300) = 1{,}930$

$T_3 = \beta(F_3 - F_2) + (1 - \beta)T_2$

$\quad = 0.4(1{,}930 - 1{,}600) + (1 - 0.4)300 = 312$

$TAF_4 = F_3 + T_3$

$\quad = 1{,}930 + 312 = 2{,}242$

Thus the trend-adjusted forecast for Period 4 is 2,242.

Linear Trend Forecasting Model. The trend can be estimated using simple linear regression to fit a line to a time series of historical data. The linear trend method minimizes the sum of squared deviations to determine the characteristics of the linear equation, or

$$\hat{Y} = b_0 + b_1 x$$

where

$\hat{Y}$ = forecast or dependent variable
x = time variable,
b_0 = intercept of the line, and
b_1 = slope of the line.

The coefficients b_0 and b_1 are calculated as follows:

$$b_1 = \frac{n \sum (xy) - \sum x \sum y}{n \sum x^2 - (\sum x)^2} \text{ and}$$

$$b_0 = \frac{\sum y - b_1 \sum x}{n}$$

where

b_1 = slope of the line,
x = independent variable values,
y = dependent variable values,
$\bar{x}$ = average of the x values,
$\bar{y}$ = average of the y values, and
n = number of observations.

Example 5.5 illustrates **linear trend forecasting.**

EXAMPLE 5.5   Linear Trend Forecasting

The demand for toys produced by the Miki Manufacturing Company is shown in the following table:

Period	Demand	Period	Demand	Period	Demand
1	1,600	5	2,500	9	3,900
2	2,200	6	3,500	10	4,700
3	2,000	7	3,300	11	4,300
4	1,600	8	3,200	12	4,400

1. What is the trend line?
2. What is the forecast for Period 13?

Solution

Period (x)	Demand (y)	x^2	xy
1	1,600	1	1,600
2	2,200	4	4,400
3	2,000	9	6,000
4	1,600	16	6,400
5	2,500	25	12,500
6	3,500	36	21,000
7	3,300	49	23,100
8	3,200	64	25,600
9	3,900	81	35,100
10	4,700	100	47,000
11	4,300	121	47,300
12	4,400	144	52,800
$\Sigma x = 78$	$\Sigma y = 37,200$	$\Sigma x^2 = 650$	$\Sigma xy = 282,800$

$$b_1 = \frac{n\sum(xy) - \sum x \sum y}{n\sum x^2 - (\sum x^2)} = \frac{12(282,800) - 78(37,200)}{12(650) - 78^2} = 286.71$$

$$b_0 = \frac{\sum y - b_1 \sum x}{n} = \frac{37,200 - 286.71(78)}{12} = 1,236.4$$

The trend line is

$$\hat{Y} = 1,236.4 + 286.7x$$

To forecast demand for Period 13, we substitute $x = 13$ into the preceding trend equation.

Forecast for Period 13 = 1,236.4 + 286.7(13) = 4,963.5, or 4,964.

The solution using Microsoft Excel spreadsheet is shown in Figure 5.4.

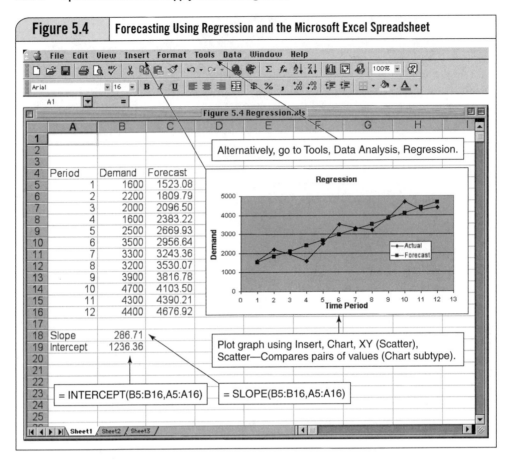

Figure 5.4 | Forecasting Using Regression and the Microsoft Excel Spreadsheet

Associative Forecasting Models. **Associative forecasting** generally uses regression analysis to estimate future demand. One or several external variables are identified that are related to demand, which are hopefully easier to determine than demand. Once the relationship between the external variable and demand is determined, it can be used as a forecasting tool. Let us review several associative models.

Simple Regression. When there is only one explanatory variable, we have a **simple regression model** equivalent to the trend model described earlier. The difference is that the x variable is no longer time but an explanatory variable of demand. For example, demand could be dependent on the size of the advertising budget. The equation is as follows:

$$\hat{Y} = b_0 + b_1 x$$

where

$\hat{Y}$ = forecast or dependent variable,
x = explanatory or independent variable,
b_0 = intercept of the line, and
b_1 = slope of the line.

Example 5.6 illustrates the associative forecasting technique.

EXAMPLE 5.6   Simple Regression

Data on sales and advertising dollars for the past six months are shown in the following table:

$ Sales (y)	$ Advertising (x)
100,000	2,000
150,000	3,000
125,000	2,500
50,000	1,000
170,000	3,500
135,000	2,750

Determine the linear relationship between sales and advertising dollars.

Solution

$ Sales (y)	$ Advertising (x)	x^2	xy
100,000	2,000	4,000,000	
150,000	3,000	9,000,000	450,000,000
125,000	2,500	6,250,000	312,500,000
50,000	1,000	1,000,000	50,000,000
170,000	3,500	12,250,000	595,000,000
135,000	2,750	7,562,500	371,250,000
$\Sigma y = 730,000$	$\Sigma x = 14,750$	$\Sigma x^2 = 40,062,500$	$\Sigma xy = 1,978,750,000$

$$\hat{Y} = b_0 + b_1 x$$

$$b_1 = \frac{n \sum (xy) - \sum x \sum y}{n \sum x^2 - (\sum x)^2} = \frac{6(1,978,750,000) - 14,750(730,000)}{6(40,062,500) - 14,750^2} = 48.44$$

$$b_0 = \frac{\sum y - b_1 \sum x}{n} = \frac{730,000 - 48.43836(14,750)}{6} = 2,589.04$$

$$\hat{Y} = 2,589.04 + 48.44x$$

The results indicate that a one-dollar increase in advertising will increase sales by $48.44.

Multiple Regression. When several explanatory variables are used to make the forecast, a **multiple regression model** is applicable. Regression analysis works well when the relationships between demand (dependent variable) and other factors (independent or explanatory variables) impacting sales are strong and stable over time. The multiple regression equation is as follows:

$$\hat{Y} = b_0 + b_1 x_1 + b_2 x_2 + \ldots + b_k x_k$$

where

$\hat{Y}$ = forecast or dependent variable,
x_k = kth explanatory or independent variable,
b_0 = constant, and
b_k = regression coefficient of the independent variable x_k.

Although the mathematics involved in determining the parameters of the equation are complex, numerous commercial software programs such as Microsoft Excel Spreadsheet and SAS and SPSS statistical packages can be used to solve the equation. Any statistics textbook should provide the formula for calculating the regression coefficient values and discussion of the assumptions and challenges of using multiple regression techniques. Multiple regression forecasting requires much more data than any of the other techniques discussed earlier, and the additional cost must be balanced against possible improvement in the level of forecast accuracy.

Forecast Accuracy

The ultimate goal of any forecasting endeavor is to have an accurate and unbiased forecast. The costs associated with prediction error can be substantial and include the cost of lost sales, safety stock, unsatisfied customers, and loss of goodwill. A recent study found that only 18 percent of those companies surveyed had forecast accuracy exceeding 90 percent.[22] Companies must strive to do a good job of tracking forecast error and taking the necessary steps to improve their forecasting techniques. The formula for **forecast error,** defined as the difference between actual quantity and the forecast, follows:

$$\text{Forecast error, } e_t = A_t - F_t$$

where

e_t = forecast error for Period t,
A_t = actual demand for Period t, and
F_t = forecast for Period t.

Several measures of forecasting accuracy follow:

- **Mean absolute deviation (MAD)** = $\dfrac{\sum_{i=1}^{n} |e_t|}{n}$, and

- **Mean absolute percentage error (MAPE)** = $\dfrac{1}{n} \sum_{t=1}^{n} \left| \dfrac{e_t}{A_t} \right| (100)$,

where e_t = forecast error for Period t,
A_t = actual demand for Period t, and
n = number of periods of evaluation.

The MAD is a widely used forecast accuracy indicator and gives the evaluator a very simple way to compare various forecasting methods. A MAD of zero indicates that the forecast exactly predicted demand over the evaluation period. A positive value indicates the forecast either over- or underestimated demand. When comparing forecasting techniques then, the evaluator looks for the technique resulting in the lowest MAD over the evaluation period.

The **mean absolute percentage error** is determined by dividing the absolute forecast error by actual demand and multiplying the outcome by one hundred to get the absolute percentage error, summing them, and then computing the average. The mean absolute percentage error has the advantage of providing the correct perspective of the true magnitude of the forecast error. For example, if the absolute forecast error is 10, the error looks a lot better when the actual demand is 1000 than when actual demand is 100.

- **Mean squared error (MSE)** = $\dfrac{\sum_{t=1}^{n} e_t^2}{n}$

where e_t = forecast error for Period t, and
n = number of periods of evaluation.

"Our forecast was only 5,000% off,
which is a 10,000% improvement
in our forecasting."

Another widely used measure of forecast accuracy is **mean squared error.** Mean squared error is a measure analogous to variance in statistics. With MSE, large forecast errors are heavily penalized because the errors are squared, summed, and then averaged. In general, forecasters do not favor models that provide forecasts with many small errors and a few very large ones.

- **Running sum of forecast errors (RSFE)** $= \sum_{t=1}^{n} e_t$

where e_t = forecast error for Period t.

The RSFE is an indicator of bias in the forecasts. Forecast bias measures the tendency of a forecast to be consistently higher or lower than the actual demand. A positive RSFE indicates that the forecasts generally were too low (they were underestimating demand and stock-outs likely occurred), whereas a negative RSFE indicates that the forecasts were too high (they were overestimating demand resulting in excess inventory carrying costs). A zero RSFE means the positive errors equaled the negative errors (it does *not* mean that the forecast was necessarily accurate, since a forecast could have significant positive and negative errors and still have a zero bias).

- **Tracking signal** $= \dfrac{\text{RSFE}}{\text{MAD}}$

The tracking signal is checked to determine if it is within the acceptable control limits. If the tracking signal falls outside the preset control limits, there is a bias problem with the forecasting method and an evaluation of the way forecasts are generated is warranted. As already stated, a biased forecast can lead to excessive inventories or stock-outs. Some inventory experts suggest using a tracking signal of ±4 for high-volume items and ±8 for lower-volume items, while others prefer a lower limit. For example, GE Silicones started off with a control limit for the tracking signal of ±4. Over time, the quality of forecasts improved and the control limits were reduced to ±3. As tighter limits are instituted, there is a greater probability of finding exceptions that require no action but it also means catching changes in demand earlier.

Eventually, with additional improvements in the forecasting system, the control limits were further reduced to ±2.2. The greater sensitivity allowed GE Silicones to quickly identify changing trends and resulted in further improvement in their forecasts.[23]

Example 5.7 illustrates the use of these forecast accuracy indicators.

EXAMPLE 5.7   Forecast Accuracy

The demand and forecast for the XYZ Company over a twelve-month period is shown in the following table. Calculate the MAD, the MSE, the MAPE, and the tracking signal. Assume that the control limits for the tracking signal are ±3. What can we conclude about the quality of forecasts?

Period	Demand	Forecast	Period	Demand	Forecast
1	1,600	1,523	7	3,300	3,243
2	2,200	1,810	8	3,200	3,530
3	2,000	2,097	9	3,900	3,817
4	1,600	2,383	10	4,700	4,103
5	2,500	2,670	11	4,300	4,390
6	3,500	2,957	12	4,400	4,677

Solution

Period	Demand	Forecast	Error (e)	Absolute Error	e^2	Absolute % Error
1	1,600	1,523	77	77	5,929	4.8
2	2,200	1,810	390	390	152,100	17.7
3	2,000	2,097	−97	97	9,409	4.9
4	1,600	2,383	−783	783	613,089	48.9
5	2,500	2,670	−170	170	28,900	6.8
6	3,500	2,957	543	543	294,849	15.5
7	3,300	3,243	57	57	3,249	1.7
8	3,200	3,530	−330	330	108,900	10.3
9	3,900	3,817	83	83	6,889	2.1
10	4,700	4,103	597	597	356,409	12.7
11	4,300	4,390	−90	90	8,100	2.1
12	4,400	4,677	−277	277	76,729	6.3
		Total	0	3,494	1,664,552	133.9
		Average		291.1667	138,712.7	11.158
				MAD	MSE	MAPE

MAD = 291.2

MSE = 138,712.7

MAPE = 11.2 percent

RSFE = 0

$$\text{Tracking Signal} = \frac{\text{RSFE}}{\text{MAD}} = 0$$

The results indicate no bias in the forecasts, and the tracking signal is well within the control limits of ±3. However, the forecasts are on average 11 percent off from actual demand each period. This situation might require attention to determine the underlying causes of the variation or to seek an alternate technique with a lower MAD using the same demand data.

In one study, researchers found that bias in the forecast could be intentional, driven by organizational issues such as motivation of staff and satisfaction of customer demands, influencing the generation of forecasts.[24] For example, sales personnel tend to favor underforecasting so they can meet or exceed sales quotas and production people tend to overforecast because having too much inventory presents less of a problem than the alternative. The key to generating accurate forecasts is collaborative forecasting with different partners inside and outside the company working together to eliminate forecasting error. A collaborative planning, forecasting, and replenishment system, which is discussed in the next section, provides for free exchange of forecasting data, point-of-sale data, promotions, and other relevant information between trading partners; this collaborative effort, rather than more sophisticated and expensive forecasting algorithms, can account for significant improvements in forecasting accuracy.

Collaborative Planning, Forecasting, and Replenishment

The American Production and Inventory Control Society (APICS) defines **collaborative planning, forecasting, and replenishment (CPFR)** as "a collaboration process whereby supply chain trading partners can jointly plan key supply chain activities from production and delivery of raw materials to production and delivery of final products to end customers. Collaboration encompasses business planning, sales forecasting, and all operations required to replenish raw materials and finished goods." The objective of CPFR is to optimize the supply chain by improving demand forecast accuracy, delivering the right product at the right time to the right location, reducing inventories across the supply chain, avoiding stock-outs, and improving customer service. Basically, this can be achieved only if the trading partners are working closely together and willing to share information and risk through a common set of processes.

The real value of CPFR comes from an exchange of forecasting information rather than from more sophisticated forecasting algorithms to improve forecasting accuracy. The fact is that forecasts developed solely by the firm tend to be inaccurate. When both the buyer and seller collaborate to develop a single forecast, incorporating knowledge of base sales, promotions, store openings or closings, and new product introductions, it is possible to synchronize buyer needs with supplier production plans, thus ensuring efficient replenishment. The jointly managed forecasts can be adjusted in the event that demand or promotions have changed, thus avoiding costly corrections after the fact.

On the surface, when decisions are made with incomplete information, it may appear that companies have "optimized" their internal processes when, in reality, inventory has merely shifted along the supply chain. Without trading partners in the supply chain collaborating and exchanging information, the supply chain will always be suboptimal, resulting in less-than-maximum supply chain profits.

CPFR is an approach that addresses the requirements for good demand management. The benefits of CPFR include the following:

- Strengthens partner relationships
- Provides analysis of sales and order forecasts upstream and downstream
- Uses point-of-sale data, seasonal activity, promotions, new product introductions, and store openings or closings to improve forecast accuracy
- Manages the demand chain by exception and proactively eliminates problems before they appear
- Allows collaboration on future requirements and plans

- Uses joint planning and management of promotions
- Integrates planning, forecasting, and logistics activities
- Provides efficient category management and understanding of consumer purchasing habits
- Provides analysis of key performance metrics (e.g., forecast accuracy, forecast exceptions, product lead times, inventory turnover, percentage stock-outs) to reduce supply chain inefficiencies, improve customer service, and increase sales and profitability

Most companies implement CPFR using some form of the Voluntary Interindustry Commerce Standards (VICS) Association CPFR Process Model (see Figure 5.5). The Global Commerce Initiative (GCI) created the GCI Recommended Standard for Globalizing CPFR by combining portions of VICS CPFR publications and adding new materials. GIC is a voluntary body created in 1999 to "improve the performance of the international supply chain for consumer goods through the collaborative development and endorsement of recommended standards and key business processes."[26] A description of the CPFR process model used by GCI follows:

- *Step 1: Develop Collaboration Arrangement*

  The buyer and seller must agree on the objective of the collaboration, ground rules for resolving disagreements, confidentiality of information to be shared, sales forecast exception criteria, review cycle, time frame, frozen time period with acceptable tolerances, resource commitments, financial incentives, and success metrics. Some examples of objectives are to improve customer service levels, reduce stock-outs, reduce inventories, increase sales, reduce costs, improve forecast accuracy, and synchronize production with the forecast.

- *Step 2: Create Joint Business Plan*

  A joint business plan is developed by sharing the companies' business strategies and plans. The plan typically involves developing a joint product category and promotional plan in which the appropriate category strategies, inventory policies, promotional activities, and pricing policies are specified. A product category is a manageable group of products perceived by consumers to be similar that can be substituted in meeting their needs. For each item in the product category, an item management profile is developed that includes the minimum order quantity, lead time, time between orders, frozen time period, and safety stock guidelines. The trading partner should be informed of changes such as store openings or closings or changes of items in each product category. It is important that trading partners be able to understand the impact new product introductions, promotions, and marketing campaigns have on demand and ultimately on the effective management of the supply chain.

- *Step 3: Create Sales Forecast*

  The trading partners use Web-based technologies to share data such as retailer point-of-sale information, distribution center withdrawals, manufacturing consumption, planned events including store openings or closings, and new product introductions. Using multiple inputs into the forecasting process including information about the future, as well as the past, results in the creation of a shared forecast that reflects the most accurate and real-time information available. Either partner or both partners may generate the sales forecast. The forecasting techniques used can be qualitative or quantitative. When both partners each generate a forecast, middleware is used to highlight the differences, based on predetermined exception criteria previously agreed upon by the partners. For example, J. D. Edwards' Demand Management software has an algorithm that can reconcile multiple forecasts by considering the historical forecast accuracy of the partners. If Company A's historical forecast is accurate

Figure 5.5 | **VICS's CPFR Process Model**

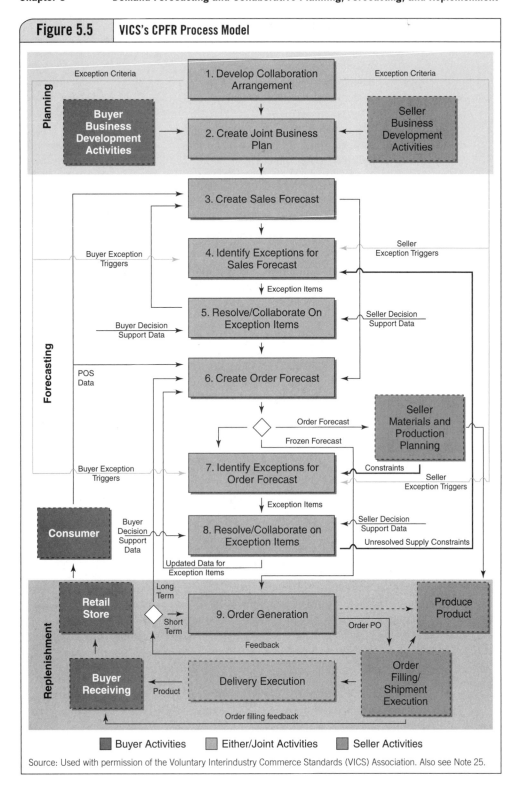

Source: Used with permission of the Voluntary Interindustry Commerce Standards (VICS) Association. Also see Note 25.

95 percent of the time compared to Company B's forecast accuracy rate of 85 percent, then the software will assign more weight to Company A's information.

- *Step 4: Identify Exceptions for Sales Forecast*

Irrespective of how the initial forecast is generated, all exceptions are identified in Step 4. Examples of sales forecast exception criteria are: retail in-stock is less than 95 percent, sales forecast error is greater than 20 percent, the difference in sales forecast from the same period of the previous year is greater than 10 percent, or any changes that have occurred in timing of promotional activities or number of active stores. The real-time joint decision making reduces the risk and increases the confidence in the single forecast.

- *Step 5: Resolve/Collaborate on Exception Items*

In Step 5, all exceptions are resolved through a collaborative process to create a single consensus forecast.

- *Step 6: Create Order Forecast*

Data are analyzed—such as point-of-sale (POS) data; historical demand; shipment data; current capacity limits; minimum order quantities; lead times; time between orders; frozen time periods; safety stock rules; impact events such as new product introductions, store openings, and store closings; and current inventory positions (on hand, on order, in transit)—to generate the order forecast consistent with the sales forecast and joint business plan developed earlier. The order forecast represents detailed time-phased ordering needs with inventory objectives by product and receiving location. The order forecast enables the manufacturer to effectively schedule production capacity based on the demand and to minimize safety stock. For the retailer, there is greater confidence that orders will be met. In effect, the real-time collaborative effort minimizes the uncertainty between trading partners, leading to reduced supply chain inventories, along with improved customer service levels.

- *Step 7: Identify Exceptions for Order Forecast*

The items that fall outside the order forecast exception criteria such as customer service measures, order fill rate, or forecast error measures, established jointly by the buyer and seller in the collaboration agreement, are identified as exception items. Examples of order forecast exception criteria are retail in-stock less than 95 percent, order forecast errors greater than 20 percent, annual inventory turnover less than agreed-upon goal, addition of new event that affects inventory/orders, or requested emergency orders greater than 5 percent of weekly forecast.

- *Step 8: Resolve/Collaborate on Exception Items*

Any order forecast exceptions are investigated by examining the shared data, e-mail, telephone conversations, meetings, and other supporting information. If the analysis justifies a change in the forecast, a revised forecast is submitted.

- *Step 9: Order Generation*

This last step involves converting the order forecast into a committed order. The actual order is expected to consume the forecast. The committed order is generated based on the product demand in the frozen time period of the order forecast.

Common performance metrics, such as gross margin percent, return on investment, and sales growth, are developed to measure the success of the relationship. Other metrics include in-stock percent at point of sale, inventory turnover, inventory level, sales forecast accuracy, potential sales lost due to stock-out, manufacturing cycle time, order cycle time, shipping cycle time, problem resolution time, rate of emergency or cancelled orders, and percent shipped or delivered on time.

Using CPFR, companies are working together to develop mutually agreeable plans and take responsibility for their actions. The collaborative effort leads to benefits that are greater than if each partner was to go at it independently. According to the VICS CPFR Pilot Project Overview, the CPFR concept and efforts are consumer driven without losing focus on best practices within the supply chain. Setting common goals for organizations pulls individual efforts together into a cohesive plan, supports better execution of the plan, and invites improved planning in the next business planning exercise. The improved planning drives sales gains through to the consumer and lowers costs throughout the supply chain.[27]

A survey on benefits carried out by the Grocery Manufacturers of America of twenty-one companies with CPFR experience shows that 57 percent of the companies improved their relationships with their trading partners, 38 percent showed an increase in service levels, 38 percent had reduced stock-outs, 38 percent had increased sales, 29 percent had reduced inventory, and 29 percent had improved forecast accuracy.[28] According to the Gartner Group, "Enterprises that collaboratively integrate disparate forecasting systems . . . will improve revenue predictability by 10 to 25 percent and decrease inventory carrying costs by more than 30 percent over a three-year period."[29]

Despite the much-heralded debut of CPFR in 1996, widespread adoption has fallen short of expectations. AMR Research estimates that while 45 to 65 retailers and 100 to 150 manufacturers were involved in some aspects of CPFR in 2002, no company was totally happy with where they were or where they expected to be in the long run with CPFR.[30] Examples of companies involved with CPFR include Eastman Kodak, Federated Department Stores, Hewlett-Packard, JC Penney, Kimberly-Clark, Kmart, Nabisco, Procter & Gamble, Target, Wal-Mart, and Warner-Lambert.

The top three challenges for CPFR implementation are difficulty of making internal changes, cost, and trust.[31] As with any major implementation, internal resistance to change must be addressed by top management. Change is always difficult; however, if top management is committed to the project, then the project is much more likely to succeed. Companies will need to educate their employees on the benefits of the process changes and the disadvantages of maintaining the status quo. Due to cost reasons, Johnson & Johnson is working on CPFR projects with its largest trading partners having high-volume SKUs only.[32] There is also the question of reducing the scale of CPFR and, therefore, the cost of implementation for smaller trading partners. While cost is an important factor, companies with no plans for adopting CPFR should determine if they are at a competitive disadvantage as more and more companies implement CPFR.

Trust, a major cultural issue, is considered a big hurdle to widespread implementation of CPFR because many retailers are reluctant to share the type of proprietary information required by CPFR. While the suppliers of Wal-Mart, for instance, may be willing to share sensitive data with Wal-Mart, they do not want other suppliers to obtain this information. However, other experts do not believe that trust is the stumbling block for mass adoption of CPFR. Jim Uchneat, of Benchmarking Partners, Inc., says, "Trust may be a catch-all phrase that covers a host of other problems, but I have never found trust between people to be the issue. CPFR won't shift the power dynamics in a retailer/buyer relationship. If people are hoping that this is the case and refer to this as 'trust,' then they are fooling themselves. Lack of trust is more often related to the unreliable data in systems and the lack of integration internal to retailers and manufacturers."[33]

The real challenge to widespread adoption of CPFR is that it requires a fundamental change in the way buyers and sellers work together. Companies must ensure that their information technology systems, organizational structures, business processes, and internal data are conducive to implementing CPFR. For instance, many organizations are hampered by legacy systems that will have to be replaced, lack of executive management support, and an unwillingness to share sensitive information.

Global Perspective

CPFR AT PROCTER & GAMBLE AND dm-drogerie markt GmbH

Procter & Gamble's German subsidiary and dm-drogerie markt GmbH implemented a CPFR six-month pilot project. Procter & Gamble has 102,000 employees in eighty countries and markets nearly 300 brands. dm-drogerie is the second-largest drugstore chain in Germany with more than 14,000 employees, 13,000 stock-keeping units, and more than 1,300 outlets in Europe. The goal of the project was to ensure that products are always available at all distribution centers as well as retail outlets. Both companies realized that high forecast accuracy had a major impact on the companies' sales, profitability, and customer service.

In the promotional business, failure to forecast correctly can result in either stockouts due to heavy unexpected demand or excessive inventory at the end of the promotional period due to poor demand. The pilot project's primary focus was the promotion of Pampers. There were three Pampers jumbo pack promotions, with each lasting two weeks. dm-drogerie was provided access to Procter & Gamble's data through Syncra XtTM, an Internet-based supply chain collaboration platform designed by Syncra Systems.

Using this data, information on demand at the point of sale flows through the entire supply chain from the end users to the manufacturer and suppliers. Forecasts for a promotional activity are exchanged thirteen weeks in advance of the event and adjusted based on additional information four weeks prior to the promotion. The two companies' order forecasts are compared to determine if the difference is within the mutually agreed-upon tolerance, and any significant exception is jointly resolved based on an agreed-upon solution process.

Preliminary results of the pilot program show improvements of 10 percent in forecast accuracy and 4 percent in product availability from the first to the second promotion. The success of the program can be attributed to a cooperative culture that builds trust and promotes communication and free information exchange. The outcome is a win-win relationship between the two trading partners.

Sources: "CPFR at Procter & Gamble and dm-drogerie in Germany: A Case Study (Part 1)," Syncra Systems, Inc. (September 2002); Procter & Gamble Web site, http://www.pg.com; dm-drogerie markt GmbH Web site, http://www.dm-drogeriemarkt.de/CDA/Home

Software Solutions

Forecasting Software

Forecasting is seldom calculated manually. If a forecaster uses a quantitative method, then a software solution can be used to simplify the process and save the time required to generate a forecast. A recent survey by the Institute of Business Forecasting shows that Forecast Pro from Business Forecast Systems, Inc., is the market leader in the forecasting software category with 32.20 percent market share, followed by Smart Software with 6.78 percent.[34] A discussion of the top two forecasting software solutions follows:

1. *Business Forecast Systems, Inc.*

The Forecast Pro software package is used by over 15,000 companies in eighty-four countries. The software is easy to use and has a built-in expert selection system that analyzes the data, selects the appropriate forecasting technique, builds the model, and calculates the forecasts. Several of the forecasting approaches discussed in this chapter such as moving average, trend, and exponential smoothing models are included in the package. The expanded packages of Forecast Pro XE and Forecast Pro Unlimited provide additional methodologies suited for advanced business needs.

2. *Smart Software, Inc.*

Major corporations using SmartForecasts™ forecasting software include Mead Corporation, Hewlett Packard, Labatt Breweries, and Bristol-Myers Squibb. SmartForecasts is designed to run under Windows 95, 98, NT, and 2000. NSK, the second largest provider of anti-friction bearings and precision products in the automotive parts industry, uses the SmartForecasts software to accurately forecast standard aftermarket products and as a result has reduced inventory by $1 million, shortened lead times, and exceeded 98 percent on-time delivery performance.

For the occasional user, Microsoft Excel and Lotus 1-2-3 are two widely used spreadsheet software programs that have basic forecasting capabilities. In addition, SAS and SPSS are statistical software packages that can be used for forecasting.

CPFR Sofware

A CPFR software solution typically includes a forecasting module and other modules for planning procurement, supply, replenishment, and so on. Examples of several leading suppliers of CPFR solutions follow:

1. *Manugistics*

The Manugistics CPFR solution enables an organization to collaborate and share critical information with partners on forecasts, inventory, replenishment plans, point-of-sale data, promotional activities, and transportation requirements. A Web-based application publishes easy-to-access information and notifies the appropriate participants when new data or deviations from defined business rules require action.[35]

2. *i2 Technologies*

i2 Demand Collaboration supports the CPFR process as defined by VICS and "enables trading partners to collaborate on both demand forecasts and capacity availability, to synchronize supply chain planning, and execute for multiple customers. Through Demand Collaboration, companies get better visibility into long-term, medium-term, and short-term customer demand so demand/supply mismatch problems can be resolved before they adversely affect the planning processes or customer satisfaction. Planners can reach forecast demands with customers, provide supply commitments, and resolve exceptions, resulting in better supply chain plans for the enterprise and its customers."[36]

3. *Syncra Systems*

SyncraXt is fully compliant with the CPFR guidelines as defined by VICS, enables easy visualization and analysis of all data required to align supply and demand, and supports the CPFR exception identification and resolution process. An optional Syncra Demand module can generate statistical demand forecasts. The software's high-performance exception process engine can compare information from several partners across multiple dimensions of products, partners, locations, and time and can alert users to critical differences such as unexpected changes in a promotional activity, a new product introduction, or an unexpected replenishment shortage.[37]

A few examples of companies using CPFR software solutions follow:

- Fujitsu Siemens Computers reported savings of over 10 million euros after implementing the i2 Demand Planner software. i2 Demand Planner is a "comprehensive management solution that enables enterprises and ultimately demand planners to accurately and effectively manage their demand by eliminating and addressing the challenges and pain points."[38] Other results are the improvement in forecasting accuracy from 50 to 70 percent, increase in inventory turns from twenty-five to forty, decrease in planning cycle time from thirty to seven days, and improvement in delivery promise reliability from 85 to 95 percent.[39]

- Ace Hardware implemented CPFR technology to manage 6,000 items and twenty-three manufacturers. Ace was able to save 20 percent in labor cost from receiving merchandise from its CPFR suppliers because Ace can make three times more "full-pallet" purchases from its CPFR partners than from its 1,500 other suppliers. Freight expenses were reduced from 7 to 2.5 percent, which allowed Ace to keep prices down.[40]

- Nabisco and Wegmans worked on a CPFR project involving Planters nuts. Although annual sales were growing at a 36 percent rate, Wegmans was able to reduce the average Planters inventory from 14.1 to 11.6 days of sales and improve the replenishment of store orders. However, the project involved a serious time commitment by the two companies. It took five months to streamline the business processes to enable sales and product promotion data to be shared.[41]

- Frequent promotions and price changes are common in the soft drink industry. Coca-Cola Bottling Company uses the Manugistics collaborative forecasting solution to generate collaborative consensus forecasts right down to the SKU level. The results are a 15 percent reduction in finished goods inventory and a one-day reduction in cycle time even with the introduction of ninety-four new SKUs. The improvements were achieved without any sacrifice in customer service.[42]

The e-Business Connection box profiles several on-line exchanges and their use of CPFR.

---

e-BUSINESS CONNECTION
ON-LINE EXCHANGES AND CPFR

Several mega on-line exchanges such as Transora, WorldWide Retail Exchange, and GlobalNetXchange understand the importance and benefits of CPFR and have incorporated this solution into their product offerings. The three exchanges that follow have each selected a different CPFR provider.

- *Transora*

In mid-2000, members of the Grocery Manufacturers of America established Transora, a business-to-business exchange for the consumer packaged goods industry. Transora's investors are leading consumer products companies, with over $600 billion in annual sales, and include Bristol-Myers Squibb, Campbell Soup, Coca-Cola, Colgate-Palmolive, Eastman Kodak, General Mills, Kraft Foods, Nestlé, PepsiCo, Procter & Gamble, and Heineken. Its CPFR provider is Syncra Systems.

- *WorldWide Retail Exchange (WWRE)*

Founded in March 2000, WWRE is an industry-sponsored marketplace for retailers and suppliers in the food, general merchandise, textile/home, and drugstore sectors. Current membership consists of sixty-two retail industry leaders worldwide with total revenues of over $845 billion dollars. Members of WWRE include JC Penney Co., Kmart, Best Buy, Gap, Target, Albertsons, CVS Pharmacy, Marks & Spencer, Walgreens, Rite Aid, and Radio Shack Corporation. Its CPFR provider is i2.

- *GlobalNetXchange (GNX)*

GNX is a retail industry exchange with equity partners such as Carrefour SA; Coles Myer Ltd.; Karstadt Quelle AG; The Kroger Co.; Metro AG; Pinault-Printemps-Redoute SA; J Sainsbury Plc; and Sears, Roebuck and Co. Its CPFR provider is Manugistics Net-WORKS.

The major retail exchanges such as Transora, WWRE, and GNX argue that CPFR is best included in an e-marketplace. Carrefour, a founding member of GNX, is an example of a company committed to the exchange-based CPFR. The WorldWide Retail Exchange reports that the launch of its CPFR product has resulted in a 32 percent decrease in excess inventory, a 25 percent improvement in lead times, and a 10 percent reduction in in-stock inventory levels.[43]

Summary

Proper demand forecasting enables better planning and utilization of resources for businesses to be competitive. Forecasting is an integral part of demand management since it provides an estimate of future demand and the basis for planning and making sound business decisions. A mismatch in supply and demand could result in excessive inventories and stock-outs and loss of profits and goodwill. Both qualitative and quantitative methods are available to help companies forecast demand better. The qualitative methods are based on judgment and intuition, whereas the quantitative methods use mathematical techniques and historical data to predict future demand. The quantitative forecasting methods can be divided into time series and associative models. Since forecasts are seldom completely accurate, management must monitor forecast errors and make the necessary improvement to the forecasting process.

Forecasts made in isolation tend to be inaccurate. Collaborative planning, forecasting, and replenishment is an approach in which companies work together to develop mutually agreeable plans and take responsibility for their actions. The objective of CPFR is to optimize the supply chain by generating a consensus demand forecast, delivering the right product at the right time to the right location, reducing inventories, avoiding stock-outs, and improving customer service. The Global Commerce Initiative and Voluntary Interindustry Commerce Standards have been instrumental in standardizing and promoting CPFR worldwide. Major corporations such as Wal-Mart, Warner-Lambert, and Proctor & Gamble are early adopters of CPFR. Although the benefits of CPFR are well recognized, widespread adoption has not materialized.

The computation involved in generating a forecast is seldom done manually. Forecasting software packages such as Forecast Pro, Microsoft Excel, SAS, and SPSS are readily available. Major CPFR solutions providers include Manugistics, i2, and Syncra. Recently, on-line exchanges such as Transora, WorldWide Retail Exchange, and GlobalNetXchange are incorporating CPFR solutions into their product offerings for their partnering companies.

Key Terms

associative forecasting, 130

business cycle, 130

collaborative planning, forecasting, and replenishment (CPFR), 143

consumer survey, 130

cyclical variations, 130

Delphi method, 129

exponential smoothing forecasting, 133

forecasting error, 140

jury of executive opinion, 128

linear trend forecasting, 136

mean absolute deviation (MAD), 140

mean absolute percentage error (MAPE), 140

mean squared error (MSE), 141

multiple regression model, 139

qualitative forecasting methods, 128

quantitative forecasting methods, 128

random variations, 131

running sum of forecast errors (RSFE), 141

sales force composite, 130

seasonal variations, 130

simple moving average forecasting, 131

simple regression model, 138

time series forecasting, 130

tracking signal, 141

trend variations, 130

trend-adjusted exponential smoothing forecasting, 135

weighted moving average forecasting, 133

Discussion Questions

1. What is demand forecasting?
2. Why is demand forecasting important for effective supply chain management?
3. Explain the impact of a mismatch in supply and demand.
4. What are qualitative forecasting techniques? When are these methods more suitable?
5. What are the main components of a time series?
6. Explain the difference between a time series model and an associative model.
7. What is the impact of the smoothing constant value on the simple exponential forecast?
8. Compare and contrast the jury of executive opinion and the Delphi techniques.
9. Explain the key difference between the weighted smoothing average and the simple exponential smoothing methods?
10. What are three measures of forecasting accuracy?
11. What is a tracking signal?
12. What are the key features of CPFR?
13. Why is widespread adoption of CPFR below expectations?

Internet Questions

1. Go to the Web sites of i2 (http://www.i2.com) and Manugistics (http://www.manugistics.com) and write a report comparing the capabilities of these two CPFR solutions.
2. The VICS Web site at http://www.cpfr.org shows the road map for CPFR implementation. What are the key success elements and roadblocks to implementation of CPFR?
3. Business Forecasts System (http://hwww.forecastpro.com) is considered one of the leading providers of the forecasting software, Forecast Pro. Compare the three versions of forecasting software: Forecast Pro, Forecast Pro XE, and Forecast Pro Unlimited.

Spreadsheet Problems

1. Ms. Winnie Lin's company sells computers. Monthly sales for a six-month period are as follows:

Month	Sales
Jan	18,000
Feb	22,000
Mar	16,000
Apr	18,000
May	20,000
Jun	24,000

a. Plot the monthly data on a sheet of graph paper.
b. Compute the sales forecast for July using the following approaches:
   (1) A four-month moving average
   (2) A weighted three-month moving average using .50 for June, .30 for May, and .20 for April

(3) A linear trend equation

(4) Exponential smoothing with α (smoothing constant) equal to .40, assuming a February forecast of 18,000

c. Which method do you think is the least appropriate? Why?

2. The owner of Chocolate Outlet Store wants to forecast chocolate demand. Demand for the preceding four years is shown in the following table:

Year	Demand (Pounds)
1	68,800
2	71,000
3	75,500
4	71,200

Forecast demand for Year 5 using the following approaches:

a. A three-year moving average

b. A three-year weighted moving average using .40 for Year 4, .20 for Year 3, and .40 for Year 2

c. Exponential smoothing with α = .30, and assuming the forecast for Period 1 = 68,000

d. The trend adjusted exponential smoothing method (Assume the smoothed average for the series in period 2 is 71,000 and the smoothed trend is 1,300. Use α = 0.2 and β = 0.4.)

3. The forecasts generated by two forecasting methods and actual sales are as follows:

Month	Sales	Forecast 1	Forecast 2
1	269	275	268
2	289	266	287
3	294	290	292
4	278	284	298
5	268	270	274
6	269	268	270
7	260	261	259
8	275	271	275

Compute the MSE, the MAD, the MAPE, and the tracking signal for each forecasting method. Which method is better? Why?

References

Andraski, J., and R. Ireland. "CPFR for Beginners: The 5 W's." Available from http://www.cpfr.org/ MembersOnly/CPFRForBeginnersFeb2003V3.pdf

Baumann, F. "The Power of an Executable Single Forecast." White Paper, The JDA Software Group (10 June 2002).

Elikai, F., R. Badaranathi, and V. Howe. "A Review of 52 Forecasting Software Packages." *Journal of Business Forecasting* 21, no. 2 (summer 2002): 19–27.

"The Evolution of CPFR." Syncra Systems Inc. (June 2003). Available from http://www.syncra.com/news/ papers/evol_CPFR.pdf

Foote, P. S., and M. Krishnamurthi. "Forecasting Using Data Warehousing Model: Wal-Mart's Experience." *Journal of Business Forecasting Methods & Systems* 20, no. 3 (fall 2001): 13–17.

Gilliland, M. "Is Forecasting a Waste of Time?" *Supply Chain Management Review* (1 July 2002). Available from http://www.manufacturing.net/SCM

"Globalization of CPFR." Sycra Systems Inc. (May 2002). Available from http://www.syncra.com/news/papers/Globalization_of_CPFR.pdf

Haugen, K. J. "Using Spreadsheets to Forecast Product Needs." *NAPM Insights* (1 November 1994): 32. Available from http://www.ism.ws

Hennel, M. J. "There's Only ONE Answer to Demand Management." *ITtoolbox Supply Chain Management Knowledge Base* (27 September 2002). Available from http://www.supplychain.ittoolbox.com/browse.asp?c=SDMPeerPublishing&r=%2Fpub%2FPB09 2502%2Epdf

Jain, C. L. "Benchmarking Forecasting Software Packages and Systems." Research Report 3, Institute of Business Forecasting. Available from http://www.forecastpro.com/rsch3.pdf

Jain, C. L. "Editorial: Which Forecasting Model Should We Use?" *Journal of Business Forecasting* 19, no. 3 (fall 2000): 2, 28, 35.

Karolefski, J. "Is Momentum Building for the Revolutionary Business Process of CPFR?" *Food Logistics* (15 June 2002): 19–30. Available from http://www.foodlogistics.com

Kauffman, R. G., and T. A. Crimi. "Supply Chain Integration and the Supply/Demand Imperative." *86th Annual International Purchasing Conference Proceedings* (May 2001).

Lawrence, M., M. O'Conner, and B. Edmundson. "A Field Study of Forecasting Accuracy and Processes." *European Journal of Operational Research* 22, no. 1 (1 April 2000): 151–60.

Makridakis, S., S. Wheelwright, and R. Hyndman. *Forecasting Methods and Applications.* New York: John Wiley & Sons, 1998.

Maslanka, B. "Demystify the Forecast." *APICS—The Performance Advantage* (March 2001): 25–27.

Portougal, V. "Demand Forecast for a Catalog Retailing Company." *Production and Inventory Management Journal* (first/second quarter 2002): 29–34.

Notes

1. "Profitably Manage Your Customer Demand," White Paper, i2 Technologies, Inc. (October 2001); available from http://www.i2.com/web505/media/9E16A575-18D3-47B0-A0B734EA8DCC5691.pdf

2. Wal-Mart "Exceeding Customer Expectations" available from: http://www.walmartstores.com/wmstore/wmstores/Mainabout.jsp?BV_SessionID=@@@@0340977454.1067474232@@@@&BV_EngineID=ccccadcjjgkkfhmcfkfcfkjdgoodg lh.0&pagetype=about&template=DisplayAllContents.jsp&categoryOID= –8276&catID=–8242

3. A. H. Johnson, "A New Supply Chain Forged," *Computerworld* (30 September 2002); available from http:www.computerworld.com/industrytopics/retail/story/0,10801,74647,00.html

4. R. J. Bretz, "Forecasting with the Report on Business," *NAPM Insights* (August 1990).

5. M. Magnier, "PlayStation2 Is Not Just Fun and Games," *Los Angeles Times* (4 March 2000).

6. "PlayStation Sales Zoom," *New York Times* (7 March 2000).

7. H. Suzuki, "PlayStation 2 Output to Double; Sony Seeks to Remedy Shortage of Video Game Consoles," *Washington Post* (16 January 2001).

8. "CPFR's Secret Benefit," *Frontline Solutions* (October 2002); available from http://www.frontlinetoday.com

9. T. Wilson, "Accuracy's in Demand," *Internet Week* (19 July 2001); available from http://www.internetweek.com/newslead01/lead071901.htm

10. Y. J. Dreazen, "Behind the Fiber Glut—Telecom Carriers Were Driven by Wildly Optimistic Data on Internet's Growth Rate," *Wall Street Journal* (26 September 2002).

11. M. Fisher, J. Hammond, W. Obermeyer, and A. Raman, "Making Supply Meet Demand in an Uncertain World," *Harvard Business Review* (May–June 1994): 83–93.

12. C. L. Jain, "Forecasting Practices in Corporate America," *Journal of Business Forecasting Methods & Systems* 20, no. 2 (summer 2001): 2–3.

13. The Marmon Group Companies, http://www.marmon.com/Companies.htm

14. Wells Lamont—Corporate Information, http://www.wellslamont.com/information_tmp.tp1?doc=info_history.txt

15. "Wells Lamont Gets a Grip on Manufacturing Forecasts," Case Study, Demand Management, Inc.; available from http://www.demandsolutions.com/articles/wells_lamont.html

16. Fisher, Hammond, Obermeyer, and Raman, "Making Supply Meet Demand": 83–93.

17. C. L. Jain, "Forecasting Process at Wyeth Ayerst Global Pharmaceuticals," *Journal of Business Forecasting Methods & Systems* (winter 2001–02): 3–4, 6.

18. "The Institute for Supply Management Manufacturing Report on Business," The Institute for Supply Management (September 2002).

19. "Honda May Ship through Mexico; Japanese Automaker Says It Is Seeking Ways to Avoid Parts Shipment Delays Such As Those Caused by Last Month's Shutdown of Ports on the West Coast," *Los Angeles Times* (7 November 2002).

20. J. D. Wisner and L. L. Stanley, "Forecasting Practices in Purchasing," *International Journal of Purchasing and Materials Management* (winter 1994): 22–29.

21. J. Malehorn, "Forecasting at Ocean Spray Cranberries," *Journal of Business Forecasting Methods & Systems* 20, no. 2 (summer 2001):6–8.

22. C. L. Jain, "Forecasting Practices in Corporate America": 2–3.

23. R. M. Duncan, "Quality Forecasting Drives Quality Inventory at GE Silicones," *Industrial Engineering* 24, no. 1 (January 1992): 18–21.

24. M. Lawrence, M. O'Conner, and B. Edmundson, "A Field Study of Forecasting Accuracy and Processes," *European Journal of Operational Research* 22, no. 1 (1 April 2000): 151–60.

25. "The CPFR Process Model," Voluntary Interindustry Commerce Standards (VICS) Association; available from http://www.cpfr.org/ProcessModel.html. See also Global Commerce Initiative, Global Working Group on Globalization of CPFR; available from http://www.globalcommerceinitiative.org/oas/gci/gci.wwv_main.main?p_language=us&p_cornerid= 10000&p_currcornerid=1&p_full=1

26. Global Commerce Initiative Website, available from http://www.gci-net.org/QuickPlace/home/ Main.nsf/h_Toc/79a7bf70c3e3319b48256d8a000f3d3b/?OpenDocument

27. "CPFR Pilot Project Overview," VICS CPFR; available from http://www.cpfr.org/documents/ pdf/07_4_0_CPFR_pilot_Overview.pdf

28. C. Sliwa, "CPFR Clamor Persists, but Adoption Remains Slow," *Computerworld* (1 July 2002); available from http://www.computerworld.com/softwaretopics/erp/story/0,10801,72394,00.html

29. M. J. Hennel, "There's Only ONE Answer to Demand Management," *ITtoolbox Supply Chain Management Knowledge Base* (27 September 2002); available from http://www.supplychain. ittoolbox.com/browse.asp?c=SCMPeerPublishing&r=%2Fpub%2FPB092502%2Epdf

30. C. Sliwa, "CPFR Clamor Persists."

31. "The Next Wave of Supply Chain Advantage: Collaborative Planning, Forecasting, and Replenishment," Industry Directions Inc. and Syncra Systems, Inc. (April 2000).

32. B. Albright, "CPFR's Secret Benefit," *Frontline Solutions* (October 2002): 31–35; available from http://www.frontlinetoday.com

33. J. Uchneat, "CPFR's Woes Not Related to Trust," *Computerworld* (22 July 2002); available from http://www.computerworld.com/news/2002/story/0,11280,72834,00.html

34. C. L. Jain, "Forecasting Practices in Corporate America."

35. The Manugistics CPFR® Solution; available from http://www.manugistics.com/solutions/cpfr.asp

36. "i2 Demand Collaboration," i2 Web site; available from http://www.i2technologies.com/web505/media/CBF9A153-1181-4C3A-822EA9C6F7C94B3E.pdf

37. "SyncraXt: Delivering Supply Chain Intelligence and Collaboration," Syncra Systems, Inc.; available from http://www.syncra.com/solutions/SyncraXt-web.pdf

38. i2 Technologies Web site; available from http://www.i2.com

39. "Profitably Manage Your Customer Demand," White Paper, i2 Technologies, Inc. (1 October 2001).

40. C. Sliwa, "Ace Has a Place for CPFR Technology," *Computerworld* (11 February 2002); available from http://www.computerworld.com

41. C. Stedman, "Retailers Face Team-Planning Hurdles," *Computerworld* (19 October 1998); available from http://www.computerworld.com

42. J. Karolefski, "Is Momentum Building for the Business Process of CPFR?" *Food Logistics* (15 June 2002): 19–30.

43. D. Barlas, "CPFR Benefits," *Line56*, The E-Business Executive Daily (29 April 2002); available from http:/www.line56.com/articles/default.asp?ArticleID=3627

Chapter 6:

AGGREGATE PLANNING AND INVENTORY MANAGEMENT

Sure, they had computerized inventory records, but Ron was too busy to enter transactions in a timely fashion. His terminal was covered with post-it notes such as "10 pc. p/n A202 issued June 4"—and this was July. It was no surprise that the physical inventory yielded 50 percent accuracy. Yet, somehow MRP was supposed to make this better.[1]

Learning Objectives

After completing this chapter, you should be able to
- Describe the hierarchical operations planning process in terms of materials planning (APP, MPS, MRP) and capacity planning (RRP, RCCP, CRP).
- Describe MRP, closed-loop MRP, MRP-II and ERP and their relationships.
- Know how to compute available-to-promise quantities.
- Know how to perform an MRP explosion.
- Distinguish dependent from independent demand inventories.
- Describe the four basic types of inventories and their functions.
- Understand the EOQ model.

Chapter Outline

SUPPLY CHAIN MANAGEMENT IN ACTION   *Inventory Management at Wal-Mart*

Sam and Bud Walton opened the first Wal-Mart store in Rogers, Arkansas, in 1962. By 1967, the company owned twenty-four stores, with $12.6 million in sales. The company was incorporated as Wal-Mart Stores, Inc., in late 1969 and was traded as a publicly held company in 1970. By 1987, Wal-Mart's twenty-fifth anniversary, the company owned 1,198 stores, with sales of $15.9 billion, and employed 200,000 associates. By its fortieth anniversary, Wal-Mart was the world's largest retailer, with $218 billion in sales for the fiscal year ending January 31, 2002. By September 2002, Wal-Mart had hired more than a million associates and owned 1,603 discount stores, 1,179 super centers, 517 SAM'S CLUB warehouses, and 36 neighborhood market stores in the United States. It also had hired 300,000 associates and operated 1,211 international units in Mexico, Puerto Rico, Canada, Argentina, Brazil, China, Korea, Germany, and the United Kingdom.

In less than forty years since its incorporation, Wal-Mart's stock split two-for-one for the eleventh time in March of 1999. A hundred shares of Wal-Mart's stock purchased in 1970 would be equivalent to 204,800 shares today. Wal-Mart Stores, Inc., plans to continue this aggressive growth in the future.

Wal-Mart owes much of its success and expectation for future growth to its knowledge management system, a vast network of strategically located modern distribution centers, and a very efficient private truck fleet. For example, sales from 2001 to 2002 increased 32 percent from $165 billion to $218 billion, but the value of its inventory increased by just 12.8 percent.[2] Wal-Mart essentially replaced the need to hold huge amounts of inventory to support its vast distribution system with an effective and efficient information system across its supply chain. This capability not only has enabled Wal-Mart to restrict inventory growth while maintaining a strong in-stock position, but it has also enabled supply chain members to lower their inventory levels. The potential benefits of reducing overall inventories or assets across a supply chain is commonly referred to as **cash spin or free cash spin.** The concept is to efficiently reduce overall supply chain assets and re-deploy the freed cash or invest in alternate projects.

Introduction

Operations scheduling and inventory management are two of the most critical activities of an organization; they directly influence how effectively the organization deploys its assets and capacity in producing goods and services. Developing feasible operations schedules and inventory control systems to meet delivery due dates and minimize waste in manufacturing or service organizations is a complex problem. The need for better operations scheduling and inventory management systems continues to challenge operations managers, especially in today's fiercely competitive global environment. In an environment fostering close buyer-supplier relationships, the challenge of scheduling operations to meet delivery due dates and eliminate waste is becoming a more complex problem. The problem is compounded in an integrated supply chain, where a missed due date or stock-out cascades downstream, affecting the entire supply chain.

Operations managers are continuously involved in resource and operations planning to balance *capacity* and *output.* Capacity may be stated in terms of labor, materials, or equipment. With too much excess capacity, production cost per unit is high due to idle workers and machinery. However, if workers and machinery are stressed, quality levels are likely to deteriorate. Firms generally run their operations at about 85 percent capacity to allow time for scheduled repairs and maintenance and to meet unexpected demand.

This chapter describes the hierarchical operations planning process in terms of materials and capacity planning. A hypothetical industrial example is used to demonstrate the hierarchical planning process. This chapter also discusses dependent and independent demand, basic types of inventories, and various inventory management approaches.

Operations Planning

Operations planning is usually *hierarchical* and can be divided into three broad categories: (1) **long-range,** (2) **intermediate or medium-range,** and (3) **short-range planning horizons.** While the distinctions among the three planning horizons can be vague, long-range plans usually cover a year or more, tend to be more general, and specify resources and outputs in terms of aggregate hours and units. Medium-range plans normally span six to eighteen months, whereas short-range plans usually cover a few days to a few weeks depending on the size and type of the firm. Long-range plans are established first and are then used to guide the medium-range plans, which are subsequently used to guide the short-range plans. Long-range plans usually involve major decisions in capacity, such as the construction of new facilities and purchase of capital equipment, whereas medium-range plans involve more minor changes in capacity such as changes in employment levels. Short-range plans are the most detailed and specify the exact end items and quantities to make on a daily or hourly basis.

Figure 6.1 shows the planning horizons and how a business plan cascades into the various hierarchical materials and capacity plans. The **aggregate production plan (APP)** is a long-range materials plan. Since capacity expansion involves the construction of a new facility and major equipment purchases, the aggregate production plan's capacity is usually considered fixed during the planning horizon. The aggregate production plan sets the aggregate output rate, workforce size, utilization and inventory, and/or backlog levels for an entire facility. The **master production schedule (MPS)** is a medium-range plan and is more detailed than the aggregate production plan. It shows the quantity and timing of the end items or services that will be produced. The **materials requirement planning (MRP)** is a short-range materials plan. The MRP, also known as *little mrp* or *MRP-I,* is the detailed planning process for components and parts to support the master production schedule. It is a system of converting the end items from the master production schedule into a set of time-phased component and part requirements.

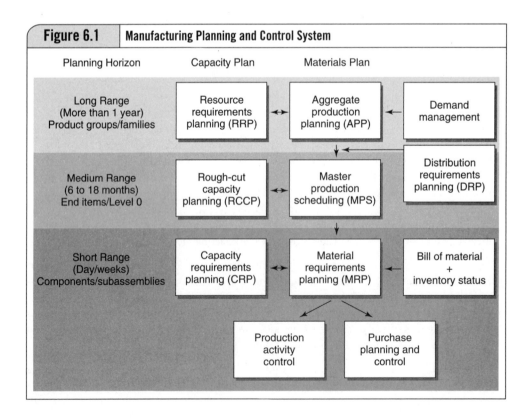

Figure 6.1	Manufacturing Planning and Control System

A **closed-loop MRP** is an MRP-based manufacturing planning and control system that incorporates the aggregate production plan, the master production schedule, the material requirements plan, and the capacity requirements plan. It is an extension of MRP. **Manufacturing resource planning (MRP-II)** is an outgrowth and extension of the closed-loop MRP system. It incorporates the business and sales plans with the closed-loop MRP system and has simulation capabilities to answer "what-if" types of planning questions. A further extension of the MRP-II system is enterprise resource planning (ERP), which is covered in Chapter 7.

Distribution requirement planning (DRP) describes the time-phased net requirements from warehouses and distribution centers. It is equal to the customer demand minus any on-hand and in-transit inventories. Distribution requirement planning links production with distribution planning by providing aggregate time-phased net requirement information to the master production schedule.

An effective manufacturing planning and control system implementation is discussed in the e-Business Connection box.

e-BUSINESS CONNECTION
INTERNATIONAL TRUCK AND ENGINE CORPORATION

International Truck and Engine Corporation (International) is a Fortune 500 manufacturer of make-to-order trucks and buses. One of its flagship products is the Navistar International brand of trucks. International sells its products, parts, and services through a huge network of dealers in more than fifty countries worldwide, including the United States, Canada, Mexico, and Brazil. The company employed approximately 16,500 employees in 2001, with annual sales of $6.7 billion. It operated eight manufacturing facilities and sold about half a million trucks annually as of 2001.

An important aspect of International's core competencies is its ability to offer make-to-order (MTO) trucks tailored to customers' specifications. Make-to-order operations enable International to lower costs by reducing finished goods inventory and provide the opportunity to charge a price premium for its trucks. However, managing the complexity of truck product variations and options is an enormous task. By the mid-1990s, management realized that its operations systems and business processes needed to change in order to effectively and efficiently manage the complexity of truck product variations. It required a system that could handle more than 173,000 model and feature combinations. The new system needed to handle all aspects of product change effectively and efficiently, including the ability to interface and communicate with existing systems.

International evaluated more than thirty solutions, including configuration modules of ERP systems and stand-alone solutions. The company opted for the Trigent Configuration Solution (TriCon) as its core manufacturing planning and control system to enable custom truck manufacturing. TriCon's product-driven approach to configuration management allowed product engineers to share and integrate truck configuration information with sales, engineering, manufacturing, and other enterprise applications. This information was also subsequently used to process truck orders. Dealers are connected to the system via a Web-based tool. Thus, dealers can quickly assist customers in ordering MTO trucks, while the company ensures that it meets customer expectations.

The TriCon system reduced International's BOM records from 7.2 million to 250,000. The system enabled International to differentiate its products and compete effectively in a market plagued by an oversupply of used trucks.[3]

The Aggregate Production Plan

Aggregate production planning is a hierarchical planning process that translates annual business and marketing plans and demand forecasts into a production plan for all products in a plant or facility. As shown in Figure 6.1, *demand management* includes determining the aggregate demand based on forecasts of future demand, orders received from internal and external customers, special promotions, and safety stock requirements. This forecast of demand then sets the aggregate utilization, production rate, workforce levels, and inventory balances or backlogs. Aggregate production plans are typically stated in terms of product families or groups. A product family consists of different products that share similar characteristics, components, or manufacturing processes. For example, an all-terrain-vehicle (ATV) manufacturer who produces both automatic and manual drive options may group the two different types of ATVs together, since the only difference between them is the drive option. Production processes and material requirements for the two ATVs can be expected to be very similar and, thus, can be grouped into a family.

The planning horizon covered by the APP is usually at least one year and is usually extended or rolled forward by three months every quarter. This allows the firm to see its capacity requirements at least one year ahead on a continuous basis. The APP *disaggregates* the demand forecast information it receives and links the long-range business and market-

---

EXAMPLE 6.1   An aggregate production plan for the ATV Corporation

The ATV Corporation makes three models of all-terrain vehicles—Model A, Model B, and Model C. Model A uses a 0.4-liter engine, Model B uses a 0.5-liter engine, and Model C uses a 0.6-liter engine. The aggregate production plan is the twelve-month plan that lumps all three models together in total monthly production. The planning horizon is twelve months. The aggregate production plan sets the size of the workforce, which is the constrained resource. Table 6.1 shows the annual aggregate production plan from January to December, assuming the beginning inventory for January is 100 units (thirty units each of Model A and Model B, and 40 units of Model C), and the firm desires to have an inventory of forty units at the end of the year. On average, one unit of ATV requires eight labor hours to produce, and a worker contributes 160 (8 hours × 5 days × 4 weeks) hours per month.

Table 6.1	ATV Corporation's Aggregate Production Plan		
		Capacity (Labor Hours)	
Period	**Forecast Demand**	**Needed**	**Planned**
January	120 units	960 hrs	10 workers
February	100 units	800 hrs	10 workers
March	300 units	2,400 hrs	12 workers + overtime
April	460 units	3,680 hrs	18 workers + overtime
May	600 units	4,800 hrs	25 workers + overtime
June	700 units	5,600 hrs	25 workers + overtime + subcontracting
July	760 units	6,080 hrs	25 workers + overtime + subcontracting
August	640 units	5,120 hrs	25 workers + overtime
September	580 units	4,640 hrs	25 workers + overtime
October	400 units	3,200 hrs	20 workers
November	200 units	1,600 hrs	10 workers
December	140 units	1,120 hrs	10 workers
	5,000 units	40,000 hrs	

ing plans to the medium-range master production schedule. The objective is to provide sufficient finished goods each period to meet the sales plan while meeting financial and production constraints.

Costs relevant to the aggregate planning decision include inventory cost, setup cost, machine operating cost, hiring cost, firing cost, training cost, overtime cost, and costs incurred for hiring part-time and temporary workers to meet peak demand. There are three basic production strategies for addressing the aggregate planning problem: (1) the *chase strategy*, (2) the *level strategy*, and (3) the *mixed strategy*. Example 6.1 provides a detailed illustration of an APP.

The Chase Production Strategy

The pure **chase production strategy** adjusts capacity to match the demand pattern. Using this strategy, the firm will hire and lay off workers to match its production rate to demand. The workforce fluctuates from month to month, but finished goods inventory remains constant. Using Example 6.1, the ATV Corporation will use six workers to make 120 units in January, and then lay off a worker in February to produce 100 units, as shown in Table 6.2. In March, the firm must hire ten additional workers so that it has enough labor to produce 300 units. An additional eight workers must be hired in April. The firm continues its hiring and lay-off policy to ensure its workforce matches demand. In December, 180 units will be produced (although the demand is 140) because of the firm's desire to increase its ending inventory by 40 units. This strategy obviously has a negative motivational impact on the workers, and it assumes that workers can be hired and trained easily to perform the job. In a chase strategy, the finished good inventories always remain constant but the workforce fluctuates in response to the demand pattern.

This strategy works well for **make-to-order manufacturing firms** since they cannot rely on finished goods inventory to satisfy the fluctuating demand pattern. Make-to-order firms generally produce one-of-a-kind, specialty products based on customer specifications. Make-to-order firms cannot build ahead of orders since they do not know the actual specifications of the finished goods.

Table 6.2	An Example of Chase Production Strategy				
		Capacity (Labor)			
Period	Forecast Demand	Hours	Workers	Production	Ending Inventory
January	120 units	960	6	120 units	100 units
February	100 units	800	5	100 units	100 units
March	300 units	2,400	15	300 units	100 units
April	460 units	3,680	23	460 units	100 units
May	600 units	4,800	30	600 units	100 units
June	700 units	5,600	35	700 units	100 units
July	760 units	6,080	38	760 units	100 units
August	640 units	5,120	32	640 units	100 units
September	580 units	4,640	29	580 units	100 units
October	400 units	3,200	20	400 units	100 units
November	200 units	1,600	10	200 units	100 units
December	140 units	1,120	9	180 units	40 units
	5,000 units	40,000	252	5,040 units	

Table 6.3	An Example of Level Production Strategy				
		Capacity (Labor)			
Period	Forecast Demand	Hours	Workers	Production (Units)	Ending Inv./Backlog
January	120 units	960	21	420	300 units
February	100 units	800	21	420	620 units
March	300 units	2,400	21	420	740 units
April	460 units	3,680	21	420	700 units
May	600 units	4,800	21	420	520 units
June	700 units	5,600	21	420	240 units
July	760 units	6,080	21	420	(100) units
August	640 units	5,120	21	420	(320) units
September	580 units	4,640	21	420	(480) units
October	400 units	3,200	21	420	(460) units
November	200 units	1,600	21	420	(240) units
December	140 units	1,120	21	420	40 units
	5,000 units	40,000	252	5,040	

The Level Production Strategy

A pure **level production strategy** relies on a constant output rate and capacity while varying inventory and backlog levels to handle the fluctuating demand pattern. Using this strategy, the firm keeps its workforce levels constant and relies on fluctuating finished goods inventories and backlogs to meet demand. Since the level production strategy keeps a constant output rate and capacity, it is more suited for firms that require highly skilled labor. The workforce can be expected to be more efficient, and morale is likely to be better when compared to the chase strategy. Again using Example 6.1, a pure level production strategy calls for a monthly production rate of 420 units [(5,000 units yearly demand + 40 units additional ending inventory) ÷ 12 months]. Thus, this strategy requires a constant workforce of twenty-one workers, as shown in Table 6.3.

The firm allows finished goods inventories to accrue while cumulative demand remains less than cumulative production and then relies on a series of backlogs to handle the demand from July through November. This strategy works well for **make-to-stock manufacturing firms,** which typically emphasize immediate delivery of off-the-shelf, standard goods at relatively low prices compared to the chase strategy. Thus, firms whose trading partners seek the lowest prices of stock items might select this type of production strategy.

The Mixed Production Strategy

Instead of using either the pure chase or level production strategy, many firms use a **mixed production strategy** that strives to maintain a stable core workforce while using other short-term means such as overtime, an additional shift, subcontracting, or the hiring of part-time and temporary workers to manage short-term high demand. Usually, these firms will then schedule preventive maintenance, engage in producing complementary products that require similar resources but different demand cycles, or continue to produce the end items, holding these as finished goods inventory during the off-peak demand periods.

For example, an all-terrain-vehicle manufacturer can produce snowmobiles to smooth out the seasonal effect of the two products. Table 6.1 shows a mixed strategy in which the firm strives to maintain a minimum core workforce of ten workers while avoiding hiring above twenty-five workers during peak season. Hiring above twenty-five workers may strain other capacities, such as machine capacity and the availability of component parts. Instead, the mixed strategy uses overtime and subcontracting to cope with excessively high demand.

If labor is the only constrained capacity, it may even hire enough workers to run an additional shift to cope with exceptionally high demand. We can see here that firms with multiple products and with customers seeking both low-cost and make-to-order items may opt for this type of production strategy to minimize stock-outs and cycle time.

Master Production Scheduling

The master production schedule is a detailed disaggregation of the aggregate production plan, listing the exact end items to be produced by a specific period. It is more detailed than the aggregate production plan and is easier to plan when demand is stable. Its planning horizon is shorter than the aggregate production plan but longer than the lead time to produce the item. Otherwise, the end item cannot be completed within its MPS planning horizon.

For example, disaggregating ATV Corporation's January and February aggregate production plans may yield the master production schedule shown in Table 6.4. The plan results in time-phased production requirements of the specific model of ATV to produce for every week in January and February. The sum of the master production schedule is equal to the total of the aggregate production plan. For example, the master production schedule for January and February in Table 6.4 equals 120 and 100 units, respectively. The master production schedule also provides more detail by breaking down the aggregate production plan into specific weekly demand of Model A, Model B, and Model C.

For the service industry, the master production schedule may just be the appointment log or book, which is created to ensure that capacity in the form of skilled labor or professional service is balanced with demand. Appointments (or the MPS) are not overbooked to ensure capacity is not strained, but operations continues to revise and add appointments to the MPS until it obtains a schedule that is optimal. An example of an MPS in the service sector is the appointment book of a clinic for scheduling patients' appointments for the next three months.

Master Production Schedule Time Fence

The master production schedule is the production quantity required to meet demand from all sources and is the basis for computing the requirements of all time-phased end items. The material requirements plan uses the MPS to compute component part and subassembly requirements. Frequent changes to the MPS can be costly and may create *system nervousness.*

System nervousness is defined as a situation where a small change in the upper-level production plan causes a major change in the lower-level production plan. For example, in the case of the clinic booking new appointments, it is very difficult for the clinic to book additional appointments for the current period because it is very likely that the appointment

Table 6.4	ATV's Master Production Schedule for January and February		
Period	Model A	Model B	Model C
January—Week 1	10	10	10
January—Week 2	10	10	10
January—Week 3	20	0	10
January—Week 4	0	20	10
February—Week 1	20	0	0
February—Week 2	0	20	0
February—Week 3	0	0	20
February—Week 4	20	20	0
Total	80	80	60

book is already fully booked. If a patient insists that she must see the doctor immediately, it is likely that another patient's appointment may have to be delayed or the clinic would need to work overtime to see an additional patient. However, it is much easier for the clinic to book new appointments farther into the future.

System nervousness can also create serious problems for manufacturing firms. For example, if the January production plan for the ATV Corporation is suddenly doubled during the second week of January, the firm would be forced to quickly revise purchase orders, component assembly orders, and end-item production orders, causing a ripple effect of change within the firm and up its supply chain to its suppliers. The change would also likely cause missed delivery due dates. The firm needs sufficient lead time to purchase items and manufacture the end items, especially if manufacturing lead times and lot sizes are large.

Many firms use a *time fence system* to deal with this problem. The time fence system separates the planning horizon into two segments—a *firmed* and a *tentative segment*. A *firmed segment* is also known as a **demand time fence,** and it usually stretches from the current period to a period several weeks into the future. A firmed segment stipulates that the production plan or master production schedule cannot be altered except with the authorization of senior management. The *tentative segment* is also known as the **planning time fence,** and it typically stretches from the end of the firmed segment to several weeks farther into the future. It usually covers a longer period than the firmed segment, and the master scheduler can change production to meet changing conditions. Beyond the planning time fence, the computer can schedule the MPS quantities automatically, based on existing ordering and scheduling policies.

Available-to-Promise Quantities

In addition to providing time-phased production quantities of specific end items, the MPS also provides vital information on whether additional orders can be accepted for delivery in specific periods. This information is particularly important when customers are relying on the firm to deliver the right quantity of products purchased on the desired delivery date. This information is the **available-to-promise (ATP) quantity,** or the uncommitted portion of the firm's planned production (or scheduled MPS). It is the difference between confirmed customer orders and the quantity the firm planned to produce, based on the MPS. The available-to-promise quantity provides a mechanism to allow the master scheduler or sales personnel to quickly negotiate new orders and delivery due dates with customers or to quickly respond to a trading partner's changing demands. The three basic methods of calculating the available-to-promise quantities are: (1) *discrete available-to-promise,* (2) *cumulative available-to-promise without look ahead,* and (3) *cumulative available-to-promise with look ahead.* The discrete available-to-promise (ATP:D) computation is discussed next. Readers who are interested in the other two methods are referred to Fogarty, Blackstone, and Hoffmann (1991).[4]

The ATV Corporation's January and February master production schedule for Model A, Model B, and Model C is used in Table 6.5 to demonstrate the ATP:D method for computing the ATP quantities. Let us assume that there are four weeks each in January and February, which is shown in the first row and are labeled Week 1 to Week 8. The MPS row indicates the time-phased production quantities derived from the master production schedule in Table 6.4. These are the quantities to be produced by manufacturing as planned. The number labeled "BI" is the beginning inventory for the first week in January. *Committed customer orders* are orders that have already been booked for specific customers.

Calculating Discrete Available-to-Promise

The discrete available-to-promise (ATP:D) is calculated as follows:

1. Begin by adding the Beginning Inventory to the MPS for Period 1, then subtracting the Committed Customer Orders. The remainder becomes the Period 1 Available-to-Promise.

Table 6.5	Discrete ATP Calculation for January and February							
Week	**1**	**2**	**3**	**4**	**5**	**6**	**7**	**8**
Model A—0.4-Liter Engine								
MPS BI = 30	10	10	20	0	20	0	0	20
Committed Customer Orders	10	0	30	10	0	20	0	10
ATP:D	20	0	0	0	0	0	0	10
Model B—0.5-Liter Engine								
MPS BI = 30	10	10	0	20	0	20	0	20
Committed Customer Orders	20	10	10	0	0	20	20	0
ATP:D	10	0	0	0	0	0	0	20
Model C—0.6-Liter Engine								
MPS BI = 40	10	10	10	10	0	0	20	0
Committed Customer Orders	20	10	20	0	0	10	0	15
ATP:D	20	0	0	0	0	0	5	0

2. For the next period, subtract the Committed Customer Orders from the MPS. If the result is positive, this becomes the Period 2 ATP. If the result is negative, subtract enough from the previous period's ATP to make the current period's ATP zero, and revise the previous period's ATP to reflect this change.

3. For all subsequent periods, follow Step 2. However, if the ATP for any previous period is not large enough to accommodate a desired change, then subtract the desired units from earlier periods until all Committed Customer Orders are satisfied, updating the ATP in each period.

Using these guidelines, the ATP:D quantities in Table 6.5 are computed as follows:

Model A

Period 1: $ATP_1 = BI + MPS_1 - CCO_1 = 30 + 10 - 10 = 30$
Period 2: $ATP_2 = MPS_2 - CCO_2 = 10$
Period 3: $ATP_3 = MPS_3 - CCO_3 = -10$ (need to use 10 units from ATP_2)
        Revising, $ATP_2 = 0$ and $ATP_3 = 0$.
Period 4: $ATP_4 = MPS_4 - CCO_4 = -10$ (need to use 10 units from ATP_1)
        Revising, $ATP_1 = 20$ and $ATP_4 = 0$.
Period 5: $ATP_5 = MPS_5 - CCO_5 = 20$
Period 6: $ATP_6 = MPS_6 - CCO_6 = -20$ (need to use 20 units from ATP_5)
        Revising, $ATP_5 = 0$ and $ATP_6 = 0$.
Period 7: $ATP_7 = MPS_7 - CCO_7 = 0$
Period 8: $ATP_8 = MPS_8 - CCO_8 = 10$

As a check on the calculations, the CCO quantities can be summed and subtracted from the sum of the BI and the MPS quantities for the eight periods, which should result in the sum of the ATP quantities. The computation shows that twenty units of the Model A ATV can be promised for delivery in the first week of January or later, and another ten units can be promised for delivery in Week 8 or later. The total of thirty ATP units is the difference between the sum of the BI and MPS (110) and the sum of the Committed Customer Orders (80) for the first eight weeks.

Model B

Period 1: $ATP_1 = 20$
Period 2: $ATP_2 = 0$
Period 3: $ATP_3 = -10$
        Revising, $ATP_1 = 10$ and $ATP_3 = 0$.
Period 4: $ATP_4 = 20$
Period 5: $ATP_5 = 0$
Period 6: $ATP_6 = 0$
Period 7: $ATP_7 = -20$
        Revising, $ATP_4 = 0$ and $ATP_7 = 0$.
Period 8: $ATP_8 = 20$

The computation shows that ten units of the Model B ATV can be promised for delivery in the first week of January or later, and another twenty units can be promised for delivery in Week 8 or later. The total of thirty ATP units is the difference between the sum of the BI and MPS (110) and the sum of the Committed Customer Orders (80) for the first eight weeks.

Model C

Period 1: $ATP_1 = 30$
Period 2: $ATP_2 = 0$
Period 3: $ATP_3 = -10$
       Revising, $ATP_1 = 20$ and $ATP_3 = 0$.
Period 4: $ATP_4 = 10$
Period 5: $ATP_5 = 0$
Period 6: $ATP_6 = -10$
       Revising, $ATP_4 = 0$ and $ATP_6 = 0$.
Period 7: $ATP_7 = 20$
Period 8: $ATP_8 = -15$
       Revising, $ATP_7 = 5$ and $ATP_8 = 0$.

The computation shows that twenty units of Model C ATV can be promised for delivery in the first week of January or later, and another five units can be promised for delivery in Week 7 or later. The total of twenty-five ATP units is the difference between the sum of the beginning inventory and MPS (100) and the sum of the committed orders (75) for the first eight weeks.

While the total uncommitted production quantity can easily be computed by subtracting all committed customer orders from the scheduled MPS, it lacks time-phased information. For this reason, the ATP quantities must be determined as we have shown. This enables the master scheduler or salesperson to quickly book or confirm new sales to be delivered on specific due dates. Reacting quickly to demand changes and delivering orders on time are necessities in high-performing supply chains, and the tools we have discussed here enable firms to effectively meet customer needs. In supply chain relationships, using the MPS and ATP information effectively is essential to maintaining speed and flexibility throughout the supply chain as products make their way to end users.

Dependent Demand and Independent Demand

Inventory management models are generally separated by the nature and types of the inventory being considered and can be classified as *dependent demand* and *independent demand models*.

Dependent demand is a term used to describe the internal demand for parts based on the demand of the final product in which the parts are used. Subassemblies, components, and raw materials are examples of dependent demand items. Dependent demand may have a pattern of abrupt and dramatic changes because of its dependency on the demand of the final product, particularly if the final product is produced in large lot sizes. Dependent demand can be calculated once the demand of the final product is known. Therefore, material requirements planning (MRP) software should be used to compute exact material requirements instead of relying on forecasting techniques. For example, the ATV Corporation's MPS (Table 6.4) shows that 120 ATVs will be produced in January. The firm thus knows that 120 handlebars and 480 wheel rims will be needed.

The demand for handlebars, wheel rims, and other dependent demand items can be calculated based on the bill of materials (BOM) and the demand of the final product as stated on the MPS. A bill of materials is an engineering record showing all the component parts and assemblies needed for making a unit of the final product.

Independent demand is the demand for final products and has a demand pattern affected by trends, seasonal patterns, and general market conditions. For example, the demand for an ATV is independent demand. Seals and gaskets originally used in assembling the ATVs at the ATV Corporation are dependent demands; however, the same seals and gaskets would be classified as independent demand to the manufacturers of seals and gaskets (these would be that company's final products). Independent demand cannot be derived from demand for other items and, thus, must be forecasted based on market conditions.

The Bill of Materials

The bill of materials (BOM) is an engineering document that shows an inclusive listing of all component parts and assemblies making up the final product. Figure 6.2 is an example of a *multilevel bill of materials* for the ATV Corporation's all-terrain vehicles. It shows the parent-component relationships and the specific units of components—known as the **planning factor**—required for making a higher-level part or assembly. For example, "engine assembly" is

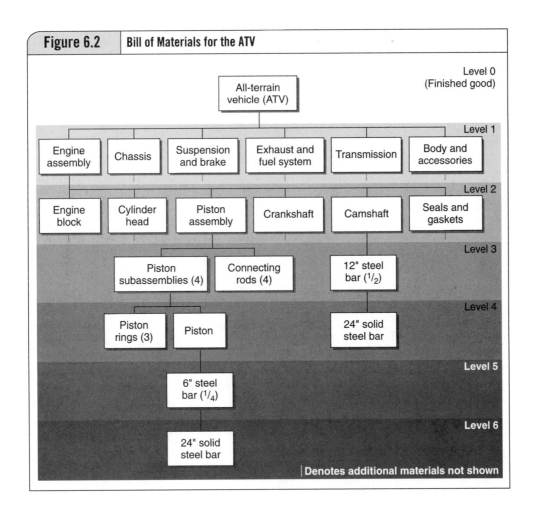

Figure 6.2   **Bill of Materials for the ATV**

Table 6.6	Indented Bill of Materials—All-Terrain Vehicles	
Part Description	**Level**	**Planning Factor**
Engine assembly	1	1
Engine block (components not shown)	2	1
Cylinder head (components not shown)	2	1
Piston assembly	2	1
Piston subassembly	3	4
Piston rings	4	3
Pistons	4	1
6" steel bar	5	¼
24" solid steel bar	6	1
Connecting rods	3	4
Crankshaft (components not shown)	2	1
Camshaft	2	1
12" steel bar	3	½
24" solid steel bar	4	1
Seals & gaskets (components not shown)	2	1
Chassis (components not shown)	1	1
Suspension & brake (components not shown)	1	1
Exhaust & fuel system (components not shown)	1	1
Transmission (components not shown)	1	1
Body & Accessories (components not shown)	1	1

an immediate *parent* of "engine block," and "engine block" is an immediate *component* of "engine assembly." "24-inch solid steel bar" is a *common component part,* because it is a component of "6-inch steel bar" and "12-inch steel bar." The *planning factor* of "connecting rods" shows that four pieces of connecting rods are needed to make a "piston assembly." Twelve "piston rings" (3×4) are needed to assemble one unit of ATV since there are three "piston rings" in each "piston subassembly," and there are four "piston subassemblies" in each "piston assembly."

The BOM is shown in various levels, starting from Level 0. Level 0 is the final product, which is the independent demand item. In this case, it is the ATV. Requirements of Level 0 items come from the master production schedule (i.e., Table 6.4 in the ATV Corporation example). The next level in the BOM is Level 1, which consists of all the components and subassemblies required for making one unit of the ATV. The requirements of Level 1 components and subassemblies are computed based on the demand of ATVs as specified in Level 0. The level numbers increase as one moves down on the BOM.

Correspondingly, the multilevel bill of materials can also be presented as an **indented bill of materials** as shown in Table 6.6. At each level of indentation, the level number increases by one. The indented bill of materials in Table 6.6 can be seen as a representation of the multilevel bill of materials (Figure 6.2) rotated 90 degrees counterclockwise.

Another type of bill of materials is the **super bill of materials,** which is useful for planning purposes. It is also referred to as a *planning bill of materials, pseudo bill of materials, phantom bill of materials,* or *family bill of materials.* Using the ATV Corporation's BOM in Figure 6.2 as an example, a simplified product structure diagram can be created for the family of ATVs that consists of different engine sizes (i.e., models) and transmission options.

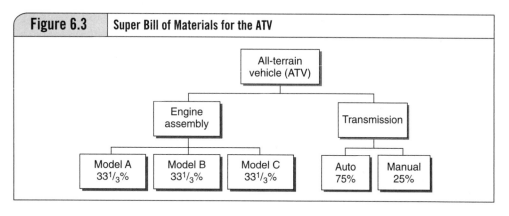

Figure 6.3 | Super Bill of Materials for the ATV

Instead of stating the planning factor, the percentage of each option is used. Figure 6.3 shows that 33⅓ percent of the ATVs are Model A, Model B, and Model C, respectively. Similarly, 75 percent of the ATVs use automatic transmissions and the remaining 25 percent use manual transmissions. Therefore, ATV Corporation's January planned production (120 units) consists of forty units each of Model A, Model B, and Model C (see Table 6.4). Similarly, ninety (75 percent × 120) units of the ATVs will be manufactured with automatic transmissions and the remaining thirty (25 percent × 120) units will be manufactured with manual transmissions.

The super bill of materials enables the firm to forecast the total demand of ATVs and then break down the forecast into different models and transmission options using the proper percentage, instead of forecasting the demand of each option individually. It provides quick information on the quantity of components for each option needed for the scheduled production. In addition, it also reduces the number of master production schedules. For the ATV Corporation example, the number of master production schedules was reduced from six (3 models × 2 transmission options) to one.

When the exact proportion of each option is uncertain, the percentage can be increased slightly to cover the uncertainty. For example, the ATV Corporation may increase its automatic transmission option to 78 percent and manual option to 27 percent, for a total of 105 percent. The firm increases its total planned production by 5 percent to cover uncertainty. This is known as **option overplanning.**

Materials Requirement Planning

Materials requirement planning (MRP) systems have been used widely by manufacturing firms for computing dependent demand. MRP is a computer-based materials management system. With the advent of computer and information technologies, the span of MRP evolved to include aggregate production planning, master production scheduling, and capacity requirements planning to become *closed-loop MRP*. It further evolved into *manufacturing resource planning (MRP-II)* by including other aspects of materials and resource planning, demand management, and the ability to perform "what-if" analyses. A complete MRP-II system consists of many modules that enable the firm to book orders, schedule production, control inventory, and perform accounting and financial analyses.

While there are hundreds of suppliers still selling and supporting their original MRP systems, some suppliers have expanded their systems to enable the users to perform more sophisticated analyses and integrate organization-wide activities, including operations and facilities that are located in different countries from the head office. This new generation of MRP system is known as the *enterprise resource planning (ERP)* system (the topic of Chapter 7).

The materials requirement plan is used to calculate the exact quantities, need dates, and planned order releases for subassemblies and materials required to manufacture the final products listed on the MPS. MRP begins the computation process by first obtaining the requirements of the final product (the Level 0 item on the BOM) from the MPS to calculate the requirements of Level 1 components and materials, and then working its way down to the lowest level components, taking into account existing inventories and the time required for each processing step. While these manufacturing and delivery lead times are ignored in the MPS, they are considered in the MRP computation process. For example, if a parent item requires an immediate component with a three-week lead time, the component must be ordered three weeks ahead of the need date.

For MRP, a dependent demand management system, to work effectively, it requires: (1) the independent demand information (the demand for the final product or service part) from the master production schedule; (2) parent-component relationships from the bill of materials, including the planning factor and lead-time information; and (3) inventory status of the final product and all of the components. MRP takes this information to compute the net requirements of the final product and components, and then offsets the net requirements with appropriate lead times to ensure orders are released on time for fabricating higher-level components. This information is a major output of the MRP system, known as **planned order releases.**

A major advantage of the MRP system is that it provides planning information. Production information—such as scheduled receipts, on-hand inventories, net requirements, and planned order releases—is available for the entire planning horizon, enabling schedulers and operators to plan ahead. However, a major disadvantage of the MRP system is its *loss of visibility,* due to the requirement of offsetting net requirements by the appropriate lead time to obtain planned order releases. This problem is especially acute for products with a deep bill of materials. Another drawback of MRP systems is that they ignore capacity and shop floor conditions.

Terms Used in Materials Requirement Planning

Prior to examining how the dependent demand system works, let us look at some terms as they apply to MRP:

1. *Parent:* The item generating the demand for lower-level components. Level 0 is the final product. It is the parent of all Level 1 components. Similarly, each Level 1 item becomes the parent of the Level 2 components used to make the item. For example, Figure 6.2 shows that "piston assembly" is a parent of "piston subassemblies" and "connecting rods."

2. *Components:* The parts demanded by a parent. For example, Figure 6.2 shows that "piston assembly" is a component of "engine assembly."

3. *Gross requirement:* A time-phased requirement prior to netting out on-hand inventory and the lead-time consideration. The gross requirement is satisfied from inventory and/or production.

4. *Net requirement:* The unsatisfied item requirement for a specific time period. It equals the gross requirement for that period minus the current on-hand inventory and any scheduled receipts.

5. *Scheduled receipt:* A committed order awaiting delivery for a specific period. It is an order released in a past period and due to be received in a specific later period. This information is updated automatically by the MRP computer logic system once an order has been placed. For example, an item with a two-week delivery lead time ordered on the first week of the month automatically becomes a scheduled receipt on the third week.

6. *Projected on-hand inventory:* The projected closing inventory at the end of the period. It equals the beginning inventory minus the gross requirement, plus the scheduled receipt and planned receipt from planned order releases.

7. *Planned order release:* A specific order to be released to the shop (if the component is made in-house) or to the supplier (if the component is purchased) to ensure that it is available on the need date. Planned order releases of the parent become gross requirements of the components.

8. *Time bucket:* The time period used on the MRP. It is usually expressed in days or weeks. The current period is the *action time bucket.*

9. *Explosion:* The common term used to describe the process of converting a parent item's planned order releases into component gross requirements.

10. *Planning factor:* The number of components needed to produce a unit of the parent item. For example, Figure 6.2 shows that four units of "connecting rods" are needed to produce a unit of "piston assembly."

11. *Firmed planned order:* A planned order that the MRP computer logic system does not automatically change when conditions change. The primary purpose of a firmed planned order is to prevent system nervousness, similar to the time fence system discussed earlier in the master production schedule discussion.

12. *Pegging:* Relates gross requirements for a part to the planned order releases that created the requirements. It is essentially the reverse of the explosion process.

13. *Low-level coding:* Assigns the lowest level on the bill of materials to all common components to avoid duplicate MRP computations. For example, Figure 6.2 shows that "24-inch solid steel bar" is a common component that appears in Level 4 and Level 6. Instead of computing its planned order releases at Level 4 and Level 6 separately, a low-level code of 6 is assigned to the item. Its net requirements at Level 4 are added to those at Level 6, and the MRP explosion logic is performed at Level 6 only.

14. *Lot size:* The order size for MRP logic. Lot size may be determined by various lot-sizing techniques, such as EOQ (a fixed order quantity) or *lot-for-lot* (order whatever amount is needed each period). A lot size of fifty calls for orders to be placed in multiples of fifty. With a net requirement of eighty-five units, using lot-for-lot (LFL) order sizing will result in an order of eighty-five units; however, an order of 100 units would be placed when using a fixed order quantity of fifty.

15. *Safety stock:* Protects against uncertainties in demand, supply, quality, and lead time. Its implication in MRP logic is that the minimum projected on-hand inventory should not fall below the safety stock level.

A materials requirement planning example is provided in Example 6.2.

EXAMPLE 6.2   An MRP example at the ATV Corporation

Model A's production schedule for the ATV Corporation is used to illustrate the MRP logic. Its gross requirements are first obtained from the master production schedule in Table 6.4, and the inventory status shows that thirty units of Model A are available at the beginning of the year. The parent-component relationships and planning factors are available from the BOM in Figure 6.2. Assuming the following lot sizes (Q), lead times (LT), and safety stocks (SS) are used, the MRP computations of the Model A ATV and some of its components are as follows:

Model A ATV—Level 0	1	2	3	4	5	6	7	8
Gross requirements	10	10	20	0	20	0	0	20
Scheduled receipts		10						
Projected on-hand inventory 30	20	20	20	20	20	20	20	20
Net requirements			15		15			15
Planned order releases	20		20			20		

Q = 10; LT = 2; SS = 15

×1   ×1   ×1

Engine Assembly—Level 1	1	2	3	4	5	6	7	8
Gross requirements	20		20			20		
Scheduled receipts	20							
Projected on-hand inventory 2	2	2	0	0	0	0	0	0
Net requirements			18			20		
Planned order releases	18			20				

Q = LFL; LT = 2; SS = 0

×1   ×1

Piston Assembly—Level 2	1	2	3	4	5	6	7	8
Gross requirements	18			20				
Scheduled receipts	20							
Projected on-hand inventory 10	12	12	12	22	22	22	22	22
Net requirements				18				
Planned order releases			30					

Q = 30; LT = 1; SS = 10

×4

Connecting Rods—Level 3	1	2	3	4	5	6	7	8
Gross requirements			120					
Scheduled receipts								
Projected on-hand inventory 22	22	22	52	52	52	52	52	52
Net requirements			118					
Planned order releases		150						

Q = 50; LT = 1; SS = 20

Level 0 MRP Computation—Model A ATV

The first row is the planning horizon for the eight weeks in January and February. The gross requirements are derived directly from the MPS. The scheduled receipt of ten units in Week 2 is due to an order placed last week, which automatically becomes a scheduled receipt two weeks later (note that scheduled receipts are only shown for orders that were placed in periods previous to the current period). The order size for the Model A ATV is in multiples of ten units, the lead time is two weeks, and the desired safety stock is fifteen units. The projected on-hand inventory of twenty units for the first week is computed by taking the beginning inventory of thirty units and subtracting the gross requirement of ten units in that week. The projected on-hand inventory of twenty units in Week 2 is computed by taking the previous balance of twenty units, adding the scheduled receipt of ten units, and subtracting the gross requirement of ten units.

During the third week, additional Model A ATVs must be received to ensure the on-hand balance is above the safety stock level of fifteen units. The net requirement here is fifteen

EXAMPLE 6.2   *Continued*

units (since all of the incoming inventory is consumed to satisfy the gross requirement of twenty units). Since orders must be in multiples of ten, twenty units must be ordered in the first week to satisfy both the lead time and the safety stock requirements. Simply stated, if twenty units are needed in the third week, the two-week lead time requires the order to be placed two weeks ahead, which explains why there is a planned order release of twenty units in the first week. The on-hand inventory balance of twenty units at the end of the third week is computed by taking the previous balance of twenty units, adding the planned order receipt of twenty units (due to the planned order release in the first week), and subtracting the gross requirement of twenty units.

Similarly, the gross requirements of twenty units each in the fifth and eighth week consumed the beginning of period inventory, triggering a net requirement of fifteen units for those periods and a planned order release of twenty units each during the third and sixth week, respectively.

Level 1 MRP Computation—Engine Assembly

The BOM in Figure 6.2 indicates that the gross requirements for the engine assembly are derived from the planned order releases of the Model A ATV. Since the planning factor is one unit, Model A ATV's planned order releases translate into gross requirements for engine assembly in the first, third, and sixth weeks. The scheduled receipt of twenty units in the first week is due to an order placed two weeks earlier (although it could also be a rescheduled delivery from some earlier week). The gross requirements of twenty units each for the third and sixth week triggered net requirements in the same weeks and planned order releases of eighteen and twenty units, respectively, for the first and fourth week (note here that since no safety stock is required and the lot size is LFL, the planned order releases equal the net requirements, and the inventory balances are allowed to stay at a projected level of zero once the on-hand inventory is consumed).

Level 2 MRP Computation—Piston Assembly

The gross requirements for the piston assembly are derived from the planned order releases of engine assembly. Therefore, the gross requirements of piston assembly are eighteen and twenty units, respectively, for the first and fourth week. Computations of its projected on-hand balances and planned order releases are similar to earlier examples (note again here that inventories must not drop below ten and order quantities must be made in multiples of thirty).

Level 3 MRP Computation—Connecting Rods

The BOM in Figure 6.2 indicates that four connecting rods are required for each piston assembly. Therefore, the gross requirement for connecting rods in the third week is obtained by multiplying the planned order releases for piston assemblies by four. Note that due to the requirement to offset the lead times in each MRP computation, the planned order release for connecting rods can be determined only up to the second period, although the gross requirements of the Model A ATV are known for the first eight weeks. This is referred to as *loss of visibility,* as discussed earlier.

Since there are no lower-level components shown for the connecting rods, we can assume that the ATV Corporation purchases this component. Thus, the planned order releases would be used by the purchasing department to communicate order quantities and delivery dates to its connecting rod supplier. In supply chain settings, manufacturing firms share their planned order release information with their strategic suppliers either through EDI communications, FAX transmissions, or their ERP system. Since the firm manufactures its own piston assemblies, the planned order release information for this part is communicated to shop floor operators and used to trigger production. We can see, then, that planned order releases for purchased items eventually become the independent demand gross requirements for the firm's suppliers. Communicating this information accurately and quickly to strategic suppliers is a necessary element in the supply chain information system.

Capacity Planning

The material plans (the aggregate production plan, the master production schedule, and the material requirements plan) discussed so far have focused exclusively on production and materials management but must also address capacity constraints. Excess or insufficient capacity prevents a firm from fully taking advantage of the efficiency and effectiveness of the manufacturing planning and control system. Thus, a set of capacity plans is used in conjunction with the materials plan to ensure capacity is not overstressed or underutilized.

Capacity planning follows the basic hierarchy of the materials planning system as shown in Figure 6.1. At the aggregate level, **resource requirement planning (RRP),** a long-range capacity planning module, is used to check whether aggregate resources are capable of satisfying the aggregate production plan. Typical resources considered at this stage include gross labor hours and machine hours. Generally, capacity expansion decisions at this level involve a long-range commitment, such as new facilities or additional capital equipment. If existing resources are unable to meet the aggregate production plan, then the plan must be revised. The revised aggregate production plan is reevaluated by the resource requirement plan until a feasible production plan is obtained.

Once the aggregate production plan is determined to be feasible, the aggregate production information is disaggregated into a more detailed medium-range production plan, the master production schedule. Although resource requirement planning has already determined that aggregate capacity is sufficient to satisfy the aggregate production plan, medium-range capacity may not be able to satisfy the master production schedule. For example, the master production schedule may call for normal production quantities when much of the workforce typically takes vacation. Therefore, the medium-range capacity plan, or **rough-cut capacity plan (RCCP),** is used to check the feasibility of the master production schedule.

The rough-cut capacity plan takes the master production schedule and converts it from production to capacity required, then compares it to capacity available during each production period. If the medium-range capacity and production plans are feasible, the master production plan is firmed up. Otherwise, it is revised or the capacity is adjusted accordingly. Options for increasing medium-range capacity include overtime, subcontracting, adding resources, and an alternate routing of the production sequence.

Capacity requirement planning (CRP) is a short-range capacity planning technique that is used to check the feasibility of the material requirements plan. The time-phased material requirement plan is used to compute the detailed capacity requirements required at each workstation during specific periods to manufacture the items specified in the MRP.

Independent Demand Inventory Systems

Savvy operations managers are concerned with controlling inventories throughout the entire supply chain. An effective independent demand inventory system ensures smooth operations and allows manufacturing firms to store up production capacity in the form of work-in-process and finished goods inventories. While service organizations are unable to inventory their output, such organizations may use appointment backlogs, labor scheduling, and cross-training to balance supply and demand.

The four broad categories of inventories—raw materials; work-in-process; finished goods; and maintenance, repair, and operating (MRO) supplies—are briefly discussed next:

- *Raw materials* are defined as unprocessed purchased inputs or materials for manufacturing the finished goods. Raw materials become part of finished goods

Global Perspective

GARRETT ENGINE BOOSTING SYSTEMS

Garrett Engine Boosting Systems, a division of Honeywell, Inc., is a leading manufacturer in the turbocharger industry. Garrett turbochargers provide sophisticated engine boosting systems to automotive and industrial original equipment manufacturers (OEMs), including Audi, BMW, DaimlerChrysler, Fiat, Ford, Peugeot, Renault, Saab, Volkswagen, and Caterpillar. In addition to a global network of more than 200 distributors, Garrett maintains manufacturing plants in fourteen countries. The company employs more than 6,000 people worldwide.[5]

Intense global competition, shrinking product life cycles, and the ever-increasing demand for shorter lead times have posed a challenge for Garrett. OEM customers have demanded more complex products and improved delivery performance without sacrificing product quality.

Garrett assessed the situation and realized that it needed to implement a system that would (1) provide easy and flexible integration with its existing enterprise resource planning and other systems, (2) increase productivity, (3) improve all aspects of delivery performance, and (4) reduce expediting costs due to premium freight or overtime production.

Garrett turned to Apexon's Web-based solution, which was capable of providing real-time visibility, collaboration, and exception management across key supplier-facing functions. The Apexon solution was completely integrated with Garrett's North American enterprise systems within ninety days, and it was subsequently implemented in Europe. The company also planned to implement the Apexon solution in Asia and Latin America to fully integrate its global operations.[6]

Some tangible results of the Apexon solution at Garrett include:

1. Materials planners eliminated fourteen hours per week that were spent on reconciling supplier production capabilities with MRP requirements and providing inventory information.

2. Quality engineers achieved a 20 percent productivity increase.

3. Suppliers were able to log on to the Web-based system to access real-time inventory and consumption information at any time.

4. The company was able to reduce its safety stock levels and both inbound and outbound premium freight costs.

---

after the manufacturing process is completed. There are many reasons for keeping raw material inventories, including volume purchases due to quantity discounts, stockpiling in anticipation of future price increases, safety stock to guard against supplier delivery or quality problems, volume purchases to create transportation economies, and stockpiling to avoid a possible short supply in the future.

- *Work-in-process* describes materials that are partially processed but not yet ready for sales. One reason to keep excess work-in-process inventories is to *decouple* processing stages or to break the dependencies between work centers.

- *Finished goods* are completed products ready for shipment. Excess finished goods inventories are often kept to buffer against unexpected demand changes and in anticipation of production process downtime; to ensure production economies when the setup cost is very high; and/or to stabilize production rates, especially for seasonal products.

- *Maintenance, repair and operating (MRO) supplies* are materials and supplies used when producing the products but are not parts of the products. Solvents, cutting tools, and lubricants for machines are examples of MRO supplies. The two main reasons for storing MRO supplies are to gain purchase economies and to avoid material shortages that may shut down production.

Some of the common independent demand inventory management systems are discussed in the following sections.

The ABC Inventory Control System

A common problem with many inventory management systems is the inability to maintain accurate inventory records. **Cycle counting** is a commonly used technique in which physical inventory is counted on a periodic basis to ensure that physical inventory matches current inventory records. However, cycle counting can be costly and time-consuming and can disrupt operations. The **ABC inventory control system** is a useful technique for determining which inventories should be counted more frequently and managed more closely and which others should not.

The ABC inventory control system prioritizes inventory items into Groups A, B, and C. A items are given the highest priority, while C items have the lowest priority and are typically the most numerous. Greater attention, safety stocks, and resources are devoted to the high-priority or A items. The priority is most often determined by annual dollar usage. However, priority may also be determined by shelf life, sales volume, whether the materials are critical components, or other criteria.

When prioritizing inventories by annual dollar usage, the ABC system suggests that approximately 20 percent of the items make up about 80 percent of the total annual dollar usage and these items are classified as the A items. The B items make up approximately 40 percent of the items and account for about 15 percent of the total annual dollar usage, while the C items are the remaining 40 percent of the items making up about 5 percent of the total annual dollar usage of inventory. Since the A items are the highest annual dollar usage items, these items should then be monitored more frequently and may have higher safety stock levels to guard against stock-outs, particularly if these items are used in products sold to supply chain trading partners. C items would then be counted less frequently, and stock-outs may be allowed to save inventory space and carrying costs. An illustration of an ABC inventory classification is shown in Example 6.3.

EXAMPLE 6.3   An ABC inventory classification example

Inventory Item Number	Item Cost ($)	Annual Usage (Units)	Annual Volume ($)	Percent of Total Volume	Class
A246	1.00	22,000	22,000	35.2	A
N376	0.50	40,000	20,000	32.0	A
C024	4.25	1,468	6,239	10.0	B
R221	12.00	410	4,920	7.8	B
P112	2.25	1,600	3,600	5.8	B
R166	0.12	25,000	3,000	4.8	B
T049	8.50	124	1,054	1.7	C
B615	0.25	3,500	875	1.4	C
L227	1.25	440	550	0.9	C
T519	26.00	10	260	0.4	C

Note that the A items only account for about 67 percent of the total annual dollar volume, while the B items account for about 28 percent. This illustrates that judgment must also be applied when using the ABC method and the 80/20 rule should only be used as a general guideline.

The Economic Order Quantity Model

The **economic order quantity (EOQ)** model is a classic independent demand inventory system that provides many useful ordering decisions. The basic order decision is "What is the correct order size to minimize total inventory costs?" The issue revolves around the trade-off between annual inventory holding costs and annual order costs. When order sizes for an item are small, orders have to be placed on a frequent basis, causing high annual ordering costs. However, the firm has a low average inventory level for this item, resulting in low annual inventory holding costs. When order sizes for an item are large, orders are placed less frequently, causing lower annual order costs. Unfortunately, this also causes the average inventory level for this item to be high, resulting in higher expenses to hold the inventory. The EOQ model seeks to determine an optimal order quantity, where the sum of the annual order cost and the annual inventory holding cost is minimized.

Order cost is the direct variable cost associated with placing an order with the supplier, whereas **holding cost or carrying cost** is the cost incurred for holding inventory in storage. Order costs include managerial and clerical costs for preparing the purchase, as well as other incidental expenses that can be traced directly to the purchase. Examples of holding costs include warehousing expenses, handling charges, insurance, pilferage, shrinkage, taxes, and the cost of capital.

Assumptions of the Economic Order Quantity Model

Users must carefully consider several assumptions when determining the economic order quantity:

1. *The demand must be known and constant.* For example, if there are 360 days per year and the annual demand is known to be 720 units, then daily usage must be exactly two units throughout the entire year.

2. *Delivery time is known and constant.* For example, if the delivery time is known to be ten days, each and every delivery will arrive exactly ten days after the order is placed.

3. *Replenishment is instantaneous.* The entire order is delivered at one time, and partial shipments are not allowed.

4. *Price is constant.* Quantity or price discounts are not allowed.

5. *The holding cost is known and constant.* The cost or rate to hold inventory must be known and constant.

6. *Ordering cost is known and constant.* The cost of placing an order must be known and remains constant for all orders.

7. Stock-outs are not allowed. Inventory must be available at all times.

Deriving the Economic Order Quantity

The economic order quantity can be derived easily from the total annual inventory cost formula using simple calculus. The total annual inventory cost is the sum of the annual purchase cost, the annual holding cost, and the annual order cost. The formula can be shown as:

$$TAIC = APC + AHC + AOC = (R \times C) + \left(\frac{Q}{2} \times k \times C \right) + \left(\frac{R}{Q} \times S \right)$$

where

$TAIC$ = total annual inventory cost
APC = purchase cost
AHC = annual holding cost
AOC = annual ordering cost
R = annual requirement or demand
C = purchase cost per unit
S = cost of placing one order
k = holding cost rate, where annual holding cost per unit = $k \times C$
Q = order quantity

Since R, C, k, and S are assumed to be constant, Q is the only unknown variable in the TAIC equation. The optimum Q (the EOQ) can be obtained by taking the first derivative of TAIC with respect to Q and then setting it equal to zero. A second derivative of TAIC can also be taken with respect to Q to prove that the TAIC is at the minimum.

$$\Rightarrow \frac{dTAIC}{dQ} = 0 + \left(\frac{1}{2} \times k \times C\right) + \left(-1 \times R \times S \times \frac{1}{Q^2}\right)$$

$$= \frac{kC}{2} - \frac{RS}{Q^2}$$

then setting equal to zero,

$$\frac{kC}{2} - \frac{RS}{Q^2} = 0$$

or

$$\frac{kC}{2} = \frac{RS}{Q^2}$$

or

$$Q^2 = \frac{2RS}{kC}$$

then

$$EOQ = \sqrt{\frac{2RS}{kC}}$$

The second derivative of TAIC is:

$$\frac{d^2 ATC}{dQ^2} = 0 - \left(-2 \times \frac{RS}{Q^3}\right) = \left(\frac{2RS}{Q^3}\right) \geq 0$$

implying the TAIC is at its minimum.

The annual purchase cost drops off after the first derivative is taken. The managerial implication here is that purchase cost does not affect the order decision if there is no quantity discount (the annual purchase cost remains constant as long as the same annual quantity is purchased). Thus, the annual purchase cost is ignored in the classic EOQ model. Example 6.4 provides an illustration of calculating the EOQ.

EXAMPLE 6.4   Calculating an EOQ at the Las Vegas Corporation

The Las Vegas Corporation purchases a critical component from one of its strategic supply chain partners. The two companies want to determine the optimal order quantity, along with when to reorder, to ensure the annual inventory cost is minimized. The following information was obtained from historical data:

Annual requirements (R) = 7,200 units

Order cost (S) = $100 per order

Annual holding rate (k) = 20 percent

Unit purchase cost (C) = $20 per unit

Lead time (LT) = 6 days

Number of days per year = 360 days

Thus,

$$EOQ = \sqrt{\frac{2RS}{kC}} = \sqrt{\frac{2 \times 7,200\,\text{units} \times \$100}{0.20 \times \$20}} = 600\,\text{units}$$

EXAMPLE 6.4   *Continued*

The annual purchase cost = $R \times C = 7{,}200 \times \$20 = \$144{,}000$.

The annual holding cost = $\dfrac{Q}{2} \times k \times C = (600/2) \times 0.20 \times \$20 = \$1{,}200$.

The annual order cost = $\dfrac{R}{Q} \times S = (7{,}200/600) \times \$100 = \$1{,}200$.

The total annual inventory cost = $\$144{,}000 + \$1{,}200 + \$1{,}200 = \$146{,}400$.

(Note that when ordering the EOQ, the annual holding cost equals the annual order cost.)

For an order lead time of six days, the reorder point (ROP) would be:

$$\text{ROP} = (7{,}200/360) \times 6 = 120 \text{ units}.$$

Thus, the purchasing manager should reorder the component from supplier whenever the stock on hand is down to 120 units and 600 units at a time should be ordered. Several other statistics can also be generated:

Number of orders placed per year = $7{,}200/600 = 12$ orders.

Time between orders = $360/12 = 30$ days.

Figure 6.4 shows the relationships between annual holding cost, annual ordering cost, and total annual holding plus order cost. At the EOQ (600 units), annual holding cost ($1,200) equals annual ordering cost ($1,200). At or close to the EOQ, the total cost curve is rather flat, indicating that it is not very sensitive to small variations in the economic order quantity. Therefore, the classic EOQ model is said to be very *robust* to minor errors in estimating cost parameters, such as holding rate, order cost, or annual usage. Table 6.7 compares the annual total cost at an EOQ of 600 units and at 10 percent below and above the EOQ. The analysis shows that the cost variations range from only 0.01 percent to 0.56 percent above the minimum cost.

Figure 6.4	**The Economic Order Quantity and Total Costs**

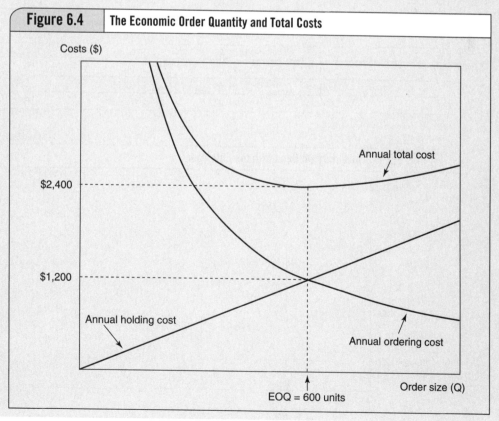

EXAMPLE 6.4   *Continued*

Figure 6.4 and Table 6.7 show that if the order size is smaller than the EOQ, the annual holding cost is slightly lower, whereas the annual ordering cost is slightly higher. The net effect is a slightly higher annual total cost. Similarly, if the order quantity is slightly larger than the EOQ, the annual holding cost is slightly higher, whereas the annual ordering cost is slightly lower. The net effect is a slightly higher annual total cost.

Figure 6.5 shows the movement of on-hand inventory and the relationships of EOQ, average inventory, lead time, reorder point, and the order cycle. At Time 0, the firm is assumed to start with a complete order of 600 units. The inventory is consumed at a steady rate of twenty units per day. On the twenty-fourth day, the firm places its first order of 600 units, and it arrives six days later (on the thirtieth day). On the twenty-fourth day, 120 units of inventory are left, which will be totally consumed immediately prior to the arrival of the first order. The vertical line on the thirtieth day shows that all 600 units are received (this is the instantaneous replenishment assumption of the EOQ model). A total of twelve orders (including the initial 600 units) will be placed during the year to satisfy the annual requirements of 7,200 units.

Table 6.7	Percent Variation in Total Annual Cost			
Q (units)	**AHC ($)**	**AOC ($)**	**ATC ($)**	**Variation (%)**
540	1080.00	1333.33	2413.33	0.56%
550	1100.00	1309.09	2409.09	0.38
560	1120.00	1285.71	2405.71	0.24
570	1140.00	1263.16	2403.16	0.13
580	1160.00	1241.38	2401.38	0.06
590	1180.00	1220.34	2400.34	0.01
600	1200.00	1200.00	2400.00	*
610	1220.00	1180.33	2400.33	0.01
620	1240.00	1161.29	2401.29	0.05
630	1260.00	1142.86	2402.86	0.12
640	1280.00	1125.00	2405.00	0.21
650	1300.00	1107.69	2407.69	0.32
660	1320.00	1090.91	2410.91	0.45

*indicates minimum total cost at EOQ.

Figure 6.5	Inventory On Hand with the EOQ Model

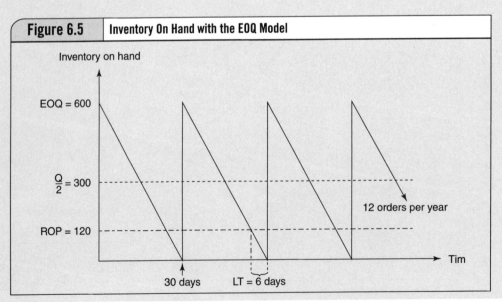

Allowing the Purchase Price to Vary in the Economic Order Quantity Model

The **quantity discount model** or **price-break model** is one variation of the classic EOQ model. It relaxes the constant price assumption by allowing purchase quantity discounts. In this case, the unit price of an item can vary with the order size. Unlike the EOQ model, the purchase cost now becomes an important criterion in determining the optimal order size and the corresponding total annual inventory cost. With the quantity discount model, there are two unknowns in the TAIC equation (the purchase price C, and the order quantity Q). A fairly straightforward procedure is then used when solving the quantity discount model.[7] Briefly, the steps can be stated as follows:

1. For each purchase price C, calculate the corresponding EOQ.

2. If any EOQ is too low to qualify for the discounted price C, then adjust the purchase quantity upward to the minimum quantity to qualify for that purchase price.

3. Using the TAIC equation, calculate the total cost for each price C and its corresponding purchase quantity (either the EOQ or the minimum purchase quantity for each price).

4. Select the price and quantity combination resulting in the lowest TAIC.

Example 6.5 illustrates the quantity discount model.

EXAMPLE 6.5   Purchasing soccer balls at Blake's Sports Emporium

Blake's Sports Emporium sells soccer balls. Recently, its soccer ball supplier had excess soccer balls and was willing to discount the purchase price for large orders. For orders under 1,000 balls, the standard price of $5.00 per ball applied. For orders between 1,001 and 2,000, the supplier was willing to drop the unit price to $4.50, and for orders over 2,000, the unit price would be $4.00. The purchasing manager at Blake's knew Blake's had some excess space in its warehouse, so she wanted to determine which purchase quantity and price would generate the greatest savings. Using the standard order cost of $40; a forecasted annual demand of 15,000 soccer balls; and an annual holding rate, k, of 25 percent, the purchasing manager determined the most favorable option as follows:

$$EOQ_{\$5} = \sqrt{\frac{2(40)(15,000)}{.25(5)}} = 980 \, units$$

$$EOQ_{\$4.50} = \sqrt{\frac{2(40)(15,000)}{.25(4.5)}} = 1,032 \, units$$

$$EOQ_{\$4} = \sqrt{\frac{2(40)(15,000)}{.25(4)}} = 1,095 \, units$$

Since the EOQ for the $5.00 purchase price is less than 1,000 soccer balls, this is a valid order size and will be compared to the other alternatives. The second EOQ is also a valid quantity, since it is greater than the minimum required to obtain a $4.50 purchase price. The third EOQ, though, will not work since, if the firm ordered 1,095 soccer balls, it would have to pay $4.50 per unit. Instead, the firm must use the alternative of ordering 2,001 soccer balls and paying $4.00 per unit in the cost comparison. The three total annual inventory costs are then:

TAIC$_{\$5}$ = 15,000(5) + (980/2)(.25)(5) + (15,000/980)(40) = $76,225

TAIC$_{\$4.50}$ = 15,000(4.5) + (1,032/2)(.25)(4.5) + (15,000/1,032)(40) = $68,662

TAIC$_{\$4}$ = 15,000(4) + (2,001/2)(.25)(4) + (15,000/2,001)(40) = $61,300

So, the purchasing manager at Blake's decides to order the minimum quantity (2,001 soccer balls) and pay the discounted price of $4 per soccer ball since it would result in the lowest total annual inventory cost, even though it is not the calculated EOQ.

Summary

While both manufacturing and service organizations rely on effective production and capacity planning to balance demand and capacity, manufacturers have the added advantage of being able to build up inventory as stored capacity. Service firms are unable to inventory their services, so they rely upon backlogs or reservations, cross-training, or queues to match supply with demand. However, excess capacity results in underutilized equipment and workforce and eventually leads to unnecessary cost, adversely impacting all firms along the supply chain.

This chapter covers materials planning, capacity planning, and various inventory management techniques that are widely used for balancing demand with supply. An example was used to demonstrate how the aggregate production plan, the master production schedule, and the material requirements plan are related to each other. This chapter also briefly discusses how the various materials plans are related to the capacity plans. A central piece of the materials plan is the material requirements plan, which takes information from the master production schedule, the bill of materials, and inventory status to compute planned order releases. For items that are produced in-house, planned order releases are released to the shop floor to trigger production. For purchased items, planned order releases are released to suppliers.

Key Terms

ABC inventory control system, 176

aggregate production plan (APP), 158

available-to-promise (ATP) quantity, 164

capacity requirement planning (CRP), 174

cash spin or free cash spin, 157

chase production strategy, 161

closed-loop MRP, 159

cycle counting, 176

demand time fence, 164

dependent demand, 166

distribution requirement planning (DRP), 159

economic order quantity (EOQ), 177

holding cost or carrying cost, 177

indented bill of materials, 168

independent demand, 167

intermediate or medium-range planning horizon, 158

level production strategy, 162

long-range planning horizon, 158

make-to-order manufacturing firms, 161

make-to-stock manufacturing firms, 162

manufacturing resource planning (MRP-II), 159

master production schedule (MPS), 158

materials requirement planning, 158

mixed production strategy, 162

option overplanning, 169

order cost, 177

planned order release, 170

planning factor, 167

planning time fence, 164

quantity discount model or price-break model, 181

resource requirement planning (RRP), 174

rough-cut capacity plan (RCCP), 174

short-range planning horizon, 158

super bill of materials, 168

system nervousness, 163

Discussion Questions

1. Why is it important to balance capacity with output?
2. Describe aggregate production planning, master production planning, and material requirements planning. How are these plans related?
3. Describe the relationships among MRP, closed-loop MRP, MRP-II, and ERP.
4. Compare and contrast chase versus level production strategies. Which is more appropriate for an industry where highly skilled laborers are needed? Why?
5. Is a level production strategy applicable for a pure service industry, such as professional accounting and tax services or law firms? Can these firms inventory their outputs?
6. What is system nervousness? Discuss how it can be minimized or avoided.
7. Compare and contrast dependent versus independent demand. Give at least two examples of each.
8. What are the crucial inputs for material requirements planning?
9. What is a BOM, and how is it different from the super BOM?
10. Is manufacturing or purchasing lead time considered in the MPS or the MRP?
11. What is the difference between scheduled receipts and planned order releases?
12. Briefly describe resource requirements planning, rough-cut capacity planning, and capacity requirements planning. How are these plans related?
13. How are the various capacity plans (ERP, RCCP, CRP) related to the material plans (APP, MPS, MRP)?
14. What is an ABC inventory system, and how is it used to manage inventory?
15. Why is it important to conduct cycle counting?
16. What is the purpose of the economic order quantity and the reorder point?
17. What are the two major costs considered in the classic EOQ model? Why is the purchase price not a factor affecting the order quantity?
18. Discuss whether the EOQ model is still useful if a small error was made while estimating one of the cost parameters used in the EOQ computation.
19. Assume you have used the classic EOQ model to compute the optimal order quantity for an A item, and the answer was twenty-three units. Unfortunately, the minimum lot size for the item is forty-eight units. Discuss how this is going to impact your annual holding cost, annual ordering cost, and annual total cost.
20. Why are aggregate planning and inventory management important to SCM?

Problems

1. Given the following production plan, use (a) chase production strategy, and (b) level production strategy to compute the monthly production, ending inventory/(backlog), and workforce levels. A worker is capable of producing 100 units per month. Assume the beginning inventory at January is zero, and the firm desires to have zero inventory at the end of June.

Month	Jan	Feb	Mar	Apr	May	Jun
Demand	2,000	3,000	5,000	6,000	6,000	2,000
Production						
Ending inventory						
Workforce						

2. Given the following production schedule, compute the available-to-promise quantities.

Week		1	2	3	4	5	6	7	8
Model A									
MPS	BI = 60	20	30	20	20	20	50	0	20
Committed customer orders		50	10	30	10	20	20	10	0
ATP:D									

3. Given the following production schedule, compute the available-to-promise quantities.

Week		1	2	3	4	5	6	7	8
Model B									
MPS	BI = 20	20	0	20	20	0	20	20	20
Committed customer orders		10	10	10	10	10	0	0	10
ATP:D									

4. The bills of materials for two finished products (D and E), inventory status, and other relevant information follow. Compute the planned order releases and projected on-hand balances for Part D, Part E, and Part F.

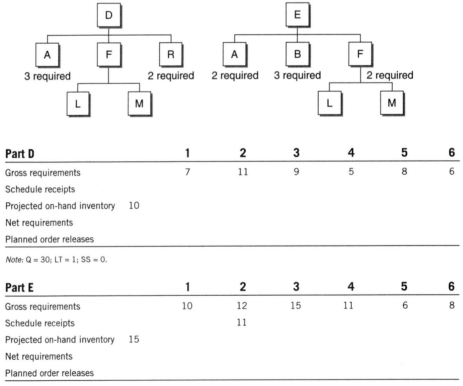

Part D		1	2	3	4	5	6
Gross requirements		7	11	9	5	8	6
Schedule receipts							
Projected on-hand inventory	10						
Net requirements							
Planned order releases							

Note: Q = 30; LT = 1; SS = 0.

Part E		1	2	3	4	5	6
Gross requirements		10	12	15	11	6	8
Schedule receipts			11				
Projected on-hand inventory	15						
Net requirements							
Planned order releases							

Note: Q = LFL; LT = 2; SS = 3.

Part F	1	2	3	4	5	6
Gross requirements						
Schedule receipts	60					
Projected on-hand inventory 20						
Net requirements						
Planned order releases						

Note: Q = 60; LT = 1; SS = 0.

Spreadsheet Problems

1. Given the following information for an important purchased part, compute the (a) economic order quantity, (b) total purchase cost, (c) annual holding cost, (d) annual ordering cost, (e) annual total cost, (f) reorder point, (g) number of orders placed per year, and (h) time between orders. Use a spreadsheet to plot the cost curves (annual holding cost, annual ordering cost, and annual total cost) on the vertical axis, and the order quantity on the horizontal axis.

   Annual requirements (R) = 5,000 units
   Setup cost (S)   = $100 per order
   Holding rate (k)   = 20 percent
   Unit cost (C)   = $20 per unit
   Lead time (LT)   = 6 days
   Number of days per year = 360 days

2. Given the following information, compute the economic order quantity, annual holding cost, annual ordering cost, and annual total cost.

   Annual requirements (R) = 50,000 units
   Setup cost (S)   = $150 per order
   Holding rate (k)   = 15 percent
   Unit cost (C)   = $100 per unit

3. Given the following inventory information, perform an ABC analysis.

Item Number	Annual Usage	Unit Cost ($)
2215	8,000	1.50
6128	1,000	32.00
3651	3,500	4.00
8921	2,000	5.50
2650	500	70.00
1285	100	6.00
4122	4,000	0.25
5596	1,500	1.00
6840	6,500	5.25
9538	800	0.75

4. Stan and Laurie's Surf Shop has an annual demand for 800 surfboards. Their purchasing cost for each board is $200. It costs about $50 to place an order, and the holding cost runs approximately 35 percent of the unit cost. If surfboards are ordered in quantities of at least 200, Stan and Laurie can get a 7 percent discount. Should they order 200 boards at a time and get the discount?

References

Chase, R. B., N. J. Aquilano, and F. R. Jacobs. *Production and Operations Management: Manufacturing and Services,* 8th ed. Boston: Irwin-McGraw-Hill, 1998.

Fogarty, D. W., J. H. Blackstone, and T. R. Hoffmann. *Production and Inventory Management,* 2d ed. Cincinnati: South-Western, 1991.

Hax, A., and D. Candea. *Production and Inventory Management.* Englewood Cliffs, N.J.: Prentice-Hall, 1984.

Krajewski, L. J., and L. P. Ritzman. *Operations Management: Strategy and Analysis,* 5th ed. Reading, Mass.: Addison-Wesley, 1999.

Vollmann, T. E., W. L. Berry, and D. C. Whybark. *Manufacturing Planning and Control Systems,* 3d ed. Burr Ridge, Ill.: Irwin, 1992.

Notes

1. M. D. Ford, "Hey, It Worked at the Shoe Factory!" *APICS—The Performance Advantage* 12, no. 8 (September 2002): 80.

2. 30 September 2002; available from http://www.walmartstores.com

3. Anonymous, "Configure This: Managing the Complexity of Truck Product Variations," *APICS—The Performance Advantage* 12, no. 8 (September 2002): 34–36.

4. D. W. Fogarty, J. H. Blackstone, and T. R. Hoffmann, *Production and Inventory Management,* 2d ed. (Cincinnati: South-Western, 1991).

5. 3 November 2002; available from http://www.egarrett.com

6. Anonymous, "Getting a Boost from SRM," *APICS—The Performance Advantage* 12, no. 8 (September 2002): 46, 48.

7. R. B. Chase, N. J. Aquilano, and F. R. Jacobs, *Production and Operations Management: Manufacturing and Services,* 8th ed. (Boston: Irwin-McGraw-Hill, 1998).

Chapter 7:

ENTERPRISE RESOURCE PLANNING SYSTEMS

Enterprise resource planning software, or ERP, doesn't live up to its acronym. Forget about planning—it doesn't do that—and forget about resource, a throwaway term. But remember the enterprise part. This is ERP's true ambition. It attempts to integrate all departments and functions across a company to create a single software program that runs off one database.[1]

Learning Objectives

After completing this chapter, you should be able to

- Describe an ERP system.
- Understand the limitations of legacy MRP systems.
- Understand why manufacturers and service firms are migrating from legacy MRP systems to integrated ERP systems.
- Understand the advantages and disadvantages of ERP systems.
- Describe the various modules of an integrated ERP system.
- Understand best-of-breed versus single integrator ERP implementations.
- Understand why many ERP implementations fail.
- Understand how an integrated ERP system works.

Chapter Outline

SUPPLY CHAIN MANAGEMENT IN ACTION   *Raytheon Aircraft Company*

The Raytheon Aircraft Company (RAC), a division of the Raytheon Company, is headquartered in Wichita, Kansas. RAC manufactures more than 600 business and special mission aircraft annually at its manufacturing facilities in Wichita and Salina, Kansas, and Little Rock, Arkansas. The company's products include the single-engine Bonanza series, the Beech King turboprop, the Hawker 800XP and Beech jet 400A business jets, and the TIA Jayhawk special mission aircraft. RAC also maintains a worldwide network of service facilities, including Raytheon Travel Air, Raytheon Aircraft Services, Raytheon Aerospace, and Raytheon Part Inventory, to serve its customers. RAC hired more than 11,000 employees and had record sales of $3.2 billion in 2000.

In the mid-1990s, RAC introduced a new twin jet engine aircraft featuring a composite body with aluminum alloy wings. The company relied on its complex group of thirty-year-old legacy software systems for coordinating its manufacturing planning and control functions. Unfortunately, the legacy systems were unable to efficiently and effectively integrate its purchasing, manufacturing, sales, customer support, financials, and other functional areas.

RAC management decided to replace its legacy systems with a completely new enterprise resource planning (ERP) system that would allow the company to utilize the Internet to manage its supply chain activities, including e-commerce capabilities. An important criterion was to implement an off-the-shelf solution to minimize cost. Eventually, RAC implemented SAP's R/3 system on Sun clustered servers running under the UNIX operating system.

Complete implementation of the new ERP system was expected to take sixteen months, including a six-month testing period. The company was committed to training its employees for the transition. In January 2000, RAC discontinued the old legacy MRP systems and switched over to SAP's R/3 system for handling its finance, manufacturing, sales, distribution, tooling, human resources, service management, Web site, and other related functions across the entire organization.

An immediate important benefit of the newly implemented ERP system was that excess queue time in the bills of materials of the legacy systems was removed, thus resulting in a two-month reduction in the cycle time for its make-to-stock fabrication facilities. The new system also transformed the company's push material flows to a pull system. However, the most significant benefit was the capability of the new ERP system in consolidating its various databases into a single central database that could be accessed in real time by the entire organization.

SAP's Internet Transaction Server also allowed RAC to establish a robust e-commerce presence. Indeed, since the implementation of the new ERP system, RAC sold more than 80 percent of its spare parts on the Internet. The server also allowed customers to submit warranty claims and return parts on the Internet. RAC's top management felt that the new ERP system was very effective and planned to expand the system to include its remote service facilities.[2]

Introduction

For over four decades, a material requirements planning (MRP) system was the first choice among manufacturing firms in the United States for planning and managing their purchasing, production, and inventories. Material requirements planning uses the master production schedule (MPS), bills of material (BOM), and inventory status to compute planned order releases for lower-level materials, components, and subassemblies. For items manufactured in-house, planned order releases are transmitted to the shop floor, whereas for purchased items, planned order releases are transmitted to the suppliers directly or via the purchasing department. To improve the efficiency and effectiveness of the production planning system, many manufacturers have utilized **electronic data interchange (EDI)** to relay planned order releases to their suppliers. This simple information system has worked well for coordinating internal production, as well as purchasing.

By the end of the twentieth century however, the U.S. business environment was rapidly changing. Many savvy manufacturers and service providers were building multiplant international sites, either to take advantage of cheaper raw materials and labor or to expand their market. Thus, business executives found themselves spending more time dealing with international subcontractors using different currencies and languages among varying political environments. The need to access real-time information on customers' requirements, production levels and available capacities, company-wide inventory levels, and plants capable of meeting current order requirements increased. The existing material requirements planning systems simply could not handle these added tasks.

To fully coordinate the information requirements for purchasing, planning, scheduling, and distribution of an organization operating in a complex global environment, an *enterprise-wide* information system was needed. Thus, enterprise resource planning (ERP) systems that operated from a single database were engineered to replace the older legacy MRP systems.

The Development of Legacy Materials Requirement Planning Systems

The term **legacy MRP system** is a broad label used to describe an older information system that usually works at an operational level to schedule production within an organization. Many legacy systems were implemented in the 1960s, 1970s, and 1980s and subjected to extensive modifications as requirements changed over the years. Today, these systems have lasted beyond their originally intended life span. The continuous modifications of these systems made them complex and cumbersome to work with, especially when considering they were not designed to be user friendly in the first place. Legacy systems were designed to perform a very specific operational function and were programmed as independent entities with little regard for meeting requirements or coordinating with other functional areas. Communication between legacy systems is often limited, and visibility across functional areas is severely restricted. Legacy systems were implemented to gather data for transactional purposes and, thus, lacked any analytical capabilities.

The development of the legacy system can be traced back to the evolution of the MRP system, the closed-loop MRP system, and the manufacturing resource planning (MRP II) system. These terms are briefly reviewed in the following sections.

Materials Requirement Planning

Materials requirement planning was the initial software development in manufacturing information systems. MRP systems use information from bills of material, master production schedules, and on-hand inventories to compute time-phased planned order releases of dependent demand items. MRP links the internal operations of an organization, such as purchasing, production, inventory control and material planning, to improve purchasing, production, and delivery performance. MRP systems do not provide feedback information, nor do they analyze the impact of changes in production levels on financial results. MRP systems were discussed in detail in Chapter 6.

The development of closed-loop MRP was a natural extension of the MRP system. It was an attempt to further develop the MRP into a formal and explicit manufacturing planning and control system by adding capacity requirements planning and feedback to describe the progress of orders being manufactured. Today, the originally developed MRP is a part of the closed-loop MRP system.

Figure 7.1	**MRP II System**

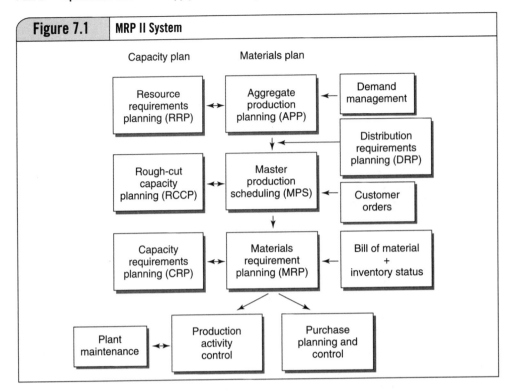

Manufacturing Resource Planning

Manufacturing resource planning (MRP-II) was the next development in MRP and was an outgrowth of the closed-loop MRP system. Business and sales plans were incorporated, and a financial function was added to link financial management to operations, marketing, and other functional areas. The concept of manufacturing resource planning was that the information system should link internal operations to the financial function to provide management with up-to-date data, including sales, purchasing, production, inventory, and cash flow. It should also be able to perform "what-if" analyses as internal and external conditions change. For example, MRP-II enables the firm to determine the impact on profit and cash flow if the firm is only able to fill 85 percent of its orders due to late deliveries of raw materials. MRP-II is an explicit and formal manufacturing information system that integrates the internal functions of an organization, enabling it to coordinate manufacturing plans with sales, while providing management with essential accounting and financial information. A typical MRP-II system is illustrated in Figure 7.1.

Today, manufacturing resource planning has further evolved to include other functional areas of the organization. Although it synchronizes an organization's information systems and provides insight into the implications of aggregate production plans, master production schedules, capacities, materials plans, and sales, it primarily focuses on one unit's internal operations. It lacks the capability to link the many operations of an organization's foreign branches with its headquarters. It also lacks the capability to directly interface with external supply chain members, such as suppliers and customers. Thus, enterprise-wide information systems began to be developed for this reason.

The Development of Enterprise Resource Planning Systems

While traditional or legacy MRP systems continue to be used and modified to include other functional areas of an organization, the emergence and growth of supply chain management, e-commerce, and global operations have created the need to exchange information directly with

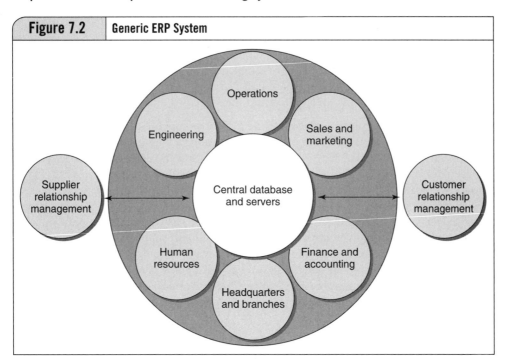

Figure 7.2 | **Generic ERP System**

suppliers, customers, and foreign branches of organizations. The concept of the manufacturing information system thus evolved to directly connect all functional areas and operations of an organization and, in some cases, its suppliers and customers via a common software infrastructure and database. This type of manufacturing information system is now commonly referred to as ERP.

The typical ERP system is an umbrella system that ties together a variety of specialized systems, such as production and inventory planning, purchasing, logistics, human resources, finance, accounting, customer relationship management, and supplier relationship management. However, exactly what is tied together varies on a case-by-case basis, based on the vendor and the selected system. Figure 7.2 illustrates a generic enterprise resource planning system, where a common centralized database and software infrastructure are used to drive a firm's information systems and to link the operations of its branches with the firm's headquarters.

Enterprise resource planning is a broadly used industrial term to describe the multimodule application software for managing an enterprise's suppliers, customers, and functional activities. Initially, ERP software focused on integrating the internal business activities of a multifacility organization, or *enterprise,* to ensure that it was operating under the same information system. With the onset of supply chain management, ERP vendors today are designing their products to include the capabilities of managing suppliers and customers. For example, ERP enables an organization to deal directly with suppliers to assess the availability of their resources, as if they are an external process of the firm. Similarly, ERP also allows business customers to access the firm's inventory information and manufacturing and delivery schedules directly.

ERP utilizes the idea of a centralized and shared database system to tie the entire organization together, as opposed to the traditional legacy MRP system that uses multiple databases and interfaces that frequently result in duplicate and inconsistent information across different branches or even departments within an organization. With ERP, information is entered once at the source and made available to all users. It eliminates the inconsistency and incompatibility created when different functional areas use different systems with overlapping data. The legacy MRP system typically utilizes multiple software packages and databases for different functional areas. Usually, each functional area implements its information system based on its unique needs, with very little input or coordination from the other functional areas. The different packages within an organization often are incompatible with each other and prevent transactions from taking place directly between systems. The multiple databases also cause the same information to be stored in multiple locations; thus, multiple entries of the same data are required. This need to enter the same data repeatedly is a major cause of inconsistency in database management. For example, a customer, ATV Inc., may be entered as ATV Inc. in one database and ATV Incorporated in another database. From an information system's perspective, ATV Inc. and ATV Incorporated are two distinct customers.

With a shared centralized database system, ERP is capable of automating business processes rapidly and accurately. For example, when taking a sales order, a sales agent has all the necessary information of the customer (for example, the credit history, rating, and limit from the finance and accounting module), the company's production and inventory levels (from the operations module), and the delivery schedule (from the sales and marketing module) to complete the sale. After the sale is confirmed and entered into the centralized database, other supply chain partners affected by the transaction can directly utilize the same information system to take appropriate proactive actions. For example, suppliers can find out the production schedules planned by upstream supply chain members so that appropriate raw materials and components can be produced accordingly to support sales. Similarly, downstream companies can also utilize the same information system and database to access delivery schedules of raw materials and components ordered from their upstream supply chain members.

Thus, ERP integrates the internal operations of an enterprise with a common software platform and centralized database system. It also ties together supply chain members through the same information system. ERP provides the mechanism for supply chain members to efficiently share information so that scarce resources can be fully utilized to meet demand, while minimizing supply chain inventories. Production changes and other modifications can also be executed efficiently and quickly to minimize delivery lead times. Example 7.1 illustrates a typical ERP transaction.

The Rapid Growth of Enterprise Resource Planning Systems

The use of ERP systems has gradually spread from manufacturing to the service sector and has become commonly used in many university classrooms. Many universities in the United States, for instance, have cooperated with major ERP software providers to integrate ERP training into their business curricula. There are many reasons, some of which are discussed in the following information, that have contributed to the rapid growth of ERP since the early 1990s.

At the turn of the century, many firms were uncertain as to how the *Year 2000 Millennium Bug* or Y2K bug (conversion of the year from 1999 to 2000) would affect their information systems. Most information systems installed were programmed to use the last two digits of the year (the year 1998 would be shown as 98). Using the same logic, the year 2000 would be recorded as 00, which is ninety-eight years prior to 1998. This could adversely affect time-sensitive programming logic (for example, interest calculations). In addition, the legacy MRP systems had been modified so extensively over the years that the many layers of program codes made it too complex and redundant to correctly assess the true impact of Y2K. The extensive modifications to the legacy systems had also made them too expensive to maintain. Thus, many savvy business managers took a proactive approach to set aside sufficient budgetary funds to replace their legacy MRP systems with the more efficient ERP systems to reduce costs and deal with the Y2K problem.

The rapid development of computer and information technology over the last two decades has also contributed positively to the growth of ERP. Tasks that were previously limited to mainframe computers are today easily implemented on servers and desktop computers that cost only a fraction of the capital investment previously needed. Information systems that were previously off limits are now accessible to many smaller organizations.

EXAMPLE 7.1   A hypothetical ERP transaction

The following example demonstrates a hypothetical ERP transaction for the ATV Corporation (as discussed in Chapter 6). The ATV Corporation makes three models of all-terrain vehicles—Model A, Model B, and Model C. Model A uses a four-liter engine, Model B uses a five-liter engine, and Model C uses a six-liter engine. The corporation is headquartered in the United States with manufacturing facilities in the United States and Mexico. ATV sells its products in the United States, Canada, and Mexico. Its sales representatives make quarterly visits to customers to take sales orders and provide necessary customer services. The following steps describe a sales transaction by a sales rep during a typical visit to a retail customer in Canada. We assume here that the retailer ordered 100 units of Model A and 150 units of Model B, to be delivered within thirty days.

1. *Ordering*

    The field sales representative takes the order of 100 units of Model A and 150 units of Model B. Using the Internet, the sales rep accesses the sales and marketing module of the ERP system at the U.S. headquarters to check the price and other related information, such as quantity discounts, guarantees, and rebates. The sales rep also accesses the customer's credit history and rating from the finance and accounting module.

2. *Availability*

    Simultaneously, the ERP system checks the inventory status and the available-to-promise quantities of its manufacturing facilities in the United States and Mexico and notifies the sales rep whether the order can be filled on time. The sales rep finds that the Mexico factory has sufficient inventory to fill the Model A order immediately, while the Model B order can be manufactured in ten days from the U.S. factory. Logistics information shows that shipping from Mexico to Canada takes two weeks, and delivery time from the U.S. factory takes one week. Thus, the entire order is accepted and the factory in Mexico receives instructions to ship 100 units of Model A to Canada immediately. Its inventory status is updated accordingly. An invoice in English will be printed, and the finance and accounting module will be updated to reflect the partial delivery upon shipment of the goods from Mexico.

3. *Manufacturing*

    The operations module immediately schedules the production of 150 units of Model B at the U.S. factory. All dependent demand items and labor necessary to produce 150 units of Model B are scheduled to meet the due date. For items and components manufactured in-house, planned order releases are transmitted to the shop floor. For purchased items, the information is sent to the suppliers.

    The human resource module checks to ensure that there are sufficient workers in the U.S. factory to complete the order. If not, the personnel manager will be notified and part-time or temporary workers may be employed.

4. *Order Tracking*

    The customer relationship management module allows the customer to access certain parts of ATV Corporation's ERP system to track the status of its order. Thus, the customer knows the exact status of the order and its shipping schedule.

According to a report from AMR Research,[3] despite the slowdown in the economy, companies still invested more than $54 billion implementing ERP systems between 2000 and 2003. This figure was expected to grow to $64 billion over the next four years. AMR Research claimed that ERP would remain to be the key building block of global business management information systems over the next five years. As the business environment continues to change, ERP is evolving to become more flexible to adapt to mergers and acquisitions and to provide more real-time monitoring and response. Using ERP in a small manufacturing business is illustrated in the e-Business Connection box.

e-BUSINESS CONNECTION
ERP AT HICKS PLASTICS, INC.

Hicks Plastics, Inc.,[4] was founded in 1988 by Carl Hicks, a pioneer in the use of thermoplastic components in automotive manufacturing. Hicks Plastics, Inc., is QS 9000 certified and owns two manufacturing facilities in Macomb Township, Michigan. The company employs more than 100 employees, with annual sales of approximately $20 million. It is a supplier specializing in manufacturing plastics components, such as headlights, taillights, and interior lighting assemblies, for the automotive industry.

Under Mr. Hicks's leadership, the company grew from a tiny job shop into a mid-sized contract manufacturer. Based on his extensive experience, Carl knew that the automotive industry was very volatile and easily affected by a sluggish economy. Thus, he marketed to a diverse customer base to expand his business in other industries, such as marine products, medical, consumer electronics, and sporting goods, to sustain a steady growth for the company.

As Hicks Plastics, Inc., continued to grow, it struggled to fully utilize its manufacturing capacity to meet demand and delivery due dates. Despite its rapid growth from a tiny job shop to a multiplant enterprise over the last decade, Hicks Plastics used relatively primitive management information systems. For example, manufacturing jobs were scheduled on spreadsheets, whereas accounting and sales were maintained on a small bookkeeping program. An independent audit revealed that the company was only utilizing 60 percent of its capacity, due to its inabilities to integrate processes and manage resources. The existing information system was severely lacking and unable to provide visibility for integrating manufacturing and financial operations.

The management team realized that they needed to replace the outdated information system with an ERP system to tie together manufacturing, financials, and supply chain management processes. A cross-functional ERP selection team with representatives from the accounting, production, quality, and warehouse departments was assembled to identify the best ERP software for the company. The team identified five key objectives of the new ERP system. These objectives were (1) to increase capacity utilization, (2) to increase on-time deliveries, (3) to reduce inventory, (4) to more efficiently use resources, and (5) to provide accurate accounting information.

The ERP team asked fellow manufacturers for referrals and narrowed down their selections to four possible vendors. Eventually, Hicks Plastics chose the EnterpriseIQ system from IQMS. IQMS is a privately owned company that provides real-time ERP and supply chain software for manufacturing firms. IQMS was founded in 1989 as an enterprise software provider for the plastics industry. Its flagship product, EnterpriseIQ, has evolved into a robust enterprise solution for repetitive manufacturers.

Hicks Plastics' customized implementation plan with IQMS consisted of a combination of classroom training at IQMS training facilities, Internet-based training, and on-site training. The ERP system was successfully implemented within six months. After the implementation of EnterpriseIQ, Hicks Plastics saw its annual sales jump from $7 million in 1998 to more than $15 million in 2001, with an annual projected growth of about 15 percent. Hicks Plastics also documented the following benefits:

- 10 percent annual increase in capacity utilization,
- reduction in inventories and 40 percent increase in inventory turns,
- 15 percent improvement in delivery lead times,
- elimination of late deliveries, and
- a steady decrease in the cost of goods sold.

Implementing Enterprise Resource Planning Systems

ERP systems have continued to evolve, and integration of e-commerce, customer relationship management (CRM), and supplier relationship management (SRM) applications are now considered ERP requirements by most organizations. While many firms believe a well-designed and implemented ERP system can translate into a substantial competitive advantage, research analysts and industrial practitioners are still debating the usefulness of ERP, as well as the advantages and disadvantages of using a **best-of-breed solution** versus a **single integrator solution.**

The best-of-breed solution picks the best application or module for each individual function in the supply chain (thus, best of breed). The resulting system includes several different applications that must be integrated to work as a single coordinated system to achieve the global scope required of the ERP. A major criticism of the best-of-breed solution is that multiple databases may have to be used to link the multiple applications obtained from different vendors. This may severely affect the ability of the system to update the databases rapidly and efficiently—a very similar problem of the legacy MRP systems.

The single integrator approach picks all the desired applications from a single vendor for the ERP system. Obvious advantages are that all of the applications should work well together and getting the system up and running should be easier. On the other hand, as information technology continues to evolve and as competition increases in the ERP software market, ERP vendors are designing their products to be more compatible with each other. Therefore, implementing an ERP system using the best-of-breed solution approach is becoming easier. Let us look at a few examples:

- Bookham Technology,[5] an integrated optical component firm based in the United Kingdom with sales offices in the United States, the United Kingdom, France, Italy, Japan, and China, recently started a £2 million project to improve its information systems to better link its customers, partners, and employees together. The new project was designed to replace its seven legacy business systems with a single global enterprise solution. Bookham Technology applied the single integrator approach to ERP by selecting an SAP-packaged solution.

- General Motors Corp.[6] was confronted with the problem of how to implement ERP applications while utilizing several software providers they felt had the best capabilities for the automobile industry. So, GM utilized the best-of-breed ERP implementation approach by selecting the financials and indirect materials modules from SAP and a human resources module from PeopleSoft. GM then linked their SAP and PeopleSoft applications using integration software from TSI International Software Ltd.

Implementing an ERP system has been proven to be a real challenge for many companies. Most ERP systems are written based on the best practices of selected firms. Thus, a condition required for implementation of the system is that the user's business processes must conform to the approaches used in the software logic. These processes can be significantly different from those currently used within the company. Adapting a company's business processes to conform to a software program is a radical departure from the conventional business practice of requiring the software to be designed around the business processes.

Two primary requirements of successful implementation of ERP are computer support and accurate, realistic inputs. Instead of complete implementation of the entire system at once, some firms choose to implement only those applications or modules that are absolutely critical to operations at that time. Additional modules are then added in a preplanned second phase. This ensures that the system can be implemented as quickly as possible while minimizing interruption of the existing system. However, many implementations have still failed due to a variety of reasons. Some of the more common reasons for failed ERP implementations follow:

- *Lack of top management commitment:* While management may be willing to set aside sufficient funds to implement a new ERP system, it may not take an active role in providing ongoing encouragement during the implementation process. Often, this leads users to revert to the old processes or systems because of their lack of knowledge and interest to learn the capabilities of the new ERP system.

- *Lack of adequate resources:* Implementing a new ERP system is a long-term commitment requiring substantial capital investment. Although the cost has become more affordable due to the rapid advent of computer technology, full implementation may still be out of reach for many small organizations. In addition, small firms may not have the necessary workforce and expertise to implement the complex system.

- *Lack of proper training:* Many employees may already be familiar with their legacy MRP systems. Thus, when a new ERP system is implemented, top management may assume that users are already adequately prepared and underestimate the training required to get the new system up and running. Lack of financial resources can also reduce the amount of training available for its workforce.

- *Lack of communication:* Lack of communication within an organization and/or between the firm and its ERP software provider can also be a major hindrance for successful implementation. Lack of communication usually results in the wrong specifications and requirements being implemented.

- *Incompatible system environment:* In certain cases, the firm's environment does not give ERP a distinct advantage over other systems. For example, there is no distinct advantage for a small family-owned used car dealer in a small town to implement an expensive new ERP system.

The Global Perspective box illustrates the use and convenience of e-learning when training global users of ERP systems.

Advantages and Disadvantages of Enterprise Resource Planning Systems

When properly installed and operating, an ERP system can provide a firm and its supply chains with a significant competitive advantage, which can fully justify the investments of time and money in ERP. A fully functional ERP system is capable of enhancing the firm's capability to fully utilize capacity, accurately schedule production, reduce inventory, meet delivery due dates, and enhance the efficiency and effectiveness of the supply chain. Let us look at some specific advantages and disadvantages.

Enterprise Resource Planning System Advantages

As mentioned earlier, the primary advantage of ERP over the legacy MRP systems is that ERP uses a single database and a common software infrastructure to provide a broader scope and up-to-date information, enabling management to make better decisions that can benefit the entire supply chain. ERP is also fairly robust in providing real-time information and, thus, is able to communicate information about operational changes to supply chain members with

Global Perspective

e-LEARNING AND ERP

Implementing an ERP software system is inherently a very complex task that involves ongoing training of employees to use the new system. However, the traditional methods of ERP training and education present many problems. Traditionally, most ERP classes are very structured and normally last from two days to two weeks per session. Each user can be expected to attend at least a couple of sessions to gain sufficient knowledge to run the new ERP application. Attending a traditional ERP training session posts many challenges to both the employees and the organization. For example, training is usually available at a specific time and location and employees must attend the class whether it is convenient or not. In addition, employers must incur substantial costs, including transportation, lodging, and allowances, for sending employees to training. Most classes also require a minimum number of students.

A new form of training, **e-learning,**[7] has emerged. e-Learning is the electronic delivery of training materials and interactions with students over the Internet. It has also been referred to as Web-based training, distance learning, and Internet-based training. e-Learning enables trainees to sign on to a class without the restriction of time, distance, and classroom availability.

Manufacturing companies such as Gateway, Dell, Northrop Grumman, Magee Rieter, and L'OREAL are utilizing e-learning to reduce training costs and to maximize its impact. Similarly, ERP software companies like SAP, Oracle, PeopleSoft, Baan, and J. D. Edwards (recently acquired by PeopleSoft) have also adopted e-learning for delivering parts of their training. A unique feature of e-learning is that it is *interactive.* That is, students can ask questions at remote locations and the instructor can respond almost instantaneously through virtual chats or e-mails. e-Learning reduces travel time, increases access to experts, provides on-demand education, and enables employees to learn at their own pace, regardless of their geographical locations.

In 1998, SAP began to use e-learning to train its worldwide employees in the various ERP modules that it offered. Students simply needed to log in to the class using an Internet browser and were able to interact with the instructor. Instructors are able to administer tests globally over the Internet. e-Learning has enabled SAP to noticeably reduce its costs for supplying training to an international client base. A very useful e-learning feature is application sharing, which allows the instructor to totally control the applications on students' computers. This enables the instructor to deliver training sessions to any part of the world.

Magee Rieter Automotive Systems of Bloomsburg, Pennsylvania, is a large manufacturer of carpets and other textile products for the automotive industry. The company uses a fully integrated ERP system to control almost every facet of its manufacturing environment. Data entry errors can severely affect the accuracy of the ERP system. Thus, top management at Magee Rieter Automotive Systems wanted to ensure that its employees were property trained in using the ERP system. In spring 2001, the company worked with a local university to utilize e-learning to deliver training materials to its employees.

With the rapid development of information technology, especially in the area of instructor and student real-time interactions, e-learning is becoming a very popular, efficient, and effective method of delivering training sessions. Some specific benefits of e-learning follow:

- The need to travel to the training location is eliminated. Students from different parts of the world can attend the same training session at their own pace. Thus, travel time and expense can be drastically reduced.

- Training can commence anytime a student signs on. There is no need to wait for other students to sign up for the class. Each student can attend the same training on a different time schedule.

- Learning can be self-paced and adapted to each student's learning strengths and weaknesses.

- Training is more consistent because each student goes through the same materials.

little delay. ERP systems are also designed to take advantage of Internet technology. Thus, users are able to share information and communicate via the Internet.

ERP helps organizations reduce supply chain inventories due to the added visibility throughout the entire supply chain. It enables the supply, manufacturing, and logistics processes to flow smoothly by providing visibility of the order fulfillment process throughout the supply chain. **Supply chain visibility** leads to reductions of the bullwhip effect (the buildup of supply chain safety stock inventories) and helps supply chain members to better plan production and end-product deliveries to customers.

ERP systems also help organizations to standardize manufacturing processes. Manufacturing firms often find that multiple business units across the company make the same product using different processes and information systems. ERP systems enable the firm to automate some of the steps of a manufacturing process. Process standardization eliminates redundant resources and increases productivity.

ERP enables an organization, especially a multi-business-unit enterprise, to efficiently track employees' time and performance and to communicate with them via a standardized method. Performance can be monitored across the entire organization using the same measurements and standards. The use of a single software platform and database also allows the ERP system to integrate financial, production, supply, and customer order information. By having this information in one software system rather than scattered among many different systems that potentially cannot communicate with one another, companies can keep track of materials, orders, and financial status efficiently and coordinate manufacturing, inventory, and shipping among many different locations and business units at the same time.

In a formalized attempt to determine the benefits of ERP systems, Accenture Institute for Strategic Change[8] surveyed 163 organizations that had implemented ERP systems. Accenture wanted to determine the specific up-front benefits firms wanted to achieve by implementing ERP systems, as well as the actual outcomes achieved after implementation. The ten most frequently cited benefits targeted by the firms prior to the actual implementation of the ERP systems are listed in Table 7.1 in descending order. The most commonly targeted benefit was the opportunity for *better managerial decision making.* However, after the ERP systems were implemented, responding firms realized that the actual benefits achieved, while in many cases impressive, did not necessarily match up with what originally had been targeted. For example, *improved financial management* was the most often cited after-implementation benefit. This has led firms in some cases to reevaluate and revise their ERP systems.

Table 7.1	ERP Benefits		
ERP Benefits		**Targeted**	**Achieved**
Better managerial decision making		1	3
Improved financial management		2	1
Improved customer service and retention		3	8
Ease of expansion/growth and increased flexibility		4	5
Faster, more accurate transactions		5	2
Head count reduction		6	9
Cycle time reduction		7	7
Improved inventory and asset management		8	4
Fewer physical resources and improved logistics		9	6
Increased revenue		10	10

Enterprise Resource Planning System Disadvantages

While it is obvious from Table 7.1 that the benefits of ERP systems can be impressive, ERP is not without shortcomings. For example, a substantial capital investment is needed to implement the system. Considerable time and money must be set aside to evaluate ERP software applications and their suppliers, to purchase the necessary hardware and software, and then to train employees to operate the new system. A recent study[9] revealed that the average total cost of ERP ownership was $15 million, with the highest at $300 million and the lowest at $400,000. Total cost of ERP ownership includes hardware, software, professional services, and internal staff costs. ERP is also very complex and has proven difficult to implement.

However, the primary criticism of ERP is that the software is designed around a specific business model based on specific business processes. Although business processes are usually adopted based on best practices in the industry, the adopting firm must change its business model and associated processes to fit the built-in business model designed into the ERP system. Thus, the adopting firm must restructure its processes to be compatible with the new ERP system. This has resulted in a very unusual situation where a software system determines the business practices and processes a firm should implement, instead of designing the software to support existing business practices and processes.

Enterprise Resource Planning Software Applications

ERP systems typically consist of many modules that are linked together to access and share the same database. Each module performs different functions within the organization and is designed so that it can be installed on its own or with a combination of other modules. Most ERP software providers design their products to be compatible with their competitors' products, so that modules from different providers can be combined. Integration of customer relationship management, supplier relationship management, and e-procurement modules into the ERP system is now becoming relatively commonplace. Although each ERP software provider configures its products differently from its competitors, some common modules of ERP systems are described here:

- *Accounting and finance:* This module assists an organization in maintaining financial control and accountability. It tracks accounting and financial information such as revenues, costs, assets, liabilities, and other accounting and financial information of the company. It is also capable of generating routine and advanced accounting and financial reports, product costing, budgeting, and analysis.

- *Customer relationship management:* This module provides the capability to manage customers. It enables collaboration between the organization and its customers by providing relevant, personalized, and up-to-date information. It also enables customers to track sales orders. The customer relationship management module enables the user to communicate effectively with existing customers and acquire new customers through sales automation and partner relationship management. Finally, it allows the firm to segment its customers and design customized promotions appealing to each customer segment.

- *Human resource management:* It assists an organization to plan, develop, and control its human resources. It allows the firm to deploy the right people to support its overall strategic goals and to plan the optimal workforce levels based on production levels.

- *Manufacturing:* It schedules materials and tracks production, capacity, and the flow of goods through the manufacturing process. It may even include the capability for quality planning, inspection, and certifications.

- *Supplier relationship management:* This module provides the capability to manage all types of suppliers. It automates processes and enables the firm to more effectively collaborate with all its suppliers corporate-wide. It also monitors supplier performance and tracks delivery of goods purchased. It enables the user to effectively manage business processes through real-time collaboration during design, production, and distribution planning with suppliers. Supplier relationship management adds value to the supply chain by reducing supply chain inventory, decreasing delivery lead times, and improving inventory turns while increasing customer satisfaction.

- *Supply chain management:* This module handles the planning, execution, and control of activities involved in a supply chain. It assists the firm to strengthen its supply chain networks to improve delivery performance. It may cover various logistics functions, including transportation, warehousing, and inventory management. In this context, supply chain management refers to logistics management in which the focus is the distribution of finished goods. The supply chain management module creates value by allowing the user to optimize its internal and external supply chains. Effective supply chain management requires the organization to have comprehensive management information systems to synchronize plans with customers and suppliers, collaborate in real time, execute plans, handle changes, and measure supply chain performance.

ERP systems have continued to evolve in the twenty-first century. One of the latest developments is the integration of e-business capabilities to use the Internet to conduct business transactions, such as sales, purchasing, inventory management, and customer service. Customers and suppliers are demanding access to certain information, such as order status, inventory levels, and invoice reconciliation through the ERP system. As information technology continues to become more complex and sophisticated, ERP software providers continue to add new functions and capabilities to their systems. Let us look now at several of the more popular ERP software providers.

Enterprise Resource Planning Software Providers

There are hundreds of ERP software providers, each targeting a specific market segment and industry type. Thus, choosing an appropriate ERP software package can be a very challenging task. SAP, Oracle, PeopleSoft, J. D. Edwards, and Baan are among the most popular ERP providers. These companies are profiled in the following sections. (At the time this text was published, there appeared to be a consolidation trend occurring in this industry. On July 18, 2003, PeopleSoft acquired J. D. Edwards; and on July 24, 2003, Oracle filed an amended offer with the SEC to purchase PeopleSoft.) In addition to these mainstream ERP software systems, there are also many specialized software companies in the business of producing add-on software to provide specific functions or interact with preexisting legacy systems.

SAP AG

SAP AG,[10] a German firm, is the world's leading ERP software provider and the world's third-largest software provider. Its flagship product is known as R/3. More than 17,500 organizations in 120 countries have used its products—including major multinational firms such as Baxter Healthcare, Chevron, Colgate-Palmolive, Exxon, IBM, and Microsoft. Five former IBM system engineers founded SAP in 1972. The company employs about 28,000 people in more than fifty countries. It is headquartered in Walldorf, Germany, with U.S. operations headquartered in Newtown Square, Pennsylvania.

SAP launched its first version of the ERP software, known as R/1, in 1973 and subsequently released its R/2 software in 1979. The now famous R/3 software was first released in 1992. R/3 has had a remarkable acceptance among ERP users, and it has reigned as the dominant ERP product for almost a decade. An Internet-enabled version of R/3, Release 3.1, was launched in 1996 to take advantage of Internet technology. In the same year, SAP expanded its market segment to include other business functions to its software applications by launching customer relationship management and supply chain management applications. It also began to develop industry-specific software.

The core functions in R/3 include financial accounting, asset accounting, cash management, fund management, personnel administration and payroll, investment management, plant maintenance, treasury, real estate management, materials management, production planning, logistics, sales and distribution, quality management, service management, plant management, human resources, product life cycle, and workflow. Other SAP offerings include business warehouse, customer relationship management, advanced planner and optimizer, ABAP programming language, and strategic enterprise management.

In 1995, SAP started to form an education alliance program with universities. Currently, there are over 400 members in the SAP education alliance program around the world, with more than 100 members in the United States. A primary goal of the SAP education alliance is to promote the teaching and understanding of integrated business processes and e-business, particularly in the use of SAP's products.

In early 2003, SAP introduced a new product configuration known as *mySAP ERP*. mySAP ERP offers an additional alternative for new customers and existing SAP users. In addition to offering a very competitive set of traditional ERP functions, mySAP ERP also includes support for corporate services, such as real estate management and travel management. The software features extensive business intelligence and strategic planning capabilities, a full portal infrastructure, and excellent e-business and integration capabilities. mySAP ERP is a very comprehensive product, and it is capable of replacing most legacy systems to provide a foundation for future extensions.

One of SAP's latest product offerings is the *mySAP Business Suite*, a family of business solutions, and an integration and application platform. mySAP Business Suite includes the following modules: ERP, Enterprise Portal, Supply Chain Management, Customer Relationship Management, Supplier Relationship Management, Product Life Cycle Management, Marketplace, Business Intelligence, Financials, Human Resources, Mobile Business, NetWeaver, and Industrial Solutions. It consists of twenty-three different industry-specific applications, including the aerospace and defense, automobile, banking, chemical, consumer products, health-care, mining, and pharmaceuticals industries.

Oracle

The Oracle Corporation[11] was founded in the late 1970s by Larry Ellison, Bob Miner, and Ed Oates. The focus of the company has been to provide business applications that utilize relational databases for storing information. Oracle technology is used in nearly every industry around the world and in almost all Fortune 100 companies. Today, Oracle continues to be the world's leading supplier of information management software. It is the world's second-largest independent software company, after Microsoft. However, it is ranked behind SAP in the sales of ERP applications. Oracle was one of the first software companies to develop and deploy 100 percent Internet-enabled enterprise software across its entire product line. Today, Oracle serves over 13,000 customers running its applications.

Oracle's product strategy focuses on five fundamental principles, that is, globalization, simplification, standardization, automation, and innovation. The company offers five comprehensive product lines: Oracle9i Database, Oracle9i e-Business Suite, Oracle9i Application Server, Oracle9i Collaboration Suite, and Oracle9i Developer Suite.

The Oracle e-Business Suite offers solutions in product life cycle management, supply chain planning, procurement, manufacturing resource management, and order fulfillment. For example, firms can track purchases against contracts, map purchasing policies to streamline the procure-to-pay process, match invoices to purchase orders and use electronic fund transfers to pay invoices, and allow their suppliers to review purchase agreements, track inventories, verify receipts, and generate invoices.

PeopleSoft

PeopleSoft, Inc.,[12] headquartered in Pleasanton, California, was founded by Dave Duffield and Ken Morris in 1987. The primary focus of the company has been to build client/server business applications instead of focusing on applications for the traditional mainframe computers. PeopleSoft's first product was a human resources application on a client-server platform introduced in 1988. Today, the company is a leader in the human resources application market. PeopleSoft serves customers around the globe, including Analog Devices, Corning, Cybex International, PepsiAmericas, and Sprint.

In 1998, PeopleSoft shifted its product focus to Internet-based business applications. The company halted development of all non-Internet applications and directed the bulk of its resources to develop its flagship product, *PeopleSoft 8,* a family of pure Internet-based enterprise business applications. PeopleSoft 8 was introduced in 2000 and includes the following applications: Human Resources Management, Financials, Supply Chain Management, Customer Relationship Management, and Supplier Relationship Management.

J. D. Edwards

J. D. Edwards,[13] founded in 1977 by Jack Thompson, Dan Gregory, and Ed McVaney, is headquartered in Denver, Colorado. It is one of the world's leading developers of agile software solutions, providing cutting-edge, collaborative technology that runs global businesses and integrates processes across multiple systems and supply chain partners. J. D. Edwards designs all of its software solutions to be open, scalable, and flexible, so that they can be integrated with software applications from other vendors. Their business-to-business software applications enable users to engage in collaborative commerce with their customers, suppliers, and other supply chain partners.

J. D. Edwards operates corporate offices in the United States, the United Kingdom, and Singapore to serve customers in North America, Europe, the Middle East, Africa, Latin America, the Caribbean, and Asia Pacific. Its 2002 annual revenues from software licenses and services were approximately $1 billion. It has over 6,500 customers worldwide, which include Boston Properties, Casio Computer Co. Ltd., Chevron Chemical Company, City of Orlando, Swiss Army, and Turner Industries. In August 2003, J. D. Edwards was acquired by PeopleSoft.

The company started as a software designer for small- and medium-sized computers and eventually moved on to focus on the IBM System/38 in the early 1980s. J. D. Edwards was soon recognized as an industry-leading supplier of application software for the widely accepted IBM AS/400 computer, which was designed to replace the System/38.

J. D. Edwards has developed a number of ERP applications, the most recent of which is known as *J. D. Edwards 5,* the company's fifth generation of ERP software. It is a family of modular, Web-enabled, collaborative enterprise software products and services. It was designed to enable customers to match specific software components to specific business requirements. This family of modular enterprise software products and services consists of seven product lines: Enterprise Resource Planning, Supply Chain Management, Customer Relationship Management, Supplier Relationship Management, Business Intelligence, Collaboration and Integration, and Tools and Technology.

Baan

Baan[14] was founded in 1978, with headquarters in the Netherlands and a current workforce of approximately 2,800 employees serving a worldwide customer base. It is part of the Production Management division of Invensys PLC, a global provider of e-business and automation solutions. Baan designed its applications based on a framework of open, flexible, and easy-to-configure components that allow individual applications to be configured to different industry processes.

Baan provides application solutions to more than 15,000 customer sites worldwide, many of which are world leaders in the manufacturing industry, including Del Monte, Volvo, Solectron, Flextronics, Landini, Komatsu, Boeing, and British Aerospace. For example, Komatsu Mining implemented Baan's e-procurement solution to establish a private exchange that successfully reduced purchase order placement lead times from five days to a fraction of a day.

The company's latest comprehensive business solution portfolio, known as the iBaan solutions, includes the following applications: Enterprise, Customer Relationship Management, Product Life Cycle Management, Supply Chain Management, Business Intelligence, OpenWorldX, and Dynamic Enterprise Modeling. Del Monte, for instance, has used iBaan to link its production facilities in the United Kingdom, Belgium, and Luxembourg to streamline and integrate key production, distribution, and financial processes throughout the enterprise.

Summary

The goal of ERP development was to build a single software application that runs off a common shared database to serve the needs of an entire organization, regardless of its units' geographical location and the currency used. Despite its complexity and considerable implementation costs, ERP provides a way to integrate different business functions, of different businesses, on different continents. The integrated approach can have a tremendous payback if companies select the right applications and implement the software correctly. Unfortunately, many companies that have installed these systems have failed to realize all of the initial benefits expected.

Implementing ERP should be viewed as a long term, ongoing project. No matter what resources a firm has initially committed to replacing legacy systems, selecting and implementing ERP applications, and training users, ERP requires ongoing management commitment and resources. As needs and technologies change and new applications are designed, new functionality and business processes will need to be continuously revisited and improved.

Key Terms

best-of-breed solution, 195	electronic data interchange (EDI), 188	single integrator solution, 195
e-learning, 197	legacy MRP system, 189	supply chain visibility, 198

Discussion Questions

1. Why have so many companies rushed to implement ERP over the past five or six years?
2. Describe the limitations of a legacy MRP system.
3. What are the advantages of an ERP system over the legacy MRP system?
4. Explain best-of-breed and single integrator ERP implementations. What are the advantages and disadvantages of the best-of-breed implementation?
5. Explain why many ERP implementations have failed to yield the expected benefits.
6. Briefly describe how an integrated ERP system works.

Internet Questions

1. The Food and Drug Administration (FDA) has started to utilize e-learning to train investigators in specific areas of regulatory responsibility. Go to http://www.fda.gov, click on "About the Food and Drug Administration," and then click on "A Tour of the FDA." Review the e-learning course titled "Tour of the FDA," and write a brief two-page report to summarize the training session. How is this e-learning session different from a traditional classroom lecture?
2. Visit the Web sites of at least three prominent ERP providers and write a brief report of their products. Do their products offer the same configuration or functionality?

3. Visit the Web sites of at least three prominent ERP providers and write a brief report to discuss whether customer relationship management (CRM) and supplier relationship management (SRM) are included in their ERP system.

4. Use the Internet and the American Production and Inventory Control Society's (APICS) Web site to find out how many ERP system providers there are. How would you categorize the list of ERP system providers?

5. Use the Internet to find out if there is any other government agency, besides the FDA, that offers e-learning for the public.

References

Brady, J. A., E. F. Monk, and B. J. Wagner. *Concepts in Enterprise Resources Planning.* Boston: Course Technology, 2001.

Chase, R. B., N. J. Aquilano, and F. R. Jacobs. *Production and Operations Management: Manufacturing and Services,* 8th ed. Boston: Irwin-McGraw-Hill, 1998.

Chopra, S., and P. Meindl. *Supply Chain Management: Strategy, Planning, and Operations.* Upper Saddle River, N. J.: Prentice-Hall, 2001.

Davis, M. M., N. J. Aquilano, and R. B. Chase. *Fundamentals of Operations Management,* 4th ed. Boston: Irwin-McGraw-Hill, 2003.

Duffy, R. J., and M. Gorsage. "Facing SRM and CRM." *Inside Supply Management* 13, issue 8 (August 2002): 30–37.

Fogarty, D. W., J. H. Blackstone, and T. R. Hoffmann. *Production and Inventory Management,* 2d ed. Cincinnati: South-Western, 1991.

Gaither, N., and G. Frazier. *Operations Management,* 9th ed. Mason, Ohio: South-Western, 2002.

Simchi-Levi, D., P. Kaminsky, and E. Simchi-Levi. *Designing and Managing the Supply Chain: Concepts, Strategies, and Case Studies,* 2d ed. Boston: Irwin-McGraw-Hill, 2003.

Vollmann, T. E., W. L. Berry, and D. C. Whybark. *Manufacturing Planning and Control Systems,* 3d ed. Burr Ridge, Ill.: Irwin, 1992.

Notes

1. C. Koch, "What Is ERP?" printed 30 August 2001, accessed 13 November 2002; available from http://www.darwinmag.com/learn/curve/column.html?ArticleID=39

2. Anonymous, "Off-the-Shelf System Takes Flight: An ERP System's Standard Modules Deliver Significant Benefits for Aircraft Manufacturer," *APICS—The Performance Advantage* 11, no. 5 (May 2001): 60.

3. Industry Watch, "The Evolution of ERP," *APICS—The Performance Advantage* 13, no. 3 (March 2003): 8–9.

4. M. Bosse, "Hitting the Growth Ceiling," *APICS–The Performance Advantage* 12, no. 8 (September 2002): 40, 42, 44.

5. Anonymous, "New Technology," *Management Sciences* 46, no. 10 (October 2002): 24–28.

6. J. Zygmont, "Mixmasters Find an Alternative to All-in-One ERP Software," *Datamation* (February 1999).

7. K. Kapp, "Anytime, Anywhere, e-Learning Takes Off in Manufacturing," *APICS—The Performance Advantage* 12, no. 6 (June 2002): 38–43.

8. T. H. Davenport, J. G. Harris, and S. Cantrell, *The Return of Enterprise Solutions: The Director's Cut* (Cambridge, Mass.: Accenture Institute for Strategic Change, 2002).

9. C. Koch, "What Is ERP?" printed 30 August 2001, accessed 13 November 2002; available from http://www.darwinmag.com/learn/curve/column.html?ArticleID=39

10. Accessed 12 November 2002; available from http://www.sap.com/company/historytimeline.asp

11. Accessed 10 March 2003; available from http://www.oracle.com

12. Accessed 10 March 2003; available from http://www.peoplesoft.com

13. Accessed 10 March 2003; available from http://www.jdedwards.com

14. Accessed 10 March 2003; available from http://www.baan.com

Chapter 8:

PROCESS MANAGEMENT: JUST-IN-TIME AND TOTAL QUALITY MANAGEMENT ISSUES IN SUPPLY CHAIN MANAGEMENT

Customers are looking for the traditional on-time delivery. They still want cost performance and improved cost over time. And they still want quality—product quality and material quality. So those three things that I grew up with 20 years ago are still key. But there are a number of new activities that really are overlaid on these traditional expectations today. First of all, customers want flexibility. They need to be able to build to order or configure to order. They no longer want to build to a standard configuration, put whatever it is in a warehouse, and wait for an order to match what they have on hand. They want us to have a high delivery to request, request being the real order, not the forecast or plan.[1]

Learning Objectives

After completing this chapter, you should be able to
- Discuss the major elements of JIT and TQM.
- Describe why JIT and TQM are integral parts of SCM.
- List and describe the major elements of JIT and TQM.
- Understand the importance of SPC and how to apply it to various processes.

Chapter Outline

SUPPLY CHAIN MANAGEMENT IN ACTION   *Tekelec's Supplier-Managed Inventory Program*

Tekelec, a leading developer of telecommunications signaling solutions with over 1,000 employees worldwide, recently integrated a supplier-managed inventory (SMI) program into its manufacturing process. By linking the SMI program to its manufacturing information system, Tekelec created a fully integrated, closed-loop, transactionally error-free, and highly auditable process that stretches from customer shipment to supplier inventory replenishment. Tekelec is replenishing completed circuit packs shipped to its customers, and Tekelec's suppliers are replenishing all the electronics required to manufacture those circuit packs. The components range from passives and miscellaneous hardware on the low end to Pentium® processors and memory modules on the high end. Over 75 percent of Tekelec's product costs are managed through this process.

The factory was ready for the migration to this new process since Tekelec had already reduced its supplier base by 70 percent and had contracts in place for over 80 percent of its components. In addition, it had just completed a review of the factory floor layout and made major changes to leverage the efficiencies of the JIT process. Completed assemblies are shipped to customers; untested assemblies are pulled through the test department to replenish finished goods; Tekelec's contract manufacturer is pulling components from the supplier's inventory to backfill the untested board inventory; and Tekelec's component suppliers are replenishing their bins of raw material from Tekelec's central warehouse. The key here is that Tekelec does not build, buy, or stock any products unless demand by its customers warrants the activity.

Before implementing the SMI process, Tekelec differed from many organizations in using a two-bin system with an auto-replenishment package furnished by one of its suppliers. (The two-bin system is a process in which there are two bins containing equal amounts of a product and the operator pulls material from the front bin until it is empty.) Prior to pulling the back bin forward and consuming material from it, the operator triggers the replenishment flag, which is a laminated card with a bar code detailing the part number, quantity, and location. The bar code is scanned, and a replenishment order is sent via EDI to the appropriate supplier. When the replenishment inventory arrives, it is placed in the empty bin and that bin becomes the back bin. Although the two-week cycle time was good, Tekelec was not comfortable with the level of redundancy and waste in this process. In addition, Tekelec realized that its growth rate demanded either a more efficient process or more manpower.

Project Objectives

The primary project objective was to reduce the cycle time required for replenishing the manufacturing inventories and to better support the JIT manufacturing method. The goal to reduce cycle time also included the support functions within the organization such as accounts payable, stores, receiving, and quality. The second objective was not to add any liabilities typically associated with increased inventories (for example, delayed implementation of engineering change orders, increased scrap risks, and increased carrying charges). The aggressive schedule for design enhancements and the need to maintain maximum flexibility eliminated going turnkey, that is, having its contract manufacturer procure material on Tekelec's behalf.

How It Works

In short, suppliers manage their own inventory warehoused at Tekelec's contract manufacturer. When the factory needs to be replenished, the contract manufacturer pulls material from the consigned location and assembles the printed circuit boards (PCBs), sometimes referred to as a printed circuit pack, identified by a pull flag. Upon delivery of completed PCB assemblies to Tekelec, the system automatically generates purchase orders for all components, receives the components to inventory, and issues them to the work order. The work order is then closed to inventory. The system goes on to generate supplier invoices, match them to the receipts, and generate payments. All records are sent via EDI to Tekelec's suppliers to update their systems.

(continued)

Internal Benefits

At the time of this news item, Tekelec had experienced the following results:

- Inventory turns for the division had increased an average of 40 percent from the preceding year to a current high of 7.8 percent annualized.

- Inventory levels for the division had been reduced by 30 percent, and on-time shipments were up 1 percent to over 98 percent year-to-date.

- Several months' supply of inventory based on forecast were down 30 percent from the previous year, and they have not had a single stock-out.

These increased efficiencies, from the combined efforts and process changes for Tekelec and its suppliers, have proven that integrated supply strategies can be successful and add to the bottom line.[2]

Introduction

As has already been discussed in earlier chapters, supply chain management is all about achieving low cost along with high levels of quality and responsiveness throughout the supply chain. Customers today expect these things, making it necessary for firms to adopt strategic responses that emphasize speed, innovation, cooperation, quality, and cost effectiveness. Just-in-time (JIT) and total quality management (TQM), two important techniques that are central to the success of supply chain management, seek to achieve these strategic imperatives, while at the same time resolving the trade-offs that can exist when simultaneously pursuing the goals of high quality, fast response, and low cost.

In the 1990s, supply chain management emerged as the paradigm that combined several initiatives that were already in use, including **Quick response (QR), efficient consumer response (ECR),** JIT, and Japanese **keiretsu relationships.** The first two are concerned with speed and flexibility, while keiretsu involves partnership arrangements. The QR program had been developed by the textile industry in the mid-1980s as an offshoot of JIT and is based on merchandisers and suppliers working together to respond more quickly to consumer needs by sharing information, resulting in better customer service and less inventory and waste. In the early 1990s, ECR was developed by a grocery industry task force charged with making grocery supply chains more competitive. In this case, point-of-purchase transactions at grocery stores are forwarded via computer to distributors and manufacturers, allowing the stores to keep stocks replenished while minimizing the need for safety stock inventories. Keiretsu networks are cooperative coalitions between Japanese manufacturing firms and their suppliers. In many cases, keiretsus are formed as the result of financial support given to suppliers by a manufacturing firm. Supply chain management is thus strongly associated with JIT.

While many may argue that Henry Ford and his company essentially invented JIT practices, the term *just-in-time* was originally associated with Mr. Taiichi Ohno and the Toyota Production System and is a philosophy or mindset encompassing continuous problem solving to eliminate waste. In the production system, items move only when they are needed by a downstream processing step. Thus, supplies and assemblies are "pulled" through the system when and where they are needed. When problems are encountered, the process is stopped until the problem is solved. Since reductions in throughput time allow things to get where they need to be on time, JIT activities are all connected to this objective. Managers work on this objective by reducing lot sizes and processing times, safety stocks, wasted worker and material movements, variabilities, and defects. These are all considered waste in the JIT philosophy. Combined, these activities tend to reduce cost and response times, while improving quality. In the early 1980s, these practices started making their way to the Western world;

today, JIT has evolved into a way of doing business for many organizations. JIT has also spawned a number of other names that also refer to at least some aspect of JIT. For instance, *lean manufacturing* is one of the more current terms used to describe JIT.

Quality is a necessary element and outcome of JIT. First, as the JIT process of waste elimination begins to shrink inventories, queues, and lead times, quality problems are typically uncovered both in production and with purchased materials. Eventually, these problems are remedied, resulting in higher levels of quality. Second, as the drive to continuously reduce throughput times continues, the need for consistent emphasis on improving quality throughout the productive system results in the need for an overall quality improvement or TQM program. TQM stresses a commitment by the firm's top management to enable the firm to identify customer expectations and excel in meeting those expectations. Since environmental changes and changes in technology and competition cause customer expectations to change, firms must then commit to a program of continual reassessment and improvement; this, too, is an integral part of TQM. Thus, to achieve the primary objectives of low cost, high quality, and reduced lead times, supply chain management requires the use of JIT and TQM throughout the supply chain.

Just-in-Time and Supply Chain Management

Simply put, the objective of supply chain management is to balance the flow of materials with customer requirements throughout the supply chain, such that costs, quality, and customer service are at optimal levels. JIT emphasizes reduction of waste, continuous improvement, and the synchronization of material flows from within the organization and eventually including the organization's immediate suppliers and customers. In many respects, then, as we described in the introduction, supply chain management seeks to incorporate JIT elements across the entire supply chain. Supply chain management encourages cross-training, satisfying internal customer demand, moving products through the production system quickly, communicating end-customer demand forecasts and production schedules up the supply chain, and seeks to optimize inventory levels across the entire supply chain. These elements of supply chain management are all supported by JIT. For example, firms practicing JIT will seek to improve the quality and delivery characteristics of their suppliers through the formation of strategic alliances. When this same firm begins to practice supply chain management with other members of a supply chain, the focus will be on **channel integration,** or extending these strategic alliances to suppliers' suppliers and to customers' customers.

JIT is an overall operating philosophy of waste reduction and value enhancement that can include a number of activities or elements, which are reviewed in subsequent sections. Many firms do not implement all of these activities but, rather, select JIT elements based on resources, product characteristics, customer needs, and supplier capabilities. Still, companies that have begun to implement JIT activities find it easier to expand these efforts into a proactive supply chain management program. In fact, in a recent survey of senior manufacturing executives, 71 percent admit to practicing some form of JIT with supply chain management and conclude that the result is more flexibility in terms of changing production runs and changes in demand.[3]

Organizations that are successfully managing their supply chains evolve through four stages, as shown in Table 8.1.[4] In Stage 1, the firm is internally focused, organizational functions are managed separately, and performance is monitored based on achieving departmental goals. This **silo effect** causes the firm to be reactive and short-term goal oriented. At this stage, no internal functional integration is occurring.

Table 8.1	Supply Chain Management Evolution		
Stage 1: Internally Focused	**Stage 2: Functional Integration**	**Stage 3: Internal Integration**	**Stage 4: External Integration**
• Functional silos • Top-down management • Internal measures used to monitor performance • Reactive, short-term planning • No internal integration	• Focus on internal flow of goods • Emphasis on cost reduction • Realization of efficiencies gained by internal integration	• Realization of integration of goods flow throughout firm • Focus on logistics and JIT activities to manage flow of goods and information • Measurement of supplier performance and customer service performance	• Extending integration efforts to suppliers and customers • Realization of need to control goods and information to second- and third-tier suppliers, customers • Emphasis on alliance development and communication capabilities

In Stage 2, the firm has begun integrating efforts and resources among internal functions. In this stage, the focus of the firm has started to shift toward an emphasis on the flow of goods and information through the firm to achieve production efficiencies and reduce throughput times.

In Stage 3, internal integration of goods and information has been achieved, and the focus begins to shift toward linking suppliers and customers to the firm's processes. Thus, at this stage, there is an emphasis on using logistics capabilities to manage the movement and storage of goods from supplier delivery to distribution to the customer. JIT activities begin to be used as the firm realizes the impact of reduced throughput times on customer service and inventory cost. As inventory levels are reduced, the need for improved quality from suppliers is magnified and firms begin to take a more proactive approach to managing and developing their suppliers. Successful use of JIT also impacts the firm's customers in terms of better-quality products, more flexibility, and faster delivery times; and firms begin to realize the need to proactively manage their customer relationships as well.

Stage 4 is characterized by efforts to broaden the firm's supply chain influence beyond immediate or first-tier suppliers and customers, as well as strengthening relationships with existing key suppliers and customers. Firms have become comfortable with JIT processes and are seeking ways to further improve the flow of information, as well as quality, flexibility, and processing efficiencies. They begin to work with their most important suppliers and customers to aid in their respective JIT implementation efforts. Supply chain management and external integration have become legitimate concerns at this stage.

Thus, throughout Stage 3 and Stage 4, we see an emphasis on JIT methods to integrate the firm's processes with its trading partners. Following is a discussion of the JIT philosophy and its component parts.

The Elements of Just-in-Time

Table 8.2 shows the major JIT elements that are discussed in this section of the chapter, along with a short description of each element. Readers should note that JIT and other lean-oriented programs can vary significantly, based on their resource capabilities, product and process orientation, and past failures or successes with other improvement projects. Firms with a mature JIT implementation status will most likely be practicing a significant number of these elements.

Waste Reduction

One of the program-wide goals of all JIT endeavors is waste reduction. Firms reduce costs and add value to the products and services they provide by eliminating waste from the productive system. Waste is a term that encompasses excess wait times, inventories, material and people movements, processing steps, variabilities, and *any other non-value-adding activity*. Syncra

Table 8.2	JIT Elements
Elements	**Description**
Waste Reduction	Eliminating waste is the overriding concern within the JIT philosophy. Includes reducing excess inventories, material movements, production steps, scrap losses, rejects, and rework.
JIT Partnerships	Firm works with buyers and customers with the mutual goal of eliminating waste, improving speed, and reducing cost. Suppliers are considered partners, and close customer relationships are also sought.
JIT Layouts	WIP inventories are positioned close to each process, and layouts are designed where possible to reduce movement of people and materials. Processes are positioned to allow smooth flow of work through the facility.
JIT Inventories	Inventories are reduced by reducing production batch sizes, setup times, and safety stocks. Tends to create or uncover processing problems, which are then managed and controlled.
JIT Scheduling	Firm produces frequent small batches of product, with frequent product changes to produce a level production schedule. Smaller, more frequent purchase orders are communicated to suppliers, and more frequent deliveries are offered to customers. Kanbans are used to pull WIP through the system.
Continuous Improvement	As queues and lead times are reduced, problems surface more quickly causing the need for continual attention to problem solving and process improvement. With lower safety stocks, quality levels must be high to avoid process shutdowns. Attention to supplier quality levels is high.
Workforce Commitment	Employees are cross-trained to add processing flexibility and to increase the workforce's ability to solve problems. Employees are trained to provide quality inspections as parts enter a process area. Employee roles are expanded, and they are given top management support and resources to identify and fix problems.
JIT II	An extension of supplier alliance development, popularized by the Bose Corp. Supplier representative is housed at buyer facility and acts as a buyer. Representative has access to all of buyer's facilities and data.

Systems, an organization specializing in fixing supply chain inefficiencies, estimates that 20 to 30 percent of all inventory in a typical supply chain is "mis-deployed."[5] Workers and managers must therefore be continually assessing processes, methods, and materials for their value contributions to the firm's salable products and services. This is accomplished through worker-management interactions and commitment to the continued elimination of waste, and frequent solicitation of feedback from customers. Significant waste reduction results in a number of positive outcomes including lower costs, shorter lead times, better quality, and greater competitiveness. The waste reduction theme runs through all of the JIT elements.

Just-in-Time Partnerships

Quite commonly, firms must hold safety stocks of purchased products because suppliers' delivery times are inconsistent or the quality of purchased goods does not always meet specifications. On the distribution side, firms hold stocks of finished goods in warehouses prior to shipment to customers, in some cases for months at a time. Holding these inventories costs the firm money and does not add value to the products; thus, it is considered a waste.

When the focal firm, its suppliers, and its customers begin to work together to remove waste, reduce cost, and improve quality and customer service, this marks the beginning of JIT partnerships. Through its supplier cost reduction effort (SCORE) program, Daimler-Chrysler encourages its suppliers to identify ways of eliminating waste in its manufacturing processes. Suppliers submit proposals designed to reduce costs in areas like logistics, design, manufacturing, sourcing, and administration. Over the years, the automaker has saved billions of dollars from the SCORE program.[6] JIT partnerships can thus exist between a firm and its most valued suppliers, and between a firm and its key customers (in this case, the firm is the valued supplier). When developing JIT partnerships with suppliers, a firm identifies its best suppliers and begins to offer these suppliers training and a greater share of the firm's purchases, while reducing or eliminating business ties with the poor-performing suppliers. This allows the firm to use purchasing leverage to obtain better service and quality assurances. Ford Motor Company even has the Ford Supplier Learning Institute to help suppliers improve performance.[7]

JIT purchasing includes delivering smaller quantities, more frequently, to the point of use in the focal firm. This serves to lower average inventory levels. More frequent deliveries mean higher inbound transportation costs; to reduce these costs, suppliers are often required to distribute product from warehouses or production facilities located in close proximity to the buyer. Many distribution centers today transform and repackage products for customers as they are needed. For example, PetsMart's busiest day of the week is Saturday. During the week, warehouses serving PetsMart receive truckloads of supplies; by Thursday, they are assembling store load quantities in anticipation of that Saturday's business.[8]

Making small, frequent purchases from just a few suppliers puts the focal firm in a position of greater dependence on these suppliers. It is therefore extremely important that deliveries always be on time, delivered to the right location, in the right quantities, and be of high quality, since existing inventories will be lower. Toward this end, the Automotive Industry Action Group (AIAG) has recently published guidelines for JIT deliveries within automotive industry supply chains, with the goal of standardizing materials management using electronic data interchange (EDI).[9] The promise of greater quantities to be purchased is what makes this performance possible. With time, JIT partnerships with suppliers develop into long-term, mutually beneficial relationships as discussed in Chapter 3 and Chapter 4. Ford, for instance, has partnered with Ryder Logistics to be responsible for the total product inflow and outflow at a number of their assembly plants to maximize logistics efficiencies.[10]

Firms also strive to develop these same mutually beneficial JIT partnerships with their key customers. As these relationships develop, firms begin to reserve greater levels of capacity for a small number of large, steady customers. They locate production or warehousing facilities close to these customers and make frequent small deliveries of finished product to their points of use within the facility. It can be seen, then, that mutual dependencies and mutual benefits occur among all of these JIT partnerships, resulting in increased product value and competitiveness for all of the partners. Cadillac has a program called Custom Xpress Delivery, where Cadillacs are built to the specifications most customers desire. They are then stored in eleven regions across the United States. When customers walk into a dealership and see exactly the model they want (except for, say, the color), they can get the car they want within twenty-four hours.[11]

Just-in-Time Layouts

The primary design objective with JIT layouts is to reduce wasted movement. Moving parts and people around the production areas does not add value. JIT layouts seek to move people and materials when and where they are needed, as quickly as possible. Processing centers that move product between them should be located close together.

Group technology work cells are designed to process similar parts or components, saving duplication of equipment and labor, as well as concentrating the area where units of the same purchased part are delivered. In many cases these work cells are U-shaped to facilitate easier operator and material movements. In assembly line facilities, work cells are positioned close to the line, feeding components directly to the line instead of delivering them to a stock area where they would be brought back out when needed. Work cells are themselves small assembly lines and are designed to be flexible, allowing machine configurations to change as processing requirements dictate; machines can be mounted on wheels or moved by overhead lifts.

JIT layouts are very visual, meaning that lines of visibility are unobstructed, making it easy for operators at one processing center to monitor work occurring at other work centers. All purchased and WIP inventories are located on the production floor, and the good visibility makes it easy to spot inventory buildups as bottlenecks occur. When these and other production problems occur, they are spotted and rectified quickly. The relative closeness of the processing centers facilitates teamwork and joint problem solving and requires less floor space than conventional production layouts.

e-BUSINESS CONNECTION
JIT AT DELL COMPUTER CORP.

One of the most well-known, e-business organizations is Round Rock, Texas-based Dell Computer Corp., which does everything in one place. Product goes in and out of Dell so fast, there is barely any time to distinguish whether it is in the warehousing or manufacturing mode. Dell refers to this correctly as a just-in-time process, and e-commerce has made Dell's JIT operation extremely successful. Dell started in 1984 as a build-to-order organization based on telephone call orders, and the inventory was always low but nothing compared with today. Typically, material arrives at Dell two hours prior to assembly. "We've continually improved our operations over the years to reduce our days of supply in inventory," says Neisha Frank, company spokesperson for Dell.

The organization cannot credit the Internet entirely, but it has been a huge contributor, allowing Dell to eliminate the paper trail and develop efficiencies in the organization's transactions. Any more efficiencies gained via the Internet will require Dell to abandon the days of supply in inventory measurement of success, relying instead on a minute-by-minute supply. "The Internet can be used to compress time and that's what you're talking about when you talk about reducing inventory," Frank says. "With the Internet, we can get a better pulse on what our customers' needs are at any given time and feed that information back to our suppliers."

Those suppliers have become fewer in number and, more importantly, much closer to Dell's Round Rock, Texas, operations. The proximity contributes to Dell's just-in-time emphasis and its ability to assemble computers right in the location that receives the parts. So who is really doing the warehousing? In this case, Dell has essentially moved that function to a different spot in the supply chain, the same approach that Wal-Mart retail stores made famous. "It's all part of the supply chain efficiencies," says Jenkins, "where manufacturers recognize that a major component of cost is the cost of carrying inventory."[12]

JIT layouts allow problems to be tracked to their source more quickly as well. Since material and parts flow directly from one processing center to the next, a quality problem, when found, can generally be traced to the previous work center, provided inspections are performed at each processing stage.

Just-in-Time Inventories

In JIT parlance, inventories are considered a costly waste, since they tend to hide a number of purchasing, production, and quality problems within the organization. Just as water hides boat-damaging rocks beneath its surface, so inventory hides value-damaging problems. And, just as reducing water levels causes rocks to become detectable, so too the reduction of inventory levels causes problems to surface in the organization. Once these problems are detected, they can be solved, improving product value and allowing the system to run more efficiently. For example, reducing safety stocks of purchased materials will cause supply disruptions when late deliveries occur. Firms can then either find a way to resolve the problem with the supplier or find a better supplier. Either way, the end result is a smoother running organization with less inventory investment. The same story can be applied to production machinery. Properly maintained equipment breaks down less often, so less safety stock is needed to keep downstream production equipment fed with parts to be further processed.

Another way to reduce inventory levels is to reduce purchase order quantities and production lot sizes. Figure 8.1 illustrates this point. When order quantities and lot sizes are cut in half, for instance, then average inventories are also cut in half, assuming usage is constant.

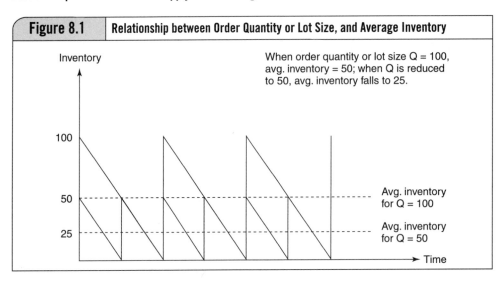

Figure 8.1   Relationship between Order Quantity or Lot Size, and Average Inventory

Unfortunately, this means that the firm must make more purchase orders and perform more production **setups.** Thus, ordering costs must be reduced and this can be accomplished by automating the purchasing process using **electronic data interchange (EDI)** and the Internet. For example, companies now are developing **virtual inventory systems** that allow distributors to feed their inventory information into one shared database, allowing small buyers to order in a JIT environment from distributors offering the quickest response times.[13]

Since setting up production equipment for the next production run takes valuable time, increasing the number of setups means the firm must find ways to reduce setup times. Setup times can be reduced in a number of ways including doing setup preparation work while the previous production lot is still being processed, moving machine tools closer to the machines, improving tooling or die couplings, standardizing setup procedures, practicing various methods to reduce setup times, and purchasing machines that require less setup time.

Finally, once inventories have been reduced and the problems uncovered and solved, the firm can reduce inventories still further, uncovering yet another set of problems to be solved. With each iteration, the firm runs leaner, cheaper, faster, and with higher levels of product quality.

Just-in-Time Scheduling

Saying that a firm should purchase small quantities, more frequently, from good suppliers and should produce small lot sizes and have more setups is one thing, but actually accomplishing this feat is something else. Many firms have tried these two things and failed, eventually returning to carrying higher levels of inventory and producing large batches to sell product, rather than dealing with the many problems accompanying lean production. Level schedules of small batches, though, communicated throughout the production process and to outside suppliers, is what is needed to support JIT efforts.

Small batch scheduling drives down costs by reducing purchased, WIP, and finished goods inventories; and it also makes the firm more flexible to meet customer demand. Figure 8.2 illustrates this point. In the same period of time, the firm with small lot sizes changes products nine times, while the firm with large lot sizes has only changed production three times and has yet to produce Product D. Maintaining a set, level, small batch production schedule will allow suppliers to anticipate and schedule deliveries also, resulting in fewer late deliveries.

Moving these small production batches through a JIT facility is accomplished with the use of **kanbans.** Kanban is a Japanese word for card, although for JIT use, it has come to mean a

Global Perspective

SYNCHRONOUS SUPPLY AT UK NISSAN

Ikeda Hoover Ltd., a synchronous seat supplier to Nissan Manufacturing UK Ltd., employs 658 staff and operates a two-shift system to supply seats for models produced at the Nissan plant. Current output is around 6,000 seating systems per week (approximately 300,000 sets per annum).

Synchronous supply is essentially a system where components supplied are matched exactly to the production requirements of the buyer. In essence, IHL's production line is a seating version of Nissan's assembly line and reflects the variation and mix requirements of each vehicle. Synchronous supply differs from traditional JIT since the latter generally accommodates the sequencing of parts that are model, rather than vehicle, specific. IHL's production is geared solely to supply the exact needs of Nissan for each of the 300 vehicles produced each day at the plant. In total there are up to 200 seating variations that Nissan may require and that IHL must be able to coordinate and deliver within the short time window available. In such a complex production environment, synchronous supply requires greater planning and control to ensure that customer requirements are met first time every time.

The synchronous supply system that operates between IHL and Nissan is activated when a painted body passes the start of the trim line at Nissan. It is at this time that an electronic message is relayed to IHL's plant detailing the precise seating requirements for the particular model to be produced during that shift. This information is the "live" version of that day's production, and it is at this stage that IHL has a time window of around two and a half hours to build, assemble, and deliver around forty seating systems (each seating system comprises front and back seats); subsequent deliveries are made at thirty-minute intervals. Each order received by IHL details the car identification number; whether the seats are for left- or right-hand drive vehicles; the type and color of material to be used; and whether the seats require height adjusters, heaters, lumbar support, or airbags. Given the high number of seating variations that Nissan may require, IHL's computing system plays an important role in ensuring that the right seating systems are supplied for the right cars at the right time.[14]

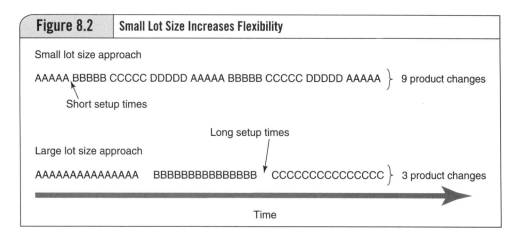

Figure 8.2	Small Lot Size Increases Flexibility

Small lot size approach

AAAAA BBBBB CCCCC DDDDD AAAAA BBBBB CCCCC DDDDD AAAAA } 9 product changes

Short setup times

Long setup times

Large lot size approach

AAAAAAAAAAAAAAAA   BBBBBBBBBBBBBBBB   CCCCCCCCCCCCCCCC } 3 product changes

Time

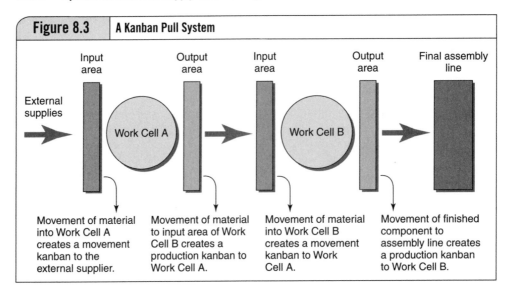

Figure 8.3   A Kanban Pull System

Movement of material into Work Cell A creates a movement kanban to the external supplier.

Movement of material to input area of Work Cell B creates a production kanban to Work Cell A.

Movement of material into Work Cell B creates a movement kanban to Work Cell A.

Movement of finished component to assembly line creates a production kanban to Work Cell B.

signal. When work cells need parts or materials, they use a kanban to signal their need for these things from the upstream work cell, processing unit, or external supplier that provides the needed material to the work cell. In this way, nothing is provided until a downstream demand occurs. That is why a JIT system is known as a *pull system*. Ideally, parts are placed in standardized containers, and kanbans exist for each container. Figure 8.3 illustrates how a kanban pull system works. When finished components are moved from Work Cell B to the assembly line, the following things happen:

1. The container holding finished parts in Work Cell B's output area is emptied, a **production kanban** (a light, flag, or sign) is used to tell Work Cell B to begin processing more components to restock the empty container in its output area.

2. During this stage, when parts are moved from Work Cell B's input area for processing, the container holding these parts is emptied and a **withdrawal kanban** (a light, flag, or sign) is used to indicate to Work Cell A that more parts are needed. This allows a full container of parts to move from Work Cell A's output area to Work Cell B's input area, and the empty container is moved to Work Cell A's output area.

3. As this movement occurs, a production kanban is now used to allow Work Cell A to begin processing parts to restock its empty container in the output area.

4. Finally, as full containers of parts are emptied and used in Work Cell A's processing area, these empty containers in Work Cell A's input area create a withdrawal kanban seen by the external supplier who then restocks Work Cell A's empty containers in the input area.

Thus, it can be seen that kanbans are used to control the flow of inventory through the facility. Inventories are not allowed to accumulate beyond the size of each container and the number of containers in the system. When containers are full, production stops until another production kanban is encountered. A simple relationship can be used to determine the number of containers for a JIT system:

$$\text{\# of containers} = \frac{DT}{C},$$

where

D = the demand rate of the assembly line;
T = the time for a container to make an entire circuit through the system, from being filled, moving, being emptied, and returning to be filled again; and
C = the container size, in number of parts.

For example, suppose the assembly line demand is twenty parts per hour for Work Cell B, and the standard container used in this processing area holds five parts. If it takes two hours for a container to make a circuit from Work Cell B to the assembly line and back again, then the number of containers needed in the system is eight:

$$\text{\# of containers} = \frac{20(2)}{5} = 8.$$

The maximum inventory for this system would then be the total number of containers times the container size, or forty units. Finally, reducing inventory in the system (one of the objectives of JIT) occurs by reducing the number of containers. Of course, when this is done, the circuit time for a container would also have to be reduced to enable the demand rate to be met. This can be done by reducing setup time, processing time, wait time, or move time.

Continuous Improvement

As alluded to already, JIT systems are never-ending works in progress. Compact layouts are designed to allow work to logically flow through the facility. Inventory is moved from storage areas to the shop floor and placed in containers in designated work cell storage areas. Purchasing and production are performed in small batch sizes. In this system, problems often will surface, at least initially, as suppliers struggle to deliver more frequently and on time, and as workers struggle to maintain output levels while spending more time setting up machines for small production runs. To make the JIT system work better, employees are continuously seeking ways to reduce supplier delivery and quality problems, and in the production area to improve movement problems, visibility problems, machine breakdown problems, setup problems, and internal quality problems. In Japanese manufacturing facilities, this is known as **kaizen.** Once the existing problems are solved, removal of an inventory container from one of the work cells starts the problem-solving cycle all over again—thus, the need for continuous improvement in all JIT systems. Until things are always where they need to be, at the expected time and in the right quantity and quantity, improvements must be sought out.

Quality improvement is certainly part of the ongoing continuous improvement efforts in JIT systems. For instance, receiving a batch of goods from an external supplier or internal supplying work cell that does not satisfy design specifications is like not getting a shipment at all. In short order, processing areas needing these supplies will be out of stock and unable to work. Higher quality is then necessary throughout the production system to meet demand with lower safety stocks and WIP inventories. We talk in greater detail about quality in the next section of this chapter.

Workforce Commitment

Since JIT depends on so much waste reduction and continuous improvement for its success, dedicated people must play a significant role in this process. Managers must show strong support for JIT efforts by providing subordinates with the skills, tools, time, and other necessary resources to identify problems and implement solutions. Top managers of JIT companies need to create a culture in which workers are encouraged to speak out when problems exist. For example, to improve productivity at DaimlerChrysler's distribution centers, management personnel rely on warehouse workers for suggestions. By working closely with workers to develop ideas, the company is able to improve throughput, efficiency, and morale.[15] And, as W. Edwards Deming so eloquently pointed out in his theory of management, eliminating fear in the workplace is one of the primary requirements for creating a successful company.[16]

Employees are cross-trained in many of the production processes to enable shop capacities to be adjusted at different work cells as needed when machines break down or workers are absent. Employees are given time during their workday to work on reducing setup times as well as solving other production problems as they occur. They are also expected to perform a number of quality checks on processed items coming in to the work cell. When quality problems are found, workers are empowered to shut down the production process until the source of the problem can be found and corrected. Most employees who work for JIT companies enjoy their jobs; they are given a number of responsibilities and are considered one of the most important parts of a successful JIT organization.

Just-in-Time II

A relatively new concept, JIT II is an extension of supplier partnerships and *vendor-managed inventories.* Mr. Lance Dixon, director of the Bose JIT II Education and Research Center, is credited with creating the JIT II concept in the late 1980s. Today the phenomenon is exploding, with many of the largest U.S. corporations using dozens of JIT II partners. It refers to a situation wherein a supplier's employee is housed in the purchasing department of the buyer's organization, acting as both buyer and supplier representative. This person is given all the rights and duties of an employee for the buyer firm—he (or she) monitors inventory levels, places purchase orders, participates on product design and **value analysis** teams, and has access to all of the files and records of the buyer firm. For instance, the JIT II team handling just Bose's transportation function includes a less-than-truckload carrier, a truckload carrier, an import/export brokerage firm, and a major ocean carrier. These representatives are each linked to their respective firm's information systems and work daily with Bose's transportation group and each other to assure that parts and products arrive at Bose facilities when they are needed. The system has reduced late shipments by 50 percent, transportation costs by 37 percent, and shipping errors by 87 percent.[17]

Several advantages exist for both sides of a JIT II relationship. First, the buyer gets the use of a costless employee, while the supplier gets the security of future purchases. Communication between both firms also improves with this arrangement. The supplier learns very quickly about new products and design changes that are going to impact the organization. The supplier soon learns about production problems potentially caused by the supplier's products and customer service performance and can help to more quickly alleviate these problems. The arrangement serves both sides and creates a much closer working relationship between the two companies. This can greatly benefit a JIT implementation effort.

As we have shown, JIT is a necessary element in successful supply chain management. A second, equally necessary element is total quality management. While we introduced the concept of total quality management and its relationship to JIT earlier in the chapter, we would like to now more fully explore the concept of TQM and its relationship to supply chain management.

Total Quality Management and Supply Chain Management

By now, the supply chain management outcomes of better customer service, lower costs, and higher quality should be starting to sound familiar. To sustain and improve competitiveness, firms must offer higher-quality products and services than their competitors. Through better process integration and communication, trading partners along the supply chain realize how poor-quality products and services can cause negative chain reactions to take place, such as greater levels of safety stock throughout the supply chain, lost time and productivity due to product and component repairs, the increased costs of customer returns and warranty repairs, and, finally, loss of customers and damage to reputations. The impact of better quality can be felt throughout the supply chain and ultimately by end customers. Thus, no discussion of supply chain management would be complete without a discussion of quality and the total quality management philosophy.

Like JIT, TQM is an enterprise-wide philosophy, encompassing suppliers and customers. It emphasizes a commitment by the organization to strive toward excellence in the production of services and products that customers want. Firms implementing a TQM program

© 1996 Ted Goff

"We could only afford half a quality program."

have made a proactive decision to understand, meet, and then strive to exceed customer expectations; and this is the overriding objective in all TQM programs. Since TQM is all about pleasing the customer, a very straightforward customer-oriented definition of quality is employed here: "The ability to satisfy customer expectations." This definition is echoed by the American Society for Quality when it states: "Quality is defined by the customer through his/her satisfaction." In this sense, the quality of both a fast-food hamburger and a steak-house chopped sirloin sandwich can be considered to possess equally high quality, if they meet or exceed the expectations of their customers.

In a supply chain setting, quality is exemplified, for instance, by a machine tool manufacturer identifying its industrial customers, determining their tooling needs and requirements, and then setting out to meet those requirements and make the sale. With worldwide competition expanding, the desire to practice TQM can be seen in all industries and all sizes of organizations. In countries like China for instance, where their competitive advantage has largely been their low cost of labor, many Chinese firms are now paying more attention to quality management to compete in global markets.[18] Further, in a survey of small- to medium-sized firms, 82 percent of the respondents regarded product and service quality as a very important measure of firm success.[19]

TQM programs aim to assure that the firm is capable of satisfying customers now and into the future. Good supply chain trading partners use TQM methods to assure that their customers' needs are met. Ultimately, this translates into final customers getting what they want. While TQM programs tend to vary somewhat in the details from one organization to another, all tend to employ a mix of qualitative and quantitative elements aimed at achieving customer satisfaction, and we will see that—on the qualitative side at least—there is some overlap in JIT and TQM programs. The most common elements addressed in most TQM programs are discussed in the following section.

The Elements of Total Quality Management

The philosophy and tools of TQM are borrowed from a number of resources including the philosophies of a number of quality professionals such as W. Edwards Deming, Philip Crosby, and Joseph Juran, the Malcolm Baldrige National Quality Award, the International Organization for Standardization's ISO 9000 quality standards, and statistical process control techniques developed by Walter Shewhart. From these resources, a number of commonly used elements emerge that are collectively known today as total quality management. The more philosophical elements are discussed next, followed by the TQM tools, or the more quantitative elements.

Two elements are mentioned in almost every TQM paper, booklet, article, or how-to book, and these are (1) a focus on the customer and (2) workforce involvement. For this reason and because of their importance, these two items are discussed first.

Focus on the Customer

Since the practice of TQM is all about meeting customer expectations, then all of the TQM elements must be focused ultimately on the customer; in the supply chain sense, this focus must extend to the end-product consumer. Additionally, all employees in an organization have internal customers. Thus, the concept of meeting customer expectations applies to internal suppliers and customers as well: the customers of the secretarial pool are the staff members asking them for secretarial services; the computer technician's customers are the users of the computer equipment; and the customers of the purchasing department are the users of the items they purchase. Meeting the needs of internal customers allows firms to meet the needs of external customers and, finally, end-product consumers. (Who are the customers of the professor teaching this course?)

Today more than ever before, companies are asking their employees to take responsibility for providing high levels of customer service, to identify customer service failures, and to work as a team to effectively remedy these problems. Customers and potential customers need to be identified, observed, and surveyed to determine their buying habits and product or service requirements. Savvy companies are doing this and developing new products and services aimed at rapidly responding to their customers' ever-changing needs. (When was the last time you were asked for feedback regarding a product or service?) For example, PB and NRS Corp., a Madison, Wisconsin-based research firm, developed the National Homeowner Satisfaction Awards to highlight the critical role customer satisfaction plays in profitability. U.S. homebuilders are ranked according to responses from a home buyer survey seeking information on satisfaction with things like layout, material quality, workmanship, price/value, and warranty service, as well as their willingness to recommend their builder. Winners for 2002 were Ginsburg Development Corp., Hawthorne, New York (100 to 500 closings per year), and Engle Homes/Arizona, Phoenix, Arizona (more than 500 closings per year).[20]

The ability of the firm to meet customer requirements must also continually be measured. Firms should develop measures of customer service and satisfaction for all of their products and services and make a point of reviewing and updating these measures as products and customer needs change. Firms can track, for instance, things like on-time deliveries, customer complaints, customer returns, warranty repairs, wait time, and other similar measures that will link firms to their customers.

Workforce Involvement

First and foremost, the organization's top managers must be committed to quality improvement; this commitment manifests itself in a number of ways. When managers give their subordinates the resources, encouragement, and responsibility to contribute to quality assessment and improvement, the firm will see the results of these efforts in terms of better processes, morale, products, and competitiveness. Managers at all levels of the organization must view their roles as facilitators: formulating procedures, matching people to job requirements, providing training where needed, designing teams for problem-solving purposes, providing time and resources to solve problems, rewarding employee successes, and encouraging employee involvement. Employees should be encouraged to think "out of the box" to identify new and better ways of doing things, everywhere in the organization. Managers must also serve as role models; employees notice immediately if managers say one thing ("Quality and customers are our main priorities!") while rewarding something else ("Hit your goal this month or you won't get your bonus."). A great example of a company that turns employee involvement into success is Coco-Mat, a family-owned mattress company headquartered in

Athens, Greece. They reward employees for participating in everything from TQM programs to company sporting events. The result is products that won the prestigious European Quality Award in 2001 and over a 50 percent growth rate in annual sales.[21]

Empowering employees to make decisions to solve problems or satisfy customers is one way managers can build a company culture of support and trust. Employees view jobs at companies such as this as dream jobs and rarely want to leave. When employees are devoted and focused on serving internal and external customers and are rewarded for improving customer satisfaction, the firm is well on its way to embracing the total quality concept.

Teamwork is also an important aspect of workforce involvement. Managers create functional and cross-functional teams to allow workers to solve complex problems, to break down barriers and competition between departments, and to foster cooperation, leading to concrete results. Self-directed work teams aimed at solving quality problems are rooted in the **quality circle concept,** which originated in Japan in the 1960s and is in widespread use today in many companies around the United States.

Deming's Way

Deming's Theory of Management essentially holds that since managers are responsible for creating the systems that make organizations work, they must also be held responsible for the organization's problems. Thus, only management can fix problems, through application of the right tools, resources, encouragement, commitment, and cultural change. Deming's Theory of Management was the centerpiece of his teachings around the world (Deming died in 1993) and includes his Fourteen Points for Management, shown in Table 8.3.

Table 8.3	**Deming's Fourteen Points for Management**
1. Create constancy of purpose toward improvement of product and service.	Define values, mission, and vision to provide long-term direction for management and employees. Invest in innovation, training, and research.
2. Adopt the new philosophy.	Adversarial management-worker relationship and quota work systems no longer work in today's work environment. Management must work toward cooperative relationship aimed at increasing quality and customer satisfaction.
3. Cease dependence on inspection to improve quality.	Inspecting products does not create value or prevent poor quality. Workers must use statistical process control to improve quality.
4. End the practice of awarding business on the basis of price.	Purchases should not be based on low cost; buyers should develop long-term relationships with a few good suppliers.
5. Constantly improve the production and service system.	Significant quality improvement comes from continual incremental improvements that reduce variation and eliminate common causes.
6. Institute training on the job.	Employees should receive adequate job training and statistical process control training.
7. Institute leadership.	Managers are leaders, not supervisors. They help, coach, encourage, and provide guidance to employees.
8. Drive out fear, so that everyone may work effectively.	A supportive organization will drive out fear of reprisal, failure, change, the unknown and loss of control. Fear causes short-term thinking.
9. Break down barriers between departments.	Teamwork focuses workers, breaks down departmental barriers, and allows workers to see the big picture.
10. Eliminate slogans, exhortations, and targets for the workforce.	Slogans and motivational programs are directed toward workers, and they are not the cause of poor quality. These cause worker frustration when slogans don't work.
11. Eliminate quotas and MBO and substitute leadership.	Quotas are short-term thinking and cause fear. Numerical goals have no value unless methods are in place that will allow them to be achieved.
12. Remove barriers to pride of workmanship.	Too often, workers are given boring tasks with no proper tools and performance appraisals by supervisors that know nothing about the job.
13. Institute a vigorous program of education and self-improvement.	All employees should be encouraged to further broaden their skills through continuing education.
14. Put everyone to work to accomplish the transformation.	Management must have the courage to break with tradition and explain to a critical mass of people that the changes will involve everyone. Management must speak with one voice.

Table 8.4	Crosby's Four Absolutes of Quality
1. The definition of quality is conformance to requirements.	Adopt a do-it-right-the-first-time attitude. Never sell a faulty product to a customer.
2. The system of quality is prevention.	Use SPC as part of the prevention system. Make corrective changes when problems occur. Take preventive action.
3. The performance standard is zero defects.	Insist on zero defects from suppliers, workers. Education, training, and commitment will eliminate defects.
4. The measure of quality is the price of nonconformance.	The price of nonconformance is the cost of poor quality. Implementing a prevention program will eliminate this.

Table 8.5	Crosby's Fourteen Steps to Quality Improvement
1. Management commitment	Senior management must change the culture, initiate a hassle-free style, insist on strict conformance to requirements.
2. The quality improvement team	Form a team to guide, coordinate, and support the quality process. Team must all be educated in the quality improvement process.
3. Measurement	Measure the quality team's progress. Measure the quality process.
4. The cost of quality	Measure the costs of nonconformance before the quality effort begins. Then continuously track the costs of the quality effort.
5. Quality awareness	Communicate to employees the effort and successes associated with the quality program, quality policies, management commitment.
6. Corrective action	Use SPC and problem-solving tools to identify and eliminate quality problems.
7. Zero defects planning	Commit to zero defects. Start planning a ZD day to commit to the quality improvement process.
8. Employee education	Educate everyone on the quality process.
9. ZD day	Have a public commitment by the firm to quality improvement. Invite employees, officials, customers.
10. Goal setting	Set goals for the quality team and display them to employees.
11. Error-cause removal	Collect statements about quality problems from everyone. Analyze each response.
12. Recognition	Create a recognition program for management and employees. Have them chosen by their peers.
13. Quality councils	Bring the quality professionals together and let them learn from each other.
14. Repetition	Do Steps 1–13 over again. Choose a new quality team.

Deming's Fourteen Points are all very closely related to TQM principles, covering the qualitative as well as the quantitative aspects of TQM. He was convinced that quality was the outcome of an all-encompassing philosophy geared toward personal and organizational growth. He argued that growth occurs through top management vision, support, and value placed on all employees and suppliers. Value is demonstrated through investments in training, equipment, continuing education, support for finding and fixing problems, and teamwork both within the firm and with suppliers. Use of statistical methods, elimination of inspected-in quality, and elimination of cost-based decisions are also required to improve quality. Today, Deming's work lives on through the Deming Institute, and companies all over the world have adopted Deming's Fourteen Points as an integral part of their firm's operating philosophy.

Crosby's Way

Philip Crosby, a former vice president of quality at IT&T, was a quality consultant during the latter part of his life and wrote several books concerning quality and striving for zero defects, most notably *Quality Is Free* and *Quality without Tears* (he died in 2001). His findings about quality improvement programs as discussed in *Quality Is Free* were that these programs invariably more than paid for themselves. In *Quality without Tears,* Crosby discussed his four Absolutes of Quality, shown in Table 8.4, and his Fourteen Steps to Quality Improvement shown in Table 8.5. Industrial giants like IBM, General Motors, and Mattel have

Table 8.6	Juran's Quality Trilogy
1. Quality planning	The process of preparing to meet quality goals. Identify internal and external customers, determine their needs, and develop products that satisfy those needs. Managers set short- and long-term goals, establish priorities, compare results to previous plans.
2. Quality control	The process of meeting quality goals during operations. Determine what to control, establish measurements and standards of performance, measure performance, interpret the difference between the actual measure and the standard, and take action if necessary.
3. Quality improvement	The process of breaking through to unprecendented levels of performance. Show the need for improvement, identify projects for improvement, organize support for the projects, diagnose causes, implement remedies for the causes, provide control to maintain improvements.

benefited greatly from implementing Crosby's ideas (Mattel, for instance, saved $7.5 million in two years after implementing Crosby's fourteen steps).[22]

Crosby emphasized commitment to quality improvement by top management, development of a prevention system, employee education and training, and continuous assessment—all very similar to the teachings of Deming. Crosby, though, was somewhat more prescriptive in his fourteen steps, and some of his recommendations even conflicted with those of Deming. For instance, Deming was opposed to slogans, posters, and work standards like zero defects, and these are a significant part of Crosby's steps. When viewed, though, in their entireties, both programs recommend a combination of management and statistical methods to assess and improve quality over the long run.

Juran's Way

Joseph Juran, founder of the Juran Institute, helped to write and develop the *Quality Control Handbook* in 1951; like Deming, he helped to engineer the Japanese quality revolution starting in the 1950s. Juran, like both Crosby and Deming, has strived to introduce new types of thinking about quality to business managers and employees, but Juran's recommendations were a little different from both Crosby and Deming. Juran did not seek cultural change but sought to work within the system to instigate change. He felt that to get managers to listen, your message had to be spoken in dollars. To get workers to listen, you had to speak the language of things. So, he advocated the determination of the costs of poor quality to get the attention of managers, and the use of statistical control methods for workers.

Juran's recommendations are focused on his Quality Trilogy, as shown in Table 8.6. He found in his dealings with companies that most gave priority to quality control but paid little attention to quality planning and improvement. Thus, while both Japan and the United States were using quality control techniques since the 1950s, Japan's overall quality levels grew faster than those of the United States because Japan's quality planning and improvement efforts were much greater.

Many characteristics of the Deming, Crosby, and Juran philosophies are quite similar. All three focus on top management commitment, the need for continuous improvement efforts, training, and the use of statistical methods for control purposes.

The Malcolm Baldrige National Quality Award

The Baldrige Quality Award was signed into law on August 20, 1987, and is named after President Reagan's Secretary of Commerce, who was killed in an accident shortly before the award was enacted. The objectives of the award, given only to U.S. firms, are to stimulate American firms to improve quality and productivity, to recognize firms for their quality achievements, to establish criteria and guidelines so that organizations can independently evaluate their quality improvement efforts, and to provide examples and guidance to those

Table 8.7	Malcolm Baldrige National Quality Award Recipients			
Year	Small Business	Manufacturing	Service	Education (1999)	Health Care (1999)
1988	Globe Metallurgical	Motorola Westinghouse—Comm. Nuclear Fuel Div.			
1989		Xerox—Bus. Products and Systems Milliken & Co.			
1990	Wallace Co.	Cadillac Motor Car Co. IBM—Rochester	FedEx Corp.		
1991	Marlow Industries	Solectron Corp. Zytec Corp.			
1992	Granite Rock Co.	AT&T—Network Sys. Texas Instruments— Def. Sys. & Elec. Grp.	AT&T—Universal Card Svcs. The Ritz-Carlton Hotel Co.		
1993	Ames Rubber Corp.	Eastman Chemical Co.			
1994	Wainwright Indus.		AT&T—Consum. Commun. Svcs.		
1995		Armstrong World Ind.— Bldg. Prod. Ops. Corning—Telecomm. Prod. Div.			
1996	Custom Research Trident Precis, Mfg.	ADAC Laboratories	Dana Comm. Cred.		
1997		3M—Dental Prod. Div. Solectron	Merrill Lynch Cred. Corp. Xerox—Bus. Svcs.		
1998	Texas Nameplate Co.	Boeing—Airlift and Tanker Programs Solar Turbines			
1999	Sunny Fresh Foods	STMicroelectronics— Region Americas	BI The Ritz-Carlton Hotel Co.		
2000	Los Alamos Nat'l. Bank	Dana Corp.—Spicer Driveshaft Div. KARLEE Co.	Operations Mgt. Int'l.		
2001	Pal's Sudden Service	Clarke American Checks		Chugach Sch. Dist. Pearl River Sch. Dist. Univ. of Wisc-Stout	
2002	Branch-Smith— Printing Div.	Motorola—Comm., Gov't., and Indus. Sol. Sector			SSM Health Care

companies wanting to learn how to manage and improve quality and productivity. The Baldrige Award is administered by the National Institute of Standards and Technology (NIST) and is given to, at most, two organizations in each of five categories: small business, manufacturing, service, education, and health care (the final two categories were added in 1999). Table 8.7 shows the winners from 1988 through 2002.

Applications are reviewed by professional volunteers from the private sector in seven categorical areas:[23]

1. *Leadership:* How senior leaders address values, short- and long-term directions, and performance expectations; create value for customers and other stakeholders; create an environment for empowerment, innovation, organizational agility, and employee

learning; ensure two-way communication; address organizational governance; measure, review, and assess organizational performance and success, and then translate these findings into priorities for continuous improvement; are evaluated; and how they use these findings to improve their effectiveness. Also assesses how the organization addresses its responsibilities to the public, ensures ethical behavior, and practices good citizenship.

2. *Strategic planning:* How the organization establishes its strategic objectives and enhances its competitive position, overall performance, and future success; ensures that the strategic planning process addresses customer needs, the competitive environment, and technological changes, and how these might impact products and services, internal strengths and weaknesses, potential risks, and economic changes; converts its strategic objectives into short- and long-term action plans.

3. *Customer and market focus:* How the organization determines requirements, expectations, and preferences of customers and markets to assure continuing relevance of products and services and to develop new opportunities; builds relationships to acquire, satisfy, and retain customers to increase customer loyalty and to develop new opportunities; determines customer satisfaction.

4. *Information and analysis:* How the organization measures, analyzes, aligns, and improves its performance data and information throughout the organization; ensures the quality and availability of needed data and information for employees, suppliers, partners, and customers; builds and manages its knowledge assets.

5. *Human resource focus:* How the organization's work, jobs, compensation, career progression, and other workforce practices enable employees to achieve high performance; employee education, training, and career development support the achievement of overall objectives, contribute to high performance, and build employee knowledge, skills, and capabilities; work environment and employee support climate contributes to the well-being, satisfaction, and motivation of all employees.

6. *Process management:* How the organization identifies and manages its key processes for creating customer value and achieving business success, profitability, and growth; incorporates input from customers, suppliers, and partners to determine process requirements; incorporates efficiency and effectiveness factors into process design; designs and implements processes to ensure they meet requirements; measures performance for the control and improvement of value-creation processes; minimizes cost while preventing defects and rework; identifies and manages its key support processes.

7. *Business results:* Describes the organization's key customer-focused results, including customer satisfaction and customer-perceived value; customer satisfaction compared to that of its competitors; measures of customer retention and relationship building; key product and service performance results, key financial performance results, key human resource results, key operational performance results, and key governance and social responsibility results compared to its competitors.

Organizations are encouraged by NIST to obtain a copy of the Baldrige Award criteria and perform self-assessments using the form and its point valuations. Completing a self-assessment process using the Baldrige Award criteria identifies a firm's strengths and weaknesses and aids the firm in implementing various quality and productivity improvement initiatives. Reviewing the criteria reveals a number of areas consistent with the TQM philosophy; and, to date, thousands of firms have requested copies of the application criteria.

The International Organization for Standardization's ISO 9000 Quality Standards

In an effort to standardize quality requirements for European countries within the Common Market and for other countries wanting to do business in the Common Market, the International Organization for Standardization (ISO), established in 1947 and today with over 140 member countries, adopted the ISO 9000 series of quality standards in 1987 and revised them in 1994 and again in 2000.[24] The standards have been adopted in the United States by the American National Standards Institute (ANSI) and the American Society for Quality (ASQ) and also by Japan. To date, over 400,000 organizations worldwide have received ISO 9000 certifications. The standards apply to all types of businesses. In many cases worldwide, companies will not buy from suppliers who do not possess an ISO 9000 certification.

The three ISO 9000 standards are as follows:

1. *ISO 9000:2000:* Provides the fundamentals and vocabulary necessary to establish the requirements for a quality management system for any organization that needs to demonstrate its ability to meet customer and regulatory requirements and aims to enhance customer satisfaction.

2. *ISO 9001:2000:* Specifies activities that will be needed to be documented and performed to assure that the quality management system is implemented successfully and to assure that customer and regulatory requirements are consistently met, resulting in continuous improvement in the quality management system and its ability to satisfy customers.

3. *ISO 9004:2000:* Standards used to extend the benefits of ISO 9001:2000 to all parties that are interested in or affected by the organization's operations, including employees, owners, suppliers, and society in general.

The quality management system discussed in the ISO 9000 series of standards is based on eight Quality Management Principles, derived from the collective experiences of the international member-experts who participate on the ISO Technical Committee, the body responsible for developing and maintaining the ISO 9000 standards. The eight principles are shown in Table 8.8. Once again, we see the recurring themes of customer focus, top management commitment, workforce involvement, and measuring and evaluating system performance, evident in the quality management approaches discussed earlier. Let us now move on to the TQM tools and statistical approach section.

Table 8.8	ISO's Eight Quality Management Principles
1. Customer focus	Understand current and future customer needs, meet customer requirements, and exceed customer expectations.
2. Leadership	Establish unity of purpose and direction for the organization; create and maintain the internal environment so that people become involved in achieving the organization's objectives.
3. Involvement of people	Understand the importance of fully involving people at all levels in the organization so their abilities can be used to the organization's benefit.
4. Process approach	Identify and manage all key activities and related resources as a process to achieve the desired results.
5. System approach to management	Identify, understand, and manage interrelated processes as a system to effectively and efficiently achieve organization's objectives.
6. Continual improvement	Employment of a consistent organization-wide approach to continual improvement of the organization's performance.
7. Factual approach to decision making	Analyze accurate and reliable data and information using valid methods to obtain more effective decisions.
8. Mutually beneficial supplier relationships	Recognize that an organization and its suppliers are interdependent and that mutually beneficial relationships enhance the ability of both to create value.

The Tools of Total Quality Management

Flow Diagrams

Also called process diagrams or maps, this tool is the necessary first step to evaluating any manufacturing or service process. Flow diagrams use annotated boxes representing process action elements and ovals representing wait periods, connected by arrows to show the flow of products or customers through the process. Once a process or series of processes is mapped out, potential problem areas can be identified and further evaluated for excess inventories and wait times and capacity problems, for instance. An example of a flow diagram is shown in Figure 8.4. Managers should be mapping, observing, and analyzing each process action and wait period element for potential problems.

Check Sheets

Check sheets allow users to determine frequencies for specific problems. For the restaurant example shown in Figure 8.4, managers could make a list of potential problem areas based on experience and then direct employees to keep counts of each problem on check sheets for a given period of time (long enough to allow for problem discrimination). At the end of the data-collection period, problem areas can be reviewed and compared. Figure 8.5 shows a typical check sheet that might be used in a restaurant.

Pareto Charts

Pareto charts, useful for many applications, are based on the work of Vilfredo Pareto, a nineteenth-century economist. For our purposes here, the charts are useful for presenting data in an organized fashion, indicating process problems from most to least severe. It only makes sense when utilizing a firm's resources to work on fixing the most severe problems first (Pareto theory applied here suggests that most of a firm's problem "events"—maybe 80 percent—are accounted for by just a few of the problems). Figure 8.6 shows two Pareto charts for the problems counted in Figure 8.5. Note that we could look at the total problem events either from a problem-type or day-of-the-week perspective and see that *long wait* and *bad server* are the two most troublesome problems, while Saturdays and Fridays are when the most problem events occur. Solving or fixing the top two problems in this case would eliminate approximately 40 percent of all the problem events.

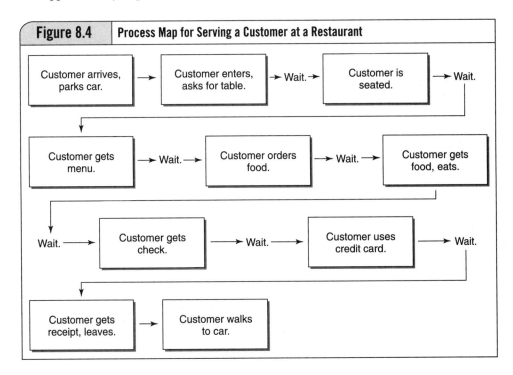

| Figure 8.4 | Process Map for Serving a Customer at a Restaurant |

Figure 8.5	Check Sheet for a Restaurant

Problem	Mon.	Tues.	Wed.	Thurs.	Fri.	Sat.	Sun.	Totals	% of Total
Long wait	//////	/////	////////	//////	/////////	//////////	////	48	26.5
Cold food		//	/	/	///	//		9	5.0
Bad food	//	/	///		/	////		11	6.1
Wrong food	/////	//	/	//	/////	///	/	19	10.5
Bad server	//////	///	/////	/	//////	//	/	24	13.3
Bad table		/	//		/	///	/	8	4.4
Room temp.			//	///	/////	/////		15	8.3
Too expensive	/	//	/	/	///	///		11	6.1
No parking			//		/////	///////		14	7.7
Wrong change	//////	/	////		////	///		18	9.9
Other		/	//			/		4	2.2
Totals	26	18	31	14	42	43	7	181	100

Figure 8.6	Pareto Charts for Restaurant Problems

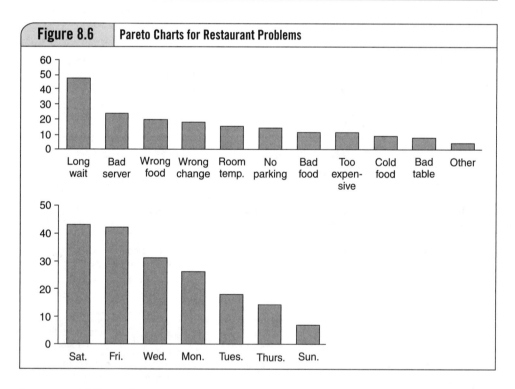

Cause-and-Effect Diagrams

Once a problem has been identified, **cause-and-effect diagrams** (also called **fishbone or Ishikawa diagrams**) can be used to aid in brainstorming and isolating the causes of a problem. Figure 8.7 illustrates a cause-and-effect diagram for the *long wait* problem of Figure 8.5. The problem is shown at the front end of the diagram. Each of the four diagonals of the diagram represents potential groups of causes. The four groups of causes shown, Material, Machine, Methods, and Manpower, or the 4 Ms, are the standard classifications of causes and provide a very good checklist for problem-cause analyses. Typically, workers will gather together and brainstorm causes for a problem in these four areas. Each branch on the diago-

Figure 8.7	Cause-and-Effect Diagram for the Long Wait Problem

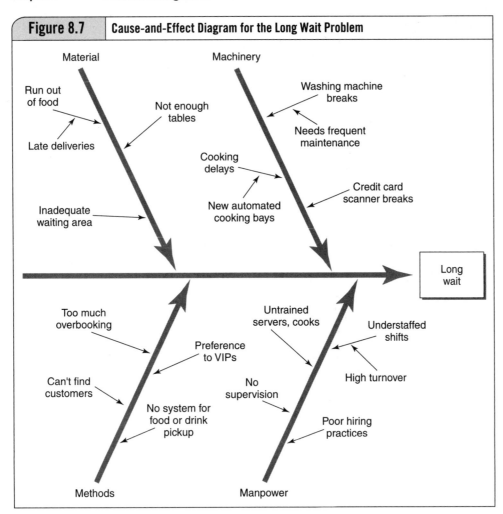

nals represents one potential cause. Subcauses are also part of the brainstorming process and are shown as smaller branches attached to each of the primary causes. Breaking a problem like this down into its causes and subcauses allows workers to then go back to the process and determine the relative significance of each cause and subcause using checklists, statistical process control techniques (discussed next), and Pareto charts once again. Eventually, the firm begins working to eliminate the sources of the problem, starting with the most significant causes and subcauses, until most of the problem's impact disappears.

A properly thought-out cause-and-effect diagram can be a very powerful tool for use in TQM improvement efforts. Without its use, workers and management risk trying to eliminate causes that have very little to do with the problem at hand or working on problems that are quite minor compared to other, more significant problems.

Statistical Process Control

A necessary part of any quality improvement effort, *statistical process control (SPC)* allows firms to visually monitor process performance, compare the performance to desired levels or standards, and take corrective steps quickly before process variabilities get out of control and damage products, services, and customer relationships. Once a process is working correctly, firms gather process performance data, create **control charts** to monitor process variabilities, then collect sample measurements of the process over time. The means of these sample measures are plotted on control charts. If the sample means fall within acceptable limits and appear *normally distributed* around the desired measurement, we say the process is in *statistical control* and the process is permitted to continue; sample measurements also continue. When a sample plot falls out of the acceptable limits or when the plots no longer appear normally distributed around the desired measurement, the process is deemed to be *out of control.* The process is then stopped, problems are identified, and causes are determined and eliminated. Control charts are graphic representations of process performance over time, showing the desired measurement (the center line of the control chart) and the process's upper and lower control limits. This visual aid makes it very easy for operators or other workers to plot data and compare performance over time.

Variations. Variations in process measurements can be either **natural variations** or **assignable variations.** All processes are affected by these variations, and environmental noise or natural variations are to be expected. When only natural variations are present, the process is in statistical control. Assignable variations are those that can be traced to a specific cause (such as the causes shown in Figure 8.7). These assignable variations are created by causes that can be identified and eliminated and thus become the objective of statistical process control efforts.

Samples. Because of the presence of variations in process measures, samples of data are collected and their means are then plotted onto control charts. Sample measures can be either **variable data** or **attribute data,** and each requires a different type of control chart. Variable data are continuous, such as weight, time, and length (as in the weight of a box of cereal, the time to serve a customer, or the length of a steel girder). Attribute data indicate the presence of some attribute such as color, satisfaction, workability, or beauty (for instance, measuring whether or not a car was painted the right color, if a customer liked the meal, if the light bulb worked, or if the dress was pretty).

Variable data samples are shown as an average of the sample's measures (for instance, an average of 12.04 ounces in five boxes of cereal), whereas attribute data are shown as the percent defectives in a sample (for instance 10 percent, or 0.10 of the light bulb sample that did not work). Let us look at the two types of control charts next.

Variable Control Charts. When measuring and plotting variable process data, two types of control charts are needed: the **x̄-chart** and the **R-chart.** The x̄-chart is used to track the central tendency of the sample means, while the R-chart is used to track sample ranges, or the variation of the measurements within each sample. A perfect process would have sample means equal to the desired measure and sample ranges equal to zero. It is necessary to view both of these charts in unison, since a sample mean might look fine even though, for instance, two of the five measures are far from the desirable measure, making the sample range very high. It could also be the case that the sample range looks fine (all measures are quite close to one another), even though all five measures are far from the desirable measure, making the sample mean look bad. For variable data then, both the x̄-chart and the R-chart must show that the samples are in control before the process itself is considered in control. Constructing the x̄-chart and the R-chart is discussed next.

The first step in constructing any control chart is to gather data (provided the process is already in control and working well). Typically, about twenty-five or thirty samples of size five to ten are collected, spaced out over a period of time. Then, for each sample, the mean ($\bar{x}$) and the range *(R)* are calculated. Next, the *overall mean* ($\bar{\bar{x}}$) of all the samples and the *average range (R̄)* of all the samples are calculated. The $\bar{\bar{x}}$ and $\bar{R}$ measures become the center lines (desirable measures) of their respective charts. Example 8.1 provides the data used to illustrate the calculation of the center lines of the x̄-chart and the R-chart. The formulas used to calculate the center lines $\bar{\bar{x}}$ and $\bar{R}$ are

$$\bar{\bar{x}} = \frac{\sum_{i=1}^{k} \bar{x}_i}{k} \quad \text{and} \quad \bar{R} = \frac{\sum_{i=1}^{k} R_1}{k},$$

where *k* indicates the number of samples and *i* indicates the specific sample.

EXAMPLE 8.1   Variable control chart data for soup cans at Hayley Girl Soup Co.

The Hayley Girl Soup Co., a soup manufacturer, has collected process data in order to construct control charts to use in its canning facility. Hayley Girl collected twenty-four samples of four cans each hour over a twenty-four-hour period, and the data follow for each sample:

Hour	1	2	3	4	$\bar{x}$	R
1	12	12.2	11.7	11.6	11.88	0.6
2	11.5	11.7	11.6	12.3	11.78	0.8
3	11.9	12.2	12.1	12	12.05	0.3
4	12.1	11.8	12.1	11.7	11.93	0.4
5	12.2	12.3	11.7	11.9	12.03	0.6
6	12.1	11.9	12.3	12.2	12.13	0.4
7	12	11.7	11.6	12.1	11.85	0.5
8	12	12.1	12.2	12.3	12.15	0.3
9	11.8	11.9	12	12	11.93	0.2
10	12.1	11.9	11.8	11.7	11.88	0.3
11	12.1	12	12.1	11.9	12.03	0.2
12	11.9	11.9	11.7	11.8	11.83	0.2
13	12	12	11.8	12.1	11.98	0.3
14	12.1	11.9	12	11.7	11.93	0.4
15	12	12	11.7	11.2	11.73	0.8
16	12.1	12	12	11.9	12.00	0.2
17	12.1	12.2	12	11.9	12.05	0.3
18	12.2	12	11.7	11.8	11.93	0.5
19	12	12.1	12.3	12	12.10	0.3
20	12	12.2	11.9	12	12.03	0.3
21	11.9	11.8	12.1	12	11.95	0.3
22	12.1	11.8	11.9	12	11.95	0.3
23	12.1	12	11.9	11.9	11.98	0.2
24	12	12.3	11.7	12	12.00	0.6
Means					**11.96**	**0.39**

For the data shown for Hayley Soup Co., we see that $\bar{\bar{x}} = 11.96$ and $\bar{R} = 0.39$. If these measures are seen as acceptable by Hayley Soup Co., then it can use these to construct its control charts. These means are also used to calculate the upper and lower control limits for the two charts. The formulas are:

$$\text{UCL}_{\bar{x}} = \bar{\bar{x}} + A_2\bar{R} \text{ and } \text{LCL}_{\bar{x}} = \bar{\bar{x}} - A_2\bar{R}$$
$$\text{UCL}_R = D_4\bar{R} \text{ and } \text{LCL}_R = D_3\bar{R},$$

where A_2, D_3, and D_4 are constants based on the size of each sample and are shown in Table 8.9 (the constants used are based on an assumption that the sampling distribution is normal and that the control limits are ± three standard deviations from the population mean, which contains 99.73 percent of the sampling distribution). The constants for various sample sizes are shown in Table 8.9.

Table 8.9	Constants for Computing Control Chart Limits ($\pm\,3\sigma$)		
Sample Size, n	Mean Factor, A_2	UCL, D_4	LCL, D_3
2	1.88	3.268	0
3	1.023	2.574	0
4	0.729	2.282	0
5	0.577	2.115	0
6	0.483	2.004	0
7	0.419	1.924	0.076
8	0.373	1.864	0.136
9	0.337	1.816	0.184
10	0.308	1.777	0.223

Source: Adapted from Table 27 of the ASTM STP 15D ASTM *Manual on Presentation of Data and Control Chart Analysis,* © 1976 American Society for Testing and Materials, Philadelphia, Pa.

Using the data in Example 8.1 and Table 8.9, we can determine the upper and lower control limits for both the $\bar{x}$-chart and the R-chart for the Hayley Soup Co.:

$$\text{UCL}_{\bar{x}} = \bar{\bar{x}} + A_2\bar{R} = 11.96 + 0.729(0.39) = 12.24$$
$$\text{LCL}_{\bar{x}} = \bar{\bar{x}} - A_2\bar{R} = 11.96 - 0.729(0.39) = 11.68$$
$$\text{and}$$
$$\text{UCL}_R = D_4\bar{R} = 2.282(0.39) = 0.89$$
$$\text{LCL}_R = D_3\bar{R} = 0(0.39) = 0$$

Next, we can use the means and control limits to construct our two control charts. In Figure 8.8, we have plotted the original data sample means and ranges onto the two variable data control charts, showing the center lines and the control limits. From these plots, it appears that the process is indeed in statistical control, and the Hayley Soup Co. can begin using these charts to monitor the canning process. If the process appears out of control on either chart, the control charts would not be useful and should be discarded until problems are eliminated and the process is once again in statistical control.

Once control charts have been created and samples from the process are being statistically monitored, the following steps should be followed:

1. Collect samples of size four to five periodically (depending on the type of process and ease of data collection).

2. Plot the sample means on both control charts, monitoring whether or not the process is in control.

3. When the process appears out of control, use check sheets, Pareto charts, and fishbone diagrams, if necessary, to investigate causes and eliminate process variations.

4. Repeat Step 1 through Step 3.

Attribute Control Charts. When collecting data on whether or not a process is producing good or bad (nondefective or defective) output, use of $\bar{x}$- and R-charts no longer apply. In these cases, we use either ***P-charts,*** which monitor the *percent defective* in each sample, or ***C-charts,*** which count the *number of defects* per unit of output. Discussion of each of these follows.

P-charts are the most commonly used attribute control charts. If we use large sample sizes when collecting data samples, we can assume they are normally distributed and use the following formulas to calculate the center line ($\bar{P}$) and the upper and lower control limits for the P-chart:

$$\bar{P} = \frac{\sum\limits_{i=1}^{k} P_i}{k},$$

| Figure 8.8 | $\bar{x}$-Chart and R-Chart for the Hayley Girl Soup Co. |

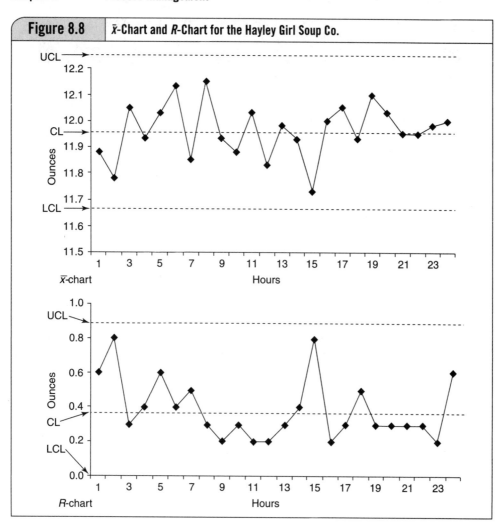

where $\bar{P}$ is the mean fraction defective for all samples collected, k represents the number of samples, P is the fraction defective in one sample, and i represents the specific sample; and

$$\text{UCL}_\text{P} = \bar{P} + z\sigma_p$$
$$\text{LCL}_\text{P} = \bar{P} - z\sigma_p,$$

where z is the number of standard deviations from the mean (recall when $z = 3$, the control limits will contain 99.73 percent of all the sample data plots) and σ_p is the standard deviation of the sampling distribution. The sample standard deviation is calculated using

$$\sigma_P = \sqrt{\frac{(\bar{P})(1 - \bar{P})}{n}}$$

where n is the size of each sample. Example 8.2 provides the data used to determine $\bar{P}$, σ_P, and the control limits for the P-chart.

As shown in Example 8.2, $\bar{P} = 0.014$. Calculating σ_p, we get

$$\sigma_P = \sqrt{\frac{(0.014)(0.986)}{100}} = 0.012.$$

EXAMPLE 8.2   Attribute control chart data for the Blakester Lightbulb Co.

The Blakester Lightbulb Co. makes 100-watt light bulbs, and it has decided to begin monitoring their quality using a P-chart. So, over the past thirty days, Blakester has collected and
tested 100 bulbs each day. The following chart shows the fraction defectives for each sample
and the overall average fraction defective, or $\bar{P}$.

Day	Fraction Defective	Day	Fraction Defective
1	0.01	16	0.04
2	0.02	17	0
3	0	18	0
4	0.03	19	0.01
5	0	20	0.03
6	0.01	21	0.02
7	0.04	22	0
8	0	23	0.01
9	0	24	0.02
10	0.02	25	0.01
11	0.02	26	0.03
12	0.03	27	0
13	0	28	0.02
14	0.04	29	0.01
15	0.01	30	0
			$\bar{P} = 0.014$

Now the control limits can be calculated (assuming we want limits containing 99.73 percent of the data points, or $z = 3$):

$$UCL_P = 0.014 + 3(0.012) = 0.05, \text{ and}$$
$$LCL_P = 0.014 - 3(0.012) = 0.$$

Note that the lower control limit is truncated at zero, as is the case in most P-charts. Figure 8.9 shows the P-chart for the Blakester Lightbulb Co. with the fraction defectives from
Example 8.2. Viewing the chart, we see that the process appears to be in control, since the
data points are randomly dispersed around the centerline and about half the data points are
on each side of the centerline. Thus, the Blakester Lightbulb Co. can continue using the control chart to monitor its lightbulb quality.

When multiple errors can occur in a process resulting in a defective unit, then we can use
c-charts to control the *number* of defects per unit of output. c-charts are useful when a number of mistakes or errors can occur per unit of output but they occur infrequently. Examples
can include a hotel stay, a printed textbook, or a construction project. The control limits for
c-charts are based on the assumption of a Poisson probability distribution of the item of interest (commonly used when defects are infrequent). In this case, the distribution variance is
equal to its mean. For c-charts, then,

$$\bar{c} = \text{mean errors per unit of measure (and also the sample variance),}$$
$$\sqrt{\bar{c}} = \text{sample standard deviation, and}$$
$$\bar{c} \pm 3\sqrt{\bar{c}} = \text{control limits.}$$

Example 8.3 can be used to illustrate the calculation of the c-chart's control limits. In the
example, the units of measure are days; thus, the average daily defects are 29.1 (the centerline
and also the variance). The upper and lower control limits are 45.3 and 12.9, respectively.

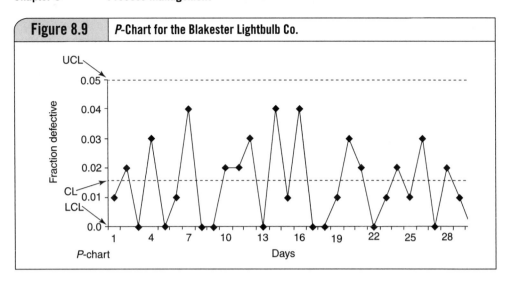

Figure 8.9 | *P*-Chart for the Blakester Lightbulb Co.

EXAMPLE 8.3   Monitoring editorial defects at Taney Publishing, Inc.

Eight editorial assistants are monitored for defects in the firm's printed work on a monthly basis. Over the past thirty days, a total number of 872 editorial mistakes were found. Computing the centerline and control limits, we find:

$$\bar{c} = \frac{872}{30} = 29.1 \text{ mistakes per day}$$

$$\text{UCL}_c = 29.1 + 3\sqrt{29.1} = 45.3, \text{ and LCL}_c = 29.1 - 3\sqrt{29.1} = 12.9.$$

The Taney Publishing Co. can now use the *c*-chart centerline and control limits based on the thirty-day error data to monitor its daily editorial error rate.

Process Capability. Statistical process control is all about monitoring processes so that we can isolate and then reduce process variations, resulting in higher levels of product and service quality. If our organization, our suppliers, and our industrial and retail customers can do this effectively, the products and services from our supply chains can create tremendous competitive advantage for all the firms involved. As time progresses and process improvements occur, the range of variations within each process narrows, which in turn allows control limits to narrow. This reduction in variation and control limits thus coincides with quality improvement and results in benefits to the firm and its supply chains.

Firms can monitor the current process variation and its future changes using a *process capability index*, or C_{pk} **index.** For each process, C_{pk} measures the ratio of the desired process variation to the actual process variation. Two assumptions accompany use of the C_{pk}:

1. The process must be under control (only natural variations are present).

2. The process is normally distributed.

The formula for the C_{pk} is

$$C_{pk} = \frac{[\text{the smallest difference between the UCL or LCL and the center line}]}{3\sigma}$$

Thus, a C_{pk} of 1.0 indicates that the process is capable of producing within the control limits 99.73 percent of the time, resulting in no more than three data points outside the control limits for every thousand. A C_{pk} greater than 1.0 indicates even fewer defects, while a C_{pk} of less than 1.0 is potentially troublesome and indicates that the process may be incapable of producing within the control limits.

An extension of process capability is the **six sigma program,** a type of TQM program centered around statistical process control, popularized by Motorola, and referring to just over three data points outside the control limits for every million. General Electric, among many others, has embraced the six sigma program, saving billions of dollars in poor-quality costs.[25]

Acceptance Sampling. When shipments of product are received from suppliers, or before they are shipped to customers, samples can be taken from the batch of units and measured against some quality acceptance standard. The quality of the sample is then assumed to represent the quality of the entire shipment (particularly when shipments contain many units of product, sampling is far less time-consuming than testing every unit to determine the overall quality of an incoming or outgoing shipment). Ideally, if strategic alliance members within a supply chain are using SPC and the quality improvement tools to build quality into the products they provide, acceptance sampling can be eliminated and used only when new or nonalliance suppliers furnish products or materials to the firm. In these situations, acceptance sampling can be used to determine whether or not a shipment will be accepted, returned to the supplier, or used for billback purposes when defects are fixed or units are eliminated by the buyer.

One topic that arises is how big to make the test sample. One way to assure that the quality of the sample is identical to the quality of the entire shipment is to make the sample size equal to the size of the shipment (in other words, examine every unit). Since this is usually impractical, we assume the risk of incorrectly judging the quality of the shipment based on the size of the sample: the smaller the sample size, the greater the risk of incorrectly judging shipment quality.

There is a cost to both the supplier and buyer when incorrect quality assessments are made. When a buyer rejects a shipment of good-quality units because the sample quality level did not meet the acceptance standard, this is termed **producer's risk.** When this happens, it is called a **type-I error.** Conversely, when a buyer accepts a shipment of poor-quality units because the sample did meet the acceptance standard, this is termed **consumer's risk** and results in a **type-II error.** Obviously, trading partners wish to avoid or minimize the occurrence of both of these outcomes. To minimize type-I and type-II errors, buyers and sellers must derive an acceptable sampling plan by agreeing on unacceptable defect levels and a sample size big enough to result in acceptable levels of type-I and type-II errors.

Statistical Process Control and Supply Chain Management. Ideally, strategic supply chain partners would not need to monitor their own process quality; quality would already be extremely high, and employees could spend their time in more productive pursuits. However, most processes are not yet perfect, and the level of competition is so fierce in most industries that firms find they must continually be assessing and reassessing process quality levels and capabilities. Managers should identify processes that are critical to achieving the firm's objectives, decide how to monitor process performance, gather data and create the appropriate control charts, and create policies for collecting process samples and monitoring quality over time. Managers must also work to create a culture where quality improvements are encouraged and employees are empowered to make the changes that will result in improved product and service quality.

Summary

Supply chain management, the just-in-time philosophy, and total quality management make up a hierarchy for breakthrough competitive advantage. In order for supply chain management to reach its full potential and provide benefits to its members, trading partners must adopt a JIT operating philosophy. Similarly, the primary ingredient in the success of a JIT program is the use of TQM and its improvement tools. There are a number of practices mentioned within each of the three topics that overlap or are very similar such as top management and workforce involvement and continuous improvement. This is not surprising given the close ties between supply chain management, JIT, and TQM. We have spent considerable time covering JIT and TQM because of their critical importance in achieving successful supply chain management, and we hope you have gained an appreciation for the topics presented here.

Key Terms

assignable variations, 230
attribute data, 230
cause-and-effect diagrams, 228
c-chart, 232
channel integration, 209
consumer's risk, 236
control charts, 229
C_{pk} index, 235
efficient consumer response (ECR), 208
electronic data interchange (EDI), 214

fishbone or Ishikawa diagrams, 228
group technology work cells, 212
kaizan, 217
kanban, 214
keiretsu relationships, 208
natural variations, 230
P-chart, 232
producer's risk, 236
production kanban, 216
quality circle concept, 221
quick response (QR), 208

R-chart, 230
setup, 214
silo effect, 209
six sigma program, 236
type-I error, 236
type-II error, 236
value analysis, 218
variable data, 230
virtual inventory systems, 214
withdrawal kanban, 216
$\bar{x}$- chart, 230

Discussion Questions

1. Explain why JIT is so important to successful supply chain management.
2. Briefly explain the primary concerns and objectives of JIT.
3. Looking at Table 8.1, which stage would you say Wal-Mart is in? How about a locally owned sandwich shop?
4. What are the advantages and disadvantages of making small, frequent purchases from just a few suppliers? How do we overcome the disadvantages?
5. What are group technology work cells, and why are they important in JIT?
6. Why should JIT layouts be "visual"?
7. Reducing lot sizes and increasing setups are common practices in most JIT firms. Why?
8. What are kanbans and why are they used in JIT?

9. What is kaizen, and why is it so important to successful JIT?

10. What are the advantages and disadvantages of using JIT II supplier relationships?

11. Why is the customer so important in TQM?

12. How does your definition of quality compare to that of the American Society for Quality?

13. Describe three ways that your university could improve quality.

14. What does Deming's Theory of Management have to do with quality?

15. How do Deming's fourteen points and Crosby's fourteen steps differ?

16. In looking at the list of Baldrige Award winners (Table 8.7), do you think these firms have high-quality products? How successful are they now?

17. In viewing the Baldrige Award's seven information categories, how would your firm stack up in these areas (use the university or your most recent job if you are not currently employed).

18. Construct a flow diagram of the registration process at your university.

19. Construct a cause-and-effect diagram for the following problem: The registration process is too long.

20. Can a process exhibit sample measurements that are all within the control limits and still be considered out of control? Explain.

21. Can organizations control and reduce natural variations? If so, how?

22. What are some variable data and attribute data that could be collected to track the quality of education at your university?

23. When monitoring variable process data, why do we need to monitor both the $\bar{x}$-chart and the R-chart simultaneously?

24. How could P-charts be used in a manufacturing facility?

25. Can a process be considered in control but incapable?

26. Using the table in Appendix I, find out exactly how many defective samples out of 1 million you would expect if you successfully reached the six sigma goal.

27. If a goal of a supplier partnership is to eliminate acceptance sampling, then who does it?

Internet Questions

1. Search on-line for the term *JIT II* and report on several firms that have used JIT II.

2. Go to the Baldrige Award Web site (http://www.quality.nist.gov) and find out what organizations have won the award since this book was published.

3. Why isn't the International Organization for Standardization called the IOS? (*Hint:* There is a discussion of this topic at the ISO Web site, http://www.iso.ch.)

Problems

1. Stanley Compressors uses a JIT assembly line to make its compressors. In one assembly area, the demand is 100 parts per eight-hour day. It uses a container that holds eight parts. It typically takes about six hours to round-trip a container from one work center to the next and back again. How many containers should Stanley Compressors be using?

2. Eakins Enterprises makes model boats, and it is switching to a JIT manufacturing process. At one assembly area, Eakins is using one parts container that holds 250 parts, and it wants the output to be approximately 100 finished parts per hour. How fast will the container have to make it through the system to accomplish this?

3. The following sample information was obtained by taking four doughnuts per hour for twelve hours from the Grebson Bakery doughnut process and weighing them:

Hour	Weights (Grams)
1	110, 105, 98, 100
2	79, 102, 100, 104
3	100, 102, 100, 96
4	94, 98, 99, 101
5	98, 104, 97, 100
6	104, 97, 99, 100
7	89, 102, 101, 99
8	100, 101, 98, 96
9	98, 95, 101, 100
10	99, 100, 97, 102
11	102, 97, 100, 101
12	98, 100, 100, 97

For the data shown, find:

a. $\bar{x}$ and R for each sample

b. $\bar{\bar{x}}$ and $\bar{R}$ for the twelve samples

c. the three-sigma UCL and LCL for the mean and range charts

d. Does the process look to be in statistical control. Why or why not?

4. Through process sampling of cooking and delivery times, Mary Jane's Pizzeria finds the mean of all samples to be 27.4 minutes, with an average sample range of 5.2 minutes. The pizzeria tracked four deliveries per hour for eighteen hours to obtain its samples.

a. Is this an example of variable or attribute sampling data?

b. Find the UCL and LCL for both the $\bar{x}$ and R charts.

5. Ten customers per hour were asked by the cashier at Pearson's Deli if they liked their meal, and the fraction that said "no" are shown in the following table for a twelve-hour period.

Hour	Fraction Defective
1	0
2	.2
3	.4
4	.1
5	.1
6	.2
7	.1
8	0
9	0
10	.2
11	0
12	.1

For the data shown, find:

a. $\bar{P}$

b. σ_P

c. the three-sigma UCL and LCL

d. Does customer satisfaction at Pearson's appear to be in statistical control? How could we improve the analysis?

6. Le Robert's Steakhouse tracks customer complaints every day and then follows up with its customers to resolve problems. For the past thirty days, it received a total of twenty-two complaints from unhappy customers. Using this information, calculate:

   a. $\bar{c}$

   b. the three sigma control limits

7. What would the C_{pk} index be for Problem 3 if we desired the doughnuts to be 100 grams ±5 percent? Is the process capable of this?

References

Burt, D. N., D. W. Dobler, and S. L. Starling. *World Class Supply Management: The Key to Supply Chain Management,* 7th ed. New York: McGraw-Hill, 2003.

Crosby, P. B. *Quality Is Free.* New York: McGraw-Hill, 1979.

Crosby, P. B. *Quality without Tears.* New York: McGraw-Hill, 1984.

Deming, W. E. *Out of the Crisis.* Cambridge, Mass.: MIT Center for Advanced Engineering Study, 1986.

Evans, J. R., and W. M. Lindsay. *The Management and Control of Quality,* 4th ed. Cincinnati: South-Western, 1999.

Heizer, J., and B. Render. *Principles of Operations Management,* 4th ed. Upper Saddle River: Prentice-Hall, 2000.

Smith, G. *Statistical Process Control and Quality Improvement.* New York: Macmillan, 1991.

Vokurka, R. J., and R. R. Lummus. "The Role of Just-in-Time in Supply Chain Management." *International Journal of Logistics Management* 11, no. 1 (2000): 89–98.

Notes

1. V. Cooper and M. Cohen, "Inside Outsourcing at Celestica: An Interview with Celestica's Supply Chain Chief, Andrew Gort," *Insight Magazine* 13, no. 2 (2001): 6–10.

2. Reprinted with permission from the publisher, the Institute for Supply Management™, "Integrated Supply Successes," by J. V. Veronesi, A. MacLea, and R. P. Zigas, Ph.D., C.P.M. *Purchasing Today*® 10, no. 2 (February 1999): 60–64.

3. J. S. McClenahan, "JIT Inventory Systems Hold Appeal," *Industry Week* 250, no. 7 (2001): 11.

4. Adapted from G. C. Stevens, "Integrating the Supply Chain," *International Journal of Physical Distribution and Logistics Management* 19, no. 8 (1989): 3–8.

5. Reprinted with permission from the publisher, the Institute for Supply Management™, "Warehouse Changes are Just in Time," by S. Caulk, *Purchasing Today*® (March 2000 Supplement).

6. C. Gourley, "What's Driving the Automotive Supply Chain?" *Warehouse Management* 5, no. 10 (1998): 44–48.

7. T. Andel, "Profitablity Reflects Well on the Big Three," *Material Handling Management* 56, no. 7 (2001): 44–48.

8. S. Caulk, "Warehouse Changes Are Just in Time," *Purchasing Today*® (March 2000 Supplement).

9. T. Andel, "Auto Makers May Teach You a Lesson," *Transportation & Distribution* 39, no. 8 (1998): 45–49.

10. C. Gourley, "What's Driving the Automotive Supply Chain?" *Warehouse Management* 5, no. 10 (1998): 44–48.

11. T. Andel, "Auto Makers May Teach You a Lesson," *Transportation & Distribution* 39, no. 8 (1998): 45–49.

12. Reprinted with permission from the publisher, The Institute for Supply Management,® "Warehouse Changes are Just in Time," by S. Caulk, *Purchasing Today*® (March 2000 Supplement).

13. L. J. Aaron, "From Push to Pull: The Supply Chain Management Shift," *Apparel Industry Magazine* 59, no. 6 (1998): 58–59.

14. D. Doran, "Synchronous Supply: An Automotive Case Study," *European Business Review* 13, no. 2 (2001): 114–20. Reprinted with permission of www.emeraldinsight.com.

15. C. Gourley, "What's Driving the Automotive Supply Chain?" *Warehousing Management* 5, no. 10 (1998): 44–48.

16. W. E. Deming, *Out of the Crisis* (Cambridge, Mass.: MIT Press, 1993).

17. B. Deierlein, "JIT: Zero Tolerance for Late Deliveries," *Fleet Equipment* 26, no. 1 (2000): 36–39.

18. C. Y. Lee and X. Zhou, "Quality Management and Manufacturing Strategies in China," *The International Journal of Quality and Reliability Management* 17, no. 8 (2000): 876–98.

19. H. Sun and T. Cheng, "Comparing Reasons, Practices, and Effects of ISO 9000 Certification and TQM Implementation in Norwegian SMEs and Large Firms," *International Small Business Journal* 20, no. 4 (2002): 421–35.

20. B. Lurz, P. Cardis, and M. Stromberg, "Cementing Relationships," *Professional Builder* 67, no. 9 (2002): 66–75.

21. T. Mudd, "Sleeping Beauty," *Industry Week* 251, no. 7 (2002): 64–65.

22. E. John, "Quality Is . . .," *Management Services* 46, no. 9 (2002): 8–11.

23. Criteria and other Baldrige Award information are available from the National Institute of Standards and Technology; available from http://www.nist.gov (criteria for education and health-care categories vary somewhat from what is shown here).

24. Information about the International Organization for Standardization and the ISO certification standards can be obtained from the ISO Web site; available from http://www.iso.ch

25. G. Lucier and S. Seshadri, "GE Takes Six Sigma Beyond the Bottom Line," *Strategic Finance* 82, no. 11 (2001): 40–46.

PART 3 CASES

Case Study 6

JIT Implementation Issues at the Oak Hills Production Facility

Industry and Company Overview

The Oak Hills facility is a unit of The Oil and Gas Services (TOGS) Company, an integrated oil and gas industry services company headquartered in Houston, Texas. Primarily, TOGS provides services to public and government-owned energy companies. Currently, oil prices and demand are at a low point in an industry-wide cyclical slump, with no upturn in oil prices or demand in the foreseeable future. TOGS recently acquired a competitor, Triangle Corp. Triangle manufactures the same types of service products as the Oak Hills facility. In turn, TOGS was acquired by Pasadena Services. Press releases by Pasadena Services indicated that the company intended to reduce operating expenses by consolidating redundant operations. Pasadena Services also expected that revenues would increase since the combined companies would now offer a full array of upstream services that could be marketed as a complete service package.

The Oak Hills Facility and Product Line

A project team of students in a Supply Chain Management class had been assigned the task of assisting the Oak Hills manufacturing facility to implement a pull system to replace the existing push system. Due to industry conditions, the facility was under intense pressure from headquarters to reduce costs. The managers of the plant had decided the best way to accomplish this was to implement a just-in-time (JIT) inventory system to reduce inventory costs and delivery costs and to improve customer service. The semester was only two weeks old when the project team met Pauline Zhang, special projects coordinator at the Oak Hills facility. Oak Hills was a separate facility located close to TOGS headquarters, and Pauline had recently been assigned to the Oak Hills plant. The agenda for the visit was to provide an overview of the facility and the product line under consideration for conversion to a JIT system. A full tour of the facility and a short question-and-answer session would conclude the visit. The facility layout is shown in Figure C.1.

The main product manufactured at the Oak Hills facility was a testing instrument used in oil and gas exploration. The facility sold to other oilfield supply companies and to large foreign government-owned companies that did not own manufacturing facilities for the testing instrument. Due to the depressed price of oil, exploration activities were at an all time low and product demand was anticipated to drop from an estimated 2.5 million units this year to less than half that amount next year.

Demand for testing instruments was both local and global and, as seen in Table C.1, was highly erratic within product lines. Large-volume orders with lead times of up to three months were the norm for foreign orders, so months could go by before a product line was manufactured again. The reason for the large international orders was the complicated and voluminous export paperwork requirement of the U.S. government. Domestic order volumes were smaller, and lead times were around one week. Many domestic orders were rush jobs and had to be expedited on the shop floor since the daily cost of an idle exploration well could range from $50,000 to $100,000 per day.

Source: © John K. Visich, Ph.D., Bryant College; Angela M. Wicks, Ph.D., Bryant College; and Tarek M. Amine, MBA and Six Sigma Black Belt, Bechtel Global Engineering and Construction Co. Reprinted with permission.

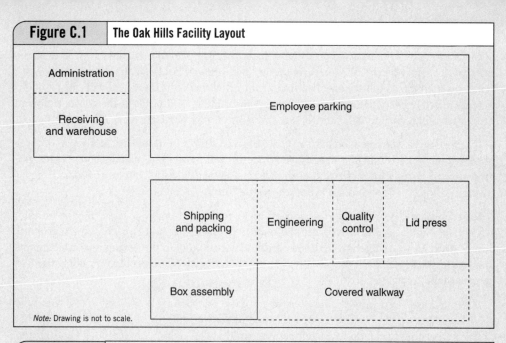

Figure C.1	The Oak Hills Facility Layout

Administration

Receiving and warehouse

Employee parking

Shipping and packing

Engineering

Quality control

Lid press

Box assembly

Covered walkway

Note: Drawing is not to scale.

Table C.1	Pilot Line and Demand Projections					
Product No.	Sensor	Case No.	Lid No.	12M Total	Survey	Forecast
1	G1	595	1-633	42,000	11,000	28,000
2	B1	725	1-779	4,000	0	2,600
3	R1	725	1-779	0	0	0
4	R1	725	1-102	0	6,000	4,000
5	B1	725	1-102	76,000	100	22,000
6	G1	669	1-102	16,000	26,000	17,500
7	R1	595	1-129	3,600	54,000	28,000
8	B1	595	1-129-5	295,000	88,000	216,000
9	R1	056	1-129-5	6,400	4,800	4,500
10	R1	576	1-521	4,7000	0	3,000
11	B1	576	1-521	7,600	1,200	4,000
12	R1	818	1-5460	25,000	44,000	16,000
13	R1	818	1-5460	63,000	48,000	46,000
14	R1	757	1-5460	80,000	3000	45,000
15	B1	757	1-5460	69,000	11,000	44,000
16	R1	117	1-601	161,000	12,000	98,000
17	B1	117	1-601	97,000	15,000	24,500
18	R1	930	1-622	158,000	6,000	80,000
19	B1	930	1-622	92,000	9,500	56,000
20	R1	233	1-622	3,600	750	2,500
21	B1	233	1-622	0	0	0
22	G1	233	1-622-5	56,000	21,000	35,500
23	G1	232	1-6320	42,000	0	28,000
24	R1	932	1-6320	234,000	48,000	142,000
25	R1	618	1-852	92,000	22,000	56,000
26	B1	002	1-896	215,000	38,000	120,000
27	R1	752	1-896	9,000	0	6,000
28	B1	134	1-906	100,000	26,000	72,000
29	G1	386	1-906-5	21,000	25,000	14,000

Notes: 12M Total is the most recent twelve months of demand. Forecast data have been adjusted to reflect the downturn in the industry and are projected out twelve months. Product Numbers 3, 4, and 21 have been recently developed and not all customers are aware they are available. Temperature sensors are categorized as: G (325= C); B (400= C); and R (500= C).

Since rush jobs were expected on a weekly basis, the plant had to maintain a high level of raw materials inventory on site. This, in turn, meant that inventory holding costs were quite high; inventory was estimated to turn over five times annually. Other costs associated with the rush jobs were increased delivery costs and overtime pay. In addition, as a result of the constant flow of rush orders, employee morale suffered and expected customer service levels were not maintained.

The testing instrument produced by Oak Hills was simple in design and consisted of three primary components that comprised over 80 percent of the cost. A machined case acted as a protective receptacle for a sensor board. A lid made from a composite of powdered metals covered the case. This combination was called the "box."

Cases were purchased from Precision Milling, an outside vendor located in San Antonio, Texas (about a three-hour drive from the plant). The cases had to be machined to specification in order to fit a matching sensor board and accommodate the wiring and attachments that would go out the back of the case and up the drill shaft. Case production comprised 48 percent of the cost of the box.

The purchased sensor board was 20 percent of the cost. Sensor boards came in a variety of sizes depending on the variables to be measured in the well and three material variations that differed according to the expected temperature in the well. Sensor boards built to withstand temperatures up to 500° Celsius were more expensive than those built for 400° and 325°.

The lid was manufactured by Oak Hills. A different lid was required for each type of box, and the lids could not be inventoried due to the properties of the composite. The manufacturing process and the placement of the lids were critically important; management estimated that these factors accounted for 75 percent of the variation in the box production process.

Other important factors were labor costs and the manufacturing system utilized at the facility. The cost of labor for the entire process was less than 10 percent of the total production and packaging costs. The plant had a working materials requirements planning (MRP) system in place and used MRP for ordering all raw materials except the cases purchased from Precision Milling. The MRP system was not used to schedule production.

The Strategic Plan

Since the majority of the manufacturing costs were associated with the box, management was primarily interested in decreasing costs associated with box production. The central tactic in the strategic plan was to move to a pull system in order to reduce inventories and improve customer service. Management had selected a pilot line of twenty-nine boxes that accounted for 80 percent of the sales volume in units. Table C.1 shows the bill of material numbers of the three common components of the product line as well as the forecast projections made by the company. Precision Milling had agreed to provide up to 3,000 units of each case size within twenty-four hours of Oak Hills placing an order. Precision Milling intended to meet this customer service level by maintaining cases for the pilot line as finished goods inventory. Currently, Oak Hills received shipments of 5,000 units for the cases and 10,000 for the sensor boards. Management wanted to know what advice the project team could give them in changing over to a pull system.

The Plant Tour

As the team entered the building for a plant tour, Sam McNeel, the manager in charge of manufacturing and shipping, met them. Sam casually mentioned they were waiting for a delivery truck that would take a rush order to a freight forwarder for next-day delivery to a drilling rig in Louisiana. The shipping department was a rush of activity as teams of employees worked frantically to have the order ready when the truck arrived. Due to the business slowdown, some employees had already been laid off and those remaining were concerned about their jobs.

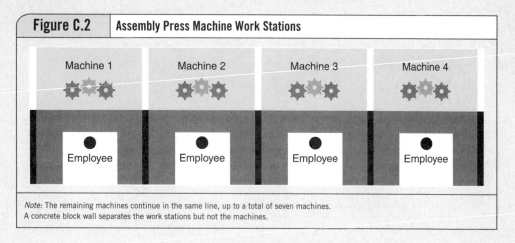

Figure C.2 | **Assembly Press Machine Work Stations**

Machine 1   Machine 2   Machine 3   Machine 4

Employee   Employee   Employee   Employee

Note: The remaining machines continue in the same line, up to a total of seven machines.
A concrete block wall separates the work stations but not the machines.

The employees in the shipping department were all part of a four-person team where team members rotated between four jobs. Because employees were cross-trained, they were often pulled from their team to assist other teams that had rush jobs; however, productivity and quality bonuses were team based.

Seven assembly press machines were set up as parallel lines with the assembler sitting in the middle of a U-shaped table centered at each machine. Workflow moved in a clockwise direction with raw materials on the left side and finished boxes on the right. Figure C.2 shows the machine layout for the assembly work area. When a box was completed, the assembler put the box into a sectioned tray that could hold twenty-five boxes.

Setup procedures were a major problem of this production. In order to change the die set and recalibrate the pressure on one machine, all seven machines had to be stopped. Press setups took ten to fifteen minutes during which time employees either helped with packing or built up materials on the assembly table. When the presses were running, the level of employee movement was similar to that of a fast-food restaurant during a lunch rush. Organized chaos was the impression the group members had. The assembly press machines themselves looked rather worn, and indeed they were after twenty years of use.

A small storage area behind the press machines held the sensor boards. All the sensor boards were packaged to prevent damage; however, because of the space constraints, only a limited number could be held in the area. Often one of the team members would have to go to the warehouse to restock the supply of sensor boards that the team needed for a particular assembly. Cases were kept in the packing area by a large worktable where the assistant could load trays.

Lids were manufactured in a separate area of the building. The lid manufacturing area was approximately 120 feet away from the box assembly area, and the only way to the reach the area was to exit the building and travel under a covered walkway and re-enter the building (see Figure C.1.). The lid machine room had the same layout of seven machines in a line, with a single operator sitting in front of each machine around a much smaller U-shaped table. Figure C.3 shows the machine layout for the lid work area.

Lids were made from a composite of powdered metals that included lead. Because of the health hazards of working with lead, the room had an extensive vacuum system and the operators wore facemasks and gloves. The room was sealed off from the rest of the building, and the only way in was through the outside door. Each lid machine was correlated with an assembly press machine, and enough lids were made to meet the requirements of the production run.

When lid pressing was complete, a suction device lifted the lid out of the die and the door opened. The lid maker reached inside the machine with one hand placed under the lid and

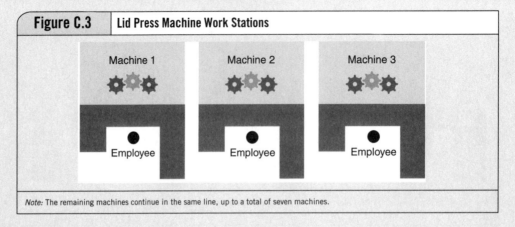

Figure C.3 | **Lid Press Machine Work Stations**

Note: The remaining machines continue in the same line, up to a total of seven machines.

stepped on a foot pedal to release the lid. The newly formed lid was then placed in a holding rack and the process repeated. The rack could hold forty lids. When the rack was full, the lid maker walked the lids to the assembly room. If it was raining, a plastic cover was used to protect the lids.

Two methods were used to control quality. The first method was to weigh the first scoop of powdered metal used for lids and then every fiftieth scoop. The second method was to fit the first lid into the fitting rectangle, which acted as a poka-yoke to make sure the lid was the correct size and thickness. Every tenth lid was checked this way. Lids were not weighed. The lid maker kept a written log of these results and used a handheld click counter to keep track of how many lids were made. At the end of each hour there was a five-minute cleanup period during which the lid maker used a portable vacuum cleaner to remove powder inside the machine and around the work area.

The lid makers were busy helping the packers get the rush jobs ready for shipment. A large case with glass doors and rubber seals was used to hold a buffer supply of lids that would be used to start the next day's production. On a table by the door was a small pile of defective lids. Sam demonstrated how fragile the lids were by crumbling one of the defects in his hand.

The next stop on the plant tour was the quality control department, which was next to the lid press room. Boxes were tested by sending an electronic shock through the lid; the shock fragmented the lid and exposed the sensor to the environment in a typical well. The first box of each production run was tested; if the box passed, then the assembler could initiate the production run. If the box failed, the assembler had to wait while quality control determined the cause of the failure. The main causes of box failure were related to the lid. If the lid was too thick or the wrong density, the electronic shock would not be strong enough to fragment the lid. If the lid was too thin, it tended to fracture while being pressed into the case, and the defect was immediately apparent to the assembler whose job it was to visually inspect each lid after assembly. The box test took about ten minutes, including the travel time to the quality control room. There was always a backlog of work in the quality control department in the morning.

During testing, the lid maker was still busy making lids while the rest of the work team was either idle or setting up the packing area. Management felt it was cheaper to scrap defective lids than to slow down production. Boxes that were defective after the assembly process were not salvaged since the labor cost for rework was higher than the purchase cost of the case and sensor. In addition, the technician was very busy at the start of the day since all seven assembly press machines tended to start production at the same time.

Completed trays of boxes were delivered to the packer who worked inside the open end of a large U-shaped conveyor belt. The packer applied a coating to each lid, and the tray of boxes then proceeded along the conveyor belt to a low-temperature oven that dried the coating. After the tray emerged from the oven, the packer attached the packet of wires to the box and packaged and labeled the carton of boxes. The packer did not monitor for quality problems since the assembler was supposed to check the lid surface for damage. However, boxes did arrive at customer destinations with damaged lids. Management could not be sure if the damage occurred during transportation, even though the boxes were shipped in a sturdy carton with cushioning.

The Question-and-Answer Session

Upon completion of the plant tour, the project team had a short question-and-answer session with Pauline. The following information was gathered:

- End-product cycle time averaged thirty seconds, with a range from twenty-five to forty seconds. The average was used for all planning periods except daily production.

- The daily production schedule was fixed, while the weekly production schedule was more fluid due to the need to expedite rush orders. In some instances the plant manager disrupted the daily production schedule to meet an important delivery.

- Sensor boards were purchased from a nearby plant that also supplied other TOGS manufacturing facilities with electronic equipment. The plant preferred to manufacture large batches of components.

- Oak Hills did not know the inventory positions of internal customers in the field and did not correlate current service jobs with future demand. The survey results in Table CS6.1 are based on phone calls to internal departments of TOGS. Not all project managers were contacted, and those on foreign assignments were the most difficult to reach.

- Employees were not trained in statistical process control techniques, nor were they empowered to stop the production process.

- Some lids took longer to make than it did to assemble the box. This created a shifting bottleneck, which had the effect of starving the assembly press.

- Engineers came in at 7:00 A.M. to set up the required tooling for the assembly press machines. The tooling for the lid press machines was done in the afternoon so a buffer supply of lids could be built up for the next day's production.

The Assignment

Pauline was anxious to report back to management about JIT implementation procedures. She asked the project team to help her prepare the report. The project team members decided they would have to address the following questions to determine if it was appropriate to implement a JIT system at the Oak Hills production facility.

1. What are the differences between a push and a pull system?

2. What changes need to be undertaken in order to convert from a push system to a pull system?

3. What are the quality problems Oak Hills is facing and how will they influence the company's ability to convert to a JIT system?

4. What other issues need to be considered in the conversion?

5. Develop a strategic plan that will help Oak Hills management convert its processes to a JIT system. Your plan should encompass quality, demand management, supply chain management, scheduling, facility layout, and employees.

Case Study 7
ISO 14001 Implementation at Mt. Baker Products

Joshua Perry smiled as he shook hands with the three managers from Mt. Baker Products, Inc. Josh was a junior in the Manufacturing Management Program at Western Washington University, and he had just secured a manufacturing internship position for the upcoming summer quarter. The previous year, Josh had completed an entry-level quality control internship at a Seattle-area circuit board manufacturer. While the internship had been a good experience, Josh had felt at times that his skills and knowledge were underutilized. That would not be a problem this summer at Mt. Baker Products, however: Josh had just signed on to manage the implementation of an ISO 14001–registered environmental management system for the plywood manufacturer.

Company Background

Mt. Baker Products (MBP) is a plywood manufacturer located on the waterfront of the small town of Bellingham, Washington. MBP came into existence in 1950 when a workers' co-op leased the property and began producing plywood. The enterprise was short-lived, unfortunately; the cooperative was facing shutdown due to financial problems by the end of the decade. The company's fortunes took a turn for the better when, in the early 1960s, an investor financed the turnaround of the failing company. About thirty years later, in 1992, a group of Texas investors bought MBP and promptly filed for bankruptcy the next year. The company's financial turmoil of the early 1990s set the stage for the current owner, Swaner Hardwood Company of Burbank, California, to purchase the company. At the time of Josh's internship, MBP was the one of two manufacturing entities owned by Swaner, a privately owned company that specializes in forest product wholesaling. The proximity of transportation channels (road, rail, and ship) allowed the company to purchase raw materials and ship its product all over North America.

The batch manufacturing process at MBP was fairly standard for the plywood industry. Twenty-five different species of hardwood veneers arrived from as far away as Maine and were graded by quality. Each sheet of finished plywood was composed of several layers of veneer—a hardwood face and back as well as several softwood core layers. At the beginning stage of production, plies of softwood core were "plugged"; during this process, plugs were inserted, removing voids and knots in the cores that could cause defects or discoloration later in processing. After grading and plugging, the fronts and backs were matched and sent to the spreader, where the various layers comprising a sheet of plywood were glued together. The resulting sheets were then pressed for eight minutes in a cold press followed by another eight minutes in a hot press heated to 240° F. After the presses, the ragged edges of the sheets were trimmed at the sawing station. The sheets then passed through the patching station, where knotholes and other voids in the surface veneers were removed and plugged with a wood putty. Finally, the sheets were sanded, inspected, and shipped to the customer.

The Push for "Green" Wood Products

Rod Remington, the president and general manager of MBP, had been with the Swaner Corporation for over twenty years. A graduate in forestry from Oregon State University, Rod had managed a hardwood lumber mill for Swaner before moving to Bellingham to run Swaner's latest acquisition. The ISO 14001 implementation was Rod's idea; he felt it would give MBP additional credibility with an increasingly environmentally conscious customer base. MBP had already obtained the "SmartWood" chain-of-custody certification for some of its products.

Source: © Dr. Mark C. Springer, Department of Decision Sciences, Western Washington University, Bellingham, Washington; and Joshua Perry, Project Coordinator, Mt. Baker Products, Inc., Bellingham, Washington. Used with permission.

Initiated in 1989, SmartWood was a program of the Rainforest Alliance, an international nonprofit environmental group based in New York City. For wood-harvesting companies electing to pursue SmartWood certification, SmartWood would assure that the wood was being harvested in an environmentally and socially responsible manner. For wood processors, SmartWood provided "chain-of-custody" certification to enable them to claim that their products contained wood harvested by a SmartWood-certified timber company.

A year after SmartWood was initiated, the nonprofit Forestry Stewardship Council (FSC) was established to set standards for forestry certification programs worldwide and accredit certification organizations that comply with these standards. The FSC was created by certifiers, forest products businesses, and environmental groups to monitor certification and prevent a confusing proliferation of standards. SmartWood was accredited by the FSC for natural forest management certification in early 1996 and is now accredited for plantation and chain-of-custody certifications. The future importance of FSC certification to wood processors, via either SmartWood or some other registrar, cannot be understated: Home Depot, Lowe's, and other major retailers had begun giving preference to FSC-certified lumber and had stated that in the near future they would only sell FSC-certified wood in their stores.

Rod was aware that many customers—especially those overseas—also wanted assurance that their forest product suppliers were managed in an environmentally friendly manner. Since MBP was seeking to increase its sales in Europe and Asia, dealing with these customer concerns was of vital importance.

ISO 14001 was the newly released international standard for evaluating a company's environmental management system (EMS); being certified by a third-party registrar as ISO 14001 compliant would therefore ensure these customers that MBP itself—and not just MBP's suppliers—was environmentally responsible. Another incentive for demonstrating MBP's environmental sensitivity came from the local political arena; the waterfront area surrounding the old mill had been increasingly "gentrified" with upscale development, and this had created pressure on the property owner—the city's Port Authority—to not renew MBP's expiring lease. A clean environmental bill of health could help sway the Port's decision toward one of renewing the company's lease.

The ISO Implementation Team Gets to Work

After deciding that the company would seek ISO registration, Rod handed the responsibility for the project off to Tim Shannon, the operations coordinator for MBP. As the main regulatory and public relations contact for the mill, as well the architect of a significant amount of strategic planning for MBP, Tim was the natural choice to lead the newly formed ISO Implementation Team (IIT) at MBP. Other members of the team included Ken Durland, the lean manufacturing manager; Jerry Ingram, the mill superintendent; and the HR manager, Shawn Goenen.

The IIT began work in May and June, developing an environmental policy for the mill, the backbone of an ISO-compliant EMS. The IIT then decided to hire an intern from Western Washington University to manage the EMS implementation process. MBP did not want to spend the large amounts of money typically associated with consulting and training costs; the intern, with the help of the other team members, would be responsible for developing an understanding of ISO 14001 requirements and then implementing these requirements in the mill. After a brief interview with Tim, Ken, and Jerry, Josh was offered the job and he accepted.

ISO 14001

Josh had little specific knowledge of the requirements of 14001. He did know that ISO 14001 was promulgated by the International Organization for Standardization (ISO), the same body that not only designed the quality management system standard ISO 9001 but also maintained standards for everything from fasteners to clothing labels. Josh had reasoned that the standard was probably similar to ISO 9001 with regard to its central approach: "Say what you do, and do what you say." So far, everything he read about the standard confirmed his suspicions.

Josh learned that the next step toward achieving ISO 14001 compliance was the identification of the company's "environmental aspects," which were to include any company activity, product, or service that could interact with the environment. Once the aspects were identified, they needed to be evaluated for significance. For those aspects deemed to have a significant impact on the environment, the company needed to define performance objectives aimed at lessening the negative impact of those aspects. Measurable targets quantifying those objectives then needed to be defined, and an environmental management program (EMP) with a time frame for achievement of the targets was to be specified.

For example, a shipping company might reasonably identify its large fleet of trucks as an environmental aspect and the exhaust of the trucks would then be identified as a environmental impact. The company might therefore have reduction of nitrous oxide emissions as an objective and then define the precise target in terms of kilograms per year. A plan could then be developed to achieve these objectives through fleet reduction and the purchase of newer vehicles with cleaner emission systems. In effect, companies were responsible for assessing the environmentally sensitive components of their operations and then developing plans to responsibly manage those components.

Josh found that another similarity with ISO 9001 was the emphasis on documentation. ISO 14001 was very prescriptive in requiring certain systems to maintain control of the EMS. Fortunately, a core veneer supplier, Pacific Veneer, forwarded MBP a copy of its "ISO Book" containing all of the documents comprising its EMS. This book formed a boilerplate that MBP could use to develop its own documentation. MBP's procedures were initially just copied from Pacific Veneer's book and then modified as necessary to meet MBP's needs. This approach worked well on the whole, although it did lead to some over-complications in document organization.

Aspect Identification and Evaluation

After he felt confident in his overall knowledge of ISO 14001, Josh knew that his first step needed to be the identification of all the environmental aspects at MBP. Josh realized that he would have to rely on the knowledge of those individuals who knew the inner workings of the mill. Consequently, he arranged a series of meetings with the experienced managers of the mill on the IIT and identified all of the inputs and outputs of each activity in their area. For each area, this information was gathered on a form. Since the inputs to an area could include energy and environmentally sensitive materials and the outputs might well include noise and waste products, this was a reliable if somewhat tedious approach to identifying potentially significant aspects. The sanding operation, for example, consumed electricity and generated dust; both of these were environmental aspects whose potential significance had to be determined.

To identify and evaluate the significant aspects, the IIT first developed a list of the potential environmental impacts that could be affected by each environmental aspect. Dust, for example, was an aspect that could impact air quality, while the electricity impacted energy usage. The team then went over the aspects of a specific activity (sanding, for example) and decided if any of the aspects seemed significant enough to merit evaluation. If so, each aspect was then evaluated using another form to rate the frequency and severity of the various environmental impacts on a scale from zero (lowest frequency and severity) to eight (highest frequency and severity). The frequency and severity ratings for each aspect were multiplied and summed across all significant impacts to come to a single "significance score" for that aspect. The resulting scores ranged from 116 (most significant) to 4 (least significant); an analysis of all of the scores pointed to a threshold value of ten for separating significant from insignificant aspects.

Objectives, Targets, Programs, and Controls

After all of the significant aspects for the mill were identified, objectives, targets, and environmental management programs (EMPs) had to be developed for each aspect. These programs were the means by which the company could improve its environmental performance. To deal with the dust generated by the sanding operation, for example, MBP set an objective of consistently maintaining regulatory compliance with regard to dust levels; their quantifiable target was to be in compliance 100 percent of the time, as measured by an independent contractor on a weekly basis. A well-defined maintenance and training program was part of the EMP to achieve this objective. Furthermore, MBP established a long-term plan for completely replacing the current dust-collection system.

Being relatively unfamiliar with mill operations, Josh found himself making a series of mis-steps in this part of the implementation, as detailed knowledge of the mill was required for the design of the programs. One example of this was the "operational control setting process." ISO requires procedures to be set up that will control operations and bring some degree of standardization and repeatability to the activities associated with the EMPs.

At Josh's suggestion, the team listed "job description" as the operational control for almost all of the EMPs in the mill. This seemed reasonable at first but later proved faulty, since the "job descriptions" referenced were merely job *postings* that were used to solicit employee bids. That is, there were no "job descriptions" that employees could reasonably be expected to refer to often enough to ensure that the environmental instructions contained therein would be followed. In lieu of reliable job descriptions that could be used by the employees, the IIT decided to append training sessions to the monthly safety meetings held by each department to provide guidance for the workers and operational control for the EMPs.

Another challenge for the implementation process was the extremely demanding business schedules of team members; for all of the team members except Josh, ISO 14001 was one more task added to an already full plate. Josh sometimes found this especially frustrating, as it was sometimes difficult for him to get prompt action from team members temporarily distracted by some other aspect of their job. Also, while Josh embraced the role of implementation manager, he neglected to provide training or pass on the knowledge that he was building. It was clear that this would soon become an issue, as Josh was scheduled to leave Bellingham for Colorado Springs in the upcoming fall quarter. As the time for his departure approached, he realized that transferring knowledge to the other team members would be critical for the implementation process to go forward.

Off to Colorado

As September approached, Josh looked back at the last three months with a degree of satisfaction; he had walked into an unfamiliar manufacturing process and, with the critical help of the experienced IIT, helped guide MBP well on its way to ISO 14001 registration. The significant environmental aspects and their impacts had been identified; environmental objectives had been established, and quantifiable targets had been set. The programs to achieve these targets were, for the most part, already in place and running smoothly. The quality manual documenting the EMS was nearing completion, and the training sessions for the employees had begun. Josh was aware that the "typical" time and effort for an ISO 14001 implementation was eighteen months and nine person-years, so he felt justifiably proud of his accomplishments.

As Josh looked ahead, however, he realized that his job was far from done, even though he was scheduled to leave town in a few weeks. He was headed to Colorado Springs for the fall quarter, meaning he would not be available on site to help MBP as the registration process continued. The quality manual needed to be sent in for review at the beginning of October; Josh knew he would not have it completed when he left for Colorado in early September. The training, which he had been providing, needed to continue while he was gone; someone else would need to provide it in his absence. Furthermore, if the quality manual was deemed satisfactory, an auditor would be sent for a "readiness review" or "pre-audit audit" of the mill in December. Josh would in fact be arriving back in Bellingham in late December, but he would not have much time to prepare for the readiness review. The purpose of the review was to examine whether the mill seemed to be ready to undergo a full registration audit and to check on progress made to address any documentation issues found in the quality manual. If the readiness review did not find any major issues, the full audit would occur sometime in late January.

Josh stared at the current version of the quality manual displayed on his computer screen. He figured that with a lot of conference calling he could put the finishing touches on the quality manual from his dorm room in Colorado Springs. He could also call on one of the other IIT members to lead the training sessions. Hopefully, there would be no major issues with the quality manual. If so, he would need to work on those from Colorado Springs as well. While Josh thought he and the IIT had done a pretty thorough job, he found himself wishing that he had found the time to further educate more MBP employees on ISO 14001. With his departure, following through on the implementation was now primarily outside of his control.

Questions for Discussion

1. What external pressures led Mt. Baker Plywood to seek ISO 14001 registration? How are these pressures likely to differ by industry and region?

2. How does the "SmartWood" or FSC certification differ from ISO 14001 certification?

3. What role do "aspects" and "impacts" have in ISO 14001? What did Josh discover about the "right" and "wrong" way to identify environmental aspects?

4. Who sets the environmental goals and objectives for a company under ISO 14001?

5. What was Josh's major error in the implementation process?

6. What are the various ISO certifications available, and how important are they today, in creating and maintaining global market share? Justify your answer.

Case Study 8
Service Parts Operations for General Motors Brazil

There are 472 GM dealers, nine GM authorized garages, and ten GM parts distributors in Brazil, for a total of 491 service parts points of sale. GM has 650 employees allocated to the service parts operation in Brazil, with two service parts distribution centers located in the Southeastern state of São Paulo. Currently, GM has approximately 75,000 part numbers, with 700 high-turnover parts, supporting twenty vehicle platforms.

The relationships between GM Brazil and the GM dealers have always been independent. Consistent with most supply networks, the nodes of the network were managed separately, favoring the zero-sum game. In other words, in many situations for one business to gain in a negotiation, the other business had to lose. This led to less-than-cooperative relationships and to independent management systems with undesirable effects.

The Bullwhip Effect

One such undesirable effect was the bullwhip effect in which small variations in demand downstream caused increasingly large variations toward the upstream portion of the network. The demand at the GM distribution center is dependent on the inventory management systems and inventory policies of the dealers. Considering each item, if reorder point policies are used, dealer systems will use an EOQ system to benefit from scale economies with the logistics costs between themselves and the distribution center. This means they wait until the reorder points are reached and then they issue replenishment orders using the EOQ for each part. Consequently, the somewhat stable demand of the end user becomes a lumpy demand, one tier upstream. This occurs because the distribution center will receive the orders from the dealers only at certain points in time (the points in which the dealer's "reorder point" is reached) and not on a continuous basis, as the dealer receives orders from its customers at the counter. The distribution center will receive zero orders from the dealer between replenishments and then a lump of demand (the dealer's EOQ) when the replenishments are due.

Now think about 483 points of sale with their inventory management systems issuing replenishment orders at independently defined moments, with independently defined quantities. This system causes demand at the distribution center to be significantly impacted by the bullwhip, effect in an almost random way. Now consider that each distribution center has its own inventory management system with independently defined inventory policies and parameters. Thus, the bullwhip effect is being passed on with an amplified intensity to the suppliers, suppliers' suppliers, and so on. Because the amplified effect is random, what normally happens is that all of the firms increase their safety stock levels.

The result is severe instability in production programs for the companies upstream, which negatively affect cost efficiencies in the supply chain. Plants are forced to work overtime when the bullwhip goes up and then face idleness when the bullwhip goes down. This raises costs for all of the supply chain members, which are ultimately passed on to the end customer. It should be no surprise, then, that an original part bought from the dealer's counter costs something between 50 percent and 100 percent more than a similar part bought on the

Source: © Prof. Henrique Corrêa (hcorrea@fgvsp.br), Dept. of Production and Operations Mgt., Fundação Getulio Vargas Business School, São Paulo, Brazil, with the collaboration of Denio Nogueira of GM, as a basis for class discussion only. Used with permission.

so-called gray market (parts sold direct from the part manufacturer bearing its own brand name and not GM's). This difference in price is at least partially responsible for the relatively low (estimated by GM to be around 30 percent) market share of GM original parts when compared to the overall market for GM service parts.

The GM Solution—AutoGiro

Facing all that, GM decided to launch a national initiative to substantially change the way it managed its supply network, a project called AutoGiro. The logic behind it is quite simple and can be explained by some of its principles:

1. *It is a VMI system: GM assumes the responsibility for the management of parts inventories of the dealers.*

    VMI makes sense in this situation because GM, being the common denominator of the network, is the only player in the network who can actually see the aggregated demand of the 472 dealers. GM is able to identify national patterns of demand and therefore enrich the demand forecast of each dealer with these national patterns. Since demand forecast is a great part of the task of managing inventories, GM assumes the responsibility for managing the inventories too. VMI also makes sense in this situation because GM delivers thousands of different items (each dealer has about 6,000 active inventory items, with approximately 2,500 being purchased in any month) to a defined and stable group of dealers. This means that economies of scale in logistics can be achieved if deliveries to several dealers share the transportation costs using a milk-run type of routing in which one mode of transportation makes periodic and coordinated deliveries to a group of dealers. GM is the player who can coordinate these deliveries (GM uses Emery, a logistics service provider).

    GM suggests when, how many, and what parts the dealers should buy. However, given the past relationship in which GM tried to maximize sales by pushing parts downstream in the chain, it would be understandable that the dealers would resist this idea of GM managing their inventories. To overcome this resistance:

2. *GM grants protection against part obsolescence and part stock-outs.*

    Dealers fear that GM would push parts needlessly to maximize sales and that these parts would eventually become obsolete. To avoid that, AutoGiro grants dealers who accept GM's VMI plan that any part that becomes obsolete (more than nine months without a sale) will be subject to "buyback" by GM for either the current price or the original purchased price, whichever is higher. This means that if GM overestimates the purchases, it assumes the costs of the mistake. In the same way, if the dealer accepts the GM suggestion for the replenishment and runs out of a part, GM will ship the part fast track, urgent delivery, at no extra cost to the dealer. Before the AutoGiro program, obsolete parts were the dealers' problem and urgent deliveries were costly.

3. *GM provides an internet-based "parts locator."*

    For GM to be able to manage the dealers' inventories and provide automatic replenishment, they need to have very frequently updated information on the stock position of each stock item at each dealer. GM would make this information available to the dealers. This means that in case of a stock-out, a dealer with an urgency to serve a customer can browse on the GM extranet and search for that part availability at a dealership nearby, getting the part in the same day (by comparison, depending on the dealers' location, fast-track delivery can take two days).

4. *Replenishment is done twice, three times, or five times per week depending on the dealers' demand volumes.*

    Present reorder point systems used by dealers tend to treat items independently. Therefore the logic used is to "dilute" logistics costs by transporting a large number of units of each item, and this tends to increase inventories (the less frequent the replenishment, the higher the average inventory). One of the most utilized systems limits the replenishments to a maximum of three times per month per part. This means that in the most favorable case, the replenishment will be of a quantity equivalent to 1/3 of the monthly demand. In the case of AutoGiro, in which a part is possibly delivered daily, the replenishment quantity will be approximately 1/20 of the monthly demand. AutoGiro considers that the transportation cost does not have to be "diluted" by a large number of units of one item but, rather, by a small number of units of a large number of different items. The system recognizes that different items will go from the same origin to the same destination in a joint replenishment. This makes it possible to keep delivery costs low even with small replenishment lots per item.

In addition to the joint replenishment economies of scale, the dealers in each region that receive replenishment on Mondays, Wednesdays, and Fridays will be served in a milk-run routing logic. This consolidation of loads helps keep logistics costs down.

5. *A periodic review inventory management system is used.*

To make it possible to achieve economies of scale in deliveries, it is necessary to replenish all items at regular intervals. For this type of VMI, the desired type of inventory management system is periodic review. This system makes sure that all of the service items of a dealer are checked periodically (AutoGiro does it daily). Depending on the stock position of the item at the review point, an order quantity may be generated. This quantity is calculated as the difference between a maximum pre-established level and the stock position at each review. A replenishment order is issued, and, after a period equal to the transportation lead time, the replenishment quantity arrives. Note that in this system, the reviews are done at fixed intervals, but the quantities replenished vary.

AutoGiro Information Flows

Figure C.1 shows the AutoGiro information and material flows. Descriptions of these flows follow.

- *Flow 1:* The points of sale have to send GM a file (via EDI) between 6P.M. and 10P.M. daily containing information on unit sales per day per item and the inventory positions per item. The inputted information will be used for the

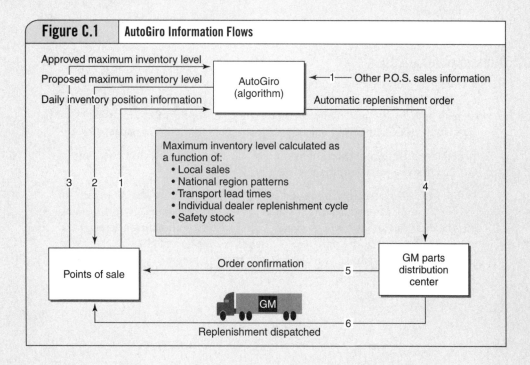

Figure C.1   AutoGiro Information Flows

short-term demand forecast per item per point of sale. GM receives sales information from all points of sale and uses this aggregated demand to enrich the individual SKU (stock-keeping unit—associated with one particular item inventoried in one particular point of sale) and the demand forecast with possible national or regional patterns.

- *Flow 2 and Flow 3:* Once per week, normally on Monday morning, AutoGiro re-calculates the demand forecast for the upcoming week and, based on the new demand forecast, re-calculates the maximum level of inventory for each SKU. The list of new maximum levels of inventory for the whole set of items of each point of sale is made available on the Extranet. The parts manager of each point of sale then analyzes the new proposed maximum inventory level on Monday morning and has the chance either to approve it or to alter it according to a qualitative analysis of the next week's demand. One possible situation to illustrate a change in demand is a promotion. Obviously an increase in demand is expected, but this increase in demand would not be captured by the quantitative method (a modified form of moving average) used by AutoGiro. Once the parts manager informs AutoGiro of the approved and modified maximum levels for the items, those are the maximum inventory levels that will be used by AutoGiro to calculate the automatic replenishments daily.

- *Flow 1 and Flow 4:* During the week, AutoGiro receives the inventory position daily and calculates the difference between the currently agreed maximum level of inventory and the stock position and automatically sends information to the GM distribution center.

- *Flow 5:* The GM parts distribution center sends the points of sale an advance notice announcing that a delivery is on its way and also informs the quantities.

- *Flow 6:* Deliveries are sorted out (picking, packing, identifying) and dispatched using the appropriate milk runs, according to the frequencies (twice a week, three times a week, or daily) defined by the demand volume of the point of sale.

These flows characterize the daily automatic replenishment system.

Questions for Discussion

1. GM expects a drastic reduction in the levels of safety stocks needed at the points of sale and in other nodes of the supply network and simultaneously expects an increase in the parts availability at each of the points of sale. Explain, using characteristics of the AutoGiro model, the rationale behind these GM expectations.

2. Explain how the AutoGiro system can help mitigate the bullwhip effect in the GM Brazil spare parts supply chain.

3. Before AutoGiro, research conducted by GM showed that around 80 percent of the work time of a dealer parts manager was spent managing inventories and making decisions about replenishment. With AutoGiro automating a great part of this, how do you see the new role of the parts manager at the dealers? What should they do, if anything, to make sure that they are prepared for this new role?

Case Study 9
A Comparative Analysis of Utility Rate Forecasting: The Cape Coral Experience

Introduction and Background Information

Cape Coral, founded over forty years ago, is described as the largest and most successful master-planned community in the country. Prior to incorporation in 1970, city designers carefully planned the location of streets, canals, parks, public areas, transportation routes, commercial zones, and industrial parks. The emphasis was always on assuring that commercial and residential growth remained orderly, controlled, and balanced. Cape Coral has grown dramatically since its incorporation. In 1960 there was virtually no population. The city's metropolitan market area grew seven times faster than the national average in the 1980s. By 1995, the population had risen to approximately 85,000. Today, it is the most populous Florida Gulf Coast city south of Tampa. With approximately 30,000 of 135,000 building parcels occupied, the city has tremendous room for future growth.

The tremendous growth of Cape Coral has presented city administrators with numerous management challenges. Among them is that of maintaining city-owned reliable water, wastewater, and reuse (irrigation) systems that deliver a high-quality product. At the same time, these systems must also be responsive to consumers, protect the environment, and ensure that the community remains self-sufficient. Coupled with this mandate is the maintenance of financial viability of the community by implementing an effective ad valorem tax structure, debt levels, user fees, and other revenue sources that are equitable and affordable to the community (Raftelis Environmental Consulting Group, Inc., 1995).

In 1991, the city of Cape Coral hired an engineering firm to conduct a utility rate update for the city water and wastewater utility system. According to the 1991 rate study, based on account data provided by the city, water accounts were predicted to reach 28,979 and wastewater accounts to reach 23,088 in 1992. The city reported that actual water accounts for 1992 reached 37,098 while wastewater accounts rose to 23,705. The study predicted that the city would make $15,470,594 during that first year. Actual revenues were $15,406,209. The difference of $64,385 that first year was insignificant. However, the larger question is how revenues could be short at all when actual accounts appeared to exceed predicted accounts by a significant margin.

The problem worsened in the second year as the real impact of a faulty forecast was realized. Projections for that year called for 35,327 water accounts and 25,009 wastewater accounts. City statistics for 1993 revealed that actual water accounts reached 38,315 while sewer accounts rose to 23,342. Projected revenues for 1993, based on the rate study, were $19,147,161. Actual utility revenues were $15,406,209, representing a difference of $3,740,952. Again, actual accounts appeared to exceed predicted accounts and, given the wide range of error in estimating revenues, there was substantial reason to doubt the ability of the forecasting study to accurately estimate utility revenues.

In 1994, city staff determined that the account data utilized in the 1991 study were flawed and corrected the account totals for future use. As evidence of how far the data were off, the

Source: © Terry A. Anderson, Ph.D., Public Administration Department, and Donald A. Forrer, D.B.A., Management Department, Troy State University Florida Region, Ft. Meyers, Fla. Used with permission.

1991 study had predicted that the city would have 37,044 water accounts and 39,933 wastewater accounts in 1994. Using the 1994 adjusted data, the prediction was for 28,891 water accounts and 17,344 wastewater accounts. The actual figures for 1994 were 28,152 water accounts and 16,203 wastewater accounts. The inflated rate study projected $24,228,719 in utility revenues for 1994. Actual revenues realized were $14,523,876, almost $10 million below the expected total.

Four issues contributed to the forecasting model used in the study producing inaccurate projections: (1) the city was installing fourteen square miles of sewer system that was completed behind schedule; (2) the city was installing an irrigation system to homes. These accounts were added at a slower-than-anticipated pace; (3) the growth rate for the city was anticipated to continue at the 8 percent level experienced in the 1980s. In fact, the rate dropped to approximately 3 percent; and (4) the data provided by the city for water and sewer accounts were inaccurate.

The combination of erroneous data, slower-than-expected growth rate, slower-than-projected wastewater construction, and delays in securing irrigation connections created revenue flow problems for the city. Compounding the issue was the fact that city planners budgeted with the projected figures. In 1994, the city of Cape Coral budgeted almost $1.6 million more than actual revenues. The 1991 rate study, in its executive summary, indicated that, "from projections of revenues and expenses at existing rates, the water system appears to be self-sufficient only through Fiscal Year 1992 in terms of meeting its operating revenue needs from the standpoint of debt coverage." As later facts became known, this turned out to be a true statement. Clearly, the efficiency and effectiveness of the rate study were handicapped by the data used and thus by the forecasting model developed.

Correcting Faulty Forecasting

Clearly, results from the 1991 rate study were flawed, leading to significant underestimating of revenues for city water, wastewater, and irrigation programs. Growth in government means changes in processes and structure. While Cape Coral accomplished this strategically with forward-thinking innovations such as a $21 million Water Reclamation Plant, a $125 million Gravity Sewer Project, and a $100 million Dual Water System, the city's data-collection system was not as responsive. In 1991, as the rate study was being conducted, the city realized that its computer system would be the key to a cost-effective solution to problems already identified with information processing, data collection, and full integration of systems. A proposal was presented to the city council to replace the WANG VS100 with an IBM AS400 and a fully integrated database provided by Harward Technical Enterprises (HTE). The AS400 and the HTE software were chosen in 1992, but the implementation process extended into 1994.

The city's first business manager was hired in January 1994. At that time, the utility module was not converted from the WANG system to the HTE system. A new utility rate study was commissioned in early 1994 but not completed until December of that year. Once completed, the new rate study was rejected by the city council after many sessions of heated public debate. The discrepancies noted between the 1991 rate study and current data in 1994 proved to be confusing to citizen groups and city council members. Basically, conversion of the WANG system to HTE highlighted data problems that contributed to inaccurate forecasting during the previous study. The business manager assumed responsibility for data conversion. It was apparent at an early stage that the HTE system was an outstanding system that would accomplish everything that the city needed in the area of data storage, management, and security. However, the HTE system was only as good as the data provided by the city and the previous system. Therefore, the first element of conversion became an analysis of data and processes. Through this process, several areas of concern developed.

In 1991, there were few processes in place that involved users in the storage and manipulation of data. This resulted in responsibility for data being maintained at a centralized level with few measurements in place for data accuracy. Additionally, property changes were the responsibility of Lee County. The county utilized a good system for joining and dividing property. However, once the action was accomplished, the county transferred the changes on a weekly basis to the city for inclusion in their database. There was no process in place for the data to be entered in the city's database; therefore, each week the data held by the city of Cape Coral were deteriorating.

Also in 1991 there was no accounts receivable database available for a water assessment. Citizens paid as they were connected, and the results were logged but not maintained so that they could be queried or analyzed. Several accounts, totaling approximately $65,000, were not billed for their annual payment. In 1993, some twenty-four months later, the properties involved were assessed liens by the city but still not billed. In 1994, the accounts were billed by the incoming business manager. However, due to the liens not being placed until 1993, several properties had new owners. This caused a huge customer service problem. Additionally, the absence of a database resulted in several homes being missed and not connected as legally required by city ordinance.

Finally, in 1991, water and wastewater accounts and housing units were tracked by a report from the WANG system. Though this report was difficult to read, the 1991 report relied primarily on this historical data for its forecasting model. This customer data obtained from internal records proved to be the Achilles' heel of the rate study. Data retrieved from historical files indicated that over time, city staff had erroneously transposed units and accounts. Each dwelling is considered a unit, while only the metered accounts are measurable for revenue purposes. The reporting system used by city staff consisted of reports from various internal forms that were consolidated in the customer service department on a written monthly report.

Compounding the issue was the fact that these reports to management were simply compiled on the monthly reporting sheet and then filed. Without the benefit of a spreadsheet, it was easy for management to miss the transposition of erroneous data. This caused customer complaints and data that were virtually useless for planning purposes. Since the reports were filed and not followed on a spreadsheet, the significant difference in the number of units was not discovered until the city converted to the new computer system in 1994.

The 1991 rate study predicted that the city would experience a 20 percent reduction in water consumption due to the implementation of Water Independence for Cape Coral, the earlier report commissioned in 1988. This projection was built into the model but did not compensate for erroneous data provided by the city. In 1994, the city business manager analyzed six months of water usage for the first 10,500 customers receiving the dual water system. This review determined that in a six-month window, 9,500 users having irrigation in 1994 and no irrigation in 1992 consumed 203 million fewer gallons of potable water. With a city average of 207 million gallons per month, this constitutes two full months of water and wastewater revenues with only 33 percent of the potential users connected. While this variable was considered, its effects on new irrigation revenues were considered to be minimal. Further analysis of accounts in preparation for the 1994 rate study revealed inaccuracies in approximately 8,000 water accounts and 5,000 wastewater accounts.

In 1991, the city was structured for a centralized information system division that allowed no ownership of data by the individual departments. The MIS manager and two programmers managed the WANG system. This was a system of centralization by necessity. The COBOL programming required to provide reports was complicated and cumbersome. While department managers controlled input through account entry at the various service counters, very little control over or responsibility for data was provided to department managers.

Therefore, many of the data-entry requirements fell on the MIS division. Managers requiring reports would request the necessary data through the programmer and wait on results. Due to the complexity of the COBOL programming, managers had to assume that the programmer understood the requirements.

In 1991, responsibility for data and processes was placed at the lowest level rather than with senior management. The engineering firm was provided data by a divisional supervisor based on reports provided by the MIS division. Measurement and accuracy checks were not in place at higher levels of the organization.

The rate study conducted in 1994 was ultimately rejected in the face of problems realized with the earlier study. In addition to inaccuracies identified in the data provided for the 1991 study, citizens blamed city officials for delays in ongoing projects and voted the 1994 study down.

Conclusion

Due to the public hearing process, the city of Cape Coral learned a valuable lesson about accurate forecasting. The 1991 rate study produced a false target resulting in overspending by city government and the need for a utility hike in 1994. Inaccurate data and the inability to explain the deficiencies led to mistrust of government staff and the voting down of the 1994 rate study.

During the public hearings, citizens were blaming everything from expensive supplies to government corruption as the problem. Laubach (1995) wrote an article titled "City Utilities Losing $200,000 a Month" in which a quote from the then public service director placed the blame for the losses with the predictions made for the 1991 utility rate study and delays in the wastewater project. The debate over utility rates resulted in demands by city council members for audits of the entire system. The city council voted to delay any rate increase until a determination of cause could be established.

Overall, pitfalls in forecasting brought budget deficits, audits, citizen committees, and criticism from the city council and the public. Along the way, resignations were tenured, thousands of dollars were spent, and trust in city staff was diminished. Following good management principles in the forecasting of utility rates would have precluded or minimized this problem.

Questions for Discussion

1. After reading this case, what processes would you implement if you were the city manager for Cape Coral?

2. What implications does the failure of the utility rate study in 1995 have for the city in regard to immediate impact?

3. What were the problems with the initial forecast and what would you suggest to improve the forecast for future rate studies?

4. What would you suggest that the city do for the future? How can this problem be avoided?

References

Hartman & Associates, Inc. "City of Cape Coral: Water and Wastewater Annual Report Fiscal Year 1995." Hai Project No. 96-347.00. Fort Myers, Fla.: Author, 1995.

Laubach, D. "City Utilities Losing $200,000 a Month." *Cape Coral Daily Breeze* (15 February 1995).

Raftelis Environmental Consulting Group, Inc. "City of Cape Coral: Performance Audit of Utilities Division." Charlotte, N.C.: Author, 1995.

Case Study 10
AMP Incorporated, 1941–1999

Introduction

This case study of AMP Incorporated provides an illustration of the importance of business strategy. It demonstrates how the correct corporate strategy can provide prosperity for a company while a poor strategy can result in dire consequences. The study also highlights how factors such as company size, economic conditions, competition, and corporate culture influence the development and the ultimate success of the business strategy. AMP Incorporated is a global company that specializes in electronic and electrical connectors. The company, which was started in 1941, quickly grew into the world's largest manufacturer of connector and interconnection devices. But in 1998, the company's stock fell resulting in a hostile takeover bid by Allied Signal and the eventual purchase of the company by Tyco International.

The Electronics Industry

During the 1950s, electronics became the fifth-largest industry in the United States. During the 1960s and 1970s, there was a trend toward miniaturization, circuit integration, and modularization. With the introduction of semiconductor technology in the early 1970s, this industry trend accelerated. The 1980s were rough. Barely rebounding from the recession of 1981–82, the electronics industry entered into a substantial downturn by 1985 when customers turned away from discrete components toward larger subassemblies, and shifted from cheap labor to advanced automation. The 1990s saw a rapid growth in global demand for electronic components. But ailing economies in the Asia/Pacific region affected foreign sales. Today one sees declining distributor inventory levels and a recovery trend in the Asia/Pacific region. The long-term industry growth prospects are good, due to growth of electronic content in industrial and consumer products. Two important issues facing electronic companies will be finding new applications for outdated products and lowering expenses.

The History of AMP

Born in Lincoln, Kansas in 1900, Uncas Aeneus Whitaker grew up in a tiny southwestern town in Missouri. In the fall of 1941, Whitaker took over a small firm called Industrial Manufacturers in Elizabeth, New Jersey. It produced solderless electrical terminations for the aircraft and shipbuilding industry. Whitaker, an electrical engineer, developed a system to crimp a terminal with a precision tool that looked like a pair of pliers, eliminating the need for skilled soldering. Industrial Manufacturers grew over time, and was renamed Aircraft-Marine Products, Inc., or AMP Incorporated, in 1956. Whitaker recruited talented engineers/technicians and gave them wide latitude. He would financially reward success. He also created competitive spirit within his workforce. He encouraged independent initiatives taken by the employees. Whitaker claimed, "We engineer the hell out of everything."

Early Strategies

Whitaker identified seven major tasks to accomplish in order to build a successful business, and they were the following:

1. Establish a modern sales organization with qualified personnel having definite ideas and territories, properly controlled, and each with a suitable compensation plan.

Source: © Krishna S. Dhir, Berry College, Mount Berry, Georgia; Keith Drumheller, Elizabethtown, Pennsylvania; David H. Klose, Enola, Pennsylvania; Stephen Sucheski, Harrisburg, Pennsylvania; Ronald M. Zigli, The Citadel, Charleston, South Carolina. Used with permission.

2. Develop an organization chart.

3. Establish a sales policy as to the prices, deliveries, and job resources, and see that it is carried out uniformly.

4. Establish a scientific survey of the sales possibilities of the country by territories and make the proper plans accordingly.

5. Provide production drawings for all parts manufactured, showing dimensions, tolerances, materials, and all other specifications.

6. Inaugurate the test program covering all of the items sold and manufactured to determine their suitability for the service intended, whether they meet customer and government specifications, and comparative performance with competitive items.

7. Maintain accurate, up-to-date records on all phases of the business so as to permit continuous analyses of the business situation.

Whitaker developed a planning model emphasizing organized project management, customer satisfaction, high quality of goods and services, and continuous quality improvement. This model, focused on territorial marketing, formed the basis of AMP strategies throughout the 1950s, 1960s and early 1970s. Three events occurred in the early history of AMP that enabled it to survive through the 1940s: (1) Boeing was persuaded by Whitaker to sign on in spite of his company being small and unknown; (2) Whitaker struck a joint venture with Hoover to tap the market in the United Kingdom; (3) AMP was continually receiving new wartime business from the government.

Although its revenues were high, wartime taxes squeezed AMP's profits. It was only able to break even during its first four years in the market. During 1946–49, despite loss of the Boeing deal in the post-war recession, AMP was able to sustain about $2.5 million annual revenue through government contracts. It increased its profitability to about 4 percent of revenue by 1949.

Whitaker recognized the post-recession opportunity for growth of his small company. In the early 1950s, he became interested in diversification and growth through new technological developments of profitable product lines. The electronics industry as a whole boomed in the 1950s and became the fifth-largest sector in the United States behind only autos, steel, aircraft, and chemicals. A major expansion project was undertaken by AMP in 1951. During this year, large additions were added to the Harrisburg and Carlisle plants and new facilities were built in Mount Joy and Shrewsbury, Pennsylvania. This expansion project more than tripled the company's total plant size to 51,000 square feet.

In 1952, AMP first entered the international market with a small facility in Paris to support IBM's European operations. The first half of the 1950s saw AMP's sales grow from $5.5 million to $21.6 million. By 1955, AMP entered Holland and Scotland and, in 1956, changed its name to AMP Incorporated and went public. By 1959, it was in Japan, Germany, and Italy. In 1960–61, AMP set up facilities in North Carolina, Florida, Virginia, and South Carolina. As always, Whitaker attributed the growth to engineering and direct sales, supported by a 500-person development staff that absorbed 14 percent of the total sales for R&D.

International expansion continued throughout the 1960s and 1970s in Europe, South America, Asia, and Australia. By 1979, AMP had subsidiaries in twenty-two countries, operating in Aerospace and Military, Industrial and Commercial Electronics, Consumer Goods, Communications, Computer and Office, Transportation and Electrical, and Special Industries. During the 1980s, larger integrated facilities were constructed to replace some of the smaller, aging plants, and over forty U.S. facilities had been eliminated, reducing the number of U.S. facilities to less than 100 plants.

Aggressive After the 1980s

Acquisitions became AMP's strategy in the 1980s. Its first acquisition was Midland Investment Co. The 1980s brought Carroll Touch Systems, Matrix Science, Garry Screw Machine Corporation, and Lytel Inc. into AMP. AMP acquired aggressively and entered joint ventures at an incredibly rapid pace in the 1990s to curb mounting risks and prohibitive costs of increasingly complex technologies while offering one-stop shopping for its customers.

Instead of discrete electrical components, AMP broadened its product lines, providing complete assemblies. Along with the acquisition of new fiber-optic, additive printed wiring boards, and cable assembly technologies, AMP expanded in Europe, Asia, and the United States. By 1997, overseas business generated 59 percent of its income, sales topped $5.7 billion, and net income was $473 million. It had increased its dividend to its shareholders forty-four years in a row, and its employee base had nearly doubled over a decade to 46,500.

The Quality Emphasis

AMP established a quality program in 1983 long before TQM was fashionable. In 1984, AMP established the 10/5 program, which was designed to reduce defects by tenfold over five years. Even as its sales grew, AMP continued to spend as much as 9 percent on research, development, and engineering even though its competitors were spending far less. In the early 1980s, AMP also switched from direct sales to distributors. By 1990, AMP had the most sales through distributors of any U.S. connector company.

In February 1990, AMP launched its Plan for Excellence program. This broad program sought continuous improvement in productivity, quality, service, delivery, and customer responsiveness. During 1991, AMP launched ISO 9000 worldwide quality and MRP-II Class A certification programs. AMP's 1990s mission was to be a customer-focused, market-driven global firm evolving into a broader-based producer of interconnection systems and value-added assemblies. Its goals of reaching a 15 percent growth rate and a 20 percent pretax profit were to be attained through market share gains, product diversification, value-added assemblies, geographic expansion, horizontal integration, strategic alliances, and acquisitions.

The second wave of acquisitions started in 1993. Within three years, AMP made fourteen major acquisitions and had minor investments in several more. The largest was of M/A-COM, a wireless component Massachusetts firm, for an estimated $270 million in stock.

Redesigning AMP

In 1993, AMP's Vision 2000 goals were to reach $10 billion sales by the year 2000, with an annual 18 percent pretax margin and an annual 20 percent return on equity. It began to redefine and restructure itself with presidents for Asia/Pacific, Europe/Middle East/Africa, Americas, and the Global Interconnect Systems business. A core competencies–based business model was developed in 1994. It leveraged global resources by aligning the organization into three sectors: technical, financial, and global operations. It recognized the need to go through a cultural transformation. A new organization, the Engineering Control Organization, was formed to bring uniformity in engineering practices and processes. In 1996 and 1997, the company was redesigned into a matrix structure around five industry-focused groups. The new structure also targeted new products and markets, expanding the potential market from $27 billion to $97 billion.

A Hostile Bid and a White Knight

In the fall of 1998, AMP's share price dropped mainly due to the Asian economic slowdown and the strong U.S. dollar. Allied Signal, a manufacturing company in the aerospace and automotive products, chemicals, fibers, plastics, and advanced materials markets worldwide, commenced a hostile takeover bid, offering $44.50 for each outstanding share. The battle was very public. Allied Signal's Bossidy criticized AMP's use of tactics available under the laws of Pennsylvania, a state that provides protections to companies within its borders. AMP requested legislation to prevent Allied Signal from restructuring its board. This found strong legislative support but was not enacted because of the legislature's decision to wait until upcoming elections.

A public relations war dragged on for months. In September, AMP announced a self-tender offer for up to 30 million shares at $55 a share. This did not seem to turn public sentiment. The Hixon family, a founding family of the company, published a letter in *The Wall Street Journal* requesting AMP to discontinue its adversarial relations with Allied Signal and begin a good faith discussion, stating that (1) AMP was preventing its shareholders from maximizing their value; (2) seeking legislative help was not good corporate policy; and (3) AMP's self-tender was not in the shareholders' best interests. This letter followed a commitment by Allied to preserve the jobs of all workers making less than $50,000 for a full year.

After over three months of jockeying, AMP announced in November that it would merge with a white knight, Tyco International's electronics operations. This agreement was a $51 per share, stock-for-stock transaction. Bermuda-based Tyco was a diversified manufacturing and service firm, with the world's largest fire protection systems and electronic security services.

The Hixon family expressed satisfaction. AMP's President Ripp joined the Tyco board of directors and kept his job. After completing the merger in April of 1999, Tyco began to trim AMP's workforce. The goal was to reduce $1 billion in costs over two years and reduce the total jobs by possibly as much as 9,000 over the period. But that is yet another story.

Questions for Discussion

1. Why, after forty years of being self-sufficient and development oriented, did AMP begin aggressively purchasing companies? Was this a good strategic move? What should AMP have done differently?

2. Was AMP's "one-stop-shopping" strategy a good strategy to pursue? Why, or why not?

3. What is the ultimate responsibility of the management and board of directors of a company? Should they follow the direction of the stockholders? Or should they attempt to bring about the best results for the stockholders? Should AMP's management and board have fought Allied Signal?

4. Why did economic conditions affect AMP so dramatically yet have little effect on its competitors? Could AMP have done anything to prevent this situation?

References

Rodengen, J. L. *The Legend of AMP.* Fort Lauderdale, Fl.: Write Stuff Syndicate, 1997.

Sharfman, B. *The AMP Story: Right Connections.* Harrisburg, Pa.: AMP Incorporated, 1992.

Value Line, 1999.

Case Study 11
Whirlpool Corporation—Giving ERP a Spin

Whirlpool Corporation is one of the world's leading manufacturers and marketers of major home appliances. The company has principal manufacturing operations and marketing activities in North and South America, Europe, and Asia. Whirlpool's primary brand names—KitchenAid, Roper, Bauknecht, Ignis, Brastemp, Consul, and its global Whirlpool brand—are marketed in more than 170 countries worldwide. In North America, Whirlpool is the largest supplier of major appliances to Sears, under the Kenmore brand. This accounts for nearly 20 percent of Whirlpool's sales. Whirlpool, which manufactures its products in thirteen countries, makes about 25 percent of its sales in Europe and is concentrating on emerging markets in Asia and Latin America.

Regional Operations Summary

North America Whirlpool operations in the United States, Canada, and Mexico together form the North American Region. The combined operations work with a unified strategy for manufacturing and marketing appliances in the three countries.

Latin America Whirlpool includes Central and South America and the Caribbean. The Latin American Appliance Group of Whirlpool and its affiliates have the largest market share and one-third of the manufacturing capacity of the region. The Latin American home appliance market is expected to expand more rapidly than that of either North America or Europe.

Asia Whirlpool has been exporting home appliances to Asia for over thirty years. From 1993 to 1995, Whirlpool moved aggressively to increase its presence throughout the region by establishing marketing and manufacturing joint ventures. In Asia, Whirlpool focuses on four key products: clothes washers, refrigerators, air conditioners, and microwave ovens. Today, the company enjoys the number one position among non-Asian competitors in the region.

With a staff of approximately 11,000 and eleven factories in six countries, Whirlpool Europe ranks as the third-largest producer and marketer in Western Europe. It commands the leading position in Central and Eastern Europe and is growing steadily in the Middle East and Africa. A strong focus on the needs of customers in each of Europe's various markets, combined with a coordinated, pan-European approach to many common operations and activities, provides Whirlpool Europe with a strong foundation to build for the future.

Company Vision, Values, and Social Responsibility

- *The Whirlpool vision:* Every Home . . . Everywhere with Pride, Passion, Performance. We create the world's best home appliances that make life a little easier and more enjoyable for all people. Our goal is a Whirlpool product in every home, everywhere. We will achieve this by creating: Pride . . . in our work and each other; Passion . . . for creating unmatched customer loyalty for our brands; and Performance . . . results that excite and reward global investors with superior returns.

- *Values:* Five fundamental values—Respect, Integrity, Teamwork, Learning to Lead, and Spirit of Winning—represent the essence of who we are as a company. They provide a framework of expectations for how we behave and relate with others. The power of these values and the behaviors that support

Source: © Dr. Helen LaVan, Dept. of Management, DePaul University, Chicago, Ill. Used with permission.

them lies in how they help us achieve a consistently high level of performance, regardless of business or economic cycles.

- *Social responsibility:* Whirlpool Corporation meets its societal obligations by extensive commitments to Habitat for Humanity International. It is donating a Whirlpool brand refrigerator and freestanding range for homes built in the United States and Canada under Habitat's new More Than Houses Program, a campaign to build 100,000 new homes by the year 2005. The company previously announced that it would donate up to $5 million in appliances for homes built by Habitat. "We are truly grateful to Whirlpool for making such a generous pledge of support," said Millard Fuller, president and CEO, Habitat for Humanity. "Literally, thousands of families will benefit from this exciting partnership."

ERP at Whirlpool

The following portions of the ERP at Whirlpool are provided for analyses: dispatcher assignment, centralized pricing, vendor interfaces, the Internet application decision, the Internet application problems, response time monitoring, and application integration.

Dispatcher Assignment

Sophisticated geographic routing software is helping Whirlpool Corp. consolidate twenty-two field service offices into a single hub operation, slashing millions of dollars in real estate costs in the process. The $200,000 Resources in Motion Management System (RIMMS) from Lightstone Group in Mineola, New York, is expected to help Whirlpool manage and coordinate its 440 appliance technicians across the United States from one service hub in Knoxville, Tennessee.

The Benton Harbor, Michigan-based appliance maker has already consolidated seven of its twenty-two field locations. The remainder will be brought into the fold by year's end. Whirlpool is replacing the colored pins and giant wall maps that have been used in its regional service centers for years. Automation will mean dispatchers may lose the intimate knowledge they had of local routes and traffic trouble spots. (With the manual system, it sometimes took dispatchers a full day to plot a daily service route for a single technician.) Using RIMMS, Whirlpool dispatchers can lay out each technician's route within an hour.

The consolidation has presented Whirlpool with some tricky personnel problems. Under the service overhaul, technicians are being asked to cover new territories and squeeze in extra work in the same amount of time. Whirlpool's technicians typically handle ten customer calls per day. The hope is that by utilizing the most efficient routes from one customer call to another, each service technician will be able to squeeze in an extra customer job each day, said Tom Mender, a senior analyst at Whirlpool's LaPorte, Indiana, parts distribution center. "Even if we can get an extra half a job a day, the [full-year] benefits are staggering," said Mender. "Our biggest challenge has been managing the expectations of our technicians," Mender said.

Whirlpool's service center consolidation also means it will probably need only five or six dispatchers, not the twenty-four it once used to support its field service centers. Downsizing "is something we've wrestled with from the beginning," Mender said. By centralizing and automating its service centers, Whirlpool loses "the quirks of knowing your hometowns," he said. Mender said the fate of its dispatchers has not been decided.

Centralized Pricing

When Frigidaire Co. drops freezer prices, a flurry of faxes and FedExes fly from Whirlpool Corps.' offices in a fight to match those prices. But soon Whirlpool will be able to match competitors' pricing with a few keystrokes, allowing the company to react quickly to market changes or launch a special promotion for a single product. Whirlpool is implementing a centralized pricing configuration system from Trilogy Development Group, Inc., in Austin, Texas. The pricing software will allow Whirlpool to cut by more than half the 110 days it now takes to reprice its entire product line of more than 2,000 models each quarter.

Most important, the application will give Whirlpool a centralized pricing structure. Previously, the company used separate pricing models and order entry systems for each Whirlpool division, from small appliances to large goods to spare parts. "The big driver for all of this is to make Whirlpool easier to do business with," said Bill Hester, a senior information systems project manager at Whirlpool.

Whirlpool's technology overhaul, which also includes implementing SAP AG's R/3 and a massive operational reorganization, is necessary to prime Whirlpool for the dishwasher wars in years to come. The entire IT overhaul is estimated to cut $160 million from Whirlpool's operational budget over five years.

Hester said the company expects the new pricing system will pay for itself within a few years. Historically, Whirlpool's customer claims usually resulted from pricing discrepancies. "We would tell trading partners we were going to sell them something at 'x' price, but the system was charging them 'y'," said Kathleen Descamps, business project manager for Whirlpool's new pricing system. "So we would have to issue them a credit. It creates dissatisfied customers. It's much easier to say we are charging them 'x' and that is what is on the invoice."

With one centralized pricing system, sales agents will be able to meet that goal. The same information will be replicated in sales agents' laptops for quick reference when making field calls to trading partners. "They will have the same sales history information that is used to make [production] forecasts," Descamps said, so they will have the same information to help meet the forecasts. Whirlpool's current pricing system is highly dependent on spreadsheets, a laborious and time-consuming system.

Bill Hester, project manager at the appliance giant, said the quarterly job of revamping the pricing of every product takes 110 days and is prone to errors. Pricing has to be entered for every product under eleven different brand names. "It took roughly 180,000 cells in the spreadsheet," Hester said. "Since pricing is formuladriven, if someone changed a formula, you wouldn't know the effects somewhere else in the spreadsheet. It took a lot of work to get the pricing masters printed."

If a marketing manager needs to change the price of dishwashers to match General Electric's pricing, that person can now enter the information; do a profitability analysis on the change; and then, if acceptable, enter the new price. "Then a message is automatically sent to the pricing administrator, who sets up any rules for the pricing, and as soon as they hit 'enter,' if the pricing is effective today, the next person that places an order gets that new price," Hester said.

Vendor Interfaces

A warehouse automation system has propelled Whirlpool Corporation's Parts Distribution Center in LaPorte, Indiana, into a new era of customer satisfaction. The system, comprised of an elaborate configuration of computers and automatic conveyors, reduces the order-processing cycle time for customers around the world. "It helps us better manage our inventories with the ultimate improvement being customer satisfaction," says Tom Harrow, customer service supervisor.

Whirlpool Corp. hopes a new e-commerce initiative, Easy EDI, will cut down supply chain expenses and enhance efficiencies. Easy EDI's goal is twofold: to eliminate the paper process used by Whirlpool's 300 smaller suppliers and to save Whirlpool up to $600,000 a year in operational costs for the electronic data interchange network used by Whirlpool's 300 largest suppliers, says David Tibbitts, manager of strategy and planning in global procurement at Whirlpool.

Initially, Easy EDI will involve four small and midsize suppliers that rely on paper transactions to conduct business with Whirlpool's fourteen North American manufacturing facilities. Four to six weeks later, the service will expand to about thirty suppliers; all small and midsize suppliers should be on-line by year's end. Whirlpool then expects to gradually roll out Easy EDI to its largest suppliers, which use a public value-added network (VAN) for EDI transactions. The company hopes to phase out VAN-based EDI, Tibbitts says, along with the $40,000 to $50,000 a month it pays for the service.

Easy EDI is an example of how the consumer-goods manufacturing industry is moving in the same direction as the automotive industry, says Susan Cournoyer, an analyst at Dataquest. "Agile, just-in-time manufacturing and its use of the Internet will cut costs and improve communications and responsiveness to customers," she says.

Whirlpool is working with integrator Litton Enterprise Solutions, a division of government contractor Litton Industries, to develop Easy EDI.

Internet Application Problems

Late this year, Whirlpool Corp. plans to turn on SAP R/3 and link it to the Internet so retailers can place and track orders on-line. But that does not mean the call-center workers who take orders over the phone will go away. In fact, their jobs will become more important—and more complex—said senior project manager Bob Briggs. He said Whirlpool plans to use SAP AG's R/3 applications to give call-center employees access to all the information they need to answer questions about pricing, promotions, and billing from retailers that sell its appliances.

Those data currently are split into stand-alone mainframe systems, forcing retailers to get answers from multiple departments, Briggs said. Whirlpool is not the only company that is still depending on its call center while moving more routine business transactions to the Web. But the call center is still vital "because the most complex problems are going to go there," he added. "The nature of the work has changed, but I think its importance goes up."

But change will not be easy. At Whirlpool, for example, call-center workers will be fielding "bigger and more sophisticated questions" on matters such as credit and pricing promotions, Briggs said. That will require them to learn both R/3 and a new set of business processes before the combination of SAP's software and Whirlpool's retailer Extranet goes into use in the fourth quarter.

Whirlpool made a risky and ultimately damaging business decision by going live with its SAP R/3 implementation over the Labor Day weekend knowing that "red flags" had been raised, according to SAP AG officials. Fixing the problem would have delayed Whirlpool's go-live date by a week, SAP said. But pressure to take advantage of the long holiday weekend and to get off of its legacy system well before 2000 pushed Whirlpool ahead.

The decision resulted in a botched shipping system that, until it was fixed November 1, left appliances sitting in warehouses. Some stores experienced six- to eight-week delays before receiving their orders. "We suspected there would be problems, but the customer made a decision to go live despite warning signals," said Jeff Zimmerman, senior vice president of customer support services at SAP.

Officials at Benton Harbor, Michigan-based Whirlpool would not discuss details of the snafu. "We have had some delays, partially due to the new [SAP] implementation and also due to record levels of orders," said Christopher Wyse, a Whirlpool spokesman.

In a statement, Whirlpool Chairman and CEO David R. Whitwam said shipping delays, "most of which are already behind us, are due as much to the strength of our North American business . . . as to issues we've already addressed with the new system." He added that the problems should not force the company to miss its fourth-quarter earnings targets.

Things seemed to be running smoothly days after the launch when 1,000 system users processed appliance orders. But by September 18, with 4,000 users placing orders, performance started to disintegrate, Zimmerman said. That was when stores selling Whirlpool appliances started feeling the pinch. Foremost Appliance in Chantilly, Virginia, which gets one-third of its revenue from Whirlpool sales, had shipments from Whirlpool's Carlisle, Pennsylvania, distribution center delayed six to eight weeks. "Some people are ordering four or five appliances, and we get one this week, none for them the next week. Then one more the week after. It's been a dilemma," said Bill Brennan, store manager. Brennan said he has been steering customers who do not want the long wait to other brands.

Whirlpool is the latest in a recent spate of enterprise resource planning (ERP) implementations in which user companies have grossly underestimated the complexity. "These implementations are like doing open-heart surgery. There was an expectation on the part of the companies that was completely unreasonable," said Chris Selland, an analyst at The Yankee Group in Boston. Selland said that SAP has recorded more implementation successes than failures and that it is common to find "a hundred little problems and ten that are major" when going live—not just two like Whirlpool had. SAP has been under pressure to change its image from that of a company whose software requires multiyear, multimillion dollar implementations to one that offers shorter, easier projects, Boulanger said. SAP's plan to bring in project overseers ninety days before going live is relatively new, he said, but users would be better served if SAP were present at the project from beginning to end. Regardless of who is fueling the impression that companies can launch an ERP application quickly, "companies have to realize that the onus is on you and the consulting firm to make it work," Selland said.

Questions for Discussion

1. How was the organization prepared for the change?

2. Was the problem with employees whose jobs had changed dealt with properly?

3. How were the customers and vendors communicated to about the changed procedures for interfacing in various transactions with Whirlpool?

4. How were IT employees prepared for interfacing with external consultants?

5. Evaluate the steps that were taken in the ERP activities. Which were done well and which could be improved?

6. Do you think SAP should be held accountable for any of the problems faced by Whirlpool? Why or why not?

References

Balu, R. "Whirlpool Gets Real with Customers." *Fast Company*, no. 30 (December 1999): 74.

Collett, S. "SAP Gets Stuck in the Spin Cycle." *Computerworld* 33, no. 45 (8 November 1999): 1, 16.

Hoffman, T. "IT Plan Has Whirlpool Spinning." *Computerworld* 31, no. 26 (10 January 2000): 41.

Liebmann, L. "Look Beyond the Enterprise." *InternetWeek*, no. 774 (19 July 1999): 39.

McGee, M. K. "Whirlpool Jumps on the Net." *InformationWeek*, no. 713 (14 December 1998) 34.

Niccolai, J. "Whirlpool Lays Delays at SAP's Door." *Network World Fusion* (4 November 1999). Available from http://www.nwfusion.com/news/1999/1104whirlpool.html

Niccolai, J., and M. LaMonica. "Whirlpool Latest to Hit ERP Production Snags." *InfoWorld* 21, no. 45 (8 November 1999): 3.

Stedman, C. "Whirlpool Plans to Spin R/3 for Call Center." *Computerworld* 33, no. 17 (10 April 1999): 10.

Tiazkun, S. "EAI Is Fast Becoming Critical Solution for Enterprise Accounts." *Computer Reseller News*, no. 841, CRN Enterprise Partner Supplement (10 May 1999): 1, 6.

Weston, R. "Appliance Firm Gives Pricing System a Whirl." *Computerworld* 32, no. 12 (23 March 1998): 1.

"Whirlpool Corporation Comments on Product Availability and Performance Expectations." *Business Wire* 12 (3 November 1999): 24.

"Whirlpool Corporation Extends and Expands Commitment to Habitat for Humanity Throughout North America." *Business Wire* (15 January 2000). Available from http://www.whirlpoolcorp.com/news/releases/release.asp?rid=137

"Whirlpool Sues CA (Computer Associates International)." *Computerworld* 32, no. 22 (1 June 1998): 12.

Wilder, C. "Automotive Net Seeks Outsiders." *InformationWeek* 728 (5 April 1999): 36.

Note: Other information available from http://www.hoovers.com, http://www.whirlpool.com

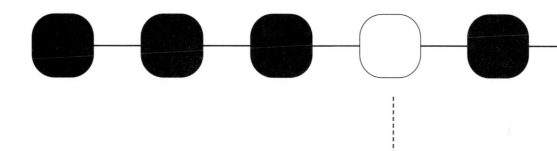

Part 4

Distribution Issues in Supply Chain Management

Case Studies

Chapter 9:

DOMESTIC AND INTERNATIONAL TRANSPORTATION

Shipments are getting to their global destinations faster every day, but boats, trains, planes, and trucks are not moving any faster. The processes among the shipping legs are getting more efficient thanks to technology. The technologies driving this trend started with bar coding and have moved to freight handling systems and shipment identification chips.[1]

Learning Objectives

After completing this chapter, you should be able to
- Understand the strategic importance of transportation.
- Identify the various modes of transportation.
- Discuss the international aspects of transportation.
- Describe how transportation impacts supply chain management.
- Examine the interrelatedness of transportation, warehousing, and material handling.
- Identify a number of third-party transportation service providers.
- Summarize the important aspects of transportation regulation and deregulation.
- Discuss some of the e-commerce issues in transportation management.

Chapter Outline

SUPPLY CHAIN MANAGEMENT IN ACTION   *Game Theory at Mars, Inc.*

You are arrested for a crime you may or may not have committed. Your best friend is locked up in a separate cell. A corrupt cop, who has no evidence, tells you with a sneer that if neither of you confesses, you will both get two years in jail. If only you confess, you will walk free while your friend will get twelve years—and vice versa. If you both confess, however, you will each get four years. What do you do? Chances are, both of you will sing like canaries, even though you would both be better off keeping your mouths shut. It is the classic "prisoner's dilemma" that sits at the heart of game theory—a branch of economics that analyzes how people interact to achieve their goals. The solution to the paradox? According to the theory, only by changing the rules of the game—allowing cooperation—can both prisoners get out of jail early.

Here is the next question: What does any of this have to do with food, trucks, and logistics? The answer: Food giant Mars Inc. is using game theory to change the rules of logistics and tease out win-win deals with manufacturers and truckers delivering goods in Europe. For the average company, hiring a trucking outfit to move finished goods or raw materials demands a phone, a pen, a Rolodex, and a trailer load of patience. But Mars, which runs up a European freight tab of more than $250 million per year, instead uses the Internet and game theory. In fact, the on-line tenders and auctions that Mars runs to select its carriers have been so successful that the company has launched a United Kingdom–based subsidiary, Freight Traders. From its headquarters in the English town of King's Lynn, Freight Traders has helped Kellogg, Lever Faberge, and Reckitt Benckiser move about $1 billion worth of goods in the past three years. Tenders that used to take months now run in weeks, and at least one shipper is banking savings of up to 50 percent on its freight costs. In classic game theory terms, Mars has changed the game to come up with win-win logistical solutions.

Transportation costs account for between 3 and 6 percent of the budget of most companies that are in the fast-moving consumer goods sector. Planning truck movements for these giant enterprises is usually a stunningly complex task. And yet, despite the scale and complexity of the operation, according to Freight Traders' managing director Garry Mansell, negotiations between shippers and carriers almost inevitably devolve into the age-old practice of haggling over price. Driving a single load between the United Kingdom and Italy may cost $1,100 or it may cost $2,300, depending on whether the shipper or the carrier has the upper hand. In the language of game theory, a "zero-sum" game is one in which somebody wins and somebody loses, period. But there is an alternative approach to competitive interactions—rivals can compete and cooperate at the same time.

To disrupt the zero-sum framework in logistics, Freight Traders uses some of the best game theorists in the world to help shippers and carriers strike deals that are mutually beneficial. The first step is for Freight Traders to create a broad "community" of shippers with cargo to move who are then introduced to a wide selection of carriers with trailers to fill at Freight Traders' Web site. After that initial step, game theory takes over. Here is how it works: Game theory helps Freight Traders decide when to end a tender or auction. Say you are bidding for a rare Eminem action doll on eBay. The deadline is midday Friday, but you are going to watch the action and wait until 11:55 A.M. before making your bid. It is no different with freight. A shipper might post a big tender on Freight Traders' Web site for seven days, but 95 percent of the bids from carriers will probably occur in the last two hours. "Sniping," or withholding bids until the last moment, suppresses competition, says Gail Hohner, a game theorist from New Jersey and Freight Traders' research director. Freight Traders has found the way to fix that problem: By introducing a "soft ending" mechanism, the company changes the rules of the bidding process so that any offer made in the last hour automatically triggers an extension of the deadline, removing the incentive for sniping.

Critics might dismiss game theory and logistics as, well, just theory. But hard economics are at work: Mansell estimates average savings to shippers in the region of 5 to 8 percent. Geoff Norris, distribution manager of babyfood manufacturer Nutricia Wells, calculates that

Freight Traders saved him $1 million in a single tender. And the on-line tenders and auctions enable carriers to allocate their trucks more efficiently: "Empty running," or the number of unloaded trailers on fruitless journeys, is down 20 percent.

In 1990, Mars appointed Mansell, an applied chemist, to Consolidated European Logistics Services, an internal organization tasked with bringing pace, power, and focus to Mars's logistics buying. Having worked with Hohner before on a crop-forecasting project, Mansell asked if game theory could be applied to logistics. Hohner's reply: "Let's find out." Over the course of the 1990s, Mars gained a reputation as a logistics pioneer. "When other companies started asking to buy our software, I smelled a business opportunity," says Mansell, who convinced Mars that it could, by creating Freight Traders, offer the service to other companies via the Internet. IBM beat four rivals in a game theory tender (of course) to build the high-powered site that can handle 3,000 to 5,000 offers in a typical twenty-minute blitz.

Freight Traders employs just ten staffers, but with more than 1,000 carriers and almost 200 shippers active in its tenders and auctions, the company is already making money by charging shippers a fee. Now Freight Traders is plunging into deep-sea freight. And by 2004, Mansell expects to introduce collaborative buying, which will allow shippers to pool their needs, giving carriers fuller loads on certain routes. John Nash, who received a Nobel Prize in 1994, waited forty years for his achievements in game theory to be recognized. Mansell and Freight Traders will not need to be so patient.[2]

Introduction

Transportation is necessary for both moving purchased goods from suppliers to the buying organization and moving finished goods to the customer. An efficient and effective transportation system is needed for commerce to occur in any industrialized society. Products have little value to the customer until they are moved to the customer's point of consumption. For supply chains in particular, transportation is what creates the efficient flow of goods between supply chain partners, allowing profits and competitive advantage to be maximized. Anytime anyone moves around a city, between cities, or between countries, it is impossible to ignore the business of transportation, whether it be the large, slowly moving truck in front of you, the train moving along next to the highway, the airplanes taking off at the airport, the container ships unloading cargo, or the barges meandering down the waterways. In the United States and other highly industrialized nations, the transportation of goods is ever-pervasive. Without it, we as consumers would never have the opportunity to find whatever we want, when we want it, at the many retail outlets we routinely visit each day.

Today, the U.S. freight transportation bill amounts to about 6 percent of gross domestic product (GDP). In Table 9.1, we can see the growth of transportation expenditures in the United States, and as of 1999, the nation's total freight cost was approximately $562 billion. Notice that since about 1980 (the time when transportation was deregulated in the United States), the nation's freight bill relative to U.S. GDP has been reduced. This is due to lower overall transportation prices as the result of deregulation. Also note the steady increase in the use of both truck and air transportation since 1980 and the steady decrease in the use of rail and water transportation. This most likely is due to the need for faster and more flexible transportation, coming from customers seeking to satisfy their own customers or increase their competitive advantage.

In this chapter we discuss the many transportation activities, nomenclature, and events that affect businesses each day. We discuss the impact of transportation on supply chain management and review the modes of transportation, transportation regulation and deregulation, transportation decisions the firm must make, the relationship between transportation and warehousing, the international issues impacting transportation, and the impact of e-commerce on transportation.

Table 9.1	Total U.S. Freight Transportation Expenditures (Current $ billions)											
	1970	1980	1990	1991	1992	1993	1994	1995	1996	1997	1998	1999
Total U.S. GDP	1,040	2,796	5,803	5,986	6,319	6,642	7,054	7,401	7,813	8,318	8,782	9,269
Total U.S. Freight Transp Costs (% GDP)	84.0 (8.1)	213.7 (7.6)	351.0 (6.0)	355.2 (5.9)	375.1 (5.9)	396.4 (6.0)	420.3 (6.0)	442.4 (6.0)	467.2 (6.0)	494.9 (5.9)	528.8 (6.0)	561.8 (6.1)
Truck Total (% Freight Total)	62.5 (74.4)	155.3 (72.7)	270.8 (77.2)	274.4 (77.3)	292.9 (78.1)	311.9 (78.7)	330.7 (78.7)	348.1 (78.7)	368.5 (78.9)	396.7 (80.2)	427.2 (80.8)	456.8 (81.3)
Rail Total (%)	11.9 (14.2)	27.9 (13.1)	30.1 (8.6)	30.0 (8.4)	30.5 (8.1)	30.8 (7.8)	33.1 (7.9)	34.4 (7.8)	35.1 (7.5)	35.3 (7.1)	35.3 (6.7)	35.9 (6.4)
Water Total (%)	5.3 (6.3)	15.5 (7.3)	20.1 (5.7)	20.3 (5.7)	19.9 (5.3)	20.8 (5.2)	21.2 (5.0)	22.7 (5.1)	24.6 (5.3)	21.0 (4.2)	22.5 (4.3)	24.5 (4.4)
Air Total (%)	1.2 (1.4)	4.0 (1.9)	13.7 (3.9)	14.4 (4.1)	15.0 (4.0)	15.8 (4.0)	17.3 (4.1)	18.8 (4.2)	20.4 (4.4)	22.8 (4.6)	24.2 (4.6)	25.3 (4.5)
Pipeline Total (%)	1.4 (1.7)	7.5 (3.5)	8.5 (2.4)	8.1 (2.3)	8.5 (2.3)	8.5 (2.1)	8.7 (2.1)	9.1 (2.1)	8.6 (1.8)	8.6 (1.7)	8.6 (1.6)	9.1 (1.6)
Other Total[a] (%)	1.8 (2.1)	3.5 (1.6)	7.8 (2.2)	8.1 (2.3)	8.3 (2.2)	8.6 (2.2)	9.4 (2.2)	10.3 (2.3)	10.0 (2.1)	10.6 (2.1)	10.6 (2.0)	10.2 (1.8)

[a]Includes freight forwarder and other shipper costs such as loading/unloading freight cars.
Source: U.S. Bureau of Transportation Statistics; available from http://www.bts.gov/publications/nts

The Impact of Transportation on Supply Chain Management

Transportation is what allows products to move from point of origin to point of consumption throughout the supply chain, and is thus responsible for creating **time utility** and **place utility.** Time utility or time value is created when customers get products delivered at precisely the right time, not earlier and not later. The transportation function creates time utility by determining how fast products are delivered and how long they are held in storage prior to delivery. Place utility is created when customers get products delivered to the desired location, and again, it is the transportation function that accomplishes this. Thus, transportation in a supply chain setting is extremely important in that products must be routinely delivered to each supply chain partner on time and to the correct location. As mistakes occur in deliveries along the supply chain, more safety stocks must be held and customer service levels deteriorate, eventually causing higher costs and lower customer satisfaction for end consumers. To make up for lost time, overnight deliveries are also frequently used, causing transportation costs to escalate.

For international supply chains, the transportation function is even more critical. Providing adequate transportation and storage, getting items through customs, delivering to foreign locations in a timely fashion, and transportation pricing can all impact the ability of a supply chain to serve a foreign market competitively. In many cases, firms are forced to use outside agents or **third-party transportation services** to move items into foreign locations effectively. International purchases are also similarly impacted by transportation. When firms consider expanding the supply side of their supply chain to include foreign suppliers, transportation cost and timing become critical factors in the decision. For instance, Chinese suppliers delivering goods to buyers along the U.S. East Coast are tending to favor an all-water route through the Panama Canal, rather than dealing with rail congestion on the U.S. West Coast. Buyers get cheaper freight rates and can plan on shipments arriving at a specific time when using an all-water route, whereas the chances of shipments being held up due to missed rail connections can be significant. All-water shipments have risen about 65 percent since the early 1990s.[3] These issues become part of the negotiating process between the buyer and the foreign supplier; and, in many cases, buyers with limited foreign purchasing experience must use a knowledgeable third-party transportation service in order to purchase from foreign suppliers efficiently.

Thus, we can see the value created for supply chains by transportation. It is what effectively links each supply chain partner. Poor transportation management can bring a supply chain to its knees literally, regardless of the production cost or quality of the products produced. Alternatively, good transportation management can be one of the elements creating competitive advantage for supply chains.

The Fundamentals of Transportation

This section reviews a number of important transportation elements including the objective of transportation, transportation classifications, the modes of transportation, pricing, third-party transportation services, regulation and deregulation, and intermodal transportation. This will provide a good foundation for discussion of the remaining topics in the chapter, and will also cultivate an appreciation for the complex nature of transportation management.

The Objective of Transportation

While you may think the overriding objective of transportation is obvious, that is, move the cargo from Point A to Point B, transportation providers can go broke doing this inefficiently. For example, at the time of this writing, a number of U.S. passenger airlines had declared bankruptcy and were seeking concessions from labor unions to keep operating.[4] Transportation managers seek to maximize the value of their services by correctly interpreting the service needs of their customers, setting or negotiating prices high enough to cover the delivery costs incurred while making an acceptable profit contribution, and then delivering the desired services as efficiently as possible. In other words, in the most general terms, transportation objectives should be centered on satisfying customers while minimizing costs and making a profit contribution. For transportation managers, this means deciding which forms of transportation, material handling, and storage—along with the most appropriate vehicle scheduling and routing—to use. Additionally, it means deciding what prices will result in profits for the firm, while maintaining competitiveness. In the airline industry, competitive prices may not be high enough to cover the firm's costs and this has created a tremendous problem for a number of carriers.

Legal Forms of Transportation

Transportation service companies are classified legally as either common, contract, exempt, or private carriers. The distinguishing characteristics of each of these classifications follows.

Common carriers offer transportation services to all shippers at published rates between designated locations. Common carriers must offer their transportation services to the general public without discrimination, meaning they must charge the same rates for the same service to all customers. Because common carriers are given the authority to serve the general public, they are the most heavily regulated of all carrier classifications. Some U.S. examples of common carriers are Southwest and American Airlines, Amtrak, Greyhound, and Carnival Cruise Lines.

Contract carriers are also for-hire carriers like common carriers; however, they are not bound to serve the general public. Instead, contract carriers serve specific customers under contractual agreements. Typical contracts are for movement of a specified cargo for a negotiated and agreed-upon price. Some contract carriers have specific capabilities that allow them to offer lower prices than common carriers might charge for the same service, although common carriers can also be contract carriers. For instance, America West Airlines might enter into a contractual agreement with the Phoenix Suns professional basketball team to provide transportation for their team's out-of-town games. Shippers and carriers are free to negotiate contractual agreements for price, commodity carried, liability, delivery timing, and types of service.

Exempt carriers are also for-hire carriers, but they are exempt from regulation of services and rates. Carriers are classified as exempt if they transport certain exempt products like produce, livestock, coal, or newspapers. The exempt status was originally established to allow farmers to transport agricultural products on public roads, but today the status has been broadened to include a number of commodities. Rail carriers hauling coal between specific locations are exempt from economic regulation, for instance. All carriers can also act as exempt carriers for these specific commodities.

A **private carrier** is not subject to economic regulation and typically transports goods for the company owning the carrier. Firms transporting their own products typically own and operate fleets large enough to make the costs of transportation less than if the firm hired the service. Flexibility and control of product movements may also play a role in the ownership of a private carrier. Wal-Mart, for instance, owns a fleet of trucks and a number of distribution centers to transport products from its distribution centers to its retail outlets.

The Modes of Transportation

The five basic modes of transportation are motor, rail, air, water, and pipeline carriers. Recall that these modes and the amount of freight they hauled were shown in Table 9.1. Each of these modes offers distinct advantages to its customers, and its choice depends on the goods transported, how quickly goods are needed, and the locations of the origination and destination.

Motor Carriers

Motor carriers—or trucks—are the most flexible mode of transportation and, as shown on Table 9.1, account for over 80 percent of all U.S. freight expenditures. Motor carriage offers door-to-door service, local pickup and delivery, and small as well as large shipment hauling. They have very low fixed and variable costs and can thus compete favorably with rail and air carriers for short- to medium-length (less than 1,000 miles) transportation and are still competitive with other forms of transportation for cross-country shipments, particularly if there are multiple delivery destinations. The primary disadvantage for motor carriers is the weather. Motor carriers can also offer a variety of specialized services from refrigerated, to livestock, to automobile hauling.

Motor carriers are most often classified as **less-than-truckload (LTL) carriers** or **truckload (TL) carriers.** LTL carriers move small packages or shipments that take up less than one truckload, and the shipping fees are higher per hundred weight (cwt) than TL fees, since the carrier must consolidate many small shipments into one truckload, then break the truckload back down into individual shipments at the destination, for individual deliveries. However, for small item shippers, using LTL carriers is still a much less expensive alternative than using a TL carrier. The LTL industry in the United States is made up of national LTL carriers like Yellow Transportation, Roadway Express, and ABF Freight System, and regional LTL carriers (specializing in shipments of less than 500 miles). Most of the regionals are small, privately owned companies that specialize in overnight and second-day deliveries. Today, they must contend with increased competition from the national carriers, since regional carriage represents the fastest-growing segment of the trucking industry. In fact, the majority of tonnage hauled by motor carriers today travels fewer than 500 miles.[5]

Motor carriers can also be classified based on the types of goods they haul. **General freight carriers** carry the majority of goods shipped and include common carriers, while **specialized carriers** transport liquid petroleum, household goods, agricultural commodities, building materials, and other specialized items.

Motor carriers offer fast, reliable, relatively inexpensive service with low levels of shipment damage. Their geographic coverage is very good; and, for short trips, no other mode can compete. Wages have been declining, though, in the U.S. trucking industry since deregulation (discussed later in the chapter) and with the current trend in deunionization.[6]

Rail Carriers

Rail carriers compete most favorably when the distance is long and the shipments are heavy or bulky. At one time in the United States, rail carriers transported the majority of goods shipped; however, since World War II, their share of the transportation market has fallen quite dramatically. Today, railroads only account for about 6 percent of the U.S. freight bill; however they carry about one-quarter of the nation's freight traffic in ton-miles because of their ability to carry very heavy shipments.

Rail service is relatively slow and inflexible; however, rail carriers are less expensive than air and motor carriers and can compete fairly well on long hauls. To better compete, railroads have begun purchasing motor carriers and can thus offer point-to-point pickup and delivery service using motor carriers and flatcars that carry truck trailers—known as **trailer-on-flatcar (TOFC) service.** Railroads are also at somewhat of a disadvantage compared with motor carriers with respect to shipment damage, equipment availability, and service frequency.

Since rail companies use each other's rail cars, keeping track of rail cars and getting them where they are needed can be problematic. However, with advances in railroad routing and scheduling software and rail car identification systems, this has become less of a problem for rail carriers. In the United States, railroad infrastructure and aging equipment have also been problems for the railroads; and, in recent years, the industry has seen a bit of a resurgence through efforts to replace worn track segments and rail cars, upgrade terminals, and consolidate through mergers and acquisitions.

Some of the latest changes occurring in rail transportation include high-speed trains. Today, they are beginning to be operated along the northeast U.S. corridor and along the Canadian Montreal-Ottawa-Toronto corridor. Bombardier Inc., a Montreal-based transportation and aerospace company, designed and manufactured the Acela, an electric high-speed train operating along the U.S. corridor, and is now designing the JetTrain, a non-electric high-speed train to be used along the Canadian corridor. High-speed rail can provide an attractive alternative to air transportation, depending on the cost and location of terminals.[7]

Air Carriers

Transporting goods by air is very expensive relative to other modes but also very fast, particularly for long distances. **Air carriers** transport about 5 percent of the U.S. freight bill, but this only accounts for about 1 percent of the total ton-miles hauled in the United States each year. This is because airlines cannot carry extremely heavy or bulky cargo. For light, high-value goods that need to travel long distances quickly, air transportation is the best of the modal alternatives. For movements over water, the only other modal alternative is water carriage, where the decision is based on timing, cost, and shipment weight. While the incidence of shipment damage is quite low and schedule frequency is good, air transportation is limited in terms of geographic coverage. Most small cities and towns do not have airports and regularly scheduled service, so motor carrier service must be combined with air transportation for these locations.

Today, about half of the goods transported by air are carried by freight-only airlines, like Fedex. This represents a significant change since the late 1960s when most air cargo was hauled by passenger airlines. A number of these freight-only airlines have also added motor carrier fleets to offer point-to-point service, since airport congestion and runway delays can reduce the advantage of air carriers for medium to long distances. The growth in air freight has been very strong since the 1980s, due to deregulation and the increased need for quick deliveries. Since 1980, the percentage of the nation's freight bill due to air transportation has grown by about 150 percent. This growth is expected to continue, as more firms implement JIT production capabilities.

Water Carriers

Shipping by **water carrier** is very inexpensive but also very slow and inflexible. Several types of water transportation include inland waterway, lake, coastal and intercoastal ocean, and international deep-sea transportation. Most of the inland waterway transportation is used to haul heavy, bulky, low-value materials like coal, grain, and sand, and competes primarily with rail and pipeline. Inland water transport is obviously limited to areas accessible by water, so growth in this area of transportation is also limited. There has actually been a slight decline in water transportation as a percentage of total freight costs over the past twenty years. Like rail and air transportation, water carriers are typically paired with motor carriers to enable door-to-door delivery.

In the United Kingdom, efforts are underway to reduce this downward trend. The United Kingdom is investing heavily in that country's canal and river system to reduce highway congestion and pollution by increasing the trade along its inland waterways. At present, 3.5 million tons of non-time-sensitive freight per year are moved via U.K. inland waterways, and the government's goal is to double that amount within the next few years.[8]

Developments in deep-sea transportation have made water transportation cheaper and more desirable, even with the slow transportation times. The development and use of supertankers and containerships have added a dimension that did not previously exist. Today's supertankers are over 1,500 feet long (that's five football fields) and 200 feet wide. Oil-producing nations can now cheaply ship large quantities of oil anywhere demand exists around the globe, and even small shippers can ship items overseas cheaply due to the ability to consolidate small shipments in containers that are placed on board containerships. Containers allow most any packaged product to be shipped overseas and add an element of protection to the cargo.

Pipeline Carriers

Pipeline carriers are very specialized with respect to the products they can carry; however, once the initial investment of the pipeline is recovered, there is very little additional maintenance cost so pipeline transportation tends to be very inexpensive. Pipelines can only haul materials in a liquid or gaseous state, so the growth potential for pipelines is quite limited. One of the items pipelines haul is coal, and they do this by first pulverizing coal into small particles, then suspending it in water to form coal slurry. When the coal slurry reaches its destination, the coal and water are separated. Other items transported include water, oil, gasoline, and natural gas. The continuous nature of pipeline flow is what makes it unique. Once the product reaches its destination, it is continuously available. As long as the world remains dependent on energy products like coal, oil, and natural gas, there will be a need for pipeline transportation.

Intermodal Transportation

Intermodal transportation, or combinations of the various transportation modes, is becoming an extremely popular method of transportation and makes the movement of goods much more efficient. Most large transportation service companies today offer one-stop, door-to-door shipping capabilities—they transport goods for one price, then determine the best intermodal transportation arrangements to meet customer requirements as cheaply as possible.

Following is a shipping example using a number of intermodal combinations:

A manufacturing company packs a standard 8' by 8' by 20' container for shipment to an overseas customer. The container is sealed and placed aboard a motor carrier trailer for transport to a nearby rail terminal. The container is then loaded onto a flatcar and double-stacked with another container where it is then transported to the U.S. West Coast. Upon arrival, the container is placed aboard a containership and transported to Japan. In Japan, the container moves through customs and then is loaded onto another motor carrier trailer for transport to its final destination, where it is unpacked. In this example, goods were only packed and unpacked one time. The container was used in three modes of transportation and remained sealed until the final destination when customs authorities unsealed, examined, and accepted the goods.

The example highlighted a number of forms of intermodal transportation. The most common are **trailer-on-flatcar (TOFC)** and **container-on-flatcar (COFC),** also called **piggyback service.** The same containers can be placed on board containerships and airliners. These combinations attempt to combine the flexibility of motor carriers with the economy of rail and/or water carriers. The Burlington Northern Santa Fe (BNSF) Corporation operates one of the largest railroad networks in North America, with 33,000 route miles covering twenty-eight states and two Canadian provinces. BNSF moves more intermodal traffic than any other rail system in the world; today, intermodal transportation accounts for about half of the number of units transported by BNSF.[9]

Another example is **ROROs** or *roll-on-roll-off* containerships. These allow truck trailers and containers to be directly driven on and off the ship, without the use of cranes. The Atlantic Container Line operates some of the largest and most versatile RORO/Containerships in the world, capable of carrying a wide variety of oversized cargo. Their RORO/Containership fleet allows all vehicles and oversized cargo to be securely parked under deck in RORO garages, providing protection. Their RORO/Container vessels are some of the most flexible ships operating today; their G-3 vessel is 958 feet long, with a capacity of 3,100 TEUs (a TEU is a 20-foot-long equivalent unit, with dimensions of 20 feet long by 8 feet high by 8 feet wide).[10]

Third-Party Logistics Services

A number of logistics service intermediaries act to facilitate better use of the transportation alternatives. Particularly for small firms with no internal transportation expertise, these third-party logistics services can help firms get what they want at reasonable prices. Today, many large firms outsource some or all of the transportation function, as well, to allow more attention to be placed on core competencies. According to an annual survey by the Georgia Institute of Technology, the most widely outsourced logistics function is outbound transportation, followed by warehousing, inbound transportation, freight bill auditing and payment, customs brokerage, and freight forwarding. Survey respondents stated that 43 percent of their current logistics expenditures were for outsourced services, and they expected that percentage to grow to 60 percent by 2007.[11] A few of these services are described in the following sections.

Freight Forwarders

Freight forwarders consolidate a large number of small shipments in order to fill entire truck trailers or rail cars that transport items at truckload or carload prices. They can also provide air transportation consolidation services. These companies pass some of the savings on to the small shippers and keep the rest of it as revenue. Thus, freight forwarders provide valuable services to both the shipper (lower prices) and the carrier (consolidation). Freight forwarders can specialize in either domestic or international shipments, as well as air or ground shipments. These companies also provide documentation services, special freight handling, and customs clearance.

Several changes are occurring in the freight-forwarding arena today, as customers seek to save money by using slower, second-day and economy shipping options. Doug Brittin, vice president of marketing and business development at Emery, says even JIT shipments can be shipped using slower, cheaper transportation alternatives if they are secure and reliable. Better software is also helping shippers by enabling them to make better shipping decisions and to obtain more shipment visibility from carriers. "Information and visibility are almost as important as transportation itself," says Brittin.[12]

Transportation Brokers

Transportation brokers are businesses that handle the transportation requirements of shippers and also find shipments for carriers for a fee. They are legally authorized to act on the shipper's or carrier's behalf; typically, these companies are hired because of their extensive knowledge of the many transportation alternatives available or the many shippers needing transportation. Typical arrangements may include small businesses using a transportation broker to handle all of their transportation needs, or trucking companies using brokers to find a back-haul job after a delivery is completed. A number of transportation broker directories exist, enabling shippers and carriers to find one meeting their needs. For instance, the Red Book Transportation Brokers Rating Service is an on-line directory of transportation brokers in the United States and Canada. The Web site provides user ratings of the various brokers as well as information about each of the brokers and their services.[13]

Shippers' Associations

The American Institute for Shippers' Associations defines **shippers' associations** as "non-profit membership cooperatives that make domestic or international arrangements for the movement of members' cargo." Thus, their job is to consolidate their members' shipments into full carloads, truckloads, or container loads to achieve volume discounts for the members and to negotiate for improved terms of service. These associations also benefit the carriers, in that they help to better utilize the carriers' equipment. Because shippers' associations do not identify themselves as carriers, they are not required to publish or adhere to tariff rates and can keep service contracts confidential. Some disadvantages are also possible for members of shippers' associations; these potentially include required minimum shipment volumes to receive the benefits of reduced rates, and some ocean carriers refusing to do business with shippers' associations. A number of shippers' associations exist for different industries. For example, the U.S. Department of Agriculture lists thirteen shippers' associations for agricultural shippers.[14]

Intermodal Marketing Companies

Intermodal marketing companies (IMCs) are companies that act as intermediaries between intermodal rail carriers and shippers. They typically purchase large blocks of flatcars for piggyback service, then find shippers to fill containers, or motor carriers with truckloads, to load the flatcars. They get volume discounts from the rail carriers and pass some of this on to the shippers. These companies facilitate intermodal shipping and have become an important intermediary. Many IMCs utilize Internet, cell-phone, and satellite transmissions to allow real-time communications between themselves, the carriers, and the shippers. This also enables accurate delivery predictions for customers.[15]

Integrated Logistics Service Providers

Integrated logistics service providers provide any and all logistics services to organizations for a fee. Typically used by very large companies with complex material handling, storage, and transportation requirements, these providers come to a firm; assess its goods handling, storage, and shipment needs from both an inbound and an outbound perspective; and then provide complete solutions that often allow the firm to both reduce its total logistics costs and increase the level of customer service it can provide. This type of service is growing rapidly as firms seek to find new ways to improve supply chain performance, profitability, and competitiveness.

Schneider Logistics, for example, coordinates the entire delivery of aftermarket parts to the North American dealerships of both GM and Ford. From 1996 to 2001, Schneider's efforts were focused on service to the dealers, optimizing transportation, and optimizing the supply chain parts network. Now the focus is more on visibility, so everyone knows what is moving and what is coming from the suppliers. Penske Logistics handles all inbound parts for Ford's twenty-one North American assembly plants. The company handles 30,000 freight bills per week for Ford. For 2002, Penske adjusted Ford's supplier network to accommodate 7,000 sourcing changes made by Ford.[16]

Transportation Pricing

Two pricing strategies used by transportation service providers are **cost-of-service pricing** and **value-of-service pricing.** Both are discussed in the following sections, along with some related pricing issues.

Cost-of-Service Pricing

Cost-of-service pricing is used when carriers desire to establish prices that vary based on their fixed and variable costs. To accomplish this, firms must be able to identify the relevant costs and then accurately allocate these to each shipment. Cost-of-service pricing varies based on volume and distance. As shipping volume increases, the portion of fixed costs that are allocated to each shipment goes down, allowing the carrier to reduce prices. Large-volume shipments also allow carriers to charge carload or truckload rates instead of less-than-carload or less-than-truckload rates. As the shipping distance increases, prices tend to rise, but not proportionally with distance, since fixed costs are essentially constant regardless of distance.

Value-of-Service Pricing

In value-of-service pricing, carriers price their services at competitive levels the market will bear. Prices are thus based on the level of competition and the current level of demand for each service. This is a profit-maximizing pricing approach. If a carrier has a service that is in high demand with little competition, prices will tend to be quite high. As other carriers notice the high profit potential of this service, competition eventually increases and prices fall. As the level of competition increases, carriers seek ways to reduce their costs to maintain profitability. In the highly competitive passenger airline industry, Southwest Airlines has been able to keep its costs low by using only one type of airplane and flying relatively short distances between stops, which has enabled it to remain profitable as of 2003, while other airlines have continued to lose money.

Terms of Sale

In many cases, suppliers' terms of sale impact transportation. When products are purchased from a supplier, the supplier may quote a price that includes transportation to the buyer's location. This is known as **FOB destination** pricing, or free on board to the shipment's destination. This also means that the supplier is the legal owner of the product until it safely reaches its destination. For high-value shipments, small shipments, or when the buyer has little transportation expertise, FOB destination is typically preferred. Otherwise, the buyer may decide to purchase goods and supply its own transportation to the shipping destination; in this case, the supplier quotes **FOB origination** prices, transferring ownership to the buyer at the supplier's location.

Pricing Negotiation

Since the deregulation of transportation in the United States, negotiating transportation prices has become much more common. Additionally, shippers today are tending to develop alliances with transportation service providers because of the key role they play in making supply chains responsive to changing demand. This has also tended to increase the use of pricing negotiations. Negotiations tend to be based on the carrier's fixed and variable costs. To maintain an equitable partnership, prices are negotiated that allow carriers to cover their fixed and variable costs and make a reasonable profit.

Rate Categories

Carrier prices or rates can be classified a number of different ways. **Line-haul rates** are the charges for moving goods to a nonlocal destination; these can be further classified as *class rates, exception rates, commodity rates,* and *miscellaneous rates.* Class rates are based on the particular class of the product transported—some products have higher published class rates than others. Exception rates are published rates that are lower than class rates for specific origin-destination locations or volumes. Commodity rates apply to minimum quantities of products that are shipped between two specified locations. Miscellaneous rates apply to contract rates that are negotiated between two parties and to shipments containing a variety of products (in this case, the rate is based on the overall weight of the shipment). Today, many of the rates carriers charge are classified as miscellaneous, since negotiated rates tend to be used very often for sizable shipments.

Transportation Regulation and Deregulation

The United States has gone through periods of regulation and deregulation with respect to the transportation industry. On the one hand, government regulation is said by many to be good in that it tends to assure adequate transportation service throughout the country while protecting consumers in terms of monopoly pricing, safety, and liability. On the other hand, transportation deregulation is argued to be good because it encourages competition and allows prices to adjust as demand and negotiations dictate. Additionally, antitrust laws already in place tend to protect transportation consumers. This debate was the subject of a study in 1994 to determine the impact deregulation had on the U.S. motor carrier industry. The study concluded that transportation deregulation has resulted in greater use of cost-of-service pricing, rising freight rates for LTL shipments, and more safety problems as operators have tended to let fleets age and to reduce maintenance.[17] Today, the U.S. transportation industry remains essentially deregulated; however, a number of regulations still exist (primarily safety regulations) that carriers must adhere to. Some of the history of transportation regulation and deregulation in the United States is reviewed next.

Transportation Regulation

Table 9.2 summarizes the transportation regulations in the United States, starting with the **granger laws** of the 1870s. Prior to this time, the railroads in the United States were charging high rates and discriminating against small shippers. So, a number of midwestern states passed laws to broadly regulate the railroads to establish maximum rates, prohibit local discrimination, forbid rail mergers (to encourage competition), and prohibit free passes to public officials. While the U.S. Supreme Court later struck down these laws, the granger movement made Congress realize the impact of railroad monopolies. This led to the passage of the **Interstate Commerce Act of 1887.**

The 1887 act created the Interstate Commerce Commission (ICC); required rail carriers to charge reasonable rates, to publish rates, to file them with the ICC, and to make these available to the public; and prohibited discriminatory practices (charging some shippers less than others for the same service). The act also prohibited agreements between railroads to pool traffic or revenues. Between 1887 and 1910, a number of amendments made to the 1887 act increased the ICC's control and enforcement power. These amendments restricted railroads from providing rates and services that were not in the public's best interest, created penalties for failure to follow published rates or for offering and accepting rebates, set maximum rates, and prevented railroads from owning pipelines or water carriers unless approved by the ICC.

By 1917, increased competition combined with the rate restrictions had created a rail system unable to offer the efficient service the U.S. government needed to pursue the war, so the federal government seized the railroads. Railroad companies were guaranteed a profit, while the government poured large sums of money into upgrading the rail system. By the

Table 9.2	U.S. Transportation Regulation	
Date	**Regulation**	**Summary**
1870s	Granger laws	Midwestern states passed laws to establish maximum rates, prohibit discrimination, and forbid mergers for railroads.
1887	Interstate Commerce Act	States cannot regulate transportation; established Interstate Commerce Commission; regulated and published rates, outlawed discriminatory pricing, prohibited pooling agreements, to encourage competition.
1920	Transportation Act	Instructed the ICC to establish rates that allowed RRs to earn a fair return; established minimum rates; gave control to ICC to set intrastate rates; allowed pooling agreements if they were in the public's best interest.
1935	Motor Carrier Act	Extended the ICA of 1887 to include motor carriers and brought them under ICC control; established five classes of operators: common, contract, private, exempt, and broker; mergers must be OK'd by ICC.
1938	Civil Aeronautics Act	Established the Civil Aeronautics Board to regulate air carriers; new entrants had to get CAB approval; CAB controlled rates; Civil Aeronautics Administration controlled air safety.
1940	Transportation Act	Extended the ICA of 1887 to include ICC control over domestic water transportation; ICC controlled entry, rates, and services.
1942	Freight Forwarders Act	Extended the ICA of 1887 to include ICC control over freight forwarders; ICC controlled entry, rates, and services.
1948	Reed-Bulwinkle Act	Amendment to the ICA of 1887 legalizing rate bureaus or conferences.
1958	Transportation Act	Amended the rule of rate making by stating that rates could not be held up to protect the traffic of any other mode.
1958	Federal Aviation Act	Created the Federal Aviation Agency to assume the mission of the CAA; FAA empowered to manage and develop U.S. airspace, and plan the U.S. airport system.
1966	Dept. of Transportation Act	Assumed mission of FAA and a number of other agencies for research, promotion, safety, and administration of transportation; organized into nine operating and six administrative divisions; also established the National Transportation Safety Board.
1970	Railway Passenger Service Act	Created the National Railroad Passenger Corporation to preserve and upgrade intercity rail passenger service; resulted in the creation of Amtrak.

end of World War I, Congress had come to realize that all of the negative controls placed on railroads were unhealthy for the industry. They wanted to return the railroads to private ownership. This brought about the first of a number of regulations aimed at positive control, the **Transportation Act of 1920.**

The 1920 act instructed the ICC to ensure that rates were high enough to provide a fair return for the railroads each year (Congress initially set this at 6 percent return per year). When companies made more than the prescribed 6 percent, half of the excess was taken and used to fund low-interest loans to the weaker operators for updating their systems and increasing efficiency. The act also allowed the ICC to set minimum rates, allowed joint use of terminal facilities, allowed railroads to enter into pooling agreements, and allowed rail company acquisitions and consolidations. Finally, to keep the railroads from becoming overcapitalized, the act prohibited railroads from issuing securities without ICC approval. The rail system thus became a regulated monopoly.

From 1935 to 1942, regulations were passed that applied to other modes of transportation, and these were similar in nature to the 1920 act. A great deal of money was spent during the 1920s and during the Depression building the U.S. highway system. The time was ripe, then, for emergence of for-hire motor carriers. The number of small trucking companies grew tremendously during this period, creating intermodal competition for the railroads, as shippers opted to use the cheaper for-hire motor carriers. The **Motor Carrier Act of 1935** brought motor carriers under ICC control, thus controlling entry into the market, establishing motor carrier classes of operation, setting reasonable rates, requiring ICC approval for any mergers or acquisitions, and controlling the issuance of securities.

In 1938, the federal government enacted another extension of the Interstate Commerce Act by including regulation of air carriers in the **Civil Aeronautics Act.** This act promoted the development of the air transportation system and promoted air safety and airline efficiency by establishing the Civil Aeronautics Board to oversee market entry, establish routes with appropriate levels of competition, develop regional feeder airlines, and establish reasonable rates. The Civil Aeronautics Administration was also established to regulate air safety.

The **Transportation Act of 1940** further extended the Interstate Commerce Act of 1887, establishing ICC control over domestic water transportation. The provisions for domestic water carriers were similar to those imposed on rail and motor carriers. In 1942, the 1887 act was once again extended to cover freight forwarders, with the usual entry, rate, and service controls of the ICC. Freight forwarders were also prohibited from owning any carriers.

A number of other congressional enactments occurred up through 1970, further strengthening and refining the control of the transportation market. In 1948, the **Reed-Bulwinkle Act** gave groups of carriers the ability to form rate bureaus or conferences wherein they could propose rate changes to the ICC. The **Transportation Act of 1958** established temporary loan guarantees to railroads, liberalized control over intrastate rail rates, amended the rule of rate making to ensure more intermodal competition, and clarified the differences between private and for-hire motor carriers. The **Federal Aviation Act of 1958** replaced the Civil Aeronautics Administration with the Federal Aviation Administration (FAA) and gave the FAA authority to prescribe air traffic rules, make safety regulations, and plan the national airport system. In 1966, the **Department of Transportation Act** created the Department of Transportation (DOT) to coordinate the executive functions of all government entities dealing with transportation-related matters. It was hoped that centralized coordination of all the transportation agencies would lead to more effective transportation promotion and planning. Finally, to preserve and improve the rail system's ability to service passengers, the **Railway Passenger Service Act** was passed in 1970, creating Amtrak.

From 1971 to 1982, over $2 billion was spent by Congress to upgrade the Amtrak rail passenger system. As of 2003, Amtrak served forty-six states on over 22,000 miles of track and operated about 265 trains per day, including the Acela high-speed rail service along the Washington to Boston northeast corridor.[18] Unfortunately, Amtrak has lost money for over thirty consecutive years and its future viability is in doubt as state governments are now being asked to pay for the cost of operations not covered by ticket revenues.

Transportation Deregulation

Commencing in 1976, Congress enacted a number of laws to reduce transportation regulation (see Table 9.3). This began the movement toward less regulation to allow market forces to determine prices, entry, and services. At this point in transportation history, consumers and politicians had the opinion that transportation regulation was administered more for the benefit of the carriers than the public. Additionally, with the bankruptcy filings of a number of railroads in the mid-1970s combined with the Arab oil embargo of the same period, regulation was receiving much of the blame for an inefficient transportation system.

The **Railroad Revitalization and Regulatory Reform Act,** commonly known as the *4-R Act,* was passed in 1976 and made several regulatory changes to help the railroads. First, railroads were allowed to change rates without ICC approval, limited by **threshold costs** on one end and **market dominance** on the other. Threshold costs were defined as the firm's variable costs, while the ICC determined if the firm was in a market-dominant position (absence of market competition). A number of ICC procedures were also sped up to aid transportation manager decision making. These same ideas appeared again in later deregulation efforts.

Air freight was deregulated in 1977. No longer were there any barriers to entry, provided the firms were deemed fit by the Civil Aeronautics Board. Size restrictions were also lifted, and carriers were free to charge any rate provided there was no discrimination. Finally, carri-

Table 9.3	U.S. Transportation Deregulation	
Date	**Deregulation**	**Summary**
1976	Railroad Revitalization and Regulatory Reform Act	The "4-R Act." Railroads were allowed to change rates without ICC approval, within limits; ICC procedures were sped up.
1977	Air Cargo Deregulation Act	Freed all air cargo carriers from CAB regulations
1978	Air Passenger Deregulation Act	Airlines freed to expand routes, change fares within limits; small community routes were subsidized; CAB ceases to exist in 1985.
1980	Motor Carrier Act	Less restrictions on entry, routes, rates, and private carriers.
1980	Staggers Rail Act	Freed railroads to establish rates within limits; legalized contract rates; shortened ICC procedure turnaround.
1982	Bus Regulatory Reform Act	Amended the 1980 MCA to include buses.
1984	Shipping Act	Partial deregulation of ocean transportation; allowed ocean carriers to pool or share shipments, assign ports, publish rates, and enter into contracts with shippers.
1994	Trucking Industry Regulatory Reform Act	Motor carriers freed from filing rates with the ICC.
1994	FAA Authorization Act	Freed intermodal air carriers from economic regulation by the states.
1995	ICC Termination Act	Eliminated the ICC and moved regulatory duties to Dept. of Transportation.
1998	Ocean Shipping Reform Act	Deregulated ocean liner shipping; allowed contract shipping; rate filing not required.

ers did not have to file freight rates with the CAB. This was followed soon after by deregulation of air passenger service in 1978. This was a phased-in approach, wherein carriers could slowly add routes to their systems while protecting other routes from competition. Fares could be adjusted within limits without CAB approval. To protect small communities from losing service, all cities with service in 1977 were guaranteed service for ten additional years. In 1981, all route restrictions were to be released, allowing any carrier to operate any route. Airline rates and mergers were to be released from regulation in 1983. Finally, the CAB was to shut down in 1985. The impact of these changes on the airline industry was significant—there were thirty-four air passenger carriers in 1977, and by 1982 the number had increased to ninety. Some fares dropped substantially, while other fares went up, and routes to low-demand areas decreased.

Motor carriers were deregulated in 1980. The objective of this act was to promote competitive as well as safe and efficient motor transportation. Entry regulations were eased to make it easier to enter the market—firms had only to show that a "useful public purpose" would be served. Route restrictions were removed; and restrictions deemed to be wasteful of fuel, inefficient, or contrary to public interest were also removed. As with the 4-R Act, a **zone of rate freedom** was also used. And, as with air passenger deregulation, a large number of new motor carriers began service. By 1981, over 2,400 new motor carriers had started up in the United States.

Railroads were further deregulated with the **Staggers Rail Act of 1980.** The financial condition of railroads was worsening, and this act was aimed at improving finances for the rail industry. With this act, rail carriers were free to change rates within a zone of rate freedom but the ceiling or market-dominance rate was established more definitively as 160 percent of variable costs and varied up to 180 percent depending on ICC cost formulas. After 1984, rate increases were to be tied to the rate of inflation. Contract rates were also allowed between railroads and shippers. A number of other financially oriented procedural changes were made, including the reduction in response times for the ICC to respond to notice of rate changes.

The **Shipping Act of 1984** marked the end of the initial push by Congress to deregulate transportation. This act allowed ocean carriers to pool or share shipments, assign ports, publish rates, and enter into contracts with shippers. More recently, with the passage of the

ICC Termination Act of 1995 and the **Ocean Shipping Reform Act of 1998,** the Interstate Commerce Commission was eliminated and the requirement for ocean carriers to file rates with the Federal Maritime Commission also came to an end.

Thus, a number of changes in the U.S. transportation industry have occurred in the past century. Economic regulation of transportation occurred for several reasons. In the future, as economic conditions, technology, political, and social changes occur, transportation regulations will also continue to change. Initial regulations were instituted to establish the ground rules as new forms of transportation developed, and to control prices, services, and routes when monopoly power existed in the industry. Later, regulations were changed to encourage competition and increase efficiency and safety.

Warehousing

Warehousing is an important topic in that it enables firms to store purchases and work-in-progress and finished goods, while providing faster and more frequent deliveries of finished product to customers, resulting in better customer service when the system is designed and managed correctly. Right now, readers may be questioning the need for warehouses, particularly since this textbook has been singing the praises of low inventories, JIT deliveries, efficient supply chains, and the like; and, in some respects, the need and uses for warehouses have changed over the past twenty years. In many cases today, warehouses are not used to store things but rather to receive, break down, repackage, and distribute components to a manufacturing location or finished products to customers. These activities are collectively referred to as **crossdocking.** In this case, the warehouse is more accurately described as a **distribution center.** In other cases, firms are moving warehouses closer to suppliers or closer to customers or to more centralized locations, depending on the storage objectives. So, warehouses are still very much in use—some just to store things, and others to provide efficient throughput of goods.

This section discusses a number of warehousing issues, including their importance, the types of warehouses, public and private warehouses, locating a warehouse, risk pooling, and JIT warehousing. The Supply Chain Management in Action box that follows describes some current trends in warehousing in the apparel industry.

© 1999 Ted Goff

"And by distorting the space/time continuum, we can move every point in this sector of the universe several inches closer to our warehouse, thereby reducing costs."

SUPPLY CHAIN MANAGEMENT IN ACTION   *Warehousing Trends in the Apparel Industry*

Managing the warehousing and distribution of apparel has always presented its own unique set of challenges. From running distribution centers (DCs) to controlling inventory to dealing with customs regulations, warehousing and distribution issues are at the heart of the supply chain. In general, the distribution of apparel has always been a dilemma, especially when it comes to the more fashion-conscious goods. The problem has always been: What do you do when you have a hit, and what do you do when you have a miss? How do you deal with it on the fulfillment level?

No one will argue that with such a challenging retail market, the biggest trend is to reduce the inventory and cycle time, improve speed and turns, and reduce cost. Companies and brands want to minimize the handoffs and make the whole process run more efficiently. "Our customers are now focusing on ordering less. There are more frequent but smaller orders. It becomes a little more service intensive that way," notes Tony Zasimovich, of APL Logistics. "What we're seeing is mostly a shortening of the cycle time where the hits and misses are identified early on," notes David Himes, senior vice president of business process solutions, for NewRoads. Because inventory management is such an important key to profitability, companies are taking extra measures to avoid a lot of unsold inventory. NewRoads' client American Eagle Outfitters (AEO) for example, has a very structured program for moving inventory. If a style does not move based on projections, it will be discounted very quickly to improve its velocity.

But the real dilemma comes when the hot-selling item is identified—how do retailers get it replenished quickly enough? "There are no secrets there. Everyone tries to identify them [the hot sellers] and get their reorders in quickly. There's no great technical breakthrough there. That's the same battle they've fought forever," adds Himes. Successful warehousing and distribution for hot-selling items or commodity goods often boil down to knowing where products are and being able to alter their course depending on demand. "[Clients] want the ability at order entry to have time and space availability and be able to discern where inventory is, where it will be, and when it will be available to customers," notes Gary Gaffney, distribution and logistics specialist of Ensemble Business Software. From there, apparel firms want to be able to make prioritizations or decisions regarding their customers and their importance and the goods that they need. "Do I have them available and do I need to maybe steal from Peter to pay Paul? Do I have it now, and if not, when will I?" he adds.

In an increasingly vertical environment, some apparel brands have chosen to ship directly to their stores rather than through a DC, and some retailers are requesting direct-to-store shipment from vendors. Yet, this trend is not a widespread as one might think. It seems to hinge on the capabilities of the individual manufacturer and retailer. Himes points to the bigger stores and chains as instigators of direct-to-store shipping trends. "They're placing bigger orders and pushing really hard for vendor compliance issues, and when they've got the clout to do that, then you can get that shipping directly to the stores," he says. APL's Zasimovich adds: "Most everyone will go to a DC. The reason for this is because going directly to stores is difficult from Asia. They don't have the store allocations that far in advance. It's possible and it does happen, but the majority of situations don't allow for that. There are a lot of demands that have to be taken care of first."

But those who do decide to go the direct-to-store route are faced with their own set of challenges. A shift of this type requires much greater visibility into the supply chain. Especially in fashion, the timing of product shipments is critical. "Currently, many retailers have not formed the tight bonds with their suppliers to enable that type of distribution model," observes Jim Oakes, director of market management, supply chain solutions at Retek. Moreover, Himes adds: "There's a problem of scale there. For example, AEO has a lot of clout with its buyers where a lot of smaller chains don't have that clout, can't get the tags done properly or the special tags that they may want for their merchandise." Having said that, he brings up the issue of store preparation as a concern in terms of moving goods directly from a manufacturer to the store. "That's going to be a continuing battle because everyone has got their own custom tagging scenario to deal with," notes Himes.

Given the globalization of manufacturing, visibility into the supply chain is key. As apparel retailers and vendors source from more countries, the need to efficiently manage distribution across all of these factories is significant. Yet even with today's technology, the challenges are huge. It is one thing to say you are going to send POs and monitor movements globally; it is another to actually do it. As Himes notes: "Once we get visibility in place, vendors can start acting on it. Just getting it in place is the biggest obstacle right now." For many apparel firms, the ultimate test of supply chain software is how well it answers one key question related to visibility. As Gaffney sums it up: "The real critical need is visibility [into] when the product is going to be available for sale."

The increased focus on security is also affecting distribution models, making visibility that much more important. Importers must examine their sourcing points to ensure their inbound logistics are as secure as possible. With security concerns and the new checks and balances put in place after September 11, 2001, knowledge is key. "You have to know when it's going to be here and what it's going to be," notes Prashant Bhatia, director of product management, Manhattan Associates.

Source: T. Haisley, "Visibility, RFID Key Trends in Warehousing & Distribution," *Bobbin* 44, no. 3 (2002): 38–42. Used with permission from *Apparel Magazine*.

The Importance and Types of Warehouses

Firms hold inventories for a number of reasons as explained in Chapter 6, wherein warehouses are used to support purchasing, production, and distribution. Firms order raw materials, parts, and assemblies, which are typically shipped to a warehouse location close to the buyer's facility and then eventually transferred to the user-facility as needed. In a retail setting, the warehouse might be regionally located, with the retailer receiving bulk orders from many suppliers, breaking these down and reassembling outgoing orders for delivery to each retail location, then using a private fleet of trucks to move the goods orders to the retail locations. Similar distribution centers are used when manufacturers deliver bulk shipments to regional market areas, then break these down and ship LTL outgoing order quantities to customers.

Conversely, firms may operate **consolidation warehouses** to collect large numbers of LTL shipments from nearby regional sources of supply, where these are then transported in TL or CL quantities to a manufacturing or user-facility located at some distance from the consolidation center. The use of consolidation warehouses and distribution warehouses allows firms to realize both purchase economies and transportation economies. Firms can buy goods in bulk at lower unit costs, then ship these goods at TL or CL rates either into a distribution warehouse or directly to a manufacturing center. They can also purchase and move small-quantity purchases at LTL rates to nearby consolidation warehouses.

Private Warehouses

Just as with the private forms of transportation, **private warehouses** refer to warehouses that are *owned by the firm storing the goods*. For firms with large volumes of goods to store or transfer, private warehouses represent an opportunity to reduce the costs of warehousing. Aside from the potential cost benefit private warehouses provide, another consideration is the *level of control* provided by private warehouses. Firms can decide what to store, what to process, what types of security to provide, and the types of equipment to use, among other operational aspects of warehouses. Private warehousing can also enable the firm to better utilize its workforce and its expertise in terms of transportation and warehousing activities. Finally, private warehouses can generate income and tax advantages through leasing of excess capacity and/or asset depreciation. For these reasons, private warehousing accounts for the vast majority of warehouse space in the United States.[19]

Owning warehouses, though, can also represent a financial risk and loss of flexibility to the firm. The costs to build, equip, and then operate a warehouse can be very high; and most small- to moderate-sized firms simply cannot afford private warehouses. Private warehouses also bind firms to locations that may not prove optimal as time passes. Warehouse size or capacity is also somewhat inflexible, at least in the short term.

Public Warehouses

As the name implies, **public warehouses** are owned by for-profit organizations that contract their services to other companies. Public warehouses provide a number of specialized services that firms can combine to create customized services for various shipments and goods:

- *Breakbulk:* Large-quantity shipments are broken down so that items can be combined into specific customer orders and then shipped out.
- *Repackaging:* After breakbulk, items are repackaged for specific customer orders. Warehouses can also do individual product packaging and labeling.
- *Assembly:* Some public warehouses provide final assembly operations to satisfy customer requests and create customized final products.
- *Quality inspections:* Warehouse personnel can perform incoming and outgoing quality inspections.
- *Material handling, equipment maintenance, and documentation services.*
- *Storage.*

Besides the services shown here, public warehouses provide the flexibility and investment cost savings that private warehouses cannot offer. If demand changes or products change, the short-term commitments of public warehouses allow firms to quickly change warehouse locations. Public warehouses also allow firms to test market areas and withdraw quickly if demand does not materialize. The cost of a public warehouse can also be very small, particularly if the capacity requirements are minimal. Nabisco spends several million dollars per year to outsource to ten major third-party warehouse providers and about 200 carriers for its warehouse-delivery business, which delivers to large food chains, mass merchants, drugstores, retailers, and grocery wholesalers.[20]

The primary disadvantage associated with public warehouses is the lack of control provided to the goods' owners. Other problems can include communication problems with warehouse personnel, lack of specialized services or capacity at the desired locations, and the lack of care and security given to products.

Firms might also find it advantageous to utilize public warehouses in some locations, while using private warehouses in others. For large established markets and relatively mature products, large firms may decide owning and operating a warehouse make the most sense, while the same firm may lease space and pay for services at public warehouses in developing markets or low demand areas.

Today, a few public warehouses are finding new ways to add value for their clients, but many are not doing enough in this highly competitive market. "We find that few public warehouses are doing enough to integrate their operations with those of the companies that use their services," says John Harold, president of Business Logistics of Scotts Valley, California. One increasing customer demand is for **reverse logistics services.** This refers to disposition of returned products—including items being designated for repair, restocking, or redistribution—or auctioning of obsolete products.[21]

Risk Pooling and Warehouse Location

One of the more important decisions regarding warehouses is where to locate them. This decision impacts the number of warehouses needed, their required size or capacity, the warehousing system inventory level, customer service levels, and the warehousing system cost. For a given market area, as the number of warehouses used increases, the system becomes more *decentralized.* Responsiveness and delivery service levels increase since goods can be delivered more quickly to customers; however, warehousing system operating and inventory costs also increase. Other costs that come into play here are outgoing transportation costs to customers and the transportation costs associated with the incoming deliveries of goods to each warehouse. Thus, the trade-off between costs and customer service must be carefully considered as the firm makes its warehousing location decisions. This brings up the very important topic of **risk pooling.**

Risk Pooling

Risk pooling (also referred to as the *square root rule* and the *portfolio effect*) describes the relationship between the number of warehouses, inventory, and customer service. It can be explained intuitively as follows: When market demand is random, it is very likely that higher-than-average demand from some customers will be offset by lower-than-average demand from other customers. As the number of customers served by a single warehouse increases, these demand variabilities will occur and offset each other more often, thus reducing overall demand variance and the likelihood of stock-outs and consequently, the amount of safety stock required to guard against stock-outs. Thus, the more *centralized* a warehousing system is, the lower the safety stock required to achieve a given system-wide customer service level (recall in inventory parlance that the customer service level is inversely proportional to the number of stock-outs per period). Risk pooling assumes that the demand at the markets served by the warehouses is negatively correlated (when demand at one market is greater than average, then demand at another market will be less than average). Thus, the greater the positive correlation between demands, the smaller the benefit due to risk pooling.

The effect of risk pooling can be estimated by the **square-root rule,** which suggests that the system average inventory as the result of adding warehouses to the system is equal to the old system inventory times the ratio of the square root of the new number of warehouses to the square root of the old number of warehouses.[22] A simple illustration of risk pooling is shown in Example 9.1. As shown in the example, reducing the number of warehouses from two to one causes a reduction in average inventory of approximately 29 percent.

EXAMPLE 9.1   Risk pooling

Perkins Western Boot Emporium currently owns two warehouses in Houston and Seattle. To store its boots prior to shipping them out to various retail customers across the western United States, Greg Perkins, the owner, is considering using a centralized warehouse in Denver to service all its retail customers, and is curious to know the impact this will have on its inventory requirements. Perkins' current average inventory level is approximately 6,000 boots at each warehouse. He has found that this level of stock will result in warehouse stock-outs about 1 percent of the time. Using the square-root rule, he calculates the new average inventory level needed at the central warehouse to maintain the 99 percent customer service level:

$$S_2 = \frac{\sqrt{N_2}}{\sqrt{N_1}} (S_1) = \frac{1.0}{1.41} (12{,}000) = 8{,}511 \text{ boots,}$$

where:

S_1 = total system stock of boots for the N_1 warehouses;

S_2 = total system stock of boots for the N_2 warehouses;

N_1 = number of warehouses in the existing system; and

N_2 = number of warehouses in the proposed system.

The differences between centralized and decentralized warehousing systems follow:

- *Safety stock and average system inventory:* As the firm moves toward fewer warehouses and a more centralized warehousing system, safety stocks and thus average inventory levels across the system are decreased. The magnitude of the reduction depends on the demand correlations in the various market areas.

- *Responsiveness:* As warehouse centralization increases, delivery lead times increase, increasing the risk of late deliveries to customers and reducing the ability of the organization to respond quickly to changes in demand.

- *Customer service:* As centralization increases, customer service levels at each warehouse increase, reducing the likelihood of stock-outs for a given level of average system inventory.

- *Transportation costs:* As centralization increases, outbound transportation costs increase, as LTL shipments must travel farther to reach customers. Inbound transportation costs decrease, since manufacturers and other suppliers are able to ship larger quantities at TL rates to fewer warehouse locations. The overall impact on transportation costs thus depends on the specific warehouse locations, the goods stored, the locations of suppliers, and the modes of transportation utilized.

- *Warehouse system operating costs:* As centralization increases, total operating costs decrease because there are fewer warehouses, fewer employees, less equipment, and less maintenance costs.

Today, some companies are moving toward the use of a hybrid centralized distribution system, using IT systems to combine a more decentralized warehousing system with a central control of stocks. One example is the integrated logistics contract between DHL Worldwide Express and Roche Diagnostics to operate Roche's distributed warehousing operation. The system consists of a DHL parts center in Hoofddorp, Netherlands, to handle Roche's routine deliveries and storage of spare parts. Deliveries are handled by DHL's air express carriers. Emergency stocks are held at DHL strategic parts centers and delivered using DHL's door-to-door couriers. The combination of storage and delivery centers allows Roche to offer reliable response to customer requests while avoiding stockpiling of spare parts inventories.[23]

Warehouse Location

A number of location models and theories have been proposed over the years to optimally locate factories, services, and warehouses. In Chapter 11, a number of location analysis tools are discussed and these can certainly be useful for locating warehouses. Early in the development of modern transportation and warehousing networks, several well-known economists posited theories regarding locations, which we discuss here.

Edgar Hoover recommended three types of location strategies: the market-positioned, product-positioned, and intermediately positioned strategies.[24] The **market-positioned strategy** located warehouses close to customers to maximize distribution service and to allow the firm to generate transportation economies by using TL and CL deliveries to each warehouse location. This strategy was recommended when high levels of distribution flexibility and service were required and when there were few sources of supply. The **product-positioned strategy** recommended locating warehouses close to the sources of supply to enable the firm to collect various goods and then consolidate these into TL or CL quantities for shipment to customers. This strategy worked well when there were many sources of supply, multiproduct factories, and assortments of goods ordered by customers. The **intermediately positioned strategy** placed warehouses midway between the sources of supply and the customers. This strategy was recommended when distribution service requirements were high and customers ordered product assortments from various locations.

Johan Heinrich von Thunen argued that transportation costs alone should be minimized when considering facility location.[25] His model assumed that market prices and production costs would be identical regardless of the location of the warehouse, so the optimum location would be the one that resulted in the minimum transportation costs. Weber's location theory was very similar to von Thunen's, in that he argued that the optimum location would be found when the sum of the inbound and outbound transportation costs were minimized.[26]

Greenhut's theory was based on profit instead of transportation costs.[27] He argued that the optimum location would be the one that maximized profits, which may not coincide with the minimum cost location, since demand and prices can potentially vary based on location.

Several location methods have been developed based on transportation costs, one of which is the center-of-gravity approach, discussed in Chapter 11. The weakness of this approach, as well as some of the ones already discussed, is that it fails to consider a number of other factors such as labor availability, labor rates, land cost, building codes, tax structure, construction costs, utility costs, and the local environment. If the firm is using a public warehouse, the location selection criteria would need to include warehouse services, lease costs, communication capabilities, reporting frequency, and reputation. These factors may best be addressed using the weighted factor location analysis, also discussed in Chapter 11.

Just-in-Time Warehousing

As more firms develop their supply chain management capabilities, more pressure will be placed on warehousing to support JIT operations from the companies and production facilities supplying the warehouse as well as the customers supplied by the warehouse. Some examples of these capabilities include:

- *A commitment to customers and service quality:* Warehouse employees must perform warehouse activities so as to meet the requirements of their inbound and outbound suppliers and customers.

- *Reduced lot sizes and shipping quantities:* Inbound and/or outbound shipping quantities are likely to be smaller and more frequent, containing mixed quantities of goods, requiring more handling.

- *Greater emphasis on crossdocking:* Warehouse employees must receive shipments and mix these quickly into outgoing shipments. Far fewer goods will be stored for any appreciable time, and average warehouse inventory levels will decrease, while the number of stock-keeping units will increase.

- *Increased automation:* To improve handling speed and reliability, more warehouse activities will become automated, from scanner/bar code computer tracking systems to automated storage and retrieval systems.

- *Increased assembly operations:* As more firms implement JIT combined with mass customization, warehouses will be called upon to perform final assembly operations to meet specific customer requirements. This will change the skill requirements of warehouse employees, along with equipment requirements.

Most hospitals have adopted JIT warehousing concepts. "Transportation plays a key role in our ability to serve our customers," says Mr. Craig Smith of Owens & Minor, a national distributor of medical supplies. "We have eighty-nine different stockless programs, each with different delivery requirements," says Smith. At UCLA's hospital, Owens & Minor delivers supplies directly to 123 different locations within the facility from its distribution center using a full-service lease with its transportation partner, Penske Truck Leasing.[28]

International Transportation Issues

For international goods movements, transportation managers must be aware of the availability, services, costs, and limitations of the various modes of transportation. In the United States, freight movement to Europe or Asia involves either air or water transportation and then most likely motor or rail transportation to the final destination. Between most contiguous countries, rail and motor shipments tend to be the most common mode of transportation.

Many transportation infrastructure differences are found as we move goods from one country to the next. In Europe, rail transportation tends to be much more prevalent and reliable than rail transportation in the United States because European track, facilities, and equipment are better maintained. This is due in part to the fact that most transportation modes are government owned and maintained in Europe. Water carriers may be the dominant mode of transportation in countries with a great deal of coastline and developed inland waterways. In under- and undeveloped countries, ports may be very poorly maintained and equipped, and the highway system may be almost nonexistent.

International Freight Security

One of the most troublesome and debated issues facing international freight transportation today is the issue of security. In particular, air freight is in the middle of a tug of war, between the U.S. government on one side, pulling the industry toward more security and restrictions for inbound international shipments, and the air freight carriers on the other, looking to cut costs and create efficiencies in the midst of a tremendous air cargo recession.

In 2003, U.S. Customs introduced the idea of mandatory electronic prenotification for all air and land cargo coming into the United States, similar to the already implemented twenty-four-hour rule for ocean freight. The rule requires Customs to be notified twenty-four hours prior to shipment, of the cargo to be shipped. This rule, combined with additional restrictions and inspections put in place after September 11, 2001, further slows down shipment times from overseas, making air transportation a less attractive option to high-end shippers. For instance, an international shipment that used to take two days to get through customs at JFK Airport in New York now typically takes four days. This, combined with the fact that many businesses have opted to use cheaper LTL trucking instead of air transportation for their domestic transportation needs, has had an enormous economic impact on the air freight industry. Perhaps the hardest hit sector of this industry is the custom shipment or air charter market. A number of operators have already gone out of business because their former customers no longer had the money to pay for these types of shipments.[29]

International Intermediaries

International intermediaries provide shipping, consolidation, and import/export services for firms and offer expertise that can prove very useful for most organizations involved in global commerce. A number of intermediaries are discussed in this section.

Customs Brokers

Customs brokers move international shipments through customs for companies, as well as handle the documentation required to accompany the shipments. These specialists are often used by companies requiring expertise in exporting goods to foreign countries; their knowledge of the many import requirements of various countries can significantly reduce the time required to move goods internationally and clear them through customs.

International or Foreign Freight Forwarders

Foreign freight forwarders move goods for companies from production origination to foreign customer destination using surface and air transportation. They consolidate small shipments into larger TL, CL, or container shipments; decide what transportation modes and methods to use; handle all of the documentation requirements; and then disperse the shipments at their destination. They also determine the best routing to use; oversee storage, breakbulk, and repackaging requirements; and provide any other logistics requirements of the seller. Use of foreign freight forwarders can reduce transportation costs, increase customer service, and allow small shippers to focus on core competencies. Most companies exporting their goods use the services of foreign freight forwarders because of their expertise and presence in various foreign markets. Some of the top-rated companies providing these services are USF Worldwide, EGL Global logistics, UPS Sonic Air, and Kintetsu World Express.[30]

Trading Companies

Trading companies put foreign buyers and sellers together and handle all of the export/import arrangements, documentation, and transportation for both goods and services. Most trading companies are involved in exporting, and they are not used extensively here in the United States.

Non-Vessel-Operating Common Carriers

Also referred to as NVOCCs, **non-vessel-operating common carriers** operate very similarly to freight forwarders but normally use scheduled ocean liners. They consolidate small international shipments from a number of shippers into full container loads and then handle all of the documentation and transportation arrangements from the shippers' dock area. NVOCCs also handle distribution to consignees at the destination dock area.

Global Logistics Service Providers

Companies like DHL, Fedex, Ryder, and UPS offer total global logistics system management for companies. They own their own transportation equipment and distribution centers at key ports and inland locations around the globe and can come in to an organization and decide how best to transport, store, package, and deliver products for them. Moderate to large firms in particular can benefit from the global logistics expertise these companies can provide, because they identify more efficient logistics methods for the firm, implement them, and then charge an ongoing operating fee that hopefully is more than paid for through logistics system cost savings. In many cases, customer service levels improve as well. Using a total logistics system service provider can free company personnel to concentrate their efforts on more of the firm's core objectives.

Land Bridges

Intermodal transportation is very common in international freight movements. Many intermodal movements between Western Europe and East Asia utilize the United States as a **land bridge.** This involves transporting containers via containership to the United States, where they are transported across the country by rail and again placed aboard a containership for transport to their destination. This can reduce time in transit by as much as two weeks, with little increase in total costs. When the final destination from Asia or Europe is an opposite coastal area of the United States, then containers move aboard containerships and rail to their U.S. destination, and this is called **mini-land-bridge traffic.** When the final destination involves water transport and then land transport to an inland area, this is called **micro-land-bridge traffic.**

Foreign Trade Zones

Foreign trade zones (FTZs) are secure sites within the United States under the supervision of the U.S. Customs Service. These sites are authorized by the Foreign Trade Zones Board, chaired by the U.S. Secretary of Commerce, and are comparable to the so-called *free trade zones* that exist in many countries today. FTZs are considered to be outside U.S. Customs territory, where foreign or domestic merchandise can enter without formal customs

Global Perspective

In Mexico, the landscape of freight transportation, which constitutes around 10 percent of the gross domestic product, has changed enormously in recent years. Until the early 1990s, the sector was highly fragmented. Most large corporations were vertically integrated, conducting their supply and distribution internally. However, stung by the high costs of managing their own fleets, firms started to outsource their basic haulage needs to third parties.

Mexico is the world's eleventh largest economy and eighth largest exporter of goods and services. For many Mexican executives, life in the delivery business is no longer simple. In this quagmire of complexity, many larger corporations find themselves out of their depths and shelling out the whole shebang to the experts. "The sector in Mexico is red hot right now," says John Price, logistics and transportation practice director at Infoamericas, a consulting firm based in Miami. "Those who offer such services are growing at twice the rate of basic haulage companies." Big foreign players (including Danzas, Exel, UPS Logistics, USCO, and Eagle) have jumped into the Mexican market. Alongside regional firms (including LINSA, Grupo TMM, and FEMSA), they are enjoying a U.S. $33 billion market, according to Infoamerica's Web site.

The North American Free Trade Agreement (NAFTA) has been a key market driver. It has encouraged huge growth in international trade. The number of trucks crossing into the United States from Mexico grew from about 2.5 million in 1997 to 4.2 million in 2001. "As the NAFTA trucking market opens up and crossborder trucking prohibitions ease, more shipments will probably be made directly to the end user, reducing the need for third-party logistics management of the shipments," says Ken Morris, director of Crossborder Business Associates, a consulting firm focused on Mexico-U.S. border affairs. U.S. government rules that prevent truckers from traveling more than twenty miles north of the border augment the need for third-party interchange, warehousing, and transnational facilities.

Under Mexican law, foreign-owned transportation firms are prohibited from owning inland transport lines and must subcontract local firms to perform the haulage. However, quality of service among the 5,000 or so Mexican road haulers is generally poor. Compared with the United States and Europe, the sector is unrestricted and unregulated. Due to the high cost of financing, many rigs are aged and uninsured. Furthermore, much of the Mexican highway network is in a sad state of disrepair. Worse still, according to Kroll, a risk consulting firm, a staggering 10 percent of all loads are robbed. The alternative, rail freight, has become a safer and cheaper option since lines were privatized in 1997. Tracks such as TFM and Ferromex, which head north, are particularly popular for transporting vehicles and heavy goods to the U.S. border. In general, however, with thin rail coverage in Mexico and the extra cost of moving cargo from truck to train, market share has remained below 20 percent.

Despite these challenges, logistics firms in the region offer far more value than the incumbent transportation firms would have us believe. How so? First, by lending their weight, they can both reduce customers' transportation costs and also improve basic quality of service. "We leverage our economies of scale," says Eugenio Sevilla Sacasa, vice president of Ryder Latino America. His firm, which entered Mexico in 1994 and now has 1,100 local employees, enjoyed 23 percent growth in the region in 2002. "A customer who sends three crates a week between Mexico City and Monterrey does not have our buying power. We also train drivers and lease quality equipment to ensure that subcontractors provide the best service."

Second, with their extended reach, large carriers can remove the headache of handling different providers for each and every leg of the trip. "We used to be an entirely port-to-port based business," says Ashley Mawby, manager of Inland Services at P&O Nedlloyd. "Now, due to customer demand, we offer a fully integrated door-to-door approach." Once upon a time, an international shipping line's operations were confined to Manzanillo, Veracruz, and Altamira, Mexico's major containerized ports. Now, they handle customs, warehousing, and intermodal delivery right to the doorstep on behalf of their customers.

In Mexico, the logistics business is certainly going places. Large multinational firms are working hand in hand with midsized local haulage providers. It could be the beginning of a beautiful journey.[31]

entry or payment of duties or excise taxes. FTZs bring goods and materials into the site and offer storage, exporting, manufacturing, assembly, repacking, testing, and repairing services. If the final product is exported, no duty or excise taxes are levied. If the final product is imported, duties and taxes are paid at the time of formal entry to U.S. Customs.

Congress established the Foreign Trade Zones Board in 1934 to encourage U.S. firms to participate in international trade. By 1970, there were seven general-purpose free trade zones in the United States, handling about $200 million per year in merchandise value. As of 2001, there were 240 active FTZs with over $225 billion in merchandise throughput per year.[32] FTZs are typically located in industrial parks in close proximity to seaports or airports.

The North American Free Trade Agreement

Implementation of the **North American Free Trade Agreement (NAFTA)** began on January 1, 1994, and removed (or will eventually remove) most barriers to trade and investment among the United States, Canada, and Mexico.[33] Many **tariffs** (published import fees) and quotas were eliminated immediately, and most others will be eliminated by 2008. NAFTA forms the world's second-largest open market, somewhat smaller in size than the European Union.

Today, due in part to NAFTA, Canada and Mexico purchase over 27 percent of U.S. agricultural exports. Other product categories impacted by NAFTA include motor vehicles and parts, computers, and textiles. The treaty also protects patents and trademarks and removes restrictions on investments in the three countries. In 1993, the average tariff at the Mexican border for U.S. goods was about 10 percent, while the average tariff for Mexican goods coming in to the United States was just over 2 percent. With NAFTA, Mexico's average tariff has fallen to about 2 percent. Now, more than two-thirds of U.S. exports to Mexico enter duty-free. Several other notable changes that have occurred include:

- From 1993 to 2001, trade among the three nations went from U.S. $297 billion to U.S. $622 billion.
- U.S. exports to Canada and Mexico nearly doubled from 1993 to 2001, compared to a 44 percent growth in exports to the rest of the world.
- U.S. employment from firms exporting to Canada and Mexico grew from 914,000 jobs to 2.9 million jobs from 1993 to 2001.
- Foreign direct investment inflows in the NAFTA countries reached U.S. $1.3 trillion or 28 percent of the world's total between 1994 and 2000.
- Prior to 1993, U.S. agricultural products were losing market share in Mexico; today, because of the prices and preferential advantage the products enjoy in Mexico, U.S. products account for more than 75 percent of Mexico's total agricultural imports.

NAFTA has not been without its detractors. U.S. labor groups have argued that jobs are being lost as companies move to Mexico to take advantage of cheap foreign labor, undermining labor union negotiating power. Environmental groups have been concerned that pollution and food safety laws have become more difficult to enforce. Others argue that because of subsidized agricultural exports to Mexico, the small Mexican farmer is being run out of business. In response to these concerns, supplementary agreements have been added to NAFTA that address these and other issues.

As of 2003, the United States had free trade agreements with four trading partners—Canada, Mexico, Israel, and Jordan. Recently, the United States and Chile reached an agreement to establish a free trading market, the first between the United States and a South American country, which was on its way to Congress for approval at the time this textbook was being published. Additionally, negotiations are ongoing to establish the Free Trade

Agreement of the Americas by 2005 (including the thirty-four democratic nations in the Western Hemisphere) and to establish free trade agreements with Singapore, Australia, Morocco, and several African countries.

Transportation Management

Transportation is a vital strategic link between organizations in a supply chain and must therefore be managed effectively to meet customer due dates and other shipping requirements at a reasonable cost. Thus, suppliers, customers, end users, and transportation providers all have a stake in good transportation management. Because of the important role transportation plays within the supply chain, the job of managing the transportation function within an organization has been elevated and enlarged to include a number of issues such as transportation supply base reduction, mode and carrier selection, contracting, outsourcing the transportation function, measuring transportation performance, creating strategic carrier alliances, and performing transportation audits. Each of these issues is briefly discussed in the following sections.

Transportation Supply Base Reduction

As was discussed in Chapter 4, reducing the supply base can provide a number of advantages to the organization. Here, the discussion is very similar—using fewer transportation providers enables the firm to select and use only the best-performing suppliers, resulting in better overall levels of service. Additionally, the transportation providers remaining will see an increase in shipping demands from the firm, allowing this extra business to be used as leverage when negotiating prices, shipping schedules, and services. Thus, transportation supply base reduction should become an integral part of an effective transportation management strategy in markets characterized by numerous transportation supplier choices, combined with frequent shipments into or out of the firm.

Mode and Carrier Selection

When attempting to minimize transportation and costs and/or improve customer service along the supply chain, firms must identify the most desirable transportation modes and carriers available for the various markets they serve as well as for their inbound purchased materials. Other costs will also be impacted by this decision including inventory-in-transit carrying costs, packaging costs, warehousing costs, and shipment damage costs. Chapter 2 and Chapter 3 both discussed the topic of evaluating and selecting suppliers; again, the topic here is very similar. Firms use a mix of quantitative and qualitative factors to evaluate and select transportation providers, and there are a number of comparative methods available to aid in the decision process, the most common of which is the weighted factor analysis. In a number of surveys conducted, important carrier selection factors were found to be transit-time reliability, transportation rates, total transit time, willingness to negotiate rates and services, damage-free delivery frequency, financial stability, use of electronic data interchange, and willingness to expedite deliveries.[34]

Contracting Transportation Services

Since transportation deregulation in the United States, contracting transportation services with carriers has become commonplace for many shippers with recurring transportation needs. There are benefits to both sides when contracts for transportation services are entered into. For the shipper, a contract assures a specific package of services and prices and increases the ability of the shipper to control delivery dates, damage payments, or problem remedies. For the carrier, a contract allows the firm to plan capacity and staffing requirements, assure payment for services rendered, and build a reputation to assure continued use by the shipper. Contracts also form the basis for developing a relationship between the two parties.

Outsourcing the Transportation Function

Outsourcing transportation and other related services like warehousing, customs clearance, and shipment consolidation has become more widespread today, as firms seek to increase service levels, decrease costs, reengineer internal processes, and concentrate more resources on core functions. In small firms, transportation services may be outsourced simply because the firm's personnel lack transportation experience; for large firms, outsourcing can represent potential cost savings or service improvements when the entire function is turned over to a third party. Other firms may opt to perform this function internally and use private carriers to haul their own goods. Thus, a number of transportation service alternatives exist and the firm must assess each of them in terms of the impact on cost and service. For instance, in 2000, GM formed a joint venture with CNF, Inc., a logistics services provider, to manage the automaker's entire supply chain, integrating all third-party logistics providers for both inbound and outbound movements over a three-year transition period. Eventually, the joint venture company, Vector SCM, will manage all of GM's worldwide logistics providers. GM's goal is to reduce vehicle order cycle time from eighty-five days to the fifteen-to-twenty-day range.[35]

Measuring Transportation Performance

Measuring transportation performance allows the firm to identify problem areas and then make changes, resulting in improved transportation services. Measures of performance can be compared against predetermined standards, competitive benchmarks, or previous period performance to identify problems. The measures themselves are very similar to those used to initially select carriers: transportation cost, percent on-time deliveries, average transit time, service flexibility, billing accuracy, and damage-free delivery frequency, to name a few. Companies like Tenneco and United Sugars, for example, have implemented programs to manage compliance documentation, track shipments, and measure carrier performance, with the goal of better managing relationships with their carriers, enhancing customer service, and reducing transportation costs.[36]

Creating Strategic Carrier Alliances

Building and managing an effective supply chain network often includes the creation of alliances with providers of transportation services. In fact, in several surveys of various businesses and industries, transportation and warehousing companies were included as supply chain partners in over 50 percent of the survey respondents who were actively managing their supply chains.[37] These partnerships underscore the importance and role played by transportation in supply chain management.

Partnerships between railroads and automakers in the United States have resulted in seven out of every ten vehicles produced being moved by rail to the dealerships, and a large portion of the vehicle parts moving to assembly plants by rail. Railroads have invested billions of dollars fabricating special boxcars designed to the automakers' specifications; for fleets of autorack rail cars with premium cushioning; for fleets of auto-carrier trucks; for a vast network of vehicle distribution centers; and for information systems technologies to make railroad companies function as an integral part of the automakers' organizations. In 2002, the BNSF Railroad was named a Premier Partner by Honda for the fourth year in a row.[38] In 2000, Wal-Mart piloted a **collaborative transportation management** project with partners Proctor & Gamble and carrier J. B. Hunt. By working together and sharing forecasting, planning, and replenishment information, J. B. Hunt has been able to act on information sooner and keep trucks full and moving, resulting in a 16 percent decrease in unloading time and a 3 percent drop in empty miles, while Wal-Mart significantly reduced the number of steps to process goods for its promotions.[39]

Performing Transportation Audits

Each organization has a unique set of inbound and outbound transportation system requirements based on customer and supplier location, requirements for specific services, products purchased and sold, warehouse locations, manufacturing site locations, and the modes and carriers available. With the passage of time, these characteristics all tend to change, requiring firms to periodically audit their transportation system with the objective of finding an optimal mix of both cost and service. Since the transportation system impacts a number of functional areas within the firm as well as supply chain partners, it is wise to include personnel from various areas of the firm to participate in an audit and to develop recommendations for changes to the transportation system. This audit team might include personnel from customer service, traffic, warehousing, purchasing, production, and quality, as well as representatives of supply chain partners.

When conducting a transportation audit, firms must consider system constraints such as facility, customer locations, and the existing transportation infrastructure of domestic and international locations. Given these constraints, an audit seeks to determine the most effective way to move products to the firm from suppliers, and then from the firm to customers. Complicating factors include JIT requirements that the firm or its customers may have; special services, quantities, or packaging needs of customers; and any legal aspects of transporting goods. Given these factors, there are typically a large number of transportation system options available and the firm must evaluate each of these options to determine the most optimal system configuration.

e-Commerce and Transportation

Electronic transactions using the Internet or private EDI connections have been increasing at the very rapid pace of about 20 percent per year; and by 2005, e-commerce sales among nonstore retailers is predicted to reach $60 billion per year. Less than one-quarter of e-commerce revenues, though, are generated by the retail trade sector. The service and financial sectors account for about one-third of e-commerce-generated revenues, and this includes transportation services.[40] Business-to-business (B2B) e-commerce has also become a major trend and was expected to account for over $4 billion per year in global trade by the end of 2003.[41]

For many carriers, the growth in e-commerce has opened up a new distribution channel for their services. For shippers, the Internet has reduced the time to find carriers, enabled quicker price comparisons, and allowed companies to automate their transportation management system needs. Thus, for carriers, e-commerce capabilities are quickly becoming a requirement. Customers are demanding Web-enabled shipment execution capabilities, online payment capabilities, and real-time shipment status information. Some of the specific e-commerce issues that are impacting transportation today include electronic invoice presentment and payment, supply chain visibility technologies, third-party electronic transaction platforms, and offshore IT outsourcing. These topics are briefly discussed in the following sections.

Electronic Invoice Presentment and Payment

Electronic invoice presentment and payment (EIPP) technology, or sending and receiving invoices and payments on-line, represents one of the more recent developments in B2B transactions and is designed to create greater efficiencies among the companies using this technology. Companies like AT&T Wireless, Con-Way Transportation Services, and General Electric have been able to lower their invoice processing costs, reduce billing errors, improve cash flow, and provide better customer service using EIPP. Today, software suppliers of EIPP applications are generating even more value for their customers by enabling their EIPP software to be integrated with existing ERP, purchasing, accounts payable, and call center systems.

Con-Way Transportation Services hopes to cut invoicing costs by 90 percent, using electronic billing. Con-Way's customers, though, see the benefits of EIPP from the ability to get copies of their shipping manifests on-line, being able to check the status of their shipments, and being able to reconcile invoices with purchase orders and delivery records without having to pick up the phone. The reductions in phone calls have also reduced the need for call center representatives.[42]

Supply Chain Visibility Technologies

For supply chains to be successful, time is definitely a factor that must be managed, and e-commerce technologies are helping companies to achieve tremendous time-related benefits by providing supply chain visibility for customers, shippers, and transportation providers. The BNSF Railway Web page, for instance, allows shippers to plan the movement of their freight; get immediate rates and special service fees; make orders; trace their shipments; manage other elements of their shipments such as demurrage, storage, and diversion needs; and pay invoices on line.[43] BNSF has taken the lead in Internet-based rail transportation management systems and is profiled in the e-Business Connection box. Fairchild Semiconductor conducts trade in over forty-five countries and uses advanced transportation technologies to track its inbound and outbound shipments across borders. Its on-line system also allows Fairchild to obtain advance customs approvals and compliance for work-in-progress shipments as they move around the world for completion.[44] Finally, Japanese-based NNR Aircargo Service, a global freight forwarder, uses Web-based applications to connect its eighty-five locations in eleven countries, supporting international air and ocean freight transactions, including the creation of airway bills and bills of lading, cargo order tracking, and the creation of on-line reports.[45]

Third-Party Electronic Transaction Platforms

A number of software application providers are developing specialty Web platforms to allow shippers and carriers to perform various transactions over the Web. There are literally hundreds of Web portals and exchanges today dealing with transportation. These sites provide freight-matching services, auctions, and on-line communities or marketplaces. Most on-line transportation sites provide a mixture of portal, exchange, and catalog offerings.[47] One example is a Web site designed to help shippers, freight forwarders, and ocean carriers comply with the U.S. Customs Service's Advance Manifest Regulation, more commonly known as the "twenty-four-hour rule." GTN, operated by GT Nexus, Inc., helps companies achieve compliance with the new U.S. Customs rules by allowing shippers to prepare and transmit key shipping documents to their carriers, thereby reducing system delays.[48] Flagship Customs Services also offers a number of on-line services aimed at helping shippers comply with U.S. Customs regulations. NVOCCs for instance, are using Flagship's software to file their import manifests with the U.S. Customs Service. Flagship also offers cost-effective electronic integration into the U.S. Customs' Automated Export System, exporter/freight forwarder integration, and export compliance tools.[49]

NTE, formerly the National Transportation Exchange, offers a number of transportation management applications, including an on-line marketplace for buyers and sellers of ground transportation. Buyer and seller members interactively trade ground transportation capacity at market-driven prices in a neutral exchange, somewhat like the stock market. The exchange offers complete execution processing, shipment tracking, and guaranteed payment.[50]

Time and the railroads have been inseparable for 150 years—Standard Time itself was a railroad invention. Today, the railroads can actually create time. Here is how it works, from a railroad perspective.

Time is money: There are three parts to any rail transaction—rates, cars, and transportation. Railroads now use powerful e-commerce applications to simplify and speed up each of these. Take rates. BNSF calls its "iPOWER" approach to pricing "real rates in real time for real markets." Posted prices are market responsive, immediately available, and designed to move product now.

The best car supply model is the one that guarantees the right number of empties when and where they are wanted. Again, BNSF has taken the lead with its LOGS (loading origin guarantees), COTs (certificates of transportation), and similar programs. Trip plans tell the customer when the shipment is due at the destination dock or ramp. There is no need to trace cars as they go across the railroad.

Time is productivity: The real elegance of the Web-based rail transaction lies in the way rates, event reporting, car inventory management, carload trip plans, and performance-to-plan are linked together to shape the rail transportation product. This represents a 180-degree culture shift away from the classic rail management model and toward the on-demand world of transportation buyers everywhere.

Traditional railroad thinking was organized around the operating department. The railroad was seen as a high-fixed-cost business, and return on those sunk costs drove everything. Now, railroads use e-commerce tools for the routine stuff and use their creative energies to manage the variable costs that directly affect customer satisfaction. If it does not generate revenue, they will not do it.

Time is quality: Choice is one reason the truckers are eating the railroads' lunch. If a shipper needs empty trailers at origin today and loads at destination tomorrow, no problem. If one trucker cannot deliver, others can. We live in an on-demand world in which today's needs are met by nimble suppliers.

Being bogged down by fixed costs that limit flexibility will not work. Every foot of track, gallon of fuel, car day, and crew start must go directly to support a revenue-generating activity. And so one sees trains of mixed intermodal, merchandise, and autoracks. They in turn take out yard dwell time, cut car cycle time, and increase revenue per locomotive horsepower day. It means getting a load to the destination dock on time—customer satisfaction from quality delivered.

Time is innovation: The railroad's traditional silo-based, vertically integrated management system was never meant to be very innovative. The "cover the fixed cost" mentality left no room for customizing service design to meet shipper needs: Customers took what they got or went elsewhere—in droves, to the point that railroads now have less than $30 billion of the $500-billion-plus noncoal intercity freight transportation market. Over the last five years, railroad managers started to realize they had to compete in real time, and that was a step in the right direction. However, first attempts to do so simply laid new information technology over old operating plans.

Today, forward-thinking railroad managers know the way to manage change is to manage time. That means creating innovative products supported by business procedures that exist to improve customer satisfaction. And so it is we have high-powered tools that put the entire transportation process from car order to delivery in the customer's hands—and do it via the railroads' Web sites.

The BNSF iPOWER suite is the best of the bunch. With a few mouse clicks, even the newest user can check transit times, get rates, and order cars. More important, business processes within BNSF are being reshaped to support iPOWER's customer tools. Is it working? BNSF has identified more than 600 potential new carload customers and is hiring fifteen sales reps to convert these opportunities into revenue.

In short, railroaders use these e-commerce suites to give back and create time and get paid for it. Customers and railroads alike have more useful things to do with their time than to fritter it away on rates or cars.[46]

Offshore Information Technology Outsourcing

The growing demand for e-commerce applications has created a demand for inexpensive but competent Information Technology (IT) workers; and, as a consequence, U.S. IT service providers are contracting with offshore IT providers for software development services. India is the largest and most mature location for offshore outsourcing of programmers and project managers, with about 445,000 IT workers as of 2002. Typically, U.S. companies assign liaisons to work with overseas staff, and still can manage to save about 25 percent when compared to domestic IT service contracts. As of 2003, domestic IT service providers were expected to spend 25–30 percent of their IT budgets on offshore IT services.

For example, Cognizant, with four development facilities in India, has built a Web-based transportation management system for U.S. Cold Storage, a provider of refrigerated warehousing and storage. The system will control U.S. Cold Storage's interactions with its carriers to ensure that shipments are loaded and dispatched properly. The Cognizant personnel added a variety of development talent to the mix when combined with the U.S. Cold Storage IT personnel.[51]

Companies like Accenture, EDS, and IBM Global Services have recently opened offshore IT facilities in India, the Czech Republic, and Spain to bring their prices down and maintain profit margins during tight economic times. EDS for instance, has seventeen offshore facilities and has been offering offshore development contracts since 1998. In one large contract for DuPont, Accenture will do about 40 percent of the development work from its facilities in India and Spain.[52]

Summary

    This chapter has discussed the important role of transportation to any industrialized society—and to supply chains in particular. While this is a very broad topic, we have attempted to review the elements within transportation to give the reader an adequate understanding of the entire field of transportation. These elements included the modes of transportation, transportation pricing, regulation and deregulation of transportation, third-party transportation providers, warehousing, international transportation, transportation management, and e-commerce issues in transportation. It is hoped that readers have gained an understanding of the many elements within the broad topic of transportation and why these are so important to the management of supply chains.

Key Terms

air carriers, 279
Civil Aeronautics Act, 286
collaborative transportation management, 300
common carriers, 277
consolidation warehouses, 290
container-on-flatcar (COFC) service, 281
contract carriers, 277
cost-of-service pricing, 283
crossdocking, 288
customs brokers, 295
Department of Transportation Act, 286
distribution center, 288
electronic invoice presentment and payment (EIPP), 301
exempt carriers, 278
Federal Aviation Act of 1958, 286
FOB destination, 283
FOB origination, 283
foreign freight forwarders, 295
foreign trade zones (FTZs), 296
freight forwarders, 281
general freight carriers, 278
granger laws, 284

ICC Termination Act of 1995, 288
integrated logistics service providers, 282
intermediately positioned strategy, 293
intermodal marketing companies (IMCs), 282
intermodal transportation, 280
Interstate Commerce Act of 1887, 284
land bridge, 296
less-than-truckload (LTL) carriers, 278
line-haul rates, 284
market dominance, 286
market-positioned strategy, 293
micro-land-bridge traffic, 296
mini-land-bridge traffic, 296
Motor Carrier Act of 1935, 285
motor carriers, 278
non-vessel-operating common carriers (NVOCCs), 296
North American Free Trade Agreement (NAFTA), 298
Ocean Shipping Reform Act of 1998, 288

piggyback service, 281
pipeline carriers, 280
place utility, 276
private carrier, 278
private warehouses, 290
product-positioned strategy, 293
public warehouses, 291
rail carriers, 279
Railroad Revitalization and Regulatory Reform Act, 286
Railway Passenger Service Act, 286
Reed-Bulwinkle Act, 286
reverse logistics services, 291
risk pooling, 292
ROROs, 281
shippers' associations, 282
Shipping Act of 1984, 287
specialized carriers, 278
square-root rule, 292
Staggers Rail Act of 1980, 287
tariffs, 298
third-party transportation services, 276
threshold costs, 286
time utility, 276
trading companies, 296
trailer-on-flatcar (TOFC) service, 279

Discussion Questions

1. Why are transportation and warehousing important issues in supply chain management?
2. List the legal forms and modes of transportation. Which mode is the least expensive? Which mode carries the most freight? Which mode is growing the fastest?
3. What are some intermodal transportation alternatives?
4. Describe several third-party logistics services. What role do they play in supply chain management?
5. Describe when a shipper would want to use FOB origination pricing and when they would want to use FOB destination pricing.
6. Which has been best for all concerned, transportation regulation or deregulation? Why?
7. Describe three different types of warehouses and the advantages of each.
8. Why do you think most warehouses are private warehouses and not public warehouses?
9. Define risk pooling and the advantages and disadvantages of centralized warehousing.
10. **Discussion Problem:** For the following warehouse system information, determine and compare the average inventory levels using three warehouses, or just one warehouse, using the square-root rule: the current warehouse system is six warehouses, with 3,000 units at each warehouse.
11. How has the terrorism threat since 9/11/2001 impacted international freight coming in to the United States?
12. Describe the different types of land bridges in international shipping.
13. How has NAFTA impacted trade between the United States, Canada, and Mexico?
14. How has e-commerce impacted the management of transportation?
15. Why is supply chain visibility an important consideration?

Internet Questions

1. Go to the BNSF Web site (http://www.bnsf.com) and describe the types of intermodal services offered.
2. What is a foreign trade zone and how many are there today in the United States?
3. Go to the NTE Web site (http://www.nte.com) and find two highly rated carriers and two poorly rated carriers.

References

Bloomberg, D. J., S. LeMay, and J. B. Hanna. *Logistics.* Upper Saddle River, N.J.: Prentice-Hall, 2002.

Coyle, J. J., E. J. Bardi, and C. J. Langley. *The Management of Business Logistics.* 6th ed. St. Paul, Minn.: West, 1996.

Lambert, D. M., J. R. Stock, and L. M. Ellram. *Fundamentals of Logistics Management.* New York: McGraw-Hill, 1998.

Sampson, R. J., M. T. Farris, D. L. Shrock. *Domestic Transportation: Practice, Theory, and Policy,* 5th ed. Boston: Houghton Mifflin, 1985.

Stock, J. R., and D. M. Lambert. *Strategic Logistics Management,* 4th ed. New York: McGraw-Hill, 2001.

Notes

1. D. Hannon, "Transportation Tech Helps Companies Buy and Sell Globally," *Purchasing* 131, no. 10 (2002): 37–38.

2. I. Wylie, "Mars Wins the Shipping Game," *Fast Company* (April 2003): 38–39. Reprinted with permission from *Fast Company.*

3. M. Fabey, "Changing Trade Winds," *Traffic World* 263, no. 8 (2000): 41–42.

4. "War Would Pile Big Losses on Airlines," *The Wall Street Journal* (20 March 2003): A3.

5. R. Rohman, "Regional LTLs Stake Out New Turf," *Logistics Management* 42, no. 2 (2002): 33–36.

6. D. L. Belman and K. A. Monaco, "The Effects of Deregulation, De-unionization, Technology, and Human Capital on the Work Lives of Truck Drivers," *Industrial & Labor Relations Review* 54, no. 2A (2001): 502–524.

7. K. Macklem, "Is There a Fast Train Coming?" *MacLean's* 116, no. 8 (2003): 24–25.

8. L. Hibbert, "Out of the Backwater," *Professional Engineering* 15, no. 7 (2002): 26–27.

9. BNSF Website; available from http://www.bnsf.com

10. Atlantic Container Line Web site; available from http://www.aclcargo.com

11. H. L. Richardson, "A Shift in Freight Forwarding," *World Trade* 16, no. 2 (2003): 22–26.

12. Ibid.

13. Obtained from Red Book Web site; available from http://www.redbooktrucking.com

14. Available from http://www.ams.usda.gov/tmd/shipping/existing.htm

15. H. L. Richardson, "Intermodal Update: Industry Is Meeting Customer's Demands," 16, no. 4 (2003): 40–41.

16. D. Drickhamer, "Special Delivery: Logistics Service Providers Want to Manage Your Supply Chain. Are They Ready?" *Industry Week* 252, no. 2 (2003):24–26.

17. R. E. Jerman and R. D. Anderson, "Regulatory Issues: Shipper versus Motor Carrier," *Transportation Journal* 33, no. 3 (1994): 15—23.

18. Amtrak fact sheet found on Amtrak's Acela high-speed rail Web site; available from http://www.acela.com/about/amtrakfactpage

19. T. Feare, "Jazzing Up the Warehouse," *Modern Material Handling* 56, no. 7 (2001): 71–72.

20. A. Terreri, "The Course to Outsource," *Warehouse Management* 8, no. 9 (2001): 35–38.

21. W. Atkinson, "Value-Added Services from 3PLs and Public Warehouses: What to Look For," *Logistics Management* 41, no. 10 (2002): W8–W10.

22. D. H. Maister, "Centralization of Inventories and the 'Square-Root Law,' " *International Journal of Physical Distribution and Materials Management* 6, no. 3 (1976): 124–34.

23. R. Schipper, "Centralized vs. Distributed Warehousing in Europe: From Make-Hold-Sale to Sell-Source-Deliver," *World Trade* 13, no. 1 (2000): 64–66.

24. E. M. Hoover, *The Location of Economic Activity* (New York: McGraw-Hill, 1948).

25. C. M. Warnenburg, trans., and P. Hall, ed., *von Thunen's Isolated State* (Oxford: Pergamon Press, 1966).

26. C. J. Friedrich, trans., *Alfred Weber's Theory of the Location of Industries* (Chicago: University of Chicago Press, 1929).

27. M. L. Greenhut, *Plant Location in Theory and in Practice* (Chapel Hill, N.C.: University of North Carolina Press, 1956).

28. H. L. Richardson, "Make Time an Ally," *Transportation and Distribution* 36, no. 7 (1995): 46–52.

29. D. Hannon, "Proposed Customs Regulations Weigh on Air Freight Market," *Purchasing* 132, no. 3 (2003): 35–37.

30. Meeting the Challenge," *Logistics Management* 41, no. 8 (2002): 59–60.

31. R. Messenger, "On the Road Again," *Business Mexico* 13, no. 2 (2003): 42–45. Reprinted with permission of *Business Mexico.*

32. D. Puccinelli, "Foreign Trade Zones: U.S. Customs Procedures and Requirements," *Advertising & Marketing Review* (February 2003); available from http://www.ad-mkt-review.com

33. NAFTA information was obtained from the U.S. Trade Representative Web site; available from http://www.ustr.gov

34. See, for example, R. D. Abshire and S. R. Premeaux, "Motor Carrier Selection Criteria: Perceptual Differences between Shippers and Carriers," *Transportation Journal* 31, no. 1 (1991): 31–35; E. J. Bardi, P. K. Bagchi, and T. S. Raghunathan, "Motor Carrier Selection in a Deregulated Environment," *Transportation Journal* 29, no. 1 (1989): 4–11; J. R. Foster and S. Strasser, "Carrier/Modal Selection Factors: The Shipper/Carrier Paradox," *Transportation Research Forum* 31, no. 1 (1990): 206–212; and P. R. Murphy, J. M. Daley, and P. K. Hall, "Carrier Selection: Do Shippers and Carriers Agree, or Not?" *Transportation Research* 33E, no. 1 (1997): 67–72.

35. D. Hannon, "GM Hatches Plan to Cut 70 Days from Order Cycle Time," *Purchasing* 130, no. 13 (2001): 61–62.

36. K. A. Dilger, "From Ship To Shore," *Manufacturing Systems* 17, no. 2 (1999): 83–90.

37. M. C. Mejza and J. D. Wisner, "The Scope and Span of Supply Chain Management," *The International Journal of Logistics Management* 12, no. 2 (2001): 37–56; K. C. Tan and J. D. Wisner, "A Comparison of the Supply Chain Management Approaches of U.S. Regional and Global Businesses," *Supply Chain Forum* 2, no. 2 (2001): 20–28.

38. L. S. Miller, "Riding High," *Railway Age* 203, no. 5 (2002): 35–37.

39. G. Dutton, "Collaborative Transportation Management," *World Trade* 16, no. 2 (2003): 40–43.

40. F. Yohn, "As e-Commerce Expands, So Do Insurable Expenses," *National Underwriter* 106, no. 16 (2002): 10–11.

41. C. Peralta, "The Shape of Digital Things to Come," *Planning* 68, no. 9 (2002): 24–25.

42. E. Varon, "To Bill or Not to Bill (on-line): Digital Invoicing Is the Next Big Step in e-Business Transactions," *CIO* 16, no. 3 (2002): 91–94.

43. BNSF's Web site; available from http://www.bnsf.com

44. D. Hannon, "Transportation Tech Helps Companies Buy and Sell Globally," *Purchasing* 131, no. 10 (2002): 37–38.

45. K. Hickey, "The Road Less Traveled," *Traffic World* (27 January 2003): 19–20.

46. R. Blanchard, "Shipper Satisfaction: It's About Time," *Railway Age* 203, no. 12 (2002): 10–12. Reprinted with permission.

47. B. Arntzen, "Fulfillment Partners in the Internet-Driven Supply Chain," *Transportation & Distribution* 41, no. 11 (2000): S19–S22.

48. L. Rosencrance, "Shippers Face Automation Task for Customs Deadline," *Computerworld* 37, no. 4 (2003): 10.

49. Flagship Customs Services, Inc., Web site; available from http://www.fcservices.com

50. NTE Web site; available from http://www.nte.net

51. L. Greenemeier, "Offshore Outsourcing Grows to Global Proportions," *Information Week* (11 February 2002): 56–58.

52. Ibid.

Chapter 10:

CUSTOMER RELATIONSHIP MANAGEMENT

Strategically effective CRM requires the intelligent application of technology. It must be remembered that effective CRM is more than a software solution; it is about how customer information is used to create an ongoing relationship with the customer.[1]

Learning Objectives

After completing this chapter, you should be able to

- Discuss the strategic importance of CRM.
- Describe the components of a CRM initiative.
- Discuss the implementation procedures used for CRM programs.
- Describe how information is used to create customer satisfaction and greater profits for the firm.
- List some of the popular CRM applications and their suppliers.

Chapter Outline

SUPPLY CHAIN MANAGEMENT IN ACTION   *Procter & Gamble Co.*

They are spoken of in almost reverential tones as the Two Moments of Truth: that moment when a shopper decides what product to purchase, and the one when the consumer first puts that product to use. Robert Dixon takes the Two Moments very seriously. "They're our primary reason for being," he says. Which would make sense if Dixon were in sales or marketing. But he is vice president of IT for Procter & Gamble Co.'s baby, feminine, and family-care business.

Procter & Gamble has long been a leader in the innovative use of IT. Still, its technology reputation is built on having killer supply chain optimization, rather than on driving another key aspect of its business: new product development. In fact, creating new products and getting them quickly to market had been a weak spot for the company, something CEO A. G. Lafley has made a top priority in recent years.

One example is Marta Foster, manager of IT for the global beauty-care and health-care unit. Like Dixon, Foster is responsible for the technology and strategies of her business unit's interactive marketing, from Web sites to e-mail newsletters to in-store kiosks. "We use virtual tools and capabilities from ideation to the store," she says. One such tool is Club Olay, an on-line community built around the company's venerable skin-care lotion, which Foster says has about 4 million members. The Web site collects information on who customers are and how much they use a product. In return, the site offers beauty tips, coupons, and special offers. Foster says participants in Club Olay are 20 percent more loyal to the brand and that Club Olay has been "skewing younger." That prompted the company to start a beauty line, called Ohm, specifically for a younger generation that thinks of Olay as something their grandmothers used. "If we can get teens early, we keep them for life," she says.

Foster and other managers also use customer relationship management technology from Epiphany Inc. At the core of P&G's CRM strategy is a customer data mart that spans brands and geographies, says Paul Rodwick, vice president of corporate marketing at Epiphany. The system helps managers analyze information from multiple sources: focus groups, surveys, syndicated data, inventory data, and consumer feedback from the Web or call centers.

Foster and her group are experimenting with new marketing techniques, such as putting interactive skin and hair analysis systems developed for use in P&G's lab inside stores. "This technology was developed in R&D for R&D," Foster says. The program would commercialize the technology and let P&G "become a beauty-services consulting arm" to retail customers.

Procter & Gamble is also putting technology to work on the idea and research end of the product-development cycle. P&G employs more than 1,200 Ph.D.-level scientists in eighteen technical centers in eight countries. To better leverage that community, P&G created InnovationNet, an internal portal for P&G's scientists and research community to share ideas and, it is hoped, create new products.

But it is not enough. "We continue to struggle to find enough big ideas to fill the pipeline," says Geoffrey Smith, IT director for global consumer applications and IT strategy/architecture. "And we're under pressure to do more with less." That prompted the company two years ago to create a "connect-and-develop" program, inviting outsiders onto its network. P&G gives access to Innocentive and 9Sigma, two far-flung networks of research scientists, as well as about 150 individual entrepreneurs scanning the world for innovative products. Once P&G has a new product idea, it uses Web technology in testing and marketing, largely replacing live focus groups for early-stage analysis. "We do almost 100 percent of our concept testing on-line now, at literally one-hundredth of the cost in one-hundredth of the time," CIO David says.

One area in which Procter & Gamble has been particularly aggressive is in using technology for product life cycle management, the art of creating and nurturing a brand. The reason is simple. While something of a moving target, product life cycle management is "mechanizing and automating the knowledge components, and the flow components, within the bringing-a-product-to-market phases," CIO David says. "We're doing that tremendously well right now."

While it is speeding up product development, P&G has not stopped honing its vaunted supply chain. "Full data synchronization—that's the vision," David says. P&G wants to ship products based on actual sales results, not forecasts. To get closer to that kind of real-time business, P&G is working on two fronts. First, it is looking to create electronic product catalogs that suppliers and customers, the Wal-Marts and Kmarts of the world, can tap into globally. Second, P&G and David are working with standards bodies such as the UCCNet product-registry system, with the Transora on-line exchange for consumer goods, and with retailers to advance supply chain and data synchronization standards. "We want every kind of transaction we do with our customers pulling through the supply chain to be synchronized," David says.

Like everything at P&G, these initiatives come back to understanding the customer. Thirty million times a day, a shopper looks at a P&G product—then buys it or a rival's. That works out to a million or more Moments of Truth every hour. For Dixon and his IT colleagues, that is a good reason for being.[2]

Introduction

Customer relationship management is necessary once a supplying company first establishes a relationship with a customer. To keep customers satisfied and coming back, firms must demonstrate their capabilities and the value these capabilities provide to customers. The often-told story that "finding a new customer costs five times as much as keeping an old customer" is the motivation behind customer relationship management. In the long term, value continues to be demonstrated to customers through reliable, on-time delivery, high-quality products and services, competitive pricing, innovative new products and services, attention to customer needs, and the flexibility to respond to those needs adequately. First and foremost, managing customer relationships starts with building core competencies that focus on customer requirements, and then delivering products and services in a manner that results in high levels of customer satisfaction.

Today, customer relationship management, or CRM, has come to be associated with automated transaction and communication applications—a suite of software modules or a portion of a larger enterprise resource planning system as described in Chapter 7. Firms have made tremendous investments in CRM software applications or Internet Web page sections in an effort to automate the customer relationship process; and, in some respects, this has provided a significant benefit to customers. In many cases, though, the monetary benefits from these automated applications have proven to be elusive. Studies indicate that up to 70 percent of all CRM software implementations in recent years have failed to meet the original objectives of the adopting firms. Customers today may like the convenience of communicating or transacting over the Internet; however, individualized contact between a company and its customers also needs to occur to keep customers satisfied and coming back. American Airlines, a heavy user of CRM applications, knows exactly who their profitable customers are, and they use this information to create mutually beneficial relationships. If, for example, the flight of a valued customer is going to be delayed, a personalized text message is sent to the customer so his departure for the airport can be delayed.[3]

Businesses today are rediscovering the need to provide personalized services to their customers. Many businesses have come full circle with Internet B2B and B2C transactions; today we see that a firm's Internet presence, while desirable for many types of information or product transfers, is not sufficient to satisfy most customers in a wide range of industries. Touching products and talking face-to-face with company representatives remains an integral part of the supplier/customer interface. Thus CRM must still include talking to customers, understanding their behavior and their requirements, and then building a system to satisfy those requirements.

With technological changes occurring as rapidly as they are today, many new and exciting ways to obtain and utilize customer information have been developed and many of these are highlighted in this chapter. As supplier/customer interactions become more automated and more e-services are created, though, organizations will find they must continue to identify and develop new ways to add value to customer relationships in order to maintain a competitive advantage. Managing the human elements in customer relationships will always remain a necessary element in creating that value.

Defining Customer Relationship Management

Customer relationship management (CRM) can actually be a confusing term, since in many circles CRM stands for *customer relationship marketing,* while in others it is customer relationship management. Many other terms have also popped up in recent years, and they all ultimately refer to the same thing. These days it appears that customer relationship management is winning out as the term of choice to describe building and maintaining profitable long-term customer relationships. The elements comprising CRM, though, vary based on whose definition is considered; and, as mentioned in the introduction, the advent of CRM software and modules within ERP systems has made the water even muddier. In the final analysis, though, all forms of CRM seek to keep customers continually satisfied, creating profit or benefits for the selling organization. Let us look at a few specific definitions of CRM:

- "The infrastructure that enables the delineation of and increase in customer value, and the correct means by which to motivate valuable customers to remain loyal—indeed to buy again"[4]

- ". . . [A]n interactive process for achieving the optimum balance between corporate investments and the satisfaction of customer needs to generate the maximum profit"[5]

- ". . . [M]anaging the relationships among people within an organization and between customers and the company's customer service representatives in order to improve the bottom line"[6]

- ". . . [A] core business strategy for managing and optimizing all customer interactions across an organization's traditional and electronic interfaces"[7]

- ". . . [T]o keep track of customers, learning about each one's likes and dislikes from various sources like transaction records, call center logs, Web site clicks, and search engine queries"[8]

Because of the intense competitive environment in most markets today, CRM has become the leading business strategy of the new millennium—and potentially one of the most costly. CRM expenditures worldwide are expected to reach \$148 billion by 2005.[9] And, as stated in the introduction, it appears that much of this investment is not fundamentally improving customer relationships or resulting in positive returns for the companies investing in CRM. So, why aren't CRM programs working in so many cases? Perhaps it is because some companies do not understand what constitutes a genuine relationship. While corporations may collect a customer's purchase, credit, and personal information; place it on a database for mining purposes; use it to initiate some type of direct marketing opportunity; and, finally, sell the database information to other companies, no efforts are put forth to engender a customer's trust and loyalty—*to build a relationship.* If building and maintaining relationships were truly what companies were seeking, they would, for instance, return phone messages, make it easy to return or service products, and make it easy for customers to get information and contact the right people inside the organization. Consider this—how often, in your dealings with organizations as a customer, have you been made to feel valued?

Too often, companies today have delegated customer relationship management, certainly one of the most important activities of the firm, to third-party CRM services, software developers, and internal IT departments whose goal is to design databases and use models to predict buying patterns. While a potentially valuable support element in CRM programs, data mining alone does not build the customer relationship. These kinds of activities should be used in tandem with individual attention to build genuine long-term customer relationships. Successful CRM programs require cultural change in many organizations, leading to strategies that are focused on cultivating long-term relationships with customers, aided by the software capabilities found in CRM applications.

Simply put, firms need to treat customers right. Not only does this mean providing the products and services customers want at competitive prices, but it also means providing support services and other offerings that add value and create real satisfaction for customers. Since customers are not all the same, this means the firm must segment its customers and provide different sets of products and value-enhancing services to each segment. Thus, a successful CRM program is both simple and complex—it is simple in that it involves treating customers right and making them feel that they are valued. It is complex in that it also means finding ways to identify the firm's (potentially millions of) customers and their needs and then designing the firm such that all customer contact activities are geared toward creating customer satisfaction and loyalty.

Customer Relationship Management's Role in Supply Chain Management

In Chapter 2, Chapter 3, and Chapter 4, we discussed the importance of building and maintaining strong relationships with good suppliers in order to enhance value along the supply chain and create profits for supply chain participants. In those chapters, the firm was the customer and saw the value that could be created when high-quality suppliers—and their suppliers—were found that were willing to design their services and products around the firm's and the firm's customers' needs. The buying firm had requirements that needed to be met. The distribution side of the supply chain, though, is equally important. Here, the firm is now the supplier, seeking to be a key and value-enhancing supplier to its customers. To be successful, the firm must find ways to meet its customers' needs; otherwise, just as any firm would react with a nonperforming supplier, the customers leave and take years of future purchases with them. Regardless of a firm's place in the supply chain—retailer, distributor, manufacturer, or service provider—the importance of meeting and exceeding the needs and expectations of customers cannot be understated.

In an integrated supply chain setting, the need to be a good supplier, to adequately meet the needs of supply chain customer-partners is paramount to the success of supply chains. As products make their way along the supply chain to the end user, close, trusting, and high-performance relationships must be created among all of the supplier-customer pairs along the way. Thus, just as firms must create methods for finding and developing good suppliers, they must also create methods for becoming and staying good suppliers themselves.

As was shown in the opening discussion of Proctor & Gamble, customer relationship efforts are an integral part of supply chain management. Since many firms do not sell directly to the end consumer, CRM in supply chain settings should also include first-tier customer training and education to ensure proper use of purchased products and maximum end-customer benefit. In many cases, care should also be used when establishing business-to-business relationships. These customers are, in many cases, representing their suppliers' products to their customers. In these situations, customers have a significant influence on the brand and reputation of their suppliers' products. Just as with suppliers, it may be necessary for a firm to certify its customers as to their ability to adequately represent their firm's products. Automakers, for instance, go to great lengths to establish and maintain strong end-customer-focused relationships with dealers to make sure their products are represented adequately. Pillowtex has aligned its sales teams by retail customer segment to work more closely with each retailer as a partner. In this way, they are better positioned to understand each customer's business interests and to respond to their needs and the needs of their customers.[10]

As discussed in Chapter 7, electronic CRM modules of ERP systems are one way to connect customers to the supply chain. As a software tool, CRM was developed in the late 1990s to track customer activity. Because of their high cost though, these systems have gone to only the largest firms. Again, as shown with Proctor & Gamble in the chapter opening, one of its electronic CRM capabilities was to offer an on-line catalogue to its direct customers, like Wal-Mart and Kmart. This is but one aspect of a very sophisticated and complex CRM initiative for P&G. On the one hand, it has B2B customers it must keep satisfied through timely deliveries, automated ordering systems, and competitive prices. On the other hand, its products also are the end products of its supply chains, and it must also worry about the satisfaction of the end consumer, so its CRM efforts must include these customers as well. Proctor & Gamble's reliance on technology in CRM efforts is extremely useful because of the sheer volume of business it does.

Key Tools and Components of Customer Relationship Management

A number of elements are required for companies when developing effective CRM initiatives; these include segmenting customers, predicting customer behaviors, determining customer value, personalizing customer communications, automating the sales force, and managing customer service attributes. Each of these elements is discussed in detail in the following sections.

Segmenting Customers

One of the primary elements of CRM is to **segment customers.** Companies seek to group customers in a variety of ways to create more specialized communications about their products. Customer segmentation can occur based on sales territory or region, preferred sales channel, profitability, products purchased, sales history, demographic information, desired product features, and service preferences, to name a few. Analyzing this type of customer information can tell companies something about customer preferences and the likelihood they will respond to various types of **target marketing efforts** via e-mail or direct mail. By targeting specific customer segments, a firm can save labor and postage costs with respect to these efforts, as well as avoid becoming a nuisance to customers. Chase Manhattan Bank uses its CRM system to segment its 3.5 million customers by current and potential value. They report that the CRM program is directly responsible for a 4 percent increase in retention of high net worth customers, as well as a large increase in the assets managed for these affluent customers.[11]

Permission Marketing

An extension of target marketing is **relationship marketing** or **permission marketing.** The idea here is to let customers select the type and time of communication with organizations. Customers can choose to be placed on and then taken off specific e-mail or traditional mailing lists for information about new products, or they can be reminded of upcoming sales or other events. This kind of customer contact requires software capabilities to track individual customers and their interaction preferences as well as the capability to update these preferences over time. With this capability, firms can better design multiple, parallel marketing campaigns around small, specific segments of their customer base, automate portions of the marketing process, and simultaneously free up time previously spent manually managing the marketing process.

e-BUSINESS CONNECTION
SEGMENTING CUSTOMERS AT HARRY & DAVID

Harry & David, a gourmet food marketer with annual sales of $450 million, got its start as a B2B supplier but cultivated its business over the years through a consumer-oriented gift catalogue. Recently, it has taken steps to target its most profitable customer segment: corporate clients. The company created a new division with an emphasis on customer relationship management. "The strategy was to identify and recognize valuable customers and integrate cross-channel strategies," said David Giacomini, director of the customer value management group at Harry & David.

Taking its existing marketing database, the company divided customers into segments. It found that its B2B clientele, which represents 10 percent of its database, generates much higher sales and profits at a much lower advertising-as-a-percent-of-sales ratio than consumers. Since recognizing that fact, the company has increased B2B spending by about 15 percent, including hiring additional salespeople. The marketer uses information derived from segmentation analysis and applies it to marketing tactics such as trade shows, telemarketing, and e-mail and direct mail efforts. "Instead of going to broadbased trade shows, we identify vertical industries that respond well," Giacomini said.

One challenge Harry & David encountered was retaining and up-selling current customers, so the company recently created a specific group to focus on retention. A change in compensation packages for sales employees was deemed necessary, as com-

missions had been based almost exclusively on generating new sales. "The sales team was more skewed to acquisition rather than retention," Giacomini said. "There was little incentive to retain or grow an account." After the company increased commissions for retained and reactivated sales, the effect was significant and immediate. "Two months ago, we were below plan for the year. Right now, we're at plan, and we're optimistic that we'll exceed sales goals for the year," Giacomini said. "I didn't think changing compensation would have an effect that quickly."

Another development was the creation of Gift Express On-line, a corporate gift program that features a co-branded Web page with the corporate customer's logo and direct ordering links. Alliance Capital Management L.P., Wells Fargo & Co.'s Phone Bank Service Center, and Nanogen Inc. are among the twelve clients currently participating in this program, which can be customized with features such as predetermined gifts, direct billing, and corporate accounting codes.

Harry & David, a category leader that mails 40 million catalogues yearly, continues to market to business customers through its folksy consumer catalogue. About ten years ago, it created a dedicated B2B catalogue but later decided to scrap it. "We found the consumer catalogue worked just as well for business," Giacomini said. Its corporate direct mail package contains the consumer catalogue, along with a personalized letter and a sixteen-page brochure containing gift ideas.[12]

Cross-Selling

Cross-selling occurs when customers are sold additional products as the result of an initial purchase. E-mails from Amazon.com that describe other books bought by people that have also purchased a book the customer just bought is an attempt at cross-selling. If the additional products or services purchased are more profitable than the original purchase, this can provide significant profit potential for the firm. Additionally, if firms are successful at selling the right products to the right people through cross-selling, customers are left feeling they have received individualized attention, resulting in loyal, satisfied customers. The Haddad Group, for instance, uses loyalty cards at four Kansas City–area restaurants. Users' cards are scanned and updated at each location, and the fronts of the cards display the user's loyalty point total after each transaction, along with regularly changing marketing or promotional messages. This concept at the Haddad Group is profiled in the following e-Business Connection box.[13]

Multiconcept operator Haddad Restaurant Group, Inc., of Kansas City, Missouri, never would say it wrote the book on customer relationship management and gift card strategies, but it rightfully can claim to be rewriting it on a regular basis thanks to emerging technology.

Since mid-2001, the Haddad Group has been using rewritable loyalty and gift card systems at four Kansas City–area Fred P. Ott's Bar & Grill casual-dining restaurants. The systems from Kansas City–based Visible Results feature a stand-alone card reader-writer that updates and stores card users' information after each transaction and writes changes to a magnetic strip on the back of the loyalty or gift card. That function creates what amounts to a portable, self-contained transaction database.

Moreover, Visible Results' thermochromic process enables the front of the cards to display the user's loyalty program point total or remaining gift balance after each transaction, along with regularly changing marketing or promotional messages created by the restaurant operator. "Our average check at Fred P. Ott's is $15, but card users spend noticeably more . . . several dollars more," Haddad's director of marketing, Bruce Campbell, said. "We believe the way to go right now is to take care of customers who want to be here, to get them to come back a little more often and spend a little more while they are here."

More than 1,400 customers now carry "Ott Cards" to accumulate points good for a $5 credit after each $100 in purchases, Campbell said. Card users receive promotional messages and have a shot at enjoying "Random Acts of Kindness" gifts, such as logo hats or free food. Campbell said there is a "wow" factor in terms of guest reactions to the rewritable card technology, but he acknowledged that "it took a little time" for that "buzz" to get established, as some customers were slow to notice that messages changed and point totals were updated visibly.

In 2002 the messages uploaded by the card writer changed about every six weeks and alerted guests to such things as live music schedules, karaoke nights, or offers of "double [loyalty] points" on slower days of the week. "We were not really strong on gift certificates" in the past, Campbell said. "Over the past year [gift card sales have] really accelerated through the use of this."

Because Visible Results' technology also permits Fred P. Ott's restaurants to show the updated balance on gift cards after each purchase, the small chain no longer gives cash back when purchases are below the premiums' face value. Campbell said the policy change would ensure that the chain benefits fully from gift card sales and would not serve more as a bank than as a restaurant company. The new policy also gives gift recipients an incentive to return to a Fred P. Ott's to spend any balances remaining after their initial visits.

The ability of the rewritable technology to add value to a gift card after it has been issued or its stored-dollar value is exhausted has prompted some people, such as the parents of college students, to use it as they might a debit card, Campbell said. He noted that the chain has been able to convert some gift card users into loyalty program participants.

Visible Results indicated that gift card and loyalty card users accounted for about 9 percent of total monthly sales at the Fred P. Ott's group by the end of 2002. Haddad recently installed the gift and loyalty system in its Figlio, the Italian Restaurant, and plans to do the same soon at its Ribster's barbecue concept. "This [technology] does what it says it does," Campbell said. "You [card users] are not waiting until the end of the month for a statement to see your point totals because that information is in your wallet and it's a done deal."

Through its use of rewritable loyalty cards, Haddad Restaurant Group can customize promotional messages by restaurant and, if necessary, alter promotions on the fly if the response rate is too low or too high and "we're getting killed," Campbell pointed out. For a relatively small restaurant group like Haddad Group, with about forty units spread across several concepts, the stand-alone nature of the card system is not a major concern, Campbell said. "You can set it up about anywhere where you have electricity and a phone line," he added.[14]

Predicting Customer Behaviors

By understanding customers' purchasing behavior, future behaviors can be predicted. These predictions allow firms to forecast which products customers are likely to purchase, which ones they will purchase next, and how much they are likely to pay. In this way, companies can revise pricing policies, offer discounts, and design promotions to specific customer segments. Hilton Hotels' CRM software analyzes demographic information from its Hilton Honors program, and behavioral patterns are used to help create direct mail campaigns and to help hotel managers plan for upcoming seasonal activity by business travelers.[15] One of the more desirable CRM attributes in this category is **customer defection analysis.**

Customer Defection Analysis

Knowing which customers have quit purchasing and why can be very valuable information for organizations. Not only can these customers be approached to encourage additional purchases, but the information can teach the organization things that can be used to retain future and existing customers. Offers of money or free phone minutes from telephone service companies are examples of efforts to regain customers that have switched to a competitor's phone service. In some cases, organizations may want some customers (unprofitable ones) to leave. By determining the value of each of the defecting customers, firms can gain feedback from policies geared toward retaining or regaining customers as well as policies to discourage more purchases. In some department stores, for instance, customers who repeatedly return merchandise are at some point given only store credit instead of cash. By monitoring purchase histories, these firms can see if this type of discouragement makes customers quit returning merchandise.

Companies can employ sophisticated modeling technologies that can match the characteristics of customers who have quit purchasing to those customers who are still active. Personalized interactions or marketing efforts can then be geared toward these customers with the aim of reducing customer defections to competitors, also called **churn reduction.** By assigning profit value to customers, firms can determine the level of rewards to offer customers for repeat purchases, particularly those fitting the profile of a churned customer. Frequent buyer programs, customer reward programs, and other similar programs have all come about with this ability to further segment customers.

Customer Profitability Determination

Until recently, determining customer profitability, as already mentioned, was extremely difficult for all but the most expensive CRM systems. Today, though, capturing customer profitability information is possible for many businesses; however, use of this information can potentially cause poor decisions to be made regarding some customers. For instance, customers that are unprofitable now may be profitable later. A health club, for instance, may have some unmarried members who rarely make other purchases at the club but frequently visit and use the facility. While this type of member may be seen as unprofitable, it is likely that if they are satisfied with the club, they will tell others; at some point they may marry and upgrade to a family membership. Thus, it is necessary to determine customer lifetime value or profitability and then direct specific benefits, communications, services, or policies toward each customer.

Personalizing Customer Communications

Knowledge of customers, their behaviors, and their preferences allows firms to customize communications aimed at specific groups of customers. Referring to customers by their first name or suggesting services used in the past communicates value to the customer and is likely to result in greater levels of sales. The Ritz-Carlton Hotel, for instance, profiles its customers so it can offer the accommodations each person prefers on subsequent visits. Web sites can remember a customer's credit card number, name, **clickstreams,** and items purchased to personalize future site visits by offering products, ads, and shipping preferences that fit that customer's profile.

CRM software that can analyze a customer's clickstream, or how they navigate a Web site, can tailor a Web site's images, ads, or discounts based on past usage of the site. Web site businesses may also send personalized e-mails, for instance, with incentives to lure customers back, if it has been a while since their last purchase. A quick-change oil and lube shop might send a postcard to a customer's address every ninety days, reminding them it is time for an oil change and offering a discount on the next visit. On the same card, it may also offer discounts on other services that customer has used in the past, such as a radiator flush, a tune-up, or a tire rotation. With time, this customization capability improves, as the firm learns of additional services, products, and purchasing behaviors exhibited by various customers.

Event-Based Marketing

Another form of personalized communication comes with the ability to offer individual promotions tied to specific events. Banks, for example, may try to market automated mortgage payment services to all of their customers who have recently applied for and received a home mortgage loan. The same bank might offer home improvement loans to customers once their mortgages reach an age of five years. The idea with **event-based marketing** is to offer the right products and services to customers at the right time. When entertainment venues ask for the birth dates of their customers as they buy season passes or day passes, for instance, they can direct future discounts to occur on days they are likely to be celebrating. With large volumes of customers, event-based promotion strategies are impossible without computer automation, so event-based marketing capabilities tend to be popular among firms seeking to purchase CRM systems.

Automated Sales Force Tools

Sales force automation products are used for documenting field activities, communicating with the home office, and retrieving sales history and other company-specific documents in the field. Today, salespeople need better ways to manage their accounts, their business opportunities, and communications while away from the office. To supply these capabilities, firms have been using CRM tools since the early 1990s to help management and sales force personnel keep up with the ever more complicated layers of information that are required as demand increases. When field sales personnel have access to the latest forecasts, sales, inventory, marketing plans, and account information, they can make more accurate and timely decisions in the field, ultimately increasing sales force productivity and improving customer service capabilities. Some of the desired CRM capabilities in the area of sales force automation are discussed in the following sections.

Sales Activity Management

Sales activity management tools are customized to each firm's sales policies and procedures and offer sales personnel a sequence of sales activities that guide them through the sales process with each customer. These standardized sales process steps assure that the proper sales activities are performed and put forth a uniform sales process across the entire organization. The use of a sales activity management tool reduces errors and improves customer satisfaction and productivity. Along with these prescribed sales steps, field sales reps can be reminded of key customer activities as they are needed, generate mailings for inactive customers, be assigned tasks by management, and generate to-do lists. Additionally, sales personnel can chat on-line with each other and with the home office.

Sales Territory Management

The **sales territory management tool** allows sales managers to obtain current information and reporting capabilities regarding each salesperson's activities on each customer's account, total sales in general for each sales rep, their sales territories, and any ongoing sales initiatives. Using these tools, sales managers can create sales teams specifically suited to a customer's needs, generate profiles of sales personnel, track performance, and keep up with new leads generated in the field.

Lead Management

Using the **lead management tool,** sales reps can follow prescribed sales tactics when dealing with sales prospects or opportunities to aid in closing the deal with a client. These products can generate additional steps as needed to help refine the deal closing and negotiation process. During this process, sales reps can generate product configurations and price quotes directly, using laptops or handheld devices remotely linked to the firm's server. Additionally, leads can be assigned to field sales personnel as they are generated based on the requirements of the prospect and the skill sets of the sales reps. Thus, lead management capabilities should result in higher deal-closing success rates in less time. Another common characteristic allows managers to track the closing success of sales personnel and the future orders generated by each lead.

Knowledge Management

Sales personnel require access to a variety of information before, during, and after a sale occurs including information on contracts, client and competitor profiles, client sales histories, corporate policies, expense reimbursement forms, regulatory issues and laws, sales presentations, promotional materials, and previous client correspondence. Easy access to this information through the use of a **knowledge management tool** enables quick decision making, better customer service, and a better-equipped and happy sales staff.

Customer Service Capabilities

The key element of any successful CRM initiative is the ability to provide good customer service. In fact, with any process that deals with the customer, one of the primary objectives is always to provide adequate levels of customer service. But what does customer service actually mean? In Chapter 6, customer service was discussed in terms of safety stock and filling customer orders. In Chapter 9, customer service was tied to delivering goods on time. And, as mentioned earlier in this chapter, customer service can also mean answering customers' questions and having disputes or product and service problems fixed appropriately and quickly. Thus, many definitions of customer service can be found. Today, complaints about shoddy customer service abound in many organizations and industries. This represents one area where organizations can create real competitive advantage if customer service processes are designed and operated correctly. The next segment defines customer service and discusses several elements of customer service.

Customer Service Defined

One customer service definition covers most of the elements already mentioned, and that is the "Seven Rs Rule."[16] The seven Rs stand for having the *right product,* in the *right quantity,* in the *right condition,* at the *right place,* at the *right time,* for the *right customer,* at the *right cost.* A **perfect order** is one in which all seven Rs are satisfied. This definition can be applied to any service or manufacturer and to any customer. A misstep in any of the seven Rs results in poor customer service. Consequently, competitive advantage can be created by routinely satisfying the seven Rs.

Performance measures are often designed around satisfying the seven Rs. For example, reducing stock-outs to 1 percent means that customers get the right product or service 99 percent of the time; and having an on-time delivery performance of 97 percent means that customers get their orders at the right time 97 percent of the time. Other customer service measures are typically designed to measure *flexibility* (responding to changes in customer orders), *information system response* (responding to requests for information), *recovery* (the ability to solve customer problems), and *post-sale support* (providing parts, equipment, and repairs).

Providing these kinds of services to customers (and improving it) keeps customers returning, but can come at a cost. Firms must consider the costs of improving customer service (such as faster transport, greater safety stock levels, and better communication systems) as well as the benefits (keeping customers and their future income streams). In organized supply chain relationships, firms often work together in determining (and paying for) adequate customer service, since the costs of poor customer service can be substantial.

Customer service elements can be classified as **pretransaction, transaction,** and **posttransaction elements.** Each of these is briefly discussed next.

- *Pretransaction elements:* These customer service elements precede the actual product or service and examples are customer service policies, the mission statement, organizational structure, and system flexibility.

- *Transaction elements:* These elements occur during the sale of the product or service and include the order lead time, the order processing capabilities, and the distribution system accuracy.

- *Posttransaction elements:* These elements occur after the sale of the product or service and include warranty repair capabilities, complaint resolution, product returns, and operating information.

Thus, to provide high levels of service and value to customers, firms seek to continually satisfy the seven Rs and develop adequate customer service capabilities before, during, and after the sale of products and services. Call centers have been used in many organizations to improve customer service and supply chain performance; this topic is discussed next.

Call Centers

Call or customer contact centers have existed for many years, and some organizations have used these effectively to satisfy and keep customers loyal, while others have seen them as a necessary cost of doing business and viewed them as a drain on profits. As **call centers** became automated, customer service representatives were then able to quickly see how similar questions were answered in the past, and resolve problems quickly, resulting in much greater call center effectiveness. Call center systems can now categorize all calls, determine average resolution time, and forecast future call volume. These automated systems can reduce call center labor costs and training time and improve the overall productivity of the staff, while increasing customer satisfaction levels. eMachines, Inc., has built a database of customer problems and comments to supplement its call center activities in the B2B market. Its CRM system aggregates the information and can produce reports that might reveal a defective part on a certain model.[17] Unfortunately, the call center process can still get bogged down when representatives are not hired or trained effectively. Example 10.1 represents an all-too-typical call center process.

© 2002 Ted Goff

"Now let's set up an automated
response for irate customers
demanding to speak to a real person."

EXAMPLE 10.1   A typical call center problem and solution

Mr. Donohue called his mortgage company and was not at all happy after talking to the initial customer service representative. Two months earlier, his mortgage was sold to another lender and he was notified. So, he set up his on-line bill paying service at his bank to pay the mortgage amount to the new lender every month. Four months later, in the middle of February, he received a mail notification of failure to pay his mortgage and was assessed an $80 late payment fee, due upon receipt with his payment. He noticed that the payment amount on the late payment notice was higher than the amount he was paying by about $50. Figuring there must have been a mistake, he called the institution. The customer service rep told him that because his loan escrow account was low, they had adjusted his payment two months earlier, starting with the previous January payment.

"Why wasn't I notified?" questioned Mr. Donohue.

"We notified you by mail on December 27th, Sir" was the reply.

"I never received that notice!" said Mr. Donohue.

"I'm sorry sir, but it says here that it was mailed to you on December 27th."

"OK, so what about my February payment? Did you get that?"

"Yes, Sir, but we sent it back through your bill paying service since it was an insufficient amount. We then called you, according to this record I'm looking at, two days ago."

"I never received a call or a message!" complained Mr. Donohue, very irritated.

"I'm sorry sir, but the payment is due immediately with the late payment fee" came the reply. At that point, Mr. Donohue decided he must climb up the customer service management hierarchy to resolve his problem, so he asked to speak to the representative's supervisor.

After a few minutes wait, a very friendly voice came on the line. Mr. Donohue told his story. The supervisor agreed that the initial contact letter must have become lost in the mail and also found out that, although a call was made to Mr. Donohue's phone number, no message was left. She agreed to erase the late payment charge and asked that Mr. Donohue simply pay the new mortgage amount as soon as his original check was returned to his bank account. Mr. Donohue hung up, finally satisfied with the encounter.

Today, organizations are realizing how important call centers can be in managing customer relationships. In many firms, call centers have a dedicated, well-trained staff providing 24/7 call support. And they have implemented technologies to better customize the help and information customers receive. For example, calls can be routed to various call center geographic locations based on the time of day, specialization required, or the current wait time at each of the call center locations. Call centers can quickly match the phone number of the caller to the caller's profile and then prioritize the call based on the importance of the caller or route the call to a representative in that customer's market segment.

Automated speech recognition and interactive response system capabilities offer callers options, while easing the staff required to answer routine questions like when the next show time is or when a particular airline flight is scheduled to depart. Unfortunately, these can also become very irritating if the customer wants to speak to a real person. Thus, it is important to understand which answering method, under various conditions, customers prefer.

Informational Scripting

Call center technology now allows customer problems and solutions to be compared over time, so that firms can provide service representatives with scripts to successfully guide them through many types of customer problems, while the customer is on the phone or on-line.

Global Perspective

OUTSOURCING TO LATIN AMERICAN CALL CENTERS

Tough times keep Norberto Varas busy. The CEO of Teleperformance Argentina is constantly on the road trying to convince clients like Microsoft in the United States and Tele2 in Spain that Argentina's economic penuries are their competitive advantage. Varas wishes that his native country's economic crisis had not proven such a windfall, but he is proud that his company is one of the few to be providing what Argentina needs most in these dire times—jobs.

What was once simple, in-house telephone customer service provided by corporations has boomed—particularly as cellular telephone, Internet, and pay TV service took off in the last few years, along with added demands from consumer banking. Looking for flexibility, companies have increasingly contracted out such work. Mindful of costs, they have sought out developing countries for new call center operations, especially those with educated, bilingual workers, highly developed telecommunications systems, and liberal work rules.

Not surprisingly, then, French-owned Teleperformance has expanded rapidly in Argentina, increasing its head count 65 percent to more than 700 since the beginning of 2001, when the domestic economy imploded with a sharp currency devaluation. High unemployment makes qualified staff available and motivated, while low rents ensure office space. Argentina's modern, fiber-optic telephone system is better than those found in most countries, even in the United States, and the country has capacity to spare, making phone connections cheap—an international connection from Argentina now costs U.S. $0.03 per minute. English is spoken widely, too. "Other companies would die for the amount of over-qualified talent that, in Argentina, we sadly take for granted," says Varas.

Anyone in Central America and the Southern Cone activating Microsoft's Windows XP operating software will end up talking to or e-mailing an Argentine Teleperformance agent. More than half of Varas's workforce now takes calls for products sold by companies outside Argentina.

Customer care is taking off all over Latin America. Latin America has about 100,000 call center workers, mainly in Brazil, Argentina, and Mexico; and Latin America's call center managers estimate annual growth at 25 percent, far outstripping domestic economies.

CRM products that support scripting offer the firm the capability to provide customers a standardized or unified front for disposition of particular problems. While these types of responses reduce waiting time for customers, they do not allow for much "out-of-the-box" thinking, and important customers with uncommon problems may not get the best solutions to their problems this way. Thus, even the most automated, efficient, scripted call center must be able to differentiate customers as needed, based on their value to the firm, and offer acceptable responses to customer requests or problems.

Web Site Self-Service

Web sites act as support mechanisms for call centers by making commonly requested information available to visitors of the site. Customers can, among other things, access their account information and get flight schedules, operating hours, contact information, locations, directions, and product information or return policies. On most sites, organizations provide space for e-mailing questions or complaints; some sites even offer on-line chat capabilities with company personnel or with other customers who are currently visiting the site. Well-designed Web sites can further reduce the need for call center staffers, while adequately handling most customer queries.

Going to a contractor for frontline customer service has risks, says Terry Wright, principal analyst with Gartner in London. A quarter of companies outsource the technical side of providing customer service—telephone connections, computers, and office space—quite happily. But most hire their own people for taking calls. "People like to keep that in-house, because they are talking with their own customers," Wright says. Just 5 percent of outsourcing involves hiring phone attendants.

Nevertheless, sending work offshore makes sense if cultural and technical factors make it easier, Wright says. First, flawless telephone infrastructure is a must, as is a good sense of the long-term reliability of international telephone service contracts. Speaking the language is an obvious requirement, but the job also calls for high levels of education. "If you look at India, most of the bottoms on the seats are university graduates," Wright says. "They are very proud of that."

Agustín Rubini, business development manager at Teleperformance Argentina, believes that, at the current low levels of labor costs, Argentina can even think about competing with India, now the world's largest,

low-cost call center provider for English-language customer service. Indeed, even India is looking to the region. Software maker Mphasis in Bangalore told Reuters it will spend $1 million to put a call center with space for 500 workers in Mexico.

Rubini is unequivocal. "Business has never been better" he says. When the Argentine peso was pegged to the U.S. dollar, Argentine labor costs stood at $4 per hour, compared to $8 in the United States. Now, highly educated operators are available in Buenos Aires at $1 per hour. "Our staff costs are now eight times cheaper than in the United States," Rubini says.

Demand from the U.S. Spanish-speaking market has put Hispanic Teleservices Corporation, a contact center company located in Monterrey, Mexico, into high gear, too. When customers of U.S. technology, telecom, or financial services companies dial a toll-free number for help and assistance, one of the first things they hear is a recorded voice message asking them to press one for English, or press two for Spanish. "We are the 'press two for Spanish' people: that's our business," says Teleservices CEO Mark J. Benson.[18]

Field Service Management

Those who have worked for a firm with an older copying machine may have wished that the field service process for maintaining and fixing the machine was automated. In many cases still, the field servicing process consists of calling a customer service number, having someone diagnose the problem, and then waiting for a repair technician to be dispatched for a repair. Even then, a repair may take days or weeks if parts must be ordered or if the original diagnosis was incorrect. When this process is automated, customers can communicate directly with product specialists using wireless communication devices and the right diagnosis can be made more quickly. The correct specialist can also be dispatched more effectively; and, when at the scene, the repair person is able to access repair manuals, instructions, specifications, part order forms, and other information via wireless connection to the organization's server.

Measuring Customer Satisfaction

Measuring customer satisfaction remains somewhat of a tricky proposition. Customers are frequently given opportunities to provide feedback about a product, service, or organization through customer feedback cards placed at cash registers or on tables, mailed customer surveys or surveys provided with purchased products, or surveys shown on firm Web sites. In most cases, the only time these forms are filled out is when customers are experiencing a problem. Given this, companies still can find valuable uses for this information. Responses can be analyzed and used to solve the most commonly occurring problems. In CRM programs, customer satisfaction surveys can be personalized to fit specific customer segments, and responses can be matched to the respondent's profile to provide the company direction on how to improve its communication and service capabilities for various groups of customers.

The design of the surveys themselves can be a particular problem for companies. In many cases, surveys do not ask the questions customers want to answer. On many Web site surveys, customers are more often asked about the design of the Web site instead of how the firm is performing or what the customer may be happy or unhappy about. In a study of both brick-and-mortar and Internet banks, for instance, less than half of all the banks studied even used customer comment cards or surveys and only two banks (both were Internet banks) offered service quality surveys.[19]

Customer Privacy Capabilities

Two important issues from the customer's perspective are the ability to assure privacy when information is given to businesses and the ability to minimize customer harassment resulting from unwanted solicitations. In fact, by early 2003, twenty-one states had adopted anti-spam bills to get rid of unwanted advertising messages.[20] CRM applications today are trying to determine not only the preferred channel and message but also each customer's preferred frequency of solicitation. Other features such as "opt-in" and "opt-out" policies and posted privacy policies have become very common on most Internet-oriented marketing messages.

In Conclusion

In this section, we have reviewed the common elements necessary for successful CRM programs. But having all the pieces does not necessarily guarantee success. A number of other factors come into play before, during, and after programs are implemented that must be adhered to to give the firm and its CRM program a good chance of success. This next section discusses this very important aspect of CRM.

Designing and Implementing a Successful Customer Relationship Management Program

Planning and then implementing a CRM program can be a real challenge, because it requires an understanding of and commitment to customers, adherence to CRM goals, knowledge of the tools available to aid in CRM, commitment from the firm's executives and the various departments that will be using CRM tools, and a continuous awareness of customers' changing requirements. Poor planning is typically the cause for most unsuccessful CRM initiatives because of the temptation to start working on a solution or to hire a CRM application provider prior to understanding the problems that CRM is meant to solve. The firm must first answer this question: *What are the problems CRM is going to solve?* Answering this question must involve employees from all functional groupings across the firm, as well as input from the firm's key customers. Putting together a sound CRM plan will force the organization to think about CRM needs, technology alternatives, and the providers that sell them. Selecting the right tools and providers is an important step but should not occur until a CRM plan is completed.

Aside from creating a CRM plan and getting the firm's employees to buy in to the idea and uses of CRM, firms must also look at current CRM initiatives that have already been implemented in piecemeal fashion across the firm. Integrating these functions into one enterprise-wide initiative should be part of the early objectives of the firm's CRM implementation process. Additionally, the firm must decide on specific performance outcomes and assessments for the program and provide adequate training to the CRM application users.

Creating the Customer Relationship Management Plan

Putting together a solid plan for a CRM project is crucial as an aid both to purchasing and implementing CRM applications and to obtaining executive management approval and funding for the project. The plan should include the objectives of the CRM program; its fit with corporate strategy; new applications to be purchased or used; the integration or replacement of existing methods or legacy systems; the requirements for personnel, training, policies, upgrades, and maintenance; and the costs and time frame for implementation. Once this document is completed, the firm will have a road map for guiding the purchase and implementation process, as well as the organizational performance measures to be used once the program is in place.

The objectives of the CRM initiative should be customer-focused. Examples might include increasing sales per customer, improving overall customer satisfaction, more closely integrating the firm's key customers with internal processes, or increasing supply chain responsiveness. These will vary somewhat based on the overall strategic focus of the firm. Once these objectives are in place, tactical goals and plans can be instituted at the functional level that are consistent with the CRM objectives. Finally, tactical performance measures can be used to track the ongoing performance of the CRM program. This performance will serve to justify the initial and ongoing costs of the program.

Involving Customer Relationship Management Users from the Outset

In order to get acceptance of this or any other new initiative, employee involvement and support are required. This comes about by enlisting the help of everyone impacted by the initiative from the very beginning. Employees need to understand how the CRM initiative will impact their jobs before they will buy in to the program. Creating a project team with members from sales, customer service, marketing, finance, and production, for instance, will tremendously aid in the selection, training, use, and acceptance of the initiative. The team can contact CRM application providers and collect information regarding capabilities and costs, and they can collect baseline customer service, sales, complaint, and other meaningful performance information. The team should also be heavily involved in evaluating and selecting the applications, then implementing and integrating the applications at each department. As the implementation or "burn-in" continues, closely monitoring system performance will keep users convinced of the value of the initiative and keep everyone committed to its success.

Selecting the Right Application and Provider

Once the organization has completed the plan for CRM, it should have a fairly good idea of what it is going to do and of what activities will require automation or technology. The job, then, becomes one of finding an appropriate application and deciding how much customization will be required to get the job done.

Finding the best application and supplier can be accomplished in a number of ways:

- Visiting a CRM-oriented tradeshow
- Using a CRM consulting firm
- Searching CRM or business publications such as *Call Center Magazine, Call Center News,* and *Inside Supply Management*[21]
- Using the knowledge of internal IT personnel, who already know the market
- Searching CRM supplier Web sites

Firms should seek help from a number of these alternatives, and internal IT personnel should be viewed as internal consultants in the application and supplier identification and selection process. Firms must analyze and compare the various products available. In her CRM handbook, Dychè recommends comparing the following characteristics:[22]

- Integration and connection requirements (look at hardware, software, and networking requirements and capabilities)
- Processing and performance requirements (what volume of data and number of users it can support)
- Security requirements
- Reporting requirements (preformatted and customized reporting capabilities)
- Usability requirements (ability for users to customize the software, display graphics, print information, etc.)
- Function enabling features (workflow management, e-mail response engine, predictive modeling)
- Performance requirements (quick response times for various queries)
- System availability requirements (ability to accommodate various time zones)

Comparing these CRM capabilities should narrow the list of qualified vendors substantially. When finally selecting a supplier for the application, one of the primary criteria for firms to consider is the support available from the application provider. Vendors offering implementation and after-sale user support that meets the needs of the firm (for instance 24/7 phone support) should be valued more highly than other firms. Whether suppliers offer free trial usage so the firm can verify the product's capabilities is another element firms need to consider. Finally, cost and contract negotiations should be carefully considered.

Integrating Existing Customer Relationship Management Applications

In most firms, CRM is not one single product but, rather, a collection of various applications that have been implemented over time. One of the biggest mistakes made is that departments across the firm implement various forms of CRM without communicating these actions to other departments. Eventually, these systems will interfere with each other, as they communicate with the same customer, sending confusing and irritating signals that can churn customers quickly.

Customer contact mechanisms need to be coordinated so that every CRM application user in the firm knows about all of the activity associated with each customer. Today, this lack of integration is leading to real problems as call centers and sales offices seek to please and retain customers by adopting customer loyalty programs, frequent user cards, and other types of customer satisfaction programs without making this information available firm-wide. Additionally, multiple individual applications throughout the company result in duplication of effort, incompatible formats, and wasted money. What firms need are compatible modules for each department's use, linked to one centralized database or **data warehouse** containing all customer information. Thus, from one database, users in the organization can retrieve information on a customer's profile, purchase history, promotion responses, payment history, Web visitations, merchandise returns, warranty repairs, and call center contacts.

By integrating CRM information obtained throughout the firm, decision makers in the firm can analyze the information and make much more customer-focused decisions. Using predictive models and statistical analyses, firms can identify customers most likely to purchase certain products, respond to a new promotion, or churn. This ability to track and seg-

Table 10.1	CRM Performance Measures		
Enterprise-Level Performance Measures	**Department or User-Level Performance Measures**		
	Field Sales	**Call Center**	**Marketing**
Customer/Strategic Partner Loyalty	1. % customer repurchases 2. Avg. # repurchases 3. # customer referrals	1. # customer product information requests 2. # customer praises	1. % customers responding to solicitations or promotions 2. Avg. # of campaign responses
Customer/Partner Satisfaction	1. # customer visits to resolve problems 2. # field service visits per customer	1. # logged complaints per customer 2. Customer satisfaction survey results	1. % customers who have responded more than once to promotions
Average Sales Revenue per Customer/Partner	1. # sales quotas met 2. % repeat visits resulting in sales	1. # customer calls for catalogues 2. # customer phone orders	1. # Web site visits per customer 2. Web site purchases per customer
CRM Productivity	1. % sales quotas met among FS reps 2. # new leads generated 3. % new leads closed	1. Avg. caller time 2. # complaints successfully resolved 3. Sales generated from customer calls	1. # segment catalogues produced 2. # promotional e-mails sent 3. # marketing campaigns
CRM User Satisfaction	1. Annual internal user satisfaction survey	1. Annual internal user satisfaction survey	1. Annual internal user satisfaction survey
CRM User Training	1. Hrs. training per year per rep 2. # CRM applications trained per rep	1. Hrs. training per year per rep 2. # CRM applications trained per rep	1. Hrs. training per year per user 2. # CRM applications trained per user

ment a single view of each customer at the enterprise level allows firms to truly personalize and focus their efforts and products where they will do the most good, resulting in maximum benefit for firms *and* their customers.

Establishing Performance Measures

As already stated, performance measures that are linked to what the firm hopes to accomplish with CRM allow users and managers to witness the progression of a CRM project meeting its original objectives. They also serve to keep everyone excited and informed about the benefits of a well-designed program and will identify any implementation or usage problems as they occur, allowing causes to be found and solutions to be implemented quickly.

At the organizational level, performance measures should concentrate on areas deemed strategically important, such as CRM productivity or sales generated from the CRM program. Examples of these measures are listed in Table 10.1. At the user level, other, more tactical performance measures should be developed and tracked, supporting the firm-wide strategic measures. Linking performance measures in this way will give the firm the best chance of a successful program implementation and continued revision and use of the program into the future.

Providing Training for Customer Relationship Management Users

Another important step in the implementation process is to provide and require training for all of the initial users and then provide training on an ongoing basis as applications are added or as other personnel begin to see the benefits of CRM and its use spreads through the organization. Training can also help convince key users like sales, call center, and marketing personnel of the benefits and uses of CRM applications. Training managers and users in the key customer contact areas can also help the firm decide what customizations to the CRM applications are required, before the system is put into use. This is particularly important for larger firms where supply chains and the sales and marketing processes are complex. In many cases, CRM implementation means that other systems already in place will be phased out or merged with the CRM system. Training can help personnel decide how best to phase out old systems and phase in the new ones. What firms must try very hard to avoid is having users experiment with customers, while using the CRM applications.

Some Customer Relationship Management Application Providers

A very large number of CRM software providers can be found quickly by searching the Web; two are profiled here, namely, Oracle and Siebel Systems. Just a few of the other application providers include IBM, SalesLogix, SAP, Vantive, and VISTA Computer Services.

Oracle

Oracle CRM applications for marketing, sales, service, contracts, interaction center, and e-commerce fully integrate with the Oracle e-Business Suite, as well as legacy products, to help organizations make the most of their CRM investment. Oracle CRM applications allow users to manage by fact across the entire organization while increasing customer satisfaction and loyalty. Some of the Oracle applications are described in the following sctions.

Interaction Center

Oracle's Interaction Center integrates with service, sales, contracts, and marketing applications to reduce the cost of customer contact center operations. Its common architecture and consistent customer model across all contact channels—phone, e-mail, and Web—improve customer satisfaction and give agents greater visibility into customer interactions for up-selling opportunities. Integration with existing call center hardware protects a firm's existing investment. A voiceover IP option is available for cost savings through integration of voice and data.

Oracle Sales

Oracle Sales automates business processes across all sales and customer interaction channels. From lead to order, Oracle Sales enables organizations to plan, manage, and execute sales activities that help to hit sales targets and close more deals. Firms that are an Oracle ERP or SCM customer will get the added benefits of access to invoice and payment history, real-time visibility into inventory and order status, and a streamlined order management process.

Oracle Sales On-line controls field sales costs by providing field sales representatives and sales executives with the right tools to increase sales revenue and profitability. Oracle Sales On-line brings together customer and sales information across all interaction channels to help close more business and build stronger customer relationships. Oracle Sales On-line delivers comprehensive sales and customer information to maximize every sales opportunity. It is designed for sales organizations offering ease of use and ease of information, and it offers sales forecasting capabilities for better planning with real-time global sales forecasts.

Oracle Marketing

Oracle Marketing provides automation and tools for the entire marketing process, from the initial analysis to decide what marketing is needed and who to target, to the actual campaign planning, budget management, and list creation, to automated multi-channel execution and monitoring. Oracle Marketing integrates with other Oracle e-Business Suite applications to seamlessly extend automation and support to other business processes and to help make the most of the solutions organizations may already have. Oracle Marketing helps firms go to market faster, from concept to results; it simplifies marketing, with complete information and unified operations; and it increases profits, by allowing users to understand and predict customer behavior.

Siebel Systems

One of the leading experts in CRM, Siebel has over ten years of development experience and over 3,500 deployments worldwide. Three of the tools Siebel Systems offers clients are described here.

Call Center

Call Center's enhanced usability features (Bookmarks, Smart Answer for Service Requests, Customer Dashboard) improve agent productivity by providing critical customer information quickly and easily. Embedded call center best practices enhance agent productivity, streamline business processes, and accelerate return on investment. Enhancements in the areas of call center analytics provide contact center managers and agents with real-time visibility and historical trend analyses into call statistics, employee performance, and other key operational metrics to help improve call center effectiveness while reducing overall service cost.

Siebel Sales

Siebel Sales helps selling organizations grow revenues more quickly, predictably, and profitably by providing the means to focus on the right deals at the right time. Organizations using Siebel Sales find it provides visibility into the sales pipeline, enabling sales professionals to "see" the top opportunities and enabling selling organizations to identify specific actions to better manage those opportunities, leading to more rapid closure. Sales professionals are enabled to respond more effectively to sales opportunities. Contact and opportunity management within Siebel Sales enables sales professionals to find the right piece of information to fit the sales situation, making them more effective in front of the customer. Siebel Sales also facilitates discovery of customer needs and sharing of knowledge across the entire sales force. Siebel Sales allows sales teams to analyze how customers buy, allowing them to respond to opportunities more effectively with a multi-channel sales strategy. By improving communications with comprehensive sales methodologies, Siebel Sales assists in driving best practices throughout the sales organization. Siebel Sales also enables sales organizations to implement a team-based selling strategy that facilitates better discovery of customer needs and sharing of knowledge in an effective manner across the entire sales force.

Siebel Marketing

Siebel Marketing allows users to identify and retain their most valuable customers using comprehensive next-generation customer analytics. This product optimizes targeting and improves response rates with robust segmentation capabilities based on data in the enterprise. Additionally, Siebel Marketing can execute permission-based multi-channel campaigns including automated multi-stage, recurring, and event-triggered campaigns. It allows users to engage customers in real time across any channel, and it improves conversion rates through integrated response capture and automated lead assignment, enabling rapid follow-up by direct and indirect sales teams. Siebel Marketing facilitates the use of lower-cost Web channels to acquire new customers and build loyalty. Personnel within the firm can increase revenues and grow customer lifetime value with more intelligent cross-selling and up-selling. With Siebel Marketing, firms execute high-quality, event-based marketing programs and improve marketing ROI using continuous test, real-time measurement, and analysis capabilities. Firms can enhance brand equity and customer satisfaction by engaging in a continuous dialogue with customers across all channels while eliminating conflicting, redundant, and inappropriate offers. With comprehensive functionality and scalability, Siebel Marketing delivers rapid, measurable benefits and return on investment.

Future Trends in Customer Relationship Management

A number of trends are affecting the way CRM programs are designed today, and these trends will likely continue to impact CRM programs, application providers, and the companies that use them. One of these is privacy. As the use of the Internet grows, more and more customers are becoming concerned about their personal information being shared among companies trying to find new ways to generate income. New privacy regulations are springing up as consumer protection groups continue to push for stronger Internet regulatory measures. As consumer fears mount, companies must take a proactive stand at reassuring their customers that their information will be protected, as well as convincing them to allow information to be used in the first place. Some of the ways firms can do this is to develop a privacy policy and post it on their Web site, as well as on surveys and other information-gathering forms; allow customers to opt in and opt out of mailing lists and promotional campaigns; allow customers to access their accounts on-line so they can view the information collected about them; require customers to state their privacy preferences, build this into their profiles, and use these preferences when developing one-to-one promotions; make someone in the firm (a customer privacy manager, for instance) responsible for enforcing privacy policies and communicating these to employees and customers; and periodically perform a privacy audit to assure that privacy policies are being communicated and enforced properly.

Another trend is the use of **application service providers (ASPs)**. Perhaps as many as 50 percent of all CRM programs are now designed and maintained for clients by ASPs. In many cases, firms do not have the time, knowledge, or infrastructure to buy and build effective CRM programs, so they outsource this responsibility to ASPs. Many firms prefer instead to concentrate their resources on core competencies. Besides, as technologies and Web site capabilities have become more sophisticated, customers today have no way of knowing who is answering their questions, who is maintaining their data, and who is designing marketing campaigns aimed at them. ASP clients have access to a wide array of CRM services, as well as the expertise to train internal users of the systems. Perhaps most important is the speed of implementation an ASP can offer. Clients who are in a hurry to increase their customer management capabilities most often turn to an ASP.

Adapting CRM for global uses is also increasing. Foreign locations of a firm need access to centralized customer databases, particularly when dealing with multinational business customers. Today, suppliers must cater to customer needs in the same way regardless of where those customers are located. Companies like H-P, GE, and many of Wal-Mart's major suppliers have set up global account management systems to cater to these demands. Field sales and service personnel also need access to centralized customer information when dealing with issues that may have been encountered before at other locations for the same customer. Products may be purchased, for instance, in one country, only to end up being used in yet another country. Call centers that service an array of international customers will also need to offer support in a number of languages. Privacy laws and issues will also vary from one country to the next, so firms must be cognizant of this when collecting customer information or designing marketing initiatives. Daimler Benz, for example, successfully implemented CRM across its European divisions. The justification was to understand its varied customers and offer them an individualized view of quality and a shift from mass marketing to one-to-one marketing. It was able to improve customer retention and loyalty through improved customer care and insight.[23]

Summary

In this chapter we discussed the elements of CRM, its place within the field of supply chain management, the requirements for successful CRM program implementation, and the trends in CRM; finally, we reviewed several CRM application providers. As we learned in this chapter, customer relationship management is really all about just treating customers right; for as long as there have been businesses, some firms have been very successful at keeping customers satisfied and coming back, while others have not. For the past ten or fifteen years, though, both the level of competition in the market place and the available computer technology and software capabilities have been increasing quite dramatically. Thus, we have seen a shift in CRM toward use of technology and software to better analyze, segment, and serve customers with the objective being to maximize long-term customer profitability.

Firms today are learning how to combine many channels of customer contact to better serve customers, resulting in better service and more sales. While many of the CRM applications and ASPs are very expensive, firms can use a structured approach to design an appropriate plan and then analyze and select the right applications and vendors to implement a successful CRM program.

Key Terms

application service providers (ASPs), 330

call centers, 320

churn reduction, 317

clickstream, 317

cross-selling, 315

customer defection analysis, 317

data warehouse, 326

event-based marketing, 318

knowledge management tool, 319

lead management tool, 319

perfect order, 319

posttransaction elements, 320

pretransaction elements, 320

relationship marketing or permission marketing, 314

sales activity management tools, 318

sales force automation, 318

sales territory management tool, 318

segment customers, 314

target marketing efforts, 314

transaction elements, 320

Discussion Questions

1. Define the term *customer relationship management* and describe how this definition has changed over the past twenty years.
2. Why has CRM proven to be both costly and unsuccessful in so many cases?
3. Describe how CRM can be used by firms managing their supply chains. Use an example in your discussion.
4. What is perhaps the most important activity in CRM? Why?
5. Define these terms: *permission marketing, cross-selling,* and *churn reduction.*
6. How would an analysis of customer defections help the firm become more competitive?
7. Have you ever been the recipient of an event-based promotion? Describe it or provide a fictional example.

8. How can CRM applications increase the effectiveness and productivity of a firm's sales force?

9. While call centers have been used successfully by firms for many years without the help of CRM applications, this is now a primary area of applicability for CRM products. How can CRM software aid call centers?

10. How is informational scripting used in call centers?

11. Describe the steps necessary for designing and implementing a successful CRM program.

12. Describe all of the customer service elements involved in getting an oil change at a neighborhood lube shop.

13. How are data warehouses used in CRM?

14. Why is it so important to establish performance measures when implementing a CRM application?

15. Do you think CRM applications unnecessarily invade customers' privacy? Why or why not?

Internet Questions

1. Go to *Call Center Magazine*'s Web site (http://www.callcentermagazine.com) and look at one of the recent issues of the magazine. Describe a new development in call center technology.

2. Identify a CRM service provider on the Internet, and compare its CRM applications to the two that are profiled in the chapter.

References

Barnes, J. G. *Secrets of Customer Relationship Management*. New York: McGraw-Hill, 2001.

Bergeron, B. *Essentials of CRM: A Guide to Customer Relationship Management*. New York: John Wiley & Sons, 2002.

Bloomberg, D. J., S. LeMay, and J. B. Hanna. *Logistics*. Upper Saddle River, N.J.: Prentice-Hall, 2002.

Dyché, J. *The CRM Handbook: A Business Guide to Customer Relationship Management*. Upper Saddle River, N.J.: Addison-Wesley, 2002.

Fitzsimmons, J., and M. Fitzsimmons. *Service Management for Competitive Advantage*. New York: McGraw-Hill, 1994.

Lawrence, F. B., D. F. Jennings, and B. E. Reynolds. *eDistribution*. Mason, Ohio: South-Western, 2003.

Metters, R., K. King-Metters, and M. Pullman. *Successful Service Operations Management*. Mason, Ohio: South-Western, 2003.

Notes

1. E. J. Ragins and A. J. Greco, "Customer Relationship Management and e-Business: More than a Software Solution," *Review of Business* 24, no. 1 (2003): 25–30.

2. Adapted from S. Stahl and J. Soat, "Feeding the Pipeline," *Information Week* (24 February 2003): 47. Printed with permission from *Information Week*.

3. A. Nairn, "CRM: Helpful or Full of Hype?" *Journal of Database Marketing* 9, no. 4 (2002): 376–82.

4. J. Dyché, *The CRM Handbook: A Business Guide to Customer Relationship Management* (Upper Saddle River, N.J.: Addison-Wesley, 2002).

5. R. Shaw, "CRM Definitions—Defining Customer Relationship Marketing and Management," appearing in *Customer Relationship Management,* edited by SCN Education B.V., the HOTT Guide Series (The Netherlands, 1999).

6. B. Bergeron, *Essentials of CRM: A Guide to Customer Relationship Management* (New York: John Wiley & Sons, 2002).

7. E. J. Ragins and A. J. Greco, "Customer Relationship Management and e-Business: More Than a Software Solution."

8. S. T. Cavusgil, "Extending the Reach of e-Business," *Marketing Management* 11, no. 2 (2002): 24–29.

9. J. Brewton and W. Schiemann, "Measurement: The Missing Ingredient in Today's CRM Strategies," *Journal of Cost Management* 17, no. 1 (2003): 5–14.

10. Anonymous, "Maps Out, P'tex Realigns Sales Force," *Home Textiles Today* 24, no. 20 (2003): 119.

11. S. T. Cavusgil, "Extending the Reach of e-Business."

12. Adapted from C. Krol, "Harry & David Returns to Roots," *B to B* 87, no. 13 (2002): 15. Reprinted with permission from *B to B* Magazine.

13. Adapted from A. J. Liddle, "Haddad Group Pleased by Changing Face of Card Program," *Nation's Restaurant News* 37, no. 2 (2003): 47. Reprinted with permission.

14. A. J. Liddle, "Haddad Group Pleased by Changing Face of Card Program": 47–48.

15. E. J. Ragins and A. J. Greco, "Customer Relationship Management and e-Business."

16. R. D. Shapiro and J. L. Heskett, *Logistics Strategy: Cases and Concepts* (St. Paul, Minn.: West Publishing Co., 1985).

17. E. J. Ragins and A. J. Greco, "Customer Relationship Management and e-Business."

18. Adapted from A. Thompson, J. Goodman, G. Brown, and E. Love, "Answering the Call," *Latin Trade (English)* 11, no. 1 (2003): 36–39. Printed with permission from *Latin Trade*.

19. J. D. Wisner and W. J. Corney, "Comparing Practices for Capturing Bank Customer Feedback," *Benchmarking: An International Journal* 8, no. 3 (2001): 240–50.

20. E. Vogel, "Vote on Anti-Spam Bill 41–0," *Las Vegas Review Journal* (4 March 2003): B-1.

21. Many of these references can be found at the American CRM Directory; available from http://www.american-crm-directory.com

22. J. Dyché *The CRM Handbook: A Business Guide to Customer Relationship Management.*

23. S. T. Cavusgil, "Extending the Reach of e-Business."

Chapter 11:

FACILITY LOCATION DECISIONS

Site selection must always be done to meet the corporate objectives and to integrate the factors, opportunities, and the risks that are important to a company at a particular time. Every industry out there is going through major transformations, changing the way they all do business. We are seeing higher levels of automation, changes in how companies deal with customers, and, often, manufacturing done in various parts of the world, then all brought together just-in-time. So, the location strategist needs to ask, "How will this location affect our performance by cost, access to talent, and access to customers?"

Gene DePerez
National Director, Business Location Strategies
PricewaterhouseCoopers[1]

Learning Objectives

After completing this chapter, you should be able to

- Explain the impact of facility decisions on a supply chain.
- Identify the factors influencing facility location.
- Understand the impact of the Regional Trade Agreements on facility decisions.
- Use several location evaluation models.
- Understand the advantages of business clusters.

Chapter Outline

Location Strategies

Critical Location Factors
  Regional Trade Agreements and the World Trade Organization
  Competitiveness of Nations
  Government Taxes and Incentives
  Currency Stability
  Access and Proximity to Markets/Customers
  Environmental Issues
  Labor Issues
  Right-to-work Laws

  Access to Suppliers and Cost
  Utility Availability and Cost
  Quality-of-Life Issues
  Land Availability and Cost

Facility Location Models
  The Weighted-Factor Rating Model
  The Break-Even Model
  The Center-of-Gravity Model

Helpful On-Line Information for Location Analysis

Business Clusters

SUPPLY CHAIN MANAGEMENT IN ACTION   *Foreign Auto Plants in the United States*

When Honda opened the first Japanese transplant in Marysville, Ohio, in 1982, it was to avoid political pressure and import quotas. Nissan followed shortly thereafter when they opened a plant in Smyrna, Tennessee, in 1983 to produce Sentra cars. Over the years, the Smyrna facility was expanded to include Frontier trucks and Xterra sport utility vehicles (SUVs). In 1988, Toyota built a factory in Kentucky, which has been expanded to assemble the Avalon and Camry cars and Sienna mini-vans. The landscape of the auto industry has changed as local and international auto manufacturers continue to move away from the Midwest. The South has witnessed a transformation of its agrarian economy to an industrial economy. In 1994, BMW opened a manufacturing facility in South Carolina to produce Z3 roadsters. Today, the BMW plant has been expanded to build the Z4 roadsters as well as X5 SUVs. BMW chose South Carolina because of tax and training incentives, good access to highways and ports, and a strong work ethic in the state.[2]

In the mid-1990s, Alabama pulled off a major coup by attracting Mercedes-Benz to build a sport utility factory in Vance, Alabama, with incentives amounting to $325 million. Alabama then offered Honda $158 million in economic incentives to open a $500 million auto and engine plant near Lincoln in 2001. The major incentive categories included the $16 million site, a $30 million training program, about $45 million in road improvements around the site, and $56 million in tax abatements over a twenty-year period. Honda chose Alabama because of the "outstanding community of people, excellent transportation systems, and the necessary infrastructure to support industry."[3] The Honda Odyssey minivans and Pilot SUVs are assembled at the Alabama facility.

In 2000, the state legislature in Mississippi introduced the "Advantage Mississippi" program to offer tax and job training incentives to attract industrial recruits to the state. State leaders were rewarded for their hard lobbying work when Nissan announced that it would open a $930 million plant in Mississippi by summer 2003 employing 4,000 workers. According to Emil Hassan, Nissan's senior vice president, the company had decided at the onset to locate in the south because "it is the best location for having a good, reliable, trainable workforce."[4]

The Hyundai Motor Company had previously considered sites in Kentucky, Ohio, and Mississippi but decided on Montgomery, Alabama. The $1 billion plant, scheduled to open in 2005, will build cars and SUVs and employ about 2,000 workers initially. Hyundai received incentives valued at $118 million for worker training from the state.[5] The other reasons cited by Hyundai for its decision include the "high-quality workforce, its strategic location in proximity to American population centers, the superb automotive parts supply chain available in the region, and the commitment shown by the state of Alabama and the city of Montgomery, which provided the best environment for the new plant."[6]

The money spent on incentives by state and local governments is expected to show a positive return on investment in additional employment and industry spin-offs. According to a study carried out by Michigan's Center for Automotive Research, one additional job at a new automotive plant will create 5.5 additional jobs in supplier factories or related businesses in the community.[7] The foreign-owned factories in the South have so far been able to stave off efforts at unionization by the UAW. Alabama, Mississippi, South Carolina, and Tennessee are all right-to-work states. In 2001, the UAW was unsuccessful in organizing a union at Nissan's plant in Tennessee by a two-to-one vote.[8] In summary, the South offers a supportive business environment, training and tax incentives, and a mostly nonunion workforce.

Sources: K. Jensen and G. Pompelli, "Manufacturing Site Location Preferences of Small Agribusiness Firms," *Journal of Small Business Management* (July 2002); J. Muller, K. Kerwin, and D. Welch, "Autos: A New Industry," *Business Week* (15 July 2002); K. Whitfield, "Honda's Alabama Odyssey," *Automotive Design & Production* (March 2002); D. Hakim, "Hyundai Narrows List of Sites for U.S. Plant," *New York Times* (26 February 2002); "Honda Motor Co Light-Truck Plant to Join Alabama's Auto Facilities," *Chicago Tribune* (7 May 1999).

Introduction

Locating a facility is an important decision affecting the cost of managing the supply chain, the level of service provided to customers, and the firm's overall competitive advantage. A supply chain is a network of facilities, and the location of production facilities, warehouses, distribution centers, and suppliers determines the efficient flow of goods to and from these facilities. Once a decision on locating a facility is made, it is costly to move or shut down the facility. Thus, facility location has a long-term impact on the supply chain and must be an integral part of the firm's supply chain strategy. With increased globalization and investments in technology infrastructure, faster transportation, improved communications, and open markets, companies can locate anywhere in the world—previously thought to be impossible.

On the other hand, it would appear that easy access to global markets and corporate networks makes the role of location less important as a source of competitive advantage. However, successful business clusters such as Silicon Valley, Wall Street, the California wine region, and the Italian leather fashion cluster show that location still matters. The existence of business clusters in many industries provides clear evidence that innovation and successful competition are concentrated geographically. Dr. Michael Porter suggests that the immediate business environment is just as important as those issues that impact companies internally in affecting location decisions.[9] Business clusters are discussed in detail later in this chapter.

Facility location decisions involve determining the location of the facility, defining the strategic role of the facility, and identifying markets served by the facility. For example, Honda's global strategy is to "put cost-effective plants in areas that best meet the needs of local customers."[10] The result is the establishment of more than 100 factories in thirty-three countries. Honda's "Small Born" manufacturing strategy is to start small and expand production as local demand increases. This approach allows Honda to be efficient and profitable, even when production volumes are low. In 1982 Honda built its first auto plant to assemble Accords in Marysville, Ohio. Then Honda added a second factory to produce Civics. As demand for Honda automobiles continued to increase, Honda opened its latest facility to assemble the Odyssey mini-vans in Alabama (as discussed in the Supply Chain Management in Action box at the beginning of the chapter).

The early prediction of the Internet was that Web-based business-to-business and business-to-consumer sales would transcend borders and boundaries, thus making the facility location decision somewhat irrelevant. However, the outcome has been exactly the opposite of what was predicted. While it is true that anyone can access the Internet from anywhere in the world, it is equally true that geography still affects the speed of delivery and cost in serving the customer. Dell Computers, the leader in the customized, direct-to-customer computer industry, realized that manufacturing in one location in Texas was costing the company more to transport the computers than to assemble them.[11] Consequently, Dell built a second facility in Tennessee to be closer to its customer base.

When e-commerce first emerged, the initial thought was that companies could serve customers without requiring the heavy investments in infrastructure of a Wal-Mart or a Sears. The reasoning was that these e-commerce companies could use subcontractors to manage inventory, replenish orders, and resolve customer service issues. The truth is that e-retailers have to control their own distribution centers and deliveries to reliably satisfy customer orders. For example, Peapod's outside vendors were unable to ship 8 percent to 10 percent of grocery items ordered by its on-line customers due to a lack of stock. The short-term result was an immediate loss of revenue, and the long-term impact was that Peapod likely lost early users of its on-line grocery service for good.[12]

Location Strategies

Location decisions are made to optimize the performance of the supply chain and be consistent with the firm's competitive strategy. According to Gene DePerez, National Director of Business Location Strategies for PricewaterhouseCoopers, the location strategist needs to ask, "How will this location affect our performance by cost, access to talent, and access to customers?"[13] A firm competing on cost is more likely to select a location that provides a cost advantage. Amazon.com, as profiled on the next page for instance, has located warehouses in areas that will minimize logistics and inventory costs. Many toy manufacturers have also moved their factories to Singapore, Thailand, or China because of cost advantages provided by these countries.

A firm that competes on speed of delivery such as the FedEx Corporation uses the hub and spoke approach to location determination. FedEx's first and largest hub in the United States is in Memphis, Tennessee. This site covers 300 acres and is the heart of the company's sorting operations. More than 160,000 packages and 325,000 letters an hour can be sorted at this facility. FedEx has instituted procedures to ensure that packages are moved as efficiently as possible. According to Reggie Owens, FedEx's vice president of national hub operations for day and weekend business, "Before, a package from New York going to New York left New York and went to Memphis and then went back. Now, if we have a package from the East Coast that's going to be delivered to an East Coast location, it never leaves the East Coast."[22] FedEx has smaller U.S. hubs in Anchorage, Chicago, Fort Worth, Indianapolis, Los Angeles, Newark, and Oakland, and foreign hubs in Germany, France, Japan, Philippines, China, the United Arab Emirates, and the United Kingdom. Each of the hubs has been picked for its central location and easy access to customers.

To get the most out of foreign-based facilities, managers must treat these plants as a source of competitive advantage. These foreign facilities have a strategic role to perform. Dr. Kasra Ferdows suggests a framework consisting of six strategic roles depending on the strategic reason for the facility's location and the scope of its activities:[23]

- *Offshore factory:* An **offshore factory** manufactures products at low cost with minimum investment in technical and managerial resources. These products tend to be exported. An offshore factory imports or locally acquires parts and then exports all of the finished products. The primary objective is simply to take advantage of low labor costs. Little engineering or development work is done at the factory, and local management is not involved in making decisions regarding key suppliers and outbound logistics providers. For example, in the early 1970s, Intel built a labor-intensive offshore factory to produce simple, low-cost components in Penang, Malaysia.

- *Source factory:* A **source factory** has a broader strategic role than an offshore factory with plant management heavily involved in supplier selection and production planning. The source factory's location is dictated by low production cost, fairly developed infrastructure, and availability of skilled workers. For example, Hewlett-Packard's plant in Singapore started as an offshore plant in 1970 but with significant investments over a ten-year period was able to become a source factory for calculators and keyboards.[24]

- *Server factory:* A **server factory** is set up primarily to take advantage of government incentives, minimize exchange risk, avoid tariff barriers, and reduce taxes and logistics costs to supply the regional market where the factory is located. The factory is involved in making minor improvements in products and processes. An example would be Coca-Cola's international bottling plants, each serving a small geographic region.

Global Perspective

AMAZON.COM'S FACILITY NETWORK

Jeff Bezos founded Amazon.com in 1995. Amazon's business strategy is to "offer Earth's biggest selection and to be Earth's most customer-centric company, where customers can find and discover anything they may want to buy on-line."[14] There are currently four internationally focused Amazon Web sites: http://www.amazon.co.uk, http://www.amazon.de, http://www.amazon.fr, and http://www.amazon.co.jp

The early belief in electronic commerce was that millions of customers could be served without needing the type of infrastructure of a Sears or a Wal-Mart. However, on-line retailers are finding out that without their own warehouses and shipping capabilities, customer service could suffer. For example, Peapod, Inc., an on-line grocery retailer, discovered that 8 to 10 percent of its on-line orders were not shipped to customers because its contracted supplier was out of stock.[15] In the late 1990s, Amazon.com went on a warehouse-building spree, adding new facilities in Nevada, Kentucky, and Kansas to its existing distribution system. The objective was to improve logistics and cut shipping times to customers by one day.[16]

While recognizing that distribution systems will help the company manage the delivery process better and improve customer service, there is still a need to turn a profit. With the heavy investments in distribution centers in the United States and worldwide, companies are finding that the flow of goods through the distribution system must be improved to reduce distribution costs. Amazon.com used the NetWorks Strategy module from the Manugistics e-Business suite to organize the movement of products through its transportation and facility network in the United States and Europe. The software determines which of Amazon.com's distribution centers to retain or expand and the quantity of each product to keep in stock. The resulting distribution system organization and configuration have saved Amazon.com $50 million.[17] As part of its ongoing restructuring process toward profitability, the distribution center in McDonough, Georgia, was closed. In addition, the company will operate its Seattle, Washington, distribution center only during the busy Christmas holiday season.[18] The company currently has U.S. distribution facilities in New Castle, Delaware; Coffeyville, Kansas; Campbellsville and Lexington, Kentucky; Fernley, Nevada; and Grand Forks, North Dakota. There are three European distribution centers in the United Kingdom, France, and Germany. The arrangement in Japan is a little different, with Nippon Express serving as the distribution services provider for orders from http://www.amazon.co.jp. These fulfillment centers account for a total of 4 million square feet of warehouse space.[19]

Amazon.com uses the NetWorks Transport software to schedule trucks, trains, and planes and track shipments, including expedited loads. The software also computes the shipping cost for an item from the country of origin to the Amazon.com storage location, plans the shipping of products between a supplier and an Amazon.com facility or between two company facilities, and decides which items can be delivered in the same container. As a result, inventory turns improved from twelve in 2000 to sixteen in 2001. The number of customer accounts has increased steadily from 14 million in 1999 to 25 million in 2001.[20]

According to Bezos, "Customers are now shopping at Amazon as much for our lower prices as for our selection and convenience."[21] By strategically locating its distribution centers and improving operations, Amazon.com is able to enhance its supply chain by reducing its inventory, minimizing logistics cost, and improving the speed and reliability of delivery of orders to its customers.

- *Contributor factory:* The **contributor factory** plays a greater strategic role than a server factory by getting involved in product development and engineering, production planning, making critical procurement decisions, and developing suppliers. For example, in 1973 Sony built a new server factory in Bridgend, Wales. By 1988, the factory was involved in the design and development of many of the products it produced and now serves as a contributor plant in Sony's global manufacturing network.[25]

- *Outpost factory:* The **outpost factory** is set up in a location with an abundance of advanced suppliers, competitors, research facilities, and knowledge centers to get access to the most current information on materials, components, technologies, and products. Since the facility normally produces something, its secondary role can be that of a server or an offshore factory. For example, Lego still produces molds and toys in Denmark, Germany, Switzerland, and the United States in spite of the higher manufacturing cost.[26] Lego's factories serve as outpost facilities with access to research facilities, institutions of higher learning, and sophisticated suppliers of plastic materials.

- *Lead factory:* A **lead factory** is a source of product and process innovation and competitive advantage for the entire organization. It translates its knowledge of the market, competitors, and customers into new products. The Intel factory in Penang, Malaysia, and the Hewlett-Packard factory in Singapore are examples of lead factories. In the early 1970s, both Intel and Hewlett-Packard established offshore factories in Southeast Asia. Over time, the strategic roles of these factories were upgraded to that of lead factories.

Critical Location Factors

One of the most challenging tasks as a company grows, relocates, or starts up is where to position assets strategically to create a long-term competitive advantage. Some of the questions and concerns that need to be addressed for each potential location follow:

- What will be the reaction of shareholders, customers, competitors, and employees?
- Will the location provide a sustainable competitive advantage?
- What will be the impact on product or service quality?
- Can the right people be hired?
- What will be the effect on the supply chain?
- What is the projected cost?
- What will be the impact on delivery performance?
- How will the market react?
- Is the transfer of people necessary, and, if so, are employees willing to move?

Canon Inc., for example, closed its thirteen-year ink-jet printer factory in Tijuana, Mexico, and transferred work to Thailand and Vietnam. Meanwhile, the Maytag Corporation is moving its refrigerator factory in Illinois to Reynosa, Mexico, because of its proximity to the United States and the relatively low shipping costs.[27]

There are basically three levels of location decisions: the global market or country selection, the subregion or state selection, and the community and site selection. The process starts with an analysis of the market region of the world that bears a strategic interest to the organization; and, eventually, a country is targeted. Once the country is selected, the focus shifts to finding a subregion or state within the country that best meets the company's location requirements. Finally, the community and site for the facility are selected. The weighted-factor rating model, which is discussed later in this chapter, can be used to make a location decision at each of the levels we have mentioned. A discussion of each of the location factors shown in Table 11.1 follows.

Table 11.1	**Important Factors in the Location Decision Process**		
Location Factor	**Country Selection**	**Region or State Selection**	**Community and Site Selection**
Regional trade agreements—trade barriers, tariff, import duties	X		
Competitiveness of nation—economic performance, government efficiency, business efficiency, and infrastructure	X		
Federal taxes and incentives	X		
Currency stability	X		
Environmental issues	X	X	X
Access and proximity to market	X	X	X
Labor issues	X	X	X
Access to supplies and cost	X	X	X
Transportation issues	X	X	X
Utility availability and cost	X	X	X
Quality-of-life issues	X	X	X
State taxes and incentives		X	X
Right-to-work state		X	X
Local taxes and incentives			X
Land availability and cost			X

Regional Trade Agreements and the World Trade Organization

An understanding of regional trade agreements and the **World Trade Organization (WTO)** is critical to the facility location decision process because of their impact on tariffs, costs, and the free flow of goods and services. As initially discussed in Chapter 2, the WTO[28] is the successor to the General Agreement on Tariffs and Trade (GATT), which was responsible for setting up the multilateral trading system after the Second World War. Today, the WTO is the only international organization dealing with the rules of trade between nations. Its functions include administering the WTO agreements, providing a forum for trade negotiations, handling trade disputes, monitoring national trade policies, providing technical assistance and training programs for developing countries, and cooperating with other international organizations.

On December 11, 2001, China became a member of the WTO. China's entry has resulted in faster economic, legal, and environmental reforms, a further relaxation of tariffs; and increasing economic growth. In the first nine months of 2002, China's actual foreign investment was US $41.2 billion, an annual increase of 22.55 percent. The estimated total foreign investment into China exceeded US $50 billion in 2002, making China the world's largest foreign investment destination.[29] Today, China is ranked fourth in world trade after the United States, the European Union, and Japan. According to Tony Capretta, Flextronic's general manager in China, Flextronic can produce anything in China that it makes elsewhere. The reason is the fast learning curve. Companies such as Motorola and its partners are planning to invest $6.6 billion in China over a five-year period and Intel will invest $302 million on chip assembly and testing in Shanghai.[30]

There are 162 regional trade agreements under GATT and the WTO that are in force today.[31] Examples of the better-known regional trade agreements are the **European Union (EU)**, the **North American Free Trade Agreement (NAFTA)**, the **Southern Common Market (MERCOSUR)**, the **Association of Southeast Asian Nations (ASEAN)**, and the **Common Market of Eastern and Southern Africa (COMESA)**. Several of these are discussed here:

- *The European Union (EU):* Set up after the Second World War, the European Union was officially launched on May 9, 1950, with France's proposal to create a European federation consisting of six countries: Belgium, Germany, France, Italy, Luxembourg, and The Netherlands. A series of accessions in 1973 (Denmark, Ireland, and the United Kingdom), 1981 (Greece), 1986 (Spain and Portugal), and 1995 (Austria, Finland, and Sweden) has resulted in a total of fifteen member states. The EU is also preparing for the accession of thirteen eastern and southern European countries.[32] Some highlights of the EU are the establishment of the Single Market in 1993 and the introduction of the euro notes and coins on January 1, 2002. The EU has a population of 380 million people, a GDP of US$8.7 trillion, 19.4 percent of world exports, and 18.9 percent of world imports.[33]

- *The North American Free Trade Agreement (NAFTA):* This trade agreement among the United States, Canada, and Mexico was implemented on January 1, 1994, and created the world's largest free trade area with 406 million people and producing more than US$11 trillion of goods and services annually.[34] Many tariffs were eliminated with an immediate effect, while others are being phased out over periods ranging from five to fifteen years. In a progress report made by NAFTA after the first seven years, employment had increased in all three countries, and U.S. exports to NAFTA partners had more than doubled, while Mexican exports to NAFTA partners had increased 238 percent.[35]

- *The Southern Common Market (MERCOSUR):* This agreement among Argentina, Brazil, Paraguay, and Uruguay was formed in March 1991 with the signing of the Treaty of Asuncion. The agreement was created with the goal of forming a common market/customs union between the participating countries and was based on economic cooperation between Argentina and Brazil that had been in place since 1986.[36]

- *The Association of Southeast Asian Nations (ASEAN):* This association was created in 1967 and today is comprised of the following countries in the Southeast Asian region: the Brunei, Cambodia, Indonesia, Laos, Malaysia, Myanmar, the Philippines, Singapore, Thailand, and Vietnam.[37] The primary objective of the ASEAN was to promote economic, social, and cultural development of the region through cooperative programs.

- *The Common Market of Eastern and Southern Africa (COMESA):* This treaty involves the establishment of a customs union to foster economic growth among the member countries. The member countries are Angola, Burundi, Comoros, Entrea, Ethiopia, Kenya, Lesotho, Malawi, Mauritius, Rwanda, Sudan, Swaziland, Tanzania, Uganda, Zaire, Zambia, and Zimbabwe.

Competitiveness of Nations

A nation's competitiveness is defined by the Organization of Economic Cooperation and Development (OECD) as "the degree to which a country can, under free and fair market conditions, produce goods and services which meet the rest of international markets, while simultaneously maintaining and expanding the real incomes of its people over the long term."[38] The World Competitiveness Yearbook published annually by IMD[39] features forty-nine industrialized and emerging economies and provides businesses with the basic information on

Table 11.2	2003 World Competitiveness Ranking
World Competitiveness Ranking	
1. U.S.A (1)	
2. Australia (3)	
3. Canada (2)	
4. Malaysia (6)	
5. Germany (4)	
6. Taiwan (7)	
7. United Kingdom (5)	
8. France (9)	
9. Spain (8)	
10. Thailand (13)	
11. Japan (11)	
12. China Mainland (12)	
Note: 2002 rankings are in parentheses.	
Source: Available from http://www02.imd.ch/wcy	

location decisions. There are 314 criteria, which are broadly grouped into four competitiveness factors:

- *Economic performance:* Domestic economy, international trade, international investment, employment, prices
- *Government efficiency:* Public finance, fiscal policy, institutional framework, business legislation, education
- *Business efficiency:* Productivity, labor market, finance, management practices, impact of globalization
- *Infrastructure:* Basic infrastructure, technology infrastructure, scientific infrastructure, health and environment, value system

The world competitiveness ranking of the top twelve countries in 2003 with populations greater than 20 million is shown in Table 11.2. (The complete report for 2003 is available from the Web site at http://www02.imd.ch) Each of the 321 criteria covered in the world competitiveness report are things that a company would like to know about the country before making a location decision. All things equal, a country that has a higher competitiveness ranking would potentially be a better candidate for a facility location than one that is not as competitive.

Government Taxes and Incentives

Government incentives, business attitude, economic stability, and taxes are important location factors. Several levels of government must be considered when evaluating potential locations. At the federal level, a *tariff* is a tax imposed by the government on imported goods to protect local industries, support the country's balance of payments, or raise revenue. Thus, countries with high tariffs would discourage companies from importing goods into the country. At the same time, high tariffs encourage multinational corporations to set up factories to produce locally. However, membership in the WTO requires countries to open up their markets and to reduce their tariffs imposed on imported goods. Regional trade agreements such as NAFTA, MERCOSUR, and EU also serve to reduce tariffs among member nations to promote free movement of goods.

Many countries have set up *foreign trade zones (FTZs)* where materials can be imported duty-free as long as the imports are used as inputs to production of goods that are eventually exported. If the goods are sold domestically, no duty is paid until they leave the FTZ. There are currently 252 FTZs in the United States.[40]

In the United States, forty-three states have a personal income tax and forty-six states have a corporate income tax. For example, Nevada is a business-friendly state that does not have a corporate income tax, state personal income tax, corporate franchise tax, or inventory tax. Companies such as Amazon.com have taken advantage of this by setting up warehouses in Nevada. The other states that do not have an individual income tax are Alaska, Florida, South Dakota, Texas, Washington, and Wyoming.

Location incentives at the state and local government levels are also important. In the early 1980s, Iowa turned down Ted Waitt's application for a state loan and business assistance to set up a mail-order computer company because Mr. Waitt, a budding entrepreneur, was not considered a big prospect. Consequently, Mr. Waitt moved to a neighboring state, South Dakota, and set up Gateway Computers, today one of the largest employers in the state.[41]

Currency Stability

One factor that impacts business costs and consequently location decisions is any instability in currency exchange rates. Since its introduction in 1999, for instance, the euro has depreciated in value against the U.S. dollar by more than 24 percent as of the end of 2002. In 1999, the United States had an after-tax cost advantage of between 4 and 8 percent over the euro countries. By 2002, the cost advantage had turned into a 6 to 12 percent disadvantage for the same euro countries except Germany.[42] The weakening of the euro leveled the playing field in terms of business cost for euro countries competing against the United States. Several countries such as China, Hong Kong, and Malaysia currently have fixed exchange rates and, therefore, provide for a more stable environment for investment.

Access and Proximity to Markets/Customers

According to Daniel Malachuk, partner and worldwide director of business location at Arthur Andersen in New York, "The trend in manufacturing is to be within delivery proximity of your customers. Logistics timeliness and costs are the concerns, so that reinforces a clustering effect of suppliers and producers to places that offer lower cost labor and real estate."[43] As pointed out earlier in this chapter, Honda is a global company that aims to build plants in locations that best satisfy the needs of local customers. Honda has assembly plants in the United States, Japan, Malaysia, China, and Indonesia, to name a few markets where Honda sells its vehicles.

Recently, Eli Lilly made a strategic decision to move its Asian headquarters from Singapore to Hong Kong. According to Richard Smith, president of Lilly's Asian operations, "The critical mass, the center of gravity is moving north, and the real growth industries are in China. Taiwan and the countries in Southeast Asia are becoming less important in terms of critical mass in customers. Hong Kong is a springboard for us to expand into China, one of the fastest growing pharmaceutical markets in the world."[44] For a long period of time, Singapore had been a good location for Eli Lilly, but the shifting business environment meant that the company had to rethink its long-term strategy for the Asian market; now it is closer to its rapidly growing Chinese customer base.

In the service industry, proximity to customers is even more critical. Few customers will frequent a remotely located gas station or a supermarket if another more accessible alternative is available. Similarly, fast-food restaurants are well situated next to busy highway intersections to take advantage of heavy traffic areas. Ghosh and McLafferty (1987) note that an effective location strategy is "an integral part of corporate strategy for retail firms. Whether selling goods or services, the choice of outlet location is perhaps the most important decision a retailer has to make."[45]

Wal-Mart's early super-centers were located in predominantly rural markets to avoid direct competition with major discount stores in large metropolitan areas. Many regional chains, such as Jamesway, Bradlees, Caldor, Venture, Hills, McCrory's, and Rose's, went out of business because they could not compete with the larger and smarter competitors such as Wal-Mart and Target.[46] Even Kmart is now operating under Chapter 11 protection and is closing many of its unprofitable stores. More recently, Wal-Mart has changed its location strategy to include urban locations in the west and northeast regions of the United States.

Environmental Issues

How the environment is managed has a significant impact on human health. The inability to dispose of solid and hazardous waste, plus the presence of illegal waste, contributes to high incidences of diseases such as hepatitis A and amebiasis. Global warming, air pollution, and acid rain are issues that are increasingly being debated as the price to pay for industrialization. Millions of people live in cities with unsafe air, with asthma cases at an all-time high. A study by the Environmental Working Group[47] (a not-for-profit environmental research organization based in Washington, D.C., with an office in Oakland, California) found that air pollution caused more than 16,000 admissions to hospitals each year in California at an estimated cost of $132 million and that particulate-matter-related illnesses resulted in 5 million missed workdays annually in California. The same report also attributed airborne pollution to be responsible for more deaths in California than traffic accidents, homicide, and AIDS combined.[48] The 1990 U.S. Clean Air Act strengthened efforts to reduce air pollution, airborne toxics, acid rain, and depletion of the ozone layer (a cause of global warming). In the United States, the Environmental Protection Agency (EPA) is the federal agency responsible for the enforcement of environmental laws and regulations.

The Clinton Administration negotiated the North American Agreement on Environmental Cooperation (NAAEC) to "promote sustainable development through mutually supportive environmental and economic policies" as a supplementary environmental agreement to NAFTA.[49] The agreement provides a framework for the three countries to conserve, protect, and enhance the North American environment and to effectively enforce the environmental laws.

With trade liberalization, there is a need for environmental cooperation. The WTO understands the need for sound national and international environmental policies. A WTO report on trade and the environment was prepared in 1999 to addresses three key questions: (1) Is economic integration through trade and investment a threat to the environment? (2) Does trade undermine the regulatory efforts of governments to control pollution and resource degradation? and (3) Will economic growth driven by trade help the move towards sustainable use of the world's environmental resources?[50] Several environmental trends were identified in the report:

- The increasing use of global energy resources has raised the level of greenhouse gas emissions.
- Consumption of ozone depletion substances (contributing to global warming) has gone down, but it will take another fifty years to get back to normal levels.
- Sulphur dioxide emissions (a cause of acid rain) continue to increase in developing countries.
- Excessive generation of nitrogen continues from fertilizers, human sewage, and burning of fossil fuel.
- Continued deforestation occurs in developing countries.
- The increasing global water consumption will result in water shortages in many countries without serious water conservation efforts.

The report finds that neither trade nor economic growth is the real issue. The challenge is "to strengthen the mechanisms and institutions for multilateral environmental cooperation, just like countries fifty years ago decided that it was to their benefit to cooperate on trade matters."[51]

Labor Issues

Issues such as labor availability, productivity, and skill; unemployment and underemployment rates; wage rates; turnover rates; labor force competitors; and employment trends are key factors in making facility location decisions. Mexico has long competed on cheap labor but cannot continue to depend on this source of competitive advantage because of the emergence of lower labor cost countries like China. Mexican wages today range from US $2 to $2.50 per hour and are much higher than China's labor costs, which range from US $0.35 to $1 per hour when all benefits and taxes are included.[52] For example, Flextronics, one of the world's largest contract manufacturers, is moving its plants in Malaysia and Singapore to China because of the large base of engineering students (approximately 465,000) graduating from college each year and the lower labor costs.

Due to a shortage of skilled workers, companies are likely to seek help from the community in offsetting the cost of training new employees. BMW in South Carolina and Nissan in Tennessee and Mississippi all have joint training programs with these states as part of the incentive package offered to the auto manufacturers. For example, the South Carolina state government set up the South Carolina Technical College System in 1992 to provide training programs and since its inception has reimbursed BMW for training costs in excess of $25 million.[53]

Although it is true that low labor cost is an important factor in making location decisions, true competitive advantage depends on productive use of inputs and continual product and process innovations. When Ely Lilly moved its Asian headquarters to Hong Kong, an important factor was the availability of a highly educated workforce with outstanding administrative and professional people.[54] An empirical study recently found that human capital is one of the most important determinants of foreign direct investment, and its importance has increased significantly over time.[55] The study suggests that developing countries would have to increase the level of worker skills and develop human resource capabilities if they want to be attractive as locations for foreign direct investment.

Right-to-Work Laws

In the United States today, there are twenty-two states with **right-to-work laws.** These states are Alabama, Arizona, Arkansas, Florida, Georgia, Idaho, Iowa, Kansas, Louisiana, Mississippi, Nebraska, Nevada, North Carolina, North Dakota, Oklahoma, South Carolina, South Dakota, Tennessee, Texas, Utah, Virginia, and Wyoming. A right-to-work law "secures the right of employees to decide for themselves whether or not to join or financially support a union."[56] As discussed in the Supply Chain Management in Action profile at the beginning of this chapter, there has been a shift in the U.S. auto industry to the South, with assembly plants built in Tennessee, South Carolina, and Alabama, all of which are right-to-work states.

Access to Suppliers and Cost

Many firms prefer locations close to suppliers because of material availability and transportation cost reasons. The proximity of suppliers has an impact on the delivery of materials and, consequently, the effectiveness of the supply chain. Royal Philips Electronics moved its computer monitor plant in Juarez, Mexico, to an existing plant in Suzhou, China, because of a more competitive supplier base.[57] Japanese electronics makers are finding that China is a better place to set up manufacturing facilities even though it means that the cost to transport finished products to the U.S. market is higher. Japanese companies reason that a high proportion of components needed to make finished electronic products have to be imported from outside NAFTA because U.S., Mexican, and Canadian manufacturers are not cost competitive.[58]

Utility Availability and Cost

The availability and cost of electricity, water, and gas are also important location considerations. In economically emerging countries, it is not unusual that the supply of electricity has not kept pace with the high speed of development, resulting in work stoppages from electrical outages. Even developed countries such as the United States are not immune from the energy problem. For example, California experienced rolling blackouts in January and March of 2001. Utility companies in California such as Southern California Edison and Pacific Gas & Electric are near bankruptcy, and the fear is that the cost will be passed on to corporate users.

In heavy industries such as steel and aluminum mills, the availability and cost of energy are critical considerations. The concern for companies is to have the power available when needed and at an affordable price. Consequently, areas such as upstate New York, the Tennessee Valley, and parts of Canada, which provide low-cost power, are gaining in location popularity because of their plentiful energy supply.[59]

Telecommunication costs have dropped dramatically in the last decade, resulting in many organizations setting up back office operations and call centers internationally to serve the U.S. market. For example, Sheraton Hotels offloads some of its work from its North American operations to its call center in Ireland.[60] Outsourcing International LLC services companies in the airlines, banking, insurance, and tourism industries. The customer dials a toll-free number in the United States, and the call is routed to India where the call centers are located. Labor costs in India are less than 20 percent of those in many developed countries. In addition, the working hours are off-peak hours in India, resulting in a complete synergy.[61]

Quality-of-Life Issues

Quality of life can be defined as "a feeling of well-being, fulfillment, or satisfaction resulting from factors in the external environments."[62] So what exactly are the issues affecting quality of life? While there is no definitive agreement on a set of **quality-of-life factors,** the Chamber of Commerce in Jacksonville, Florida, has annually prepared a report on the quality of life in the metropolitan area based on a comprehensive set of factors, which include the following:[63]

- *Education:* This includes the public education system comprised of pre-kindergarten through twelfth grade and higher education. Performance in terms of high-school graduation rates, college entrance test scores, teacher salaries, student-teacher ratios, and number of degrees awarded at universities and higher-education institutions provides an indicator of the quality of the education system. For example, a high student graduation rate and highly paid teachers are indicators of a high-quality education system.

- *Economy:* This includes the standard of living and community economic health. Performance indicators such as net employment growth, new housing starts, and the unemployment rate show the economic health of the community. The economy must also be sufficiently diverse to allow for long-term careers for both spouses. Thus, a low unemployment rate and an increase in the number of jobs show a vibrant local economy.

- *Natural Environment:* This category includes the quality and availability of clean water and air. Today, cities are monitoring the air-quality index and the amount of recycled waste diverted from landfills. A viable recycling program and clean air indicate a community's commitment to a green environment and the future health of the community.

- *Social environment:* Issues in this category include equal opportunity, racial harmony, emphasis on family, human services, and charitable contributions. A community where people and organizations contribute time and money to helping others in need shows a happy, affluent, and caring environment. The net result is a community that is a better place to live.

- *Culture/recreation:* A community that offers choice in terms of cultural, entertainment, recreational, and sporting activities is a more attractive location than one that offers fewer of these options. Measures of this aspect of quality of life include the number of organized sporting activities at city parks and pools, performing and visual arts events, and public parks. People feel better knowing they can go to a Swan Lake ballet, Mike Jaeger concert, or Lion King show, even if they are not fans of these types of activities.

- *Health:* The medical and health-care system is another critical element affecting the wellness of residents in the community. Measures such as infant deaths per thousand live births, number of physicians per thousand residents, and use of tobacco among residents are used to determine the health and fitness of the community. Recently, the U.S. medical profession has been facing a dramatic increase in malpractice insurance premiums in many states, with the result that many medical doctors are moving to areas with lower insurance costs. The ability to access good, affordable medical care provides residents with peace of mind and determines whether the community is a desirable place to live.

- *Government/politics:* This category examines how well the local government is performing and how involved the residents are in public affairs. Issues in this category are the percentage of registered voters, how many actually vote, approval ratings of the mayor, and how well the city government meets the needs of the residents. Since September 11, 2001, for instance, many state and local governments in the United States have been struggling to balance their budgets due to a weak economy and are considering cutting services and increasing taxes.

- *Mobility:* The ability to travel easily within the area and to other locations affects the quality of life of the residents. Issues such as the average commute time to work, the number of direct flights from the local airport, and the availability and efficiency of the public transport system provide measures of mobility. If the roads are constantly jammed with traffic, there is a huge loss of productive time. In the warehousing and distribution industry, the quality of the highways, railways, waterways, and airways has a significant impact on the performance of the supply chain in such areas as transportation cost, speed of delivery, and customer satisfaction.

- *Public safety:* Crime and accidents are two of the biggest public safety factors. The quality of law enforcement affects the crime rate. Better road systems and law enforcement are likely to lead to lower accident rates. In addition, fire protection and rescue services are issues of concern to the local residents. In the United States, there has been a trend toward suburban living because of the perception of safer neighborhoods and, therefore, a better place to live. In Mexico, especially in towns close to the U.S. border, many foreign businesses are concerned about the crime rate and the safety of expatriates working in maquiladora industries. The high-profile kidnapping of a Sanyo executive in 1996 caused Sony Mexico President Shin Takagi to warn that Japanese firms could reduce investments or withdraw from Mexico if the security situation did not improve.[64] Thus, high crime rates could frighten off firms considering a move to that area.

Land Availability and Costs

As land and construction costs in big cities continue to escalate, the trend is to locate in the suburbs and rural areas. Suburban locations can be attractive because of the cost and wide choice of land, available workforce, and developed transportation network. As mentioned earlier, when Honda first decided to set up a factory in the United States, it they located in Marysville, a small town about forty miles from Columbus, Ohio. Affordable land near the highway was readily available, and Honda could draw its workforce from several communities around Marysville. Similarly, when Honda built its assembly plant in Alabama to meet the increased demand for its Odyssey minivans and sport utility vehicles, the site was located in Lincoln, forty miles east of Birmingham. When Honeywell decided to move its manufacturing facility in Phoenix, Arizona, to China, the decision was to go to Suzhou, a city about thirty miles from Shanghai. Although the Pudong industrial zone in Shanghai was an attractive site, Suzhou had lower land and labor costs.

Facility Location Models

Several models can be used to assist companies in the facility location decision process. Three of the more common techniques are the weighted-factor rating model, the breakeven model, and the center of gravity model. These models are discussed below.

The Weighted-Factor Rating Model

The **weighted-factor rating model** is a method used to compare the attractiveness of several locations along a number of quantitative and qualitative dimensions. Selecting a facility location using this approach involves the following steps:

1. Identify the factors that are considered important to the facility location decision.

2. Assign weights to each factor in terms of their relative importance. Typically, the weights sum to 1.

3. Determine a score for each factor and for each location considered. Typically, the score varies from 1 to 100, although other scoring schemes can be used.

4. Multiply the factor score by the weight associated with each factor and sum the weighted scores across all factors.

5. The location with the highest total weighted score is the recommended location.

Since the factors, the individual weights, and the scores are subject to interpretation and bias by the analyst, it is highly recommended that a team approach be used when performing this type of analysis. Ideally, the team should include representatives from marketing, purchasing, production, finance, and transportation and possibly a key supplier and customer impacted by the location.

Determining the scores for each factor can include several intermediate steps. Comparing a labor cost score, for instance, would include determining the acceptable wage scale, along with insurance, taxes, and training costs and any other associated labor costs for each potential location. Then the total labor costs can be compared and translated into the final labor cost scores for each location by assigning the lowest cost location the maximum score and

EXAMPLE 11.1   Using the weighted-factor location model

The following factors have been identified as critical to making a location decision among the three countries of China, Singapore, and Indonesia. A group of functional managers has determined the factors, weights, and scores to be used in the analysis.

Factor	Weight	Scores (Maximum 100)		
		China	Singapore	Indonesia
Labor cost	0.20	100	40	90
Proximity to market	0.15	100	60	80
Supply chain compatibility	0.25	80	80	60
Quality of life	0.30	70	90	60
Stability of government	0.10	80	100	50

In which country should the new facility be located?

Solution

The weighted scores for the three countries are calculated as follows:

$$China = 0.20(100) + 0.15(100) + 0.25(80) + 0.30(70) + 0.10(80)$$
$$= 20 + 15 + 20 + 21 + 8 = 84.$$
$$Singapore = 0.20(40) + 0.15(60) + 0.25(80) + 0.30(90) + 0.10(100)$$
$$= 8 + 9 + 20 + 27 + 10 = 74.$$
$$Indonesia = 0.20(90) + 0.15(80) + 0.25(60) + 0.30(60) + 0.10(50)$$
$$= 18 + 12 + 15 + 18 + 5 = 68.$$

Based on the total weighted score, China would be the recommended country in which to locate the new facility.

then assigning the other locations a score based on their respective labor costs. Example 11.1 illustrates the use of the weighted-factor location model.

The Break-Even Model

The **break-even model** is a useful location analysis technique when fixed and variable costs can be determined for each potential location. This method involves the following steps:

1. Identify the locations to be considered.
2. Determine the fixed cost for each facility. The components of fixed cost are the costs of land, property taxes, insurance, equipment, and buildings.
3. Determine the unit variable cost for each facility. The components of variable cost are the costs of labor, materials, utilities, and transportation costs.
4. Construct the total cost lines for each location on a graph.
5. Determine the break-even points on the graph. Alternatively, the break-even points can be solved algebraically.
6. Identify the range over which each location has the lowest cost.

Example 11.2 illustrates the use of the break-even model.

EXAMPLE 11.2   Using the break-even model

Three locations have been identified as suitable candidates for building a new factory. The fixed and unit variable costs for each of three potential locations have been estimated and are shown in the following table.

Location	Annual Fixed Cost	Unit Variable Cost
A	$500,000	$300
B	$750,000	$200
C	$900,000	$100

The forecasted demand is 3,000 units per year. What is the best location?

Solution

First, plot the three total cost curves, represented by

$$TC_A = 500,000 + 300Q$$
$$TC_B = 750,000 + 200Q$$
$$TC_C = 900,000 + 100Q$$

The three curves are shown in Figure 11.1.

Determine the break-even points between Location A and Location B as follows:

$$TC_A = TC_B$$
$$500,000 + 300Q = 750,000 + 200Q$$
$$100Q = 250,000$$
$$Q = 2,500 \text{ units}$$

This indicates that producing less than 2,500 units per year would be cheaper at Location A, while producing more than 2,500 units per year would be cheaper at Location B.

Next, determine the break-even points between Location B and Location C as follows:

$$TC_B = TC_C$$
$$750,000 + 200Q = 900,000 + 100Q$$
$$100Q = 150,000$$
$$Q = 1,500 \text{ units}$$

This indicates that producing less than 1,500 units per year would be cheaper at Location B, while producing more than 1,500 units per year would be cheaper at Location C.

Finally, determine the break-even points between Location A and Location C as follows:

$$TC_A = TC_C$$
$$500,000 + 300Q = 900,000 + 100Q$$
$$200Q = 400,000$$
$$Q = 2,000 \text{ units}$$

This indicates that producing less than 2,000 units per year would be cheaper at Location A, while producing more than 2,000 units per year would be cheaper at Location C.

Based on the cost curves shown in Figure 11.1, Location C has the lowest total cost when producing the forecasted quantity of 3,000 units per year. If, however, the annual demand forecast was 1,000 units, then Location A would be preferred. From Figure 11.1, it can be seen that Location B would never be preferred when comparing the costs of all three locations simultaneously.

The Center-of-Gravity Model

The **center-of-gravity model** involves mapping all of the market locations on an x, y-coordinate grid and then finding a central location that is closest to the markets with the highest demand. This technique is useful for locating a manufacturing facility that will serve

Figure 11.1 | **Total Cost Curves for Location A, Location B, and Location C**

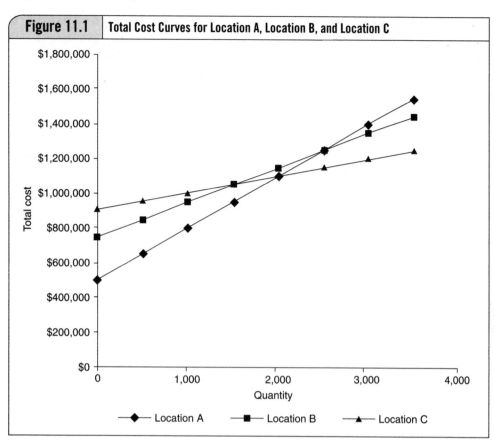

a number of different markets, or for a distribution center serving multiple facilities or markets. This model is based on the realization that markets with higher demand will require greater numbers of product deliveries; thus, the center-of-gravity model seeks to minimize total transportation costs. A weakness of this model is that it assumes that transportation costs vary linearly with distance, which is not necessarily true.

Assuming that a coordinate system is used placing all of the markets in the positive x, y quadrant, the center-of-gravity location is determined by the following:

$$\bar{X} = x\text{-coordinate of the center-of-gravity location} = \frac{\sum_{i=1}^{n} d_i x_i}{\sum_{i=1}^{n} d_i}$$

where

$$\bar{Y} = y\text{-coordinate of the center-of-gravity location} = \frac{\sum_{i=1}^{n} d_i y_i}{\sum_{i=1}^{n} d_i}$$

$x_i = x\text{-coordinate of Location } i$
$y_i = y\text{-coordinate of Location } i$
$d_i = \text{demand associated with Location } i$

Example 11.3 illustrates the use of the center-of-gravity model.

EXAMPLE 11.3   Using the Center-of-Gravity model

The XYZ Company would like to set up a distribution center to serve several key supply chain customers in the area. The annual demands and the x, y-coordinates for each customer are shown in the following table:

Customer	x, y-Coordinates (km)	Annual Demand (kg)
A	(5,12)	2,000
B	(7,8)	10,000
C	(12,10)	4,000
D	(3,9)	15,000
E	(15,4)	6,000
F	(7,15)	8,000

Solution

The locations of the customers are shown in Figure 11.2. Then,

$$\bar{X} = x-\text{coordinate of the center of gravity} = \frac{\sum_{i=1}^{n} d_i x_i}{\sum_{i=1}^{n} d_i}$$

$$= \frac{5(2,000) + 7(10,000) + 12(4,000) + 3(15,000) + 15(6,000) + 7(8,000)}{(2,000 + 10,000 + 4,000 + 15,000 + 6,000 + 8,000)}$$

$$= \frac{319,000}{45,000} = 7.09\,\text{km}$$

$$\bar{Y} = y-\text{coordinate of the center of gravity} = \frac{\sum_{i=1}^{n} d_i y_i}{\sum_{i=1}^{n} d_i}$$

$$= \frac{12(2,000) + 8(10,000) + 10(4,000) + 9(15,000) + 4(6,000) + 15(8,000)}{(2,000 + 10,000 + 4,000 + 15,000 + 6,000 + 8,000)}$$

$$= \frac{423,000}{45,000} = 9.40\,\text{km}$$

The desired x, y-coordinates for the distribution center are thus (7.09 km, 9.40 km) from the origin or (0,0) of the coordinate system.

Helpful On-Line Information for Location Analysis

Several Web sites are available that provide useful information for use in location analysis:

1. http://www.FacilityCity.com: FacilityCity.com is "a powerful, searchable platform that covers issues such as choosing a new location, managing major renovations and modernization projects, initiating facility improvements and selecting products and services."[65] The Web site also provides direct links to *Business Facilities: The Location Advisor* and *Today's Facility Manager,* as well links to resources such as:

   - Expansion/relocation news

   - Available real estate

Figure 11.2	Center-of-Gravity Location to Serve Various Customers

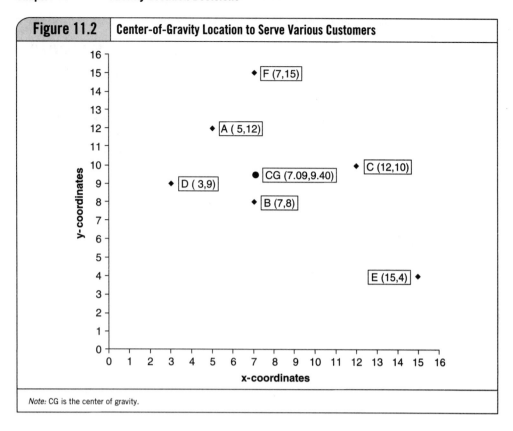

Note: CG is the center of gravity.

- Locations
- Site selectors' strategies
- Trends by industries

2. http://www.bizsitesDATA.com: The mission of bizsitesDATA is to "provide decision support tools to corporate real estate directors, site selectors, consultants, commercial realtors, and economic development professionals." The company has three objectives: (1) help corporate site analysts and their team locate ideal communities for their facilities, (2) help economic developers market their communities to these site-selection teams efficiently and effectively, and (3) help commercial real estate brokers sell their buildings and sites to the site-selection teams.

3. http://www.developmentalliance.com: The Development Alliance Web site is developed by the International Economic Development Council and Conway Data, Inc., publishers of *Site Selection* magazine (the *Site Selection* on-line Web site is located at http://siteselection.com). The Development Alliance Web site is a portal for community information that includes the following features:

a. Find a community location
    - Community demographics
    - IEDN criteria-based search
    - Community profiles
    - U.S. legislative climates

b. Find a specific site
    - Business parks directory
    - Property marketplace
    - Economic developers
    - Service provider directory

A multilingual workforce, a long history of international trade, a central location, and a government policy of encouraging high-tech development have combined to make The Netherlands one of the top places to do e-business in Europe and the world.

A number of multinational companies, noting the advantages offered in The Netherlands, have chosen to open e-commerce operations centers in or near the Dutch capital of Amsterdam. Among them is Southfield, Michigan-based Covisint LLC, the joint on-line business-to-business venture of Daimler-Chrysler AG, Ford Motor Co., General Motors Corp., Nissan Motor Co. Ltd., PSA Peugeot Citroen, and Renault. Covisint is an exchange where leaders in the automotive industry can collaborate on product development and find procurement tools in an effort to drive down costs industry-wide.

Covisint, after its launch in the United States, had its eye on Europe and Asia for some time before opening its Amsterdam headquarters on May 15, 2001. The company also has established an office in Tokyo.

"Formally establishing our European presence underscores our global vision and reinforces our stated mission to connect the automotive industry," says Kevin W. English, Covisint's chairman, CEO, and president. "Having a strong European foothold is critical to our future success."

While it was a given that Covisint would open an office in Europe, the exact location remained in question until the advantages of The Netherlands became clear. Lars Olrik, managing director of Covisint Europe BV, says his company found The Netherlands to be the best location for a variety of reasons.

"The Netherlands is the number-one spot for e-business," Olrik says. "For us it's a very good place in terms of key quality when it comes to people, very good infrastructure, high level of education."

There were also internal considerations that helped steer Covisint toward Amsterdam, Olrik says.

The Netherlands has the advantage of being seen as a somewhat neutral location, conveniently situated near the larger countries of Germany, France, and the United Kingdom, but not too close for comfort, politically speaking.

"It was driven to ensure we get the right political balance between our founding fathers," Olrik says.

"It would have been difficult to have it located in Germany due to our French-speaking partners, and it couldn't be set in Paris due to our German partners. A reasonable compromise put us in the middle, with a gateway to Detroit, Paris, Germany, Spain."

Source: C. Brown, "Netherlands Entices e-Business Companies with Location, Infrastructure," *Corporate Legal Times* 11, 120 no. (November 2001): BWB6. Reproduced with permission from *Corporate Legal Times*.

Business Clusters

Over the last decade, a number of trends have dramatically impacted the facility location process. Markets are increasingly globalized due to the liberalization of trade, technological advances, and increased demand from many regions of the world. Countries compete against one another for foreign direct investment. Having the necessary information to compare countries across a multitude of factors will help managers make better location decisions. Today, we are seeing more **business clusters** being created globally. Research parks and special economic/industrial zones serve as magnets for business clusters.

The concept of business clusters represents a new way of thinking about location decisions, challenges conventional logic on how companies should be configured, and provides a different approach to organizing a supply chain. So, what exactly are these *business clusters?* According to Dr. Michael Porter, "clusters are geographic concentrations of interconnected companies and institutions in a particular field. Clusters encompass an array of linked industries and other entities important to competition."[66] Locating research and development, component manufacturing, assembly operations, marketing, and other associated businesses in one area can improve the supply chain, technology sharing, and information sharing.

Silicon Valley and Hollywood in California are probably the two most well-known and successful clusters. Another high-tech cluster fashioned after Silicon Valley is Massachusetts' Route 128. The 1998 competitiveness study, "Our Competitive Future: Building the Knowledge Driven Economy," by the U.K. government found that "business development is often strongest when firms cluster together, creating a critical mass of growth, collaboration, and competition and opportunities for investment and knowledge sharing."[67]

Governments today recognize the need to develop existing clusters of similar businesses into world-class units. Although clusters are more prevalent in advanced economies, several emerging or newly developed economies such as Mexico, Singapore, India, and Taiwan have created high-tech clusters with the participation of foreign companies.[68] A discussion of each of these follows:

- *Mexico:* There are approximately 900 electronics firms in Mexico, with more than 40 percent located in the northwestern cities of Tijuana, Mexicali, San Luis R.C., and Tecate; 25 percent in the northern cities such as Chihuahua; 22 percent in the Northeast in Monterrey, Saltillo, Reynosa, and Tampico; and 8 percent in the West, mostly in Guadalajara. Examples of major global companies operating in Mexico are IBM, Motorola, Hewlett-Packard, Siemens, Ericsson, Sony, and Panasonic. With NAFTA, goods can be exported duty-free to North America, allowing Mexico to become an electronics manufacturing center for the Americas. Mexico produces 24 percent of the world's television receivers.

- *Singapore:* Singapore has recently replaced Japan as the most attractive country for U.S. high-tech manufacturing investment in the Asia Pacific region. Singapore has the greatest technology penetration rates in Asia, the highest per capita GDP in Asia, and a highly skilled workforce. Approximately half of the world's computer disk drives are produced in Singapore.

- *Taiwan:* Taiwan, dubbed the "Silicon Island" by Forbes in 1998, is a leading manufacturer of computer hardware and has the largest global market share for motherboards, modems, and scanners. Intel and Compaq are two major investors in Taiwan, due partly to the large pool of engineers: 6.4 percent of twenty-four-year-olds possess technical degrees.

- *India:* India is an emerging player in the software industry. With a growth rate in computer usage between 1993 and 2000 of 600 percent, India is the fastest-growing country in computer use in Asia. India has the world's third-largest pool of scientific and technical personnel. Companies such as IBM, Microsoft, Oracle, and Motorola have built facilities in India's silicon valleys: Bangalore, Hyderabad, and Mumbai (formerly Bombay).

There are many reasons why clusters are successful.[69] One is the close cooperation, coordination, and trust among clustered companies in related industries. Another reason is the fierce competition for customers among rival companies located in the cluster. Companies are more productive in their operations because of easy access to the local supplier base, information, and technology. Companies can also recruit from the local pool of skilled and experienced workers, thus reducing the recruiting transaction costs. Due to the intensity of competition, peer pressure, and constant comparison among rivals, companies respond much more quickly to customer needs and trends than do companies located outside a business cluster. Clusters thus provide the competitive environment that promotes an increasing pace of innovation, which will eventually lead to further productivity growth.

Clusters are not without their problems, though. For example, Michigan suffered through plant closings and employee layoffs in the auto industry due to the industry's over-reliance on gas-guzzling auto designs and the oil shock in the 1970s. The groupthink mentality among the cluster participants of General Motors, Ford, and Chrysler in Detroit made it more difficult for individual companies to try new ideas and see the need for radical innovation in fuel economy automobile designs. A cluster will decline unless companies continue to build capabilities using emerging technologies while attracting supporting firms and research institutions.[70]

Summary

Facility location decisions can provide organizations with a competitive advantage and, therefore, must be an integral part of their overall strategic plans. The effectiveness of a supply chain is influenced greatly by where facilities are located. Increased globalization and improved technologies have resulted in a variety of options for companies to locate their facilities. Today, companies must consider a number of factors when analyzing potential locations; several comparison methods are available when considering the country, region, and community for a facility location. Business clusters often provide for strong business development, collaboration, growth opportunities, and improved supply chain management. The existence of successful clusters suggests that innovation and competition are concentrated geographically.

Key Terms

Association of Southeast
  Asian Nations (ASEAN),
  341
break-even model, 349
business clusters, 354
center-of-gravity model,
  350
Common Market of Eastern
  and Southern African
  (COMESA), 341

contributor factory, 339
European Union (EU), 341
lead factory, 339
offshore factory, 337
outpost factory, 339
quality of life, 346
quality-of-life factors, 346
right-to-work law, 345

server factory, 337
source factory, 337
Southern Common Market
  (MERCOSUR), 341
weighted-factor rating
  model, 348
World Trade Organization
  (WTO), 340

Discussion Questions

1. What is the impact of facility decisions on a supply chain?
2. Why is demand management important for effective supply chain management?
3. What are business clusters? Provide several examples of business clusters in a variety of countries. What are the advantages of clustering?
4. What are the factors influencing facility location?
5. Discuss the major regional trade agreements in Asia, Africa, Europe, Latin America, and North America.
6. What is the World Trade Organization and what is its role in world trade?
7. What are the critical factors in making community and site decisions?
8. Discuss Wal-Mart's location strategy.
9. Define *quality of life.* Why is quality of life an important factor in facility location? Is the set of quality-of-life factors used by the Chamber of Commerce in Jacksonville, Florida, a good one? Please explain.
10. What is a right-to-work state? What are the advantages or disadvantages of doing business in a right to work state?
11. Why is China an attractive location for many businesses?
12. Discuss the six strategic roles of a foreign facility.

Internet Questions

1. What are the key factors used in the World Competitiveness Ranking? Go to the Web site of IMD—World Competitiveness Yearbook at http://www02.imd.ch/wcy
   Select any three countries in the Asia Pacific region. Prepare a report discussing the pros and cons for each of these countries to locate a business there.

2. Go to the Web site of the World Trade Organization at http://www.wto.org
   Outline the development that led to China's entry into the WTO. What is the impact of China's accession into WTO on U.S. companies?

3. Go to the Web site of STAT-US/Internet (a service of the U.S. Department of Commerce) at http://www.stat-usa.org
   First, select a country and an industry in which you are interested. Then, based on the country report, prepare an assessment of the suitability of the country for doing business in the particular industry you selected earlier.

Spreadsheet Problems

1. The Soft Toys Company has collected information on fixed and variable costs for four potential plant locations.

Location	Annual Fixed Cost	Unit Variable Cost
A	$200,000	$50
B	300,000	45
C	400,000	25
D	600,000	20

   a. Plot the total cost curves for the four plant locations on a single graph.

   b. Compute the range of demand for which each location has a cost advantage.

   c. Which plant location is best if demand is 30,000 units?

2. The Bruhaha Brewery is planning to expand internationally. The company has identified six critical location factors and their relative weights. The scores for each of the three potential sites are shown in the following table. Which site should be selected?

Factor	Weight	Scores (Maximum 100)		
		A	B	C
Proximity of market	0.25	100	90	80
Quality of life	0.30	90	60	60
Supplier base	0.20	80	100	70
Labor costs	0.15	70	90	50
Taxes	0.10	60	80	90

3. The Running Rebels Manufacturing Company is planning to locate a central facility relative to its three suppliers and two customers. The x, y-coordinates of the supplier and customer locations are shown in the following table, along with the annual volumes shipped. Use the center-of-gravity approach to determine the location for the new facility.

Location	x-, y-Coordinates (Miles)	Volume Shipped (Tons)
Supplier A	(4,8)	5,000
Supplier B	(9,12)	8,000
Supplier C	(1,10)	7,000
Customer 1	(5,2)	9,000
Customer 2	(10,4)	2,000

References

Arend, M. "Manufacturing Is On the Move." *Site Selection Magazine* (November 2002).

Barnes, N. G., A. Connell, L. Hermenegildo, and L. Mattson. "Regional Differences in the Economic Impact of Wal-Mart." *Business Horizons* (July/August 1996).

Barros, A. I. *Discrete and Fractional Programming Techniques for Location Models.* Dordrecht: Kluwer Academic Publishers, 1998.

Beckmann, M. J. *Lectures on Location Theory.* Berlin, New York: Springer-Verlag, 1999.

Brown, G., and A. McMahon. "The MATRIX: Here's the Smartest Way to Compare Factors and Narrow Your Location Choices." *Business Facilities* (April 2002). Available from http://www.facilitycity.com/busfac/bf_02_04_cover.asp

Clapp, D. "Making the Move: A Paradigm Shift in the Far East." *Business Facilities* (September 2002). Available from http://www.facilitycity.com/busfac/bf_02_09_move.asp

Clapp, D., M. E. McCandless, and K. Khan. "The World's Most Competitive Locations." *Business Facilities* (September 2001). Available from http://www.facilitycity.com/busfac/bf_01_09_cover.asp

Ferdows, K. "Making the Most of Foreign Factories." *Harvard Business Review* (March–April 1977): 73–88.

Greenhut, M. L. *Location Economics: Theoretical Underpinnings and Applications.* Aldershot, UK; Brookfield, Vt, US: Edward Elgar Publishing Limited, 1995.

Hack, G. D. *Site Selection for Growing Companies.* Westport, Conn.: Quorum Books, 1999.

Hagel, J. III, and M. Singer. "Unbundling the Corporation." *Harvard Business Review* (March–April 1999): 133–41.

Jensen, K., and G. Pompelli. "Manufacturing Site Location Preferences of Small Agribusiness Firms." *Journal of Small Business Management* (July 2002).

Khan, K. "Project Persuasion." *Business Facilities* (July 2000). Available from http://www.facilitycity.com/busfac/bf_02_07_cover.asp

Lee, H. Y. H., V. M. R. Tummala, and R. C. M. Yam. "Manufacturing Support for Hong Kong Manufacturing Industries in Southern China." Available from http://www.ism.ws/ResourceArticles/2000/winter00p35.cfm

MacCormack, A., D. Lawrence, J. Newmann III, and D. B. Rosenfield. "The New Dynamics of Global Manufacturing Site Location." *Sloan Management Review* (Summer 1994): 69–79.

MacKay, S. "The New Rules for G7 Site Selection." *Business Facilities* (September 2002). Available from http://www.facilitycity.com/busfac/bf_02_09_cover.asp

Magretta, J. "The Power of Virtual Integration: An Interview with Dell Computer's Michael Dell." *Harvard Business Review* (March–April 1998): 72–84.

Mallot, J. "Quality of Life: How to Know It When You See It." *Business Facilities* (September 2002). Available from http://www.facilitycity.com/busfac/bf_02_11_cover2.asp

Porter, M. "Clusters and Competition: New Agenda for Companies, Government, and Institutions." *Harvard Business School Press Chapter* (7 June 1999).

Porter, M. "Clusters and the New Economics of Competition." *Harvard Business Review* (1 November 1998).

Rufinni, F. "The New Face of Logistics: Technology and e-Commerce Have Reshaped the Horizons of Today's Largest Distribution Hubs." *Business Facilities* (September 2002). Available from http://www.facilitycity.com/busfac/bf_02_09_special1.asp

Scott, B. R. *Country Analysis in a "Global Village."* Harvard Business School Note #9-701-073 (12 January 2001).

Notes

1. B. Brody, "Site Selection for the 21st Century . . . and Beyond," *Business Facilities* (April 2001); available from http://www.facilitycity.com/busfac/bf_01_04_cover1.asp
2. J. Poe, "Fueling the Economy: Government Leaders in the South Liberally Use Taxpayer Funds to Attract Lucrative Auto Plants 2001 Southern Economic Survey," *The Atlanta Journal the Atlanta Constitution* (8 April 2001).
3. K. Ritzler, "It's Official: Honda Picks Alabama for Auto Plant," *The Atlanta Constitution* (7 May 1999).
4. J. Poe, "Fueling the Economy."

5. N. Shirouzu and R. Brooks, "South Korea's Hyundai Motor Chooses Alabama Site for Firm's First U.S. Plant," *Wall Street Journal* (2 April 2002).

6. D. Clapp, "Success Stories: Teamwork Drives Hyundai to Alabama!" *Business Facilities* (August 2002); available from http://www.facilitycity.com/busfac/bf_02_08_cover.asp

7. J. Poe, "Fueling the Economy."

8. C. Baird, "Unions on the Run," *Government Union Review and Public Policy Digest* 20, no. 2 (2002).

9. M. Porter, "Clusters and the New Economics of Competition," *Harvard Business Review* (November–December 1998).

10. American Honda Motor Company Web site; available from http://www.hondacorporate.com

11. L. J. Aron, "Clicks and Bricks Meet Head On in the Software/IT Location Revolution," *Site Selection Magazine* (May 2002); available from http://www.siteselection.com/features/2000/may/software

12. G. Anders, "Virtual Reality: Web Firms Go on Warehouse Building Boom," *Wall Street Journal* (8 September 1999).

13. B. Brody, "Site Selection for the 21st Century."

14. 2001 Amazon.com Annual Report; available at http://212.180.4.141/swim/files/us/US0231351067_01_Amazon_Com_Annual_Report_2001_0.42_Mo.pdf

15. G. Anders, "Virtual Reality."

16. "Amazon Coming to Nevada," *Las Vegas Review—Journal* (8 January 1999); S. Gruner, "Amazon Bets on European e-commerce—Online Retailer Builds Distribution Center in U.K." *Wall Street Journal* 27 September 2000.

17. J. Foley, S. Konicki, and G..V. Hulme, "Amazon's IT Agenda," *Information Week* (6 November 2000).

18. F. Katz, "Amazon Shuts Down McDonough Facility 442 Jobs Affected by Sudden Move," *The Atlanta Constitution* (31 January 2001).

19. 2001 Amazon.com Annual Report.

20. Ibid.

21. B. Acohido, "Amazon Posts Gain, Boosts Outlook," *USA TODAY* (24 January 2003).

22. J. B. Shah, "Fedex's Hub of Supply Chain Activity—At Its Own Operation, the Logistics Company Has Made an Art Out of the Science of Supply Chain Management," *EBN* (30 April 2001).

23. K. Ferdows, "Making the Most of Foreign Factories," *Harvard Business Review* (March–April 1997): 73–88.

24. Ibid.

25. Ibid.

26. Ibid.

27. E. Malkin, "Manufacturing Jobs Are Exiting Mexico," *New York Times* (5 November 2002).

28. World Trade Organization; available from http://www.wto.org

29. "WTO Entry Boosts China's Economy"; available from http://www.china.org.cn/english/49058.htm

30. P. Wonacott, "Talent Pool—China's Secret Weapon: Smart, Cheap Labor for High-Tech Goods—Beyond Toys and Garments, Country Raises the Bar Again in Manufacturing—View from Mr. Li's Balcony," *Wall Street Journal* (14 March 2002).

31. "Regional Trade Agreements and the Multilateral Trading System," Document 103/226 final EN (27 November 2002), Commission on Trade and Investment Policy, ICC; available from http://www.iccwbo.org/home/statements_rules/statements/2002/Regional%20trade%20agreements_multilateral%20trading%20system.asp

32. "The European Union at a Glance"; available from http://www.europa.eu.int/abc/index_en.htm

33. "More Facts and Figures on the European Union and the United States"; available from http://www.eurunion.org/profile/EUUSStats.htm

34. "NAFTA at Seven"; available from http://www.ustr.gov/naftareport/nafta7_brochure-eng.pdf

35. Ibid.

36. "The EU Relations with MERCOSUR"; available from
    http://www.europa.eu.int/comm/external_relations/mercosur/intro

37. ASEAN Secretariat; available from http://www.aseansec.org

38. D. Clapp, M. E. McCandless, and K. Khan, "The World's Most Competitive Locations," *Business Facilities* (September 2001); available from http://www.facilitycity.com/busfac/bf_01_09_cover.asp

39. IMD World Competitiveness Yearbook; available from http://www01.imd.ch/wcy

40. Foreign Trade Zone Resource Center; available from http://www.foreign-trade-zone.com

41. P. Grier, "An Economic Vision: Silicon States," *Christian Science Monitor* 91, no. 61 (24 February 1999).

42. S. MacKay, "The New Rules for G7 Sites Selection," *Business Facilities* (September 2002); available from http://www.facilitycity.com/busfac/bf_02_09_cover.asp

43. B. Brody, "Site Selection for the 21st Century."

44. D. Clapp, "A Paradigm Shift in the Far East," *Business Facilities* (September 2002); available from http:www.facilitycity.com/busfac/bf_02_09_move.asp

45. A. Ghosh and S. L. McLafferty, *Location Strategies for Retail and Service Firms* (Lexington, Mass.: Lexington Books, 1987).

46. The Supercenter Era: 1992 to 2002," *DSN Retailing Today* (New York; August 06, 2002); pp. 27–31

47. Environmental Working Group; available from http://www.ewg.org

48. B. Walker and L. Pike, "Dirty Air a Cause of Death for More Than 9,300 Californians Each Year" (15 May 2002); available from http://www.ewg.org/reports/particlecivics/newsrelease_20020515.php

49. "NAFTA 5 Years Report—Encouraging Environmental Protection"; available from http://www.ustr.gov/naftareport/encouraging.htm

50. "Trade and Environment," World Trade Organization; available from http://www.wto.org/english/tratop_e/envir_e/environment.pdf

51. Ibid.

52. E. Malkin, "Manufacturing Jobs Are Existing Mexico."

53. J. Poe, "Fueling the Economy."

54. D. Clapp, "A Paradigm Shift in the Far East."

55. F. Noorbakhsh, A. Paloni, and A. Youssef, "Human Capital and FDI Inflows to Developing Countries: New Empirical Evidence," *World Development* 29, no. 9 (2001): 1593–1610.

56. "Right-to-Work States"; available from http://www.nrtw.org/rtws.htm

57. E. Malkin, "Manufacturing Jobs Are Exiting Mexico."

58. R. Donnelly, "Dealing with the Rising Sun"; available from http://www.mexconnect.com/mex_/travel/bzm/bzmjapan.html

59. B. Brody, "Site Selection for the 21st Century."

60. Ibid.

61. "Call Centers," Outsourcing International LLC; available from http://www.outsourcingintl.com/call.htm

62. J. Mallot, "Quality of Life: How to Know It When You See It," *Business Facilities* (November 2002); available from http://www.facilitycity.com/busfac/bf_02_11_cover2.asp

63. Ibid.

64. R. Donnelly, "Dealing with the Rising Sun."

65. Available from http://www.facilitycity.com/busfac/bf_01_03_global.asp

66. M. Porter, "Clusters and the New Economics of Competition."

67. "Business Clusters in the UK—A First Assessment"; available from http://www.dti.gov.uk/clusters/map/graphics/forintro.pdf

68. B. Brody, "High-Tech Clusters Span the Globe," *Business Facilities* (March 2001); available from http://www.facilitycity.com/busfac/bf_01_03_global.asp

69. M. Porter, "Clusters and the New Economics of Competition."

70. P. Grier, "An Economic Vision: Silicon States."

Chapter 12:

SERVICE RESPONSE LOGISTICS

Nordstrom's salespeople are getting ready to throw out their little black books. Instead of filling pages with hand-scrawled notes about customers' sizes and designer preferences, 20,000 sales clerks at the Seattle chain's 137 stores soon will be using new software and mobile devices to track their customers' tastes and match them to new merchandise arrivals and store promotions.[1]

Learning Objectives

After completing this chapter, you should be able to

- Understand how supply chain management in services differs from supply chain management in manufacturing.

- Define service response logistics.

- Describe the strategies for managing capacity, wait times, distribution, and quality in services.

- Define service quality and describe how to measure it and improve it.

Chapter Outline

An Overview of Service Operations
  Service Productivity
  Global Service Issues
  Service Strategy Development
  Cost Leadership Strategy
  Differentiation Strategy
  Focus Strategy
  The Service Delivery System
  Auditing the Service Delivery System
  Service Location and Layout Strategies
  Location Strategies
  Layout Strategies

Supply Chain Management in Services

The Primary Concerns of Service Response Logistics
  Managing Service Capacity

Capacity Management When Demand Exceeds Available Service Capacity
Capacity Management When Available Service Capacity Exceeds Demand
Managing Waiting Times
Queuing System Design
Queuing System Applications
Managing Perceived Waiting Times
Managing Distribution Channels
Eatertainment, Entertailing, and Edutainment
Franchising
International Expansion
Internet Distribution Strategies
Managing Service Quality
The Dimensions of Service Quality
Recovering from Poor Service Quality

SUPPLY CHAIN MANAGEMENT IN ACTION — *The Marketplace at Putnam*

Lunchtime means showtime at The Marketplace, the corporate cafe at Boston-based Putnam Investments' Norwood, Massachusetts, offices, where an array of equipment helps sell the sizzle. In view of guests is a twelve-foot-long high-output range where busy cooks fry, saute, braise, and grill, entertaining employees of the $330 billion mutual-fund-management firm as they wait for their entrees. Nearby, pizzas flash-bake in a 700° F gas-fired pizza oven while a six-foot tall, chain-driven French rotisserie turns poultry on spits. Putnam's restaurant-inspired interactive eatery, designed and operated by Flik International, a Rye Brook, New York-based food-service-management company, serves as a prototype for future Flik accounts.

"Display cooking has naturally evolved [at our corporate food-service accounts]," says Scott Davis, president of Flik. "First there was cook-to-order, then pizza prepared from scratch in front of customers, and, now, the interactive kitchen." The goal is to present a busy food production scene to guests. "The servery is designed to have cooking activity throughout," Davis says. "People can watch pizza being baked, dough being rolled out, sauces being put on." The rotisserie and pizza oven "were specified not only for their construction quality but also for their merchandising and visual appeal," Davis adds. "They give customers a clear view of the food."

The Marketplace at Putnam serves a building population of about 1,800 people, with 65 percent to 70 percent participation; no small feat considering the large number of restaurants nearby. Marketplace food options include grill, delicatessen, antipasto bar, cook-to-order station, gelato bar, and, if the hour is late, a nearby company convenience store with its food-to-go section. At lunchtime peaks, nearly 1,000 people are served in less than an hour—a task made possible by an efficient setup. "Production is batch cooking, not a la carte," says Davis. "Only the finishing touches are added at the last minute." Smart equipment choices help display-cooking operators navigate the tricky boundary between volume efficiency and quality individual service.

Putting the twelve-foot range up front at The Marketplace keeps activity in view of customers while less showy equipment, such as steamers and ovens, is placed out of sight. Supporting equipment besides the range includes three steam-jacketed kettles, a gas grill to burn hardwood charcoal (providing better flavor and hotter cooking temperatures), and convection ovens. Such an array of equipment exemplifies the importance display cooking has achieved in the noncommercial market, from corporations and universities to hospitals and schools.

"Stations have to be flexible enough to give both preliminary production support and a la carte service while maintaining customer perceptions of 100 percent freshly prepared," says Kathleen Seelye, principal of an Englewood, Colorado, food-service design and consulting firm. "Guests watch foods being sauteed in woks or on the grill. At the same time, ready-to-serve entrees and sides wait in heated decks and hot wells. Seeing the food prepared, they think it was made just for them," she says.[2]

Introduction

While most of the concepts of supply chain management that have been discussed up to this point can be applied to service organizations, this chapter specifically introduces and discusses supply chain concepts suited particularly to services and the service arms of manufacturers. Services differ from manufacturers in a number of ways including the tangibility of the end product, the involvement of the customer in the production process, the labor content contained in the end products, and the facility location. For instance, many services are considered **pure services,** offering few or no tangible products to customers, such as consultants, legal advisors, entertainers, and brokers. Other services may have end products with a larger tangible component such as restaurants, repair facilities, transportation providers, and public warehouses. Most manufacturers, on the other hand, have only a small service component associated with their end products including maintenance, warranty repair, delivery, and other customer service tie-ins to the products.

In all of these services, customers are either directly or indirectly involved in the production of the service itself. In this sense, services are said to provide **state utility,** meaning that they do something to things that are owned by the customer, such as transport and store supplies, repair machines, cut hair, and provide health care. Managing the interactions that take place between service firms and their customers while the service is being performed is the topic of this chapter and is of paramount importance to the ultimate success of service organizations.

To maximize customer visits, service firms must be located where the customers are, they must know what their customers want, and they must be able to satisfy these needs quickly and in a cost-effective manner. This requires service firms to adequately hire, train, and schedule service representatives; acquire technologies and equipment to aid in the provision of services; and provide the right facility network and procedures to continually satisfy customers. Problems or mistakes that occur during the delivery of services most likely mean an increase in service delivery time, a reduction in customer service, lower perceived service quality, and maybe even lost current and future sales.

The important role that services play in the global economy is becoming more evident today as developed countries become increasingly service-oriented. In the United States, for instance, services account for over 80 percent of all jobs and approximately the same percentage of gross domestic product (GDP)—and these statistics are increasing. Thus, firms are all attempting to identify the customer-desired service elements in their product offerings and provide better value through attention to these elements. These efforts are at the heart of service operations and the topic of service response logistics. Let us first review service operations in general and then move on to discuss service response logistics.

An Overview of Service Operations

Services are by far the largest sector of any post-industrialized nation and include organizations like retailers, wholesalers, transportation and storage companies, financial institutions, schools, government agencies, hotels, and consulting companies. Since the 1950s, the ratio of services to manufacturing and agriculture in terms of percent of the workforce in the United States has been increasing quite dramatically; and it is extremely likely that new entrants to the job market will be employed in some service role. In the United States as productivity increased through use of technology and mass-production techniques in the manufacturing sector, fewer employees were needed to maintain the same output level. Additionally, as the nation as a whole became wealthier, people began demanding more services. Today, a much smaller workforce in the United States produces far more agricultural and manufactured products than were produced in 1950. Many services, though, require more personalized attention, thus, labor cost tends to make up a larger percentage of the service product cost when compared to manufacturing.

Some of the differences between goods and services are reviewed here:

- Services *cannot be inventoried.* Typically, services are produced and consumed simultaneously—once the mail is delivered, surgical operations are performed, and advice is given, customers have "consumed" the service. For this reason, services often struggle to find ways to utilize their service workers during slow periods and, conversely, manage demand or increase the ability to serve customers during busy periods.

- Services are often *unique.* Good service providers have the capability of customizing the service to satisfy each customer—insurance policies, legal services, and even fast-food services can be unique for each customer. Thus, training becomes an important issue for satisfying individual customer needs.

- Services have *high customer-server interaction.* Service uniqueness demands more server attention, whether it be delivering purchased product to a specific location on the manufacturing shop floor, answering customer questions, resolving complaints, or repairing machinery. Many services today are finding ways to automate or standardize services or utilize customers to provide some of their own service, in an attempt to reduce costs and improve productivity. For instance, today a growth in standardized, self-serve services can be seen such as purchasing gasoline, getting cash, and completing one's tax forms.

- Services are *decentralized.* Service facilities must be decentralized because of their inability to inventory and transport service products. Therefore, finding good locations that customers will visit is extremely important (even Web-based services must locate their signs or advertisements where they will be easily found by Web browsers).

Thus, services, whether they be stand-alone organizations or functions within goods-producing firms, must be managed in ways that will take into account these various service characteristics.

Service Productivity

The basic measure of productivity is shown by the following formula:

$$\text{Productivity} = \frac{\text{outputs produced}}{\text{inputs used}}$$

where outputs produced for services are typically shown as customers served, services produced, or sales dollars; and inputs can be shown as labor hours or labor dollars for a **single-factor productivity** measure or shown as the sum of labor, material, energy, and capital costs for a **multiple-factor productivity** measure. Productivity is useful as an ongoing measure of success. For most services, the labor component or cost is quite high; thus, increasing service productivity typically includes reduction of labor cost (this strategy can be risky since reduction of labor can adversely impact the quality or services provided as well as the ability to serve customers). Other strategies for increasing service productivity include uses of technology (better and faster equipment for service providers) and education and training (such as cross-training service providers to perform multiple services) in order to increase outputs produced for a given level of inputs. Sylvania, for instance, has begun deploying field-service logistics software to help build optimized service routes and technician schedules for managing commercial lighting and energy usage for retailers, supermarkets, office buildings, and warehouses. They expect the software to boost technician productivity.[3]

Improving service productivity can be quite challenging due to the relatively high labor content of services, the need for individual customized services, the difficulty of automating services, and the problem of assessing service quality (for instance, did the mechanic properly fix the car? Was the client properly defended?) Service quality is discussed later in the chapter. Today, service productivity constitutes the largest segment of overall U.S. productivity; thus, finding ways to improve service productivity is directly related to the growth of the United States economy. As a matter of comparison, the average service productivity growth rate in the United States from 1992 to 2002 was approximately 2 percent per year, compared to 3.7 percent per year for manufacturing.[4]

Global Service Issues

The growth and exportation of global services are increasing all over the world, as world economies improve and demand for services increase. Just a few examples of global services as of the end of 2002 include FedEx (with six delivery hubs outside of the United States and route deliveries to more than 210 countries), Deutsche Bank (serving more than 12 million customers in seventy-five countries), Wal-Mart International (operating approximately 600 foreign units while employing more than 115,000 foreign associates), and Microsoft (with subsidiary offices in twenty foreign countries accounting for 27 percent of total revenues). Today, over one-quarter of all international trade is derived from the provision of services.

Successfully managing global services involves a number of issues:

- *Labor, facilities, and infrastructure support:* Cultural differences, education, and expertise levels can prove to be problematic for firms unfamiliar with local human resources. Firms must also do a good job of locating existing support facilities, suppliers, transportation providers, communication systems, and housing.

- *Legal and political issues:* Local laws may restrict foreign competitors, limit available resources, attach tariffs to prices, or otherwise impose barriers to global service expansion. Some foreign countries require the formation of joint ventures with local business partners.

- *Domestic competitors and the economic climate:* Managers must be aware of the local competitors, the services they offer, their pricing structure, and the current state of the local economy. Firms can devise competitive strategies by modifying their services to gain competitive advantage.

- *Identifying global customers:* Perhaps most important, firms must find out where the global customers are through use of the Internet, foreign government agencies, a trading partner, or a foreign trade intermediary. Once potential customers are identified, services can begin to decide how their service products can be modified to meet the needs of these customers.

Service Strategy Development

Manufacturing and service organizations compete using three generic strategies: cost leadership, differentiation, and focus.[5] Let us briefly discuss each of these in relation to services.

Cost Leadership Strategy

Using a low-cost strategy requires a large capital investment in automated, state-of-the-art equipment and significant efforts in the areas of controlling and reducing costs, doing things right the first time, standardizing services, and aiming marketing efforts at low-cost consumers. Examples of firms employing this strategy are Southwest Airlines, McDonald's, and H&R Block. In each of these cases, we see efforts to offer routine, no-frills services at a low price. Marketing efforts are geared toward attracting cost-conscious customers with little or no service customization needs. We also see examples of efforts to reduce costs among these firms. For example, Southwest Airlines uses one type of aircraft (Boeing 737 jets) to reduce maintenance, pilot training, and purchase costs. Additionally, Southwest Airlines was named the Best Low Cost Airline in the 2001 and 2002 Official Airline Guide (OAG) Airline of the Year awards. Finally, they served over 91.7 million bags of peanuts in 2001![6]

Differentiation Strategy

Implementing a **differentiation strategy** is based on creating a service that is considered unique. The uniqueness can take many forms including customer service excellence (Ritz-Carlton hotels), brand image (McDonald's arches), variety (Wal-Mart merchandise), and use of technology (Dell's Web site), among other distinguishing factors. Differentiation is created many times as the result of companies listening to their customers. In the insurance industry, for example, many companies are partnering with financial institutions and taking on the role of financial solution provider, selling individualized financial services, including insurance, to clients.[7] Differentiation does not necessarily mean higher costs; it merely refers to the ability of the service to offer unique elements in its services. In many cases, though, it may mean the customer is willing to pay more for the service. Advertisements, logos, awards, and reputations all play a part in creating the perception of uniqueness among the service's customers.

Focus Strategy

A **focus strategy** is built around the idea that a service can serve a narrow target market or niche better than other firms that are trying to serve a broad market. Services that specialize in these market niches can provide customized services and expertise to suit the needs of their customers. For instance, a neighborhood hobby shop is more likely to serve the needs of hobby enthusiasts than a large retailer like Target, even though Target might sell some of the same merchandise. Within each market segment, firms can exhibit characteristics of differentiation or cost leadership.

The Service Delivery System

Customers actually purchase a bundle of attributes when purchasing services, including the explicit service itself (storage and use of your money) along with the supporting facility (the bank building with drive-up tellers and the on-line Web site), facilitating goods (the deposit forms, monthly statements, and the extra services provided), and implicit services (the security provided, the atmosphere in the bank, the privacy, and the convenience). Successful services are designed to deliver this bundle of attributes in the most efficient way to satisfy customer requirements. Services must therefore define their service bundle and then design the delivery system with this bundle in mind.

Service delivery systems fall along a continuum, with mass-produced, low-customer-contact systems at one extreme and highly customized, high-customer-contact systems at the other. Intermediate approaches seek to physically separate high-contact (front-of-the-house) operations from low-contact (back-of-the-house) operations in order to utilize various management techniques that will maximize the performance of each area. Back-of-the-house operations tend to be managed as manufacturing operations, where the emphasis is on maximizing output and efficiency and achieving economies of scale. Technical people are hired for specific well-defined tasks, and technology is employed to increase productivity. Front-of-the-house operations are characterized by taking care of customers, hiring front-line service providers with good pubic relations skills, and giving employees the power and resources to solve problems quickly and effectively.

Hospitals provide a good example of businesses that provide a clear separation of services requiring customer contact from those services not requiring customer contact. Administrative offices, labs, storage, laundry, and food preparation, for instance, are services typically never seen by patients in hospitals, although managing these elements of the service bundle can make a tremendous difference in the profitability of a hospital. On the other hand, nursing and physician patient care, prescription services, and emergency room services directly involve patients in the delivery of services. In each instance, the customer-server interaction must be managed so that customers get what they came for, in a quick and effective way.

Auditing the Service Delivery System

The service system should be audited periodically to assess the system's ability to meet customer expectations. Monitoring customer complaints, talking to and observing customers, and tracking customer feedback using customer comment cards and comment forms on the company's Web site are ways to continually monitor customer satisfaction. Walk-through audits should also be performed by management, covering service system attributes from the time customers initially encounter the service until they leave. Several tools have been developed and used for this purpose including service system surveys to be completed by managers, employees, and/or customers; and service process maps (as discussed in Chapter 8). The objective of the service audit is to identify service system problems or areas in need of improvement.

Service Location and Layout Strategies

Good location strategies provide barriers to entry and competitive positioning for services, as well as generating additional demand. Once a location has been secured, firms can begin to consider layout strategies to maximize customer service, server productivity, and overall efficiency. Since location strategies and analysis models are discussed in Chapter 11, only a brief discussion of location considerations is included here, followed by the design of service layouts.

Location Strategies

Location decisions are extremely important for all services, because they have a significant impact on the long-term profits of the company (how likely is it that customers would visit a clothing store, for instance, in an otherwise abandoned shopping center?) Location decisions are viewed as long-term decisions because of the typical high cost of relocation. Global market opportunities, global competitors, and technological and demographic changes contribute to the importance of using a good location strategy. In all location evaluations, it is desirable to consider a number of relevant factors to reduce the reliance on intuition. While intuition can certainly be a valuable location analysis tool, many disastrous location decisions have been made solely on the basis of intuition. A number of location analysis models can be used as an aid in the location decision, and these include the weighted-factor location model, the location break-even model, and the center-of-gravity model (refer to Chapter 11 for use of these models).

Layout Strategies

Service layout strategies work in combination with location decisions to further support the overall business strategies of differentiation, low cost, or market focus. Office layouts tend to be departmentalized to allow specialists to share resources; many retailers like Wal-Mart also tend to be departmentalized to assist customers in finding items to purchase, while others may have centers throughout the store to entice customers to try things out and buy on impulse; commercial airline layouts segment customers, reduce the time to restock and service the galleys and lavatories, and allow for fast boarding and exits (at least in theory!); casino layouts are designed to get customers in quickly and then keep them there by spacing out the attractions; and self-serve restaurant buffets are designed to process customers quickly. These are just a few examples, and many service layouts use multiple layout strategies. As customer preferences, products, technologies, and service strategies change, layouts also tend to change. Several specific service layout design tools are illustrated in the following sections.

Departmental Layouts to Reduce Distance Traveled. Service layouts can be designed to reduce the travel times of customers or service workers when moving from one area to another. An example of a layout where this might be a primary consideration would be a health clinic. The waiting area is located in front where customers enter, while the examination rooms are located nearby. The doctors' offices might be centrally located while the lab, stor-

Global Perspective

THE SAITAMA SUPER ARENA

In its first seven months of operation, the Saitama Super Arena, the US$750 million Japanese venue that has received attention mainly as a feat of engineering, has seen a wide variety of events, including a record draw of more than 13,000 for a National Hockey League game. The emblematic building opened in Saitama, a suburb north of Tokyo, in September 2001 with an international Dream Team pre-Olympic basketball series and has played host to events as disparate as Disney on Ice and the collegiate American-style football league championships. "That was one of their drivers, to be able to draw international events, make it very American style," said lead designer Dan Meis, a partner with NBBJ Design, who won the contract while he was with Ellerbe Becket. "It can hold an NFL or an NHL game without compromise."

The 1.4-million-square-foot arena converts from 20,000 seats for basketball and hockey to 30,000 for soccer and football. There are thirteen luxury suites, two VIP rooms, and a lounge. The ceilings, walls, lighting, HVAC, concessions, restrooms, clubs, and suites all move into and out of place depending upon the required configuration. Employing technologies developed for retractable roof stadiums, large seating sections are moved by motorized "bogies" on steel tracks. The floor of the facility is approximately nine feet deep to accommodate the ice for hockey.

"It's sort of redefined the concept of a flexible building. It literally transforms mechanically from as small as a 5,000-seat theater to a 20,000-seat and 30,000-seat stadium.

Seats move, toilet connections come unplugged and plug back in," Meis said. The design may be emulated but probably not copied, Meis said. "It's seen as a model but also an expensive, difficult proposition. Not every prefecture will be able to build a $750 million building," he said. "People will learn from aspects of it rather than reproduce it."

The 300,000 square feet of wrap-around retail layout at the Saitama Super Arena may be more widely copied, Meis said. Shops, restaurants, a health club, and the John Lennon Museum envelop the arena in the same way that retail wraps Staples Center in Los Angeles and the Seoul (South Korea) Dome. The retail at Saitama is open seven days a week, making the building look constantly active. There is also an attached 250,000-square-foot entertainment center.

"Saitama prefecture plans to have this arena full of activities regardless of whether it is playing host to events. For this reason, the arena needs to provide a pleasant environment filled with amusements and activities for everyone to enjoy," Nakamura said. "The John Lennon Museum is attractive enough to gather people to the arena. We have other activities, such as a cultural center, restaurant, shops, and sports gym for the same purpose."

Meis's inspirations for the look of the building were speed and movement, such as sports cars and jet airplanes. "It looks like it moves when it's standing still," he said. The arena is located near the Shinkansen bullet train terminal, which takes commuters to Tokyo in twenty minutes.[8]

age, and X-ray rooms might be located farther to the back of the clinic away from most of the patients. A primary consideration is how far nurses, doctors, and patients have to walk to reach the various areas within the clinic. The objective then, would be to place high-traffic-volume departments close to each other, to minimize total footage traveled. Example 12.1 illustrates a design tool useful for this type of layout.

EXAMPLE 12.1   Layout of Valley Health Clinic

Valley Health Clinic wants to see if there is a better layout that will reduce the time doctors and nurses spend walking throughout the clinic. The layout is shown here, along with the number of trips and the distances between each department.

Existing Layout

Storage (F)	Doctor's offices (C)		Exam rooms (B)		Lobby & waiting area (A)
Nurses (E)	Lab & X-ray (D)				

Interdepartmental Doctors' and Nurses' Trips/Day

	B	C	D	E	F
A	55	0	0	50	0
B		40	15	40	0
C			15	60	10
D				30	0
E					18

Distances between Departments (Meters)

	B	C	D	E	F
A	20	40	40	60	60
B		20	20	40	40
C			10	20	20
D				20	20
E					10

To analyze the existing layout, the distance traveled must be calculated as follows:

$$\text{Total distance traveled} = \sum_{i=1}^{n}\sum_{j=1}^{n} T_{ij}D_{ij}$$

where

n = number of departments or offices
i, j = individual departments
T_{ij} = number of trips between Department i and Department j
D_{ij} = distance from Department i to Department j

The objective is to find the layout resulting in the lowest total distance traveled. For the layout of the Valley Health Clinic, we find:

Total distance traveled = 55(20) + 50(60) + 40(20) + 15(20) + 40(40) + 15(10) + 60(20) + 10(20) + 30(20) + 18(10) = 9,130 meters

EXAMPLE 12.1   *Continued*

From the layout and distances shown, it can be seen that the nursing station needs to be closer to the lobby and waiting area, closer to the exam rooms, and closer to the doctors' offices. This can be accomplished by switching Department E and Department D (nurses and lab/X-ray). This also creates a trade-off, since now Department C, Department B, and Department A will be farther from Department D. To calculate the new total distance traveled, the distance table must be modified as shown in the following table. The asterisks denote changes made to the table.

Distances between Departments

	B	C	D	E	F
A	20	40	60*	40*	60
B		20	40*	20*	40
C			20*	10*	20
D				20	10*
E					20*

The new total distance can then be calculated as follows:

Total distance traveled = 55(20) + 50(40) + 40(20) + 15(40) + 40(20) + 15(20) + 60(10) + 10(20) + 30(20) + 18(20) = 7,360 meters

This is a better layout but only one of a large number of potential layouts. Typically, a number of layouts are evaluated until a reasonable and acceptable layout is found.

Departmental Layouts to Maximize Closeness Desirability. This is another useful type of layout analysis tool used for retail or office layouts. Here, the importance is placed on the relationship between various departments. In a convenience store, for instance, it would be extremely important to have the cashier close to the entrance and the cold food items in the back, close to the cold storage areas and the rear loading doors of the store. In an office setting, it might be desirable to have the receptionist close to the office entrance and file rooms, with the president close to the conference room. For each department pair, then, a closeness desirability rating must be determined, with the objective being to design a layout that maximizes a desirability rating for the entire office. Example 12.2 illustrates this concept.

EXAMPLE 12.2   Closeness desirability rating for an office layout

Existing Office Layout

File room (F)	Engineering offices (C)	Marketing offices (B)	Secretary & waiting area (A)
Purchasing (E)	President's office (D)	Conference room (H)	Copy room (G)

(continued)

EXAMPLE 12.2   *Continued*

Desirability Ratings

	B	C	D	E	F	G	H
A	2	0	−1	2	2	3	−1
B		0	2	1	1	0	3
C			2	2	0	0	1
D				1	−1	−1	3
E					3	1	2
F						3	1
G							0

The desirability ratings are based on a −1 to 3 scale, where −1 = undesirable, 0 = unimportant, 1 = slightly important, 2 = moderately important, and 3 = very important. To score the preceding layout, we count the closeness desirability score only when departments are adjacent to each other. For this layout:

Closeness desirability score = (A/B:2) + (A/H:−1) + (A/G:3) + (B/C:0) + (B/H:3) + (C/F:0) + (C/D:2) + (D/E:1) + (D/H:3) + (E/F:3) + (G/H:0) = 16 points

Note that department pairs are not counted twice and are also not counted if only the corners are touching. To find a better layout, we could place the department pairs with a rating of 3 adjacent to each other and place adjacent pairs with a rating of −1 such that they are not adjacent. For instance, the file room (F) could be moved adjacent to the copy room (G) and the conference room (H) could be moved farther away from the secretary/waiting area (A). The possible new layout follows:

New Office Layout

President's office (D)	Engineering offices (C)	Marketing offices (B)	Secretary & waiting area (A)
Purchasing (E)	Conference room (H)	File room (F)	Copy room (G)

The closeness desirability score for the preceding new layout follows:

Closeness desirability score = (A/B:2) + (A/F:2) + (A/G:3) + (B/C:0) + (B/E:1) + (B/F:1) + (C/D:2) + (C/H:1) + (C/E:2) + (D/H:3) + (E/F:3) + (E/H:2) + (F/G:3) = 25 points

Based on this analysis, it can be concluded that the second layout is better; like the previous example, though, there are many potential layouts so several potential new layouts should be evaluated.

Supply Chain Management in Services

In many respects, service-producing organizations are like goods-producing organizations in that they make purchases and therefore deal with suppliers, they incur inventory carrying costs, and these purchased inventories must be transported and stored somewhere. For some services, purchased items are part of the service provided and are extremely important sources of competitive advantage (such as a retailer or restaurant), while, for others, this may be a very minor concern (for instance, law offices and insurance providers). In many cases, service firms also purchase **facilitating products** such as computers, furniture, and office supplies that are not part of the services sold but, rather, are consumed inside the firm; and these materials must also be managed. Table 12.1 shows some typical transportation, warehousing, and inventory activities at several different types of services.

On the other hand, service-producing organizations are unlike goods-producing organizations, in that services typically deal with the end customer in their supply chains while most goods-producing firms deal with distributors, other manufacturers, or retailers. In other words, service products are typically not passed on to customers farther down a distribution channel. Thus, any goods that are delivered as part of the service are consumed by the immediate customers.

Typically, service firms deal very closely with their customers and the services performed in many cases require a larger labor component than manufactured products. Customers may have no idea what resources or facilitating goods were used to deliver the services they purchase; rather, customers' primary concerns are with the service itself and the way it is delivered. For this reason, the distribution elements of interest to services revolve around the customers and how they are being served. A good example of this is the transportation industry. When shippers want things moved, they want the move performed at a specific time, delivered to a specific place, delivered on time, and performed as economically as possible. Most large transportation companies today have sophisticated information systems to allow customers to track deliveries and companies to determine the best combination of warehousing, transportation method, port of entry, routing, pricing, and consolidation. In many cases, customers have no idea how things actually get to the destination. But they sure notice when the shipment is late![9] While manufacturers must also be concerned with customer service, service customers place a greater level of importance on the customer service provided.

Table 12.1	Transportation and Warehousing Activities in Services	
Services	**Transportation Activities**	**Warehousing & Inventory Activities**
Banks	• Movements of checks, coins/cash among branches and operations centers • Movement of checks to cities with Federal Reserve processing centers	• Office supplies and coins/cash • Furniture and computers • Records
Hospitals	• Movement of medical supplies to stockrooms • Transfers of patients • Movement of medical records, test results, and films among units	• Surgical/medical supplies • Pharmaceutical supplies • Office furniture • Medical equipment
Telephone companies	• Inbound transportation of switches, parts, and equipment to warehouses • Transportation of construction equipment and supplies to job sites • Routing of consumer products to retail outlets	• Parts, equipment, consumer products • Repair truck parts and equipment • Construction supplies

Source: Adapted from E. L. Drazen, R. E. Moll, and M. F. Roetter, *Logistics in Service Industries* (Oak Brook, Ill.: Council of Logistics Management, 1991), 24–26.

All the elements of supply chain management including supplier selection, transportation, warehousing, process management, distribution, and customer service hold strategic importance for the long-term success of all service organizations. While the previous chapters have presented and discussed many of these elements, the remainder of this chapter is devoted to the portion of supply chain management of greatest concern to service organizations and the service arms of goods-producing companies—namely, the activities associated with the production and delivery of the actual service.

The Primary Concerns of Service Response Logistics

Service response logistics is the management and coordination of all the organization's activities that occur while the service is being performed.[10] Managing these activities often means the difference between a successful service experience and a failure. The primary activities of concern are the management of **service capacity, waiting times, distribution channels,** and **service quality.** Since services cannot be inventoried, managing service capacity enables the firm to meet variable demand, perhaps the most important concern of all services. When demand variabilities cannot be adequately met, the firm must resort to managing queues or waiting times sufficiently to satisfy customers. **Demand management** tactics also play a role in a service firm's ability to satisfy varying demand. Customer waiting times are closely related to the customer's view of service quality and, ultimately, customer satisfaction. Since services usually must be decentralized to attract customers and provide adequate service delivery times, use of various distribution channels also becomes important to the delivery of service products. Let us discuss each of these service elements in detail.

Managing Service Capacity

Let us first start by defining the term *service capacity*. Service capacity is most often defined as the number of customers per day the firm's service delivery systems *are designed to serve,* although it could also be some other period of time such as customers per hour or customers per shift. Capacity measures can be stated somewhat differently, too, depending on the service—for instance, airline companies define capacity in terms of available seat miles per day. Most services desire to operate at some optimal capacity level (less than maximum capacity) to reduce the likelihood of having queues develop and to more effectively serve customers. For services dealing directly with customers, service capacity is largely dependent upon the number of employees providing the services and the equipment they use in providing the services.

Since service output can not be inventoried, firms are forced to either turn away customers when demand exceeds capacity or hire additional personnel. Since hiring, training, supervising, and equipping service personnel are quite costly (in many cases 75 percent of total operating costs), the decision of how many service personnel to hire greatly affects costs, productivity, and, ultimately, sales and profits. Ideally, firms want enough service capacity (service personnel) to satisfy demand, without having significant excess (and costly) capacity. This can be a tricky proposition if demand varies throughout the day, week, or month, as is typical in a great many services. So, an important part of a service manager's job is to forecast demand for various segments of time and customer service processes and then provide (or withhold) capacity to meet the forecasted demand.

When things work out right, firms operate at an optimal **capacity utilization,** as defined here:

$$\text{Capacity utilization} = \frac{\text{actual customers served per period}}{\text{capacity}}$$

As utilization approaches (and sometimes even exceeds) 1.0, services become more congested, service times increase, wait times increase, and the perceived quality of service deteriorates. With utilization close to 1.0, even a slightly greater than average service time for several customers can cause queues to become very long (some readers may recall, for instance, waiting one or two hours beyond an appointment time to see a doctor). Thus, an optimal utilization would leave some level of capacity unutilized (perhaps 15 to 25 percent depending on the volatility of demand), so that variations in service times will not severely impact waiting times.

The two most basic strategies for managing capacity are to use a **level-demand strategy** (when the firm utilizes a constant amount of capacity regardless of demand variations) or a **chase-demand strategy** (when the amount of capacity varies with demand). When a level-demand strategy is used, the firm is left to using demand management or **queue management** tactics to deal with excess customers. When a chase-demand strategy is used, effective plans must be in place to utilize, transfer, or reduce service capacity when there is excess available, and to develop or borrow capacity quickly when demand exceeds capacity. Capacity management techniques that are useful when demand exceeds available service capacity are discussed next, followed by a discussion of capacity management when service capacity exceeds demand.

Capacity Management When Demand Exceeds Available Service Capacity

An initial option may be to simply hire people when demand exceeds existing capacity (or simply let queues develop) and then lay people off when capacity exceeds demand. Most likely, though, we would like to avoid these options due to the expense of hiring, training, and supervising new workers and the loss of current and future business when letting people wait too long in queues, as well as the expense and damage to the firm's reputation when laying off workers. Instead, a number of efficient methods can be employed to minimize the expense of hiring workers and then letting them go and to minimize the cost of letting people wait in line. These include cross-training and sharing employees, using part-time employees, using customers, using technology, using employee scheduling strategies and, finally, using demand management techniques to smooth or shift demand. Each of these methods is discussed in the following sections.

Cross-Training and Sharing Employees. Have you ever been waiting to pay for items at a retail store and thought to yourself, "Why don't they use some of these other workers standing around to check people out?" Many service firms, though, do make wide use of this sharing strategy. Quite often in many service firms, some processes are temporarily overutilized while, at the same time, other processes remain under- or unutilized. Rather than hiring someone to add capacity to the overutilized processes, progressive firms have adequately hired and trained workers to be proficient in a number of different processes. Thus, when demand temporarily exceeds service capacity in one area, creating a customer queue, idle workers can quickly move to that process and help to serve customers and reduce the queue length.

By sharing employees among a number of processes, firms create the capability to quickly expand capacity as demand dictates while simultaneously minimizing the costs of poor customer service or hiring and laying off workers. This type of resource-sharing arrangement can occur in most any type of organization, from retailers to banks, hospitals, or universities.

Using Part-Time Employees. Part-time employees can also be utilized as a low-cost way to vary capacity. Their hourly wages are often lower than the wages of full-time employees, and the cost of fringe benefits is also lower. Firms use full-time employees to serve that stable portion of daily demand, while scheduling part-timers for those historically busy periods (such as lunch and dinner times, holidays, weekends, or busy seasons). Part-time employees can also be used to fill in during the vacation periods, off days, and sick days of full-time employees. Laying off part-time employees during slower periods is also more acceptable to the permanent full-time workforce and is somewhat expected by the part-time employees.

Using Customers. As the need to contain costs and improve productivity and competitiveness continues, firms are finding that customers themselves can be used to provide certain services, provided it is seen by customers as value-enhancing. The benefits for customers of self-service include faster service, more customized service, and/or lower cost. The benefits for the companies include lower labor costs and extra service capacity. In this sense, customers are "hidden" employees, allowing the firm to hire fewer workers and to vary capacity to some extent as needed. The trade-off for customers is that they expect to pay less for the service, since they are doing some of the work. This includes pumping gas, filling soda cups, filing taxes, or filing legal forms, for instance. In other cases, though, customers may actually pay the same or more for the service, as when using self-checkout at hotels or using twenty-four hour automated teller machines if they perceive the work they do as saving time or providing some other benefit. Thus, if firms can identify service process jobs that customers can perform, if they can provide process directions that are easy to understand and learn, and if they can adequately satisfy customers that are being asked to perform the work, then using customers as employees can provide yet another method for managing capacity.

Using Technology. Providing technological assistance in the form of computers or other equipment to service company personnel can improve the ability of servers to process customers, resulting in more service capacity, faster service completion times, more or better services, and the need for fewer employees. Voice-activated telephone response systems; on-line banking, purchasing, selling, and comment systems; and bar-code/scanner/computer tracking systems are just a few examples of technology helping to provide services. Some forms of technology may completely replace the need for sales or other types of customer service personnel as in the case of Amazon.com.

Technology can also enable service standardization—providing the service exactly the same way every time, as in automated teller machines or event ticket machines. In many cases, service standardization is viewed as a high-quality characteristic by customers seeking specific, periodic services. Standardization allows services to be accessed anywhere at any time without the need for re-learning the service process.

Using Employee Scheduling Policies. By properly scheduling workers during the day, service capacity can be varied to accommodate varying demand. Businesses must first forecast demand in half-hour or one-hour increments during the day and then convert the demand to staffing requirements for each period, given the average service capabilities for workers. The problem of assigning workers to shifts is complicated by the number of hours each day and the number of days each week the business is open, the timing of day off and consecutive days off, and employee shift preferences. The objective of worker scheduling is to service demand with the minimum number of employees, while also assigning equitable work shifts to employees. Employee-scheduling software is available to provide managers with multiple scheduling solutions to this problem.

Use of part-time workers, as stated earlier, makes scheduling easier and is illustrated in Example 12.3. In the example, the manager finds a need for one three-day worker, one two-day worker, and two one-day workers, in addition to the full-time workers.

Using Demand Management Techniques. Even when accurate forecasting and good capacity management techniques are used, there are still many occasions when demand exceeds available capacity. As stated earlier, forcing customers to wait in line a long period of time prior to or while purchasing a service may eventually result in lost current and future business and even damage to the firm's reputation. While waiting in line is inevitable at one time or another in most service situations, organizations try to reduce demand during busy

EXAMPLE 12.3   Use of part-time counter help at Bob's Plumbing Supply

The manager of Bob's Plumbing Supply has determined her counter help requirements as shown in the following table for the five-day workweek. Given these requirements, she sees that she needs two full-time employees working all five days, resulting in the part-time requirements as shown (found by subtracting 2 from each workday requirement). To satisfy these requirements with the fewest number of part-time employees, she begins by assigning Part-Timer No. 1 to the maximum number of workdays (Monday, Thursday, and Friday). Part-Timer No. 2 is assigned to the maximum number of workdays remaining (Monday and Friday). Then Part-Timer 3 and Part-Timer 4 are assigned to the remaining workday (Friday).

	Monday	Tuesday	Wednesday	Thursday	Friday
Workers required	4	2	2	3	6
Full-time workers	2	2	2	2	2
Part-time workers	2	0	0	1	4
Part-Timer No. 1	1			1	1
Part-Timer No. 2	1				1
Part-Timer No. 3					1
Part-Timer No. 4					1

periods using several short-term demand management techniques. These include raising prices during busy periods to curtail excess demand and shift it to less-busy periods, taking reservations or appointments to shift demand to less-busy periods, discouraging undesirable demand through use of screening procedures and marketing ads, and segmenting demand to facilitate better service (for instance, first-class versus economy-class seating, or express versus regular checkout counters). These tactics are combined with the capacity management techniques discussed earlier to provide the firm with the ability to better serve customers. Let us look now at capacity management techniques when service capacity exceeds demand.

Capacity Management When Available Service Capacity Exceeds Demand

When capacity exceeds demand, the firm is faced with the problem of how to utilize excess capacity. Too much excess capacity will increase the cost of the service provided and may also impact customers' perceptions of quality (readers may recall their perceptions when walking into a deserted restaurant). Aside from the obvious long-term solution of laying workers off and selling facilities, firms can find other uses for service capacity and they can use demand management techniques to stimulate demand.

Finding Other Uses for Service Capacity. One way to utilize excess capacity is to develop additional service products. Periodic lack of demand may be particularly troublesome for services with seasonal demand, such as hotels, airlines, and ski resorts. For these services, management may try to develop service products that the firm can provide during its characteristically slow periods. For example, this may include airlines partnering with resorts to provide vacation packages during off-peak seasonal periods, hotels booking business conferences during slow periods, or ski resorts designing mountain bike trails or building cement luge runs for summer use. Firms can also make use of cross-training to shift or transfer employees to other areas needing more capacity. For instance, swimming pool builders may train and then use their construction workers to build pool enclosures during the winter months.

Using Demand Management Techniques. Demand management techniques when capacity exceeds demand are used to stimulate additional demand. These include lowering prices during off-peak periods, as in early-bird dinner specials or mid-week hotel rates, and designing aggressive marketing campaigns for use during slow business periods.

Managing capacity in services thus involves techniques to adjust capacity and either stimulate or shift demand in order to match capacity to demand. When an oversupply or undersupply of capacity exists, service times, waiting times, cost, and service quality all suffer, all of which impact the competitiveness of the firm. The second concern in service response logistics is discussed next—managing waiting times.

Managing Waiting Times

Waiting times are encountered every day, from waiting in line at streetlights, to waiting for a table at a restaurant, to waiting on hold on the telephone. Ideally, service managers would like to design queuing systems such that customers never have to wait in line; however, the cost of maintaining enough service capacity to serve variable demand when it is significantly greater than normal is simply too expensive. Thus, managers use information they have about their customers and their service employees to design adequate queuing systems and then couple this with the management of customers' perceived waiting times to minimize the negative impact of waiting in line. Thus, good waiting line management consists of the management of *actual waiting time* and *perceived waiting time*. To accomplish this, managers must consider a number of things:

- What is the average arrival rate of the customers?
- In what order will customers be serviced?
- What is the average service rate of the service providers?
- How are customer arrival and service times distributed?
- How long will customers wait in line before they either leave or lower their perceptions of service quality?

© 2003 Ted Goff

"Did I keep you waiting long?"

- How can customers be kept in line even longer without lowering their perceptions of service quality?

Answers to these questions will allow the firm to adequately design a queuing system that will provide acceptable service to customers while minimizing service system cost and the cost of lost and disgruntled customers. Properly thought out and designed queuing systems decrease waiting times and, subsequently, the need for further managing waiting times; although, occasionally, waiting time management tactics must be utilized to decrease perceived waiting times. The design of queuing systems is discussed next, followed by a discussion of managing perceived waiting times.

Queuing System Design

The four most common queuing system configurations are shown in Figure 12.1. The choice of queuing system depends on the volume of customers to be served, the willingness of customers to wait in line, the physical constraints imposed by the service structure, and the number and sequence of services to be performed. The typical problems queuing system designers wish to solve are: the average number of customers in line and in the system, the average waiting time in line and in the system, and the average server utilization. As already alluded to, the primary elements of all queuing systems are the input process, the queue characteristics, and the service characteristics. These elements are discussed next, along with several applications.

The Input Process. The customer arrivals are referred to here as the **demand source.** The size of the demand source can be considered either infinite or finite. Many situations (along with the examples covered later) assume an unlimited demand source such as customers arriving at a retail outlet, while other situations have a finite-sized demand source, such as customers showing up for a concert at an arena.

Customers also arrive at a service according to some arrival pattern. When students show up for class, this is an example of a known or deterministic interarrival time. In many cases, customers show up in a random pattern, and the **Poisson distribution** is commonly used to

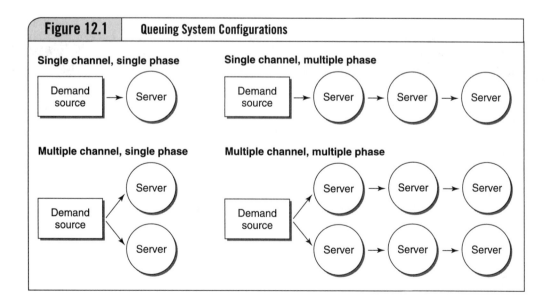

Figure 12.1   Queuing System Configurations

Single channel, single phase

Single channel, multiple phase

Multiple channel, single phase

Multiple channel, multiple phase

describe customer arrivals. Using the Poisson distribution, the probability of x customers arriving within some time period T is expressed as

$$P_{x(T)} = \frac{e^{-\lambda T}(\lambda T)^x}{x!}$$

where

λ = average customer arrivals in Time Period T
e = 2.71828 (natural log base), and
$x!$ = x factorial.

Example 12.4 illustrates the use of this formula.

If we assume the number of arrivals per time period is Poisson distributed with a mean arrival rate of λ, then the interarrival time (time between arrivals) is described by the negative exponential distribution, with a mean interarrival time of $1/\lambda$ (so if the mean arrival rate is ten per hour, then the mean interarrival time is 60 minutes/10 arrivals = 6 minutes/arrival).

Most queuing models assume that customers stay in the line once they join it. In other words, customers do not exhibit **balking**—refusing to join the queue once they see how long it is—or **reneging**—leaving the line prior to completing the service. While most people have done this at one time or another, queuing analysis becomes much more complex when these arrival characteristics are allowed.

The Queue Characteristics. Queuing models generally assume the length of a queue can grow to an infinite length, although for some situations this is not appropriate (for instance, people with tickets waiting to enter a concert). Queuing configurations can contain single or multiple lines (for example the single winding line at Wendy's versus the multiple lines at McDonald's). Another queue characteristic is the **queue discipline.** The discipline describes the order in which customers are served. The most common queue discipline is first come, first served, although other examples include most needy, first served (in emergency rooms) and most important, first served (in a VIP line at a nightclub).

The Service Characteristics. The service can be provided either by single server or by multiple servers who act in series or in parallel. Multiple servers acting in parallel is referred

---

EXAMPLE 12.4   Arrivals per hour at Jay's Quick Lube Shop

Jay's Quick Lube Shop can service an average of four cars per hour with a partial crew of three employees, and the owner Jay is interested in calculating the probability that he can handle all the customers on Saturdays with a partial crew, instead of his usual full crew of five. Given an average arrival rate of three customers per hour on Saturdays, he uses the Poisson distribution to calculate the probabilities for various customer arrivals:

Number of Arrivals, x	$P(x$ for $T = 1$ hr$) = \dfrac{e^{-3}3^x}{x!}$	Cumulative Probability
0	0.0498	0.0498
1	0.1494	0.1992
2	0.2240	0.4232
3	0.2240	0.6472
4	0.1680	0.8152

By summing the probabilities for each of the arrival levels, Jay figures that he can handle the demand per hour about 82 percent of the time. Conversely, he figures that about 18 percent of the time demand per hour will be greater than four customers, causing queues to develop.

to as a **multiple-channel queuing system.** Multiple servers acting in series is referred to as a **multiple-phase queuing system.** As already noted, Figure 12.1 shows the four most common queuing configurations.

The single-channel, single-phase configuration is the most basic. For standard distribution patterns of customer arrival and service times, the formulas to evaluate this type of system are very straightforward. An example is the one-person retailer. The single-channel, multiple-phase queuing system is the next configuration shown. For this system, customers all contact the same servers but receive more than one service and encounter a queue at each service. An example of this type of service is a dentist's office where customers are checked in by a receptionist, get their teeth cleaned by a dental hygienist, get their teeth X-rayed by a dental assistant, and then get a dental exam by a dentist. For each service, longer than average service times by the preceding customer can mean waiting line buildups within the system. The third configuration shown is the multiple-channel, single-phase system. Customers enter the system, receive one service from any one of a number of servers, then exit. Examples of this are discount store checkout stands or teller windows at a bank. These systems can have queues at each channel or one winding line where all channels receive customers from one line. The final configuration shown is the multiple-channel, multiple-phase queuing system. In this example, customers all receive more than one service in sequence from more than one set or channel of servers. An example here might be a large medical clinic where patients are checked in by one of several assistants, have their vital signs recorded by one of several nurses, and receive a medical consultation by one of several doctors.

Another characteristic of the service is the time required to complete each of the services provided. For each phase in the system, service times are described by a mean time and a probability distribution. Frequently, the negative exponential distribution is used to describe the randomness of service time distributions. To determine the probability that the service time t will be less than or equal to some specified time T, the following formula can be used:

$$P(t \le T) = 1 - e^{-\mu T}$$

where

$e = 2.71828$ (natural log base), and
μ = the average service rate.

Example 12.5 illustrates the use of this formula for calculating the probability of completing service within a specified time period.

EXAMPLE 12.5   Service times at Jay's Quick Lube Shop

Jay's shop can service an average of four customers per hour, or one customer every fifteen minutes, with a crew of three service personnel. The average customer arrival rate on Saturdays is three customers per hour, or one customer every twenty minutes. Jay is interested in calculating the probability that actual service time, t, will be within a specific time period, T, and he develops a chart showing these probabilities:

Actual Service Time	$P(t \le T \text{ hrs}) = 1 - e^{-4T}$
15 min (.25 hrs)	$1 - e^{-4(.25)} = 0.6321$
20 min (.33 hrs)	$1 - e^{-4(.33)} = 0.7329$
30 min (.5 hrs)	$1 - e^{-4(.5)} = 0.8647$
40 min (.67 hrs)	$1 - e^{-4(.67)} = 0.9314$
45 min (.75 hrs)	$1 - e^{-4(.75)} = 0.9502$

Thus, Jay thinks that almost 75 percent of the time he will service a customer in less than or equal to twenty minutes.

For single-channel systems, we can also use the average arrival and service rates to calculate average capacity utilization by dividing the customer arrival rate by the customer service rate. For example, if the arrival rate is three per hour and the service rate is four per hour, then the average capacity utilization is 75 percent; although, as can be seen in Example 12.4, there likely will be times when utilization for periods during the day approaches or exceeds 100 percent. Now that we have reviewed all of the important elements of queuing systems, let us look at several applications of the models.

Queuing System Applications

When using queuing models, managers collect arrival rate and service rate data by observing over time how many customers arrive for service and how many customers are served. Depending on the service, this may take a number of days or weeks to compile meaningful information. Following are applications of the single-channel, single-phase queuing model and the multiple-channel, single-phase queuing model. These are meant only to be introductory applications. Examples for the other queuing systems and applications can be quite complicated and are beyond the scope of this text. Interested readers are encouraged to examine management science or operations research texts for more advanced treatments of this topic. Several references are provided at the end of this chapter for this purpose.

The Single-Channel, Single-Phase Queuing Model Application. This is the most widely used and simplest of all queuing models. The assumptions in using the model follow:

- Customers come from an infinite population and are Poisson distributed over time.
- Customers are served in first-come, first-served sequence.
- No balking or reneging occurs.
- Service times are distributed according to the negative exponential distribution.
- The average service rate is greater than the average arrival rate.

The equations used to determine the operating characteristics for the single-channel, single-phase queuing model are:

λ = average arrival rate
μ = average service rate
ρ = average server utilization = λ/μ
L_s = expected number of customers in the system = $\lambda/(\mu - \lambda)$
L_q = expected number of customers in the queue = $\lambda^2/[\mu(\mu - \lambda)] = L_s - \lambda/\mu$
W_s = expected waiting time in the system = $1/(\mu - \lambda) = L_s/\lambda$
W_q = expected waiting time in the queue = $\lambda/[\mu(\mu - \lambda)] = L_q/\lambda$
P_n = probability that there are n units in the queuing system = $(\lambda/\mu)^n(1 - \lambda/\mu)$

The following example illustrates the calculation of operating characteristics for a service.

Mary Jane's Sewing Shop is a small neighborhood shop that can serve five customers per hour. For the past two weeks, she has kept track of the customer arrival rate; and the average has been four customers per hour. Mary Jane is interested in calculating a number of operating characteristics for her store. So she asks one of her customers, a business student at the local university, to help her. The student provides the following information:

λ = 4 customers per hour
μ = 5 customers per hour
ρ = 4/5 = 0.8 or 80 percent utilization
L_s = $\lambda/(\mu - \lambda)$ = 4/(5 − 4) = 4 customers
L_q = $L_s - \lambda/\mu$ = 4 − 4/5 = 3.2 customers

$$W_s = L_s/\lambda = 4/4 = 1 \text{ hour} = 60 \text{ minutes}$$
$$W_q = L_q/\lambda = 3.2/4 = 0.8 \text{ hours} = 48 \text{ minutes}$$

Mary Jane also wants to know how likely it will be that more than four customers will be in her shop at one time. So, her student-customer thinks about this and decides that the best way to calculate this is to determine the probabilities of zero, one, two, three, and four customers in the shop and then add these and subtract the sum from 1.0. So, she provides the following information:

$$\begin{aligned}
\text{For } n = 0 \quad & P_0 = (4/5)^0(1 - 4/5) = 0.200 \\
n = 1 \quad & P_1 = (4/5)^1(1 - 4/5) = 0.160 \\
n = 2 \quad & P_2 = (4/5)^2(1 - 4/5) = 0.128 \\
n = 3 \quad & P_3 = (4/5)^3(1 - 4/5) = 0.102 \\
n = 4 \quad & P_4 = (4/5)^4(1 - 4/5) = 0.082 \\
\text{For } n > 4 \quad & P_{n>4} = 1 - (P_0 + P_1 + P_2 + P_3 + P_4) \\
& = 1 - (.2 + .16 + .128 + .102 + .082) = 1 - .672 = 0.328
\end{aligned}$$

So Mary Jane can expect that there will be more than four people in her shop about 33 percent of the time.

Mary Jane can purchase a bar-code scanner with an automated cash register that will increase her service rate to ten customers per hour. She wants to know how this will change the average wait time in the queue and in the system. Her student-customer then shows her the very significant change this will make:

$$W_q = \lambda/[\mu(\mu - \lambda)] = 4/[10(6)] = 0.067 \text{ hrs} = 4 \text{ min}$$
$$W_s = 1/(\mu - \lambda) = 1/6 \text{ hr} = 10 \text{ min}$$

The Multiple-Channel, Single-Phase Queuing Model Application. All of the preceding assumptions still apply for the multiple-channel, single-phase model, except that the number of servers is now greater than 1 and the queuing system consists of multiple servers serving customers from multiple queues. The operating characteristics of this queuing system are:

λ = average arrival rate

$s\mu$ = average service rate, where s = number of service channels

ρ = average server utilization = $\lambda/s\mu$

P_0 = probability of zero customers in the system =

$$\dfrac{1}{\displaystyle\sum_{n=0}^{s-1} \dfrac{(\lambda/\mu)^n}{n!} + \dfrac{(\lambda/\mu)^s}{s!}\left[\dfrac{1}{1-(\lambda/s\mu)}\right]}, \text{ for } s\mu > \lambda$$

P_n = probability of n customers in the system = $P_0 \dfrac{(\lambda/\mu)^n}{n!}$, for $n \le s$

$\quad = P_0 \dfrac{(\lambda/\mu)^N}{s! \, s^{n-s}}$, for $n > s$

L_q = expected number of customers in the queue = $P_0 \dfrac{(\lambda/\mu)^s(\lambda/s\mu)}{s!(1-\lambda/s\mu)^2}$

L_s = expected number of customers in the system = $L_q + \lambda/\mu$

W_q = expected waiting time in the queue = L_q/λ

W_s = expected waiting time in the system = $W_q + 1/\mu$

Mary Jane's Sewing Shop has decided to hire a second worker and buy a second checkout stand with a cash register for the shop. Both Mary Jane and the second worker can serve five customers per hour, and the average arrival rate is four customers per hour. Mary Jane now wants to know all of the operating characteristics of the new configuration. Once again, her student-customer helps her out:

$$\rho = 4/10 = 0.4, \text{ or } 40 \text{ percent utilization}$$

$$P_0 = \cfrac{1}{\cfrac{(4/5)^0}{0!} + \cfrac{(4/5)^1}{1!} + \cfrac{(4/5)^2}{2!}\left(\cfrac{1}{1-(4/10)}\right)} = \cfrac{1}{1+0.8+0.32(1.67)} = \cfrac{1}{2.33} = 0.428$$

$$L_q = \cfrac{(4/5)^2(4/10)}{2(1-.4)^2}(0.428) = 0.152 \text{ customers}$$

$$L_s = 0.152 + 4/5 = 0.952 \text{ customers}$$
$$W_q = 0.152/4 = 0.038 \text{ hrs, or } 2.28 \text{ min}$$
$$W_s = 0.038 + 0.2 = 0.238 \text{ hrs, or } 14.28 \text{ min}$$

Note that because of the mean service time and distribution differences, having a two-channel, two-queue system serving customers with an average service rate of five customers per hour per channel is not the same as having a one-channel, one-queue system that serves at a rate of ten customers per hour.

Managing Perceived Waiting Times

The final topic of discussion in waiting line management is the management of perceived waiting times. Even though an admirable job may be done designing a queuing system, there are still times when the demand exceeds expectations as well as the queuing capacity (recall the earlier mention of the two-hour wait in a doctor's office). For these time periods, service firms must have other tools at their disposal to influence customers' perceived waiting times. In a very well-known paper on waiting lines, Maister presents some very interesting observations starting with his First and Second Laws of Service:[11]

> *Rule 1: Satisfaction = perception – expectation.*
> When customers expect a certain level of service and then perceive the service they actually receive to be higher, then they will be satisfied. Conversely, when customers' service expectations are higher than their perceptions once the service has been received, they are dissatisfied.

> *Rule 2: It is hard to play catch-up ball.*
> If customers start out happy when the service is first encountered, it is easy to keep them happy. If they start out disgruntled, it is almost impossible to turn things around.

Rule 1 is interesting in that expectations and perceptions are not necessarily based on reality. For example, customer expectations are formed based on previous experiences, marketing campaigns, signs, and the location; while customer perceptions can be impacted during the service encounter by a friendly server, mood music, visually pleasant surroundings, and a host of other things. A common practice coming out of Rule 1 is to "underpromise and overdeliver." Rule 2 is good for firms to remember when they are trying to improve service. Investments in service improvements might best be placed at the initial contact or early stages of the service to make sure the service encounter gets off to a good start.

Firms can manage both customer expectations and perceptions by observing and understanding how they are impacted when customers wait for service. Waiting time management techniques resulting from this understanding include keeping customers occupied, starting the service quickly, relieving customer anxiety, keeping customers informed, grouping customers together, and designing a fair waiting system.[12] Each of these is briefly discussed next.

Keep Customers Occupied. Firms must try to keep customers occupied while waiting in line. This is why magazines, televisions, and toys for children to play with are often seen in office waiting areas. Other attention keepers such as music, windows, mirrors, or menus to look at while waiting keep customers' minds off the passage of time. In amusement parks like Disneyland where long lines can be a big problem, customers waiting in line might get entertained by Mickey Mouse, a mime, or a juggler, for instance. All of these techniques try to lessen the perceived passage of time and impact customer satisfaction with the waiting experience.

Start the Service Quickly. Giving waiting customers menus, forms to complete, or drinks from the bar or seating them at a lounge all act to give customers the impression the service has started. When firms acknowledge receipt of an order via telephone, mail, or e-mail, this is another example of extending the beginning of the service. If organizations can design pre-process services that begin quickly once a customer encounters a queue, this will act to keep customers occupied and make long waits seem much shorter.

Relieve Customer Anxiety. Customer anxiety is created in many waiting situations—for example, when customers are afraid they have been forgotten, when they do not know how much longer it is going to take, when they do not know what to do, and when they fear they have entered the wrong line. Managers need to observe customers and learn what is likely to cause anxiety, then develop plans to relieve these concerns. These plans might include simply having employees reassure customers, announcing how much longer a caller on hold is likely to wait, announcing the lateness of a plane yet to arrive, or telling people they are in the wrong line.

Keep Customers Informed. Managers can derail customer anxieties before they even begin by giving customers information as their pre-process and in-process waits progress. When receptionists tell patients that their doctor was called to an emergency, when pilots tell passengers that the plane is waiting to be cleared for gate departure, when work crews place a sign on the road warning to expect delays during a period of time, and when amusement parks place signs in the queue telling customers the waiting time from that point in line, this information makes waiting customers much more patient because they know that a delay will occur and the reasons for the delay. Consequently, they are much more willing to stay in line, remain satisfied, and complete the service.

Group Customers Together. Customers would much rather wait (and commiserate) in waiting lines together than alone. Customers act to alleviate their own and others' anxieties, fears, and problems while waiting in line by talking to each other, sharing concerns, and helping out if possible. This sense of togetherness reduces perceived waiting times and may even add enjoyment to the waiting experience. Companies should think of ways to create or encourage group waiting instead of solo waiting such as closer seating, single queues instead of multiple queues, and use of numbered tickets so people do not have to stand in line.

Design a Fair Waiting System. "Taking cuts" in line is something that can cause significant irritation to others waiting in line, particularly if it is seen as unfair. In an emergency room, most people waiting will likely accept that others coming into the queue might be taken care of first (the queue discipline is most critical, first served); while taking cuts in a long queue at a retail store would result in grumbling and shouting among those waiting in line. Whenever the queue discipline is something other than first come, first served, managers need to be aware of the potential problems this causes and take steps to reduce the feeling of unfairness or segment customers such that the queue discipline is not obvious. Examples include physically separating customers such as in first-class versus economy class seating on airplanes, taking names and group sizes at a restaurant while concealing the list, and putting up signs like "six items or less" at checkout stands. In many cases, customers will understand and accept the reasons for using a particular queue discipline if they are informed of it.

This concludes the discussion of the management of waiting times. The next concern of service response logistics is the management of distribution channels.

Table 12.2	Service Distribution Channels
Service	**Distribution Channel**
Retail store	• Free standing • Mall • Internet • Mail order
Bank	• Main/headquarters • Free standing branches • Sites in malls • Sites in retail locations • ATMs • Internet • Telephone
Auto repair business	• Free standing • Attached to retailer (Wal-Mart) • Franchised outlets • Mobile repair van
University/college	• Public • Private • Specialized/general • Traditional/adult education • Main campus • Branches • Internet • Day/evening • Television

Managing Distribution Channels

This segment of service response logistics describes several distribution channels and strategies a service can use to deliver its services and products to customers. Table 12.2 lists a number of distribution alternatives for a retail store, a bank, an auto repair facility, and a university. Many of these distribution alternatives are the traditional ones everyone is used to seeing; however, services today are experimenting with other nontraditional distribution channels as customer preferences and habits change, demographics change, technology changes, and competition changes.

Some distribution channels have revolutionized the way services do business. For instance, ATMs, debit cards, and the Internet have completely changed the financial services industry; many customers never set foot inside a bank or stockbroker's office any longer. Without these distribution channels available to customers, though, financial service companies could no longer compete. Today, many people have come to expect these things.

Other distribution strategies have arisen because new technologies have made them possible and because customers were asking for them. In the grocery industry, big U.S. grocery chains like Albertson's are experimenting with home delivery of groceries ordered from the Internet. Use of the Internet is undoubtedly the most significant change in distribution channel strategy in the past twenty or thirty years. Several of the distribution channel alternatives and issues facing services today are discussed next.

Eatertainment, Entertailing, and Edutainment

As service distribution concepts change, new words have been coined to describe these concepts. **Eatertainment** is the combination of restaurant and entertainment elements. Many of these services incorporate elements of local culture or history into their design themes and offer the capabilities of eating, drinking, entertainment, and shopping all in one venue. Sports-themed restaurants such as Champs and the ESPN Zone, the jungle-themed restaurant Rainforest Café, and the kids-themed restaurant Chuck E. Cheese's are all examples of eatertainment facilities.

e-BUSINESS CONNECTION
HOWSTUFFWORKS.COM

HowStuffWorks.com explains the world from the inside out. Millions of people have described HowStuffWorks content as reliable, accurate, and entertaining. Originally founded as a Web site for curious people, the award-winning Web site now offers clear and fascinating content through various media channels to millions of visitors every month. On its Web site, viewers can click on computer stuff, auto stuff, electronics stuff, science stuff, home stuff, entertainment stuff, money stuff, and travel stuff to find out how things work in each of the categories.

Some of the other HowStuffWorks offerings include a series of books that extends How-StuffWorks' mission of delivering straightforward information about the magic behind everyday items. Four books have been published to date: *How Stuff Works, How Much Does the Earth Weigh?, More How Stuff Works,* and *What If . . . ?* There is also a HowStuffWorks newspaper feature that examines one topic per week—from MP3 players to wiretapping to hybrid cars. HowStuffWorks Video creates, produces, and directs multiple television products throughout the year. The mission of the project is to leverage the brand to create both long- and short-form video. Some of the projects include sixty-second vignettes created for local news broadcasts, a home video series, and a thirty-minute children's television program.[13]

Entertailing refers to retail locations with entertainment elements. Many shopping malls are designed today to offer entertainment such as ice skating, rock climbing, and amusement park rides. Metreon in San Francisco is a high-tech electronics-themed complex with an IMAX theater, virtual reality games, and a 3-D facility. Toy stores like Toys "R" Us are designed around centers within the stores to allow customers to try out and play with toys. Entertailing developments are designed to hold customers longer than the typical forty-five minutes, perhaps up to three or four hours. Owners are finding that these customers spend almost twice as much as the typical retail customer on merchandise and services.

Museums, parks, and a host of service providers are getting into the act with **edutainment** or infotainment to attract more customers and increase revenues. Edutainment combines learning with entertainment to appeal to customers looking for substance along with play. In the United States, state and national park employees entertain and inform tourists with indigenous animal lectures and shows or campfire stories in the evenings. Theme parks such as Legoland in San Diego offer attractions that combine fun and education aimed at the two- to twelve-year-old audience. Television shows like Sesame Street and Mr. Rogers and software aimed at teaching math and foreign languages in an engaging way, along with Web sites like HowStuffWorks.com and Learn2.com also fall into this category.

Franchising

Franchising allows services to expand quickly into dispersed geographic markets, to protect existing markets, and to build market share. When the owners have limited financial resources, franchising is a good strategy for expansion. Franchisees are required to invest some of their own capital, while paying a small percentage of sales to the franchiser in return for the brand name, start-up help, advertising, training, and assistance in meeting specific operating standards. Many services such as fast-food restaurants, accounting and tax businesses, auto rental agencies, beauty salons, clothing stores, ice cream shops, motels, and many other businesses use franchising as a strategy for growing and competing.

Control problems are one of the biggest issues in franchising. Franchisors must periodically perform financial and quality audits on the franchisees along with making frequent visits to facilities to assure that franchisees are continuing to comply with operating standards of the company.

International Expansion

The search for a larger market has driven services to expand globally. Since the world today has become essentially borderless due to the Internet and other communication mediums and the expansion that has already taken place, services today compete in a global economy.

A number of issues face firms today when they consider global expansion. At least initially, expanding overseas most likely means operating with partners who are familiar with the region's markets, suppliers, infrastructure, government regulations, and customers. For instance, when McDonald's opened its first restaurant in Moscow, an entire supply structure had to be built. McDonald's had to manufacture many of the products required by the restaurant as well as train farmers to produce the type and quality of crops needed to run the business. Exposure to foreign currency exchange rate fluctuations can also pose a problem for firms, requiring them to use financial hedging strategies to reduce exchange rate risk. Firms can also operate in several different countries to offset currency problems, since economic downturns in one country can be offset by positive economic conditions in other countries.

Language barriers, cultural problems, and the varying needs of different regional cultures also must be addressed when expanding. Local management must be allowed to vary services and their accompanying products to suit local tastes. Restaurants, for instance, typically add local favorites to menus to increase acceptability; and companies must become familiar with language translations in order to properly change the wording on signs and advertisements to increase readability and understanding. The Coca-Cola name in China was initially read as "Ke-Kou-Ke-La" meaning "bite the wax tadpole" or "female horse stuffed with wax," depending on the dialect. Coke then studied 40,000 characters to find the phonetic equivalent "Ko-Kou-Ko-Le," which translates into "happiness in the mouth."

Foreign governments and existing laws have played a large role in restricting the international growth of services. Many governments have banned the sale of insurance and financial products by foreign firms, give preferential treatment to local services, restrict the flow of information, create large delays in the processing of licensing agreements, and pass laws that make it difficult for foreign services to operate. In many Middle Eastern countries for instance, charging interest on loans is not allowable by the Muslim faith and is therefore illegal. Thus, banks must find other ways to provide income, such as charging fees for a wide range of services.

Internet Distribution Strategies

Internet-based "dot com" companies exploded on the scene during the latter part of the 1990s, pushing the NASDAQ to historic highs and promising to enrich anyone with an idea, good or bad, who could create a Web site to generate revenues on the Internet. E-commerce was touted as the coming trillion dollar revolution in retailing; but, as it turned out, many of the dot com companies of the 2000 time period are gone today. Still, Internet retailing is growing faster than traditional retailing. By the end of 2002, the e-commerce sector was accounting for over $11 billion per quarter in U.S. retail sales, or about 1.3 percent of total U.S. retail sales, and was growing at about a 30 percent per year rate, which far exceeds the 3 percent per year growth rate in overall retail sales.[14]

One of the primary advantages of the Internet is its ability to offer convenient sources of real-time information, integration, feedback, and comparison shopping. Individual consumers can use it to look for jobs, communicate with businesses, find the nearest movie the-

e-BUSINESS CONNECTION
BESTBUY.COM

You might have seen the television commercial in which a couple returns home from a trip to find that their dog has ordered an entertainment center from BestBuy.com. They pack it up and return it to a retail store without any hassles. It seems simple enough, but not many retailers have been able to integrate their physical and on-line channels. For Best Buy Co., Inc., the secret to a seamless customer interface is its robust system of e-business and supply chain management tools.

When the company first started its on-line venture, it was a separate company with its own buying organization. Now, as it integrates the dot com into the regular retail model, it must integrate the buying procedures to make the whole process more cost-effective and get product to customers any way they want it. The dot-com group started as a separate company and developed a business model that survived as many other dot coms folded, so there is a pride of ownership issue. Thus, getting the two groups together has been a challenge.

Recently, the company switched to a new value-added network (VAN) provider to process its electronic data interchange (EDI) transactions. That way, the suppliers do not need to have EDI capabilities. Best Buy sends data to the third-party service, and they convert it to HTML; so the vendor can get a purchase order with just a PC and a browser. That brought Best Buy up to almost 100 percent EDI purchase volume. The company currently uses fourteen different EDI documents with approximately 600 different trading partners, including carriers. Best Buy is also implementing an enterprise order management system to streamline its fulfillment model and provide cross-channel customer management capabilities so that order information can be shared across all channels.

Best Buy now has the systems in place to achieve seamless supply chain connectivity so that Best Buy and its suppliers can all view the same data at the same time, making on-line collaboration and quick changes a reality. Ideally, the suppliers will not be selling to Best Buy but to Best Buy's customers through the channel provided by Best Buy.[15]

ater, pay bills, shop, and barter goods—and they can do all this in the privacy of their homes. Businesses use the Internet to communicate, find and then purchase items from suppliers, and sell or provide goods and services to individual consumers and other businesses. Today, most businesses either have a Web site or are thinking about building one. Many retailers today sell products exclusively over the Internet (a *pure strategy*), while others use it as a supplemental distribution channel (a *mixed strategy*).

The pure Internet strategy can have several distinct advantages over traditional brick-and-mortar services. They can become more centralized reducing labor, capital, and inventory costs, while using the Internet to decentralize their marketing efforts to reach a vastly distributed audience of business or individual consumers. Amazon.com falls into this category. Today, though, the mixed strategy of combining traditional retailing with Internet retailing seems to be emerging as the stronger business model. Firms such as J.C. Penney sell items in retail outlets and also sell items from Internet and store catalogs. Customers can either pick up their purchases at the store or have them delivered. Southwest Airlines was the first airline to establish a home page on the Internet. By late 2002, approximately 50 percent of Southwest's passenger revenue was generated by on-line bookings via its Web site, southwest.com.

Developing good customer service capabilities can be challenging, though. J. C. Penney, for instance, must be able to perform customer service functions over the Internet, in person, and via mail and telephone. Companies are addressing this problem by developing **customer contact centers.** These centers integrate their Web site and their traditional call center to offer 24/7 support where customers and potential customers can contact the firm and each other using telephone, e-mail, chat rooms, and e-bulletin boards. These contact centers allow firms to serve a large number of geographically diverse customers with a relatively small number of customer service agents.

Just as services have to be concerned with managing service capacity and waiting lines, firms must also invest management efforts in designing the necessary distribution channels to compete in today's marketplaces. The final element of the service response logistics discussion impacts all elements of the service itself and the way it is distributed, and that is the management of service quality. Although this topic was initially addressed in Chapter 8, the quality management topics geared strictly toward services need further discussion, which is presented here.

Managing Service Quality

For services, quality occurs during the service delivery process and typically involves an interaction between a customer and a service employee. Customer satisfaction with the service depends not only on the ability of the firm to deliver what customers want but on the customers' perceptions of the quality of the service. When customer expectations are met or exceeded, the service is deemed to possess high quality; and when expectations are not met, the perception of quality is poor. In a recent survey of hundreds of consumers, Brady and Cronin found that when consumers perceived that firms were customer-oriented, their satisfaction and perceptions of service quality were also higher.[16] Thus, service quality is highly dependent upon the ability of the firm's employees and service systems to satisfy customers and on the varying expectations of the customers themselves. Because of this variable nature of customer expectations, services must continually be monitoring their service delivery systems using the tools described in Chapter 8 while concurrently observing, communicating with, and surveying customers to adequately assess and improve quality.

The Dimensions of Service Quality

Some of the more oft-quoted studies of service quality are those done by Drs. Parasuraman, Zeithaml, and Berry.[17] Studying a number of different services, they identified five dimensions of service quality generally used by customers: reliability, responsiveness, assurance, empathy, and tangibles. Reliability was consistently reported in their study as the most important quality dimension.

- *Reliability:* Consistently performing the service correctly and dependably.
- *Responsiveness:* Providing the service promptly and in a timely manner.
- *Assurance:* Using knowledgeable, competent, courteous employees who convey trust and confidence to customers.
- *Empathy:* Providing caring and individual attention to customers.
- *Tangibles:* The physical characteristics of the service including the facilities, the servers, equipment, and other customers.

Using their survey, the researchers were able to identify any differences occurring between customer expectations in the five dimensions and customer perceptions of what was actually received during a service encounter. These differences were referred to as service quality "gaps" and can be used to highlight areas in need of improvement for the service.

Organizations can develop criteria relating to the five service quality dimensions and then collect data using customer comment cards or mailed surveys on customer satisfaction with

Table 12.3	Examples of Service Quality Criteria
Service Quality Dimension	**Criteria**
Reliability	• Billing accuracy • Order accuracy • On-time completion • Promises kept
Responsiveness	• On-time appointment • Timely call-back • Timely confirmation of order
Assurance	• Skills of employees • Training provided to employees • Honesty of employees • Reputation of firm
Empathy	• Customized service capabilities • Customer recognition • Degree of server-customer contact • Knowledge of the customer
Tangibles	• Appearance of the employees • Appearance of the facility • Appearance of customers • Equipment and tools used

each of the quality dimensions to measure service quality performance. Table 12.3 presents criteria that might be used in each of the five quality dimensions. When weaknesses or gaps are encountered in any of the performance criteria, managers can institute improvements in the areas indicated.

World-class service companies realize they must get to know their customers, and they invest considerable time and effort gathering information about their customers' needs and expectations. This information is then used to design services and delivery systems that satisfy customers, capture market share, and create profits for the firm. These organizations understand that one of the most important elements affecting long-term competitiveness and profits is the quality of their products and services relative to their competitors.

Recovering from Poor Service Quality

Undoubtedly, from time to time, occasions arise when even the best organization's products and services do not meet a customer's expectations. In most cases, quickly recovering from these service failures can keep customers loyal and coming back and may even serve as good word-of-mouth advertising for the firm as customers pass on their stories of good service recoveries. Most important, when service failures occur, firms must be able to recover quickly and forcefully to satisfy customers. This involves empowering front-line service personnel to identify problems and then provide solutions quickly and in an empathetic way.

Good services offer guarantees to their customers and empower employees to provide quick and meaningful solutions when customers invoke the guarantee. In many cases, solutions to guarantee problems are designed into the process and become part of the service firm's marketing efforts. Blockbuster's guarantee of movie availability or it is free the next time a customer visits and Wal-Mart's lowest-price guarantee or customers receive the price difference are examples of this. To be effective, guarantees should be unconditional, easy to understand, and easy to implement.

Firms that anticipate where service failures can occur, develop recovery procedures, train employees in these procedures, and then empower employees to remedy customer problems can ensure that they have the best service recovery system possible.

Summary

Services constitute a large and growing segment of the world economy. Managing the supply chains of services is thus becoming an important part of an overall competitive strategy for services. Since service customers are most often the final consumers of the services provided, successfully managing service encounters involves managing productive capacity, managing waiting lines, managing distribution channels, and managing service quality. These four concerns are the foundations of service response logistics and were the primary focus of this chapter.

Service companies must accurately forecast demand, design capacity to adequately meet demand, employ waiting line systems to serve customers as quickly and efficiently as possible, utilize distribution systems to best serve the firms' customers, and then take steps to assure service quality and customer satisfaction throughout the service process. Provided that managers have selected a good location; designed an effective layout; hired, trained, and properly scheduled service personnel; and then employed effective service response logistics strategies, firms and their supply chains should be able to maintain competitiveness, market share, and profitability.

Key Terms

balking, 380

capacity utilization, 374

chase-demand strategy, 375

customer contact centers, 390

demand management, 374

demand source, 379

differentiation strategy, 366

distribution channels, 374

eatertainment, 386

edutainment, 387

entertailing, 387

facilitating products, 373

focus strategy, 367

level-demand strategy, 375

multiple-channel queuing system, 381

multiple-factor productivity, 365

multiple-phase queuing system, 381

Poisson distribution, 379

pure services, 363

queue discipline, 380

queue management, 375

reneging, 380

service capacity, 374

service quality, 374

single-factor productivity, 365

state utility, 364

waiting time, 374

Discussion Questions

1. Why is the service sector in the United States growing so much more rapidly than the manufacturing sector?
2. Describe the primary differences between goods and service firms.
3. Give an example of a single-factor productivity measure and an example of a multiple-factor productivity measure. How can you improve productivity?
4. What are the primary issues in successfully managing global services?
5. What are the three generic strategies that services use to compete? Give examples.
6. Provide some examples of front-of-the-house and back-of-the-house service operations.

7. Do services have to worry about inventories? Explain.

8. How does supply chain management differ between services and manufacturing companies?

9. What are the four concerns of service response logistics?

10. Define service capacity and explain why you would want somewhat more capacity than needed.

11. Define capacity utilization. What is an ideal utilization?

12. Describe how you would use a level- and a chase-demand capacity utilization strategy.

13. How do cross-training employees and using customers increase capacity?

14. Describe some demand management techniques that are used when demand exceeds capacity and when capacity exceeds demand.

15. How can firms make use of excess capacity?

16. Define the terms *balking* and *reneging.*

17. Explain and give examples of Maister's first and second Laws of Service.

18. If you have designed an effective queuing system, why is it still necessary to practice waiting time management?

19. What are the distribution channel alternatives for a weather service? A souvenir shop? A marriage counselor?

20. Describe the important issues in the international expansion of services.

21. How is service quality related to customer service?

22. Describe the five dimensions of service quality for a dentist's office, how performance in these dimensions might be measured, and how recoveries might be handled for failures in each of the service quality dimensions.

Internet Questions

1. Define and provide some examples that you have found from the Internet, for eatertainment, entertailing, and edutainment.

2. Describe and give examples of a pure Internet distribution strategy and a mixed Internet distribution strategy. Find your examples on the Internet.

Spreadsheet Problems

1. For the following office layout and the accompanying trip and distance matrices, determine the total distance traveled per day. Find another layout that results in a lower distance traveled per day.

Management (1)	Production (2)	Engineering (3)	Reception (4)

Files (5)	Accounting (6)	Purchasing (7)	Sales (8)

Interdepartmental Trips per Day

	(2)	(3)	(4)	(5)	(6)	(7)	(8)
(1)	6	5	2	1	7	6	15
(2)		12	4	5	2	10	5
(3)			2	9	2	10	8
(4)				18	12	4	2
(5)					0	0	0
(6)						6	14
(7)							6

Distances between Departments (Meters)

	(2)	(3)	(4)	(5)	(6)	(7)	(8)
(1)	15	30	45	10	20	35	50
(2)		15	30	20	10	20	35
(3)			15	40	20	10	20
(4)				60	50	30	10
(5)					10	30	50
(6)						20	40
(7)							20

2. For the office layout shown in Question 1, determine the closeness desirability rating using the following rating table. Treat the hallway as if it does not exist (i.e., the Production and Accounting Departments touch each other). Can you find a more desirable layout? How could you use both the distance traveled and the closeness desirability in assessing the layout alternatives?

Closeness Desirability Rating between Departments

	(2)	(3)	(4)	(5)	(6)	(7)	(8)
1)	2	2	−1	0	1	3	3
(2)		3	0	0	0	3	1
(3)			0	2	0	2	3
(4)				3	1	2	2
(5)					2	2	1
(6)						0	2
(7)							1

3. Marcia's Cat Care needs help in her grooming business as shown in the following table for the five-day workweek. Determine a full- and part-time work schedule for the business using the fewest number of workers.

	Monday	Tuesday	Wednesday	Thursday	Friday
Workers Required	2	3	3	4	5

4. Given an average service rate of twelve customers per hour, what is the probability the business can handle all the customers when the average arrival rate is ten customers per hour? Use the Poisson distribution to calculate the probabilities for various customer arrivals.

5. With an average service rate of twelve customers per hour and an average customer arrival rate of ten customers per hour, calculate the probability that actual service time will be less than or equal to six minutes.

6. Stan can handle about ten customers per hour at his one-person comic book store. The customer arrival rate averages about six customers per hour. Stan is interested in knowing the operating characteristics of his single-channel, single-phase queuing system.

7. How would Stan's queuing system operating characteristics change for Problem 6 if he added another cashier and increased his service rate to twenty customers per hour?

References

Anderson, D., D. Sweeney, and T. Williams. *An Introduction to Management Science.* Mason, Ohio: South-Western, 2003.

Davis, M., N. Aquilano, and R. Chase. *Fundamentals of Operations Management.* New York: McGraw-Hill, 1999.

Drazen, E., R. Moll, and M. Roetter. *Logistics in Service Industries.* Oak Brook, Ill.: Council of Logistics Management, 1991.

Fitzsimmons, J., and M. Fitzsimmons. *Service Management for Competitive Advantage.* New York: McGraw-Hill, 1994.

Heizer, B., and B. Render. *Principles of Operations Management.* Upper Saddle River, N. J.: Prentice-Hall, 2001.

Markland, R., S. Vickery, and R. Davis. *Operations Management.* Mason, Ohio: South-Western, 1998.

Metters, R., K. King-Metters, and M. Pullman. *Successful Service Operations Management.* Mason, Ohio: South-Western, 2003.

Rodriquez, C. *International Management: A Cultural Approach.* Mason, Ohio: South-Western, 2001.

Taha, H. A. *Operations Research An Introduction.* Upper Saddle River, N.J.: Prentice-Hall, 2003.

Taylor, B. *Introduction to Management Science.* Upper Saddle River, N. J.: Prentice-Hall, 2002.

Notes

1. A. Bednarz, "The Customer Is King," *Network World* 19, no. 48 (2002): 65–66.
2. J. Matsumoto, "The Interactive Kitchen," *Restaurants and Institutions* 112, no. 8 (2002): 99–102. Reprinted with permission from *Restaurants and Institutions.* Copyright © Reed Information, a division of Reed Elsevier, Inc.
3. S. Konicki, "Sylvania Sees the Light in Logistics," *Information Week* (9 July 2001): 49.
4. U.S. Department of Labor, Bureau of Labor Statistics Data; available from http://www.bls.gov
5. M. Porter, *Competitive Strategy: Techniques for Analyzing Industries and Competitors* (New York: The Free Press, 1980).
6. Southwest Airlines Web site information; available from http:/www.iflyswa.com/about_swa/press/factsheet.html
7. G. J. Hoeg, "Getting Together to Offer More," *Best's Review* 102, no. 8 (2001): 106–108.
8. Adapted from N. Emmons, "Flexible, $750m Arena Likely One of a Kind," *Amusement Business* 113, no. 13 (2001): 9–10. Reprint permission granted by *Amusement Business.*
9. L. L. Sowinski, "Navigating the Leading Ocean Carriers," *World Trade* 14, no. 8 (2001): 46 47.
10. E. L. Drazen, R. E. Moll, and M. F. Roetter, *Logistics in Service Industries* (Oak Brook, Ill.: Council of Logistics Management, 1991), 34.
11. D. Maister, "The Psychology of Waiting Lines," *The Service Encounter,* ed. J. A. Czepiel, M. R. Solomon, and C. F. Surprenant (Lexington, Mass.: D. C. Heath & Co., 1985).
12. Ibid.
13. Adapted from the How Stuff Works Web site; available from http://www.howstuffworks.com Reprinted with permission.
14. e-Commerce and retail sales figures were obtained from the U.S. Census Bureau's Web site; available from http://www.census.gov
15. Adapted from B. Albright, "Best Buy's Retail Secret," *Frontline Solutions* 3 no. 12 (2002): 10. Reprinted with permission from *Frontline Solutions. Frontline Solutions* is a publication of Advanstar Communications Inc. All rights reserved.
16. M. K. Brady, and J. J. Cronin Jr., "Customer Orientation: Effects on Customer Service Perceptions and Outcome Behaviors," *Journal of Service Research* 3, no. 3 (2001): 241–51.
17. See, for instance, A. Parasuraman, V. A. Zeithaml, and L. L. Berry, "SERVQUAL: A Multiple-Item Scale for Measuring Consumer Perceptions of Service Quality," *Journal of Retailing* 64, no. 1 (1988): 12–40; A. Parasuraman, V. A. Zeithaml, and L. L. Berry, "Conceptual Model of Service Quality and Its Implications for Future Research," *Journal of Marketing* 49 (Fall 1985): 41–50.

Case Study 12
Dr. Martin's Office
Seeking a Referral

The professor was not feeling well. In fact, on that Tuesday afternoon, he had felt tired and generally "down" physically. During the fifteen-minute drive home from work, he developed slight nausea and gastric discomfort. When he reached home, he headed for the bathroom. For the next several hours, he experienced severe diarrhea and recurring waves of nausea and vomiting. After a few hours, the nausea had subsided somewhat, but the gastric distress persisted through most of what proved to be a long night.

On the following morning, the professor called the office of his primary care physician, Dr. Martin. Dr. Martin's nurse, Betty, came on the line. The professor detailed his physical problems of the previous night. "Betty, the nausea is pretty much gone, but the gastric discomfort is quite severe. I really feel that I need to see a doctor." Betty replied, "Dr. Martin is booked solid all day, so it would be hard to see him."

"Betty," the professor said, "I really feel that I need to see a doctor. Suppose I go to the HealthCheck Clinic. It's close by, and I've always gotten good service there. Could the doctor refer me so that the university's insurance would cover the visit?"

Betty's voice took on a doubtful and clinical tone. "The doctor would not refer you to the clinic. However, I can ask him to prescribe something for the diarrhea. We'll call your pharmacy and place the prescription."

Slightly perturbed, the professor said, "But I don't understand. My wife and I have always gotten good service at HealthCheck. Why can't he refer me there?"

Betty's clinical tone sharpened. "The doctor would not refer you to the clinic. The medicine should help you, though. I will call it in to the pharmacy." It was obvious that it would do little good to continue the conversation; and, as he was getting a little upset by the tone that Betty used, the professor said, "Thank you," and hung up. "Thanks for nothing," he thought to himself.

Collecting Some Information

As the professor thought about the conversation, he got angrier. He did not like being told that he could not choose his own health provider, given that his primary care provider was not available. Besides, HealthCheck was much less expensive than the hospital emergency room. He decided to call the Employee Benefits Office at the university to get their views on the episode. His call was taken by Wendy, the assistant director of staff benefits.

The professor related the background of the situation to Wendy and described the results of the call to Dr. Martin's office. Wendy expressed surprise that a doctor who was an approved primary provider with the university's health plan would refuse to approve someone going to HealthCheck if the doctor could not see the patient. "If you can hold on a minute, I'll ask Candy about it," she said.

Candy was the director of the Employee Benefits Office. After a minute Wendy came back on the phone. "Candy said she was surprised and distressed that Dr. Martin would not refer

Source: Reprinted with permission from Jeffrey S. Harper, Ph.D., CFE, and William H. Moates, Ph.D., both of The School of Business, Indiana State University, Terre Haute, Indiana.

you to HealthCheck, especially since you requested this. The idea behind the recent changes in the university's health-care plan was to cut costs, and this action was certainly cheaper than the hospital's emergency room. After all, the university's plan is self-insured. The faculty and staff ultimately pay all the bills. Professor, Candy said that we could call the doctor's office if you wanted us to."

The professor replied, "No, that's not necessary at this point. I can call them myself if I need to. I'll go ahead and get the medicine that Martin prescribed and take it from there. If I need your help, I'll call." Wendy agreed, wished the professor well, and hung up.

The professor drove to the pharmacy that he used and picked up his medicine. The charge was just over $10. Returning home, he took a pill and went to bed. He did not go to work that day.

Trying Again

On Thursday, the professor felt somewhat better and the diarrhea was more under control. However, the stomach discomfort continued to be a pronounced problem. He went to work that morning. By early afternoon, however, he gave up trying to work and went home. He then called Dr. Martin's office. When Betty came on the phone, the professor explained his ongoing problem, which seemed to be getting worse. "Could the doctor see me this afternoon, Betty?" the professor asked.

"Dr. Martin is not in the office this afternoon," Betty said. The professor expressed his disappointment. Then, he repeated his earlier request to be examined by one of the other doctors in the office. Betty replied, "The doctor would not refer you another doctor for this problem." The professor replied, "But you told me yesterday that he was booked solid and I couldn't see him. Furthermore, he would not refer me to HealthCheck." Betty responded, "We would have had to have you come in yesterday and wait until we could work you in to see him."

The professor continued, "So you're telling me that he is not in the office and can't see me, yet he wouldn't refer me to another doctor or to HealthCheck. Betty, I really feel that I need to see a doctor. What would he want me to do?"

"I believe he would want you to go to the emergency room," Betty stated. The professor said in a stunned voice, "The emergency room? Why not HealthCheck? He's on the staff of the hospital, which owns HealthCheck."

"I don't think he would want you to go there," she replied.

The professor was angry and stated that he found this suggestion to be decidedly unhelpful. "Thanks for your time," he stated and hung up the telephone in disgust once again.

Taking Some Action

"To heck with this," the professor growled to himself. He stalked out of the house, got in his car, and drove the two miles to the HealthCheck clinic. Entering the facility, he explained to the receptionist the reason for his visit. She asked him to sit down in the lobby.

Almost as quickly as he sat down, a nurse called him to enter the treatment area and led him to an examination room. "What seems to be the problem?" she asked as she took his blood pressure.

The professor reviewed his experience of the last two days. "Dr. Martin is my primary care physician. When he couldn't see me, he did not want to refer me to HealthCheck. I don't understand that," he said.

The attendant looked quite surprised. "I don't understand that, either," she agreed. "You just lie down. Someone will be right in to look at you."

Within two minutes, a nurse practitioner named Hilda entered the room. She briefly explained her role in the medical hierarchy. He had seen her before and had no problem with having her conduct the exam. After looking at the professor's chart, she used a stethoscope to listen to his stomach. "Oh my," she exclaimed. "Your stomach is just gurgling." She checked a few other visible symptoms before speaking again. Then she said, "I'm going to have the nurse take a blood sample to check for bacteria or viruses."

The professor asked, "Will you have to send the sample out?"

"No," Hilda replied. "We have the equipment right here."

The nurse returned to the examination room to draw blood. Then the professor was left alone for about twenty-five minutes. Hilda then returned with the nurse. "It's a virus," she proclaimed, shaking her head. "There's nothing to do but wait it out, although it is likely close to running its course. I want to check for internal bleeding to be sure that's not a problem, though."

After checking him, Hilda told the professor that there was no sign of internal bleeding. "I'm going to prescribe some medicine for you. I want you to go home and stay there for seventy-two hours. Do not go to work tomorrow; you're contagious."

The professor gratefully thanked Hilda and the nurse. He drove home and called his wife to ask her to stop by the pharmacy and pick up his medicine on her way home from work. She came home in about an hour, and the professor immediately took the recommended dosage. Within an hour there was noticeable improvement in his condition, and within two hours he felt almost normal. He slept well that night.

A Final Discussion with Betty

By late Friday morning, the professor felt fine. His stomach problems seemed to be a thing of the past. However, he was still wondering why Dr. Martin would not send him to HealthCheck. He called Dr. Martin's office and asked to speak to Betty. When she came on the line, he told her that on the previous day he had decided to go to HealthCheck rather than to the emergency room.

"The nurse practitioner on duty examined me and took a blood sample. She determined that the problem was viral in nature and prescribed medicine. The medicine did the trick, and my stomach feels much better this morning." Betty said she was glad that he was feeling better.

The professor continued. "I'm still curious about one thing, however. Given the satisfactory treatment I received last night and the fact that the doctor is on staff at the hospital, which owns HealthCheck, why was he so unwilling to refer me to that clinic?"

Betty replied, "The doctor just didn't feel that you would get the best care there." The professor asked, "Then I suppose he won't refer me there so my insurance will pick up the bill?" Betty sounded skeptical. "I will ask him about it again, but I doubt he will approve it."

Thanking her for her time, the professor hung up. Next he called Wendy in the Staff Benefits Office at the University. He brought her up to date on his experience of the last couple of days. He then asked her for her thoughts on the situation.

"I'm really surprised that he wanted you to go to the emergency room," she said. "That is the kind of thing we hoped to avoid when we adopted the primary care plan. I would think Dr. Martin would know this since he is an approved provider. I'm sorry you had so much trouble, and I will tell Candy what happened."

The professor thanked Wendy and hung up the phone. He reflected on the events that had transpired over the last few days with mixed emotions. It seemed that he had been caught between the university's health-care plan and Dr. Martin's office and staff. He wondered about the consistency between the goals of each of the parties in monitoring and protecting his health. He also wondered how much of the cost of his treatment would come out of his own pocket.

Questions for Discussion

1. Who is the customer in this case?

2. Describe the supply chain of this health-care delivery system. Also, identify the roles of the primary players.

3. Knowing who the customer is and considering present customer service levels, what are the implications for supply chain redesign and for optimization of good customer service while keeping costs in check?

4. Discuss the ethical issues involved in the doctor's refusal of referral to the HealthCheck clinic.

Case Study 13
Mass Customization at the Gravataí Automotive Industrial Complex

Introduction

The meeting was adjourned, announced Roberto Tinoco, general director of the General Motors Brazil Gravataí (GMBG) plant, in the afternoon of November 2, 2001. The latest quarter had been the best in the company's history. The executive board was glad that 100,000 Chevrolet Celta units were produced in such a short period of time, but none of the members present was completely satisfied. Tinoco had indicated during the previous meeting the need to improve the current business model. In closing, he said, "The automotive industry's major challenge has always been finding a way to deliver a car assembled as per the consumer's own specifications in the shortest possible period of time, at a cost lower than that of the traditional make-to-stock mass-production system. For years we've been seeking the answer to this and still haven't found it. We are finally close to accomplishing this historic feat with the consolidation of the Gravataí Industrial Complex experiment, but we are not quite there yet. Our model demands improvement, and it is up to us to find a final answer. I will anxiously await suggestions to be submitted by our next meeting."

Leading up to that moment had not been easy. The Gravataí plant started operations in mid-July 2000, an event that caught the eye of professionals and academia both in Brazil and abroad. The core objective was to sell cars made-to-order for final consumers. The Gravataí plant brought about a true revolution in how cars are made, from its concept of the direct-sale model through its production management system.

Worldwide, GM has divided into small operations, a constellation of plants focused on market niches. This is the case with GMBG, charged with making compact cars for an entry-level South American market. Despite the fact that the Brazilian operation answers for less than 5 percent of GM's global business, it has gained strategic importance and has become an innovation center for opening very flexible plants and rapidly releasing new products.

The Brazilian Automotive Industry

Until 1990, the entire Brazilian automotive industry revolved around four major makers: GM, Volkswagen, Fiat, and Ford. At that time, car makers tended to limit outsourcing to the production of low-complexity individual parts, produced according to strict specifications. Car makers also used many efforts to push down the prices of parts, both by means of invitations to bid and by encouraging competition among suppliers. With the lifting of trade barriers in the early 1990s, Brazil went from a market with few choices, high prices, no credit, and known for its technologically obsolete products to become the world's new automotive phenomenon, turning into a region of significant potential sales growth.

The Gravataí Automotive Industrial Complex

The Gravataí Automotive Industrial Complex was the result of an idea by GMBG's top management to build a plant where the assembly line and an Internet-based sales system were connected and were led by a single conductor: the customer. The entire plant was to operate synchronously like clockwork.

Source: © Dr. João Mario Csillag, Titular Professor in Operations Management, EAESP-FGV (Escola de Administração de Empresas–Fundação Getúlio Vargas), São Paulo, Brazil, e-mail: csillag@fgvsp.br. Reprinted with permission.

Table C.1	General Information on the Plant
Location	Gravataí, Rio G. do Sul
Total Area	3.868 million sq. meters
Building Area	1.260 million sq. meters used by plants
Capacity	190,000 cars a year (three shifts)
Activities	Car making Automotive development
Employees	2,700 employees (only half are GM's)

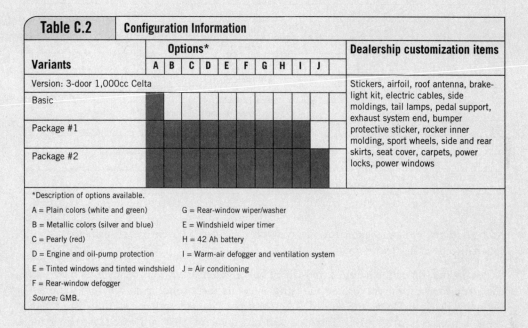

Table C.2 — Configuration Information

Variants	Options* (A B C D E F G H I J)	Dealership customization items
Version: 3-door 1,000cc Celta		Stickers, airfoil, roof antenna, brake-light kit, electric cables, side moldings, tail lamps, pedal support, exhaust system end, bumper protective sticker, rocker inner molding, sport wheels, side and rear skirts, seat cover, carpets, power locks, power windows
Basic		
Package #1		
Package #2		

*Description of options available.

A = Plain colors (white and green)

B = Metallic colors (silver and blue)

C = Pearly (red)

D = Engine and oil-pump protection

E = Tinted windows and tinted windshield

F = Rear-window defogger

G = Rear-window wiper/washer

E = Windshield wiper timer

H = 42 Ah battery

I = Warm-air defogger and ventilation system

J = Air conditioning

Source: GMB.

GM Brazil began setting up its team of suppliers in 1995, when seventeen of them were selected to work alongside the company in connection with the development of the product and process for the future Gravataí complex. In order to come up with this team, Roberto Tinoco sponsored an international bid with seventy companies participating. The enterprise required global investments of US$554 million, borne by GM, module suppliers, and the Rio Grande do Sul State Government, and employed 2,700 people at first.

The fact that suppliers and GM are in different buildings at the same site makes everything work like a single unit. The plant began selling cars on September 17, 2000. Table C.1 displays some information on the plant.

The supply chain for the Celta, which is assembled at GMBG, brings new concepts to bear on the global automotive industry: Celtas are sold over the Internet; lead time is minimal; and all suppliers are responsible for their modules of parts, in addition to being co-investors in the enterprise.

The Celta Production Concept

The Celta is a popular car with a 1,000cc engine whose platform and style was designed for the Brazilian market, with few variations. There is a choice of five colors and three versions: a basic one and two better-equipped ones with different options packages. There are, therefore, fifteen possible combinations and few hassles for the maker, as shown in Table C.2. The strategy of limiting the number of possible options was adopted by GMBG in order to more quickly respond to customers' orders. Consumers cannot change these three basic

Table C.3	System Supplier List	
	Suppliers	**Modules**
1	Valeo Térmico	Engine cooling system
2	Lear Corporation	Seats and upholstery
3	Arvin	Exhaust system
4	Indústrias Arteb	Lighting systems
5	Bosal-Gerobrás	Tool kit
6	VDO do Brasil	Instruments panel
7	Goodyear do Brasil	Tires and wheels
8	Delphi Chassis	Suspension
8	IPA-Soplast	Fuel tank
9	Ti Brasil-Bundy	Brake and fuel lines
10	Santa Marina	Windows
11	Pelzer Systems	Injected plastic parts
12	Polyprom	Pressed parts
13	Inylbra	Carpeting and insulation
14	Sogefi(Fram)	Air filters
15	FSM-Fanaupe	Car parts
16	Zamprogna*	Cut-to-size steel plates

*Supplier located outside the industrial complex.

configurations, and almost all customizations are provided by twenty accessories that can be added directly at the dealer.

For the first time in its seventy-six years of operating in Brazil, GM brought its main suppliers and their employees into an industrial site. Suppliers come from different nations—Germany, Belgium, Brazil, the United States, and France—with differing cultures and management processes, as shown in Table C.3. All take an active part in the Celta's engineering, design, logistics, and quality. They are called module suppliers, because they provide whole parts, or modules, for the car instead of separate parts. A system member is more than a supplier; instead, members act as partners in the enterprise.

All suppliers have exclusive rights to supply the modules, with no competition. They all have precise awareness of demand and receive a daily updated demand forecast for the next six months. They all maintain a contingency inventory at their plants, averaging about seven days' worth of parts. At the industrial site, some suppliers make their own modules, while others carry out assembly operations; a few of them simply receive the modules from their headquarters and store them at the plant. These suppliers are responsible for 80 percent of the car's material costs, while the other 20 percent fall to GM Brazil, who manufactures the power train (engine and transmission).

The suppliers were set up in the plant according to a planned order. The layout was developed by locating module suppliers at the closest point to the module's assembly location in the assembly line. Each supplier has a dock to offload parts or modules. Everything was conceived in such a manner as to ensure agile logistics, low production costs, and high productivity. Suppliers have an on-line connection to GMBG and have in-depth knowledge of the assembly line's needs.

Payment to each supplier is made daily at 6 P.M., when cars are cleared for invoicing by GMBG's quality control. At Gravataí, GM Brazil was able to secure a special tax policy, so instead of issuing a bill of sale for each product deployment, records are made on-line at the computer network that connects GMBG and the suppliers. This enables production to be added up at the end of the day, with a single bill of sale issued per supplier.

GMBG picked EDS as the IT support provider for Gravataí. EDS supports and manages the required IT infrastructure, as well as the services related to its use, integrating from product engineering to manufacturing process engineering, to speed up GMBG's time to market.

Inbound Logistics

GMBG uses a single logistics provider, TNT Logistics, to perform all the transportation and receiving functions for the site. TNT has three types of agreements with General Motors:

- *On-site operations:* Logistics performed within the complex; delivery of purchased materials directly to the assembly line
- *Off-site operations:* Makes collections from outside facilities
- *Material handling operations:* Moves and stores materials

TNT has two types of off-site operations for GM's Gravataí plant: the *milk-run* operation and the *line-haul* operation. Under the milk-run operation, TNT plans all pickups from the suppliers according to scheduled windows of time. Loads from approximately eighty-five suppliers in the São Paulo countryside and Minas Gerais are collected by smaller trucks and sent to a cargo consolidation center in São Paulo. The entire operation is carefully monitored from collection all the way through to delivery. TNT also has agreements with module suppliers and has implemented the milk-run system with second-tier suppliers.

Line-haul operations are between the São Paulo terminal and the Gravataí plant. Loads are optimized in express hauls toward Gravataí, which are more economic for long distances. When they get to Gravataí the merchandise is distributed among the system members.

TNT has developed software for its GMBG operation called LIRA II, a GPS-based vehicle-tracking application. All loads are tracked on-line and monitored in real time. The software is accessed over the Internet by users with pre-approved passwords who can make queries by part, criticality level, and the truck each part is on, in addition to tracking the trucks' itinerary.

As for the on-site operation, TNT Logistics is responsible for the dollies that collect materials from suppliers and for transportation to a holding area in the vicinity of the assembly line. At this point, full dollies are replaced with empty ones that are ferried back to the supplier. The dolly is essentially a Kanban packing system, a small train on wheels that is unloaded at the point of use by the GMBG production operators, who also replace them with empty ones. In some cases, production cells support an electronic pulse system (EPS) device, a type of electronic marker that enables operators to request the part needed by radio directly from the forklift operator. This system enables TNT to monitor the lead time between placement and filling of an order, thereby gauging system reliability.

Each supplier must have at least one backup dolly. The notion of backup is important and implies that an equipment operator is always available and accessible by radio in the event of a problem. There are seventeen routes and 177 points of delivery, and the average frequency is sixty minutes per route. For this purpose, TNT uses its own fleet of Toyota tractors. The tractors are TNT's property, but the dollies belong to the module suppliers since there is a specific dolly for each part type.

Plant Organization

The plant has three managerial levels: the plant director, functional managers, and supervisors, with an aim to facilitate communications and enable quick solutions to problems. The average age of employees is twenty-eight, fundamental schooling is a requirement, and most of them have completed high school. Approximately 12 percent of the workers are women. Employees change positions in the line, change islands from time to time, and change sectors. So all of the employees are multifunctional. All GMBG employees have had 440 hours of training.

Production Planning and Control

Clearance of production orders is performed according to customer orders over the Internet (70 percent) and the traditional dealer-based sales process (30 percent). GMBG only starts an Internet-ordered car's assembly after the order is placed and paid for over the Internet. As a consequence, the operation is extremely profitable, as the company receives payment for most of its cars before it has to pay its suppliers. The system is close to ideal—production is aligned with demand and relies exclusively on the ability to fill consumer orders, leading to a time-to-market period of five to fourteen days.

The Manufacturing Processes

The Press Shop

Zamprogna is the only supplier set up outside GMBG. It receives steel in spools and provides steel plates cut to size for GMBG's press. At the press line, seventeen outside panels for the auto's bodywork are made (side panels, roof panels, hoods, and doors). The press is fully automated, weighs a total of 5,600 tons, and uses a five-stage transfer process, under which a panel is moved from one side to another, until it turns out as a completed part at the far end of the press.

The Bodywork Shop

The bodywork shop is the most heavily automated sector in the plant, with 104 robots. It is divided into several islands, each responsible for one part of the car, and parts are taken from the islands to the assembly line by an aerial conveyor belt.

The Paint Shop

The world-class paint shop at Gravataí operates with five different color lines according to a process that eliminates the need for rework. Investment in this sector was about US$60 million. Operation of this system is still exceedingly expensive, costing five times more than the ordinary paint process.

At the end of the assembly line, there is an inventory of 150 bodies, which regulates the assembly line's pace. Production follows the sequence of orders received over the Internet. "This is the buffer where production says: I want a black car or a silver one, so that the automated elevators can select a car from the appropriate drawer and send it up to the assembly line" (GMBG manufacturing manager).

The General Assembly Line

The first operation performed at the assembly line is removal of the doors, as this facilitates operations inside the car. At the end of the assembly line, each door is reattached to the car it originally came from. The car is then placed on a platform whose height can be adjusted according to the employee's own height and the activity he or she is performing, thereby ensuring a comfortable working position. This is a manufacturing innovation and improves employee productivity and well-being.

Modules arrive at the assembly line at twenty- to thirty-minute intervals. The "T"-shaped assembly line facilitates replenishment, reducing the need for physical space. Inventories at the assembly line are limited to a few dollies that feed the process as needed. For more unwieldy items, such as seats, a truck is called for instead of dollies.

One of the most innovative stages found at the Celta assembly line is the installation of the VDO (a supplier) module in a single step, lasting about two minutes. The VDO module consists of sixty-five items, including plastic and metal parts such as the glove compartment, fuse-box cover, steering column, pedal modules, steering wheel, and blinker activators. In order to assemble it, VDO receives parts from two other Gravataí module suppliers: Valeo Térmico and Delphi.

Another innovation is the installation of the entire mechanical system in one single operation, which includes the engine, transmission, brakes, fuel line, exhaust, thermal protection, and rear axle. Eight components are installed in a single automated operation.

After the car passes a final quality check, if reworking is needed as a result of damage suffered during the assembly, it goes to a special line for repairs and no longer returns to the main assembly line. Less than 1 percent of the cars produced require repairs. Nineteen checkpoints certify manufacturing quality along the assembly line. The Gravataí plant is GM's worldwide benchmark: it has one of the fewest turnouts of "crippled" cars in all of General Motors (*cripple* refers to cars that are not completed because of missing parts or defective parts provided by suppliers).

The Distribution Strategy

The CELTA distribution strategy was based on four pillars:

- Direct sales to legally circumvent taxes
- e-Commerce to make consumers comfortable
- Accelerated delivery for added closeness with customers
- The same prices and freight charges apply, regardless of distance, in an effort to do away with the negotiation process between consumers and dealers

Under the traditional model, GMBG sells cars to dealers, who incorporate them into their inventories. Consumers go to the dealers, choose a car, negotiate with the salesperson, and make a purchase. However, as competitiveness increases, car buyers the world over demand more power in regard to choice and speed of delivery. Car makers need to reinvigorate their manufacturing processes to meet these demands, competing on the grounds of best service.

Under the Internet selling model, GMBG sells directly to consumers. Consumers enter the Web site and choose a configuration. The system then searches for completed cars at the Gravataí plant. The system does not place orders with the plant; instead, it finds completed cars at the distribution center. When the right configuration is found, the car is set aside. The customer then makes a small down payment to secure the car. Upon receipt of proof of payment, the car is invoiced and sent to the dealership closest to the customer's address. The customer is then called to the dealership, pays the invoice, and receives the car.

GMBG controls the entire flow of both distribution channels: the traditional one and the virtual one. At present, 30 percent of sales are made by means of the traditional model, while 70 percent take place over the Internet. Thus, 70 percent of the demand can be tracked online by GMBG, while the remaining 30 percent that consumers buy from dealers are not monitored, so a doubt remains as to whether the consumers got what they wanted, whether they bought whatever was available, or whether they simply gave up their purchase.

Relationships with Customers and Dealers

GMBG went from 500 customers, who were the brand's dealers, to direct contact with 80,000 consumers. Customer service had to be expanded with the creation of a call center to provide guidance on the sale process.

The General Motors dealership chain in Brazil has around 470 stores. One group representing the dealers studied all the processes proposed by GM Brazil. Initially, the dealers were wary and thought they might be left out. Then they learned they were not excluded from the business but quite the opposite. Each dealer was to be paid a fixed percentage of the sales channeled through its respective dealership.

For GMBG, dealerships still play a role: servicing; buying and repairing used cars; selling and installing customized items for new ones; receiving payment from customers; and delivering clean, refurbished cars to consumers. They are 100 percent involved. All direct sales involve a dealer, and dealers receive a 7 percent commission on each unit sold.

GM has set up Internet-connected kiosks in every dealership in Brazil. Each dealership has one unit for test drives and another for show. Consumers go to dealerships to see a car, they try it out, and then they can choose to buy immediately over the Internet.

The Celta Web Site

The Celta Web site allows selection of color, configuration and additional services, payment, and receipt of the car. Consumers can connect to the Celta Web site from their homes or from the nearest dealership. The main things attracting consumers to the Web site are: comfort in receiving information and sending personal and financial data for a credit check; and, secondly, the price factor. Over the Internet, a Celta sells for about R$800.00 (US$320.00) less than under the conventional dealer-based system.

GM Brazil also aims to use the Web site to develop a lifelong relationship with the customer. According to its philosophy of providing service to customers end to end, GM Brazil sells the cars, provides constant information about them, and deals with technical support and maintenance. The objective is to take care of customers from the presale process until selling the product in the used car market.

Freight

GM Brazil was able to change the traditional freight concept by implementing the notion of a set freight price for all of Brazil, due in part to the involvement of freight companies as partners from the very inception of the project. Freighters are hired by GM Brazil rather than the dealer. The freighter is actually a consortium of firms under the coordination of the National Association of Vehicles Freighters (ANTV). Hundreds of trucks are involved, each carrying eleven Celtas, delivering throughout Brazil as dictated by sales.

The Future

Roberto Tinoco still has in mind reducing time to market and increasing the customization level, while maintaining costs at competitive levels in a period of increasing competition among the major car makers. Always the pragmatist, he expects his team to provide ideas leading to the improvement of the logistics process.

Questions for Discussion

1. What are the advantages of locating each supplier in a building at the GMBG site and having their employees living in the neighborhood with their families?

2. What sort of problems do you see with this type of auto purchasing system in this and other markets such as the United States?

3. How do you think dealers typically would react to having customers order direct from the manufacturer? How do you think this will change dealers in the future?

4. What are the potential consequences of having hundreds of thousands of customers directly contacting the manufacturer? How can GMBG take advantage of this information?

5. Is GMBG a JIT facility? Why or why not?

6. What are some things that GMBG can consider doing to reduce time to market, increase customization, and maintain current cost levels?

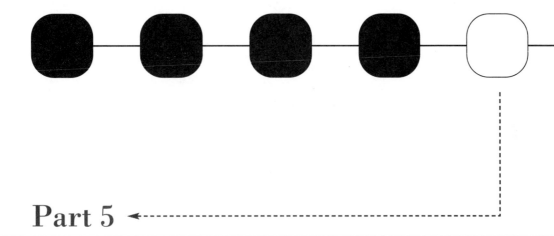

Part 5

Sustaining Competitive Advantage

Chapter 13:

SUPPLY CHAIN PROCESS INTEGRATION

Achieving visibility across a supply chain means not only being able to track the performance of a supplier, but also that of a supplier's suppliers. Such visibility enables a more agile level of demand planning, in which production and quality issues can be addressed within days, or even hours.[1]

Clear Communication between the marketer, the manufacturer, the retailer, and all the suppliers in between can be the difference in beating a competitor to the marketplace or successfully implementing a product concept. Not a minor feat in today's competitive marketplace.[2]

Learning Objectives

After completing this chapter, you should be able to

- Discuss the overall importance of process integration in supply chain management.
- Describe the advantages of and obstacles to process integration.
- Understand the important issues of internal and external process integration.
- Understand the role played by information systems in creating information visibility along the supply chain.
- Describe the various processes requiring integration along the supply chain.
- Understand the various causes of the bullwhip effect and how they impact process integration.

Chapter Outline

SUPPLY CHAIN MANAGEMENT IN ACTION   *Rexam Beverage Can Americas*

Integrating business processes brings plenty of benefits—it helps companies eliminate redundancies, reduce errors, improve efficiencies, cut costs, and speed product time to market. As companies redefine and integrate their business processes, they find that the effort pays off in important ways for customers and partners, too. But to achieve any of these benefits, companies have to start off on the right foot, going through the rigorous course of identifying all business processes; assessing which need to be eliminated, improved, or simply automated; and documenting where the value will be to get buy-in from the highest levels.

Paul Martin, vice president of information technology at Rexam Beverage Can Americas, took those steps as part of a strategic plan to boost customer service by integrating order-to-cash, order-to-supply, and procure-to-pay business processes in a redefined supply chain. The division spent four months reengineering its business processes. "We had a conscious effort going in to look at the process," Martin says. "Without doing that, you can put in a great system supporting a bad process, and that fails." All the work the company is doing around what it calls its "e-nablement" effort, based on the SAP platform, will be completed soon. Already in place are the processes and the technology to accept orders electronically via a portal and have them immediately transmitted into the division's manufacturing systems. A significant number of customers already use the portal, no longer tied to the old method of faxing, phoning, or e-mailing orders that were then keyed into a spreadsheet, held onto for a couple of hours, then faxed to a sourcing plant where the data would again be keyed into a legacy manufacturing system. "We have immediate visibility and can plan resources around the customer's requirement," Martin says. That eliminates occasional problems with transposed numbers in stock-keeping units and descriptions that in the past caused the wrong products to be shipped.

But customers are already benefiting in another key way from having access to real-time operational information. If Rexam realizes it can field an order faster than the customer indicated it would have its carrier pick it up, Martin says, "we can publish that information to the customer portal, and the customer may be able to use another common carrier or truck that might be in the area, so they can save money in the process."[3]

Introduction

The ultimate goal in supply chain management is to create value for the end customers as well as the firms in the supply chain network. To accomplish this, firms in the supply chain network must integrate process activities internally and with other firms in the network. Throughout this textbook, the integration of key business processes along the supply chain has been a recurring theme. The term **process integration** means coordinating and sharing information and resources to jointly manage a process. We have been introducing and discussing the various processes and issues concerning this somewhat daunting task throughout the text and have been alluding to the idea that key processes must be somehow coordinated, shared, or integrated among the supply chain members. In this chapter, some of these issues are revisited. Additionally, the advantages, challenges, methods, and tools used to achieve process integration both within organizations and among supply chain trading partners are discussed. More specifically, this chapter discusses the key business processes requiring integration, the impact of integration on the bullwhip effect (and vice versa), the importance of internal and external process integration in supply chain management, and the important role played by information technology (IT) in making data visible throughout the supply chain.

Process integration can sometimes be an extremely difficult task, because it requires proper training and preparedness; willing and competent trading partners; trust; and, potentially, a

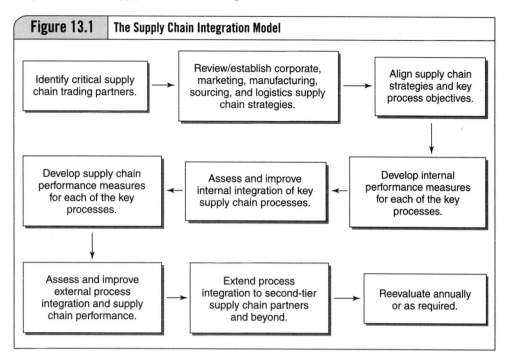

Figure 13.1 | The Supply Chain Integration Model

change in one or more organizational cultures. However, the benefits of collaboration and information sharing can be significant: reduced supply chain costs, greater flexibility to respond to market changes, less supply chain safety stock, higher quality levels, reduced time to market, and better utilization of resources. It is hoped that this chapter will allow readers to recall and consider all of the previous chapters' topics; their contributions to successful supply chain management; and the means by which collaboration, information sharing, and process integration must occur to make supply chain management a core competitive strength.

The Supply Chain Integration Model

Figure 13.1 presents a supply chain integration model, starting with the identification of key trading partners; the development of supply chain strategies; aligning the strategies with key process objectives; developing process performance measures; internally integrating these key processes; developing supply chain performance measures for each process; externally integrating key processes with supply chain trading partners; extending process integration to second-tier supply chain participants; and then, finally, reevaluating the integration model periodically. Discussion of each of the elements in the integration model follows.

Identify Critical Supply Chain Trading Partners

For each of the firm's products and services, it is important to identify the critical trading partners that will enable the successful sale and delivery of the end product to the final customer. At least initially, including a large number of supply chain businesses will be extremely difficult and cumbersome, particularly as the firm moves out to second- and third-tier suppliers and customers. Identifying only the primary trading partners allows the firm to concentrate its time and resources on managing the important process links with these companies, enabling the supply chain to perform well. Including other non-essential or supporting businesses will prove counterproductive in terms of successful supply chain management. In a landmark supply chain paper, Lambert, Cooper, and Pagh define primary supply chain members to be "all those autonomous companies or strategic business units who actually perform operational and/or managerial activities in the business processes designed to produce a specific output for a particular customer or market."[4]

Depending on where within a supply chain the firm is located (close to initial suppliers, close to end-product customers, or somewhere in between), the structure of the network of primary trading partners will vary. Mapping the network of primary trading partners is something that should be done to help the firm decide which businesses to include in its supply chain management efforts. For instance, a firm with many key suppliers and customers will most likely limit the number of integrative processes the firm can successfully manage, leading to fewer second-tier relationships.

Review and Establish Supply Chain Strategies

On an annual basis, management must identify the basic supply chain strategies associated with each of its products or services. If an end product is competing based on quality, then supply chain members should also be using strategies consistent with delivering high-quality products, along with competitive price and service levels. These strategies should then translate into internal functional policies regarding the types of parts purchased and suppliers used; the shop layout and manufacturing processes employed; the designs of the products manufactured; the mode of transportation used; the warranty and return services offered; the employee training methods used; the types of information technologies used; and, potentially, the amount of outsourcing employed. In each of these areas, policies should be geared toward supporting the overall quality-oriented strategy of the supply chain.

Similarly, if end products are competing primarily based on cost, then strategies and functional policies among each of the supply chain participants must be consistently aimed at achieving low cost as intermediate products and services are purchased, produced, and moved along the supply chain. As competition, technology, and customer requirements change, then management must also adjust supply chain and internal strategies to remain competitive.

Align Supply Chain Strategies with Key Supply Chain Process Objectives

Once the overriding strategy has been identified for each of the supply chain end products, managers need to identify the important processes linking each of the primary supply chain partners and establish process objectives to assure that resources and efforts are effectively deployed within each firm to support the overall end-product strategy. The key processes and the methods used to integrate and manage process links among supply chain partners will vary based on the internal structure of each firm, the prevailing economic conditions in the marketplace, the degree that **functional silos** exist in any of the trading partners, and the nature of existing relationships within the supply chain. In some cases, it may be best to integrate only one key process with a trading partner; while, with other partners, more processes will be integrated.

Based on the research of Lambert, Cooper, and Pagh, eight processes have been identified as important supply chain business processes. These **key supply chain processes** are shown in Table 13.1. A *process* can be defined as a set of activities designed to produce a product or service for an internal or external customer. A discussion of each of these processes follows.

Customer Relationship Management

The **customer relationship management process** provides the firm with the structure for developing and managing customer relationships. As discussed in the earlier chapter on customer relationship management, key customers are identified, their needs are determined, and then products and services are developed to meet their needs. Over time, relationships with these key customers are solidified through the sharing of information; the formation of

Table 13.1	The Eight Key Supply Chain Business Processes
Customer Relationship Management	Identifying key customer segments, tailoring product and service agreements to meet their needs, measuring customer profitability and firm's impact on customers
Customer Service Management	Providing information to customers such as product availability, shipping dates, order status and administering product and service agreements
Demand Management	Balancing customer demand with the firm's output capacity; forecasting demand and coordinating with production, purchasing, and distribution
Order Fulfillment	Meeting customer requirements by synchronizing the firm's marketing, production, and distribution plans
Manufacturing Flow Management	Determining manufacturing process requirements to enable the right mix of flexibility and velocity to satisfy demand
Supplier Relationship Management	Managing product and service agreements with suppliers; developing close working relationships with key suppliers
Product Development and Commercialization	Developing new products frequently and getting them to market effectively; integrating suppliers and customers into the process to reduce time to market
Returns Management	Managing used product disposition, product recalls, and packaging requirements and minimizing future returns

Sources: These processes are discussed in detail in D. M. Lambert, M. C. Cooper, and J. D. Pagh, "Supply Chain Management: Implementation Issues and Research Opportunities," *International Journal of Logistics Management* 9, no. 2 (1998): 1–19; and in K. L. Croxton, S. J. Garcia-Dastugue, and D. M. Lambert, "The Supply Chain Management Processes," *International Journal of Logistics Management* 12, no. 2 (2001): 13–36.

cross-company teams to improve products, deliveries, quality, and costs; the development of shared goals; and, finally, improved performance and profitability for the trading partners along with agreements on how to share these benefits. The firm should monitor the impact of customer relationship management efforts both in terms of the financial impact of these efforts and in terms of customer satisfaction.

Customer Service Management

The **customer service management process** is what provides information to customers while also providing ongoing management of any product and service agreements between the firm and its customers. Information can be provided through a number of communication channels including Web sites, personal interactions, information system linkages, and printed media. Objectives and policies are developed to assure proper distribution of products and services to customers; to adequately respond to product and delivery failures and complaints; and to utilize the most effective means of communication to coordinate successful product, service, and information deliveries. The process also includes methods for monitoring and reporting customer service performance to allow firms to understand to what extent their management efforts are achieving the process objectives.

Demand Management

The **demand management process** is what balances customer demand and the firm's output capabilities. The specific demand management activities include forecasting demand and then utilizing techniques to vary capacity and demand within the purchasing, production, and distribution functions. Various forecasts can be used, based on the time frame, the knowledge of the forecaster, the ability to obtain **point-of-sale information,** and the use of forecasting models contained in many ERP systems. The next step is to determine how to synchronize demand and productive capacity. As was discussed in Chapter 5 and Chapter 12, a number of effective techniques exist to smooth demand variabilities and increase or decrease capacity when disparities exist between demand and supply. Contingency plans must also be ready for use when demand management techniques fail or when forecasts are inaccurate. Performance measurement systems can prove quite useful here to increase the accuracy of forecasts and to track the success of various demand management activity implementations.

Order Fulfillment

The **order-fulfillment process** is the set of activities that allows the firm to fill customer orders while providing the required levels of customer service at the lowest possible delivered cost. Thus, the order-fulfillment process must integrate the firm's marketing, production, and distribution plans to be effective. More specifically, the firm's distribution system must be designed to provide adequate customer service levels, and its production system must be designed to produce at the required output levels, while marketing plans and promotions must consider the firm's output and distribution capabilities. Related order-fulfillment issues are the location of suppliers; the modes of inbound and outbound transportation used; the location of production facilities and distribution centers; and the system used for entering, processing, communicating, picking, delivering, and documenting customer orders. The order-fulfillment process must integrate closely with customer relationship management, customer service management, supplier relationship management, and returns management to assure that customer requirements are being met; customer service levels are being maintained; suppliers are helping to minimize order cycle times; and customers are getting undamaged, high-quality products.

Manufacturing Flow Management

The **manufacturing flow management process** is the set of activities responsible for making the actual product, establishing the manufacturing flexibility required to adequately serve the markets, and designing the production system to meet cycle time requirements. To be effective, manufacturing flow management activities must be interfaced with the demand management and customer relationship management processes, using customer requirements as inputs to the process. As customers and their requirements change, so too must the supply chain and the manufacturing flow process change to maintain firm competitiveness. As was shown in Chapter 8, the flexibility and rapid-response requirements in many supply chains result in the firm's use of JIT in order to continue to meet customer requirements.

Manufacturing flow characteristics also impact supplier requirements. For instance, as manufacturing batch sizes and lead-time requirements are reduced, supplier deliveries must become smaller and more frequent, causing supplier interactions and the supplier relationship to potentially change. The importance of an adequate materials planning system should become evident here, as customer requirements must be translated into production capabilities and supplier requirements. As with other processes, a good set of performance metrics should also be utilized to track the capability of the manufacturing flow process to satisfy demand.

Supplier Relationship Management

The **supplier relationship management process** defines how the firm manages its relationships with suppliers. As was discussed in Chapter 2, Chapter 3, and Chapter 4 of this textbook, firms in actively managed supply chains seek out small numbers of the best performing suppliers and establish ongoing, mutually beneficial, close relationships with these suppliers in order to meet cost, quality, and/or customer service objectives for key materials, components, and products. For other non-essential items, firms may use reverse auctions, bid arrangements, or catalogues to select suppliers. Activities in this process include screening and selecting suppliers, negotiating product and service agreements, managing suppliers, and then monitoring supplier performance and improvement. Some suppliers may have a cross-functional team to manage the supplier's progress toward meeting the firm's current and long-term requirements and establishing a record of performance improvement over time; while other suppliers may be managed little or not at all, depending on supply chain, company, or product requirements. Supplier relationship management personnel routinely communicate with production personnel to obtain feedback on supplier and purchased item performance, and with marketing personnel for customer feedback. Additionally, suppliers are frequently contacted for new product development and performance feedback purposes.

Product Development and Commercialization

The **product development and commercialization process** is responsible for developing new products to meet changing customer requirements and then getting these products to market quickly and efficiently. In actively managed supply chains, many customers and suppliers are involved in the new product development process to assure that products conform to customers' needs and purchased items meet manufacturing requirements. Activities in the product development and commercialization process include methods and incentives for generating new product ideas; the development of customer feedback mechanisms; the formation of cross-functional, inter-firm new product development teams; assessing and selecting new product ideas based on financial impact, resource requirements, and fit with existing manufacturing and logistics infrastructure; designing and testing new product prototypes; determining marketing channels and rolling out the products; and, finally, assessing the success of each new product. Successful new product development hinges on the involvement of external customers and suppliers and of internal manufacturing, marketing, and finance personnel.

Returns Management

The **returns management process,** while given little importance in some organizations, can be extremely beneficial for supply chain management in terms of maintaining acceptable levels of customer service and identifying product improvement opportunities. Returns management activities include environmental compliance with substance disposal and recycling, composing operating and repair instructions, troubleshooting and warranty repairs, developing disposition guidelines, designing an effective reverse logistics process, and collecting returns data. Returns management personnel frequently communicate with customers and personnel from customer relationship management, product development and commercialization, and supplier relationship management during the returns process.

One of the goals of returns management is to reduce returns. This is accomplished by communicating return and repair information to product development personnel, suppliers, and other potential contributors to any returns problems to guide the improvement of future product and purchased item designs. Transportation and distribution services may also be included in the returns feedback communication loop.

In Conclusion

For each of the eight processes identified, objectives or goals must be developed to help guide the firm toward its supply chain strategy. Additionally, consistent objectives within each functional area of the firm for each process help to integrate the processes internally, as well as focus efforts and firm resources on the supply chain strategy. For instance, if the supply chain strategy is to compete using low cost, marketing objectives for the customer relationship management process might be to find cheaper delivery alternatives, develop vendor-managed inventory (VMI) accounts, and to automate the customer order process. Production objectives might be to develop bulk packaging solutions consistent with the modes of transportation and distribution systems used, to increase mass production capabilities, and to identify the lowest total cost manufacturing sites for specific products; while purchasing objectives might be to identify the cheapest materials and components that meet specifications and to utilize reverse auctions whenever possible. Firms should similarly progress through each of the key processes using teams of employees from each function to develop process objectives.

Develop Internal Performance Measures for Key Process Effectiveness

As alluded to in each of the preceding key processes (and to be discussed at length in Chapter 14), procedures and metrics must be in place to collect and report internal performance data for the eight processes. Before companies can measure performance among supply chain partners, they must first build good internal performance measurement capabilities across functions. Performance measures need to drive a consistent emphasis on the overall supply chain strategy and corresponding process objectives. In order to assure that processes are supporting the supply chain strategy, performance is continuously measured using a set of metrics designed for each process.

As more companies invest in ERP systems, the ability to develop meaningful internal performance measures improves. At Dow Corning, for example, members of management are implementing consistent definitions and reporting structures for performance measurement, allowing them to find examples of best practices they can leverage across the entire organization.[5]

Continuing the discussion from the previous section in which competing based on low cost was the supply chain strategy, performance measures for the customer relationship management process would need to be designed for each of the firm's functional areas. The responsibility for designing these measures can also be assigned to the team developing objectives for each of the functional areas. Since the objectives in this case are cost driven, the performance measures should reflect this as well. For the customer relationship management process, performance measures in marketing might be the average delivery cost, the number of new VMI accounts, the average cost of ordering and carrying inventories for the new VMI accounts, and the number of new automated order systems over the period of time studied. For production, performance measures might be the average packaging cost per order, the average daily output capability for each product, and the average unit cost per order. For purchasing, the performance measures for the customer relationship management objectives might be the average purchasing cost for each of the items purchased and the percentage of time that reverse auctions were used over the period of time studied. Performance measures would similarly be designed for each of the key processes and their corresponding functional objectives. In this way, then, the firm has the capability to track its progress toward meeting each of its objectives for each of the key processes.

Assess and Improve Internal Integration of Key Supply Chain Processes

Successful supply chain management requires process coordination and collaboration internally, between the firm's functional areas, as well as externally, between the firm and its trading partners. Achieving process integration within the firm requires a transition from the typical functional silos to one of teamwork and cooperation across all business functions. To achieve this, personnel must have management support, resources, and empowerment to make meaningful organizational changes to foster the type of cooperation necessary to support the overall supply chain strategy. The formation of cross-functional teams to develop the key process objectives and accompanying performance measures is a good starting point in achieving internal process integration.

The primary enabler of integration, though, is the firm's ERP system. In Chapter 7, the importance and capabilities of ERP systems were described, along with the various software applications or modules that are used today. ERP systems provide a view of the entire organization, enabling decision makers within each function to have information regarding customer orders, manufacturing plans, work-in-process and finished goods inventories, outbound goods in transit, purchase orders, inbound goods in transit, purchased item inventories, and financial and accounting information. ERP systems thus link business processes and facilitate communication and information sharing between the firm's departments. Since the key business processes overlay each of the functional areas, the firm eventually becomes process oriented rather than functionally oriented once ERP systems are deployed. It is this visibility of information across the organization that allows processes to become integrated within the firm.

When assessing current internal integration of key processes, the firm should first develop an understanding of the **internal supply chain** of an organization. Internal supply chains can be complex, particularly if the firm has multiple divisions and organizational structures around the globe. Thus, the firm should assess the makeup of the teams used in setting process objectives and performance measures—do they include representatives from each of the organization's divisions or business units? These cross-functional teams should adequately represent the firm's internal supply chain.

Once the firm has an understanding of its internal supply chain, it can begin to assess the level of information access across the internal supply chain. Does the firm have a single, company-wide ERP system, linking all functional areas? Are all of the firm's **legacy systems** linked to its ERP system? How easy is it to extract the information needed to make effective decisions? Are **data warehouses** being used to collect data from the various divisions of the firm? Firms that are successfully integrating key business processes are using global ERP systems and data warehouses to make better, informed decisions. Data warehouses store information collected from ERP and legacy systems in one location, such that users can extract information as needed, analyze it, and use it to make decisions.

A globally linked ERP system allows the firm to use a common database from which to make product, customer, and supplier decisions. Information is captured once, reducing data input errors; information is available in real time, eliminating delays throughout the organization as information is shared; and, finally, information is visible throughout the organization—all transactions taking place can be seen and accessed by everyone on the system. As the firm moves away from legacy systems and moves toward the fully integrated ERP system—as organization-wide cross-functional teams are created to link key processes to the supply chain strategy, and as process performance is monitored and improved—the firm will become more focused on managing the key supply chain processes in an integrated fashion.

Develop Supply Chain Performance Measures for the Key Processes

As was done earlier for internal performance measures, the firm should also develop external performance measures to monitor the links with trading partners in the key supply chain management processes. And, as with the creation of internal performance measures, teams composed of members from a number of primary trading partners should be created to design these measures to be consistent with the overall supply chain strategy.

Continuing with the low-cost supply chain strategy example, trading partners should decide on monitoring a number of cost-oriented measures that are averaged across the member firms for each of the key supply chain processes. For the customer relationship management process, examples might include the average delivery cost, rush order cost, VMI carrying cost, finished goods safety stock costs, returned order costs, and spoilage costs. These measures should align closely with the internal performance measures for each process but may vary based on purchasing, production, distribution, customer service, and other variations across the participating firms.

Assess and Improve External Process Integration and Supply Chain Performance

Over time, firms eliminate poorly performing suppliers as well as unsuitable customers and try to concentrate efforts on developing beneficial relationships and strategic alliances with their remaining suppliers and customers. Building, maintaining, and strengthening these relationships is accomplished through use of external process integration. As process integration improves among supply chain partners, so, too, does supply chain performance. When firms have achieved a reasonably good measure of internal process integration, they are ready to move on to externally integrating key supply chain processes.

Supply chain trading partners must concentrate on sharing sales and forecast information, along with information on new products, expansion plans, new processes, and new marketing

Customer service drives Paul Gaffney's commitment to integration. And profits show that commitment matters. "Our most profitable customers are those who use the full range of the way we do business," says Gaffney, the CIO at Staples in Framingham, Massachusetts. He adds that customers "want to get a very consistent and seamless experience. When you do the right thing for your best customers, good things happen." The CIO of the office-supplies giant stresses that for those good things to happen, it is essential to have an overarching strategy that uses IT to advance the company's mission. Gaffney adds that "trying to be more holistic in our outlook is one of the things that separates great IT organizations from the rest of the pack."

One of the products of Gaffney's enterprise-wide focus on the customer is the on-line kiosk, dubbed Access Point, installed in all of the company's U.S. stores. Creating the kiosks required connecting the company's e-commerce Web site, http://www.Staples.com, with its point-of-sale (POS) system, order management system, distribution system, and supply chain. On the people front, staffers from the retail, catalog, on-line, finance, distribution, merchandising, and training areas—practically everyone but the cafeteria chefs—collaborated. For example, the kiosks offer customers the option of buying, say, an office chair at the kiosk using a credit card, then taking a bar-code printed receipt up front to the register to pay in real time. Customers can also use the kiosks to access a library of information about products and services, view an inventory of 45,000 on-line products, and build PCs to order (eliminating the need for more than 35 percent of stores to carry computers). "We're letting customers do business the way they want to do business, not the way we want them to," says Gaffney.

But the benefits do not go solely to customers. For Staples, the multimillion-dollar Access Point project has introduced many customers to Staples.com. The company estimates that a customer who shops in both stores and one other channel (Staples.com or catalogue) has a lifetime value of two and a half times that of a store-only shopper. And the company's approach toward integration goes beyond customer-facing systems.

Another major integration project involved consolidating the Staples and Quill fulfillment center facilities. Staples acquired Quill, a mail-order office products company, in 1998. To connect the two disparate order management systems, Staples could have gone the point-to-point route, which would have required building customized connections between the two sets of applications. But the Staples team chose instead to implement an integration layer built on IBM's MQ series. "That way, if we had a future acquisition, or needed more volume in the future, we won't have to do a new point-to-point integration project," says Gaffney.

Reducing the number of direct linkages between systems is one part of Gaffney's holistic strategy. Standardization is another. "Every IS organization is trying to deliver more business results for less money. One tool is reducing the number of different technologies that you need your staff to be proficient in. If you have four or five [technology] approaches, you've diluted your staff's proficiency. I think it's a productivity imperative," Gaffney says. Staples is just starting to look hard at how it can standardize, but Gaffney pointedly says that Web services will play a key role. Because of that, Gaffney does not feel a need to standardize his platform on either Sun's Java 2 Platform Enterprise Edition (J2EE) or Microsoft's .Net, since Web services can work with both. "We believe it's more important to focus on good semantics, for example, getting the definition of the interface right on our next generation internal pricing service, than to get hung up on whether it's a J2EE or Microsoft deployment," he says.

To ensure that his IS organization continues to maintain a big-picture integration strategy, Gaffney has appointed a team, led by two vice presidents in IS but involving people from all business areas, to help Staples get a detailed look at its business processes. They also want to determine how people and technologies map against those processes (for example, to see if there are multiple groups of people using multiple technologies, all to produce a sales forecast). They can then use the information they uncover to move ahead on the integration projects that will have the most business impact.[6]

campaigns in order to maximize profits for the entire supply chain membership, not just for themselves. Focusing on process integration will enable firms to collaborate and share this information. Again, as with internal process integration, the teams formed to design and organize process performance measures should be viewed as a key resource for external process integration. These teams can determine supply chain process objectives and the type of information that must be shared to achieve the objectives. Once the performance metrics are designed for each of the processes, they can be monitored to identify lack of process integration and supply chain competitive weaknesses. Firms should thus, periodically, jointly assess their levels of process performance and integration and collaborate on methods to improve both.

Once again, the way information is communicated plays an extremely important role in external process integration. Today, connecting buyers and suppliers in virtual companies via the Internet is the way supply chains are becoming integrated.[7] The primary companies providing this capability to supply chains are I2 Technologies, Manugistics, and SAP AG, while PeopleSoft and Oracle are busy trying to close the gap. Supply chain communication technologies have a number of issues to deal with, including handling the flows of goods between companies, negotiating and executing contracts, managing supply and demand between partners, making and executing orders, and handling financial settlements, all with a high level of security. To date, though, few standards have been widely adopted. Other companies are also becoming involved in creating Web-based collaborative infrastructures that can accommodate these communication applications using existing systems and ERP applications. For instance, IBM has launched its WebSphere application server, and BEA Systems and Sun Microsystems have their iPlanet Application Server.

Extend Process Integration to Second-Tier Supply Chain Partners

As supply chain relationships become more trusting and mature, and as the supply chain software used to link supply chain partners' ERP applications and legacy systems evolves and becomes widely used and relied upon, the tendency will be to integrate processes to second-tier partners and beyond. Today, supply chain software suppliers are developing systems that integrate more easily with other applications, allowing trading partners to exchange information on forecasts, sales, purchases, and inventories. Whirlpool, for instance, uses collaborative planning software from i2 Technologies that allows it to see sales data and work out forecasts with its retailers; and Alcatel uses Oracle's eBusiness Suite and its Advanced Planning application to share its planning and production schedules with its suppliers.[8] Using these linkages, companies can, in real time, work with suppliers and customers to compare forecasts and order commitments, determine supply/demand mismatches, and analyze supplier performance.

© 2000 Ted Goff

"We're now networked with our suppliers, our customers, our competitors, our ex-employees, our passersby, and some people having picnics in Iowa."

Every major software developer today is trying to make its supply chain tools easier to integrate with existing systems and gather data anywhere along a firm's supply chain. One of the newest developments is the **radio-frequency identification (RFID) tag.** This tiny microchip device can be attached to a product to relay information on the product's whereabouts as it moves through the supply chain. Thus, a firm's supply chain system can access real-time inventory information and instigate a replenishment order when inventories get low. The price of RFID tags have now become low enough to be used economically (about 5 cents each). For example, the Gillette Co. is using RFID tags in a test with Wal-Mart. There, "smart shelves" are capable of reading signals from the tags. When supplies of product get low on the shelves, stock clerks are alerted to refill them; when stockroom supplies get low, the store is alerted to order more.[9]

Prior to the development of these supply chain software applications, integrating processes beyond first-tier suppliers and customers was somewhat more difficult and time-consuming. As discussed in Chapter 4, firms can develop relationships with second-tier suppliers and insist that their direct suppliers use them and they can work closely with supplier alliance partners to solve second-tier supplier problems and help them to better manage their supplier alliances. To keep on the competitive edge, though, firms today must use a combination of information system linkages and old-fashioned customer and supplier teamwork to identify and manage second-tier relationships along the supply chain.

Reevaluate the Integration Model Annually

In light of the dramatic and fast-paced changes occurring with the development of supply chain information systems and the frequent changes most likely occurring with new products, new suppliers, and new markets, trading partners should revisit the integration model annually to identify changes within supply chains and to assess the impact these changes have on integration efforts. New suppliers may have entered the scene with better capabilities, more distribution choices, and better resources. Or, perhaps, the firm may be redesigning an older product, requiring different purchased components or supplier capabilities. Alternatively, the firm may be moving into a new foreign market, potentially requiring an entirely different supply chain. These examples are common and should cause firms to reevaluate their supply chain strategies, objectives, processes, performance measures, and integration levels. For example, Bulgari, the third-largest luxury goods company in the world, has introduced a number of new product lines in recent years and recently hired 4R Systems to help the company improve demand forecasting and inventory planning at its network of retail stores and independent retailers. The supply chain optimization solution provided by 4R Systems is discussed in the Global Perspective Box.

Obstacles to Process Integration Along the Supply Chain

A number of factors can impede external process integration along the supply chain, causing information distortion, longer cycle times, stock-outs, and the bullwhip effect, resulting in higher overall costs and reduced customer service capabilities. Managers can identify these obstacles and take steps to eliminate them, resulting in improved profitability and competitiveness for the supply chain's members. Table 13.2 summarizes these obstacles. Each of these are discussed in the following sections.

The Silo Mentality

Too often, firms do not consider the impact of their actions on the supply chain and its long-term competitiveness and profitability. This "I win, you lose" silo mentality manifests itself in the form of using the cheapest suppliers, paying little attention to the needs of customers, and assigning few resources to new product and service design. Eventually, these

Global Perspective

BULGARI'S SUPPLY CHAIN OPTIMIZATION SOLUTION

Fine perfumes, luxurious silks, exquisite watches, and jewelry are the hallmark products of Bulgari, the third-largest luxury goods company in the world. Bulgari sells these products through a network of retail stores and a select group of independent retailers. All of the company's products are slow-moving, high-end fashion items for which forecasting demand and planning stock levels are notoriously difficult and prone to human error.

Forecasting demand, however, is not the only trouble spot in Bulgari's day-to-day business operations. The company is very particular about where it sources its fine merchandise. Insisting on the best adds considerable complexity to the retailer's supply chain. Finished goods are shipped to a central distribution center that supplies Bulgari stores and independent retailers through regional warehouses. The company has introduced a number of new product lines in recent years, further multiplying the complexity of Bulgari's supply chain. To harness this burgeoning complexity, the retailer implemented an optimization solution from 4R Systems Inc. The solution was designed to help Bulgari improve demand forecasting and inventory planning at the store level.

Once implemented, 4R's analytics enabled Bulgari to slash jewelry and accessory inventories by 33 percent and 26 percent, respectively, while significantly enhancing its ability to meet customer demand. The solution also improved profitability on several merchandise lines by $10 million each.

Bulgari needed help in several key areas of its supply chain. The company wanted to

1. Improve the reliability and accuracy of its demand forecasting tools. Bulgari needed to make decisions well in advance on which items to manufacture and stock. However, low store item level demand, which made an accurate read of historical sales data challenging, and past stock-outs, which corrupted time-series data for Bulgari's best-selling items, complicated the decision-making process.

2. Gain a better understanding of new product demand. In the luxury goods business, new products are the lifeblood of growth. This reduces forecasting errors for accessory goods. The accessories business is driven by the seasonal launch of new collections two to four times a year. Bulgari, with the life cycle of its traditional core products typically spanning several years, was unaccustomed to this new pace when it launched its accessories product lines in 1997.

3. Improve inventory planning at the store level. As Bulgari grew, the company centralized management of its 100 retail locations to gain economies of planning, production, and distribution. This complicated the process of determining appropriate inventory levels for the stores and products.

4R Systems developed a sophisticated forecasting tool that uses point-of-sales data to take into account past sales, seasonality, and trends. It also corrects for past stock-outs. The tool enables Bulgari to better read demand signals and be more responsive to changing market conditions, increasing production for items in high demand and cutting production for others. Today, Bulgari's accessories, watches, and jewelry business units use the 4R tool to forecast demand for their products, overcoming the challenges presented by long production lead times.

The optimization solution continues to help Bulgari's business, as evidenced by the company's financial statements. In 2002, despite the uncertain political environment and unfavorable economic conditions, the retailer's revenues rose 17 percent as compared with year 2000—a testament in part to having the right product at the right place at the right time.[10]

Table 13.2	Obstacles to Supply Chain Integration
Silo mentality	Failing to see the big picture and acting only in regard to a single department within the firm or a single firm within the supply chain
Lack of supply chain visibility	The inability to easily share or retrieve trading partner information in real time, as desired by the supply chain participants
Lack of trust	Unwillingness to work together or share information because of the fear that the other party will take advantage of them or use the information unethically
Lack of knowledge	Lack of process and information system skills and lack of knowledge regarding the benefits of SCM among management and other employees, within the firm and among partners
Activities causing the bullwhip effect: Demand forecast updating	Using varying customer orders to create and update forecasts, production schedules, and purchase requirements
Order batching	Making large orders for goods from suppliers on an infrequent basis to reduce order and transportation costs
Price fluctuations	Offering price discounts to buyers, causing erratic buying patterns
Rationing and shortage gaming	Allocating short product supplies to buyers, causing buyers to increase future orders beyond what they really need

firms will create quality, cost, delivery timing, and other customer service problems that are detrimental to the supply chain. In fact, Mr. Wayne Bourne, vice president of logistics and transportation at Best Buy, noted in a recent article that the most significant obstacle to overcome in supply chain management was the silo mentality that exists in most companies.[11] Internally, the silo effect can also be present among departments. The transportation manager, for instance, may be trying to minimize total annual transportation costs while inadvertently causing safety stocks to be higher, shortages to occur, and customer service levels to deteriorate.

To overcome the silo mentality, the firm must strive to align supply chain goals and the goals and incentives of the firm. Functional decisions must be made while considering the impact on the entire firm's profits and those of the supply chain. Performance reviews of managers must include their ability to integrate processes internally and externally and to meet overall supply chain goals. Outside the firm, managers must work to educate suppliers and customers regarding the overall impact of their actions on the supply chain and its end customers. This should be an important part of the partnership creation and management process. Additionally, suppliers should be annually evaluated and potentially replaced if their performance vis-à-vis the supply chain does not improve.

Lack of Supply Chain Visibility

Lack of **information visibility** along the supply chain is also cited as a common supply chain process integration problem. In a 2002 survey, two-thirds of manufacturers had not yet successfully synchronized their supply chain operations with those of their trading partners.[12] Additionally, two-thirds of the respondents said they used different supply chain management applications than their partners, which prevented access to valuable external data, resulting in limited information visibility. If trading partners have to carve out data from their ERP or legacy systems and then send it to one another where it then has to be uploaded to other systems prior to the data being shared and evaluated, the time lost can mean lost end customers and higher costs throughout the supply chain's membership. This is the primary problem that supply chain software producers are working to overcome today.

Most of the software upgrades coming out right now allow users to share data among third-party ERP systems and other business applications and have advanced event management and integration capabilities. For instance, the Southern Company, a utility and energy services firm in Atlanta, is in the early stages of an enterprise application integration effort, aimed at providing greater visibility into all of its extensive supply chain operations. A recent application linked Southern's accounting, materials, and procurement system to seventy-five different work order and accounting applications throughout the company. In turn, those systems are tied to applications at Southern's suppliers and other business partners. Anytime a change is made to one work order system, follow-on changes are made to the systems to which it is connected.[13]

RFID technology promises to add tremendous real-time information visibility capabilities to supply chains. RFID tags can capture more accurate, specific, and timely data than UPC and bar codes offer today, while reducing or eliminating associated labor time and errors. Technology boards and user boards are being formed now to develop standards and **electronic product codes (ePCs)** for the RFID industry. An RFID tag attached to an automobile seat or engine, for example, can be used to gather and exchange work-in-process data. Additionally, product, manufacturing, and supplier information can be placed on the tag to support product warranty programs.[14]

Lack of Trust

Successful process integration between partners requires trust; and, as with the silo mentality and lack of information visibility, trust is seen as a major stumbling block in supply chain management. Trust occurs over time between supply chain partners, as each participant earns trust while it builds its reputations among the other businesses. Even though this sounds cliché, relationships employing trust result in win-win, or win-win-win for the participants. Spalding Holding collaborates with Wal-Mart, resulting in a win-win for both companies. Wal-Mart gives Spalding its forecast and point-of-sale data, which allows Spalding to keep its inventory levels down and serve Wal-Mart's needs better. As a result, Wal-Mart stocks out of Spalding goods less frequently and it now has a better understanding of Spalding's capacity and costs.[15]

Unfortunately, company practices and human nature will not change overnight. Until parties understand that it is in their own best interests to trust each other and share information, supply chain management success will be an uphill battle. Today, Boeing is running up against a trust barrier with some of its suppliers. Boeing engineers and their suppliers pass design documents back and forth as if they were in the same company. The technology that allows this is causing trust problems for Boeing. "Once you say, 'Build me the world's best overhead arch beam,' they could turn around and sell that to Airbus," says Scott Griffin, vice president and CIO at Boeing.[16] Jack Lowry's problem with the *FUD factor* in the Supply Chain Management in Action box is an interesting story dealing with trust issues.

Ethical behavior comes down to business partners setting expectations initially about the relationship and data sharing and then meeting those expectations. While reciprocal sharing of information among supply chain partners is growing in acceptance, not everyone is sold on the idea. "We still have the same issues around sharing data with supply chain vendors," says Garrett Grainger, CIO of Dixon Ticonderoga Co., a Florida pencil and crayon manufacturer. The issues involve risks created by data floating around the supply chain, which "opens us up to a lot of opportunities by competitors," he says. "As an industry, we institutionalized lying and build business practices around it," says Chris Sellers, president of Syncra Systems, Inc., a supplier of retail business collaborative software. "I don't think it was an intent to be unethical, it was just considered doing what you had to do in our business. And it increased costs for everyone."[18]

SUPPLY CHAIN MANAGEMENT IN ACTION   *The FUD Factor*

Fear, uncertainty, and doubt (FUD) have always driven people to hold information close to the vest, even among coworkers. Back when he was vice president of information technology at now-defunct Goldman Industrial Group of Vermont, an automotive capital equipment provider, Jack Lowry had a vision nearly a decade ago of how electronic collaboration would help his company and his customers work better together, cutting cost, improving quality, increasing responsiveness, and improving time to market. Back then, the technology piece was missing from the collaboration puzzle. But Lowry was convinced collaboration was so sensible that anyone could see the payoffs.

And perhaps Goldman's customers and suppliers could see potential benefits, but long-standing mistrust—both inside and outside the walls of the enterprise—proved insurmountable. Before bringing his message of collaboration to outside partners, Lowry had to start within the organization. There he found enough skepticism to sink the whole endeavor. "The reaction was, 'What's in it for me? Why should I do this? It's more work for us,'" says Lowry. With an extensive background in both manufacturing and IT, plus a boatload of charisma, he managed at last to convince people internally on the Goldman sales team that collaborating externally was the right thing to do. Then he had to wait for his salespeople to provide him the right contacts at their customer companies. Then he had to get the sales guys up to speed on collaboration, at least enough to sound marginally knowledgeable on the subject when meeting with outside parties alongside Lowry.

When Goldman reps finally met with their partners and customers, it was more of the same. "You'd need someone from the other side's IT department, the head person in charge of the plant, your sales guy, and your plant guy," says Lowry. When at last all the right people were around the table, good feelings did not exactly flow. "The arms are folded. They're shaking their heads. They're looking tired. They want to know, 'Do you really want to collaborate, or do you just want us to do something for you?'" he says. Sometimes the other side would flat out refuse to get involved. More often, and worse, the partner would agree to collaborate but then not do anything. "They'd drag their feet. They would wait it out because they knew there would be a change in management, and it would someday go away," he says.

Just months before Goldman filed for bankruptcy in February 2002, Lowry finally found a partner willing to go beyond the pilot stage on a far-reaching collaboration project in which the companies agreed to directly link their manufacturing systems. But before the venture could get going, the recession caught up with Goldman. You cannot help but wonder if Lowry had had more success earlier whether the company would be around today.[17]

Some useful advice for creating collaboration and trust are summed up nicely in a recent article appearing in *CIO* magazine, a business journal for IT and other business executives. They recommended six ways of "getting to yes":[19]

1. *Start small:* Begin by collaborating on a small scale. Pick a project that is likely to provide a quick return on investment for both sides. Once you can show the benefits of trust and collaboration, then move to larger projects.

2. *Look inward:* The necessary precondition for establishing trust with outside partners is establishing trust with internal constituents. Break down the barriers to internal communication and integration.

3. *Gather 'round:* The best way to build trust is to meet face-to-face, around a table. Listen to objections, find out the agendas, and spring for lunch. Then do it all over again, as people leave and as management changes.

4. *Go for the win-win:* Collaboration is a new way of doing business, where the biggest companies do not bully their partners but instead help create an environment that optimizes business for all supply chain members.

5. *Do not give away the store:* No one has to share all of their information. Some information should remain proprietary. The simple exchange of demand, purchase, and forecast information goes a long way.

6. *Just do it:* One of the best ways to build trust is to simply start sharing information. If all goes well, success breeds trust, allowing partners to progress to bigger things.

Lack of Knowledge

Companies have been moving toward collaboration and process integration for years, and it is just now that technology has caught up with this vision, allowing process integration across an extended supply chain. In a survey of 122 executives practicing supply chain management, 43 percent said lack of core supply chain management skills and knowledge was the greatest obstacle within their own organization, and 54 percent echoed this opinion for their trading partners.[20] Getting the network of firms to work together successfully, though, requires managers to use subtle persuasion and education to get their own firms and their trading partners to do the right things. The cultural, trust, and process knowledge differences in firms are such that firms successfully managing their supply chains must spend significant time influencing and increasing the capabilities of themselves and their partners. Change and information sharing can be threatening to people; they may fear for their job security, particularly if outsourcing accompanies integration. I2 Technologies, a supply chain systems developer, recommends a top-down approach to managing an integration project, potentially using strategic consulting partners with expertise in business process change, retraining, and change management.[21]

Additionally, as firms construct their supply chain information infrastructure, they may find themselves with multiple ERP systems, a mainframe manufacturing application, and desktop analysis and design software that all need to be integrated both internally and externally. Thus, firms must realize that the people to be using the systems must be involved early on, in terms of the purchase decision, the implementation process, and in training. Sunoco often uses temporary workers to handle employees' regular duties so those employees can concentrate on training. "We in headquarters need to understand that the people in the plant have a day job," says Bernie Campbell, vice president and CIO at Sunoco. "Just telling people to work harder is not the right answer."[22]

For all organizations, successful supply chain management requires a regimen of ongoing training. When education and training are curtailed, innovation cannot occur, and innovation fuels supply chain competitiveness. Human errors can have a rippling effect in supply chains, causing loss of confidence and trust and a magnification of the error and correction cost as it moves through the supply chain. Firms should provide learning modules to employees in mentally digestible pieces, rather than cramming every piece of information available into one program. Industry trade shows, conferences, and expos like Frontline Solutions Expo, the Institute of Supply Management's Annual Symposium on Purchasing and Supply Chain Management, and the Uniform Code Council's Annual U Connect Conference can also be valuable sources of learning, exchanging ideas, and gathering new information about supply chain management.[23]

Activities Causing the Bullwhip Effect

As discussed in Chapter 1 of this textbook, the bullwhip effect can be a pervasive and expensive problem along the supply chain and is caused by a number of factors that supply chain members must control. Recall that even though end-item demand may be relatively constant, forecasts and their corresponding orders as we move up the supply chain can become amplified, causing what is termed the *bullwhip effect.* These variations in demand cause problems with capacity planning, inventory control, and workforce and production scheduling and, ultimately, result in lower levels of customer service and higher total supply chain costs. In an important publication concerning the bullwhip effect, Dr. Hau Lee and his associates identified four major causes of the bullwhip effect.[24] These causes and the methods used to counteract them are discussed in the following sections.

Demand Forecast Updating

Whenever a buying firm places an order, the selling firm uses that information as a predictor of future demand. Based on this information, sellers update their demand forecasts and the corresponding orders placed with their suppliers. As lead times grow between orders placed and deliveries, then safety stocks also grow and are included in any orders as they pass up the supply chain. Thus, fluctuations are magnified as orders vary from period to period and as the review periods change, causing frequent **demand forecast updating.** These are major contributors to the bullwhip effect.

One solution to this problem is to make actual demand data available to the firm's suppliers. Better yet, if all point-of-sale data are made available to the upstream tiers of suppliers, all supply chain members can then update their demand forecasts less frequently, using the same data. This real-demand information also tends to reduce safety stocks among supply chain members, generating even less variability in supply chain orders. Thus, the importance of supply chain information visibility can again be seen.

Using the same forecasting techniques and buying practices also tends to smooth demand variabilities among supply chain members. In many cases, buyers allow suppliers to observe their demand, create a forecast, and determine their resupply schedules, a practice known as **vendor-managed inventory (VMI).** This practice can generally reduce inventories substantially.

Reducing the length of the supply chain can also reduce the bullwhip effect by reducing the number of occasions where forecasts are calculated. Examples of this are Dell Computers, Amazon.com, and other firms who bypass distributors and resellers and sell directly to consumers. Firms can thus see actual end-customer demand, resulting in much more accurate forecasts.

Finally, reducing the lead times from order to delivery will reduce the bullwhip effect. Developing just-in-time ordering and delivery capabilities results in smaller, more frequent orders being placed and delivered, more closely matching supply to demand patterns.

Order Batching

In a typical buyer/supplier scenario, demand draws down inventories until a reorder point is reached wherein the buyer places an order with the supplier. Inventory levels, safety stocks, and the desire to order full truckloads or containerloads of materials may cause orders to be placed monthly or even less often, or at varying time intervals. Thus, at one point in time, the supplier gets an order of some magnitude; then, until the next order is placed, there is no demand at all for the supplier's goods. This type of **order batching** amplifies demand variability and adds to the bullwhip effect. Another type of order batching can occur when salespeople need to fill end-of-quarter or end-of-year sales quotas, or when buyers desire to finish year-end budget allotments. Salespeople may generate production orders to fill future demand, and buyers may make excess purchases to spend budget money. These erratic, periodic surges in consumption and production also increase the bullwhip effect. If the timing of these surges is the same for many of the firm's customers, the bullwhip effect can be severe.

As with forecast updating, information visibility and use of more frequent and smaller order sizes will tend to reduce the order batching problem. When suppliers know that large orders are occurring because of the need to spend budgeted monies, for instance, they will not revise forecasts based on this information. Further, when using automated or computer-assisted order systems, order costs are reduced, allowing firms to order more frequently. To counteract the need to order full truckloads or containerloads of an item, firms can order smaller quantities of a variety of items from a supplier or use a freight forwarder to consolidate small shipments to avoid the high unit cost of transporting at less-than-truckload or less-than-containerload quantities.

Price Fluctuations

When suppliers have special promotions, quantity discounts, or other special pricing discounts, these price fluctuations result in significant **forward buying** activities on the part of buyers, who are stocking up to take advantage of the low price offers. Forward buying occurs between retailers and consumers, between distributors and retailers, and between manufacturers and distributors due to pricing promotions at each stage of a supply chain, all contributing to erratic buying patterns and, consequently, the bullwhip effect. If these price discounts become commonplace, firms will stop buying when prices are undiscounted and buy only when the discount prices are offered, even further contributing to the bullwhip effect. To deal with these surges in demand, manufacturers may have to vary capacity by scheduling overtime and undertime for employees, finding places to store stockpiles of inventory, paying more for transportation, and dealing with higher levels of inventory damage as inventories are held for longer periods.

The obvious way to reduce the problems caused by fluctuating prices is to eliminate price discounting among the supply chain's members. Manufacturers can reduce forward buying by offering uniform wholesale prices to its customers. Many retailers have adopted **everyday low prices (EDLP),** while eliminating sales or promotions that cause forward buying. Similarly, buyers can negotiate with their suppliers to offer EDLP, while curtailing promotions.

Rationing and Shortage Gaming

Rationing can occur when demand exceeds a supplier's finished goods available; and, in this case, the supplier may allocate product in proportion to what buyers ordered. Thus, if the supply of goods is 75 percent of the total demand, buyers would be allocated 75 percent of what they ordered. When buyers figure out the relationship between their orders and what is supplied, they tend to inflate their orders to satisfy their real needs. This strategy is known as **shortage gaming.** Of course, this further exacerbates the supply problem, as the supplier and, in turn, their suppliers struggle to keep up with these higher demand levels. When, on the other hand, production capacity eventually equals demand and orders are filled completely, demand suddenly drops to less-than-realistic levels, as the buying firms try to unload their excess inventories. This has occurred occasionally in the United States and elsewhere around the world, for instance, with gasoline supplies. As soon as consumers think a shortage is looming, demand suddenly increases as people top off their tanks and otherwise try to stockpile gasoline, which itself creates a real shortage. When these types of shortages occur due to gaming, suppliers can no longer discern the true demand; and this can result in unnecessary additions to production capacity, warehouse space, and transportation investments.

One way to eliminate shortage gaming is for sellers to allocate short supplies based on the demand histories of their customers. In that way, customers are essentially not allowed to exaggerate orders. And, once again, the sharing of capacity and inventory information between a manufacturer and its customers can also help to eliminate customers' fears regarding shortages and eliminate gaming. Also, sharing future order plans with suppliers allows suppliers to increase capacity if needed, thus avoiding a rationing situation.

Thus, it is seen that a number of rational decisions on the part of buyers and suppliers tend to cause the bullwhip effect. When trading partners use the preceding strategies to reduce the bullwhip effect, the growth of information sharing, collaboration, and process integration occurs along the supply chain. Firms that strive to share data, forecasts, plans, and other information can significantly reduce the bullwhip effect.

Summary

In this chapter, the topic of integrating processes within the firm and among supply chain partners was discussed, including the steps required to achieve process integration, the advantages of doing this, and the obstacles to overcome. Process integration should be considered the primary means to achieving successful supply chain management, but it is the one thing most firms struggle with when setting out to manage their supply chains; for, without the proper support, training, tools, trust, and preparedness, process integration most likely will be impossible to ever fully achieve.

The supply chain integration model provides the framework for integrating processes first within the firm and then among trading partners, and this model served as the foundation of the chapter. The eight primary processes that are typically integrated were presented and discussed; these are customer relationship management, customer service management, demand management, order fulfillment, manufacturing flow management, supplier relationship management, product development and commercialization, and returns management. The role played by performance measures in assessing and improving integration was also discussed. Finally, the obstacles to supply chain integration were discussed; these were the silo mentality, lack of supply chain visibility, lack of trust, lack of knowledge, and activities causing the bullwhip effect.

Key Terms

customer relationship management process, 412
customer service management process, 413
data warehouses, 417
demand forecast updating, 426
demand management process, 413
electronic product codes (ePCs), 423
everyday low prices (EDLP), 427
forward buying, 427
functional silos, 412
information visibility, 422

internal supply chain, 416
key supply chain processes, 412
legacy systems, 417
manufacturing flow management process, 414
order batching, 426
order-fulfillment process, 414
point-of-sale information, 413
process integration, 410
product development and commercialization process, 415

radio-frequency identification (RFID) tag, 420
rationing, 427
returns management process, 415
shortage gaming, 427
silo mentality, 420
supplier relationship management process, 414
vendor-managed inventory (VMI), 426

Discussion Questions

1. What does *process integration* mean?
2. What makes a supplier or customer a key or primary supply chain partner? Give some examples.
3. What are the key supply chain business processes, and why are they important?

4. Is it necessary to have internal performance measures for each of the supply chain business processes? Why or why not?

5. Why is an ERP system important for process integration?

6. Think of some supply chain performance measures for several of the eight key supply chain business processes, assuming the strategy is superior customer service.

7. Why is lack of trust an obstacle to supply chain management? How can we overcome this obstacle?

8. Define the bullwhip effect and describe how it can impact supply chain integration.

9. Describe an incidence, either personally or at work, where you have been involved in shortage gaming.

Internet Question

1. Go to the Institute for Supply Management Web site, http://www.ism.ws, and find the listing for the latest ISM Annual International Supply Management Conference. Then find the Conference Proceedings and report on a paper that was presented regarding a topic covered in this chapter.

References

Chopra, S., and P. Meindl. *Supply Chain Management: Strategy, Planning, and Operation.* Upper Saddle River, N.J.: Prentice-Hall, 2001.

Croxton, K. L., S. J. Garcia-Dastugue, D. M. Lambert, and D. S. Rogers. "The Supply Chain Management Processes." *International Journal of Logistics Management* 12, no. 2 (2001): 13–36.

Handfield, R. B., and E. L. Nichols. *Supply Chain Redesign: Transforming Supply Chains into Integrated Value Systems.* Upper Saddle River, N.J.: Financial Times Prentice-Hall, 2002.

Lambert, D. M., M. C. Cooper, and J. D. Pagh. "Supply Chain Management: Implementation Issues and Research Opportunities." *International Journal of Logistics Management* 9, no. 2 (1998): 1–19.

Simchi-Levi, D., P. Kaminsky, and E. Simchi-Levi. *Designing and Managing the Supply Chain.* New York: McGraw-Hill/Irwin, 2003.

Notes

1. D. Marabotti, "Build Supplier Metrics, Build Better Product," *Quality* 42, no. 2 (2003): 40–43.

2. S. Mason, "Innovation, Economy & Supply Chain," *Global Cosmetic Industry* 171, no. 3 (2003): 22–26.

3. B. Bachelor and J. Zaino, "Pave the Way to Success," *Information Week* (17 March 2003): 52–54. Reprinted with permission from CMP Media.

4. D. M. Lambert, M. C. Cooper, and J. D. Pagh, "Supply Chain Management: Implementation Issues and Research Opportunities," *International Journal of Logistics Management* 9, no. 2 (1998): 1–19.

5. H. Richardson, "Does Your Supply Chain Deliver Value?" *Transportation and Distribution* 44, no. 3 (2003): 58–61.

6. T. Datz, "Strategic Alignment: Your Business Processes Can't Enable Superior Customer Service or an Efficient Supply Chain without Integrated Systems. The Four Companies Profiled Here Demonstrate the Benefits of a Strategic Perspective and Long-Term Commitment to Integration," *CIO* 15, no. 21 (2002): 1–64. Reprinted through the courtesy of CIO. Copyright © 2003, CXO Media Inc.

7. J. F. Ince, "Catching Up with SCM's Vision," *Upside* 14, no. 6 (2002): 50–54.

8. B. Bacheldor, "Supply on Demand," *Information Week* (3 March 2003): 47–58.

9. Ibid.

10. L. H. Harrington, "Retail Optimization: Time for Change at Bulgari," *Transportation and Distribution* 44, no. 3 (2003): 54–57. Reprinted with permission from Penton Media Inc.

11. P. Trunick, "It's Crunch Time," *Transportation and Distribution* 43, no. 1 (2002): 5–6.

12. Anonymous, "Survey Finds Manufacturers' Supply Chains Come Up Short," *Logistics Management* 41, no. 9 (2002): 19–20.

13. T. Hoffman, "Utility Turns to EAI Tools to Revamp Supply Chain," *Computerworld* 37, no. 10 (2003): 16–19.

14. J. Fulcher, "RFID's Day Is Coming," *MSI* 21, no. 1 (2003) 24–27.

15. L. Paul, "Suspicious Minds: Collaboration Among Trading Partners Can Unlock Great Value," *CIO* 16, no. 7 (2003): 74–82. Repinted through the courtesy of CIO. Copyright © 2003 CXO Media Inc.

16. Ibid.

17. Ibid.

18. C. Wilder and J. Soat, "The Trust Imperative," *Information Week* (30 July 2001): 34–42.

19. L. Paul, "Suspicious Minds."

20. B. Bacheldor, "Implementation Imperative," *Information Week* (28 April 2003): 62–66.

21. J. Ince, "Catching Up with SCM's Vision," *Upside* 14, no. 6 (2002): 50–54.

22. B. Bacheldor, "Implementation Imperative."

23. P. Alvarez, "Your Supply Chain Management Strategy Must Include the Flow of Education," *Frontline Solutions* 2, no. 13 (2001): 36–40.

24. H. L. Lee, V. Padmanabhan, and S. Whang, "The Bullwhip Effect in Supply Chains," *Sloan Management Review* 38, no. 3 (1997): 93–102.

Chapter 14:

PERFORMANCE MEASUREMENT ALONG THE SUPPLY CHAIN

According to a recent survey, 91 percent of North American manufacturers described supply chain management as either very important or critical to their companies' success, while only 2 percent described their supply chains as world-class.[1]

Learning Objectives

After completing this chapter, you should be able to
- Describe why firms need to measure and assess performance.
- Discuss the merits of financial and nonfinancial performance measures.
- List a number of traditional and world-class performance measures.
- Describe how the balanced scorecard and the SCOR models work.
- Describe how to design a supply chain performance measurement system.

Chapter Outline

Viewing the Supply Chain as a Competitive Weapon
  Understanding End Customers
  Understanding Supply Chain Partner Requirements
  Adjusting Supply Chain Member Capabilities

Traditional Performance Measures
  Use of Organization Costs, Revenue, and Profitability Measures
  Use of Performance Standards and Variances

  Use of Firm-Wide Productivity and Utilization Measures

World-Class Performance Measurement Systems
  Developing World-Class Performance Measures

Supply Chain Performance Measurement Systems
  Specific Supply Chain Performance Measures

The Balanced Scorecard

The Supply Chain Operations Reference Model

SUPPLY CHAIN MANAGEMENT IN ACTION   *Benchmarking the Nation's Best Hospitals*

If overall performance in all acute care U.S. hospitals were the same as the nation's top hospitals, close to 57,000 more patients could survive each year and nearly $9.5 billion in annual expenses could be saved, according to a recent report from Solucient. The findings are highlighted in Solucient's 100 Top Hospitals National Benchmarks for Success, which recognizes 100 hospitals for setting national performance benchmarks across four critical areas: quality of care, operational efficiency, financial performance, and adaptation to the environment. "In short, these hospitals are able to bring increasingly better services to their patients and provide great value to their communities, despite the growing pressures of an aging population and tighter reimbursements," said Jean Chenoweth, executive director of Solucient's 100 Top Hospitals program.

Among the key findings were the following:

- The number of medical complications could decrease by more than 18 percent for patients in nonwinning or "peer" hospitals, affecting more than 150,000 patients annually, if those hospitals improved to the winning or "benchmark" performance level. If all hospitals operated at the benchmark level, a patient's average length of stay could show a marked decrease.

- Winning hospitals treated more and sicker patients than nonwinning hospitals, admitting an average of almost 16 percent more patients and maintaining higher patient-case mix than peer hospitals.

- The 100 Top Hospitals provided more successful outcomes, helping patients survive life-threatening illnesses 10 percent more often than their peers.

- Winning hospitals employed fewer staff but offered nearly $2,000 more per employee in annual salary and benefits than did peer hospitals. A recent related Solucient study indicated that benchmark hospitals tended to maintain higher ratios of registered nurses to inpatient days.

- Total profit margins for winning hospitals were twice that of their peers. However, benchmark hospital revenue tied to outpatient services was lower than at peer hospitals.

- The southern region of the United States was home to the highest number of benchmark hospitals (thirty-one), followed by the north central region (twenty-nine), the northeast region (twenty-six), and the west region (fifteen).

"Our results indicate that winning hospitals are achieving success through routine measurement of key performance indicators and collection of accurate internal and comparative information," Chenoweth said. "These hospitals appear to understand that a focus on daily organizational and clinical processes in combination with sound strategic decision making assures better patient outcomes and greater organizational efficiency." The ninth 100 Top Hospitals Benchmarks for Success study analyzed acute care hospitals nationwide using detailed empirical performance data from 1999 and 2000, including publicly available Medicare MED-PAR data and Medicare cost reports. The measures were calculated for five classes of hospitals with the following number of winners in each: major teaching, sixteen winners; teaching, twenty-five winners; large community, 250+ beds, twenty winners; medium community, 100 to 249 beds, twenty winners; and small community, 25 to 99 beds, twenty winners.

The study scored facilities according to key measures: risk-adjusted mortality and risk-adjusted complications, average length of stay, expenses, profitability, percent of outpatient revenue, total asset turnover, and data quality.[2]

Introduction

This chapter discusses the role and importance of performance measurement for both the firm and its supply chains. The old adage "You can't improve what you can't measure" is certainly true for firms as well as their supply chains. In fact, a report by the Conference Board of Strategic Performance Management in 1998 found that companies using performance measurement were more likely to achieve leadership positions in their industry and were almost twice as likely to handle a major change successfully.[3] While several types of performance measures were discussed or suggested in earlier chapters of this textbook, firms need to develop an entire system of meaningful performance measures to become and then remain competitive, particularly when managing supply chains is one of the imperatives.

Performance measurement systems vary substantially from company to company. For example, many firms' performance measures concentrate solely on the firms' costs and profits. While certainly important, managers must realize that making decisions while relying on cost-based performance alone dooms organizations to continue repeating the mistakes of the past. Even for companies like Wal-Mart that rely on low prices to attract customers, cost performance alone is not enough to succeed without assuring that products are available when needed and at acceptable levels of product quality. Attaining world-class competitive status requires managers to realize that making process decisions to create or purchase products and services customers want and then to distribute them in ways that will satisfy customers may initially cost more for the firm. Thus, it is achieving cost performance together with acceptable levels of quality and customer service performance and then continually improving on these measures that firms must aim toward. Using an adequate system of performance measures allows managers to pursue that vision. Unfortunately, many firms today are not adequately measuring performance. According to a survey by the Institute of Management Accountants' Cost Management Group, only 6 percent of its members were using customer satisfaction as an organizational performance measure.[4]

When managing supply chains, adding several tiers of suppliers and customers further complicates an already-formidable performance measurement problem. With supply chains, the system has become much larger, characterized by a range of relationships and interactions. Performance at the end-product level depends on adequate performance among the primary trading companies along the supply chain. Thus, performance measures must be visible and communicated to all participating members of the supply chain while managers continue to collaborate to achieve results that allow all supply chain members to benefit. Indeed, it will most likely be the case that some member costs will be higher than otherwise would be the case to permit supply chains to offer what end customers want. It is only through cooperation and shared planning and benefits, that an effective supply chain–wide performance measurement system can be designed.

This chapter discusses the basics of performance measurement, including cost-based and other traditional measurements, then moves on to discuss the more effective measurement systems typical of world-class organizations. From there, the discussion moves into measuring the performance of supply chains. Finally, the balanced scorecard and the SCOR model methods of performance measurement that are being utilized effectively in supply chain settings are presented and discussed.

Viewing the Supply Chain as a Competitive Weapon

The eventual and ultimate goal of a supply chain is to successfully deliver products and services to end customers. Traditionally, to meet customer service requirements, firms along the supply chain would simply load their retail shelves, warehouses, and factories with finished goods. Today, though, this strategy would ultimately lead to inventory carrying costs

Global Perspective

TOP MANAGEMENT INVOLVEMENT KEY TO SCM SUCCESS

A survey of top executives found widespread disappointment with information technology–based supply chain improvement investments. New York–based consulting firm Booz Allen Hamilton says that, globally, businesses shell out more than $19 billion annually on such improvements but nearly half of the companies surveyed were disappointed with the results. However, firms at which improvements were driven by top management saw much better results than those that put responsibility for logistics changes at a lower level.

Booz Allen surveyed manufacturing and industrial companies with assets or annual sales over $1 billion in North America, Europe, Asia, and Latin America. Respondents included CEOs, CFOs, CAOs, manufacturing/operations vice presidents and directors, and logistical/shipping directors. The survey indicated that most efforts to improve supply chain efficiency fell short because they did not challenge the fundamental structure of the supply chain but, instead, attempted to improve performance within existing limitations, often by installing expensive new technology. Companies that were able to achieve a higher level of supply chain efficiency were ones willing to break the constraints limiting performance by relocating factories, outsourcing noncore functions, or making other fundamental changes.

"Despite major advances in technology, supply chains still cost more than they should and tie up more inventory, and the underlying reasons haven't changed in twenty years," says Booz Allen vice president Dermot Shorten. "The message is clear: companies looking for improvements must break the mold, not just polish the mold."

CEO participation, the survey found, helps unlock supply chain improvement. Companies that treated supply chain management as a CEO-level item achieved annual savings improvements of 8 percent in their cost to serve customers, nearly double the 4.4 percent savings of firms where responsibility for the supply chain resided lower in the organization. In addition, purchasing savings improved significantly (5.9 percent versus 5.0 percent) for companies at which the CEO was personally engaged in setting the supply chain agenda.

"This is a wake-up call for CEOs to go 'back to basics' and pay closer attention to operations," says Shorten. "Supply chain efficiency improves when CEOs roll up their sleeves and get involved." Other best practices that emerged from the companies that were most successful in improving supply chain performance included the following:

- Involve purchasing, sales, engineering, manufacturing, and top management in supply chain decisions.

- Track well-defined metrics.

- Make explicit delivery promises to customers.

- Share forecasts with suppliers. For example, Pfizer has recently significantly improved its forecasting accuracy by developing new tools to evaluate the results of promotion events on consumption and then using this information to improve shipping effectiveness. As a result, Pfizer's consumer health-care division is an industry leader in forecast accuracy.

Companies making the biggest financial commitment to improving their supply chain management were most likely to feel they received the best return on their investment. More than a fifth, 21 percent, of companies spending $25 million or more on supply chain improvements reported that the results exceeded expectations, compared to only 5 percent for companies who reported spending $1 million or less.[5]

and product prices so high that firms would no longer be competitive. For firms and their supply chains to be effective, customers along the supply chain and the ultimate users must be satisfied. Thus, firms must invest time and effort understanding end customers and supply chain partners and then adjust or acquire supply chain competencies to satisfy the needs of these companies and end customers. To obtain the resources to accomplish these tasks, top managers must become involved and support the firm's improvement efforts. Ultimately, well-designed performance measurement systems within each supply chain partner and integrated throughout the supply chain must be implemented to control and enhance the capabilities of these firms and, thus, the supply chain. Management that stresses the importance of supply chain management while continuing to evaluate the firm and its employees using performance measurement systems that either have no effect or adversely affect the supply chain will ultimately fail in its supply chain management efforts.

Understanding End Customers

According to Anderson, Brit, and Favre, companies must first segment customers based on their service needs, then design a delivery network to meet the needs of those customers.[6] In other words, instead of taking a one-size-fits-all approach to product design and delivery, firms and their supply chains need to look at each segment of the market they serve and determine the needs of those customers. Companies must look at customer segment needs such as

- The variety of products required
- The quantity and delivery frequency needed
- The service level desired
- The product quality desired
- The price of the products

Obviously, depending on the range of customers the company and its supply chains serve, there will be a range in products desired, along with various quantities and delivery needs, product availability and response time needs, product quality demanded, and prices that customers are willing to pay. Henkel-Manco, for instance, best known for its Duck Tape, provides benefits to the customers of retailers like Wal-Mart by designing, branding, and marketing household products as the result of analyzing household buying habits and trends. Manco uses focus groups, expert advisory panels, and a consumer hotline to capture consumer ideas. This way, it can build brand loyalty, provide benefits to its retail customers, and suggest new products to its supply chain partners.[7]

Understanding Supply Chain Partner Requirements

Once firms understand end-customer needs, the next step is determining how best the supply chain can satisfy those needs. Supply chain strategies must consider the potential trade-offs existing between the cost, quality, quantity, and service requirements mentioned earlier. For instance, supply chain responsiveness (meeting due date, lead-time, and quantity requirements, providing high levels of customer service) can come at a cost. To achieve the desired level of responsiveness, companies along the supply chain may also have to become more responsive, requiring investments in additional capacity and faster transportation. Likewise, supply chain quality or reliability (providing customers with the desired levels of product quality) may require investments in newer equipment, better technology, and higher-quality materials and components among participants in the supply chain.

Conversely, increasing supply chain efficiency (enabling retailers to offer lower prices for goods) creates the need among supply chain partners to make adjustments in their production and delivery capabilities that will lower costs. This may include using slower transportation modes, buying and delivering in larger quantities, and reducing the quality of the parts and supplies purchased. Ultimately, firms within a supply chain must decide what combination of customer needs the supply chain will provide, both today and in the long term.

Adjusting Supply Chain Member Capabilities

With these capability requirements understood, supply chain members can then audit their capabilities and those of their supply chain partners to determine if what the members do particularly well is consistent with the needs of the end customers and the supply chain as a whole. Thus, some companies may be well positioned to supply the desired levels of cost,

SUPPLY CHAIN MANAGEMENT IN ACTION

Strategies and Performance at Procter & Gamble

Since early in the nineteenth century, P&G had based its strategy on delivering superior products to consumers. "Sell so that we will be filling the retail shelves as they are empty," said CEO Richard Deupree in 1911. By the late 1970s, this single-minded focus on consumers had earned P&G a reputation among wholesalers and retailers for being inflexible and dictatorial. Perceiving the growing power of these trade customers in the early 1980s, P&G revised its strategy to maintain a constant focus on reinventing the customer interface in pursuit of sustained competitive advantage.

The first step was a series of merchandising and logistics initiatives launched throughout the 1980s under the banner of "total system efficiency." Such efforts as implementing more flexible promotional policies and a damaged goods program signaled a new emphasis on trade customers. These efforts paid off. In 1990, P&G ranked fifteenth among the Fortune 500, up from twenty-third in 1979.

In the early 1990s, P&G took the next big step—a sales reorganization creating multifunctional teams with key customers, notably Wal-Mart, to address issues in such key areas as category management and merchandising, logistics, information technology, and solid waste management. P&G simultaneously developed partnerships with suppliers to reduce cycle times and costs.

P&G more recently introduced the Streamlined Logistics program to improve customer service and supply chain efficiency. The first phase consolidated ordering, receipt, and invoicing of multiple brands; harmonized payment terms; and reduced bracket pricing categories. The implications for customers? As Steven David, vice president of sales, explained: "Now they'll be able to mix a load of soap or paper or food products on a full truck to get the best possible pricing. We're going to make available common-quantity pricing brackets across all our sectors. We're going to have multisector ordering for the first time."

To ensure customer satisfaction, P&G instituted a scorecard performance system to enable both distributors and vendors to evaluate P&G's efficiency in such key areas as category management, assortment, efficient product introduction, promotion, and replenishment.[8]

quality, and customer service performance, while others may not be as well positioned. Matching or adjusting supply chain member capabilities with end-customer requirements can be a very difficult task, particularly if the communication and cooperation levels among companies are not excellent or if companies are serving multiple supply chains and customer segments requiring a different set of capabilities.

In many cases, a dominant company within the supply chain (Wal-Mart, for instance) can use its buying power to leverage demands for supplier conformance to its supply chain requirements. As customer tastes and competition change over time, supply chains can reassess and redesign their strategies for meeting customer requirements and remaining competitive. The Internet, for instance, has become a significant part of many firms' competitive strategies, allowing firms to offer much greater product variety and convenience than ever before.

Thus, matching supply chain capabilities to end-customer requirements means that firms and their supply chain partners must be continually reassessing their performance with respect to these requirements. This brings us back to the importance of performance measures and their ability to relay information regarding the performance of each member within the supply chain, along with the performance of the supply chain vis-à-vis its end customers. Now, more than ever before, successful supply chains are those that can continue to deliver the right combination of cost, quality, and customer service as customer needs change. Weaknesses in any of these areas can mean loss of competitiveness and profits for all members along the supply chain. Today, the best supply chain performers are more responsive to customer needs, quicker to anticipate changes in the markets, and much better at controlling costs, resulting in greater supply chain profits. The next section discusses traditional performance measures.

Traditional Performance Measures

Most performance measures used by firms today continue to be the traditional cost-based and financial statistics reported to the IRS and to shareholders in the form of annual report, balance sheet, and income statement data. This information is relied upon by potential investors and shareholders to make stock transaction decisions and forms the basis for many firms' performance bonuses. Unfortunately, financial statements and other cost-based information do not necessarily reflect the underlying performance of the productive systems of an organization; and, as most people witnessed with companies like Enron and WorldCom a few years ago, cost and profit information can be hidden or manipulated to make performance seem far better than it really is. Decisions that are made solely to maximize current stock prices do not necessarily reflect that the firm is performing well or will continue to perform well into the future. Success depends on the firm's ability to turn internal competencies into products and services that customers want, while providing desired availability, quality, and customer service levels at a reasonable price. Financial performance measures, while important, cannot adequately capture a firm's ability to excel in these areas.

Use of Organization Costs, Revenue, and Profitability Measures

Costs, revenues, and profits might at first glance seem to be useful types of performance measures, but several problems are associated with using them to gauge performance. Windfall profits that occur when prices suddenly rise due to supply interruptions, as is occasionally the case in the oil industry, provide one example. When this happens, firms like airline companies experience much higher costs and reductions in profits. Similarly, many tourist destinations like Las Vegas were hit hard after September 11, 2001, causing hotels to report much lower occupancies and profits in the following months. These profits, or lack thereof, were not the result of something the firms did or did not do particularly well; they were caused for the most part by uncontrollable environmental conditions. Thus, changes in these statistics may not accurately reflect the true capabilities of the firm.

Another problem with the use of costs, revenues, or profits as performance measures is the difficulty, in most cases, to attribute cost, revenue, or profit contributions to the various functional units or business units of the organization. Many departments and units are interdependent and share costs, equipment, labor, and revenues, making it extremely difficult to

© 2000 Ted Goff

"We need to cut down on productivity, quality and customer service to save money."

split out costs and revenues equitably. Additionally, using cost as a departmental or business unit performance measure can result in actions that actually raise costs for the organization. For example, rewarding the purchasing department for minimizing costs might increase product return rates and warranty repair costs due to poor quality part purchases. Minimizing transportation costs might result in lower levels of customer service, causing a loss of customers. Finally, the practice of allocating overhead costs based on a department's percentage of direct labor hours causes managers to waste time trying to reduce direct labor hours to reduce overhead cost allocations when, today, direct labor accounts for only a small fraction of total costs. In essence, these overhead costs merely get transferred somewhere else in the firm, leaving the organization no better off and perhaps in worse shape due to the loss of valuable labor resources.

Use of Performance Standards and Variances

Establishing standards for performance comparison purposes can be particularly troublesome and even damaging to an organization. Establishing output standards like 1,000 units/day or productivity standards like ten units/labor hour establishes an ultimate goal that can drive employees and managers to do whatever it takes to reach the goal, even if it means producing shoddy work or "cooking" the books. Additionally, once goals are actually reached, there is also no further incentive to improve or produce any further.

When standards are not reached, a **performance variance** is created, which is the difference between the standard and actual performance. When organizations hold managers up to performance standards, which then create performance variances, managers can be pressured to find ways to make up these variances, resulting in decisions that may not be in the long-term best interests of the firm. Decisions like producing to make an output quota regardless of current finished goods inventory levels or purchasing unneeded supplies just to use up department budgets are examples of things that can happen when performance standards are applied without considering the true performance benefits to the organization. When applied at the functional level, these standards act to reinforce the idea of functional silos. Departments are then assessed on meeting functional standards instead of optimizing firm or supply chain performance.

Use of Firm-Wide Productivity and Utilization Measures

Firm-wide total productivity measures or single-factor productivity measures, such as

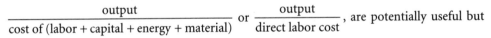

$$\frac{\text{output}}{\text{cost of (labor + capital + energy + material)}} \quad \text{or} \quad \frac{\text{output}}{\text{direct labor cost}}, \text{ are potentially useful but}$$

have the same problems as the use of revenues, costs, and profits for performance measures. These measures, while allowing firms to view the impact of one or any number of the firm's inputs on the firm's outputs (such as units produced), do not allow the firm to determine the actual performance of any of these elements.

Decisions made to increase productivity may prove to actually increase a firm's costs and reduce quality or output in the long term, ultimately reducing productivity. For example, a business unit might be tempted to produce at levels greater than demand, to increase productivity while increasing inventories and inventory carrying costs. Or, managers might be inclined to lay off workers and buy the cheapest materials to maximize their productivity ratios without considering the impact on the firm's quality, customer service, and employee morale. Productivity measures can thus prove to be damaging if used inappropriately. Example 14.1 provides a look at calculating productivity.

EXAMPLE 14.1   Productivity measures at Chris and Nancy's Ski Emporium

Chris and Nancy Heavey make top-of-the-line custom snow skis for high-end ski shops, as well as their own small retail shop, with five other employees. Chris has been adamant about finding a way to increase productivity, because their sales have been flat for the past two seasons. Given the following information, he has calculated the single-factor and total productivity values as:

$$\text{Labor productivity} = 1{,}000 \text{ skis}/10{,}800 \text{ hours} = 0.093 \text{ skis per labor hour}$$
$$\text{Material productivity} = 1{,}000 \text{ skis}/\$18{,}000 = 0.056 \text{ skis per dollar of materials}$$
$$\text{Lease productivity} = 1{,}000 \text{ skis}/\$24{,}000 = 0.042 \text{ skis per lease dollar}$$

He calculates their total productivity by first multiplying the labor hours by their average wage of $17 per hour, and finds:

$$\text{Total productivity} = 1{,}000 \text{ skis}/[10{,}800(\$17) + \$18{,}000 + \$24{,}000]$$
$$= 0.0044 \text{ skis per dollar.}$$

Inputs and Outputs	Last Year
Skis produced	1,000
Labor hours	10,800
Materials purchased	$18,000
Lease payments	$24,000

So, Chris figures he can get some great improvements in productivity by finding a cheaper supplier, moving to a cheaper location, and laying off two workers (reducing his workforce by 40 percent), making his new single-factor productivities:

$$\text{Labor productivity} = 1{,}000 \text{ skis}/10{,}800(.6) \text{ hours} = 0.154 \text{ (a 66 percent increase)}$$
$$\text{Material productivity} = 1{,}000 \text{ skis}/\$12{,}000 = 0.083 \text{ (a 48 percent increase)}$$
$$\text{Lease productivity} = 1{,}000/\$18{,}000 = 0.056 \text{ (a 33 percent increase)}$$

and his new total productivity:

$$\text{Total productivity} = 1{,}000 \text{ skis}/[10{,}800(\$17)(.6) + \$12{,}000 + \$18{,}000]$$
$$= 0.0071 \text{ skis per dollar (a whopping 61 percent increase!)}$$

So, Chris talked Nancy into making the changes for the coming year. Unfortunately, they went out of business in six months, due to poor quality materials, a bad location, and overworked employees.

Labor and machine utilization can be shown as $\dfrac{\text{actual units produced}}{\text{standart output level}}$ or $\dfrac{\text{actual hours utilized}}{\text{total hours available}}$. These performance measures can encourage the firm once again to reduce labor levels until everyone is overworked, causing queues of work or customers to develop, morale to suffer, and quality and customer service levels to erode. Additionally, as with the measures already discussed, there is a tendency to continue producing and adding to inventory just to keep machines and people busy. Less time is spent doing preventive maintenance, training, and projects that can lead to greater performance and profits in the future. While it is obviously beneficial to meet demand and keep labor costs at optimal levels, maximizing utilization can prove to be very expensive for firms.

Thus, the emphasis on overall performance in terms of generalized criteria such as the firm's financial, output, productivity, or utilization characteristics does not tell the entire story. While it certainly is important for firms to possess financial strength and high levels of productivity and utilization, these measures do not tell a detailed story of the firm's performance. Using general and internally focused measures like these do not give any clues as to specific problems that may exist or how to go about solving the problems. Managers are left to guess at what types of actions are needed and have no way of knowing if any corrections made actually had the intended effect. What is needed is a set of detailed performance measures throughout the organization and extending to supply chain partners that are consistent with firm and supply chain strategies; allow managers to find root causes of performance failures; and, finally, lead managers to problem solutions.

Traditional performance measures also tend to be short-term-oriented. To maximize profits next quarter, firms may spend considerable time delaying capital investments, selling assets, denying new project proposals, contracting out work, and leasing instead of purchasing equipment. These actions can significantly reduce a firm's ability to develop new products and remain competitive. New product research, new technology purchases, new facilities, and newly trained people all enhance the capabilities of the firm and position it to keep up with ever-changing customer requirements; but these things all initially reduce the performance measures that we have discussed. Without this infusion of ideas and capital expenditures, though, firms will ultimately perform poorly.

On the other hand, world-class organizations realize that long-term competitive advantage is created when firms' strategies are geared toward continually meeting and exceeding customer expectations of product and service cost, quality, dependability, flexibility, and innovation. These firms realize that investments to improve the firm's capabilities in these areas will eventually bear fruit and position the firm to be successful in the long term. Effective performance measurement systems link current operating characteristics to these long-term strategies and objectives.

World-Class Performance Measurement Systems

As many of the world's businesses respond to increased competitive pressures by attempting to develop and maintain a distinctive competitive advantage, the need to develop effective performance measurement systems linking firm strategy to operating decisions increases. Performance criteria that guide a firm's decision making to achieve strategic objectives must be easy to implement, understand, and measure; they must be flexible and consistent with the firm's objectives; and they must be implemented in areas that are viewed as critical to the success of the firm. Thus, an effective performance measurement system should consist of the traditional financial information for external reporting purposes along with tactical-level performance criteria used to assess the firm's competitive capabilities while directing its efforts to attain other desired capabilities. Finally, a good performance measurement system should include measures of *what is important to customers*. These measures will vary by company and through time as strategic changes occur to the firm, its products, and its supply chains.

Developing World-Class Performance Measures

Creating an effective performance measurement system involves the following steps:[9]

- Identify the firm's strategic objectives.
- Develop an understanding of each functional area's role and the required capabilities for achieving the strategic objectives.
- Identify internal and external trends likely to affect the firm and its performance over time.

Table 14.1	World-Class Performance Measures
Capability Areas	**Performance Measures**
Quality	1. No. of defects per unit produced and per unit purchased 2. No. of product returns per units sold 3. No. of warranty claims per units sold 4. No. of suppliers used 5. Lead time from defect detection to correction 6. No. of work centers using statistical process control 7. No. of suppliers who are quality certified 8. No. of quality awards applied for; no. awards won
Cost	1. Scrap or spoilage losses per work center 2. Average inventory turnover 3. Average setup time 4. Employee turnover 5. Avg. safety stock levels 6. No. of rush orders required for meeting delivery dates 7. Downtime due to machine breakdowns
Flexibility	1. Average number of labor skills 2. Average production lot size 3. No. of customized services available 4. No. of days to process special or rush orders
Dependability	1. Average service response time or product lead time 2. Percentage of delivery promises kept 3. Avg. no. of Days late per shipment 4. No. of stock-outs per product 5. No. of days to process a warranty claim 6. Avg. number of hours spent with customers by engineers
Innovation	1. Annual investment in R&D 2. Percentage of automated processes 3. No. of new product or service introductions 4. No. of process steps required per product

- For each functional area, develop performance measures that describe each area's capabilities.

- Document current performance measures and identify changes that must be implemented.

- Assure the compatibility and strategic focus of the performance measures to be used.

- Implement the new performance system.

- Periodically reevaluate the firm's performance measurement system as competitive strategies change.

Thus, world-class firms establish strategically oriented performance criteria among each of the functional areas of the firm within the categories of quality, cost, flexibility, dependability, and innovation and then revisit these measures as problems are solved, competition and customer requirements change, and supply chain and firm strategies change. Table 14.1 lists a number of performance measures that might be used in different functional areas of the firm to satisfy objectives, enhance the value of the firm's products and services, and increase customer satisfaction.

Supply Chain Performance Measurement Systems

Performance measurement systems for supply chains must effectively link the supply chain trading partners to achieve breakthrough performance in satisfying the end users. While at the local or interfirm level the performance measures discussed here are required for world-class performance, measures must also overlay the entire supply chain to assure that firms are all contributing to supply chain strategy and the satisfaction of end consumers.

In a successful supply chain, members jointly agree on a supply chain performance measurement system. The focus of the system should be on value creation for end customers, since customer satisfaction drives sales for all of the supply chain's members. While challenging to implement, supply chains are pulling it off. In a major study done by the Performance Measurement Group from 1995 and 2000, the top supply chain performers were found to be leading the way in a number of areas:[10]

- *High levels of responsiveness and flexibility:* Overall supply chain performance improved by 65 percent.

- *High levels of efficiency:* Total supply chain management costs fell by 27 percent, and cash-to-cash cycle time fell by 18 percent.

- *Use of the Internet to fundamentally alter communications among trading partners:* Orders placed via the Internet were quickly replacing telephone, mail, and FAX orders. The Internet was also being used to transmit shipment, order, and inventory status.

- *Perfect order fulfillment is becoming the new definition of reliability:* Perfect order fulfillment or complete, on-time, and damage-free orders increased by 5 percent.

Leading supply chains are achieving superior customer service levels at competitive prices, and their performance is improving continuously each year.

Specific Supply Chain Performance Measures

To achieve the type of performance shown in the preceeding section, specific measures must be adopted for the supply chain itself, allowing trading partners to adjust their specific performance to further align with supply chain objectives. A number of these are listed here.[11]

1. *Total supply chain management costs:* The cost to process orders; purchase materials; manage inventories; and manage supply chain finance, planning, and information systems. Leading supply companies are spending from 4 to 5 percent of sales on supply chain management costs, while the average company spends about 5 to 6 percent.

2. *Supply chain cash-to-cash cycle time:* The average number of days between paying for raw materials and getting paid for product for the supply chain trading partners (calculated by inventory days of supply plus days of sales outstanding minus average payment period for material). This measure shows the impact of lower inventories on the speed of cash moving through firms and the supply chain. Top supply chain companies have a cash-to-cash cycle time of about thirty days, which is far less than the average company. These trading partners no longer view "slow paying" as a viable strategy.

3. *Supply chain production flexibility:* The average time required for supply chain members to provide an unplanned, sustainable 20 percent increase in production. The ability for the supply chain to quickly react to unexpected demand spikes while still operating within financial targets provides tremendous competitive advantage. One common supply chain practice is to maintain stocks of component parts locally for supply chain customers to quickly respond to unexpected demand increases. Average production flexibility for best-in-class supply chains is from one to two weeks.

4. *Supply chain delivery performance:* The average percentage of orders for the supply chain members that are filled on or before the requested delivery date. In the top-performing supply chains, delivery dates are being met from 94 to 100 percent of the time. For average firms, delivery performance is approximately 70 to 80 percent. Updating customers on the expected delivery dates of orders is becoming a common e-service for many supply chains.

e-BUSINESS CONNECTION
MEASURING e-BUSINESS PERFORMANCE

Akamai Technologies, Inc., a leading provider of secure, outsourced e-business infrastructure services and software, and Gomez, Inc., the Internet Quality Measurement firm, have formed a strategic relationship to provide e-businesses with performance measurement solutions, providing real-time insight into end-user geo-location and network characterization data.

"Enterprises with e-business systems recognize the value of providing a consistent user experience. To do this, management vendors need to provide solutions that measure the quality of end-user interaction with business systems," says Jeb Bolding, research director at Enterprise Management Associates, a firm that specializes in management software and services. "Combining Akamai's IP intelligence capabilities with Gomez's performance measurement capabilities enables organizations to better understand the impact of specific Internet networking patterns on quality of service."

Gomez provides Internet quality measurement services that deliver competitive benchmarking, intelligence, and insight to help companies optimize their customers' on-line experiences. As part of the agreement between the two companies, Gomez has licensed the Akamai EdgeScape technology to add IP intelligence to the information available through the Gomez Performance Network, which measures Web page and transaction performance in real time. EdgeScape's IP intelligence includes characterization of individual IP addresses by measured connection speed and geo-location to the city level, enabling Gomez to enrich its analyses with data that show how end-

user location and Internet connection speed affect the quality of the on-line experience. "Gomez is committed to innovating new ways of capturing and presenting critical performance measurement information to help today's leading e-businesses better benchmark and optimize their Web site performance," said Jeff Banker, vice president at Gomez. "Akamai's proven technology and global network presence will enhance the value of our services by revealing a unique view into the quality of the end user's Internet experience based on geographic location and measured bandwidth throughput."

"Now more than ever, businesses are focusing on driving maximum benefit from their e-marketing investments," said Michael Ruffolo, executive vice president, Global Sales, Services and Marketing, Akamai. "As a leader in performance measurement, Gomez understands these challenges, and we're pleased to assist their efforts in using IP intelligence to maximize the value of their offerings and increase revenues."

With its massively distributed global platform and continuous mapping of the Internet, Akamai has an exceptional ability to provide e-businesses with real-time network knowledge for the delivery of targeted content and the protection of its digital goods and information. The EdgeScape technology correlates geographic and network information to IP addresses, enabling the customization of content without compromising end-user privacy. By leveraging the EdgeScape technology, Gomez will be able to help e-businesses measure the quality of on-line experience according to an end user's Internet connection speed or geographic location.[13]

5. *Supply chain perfect order fulfillment performance:* The average percentage of orders for supply chain members that arrive on time, complete, and damage free. This is quickly becoming the standard for delivery performance and represents a significant source of competitive advantage for top-performing supply chains and their member companies.

6. *Supply chain e-business performance:* The average percentage of electronic orders received for all supply chain members. In 1998, only about 2 percent of all firms'

purchase orders were made over the Internet. By 2000, 75 percent of purchasing professionals surveyed said their firms were using the Internet for some of their orders.[12] Today, supply chain companies are investing heavily in e-based order-receipt systems, marketing strategies, and other forms of communication and research using the Internet.

When combined with the world-class performance measures of Table 14.1, the measures shown here help supply chain trading partners align themselves with supply chain strategies, creating competencies that lead to dominant positions in their markets. Perhaps most important, this type of performance has translated into approximately 75 percent higher profits when compared to the average company.[14]

The Balanced Scorecard

The **balanced scorecard (BSC)** approach to performance measurement was developed by Kaplan and Norton in 1992, as a way to align an organization's performance measures with its strategic plan and goals, thus improving managerial decision making.[15] It has been a widely used model and, by 1998, 60 percent of the Fortune 1000 companies had experimented with the BSC.[16] Many companies have reported notable successes with the use of the BSC including Mobil Oil, Tenneco, Brown & Root, AT&T, Intel, Allstate, Ernst & Young, and KPMG Peat Marwick.[17]

The BSC is designed to provide managers with a formal framework for achieving a balance between nonfinancial and financial results across both short-term and long-term planning horizons. The BSC framework consists of four perspectives, as shown in Figure 14.1:

- *Financial perspective:* Measures that address revenue growth, product mix, cost reduction, productivity, asset utilization, and investment strategy

- *Internal business process perspective:* Focuses on performance of the most critical internal business processes of the organization including quality, flexibility, innovative elements of processes, and time-based measures

---

Figure 14.1   The Balanced Scorecard Framework

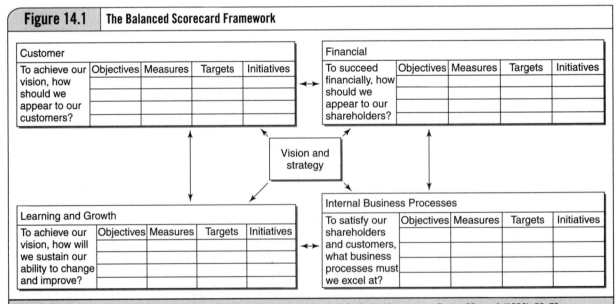

Source: R. S. Kaplan and D. P. Norton, "Linking the Balanced Scorecard to Strategy," *California Management Review* 39, no. 1 (1996): 53–79.

- *Customer perspective:* Measures that focus on customer requirements and satisfaction including customer satisfaction ratings, customer retention, new customer acquisition, customer valued attributes, customer profitability, and market share

- *Learning and growth perspective:* Measures concentrating on the organization's people, systems, and procedures including intellectual assets, re-training employees, enhancing information technology and systems, and employee satisfaction

These perspectives are all linked together through performance measures within each of the four areas. Measurements are developed for each goal in the organization's strategic plan and include both outcome measures and the performance drivers of those outcomes. In doing this, senior managers can channel the specific set of capabilities within the organization toward achieving the firm's goals. A properly constructed scorecard should support the firm's strategy and consist of a linked series of measures that are consistent and reinforcing.

The process of developing a balanced scorecard begins with defining the firm's strategy. Once the firm's strategy is understood and agreed upon by senior managers, the next step is to translate the strategy's goals into a system of performance measures. Each of the four perspectives in the BSC require four to seven performance measures, resulting in a scorecard with about two dozen measures relating to one single strategy. The potential for failure, though, does exist when using the BSC if firms are not clear about what they are hoping to achieve and are not determined to ensure that the best scorecard with the right performance measures linked to firm strategy is used.

SUPPLY CHAIN MANAGEMENT IN ACTION   *Adapting the BSC to the Public Sector*

For more than twenty-five years, Charlotte, North Carolina, measured government efficiency and effectiveness by setting objectives and tracking performance against them. Although the method served the city well, it focused primarily on the past. Therefore, the city began searching for a performance measurement system that emphasized strategic planning for the future. In the early 1990s the city manager researched the balanced scorecard and adapted the model to apply to the public sector, becoming the first U.S. city to do so.

The Charlotte City Council chose five areas on which to focus its strategic plan: community safety, transportation, economic development, neighborhoods, and restructuring government. Those priorities were later modeled to represent the "corporate" level of the city's scorecard. The council's scorecard did not include every important service delivered such as sidewalk installation, garbage pickup, or fire suppression; these were better addressed on a city department or division scorecard. Instead, the scorecard reflected the processes that must improve in order for the council to meet its strategic goals.

In late 1996, after the Charlotte City Council had established the city's corporate scorecard, the process was repeated by the planning, transportation, engineering and property management, and police departments. Department-level objectives were matched with council-level objectives to ensure that the city would achieve its highest priorities. Today, all of the city's departments have scorecards. The concept of having only a few performance indicators had been troublesome since previously there were unlimited measures. However, with the council's support and the participation of the departments, the city was able to clarify its critical objectives, identify the processes necessary to meet them, and produce a concise model to assist officials in tracking the city's progress.[18]

Table 14.2	Balanced Scorecard Measures for Supply Chains
Customer Perspective	1. Number of customer contact points in the supply chain 2. Customer order response time 3. Customer perception of supply chain value
Internal Business Processes Perspective	1. Value-added time/total time in supply chain 2. No. of choices/order cycle time
Financial Perspective	1. Supply chain costs of purchasing, carrying inventory, poor quality, and delivery failure 2. Percentage of supply chain target costs achieved 3. Percentage of supply chain profits earned 4. Cash-to-cash cycle time 5. Return on supply chain assets
Learning and Growth Perspective	1. Time between product finalization and customer delivery 2. No. of shared data sets/total data sets 3. No. of substitute technologies demanded by customers

The BSC can be also be utilized by firms in a collaborative supply chain setting by expanding the internal perspective of the scorecard to include interfunctional and partnership perspectives that characterize the supply chain.[19] In this way, for instance, the firm's employees are motivated to view their firm's performance vis-à-vis the success of the entire supply chain. The cash-to-cash cycle time is one example of an integrated measure embracing several functions across several organizations. Brewer and Speh provide a number of measures that span firm boundaries in a supply chain, and these are shown in Table 14.2. These and other supply-chain-oriented measures can thus be added to the more internally focused measures traditionally used in a balanced scorecard to help the firm, as well as its supply chains, meet its objectives.

The Supply Chain Operations Reference Model

One of the more recognized methods for integrating supply chains and measuring their members' performance is the **supply chain operations reference (SCOR)** model developed in 1996 by the Supply-Chain Council, a nonprofit global organization of more than 800 firms interested in supply chain management. The Supply-Chain Council's members continuously review and update the model for use by its members and others, who can purchase the SCOR model software. The SCOR model integrates the operations of supply chain members by linking the delivery operations of the seller to the sourcing operations of the buyer, as shown in Figure 14.2.

The SCOR model is used as a supply chain management diagnostic, benchmarking, and process improvement tool by manufacturing and service firms in a variety of industries around the globe. Some of the more notable firms to have success using the SCOR model include Intel, IBM, 3M, Cisco, Siemens, and Bayer. Striving for the best telecommunications supply chain, Alcatel used SCOR metrics following the economic downturn of 2001 to measure and benchmark its performance. Major improvements were realized in delivery performance, sourcing cycle time, supply chain management cost, and inventory days of supply.[20]

The SCOR model separates supply chain operations into five process categories—plan, source, make, deliver, and return:[21]

- *Plan:* Demand and supply planning including balancing resources with requirements; establishing/communicating plans for the supply chain; management of business rules, supply chain performance, data collection, inventory, capital assets, transportation, and regulatory requirements

- *Source:* Sourcing stocked, make-to-order, and engineer-to-order products including scheduling deliveries; receiving, verifying, and transferring product;

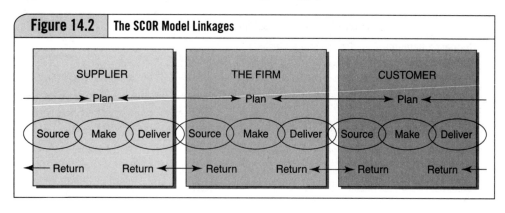

Figure 14.2 | The SCOR Model Linkages

authorizing supplier payments; identifying and selecting suppliers; assessing supplier performance; and managing incoming inventory and supplier agreements

- *Make:* Make-to-stock, make-to-order, and engineer-to-order production execution including scheduling production activities; producing, testing, packaging, staging, and releasing product for delivery; finalizing engineering for engineer-to-order products; and managing work-in-process, equipment, facilities, and the production network

- *Deliver:* Order, warehouse, transportation, and installation management for stocked, make-to-order, and engineer-to-order product including all order management steps from order inquiries and quotes to routing shipments and selecting carriers, warehouse management from receiving and picking to loading and shipping product, invoicing customer, and managing finished product inventories and import/export requirements

- *Return:* Returns of purchased materials to suppliers and receipt of finished goods returns from customers including authorizing and scheduling returns; receiving, verifying, and disposition of defective or excess products; return replacement or credit; and managing return inventories

There are three standardized levels of process detail in the SCOR model. At Level 1, users select appropriate process categories from the SCOR configuration toolkit to represent their supply chain and select from thirteen performance attributes as shown in Table 14.3. In Level 2, the SCOR processes are further described by process type. Within each process type are process categories that users specify. The process types and categories are shown in Table 14.4. In Level 3, process flow diagrams are defined with process elements or specific tasks for each of the process categories established in Level 2, showing inputs, process elements, and outputs. Additionally, specific performance measures are identified for each of the process elements within the flow diagrams. Some example measures are shown in Table 14.5. Best practices can also be identified at this level. Finally, implementation of supply chain management practices within the company occurs at Level 4 and beyond.

As can be seen in the tables, implementing the SCOR model is no simple task and requires a significant investment of time and communication within the firm and among supply chain partners. But the firms who use the model find it very helpful. For instance, Mr. Joe Williams, director of global productivity at Mead Johnson Nutritionals, a division of Bristol-Myers Squibb, says the SCOR model is playing a big role in helping its unit measure its supply chain performance against other companies. But getting those measurements "is a big job," he said. "SCOR is definitive in some respects and open to interpretation in others."[22]

Table 14.3	SCOR Level 1 Performance Categories and Attributes
Performance Category	**Performance Attribute**
Reliability	1. Delivery performance 2. Fill rates 3. Perfect order fulfillment
Responsiveness	1. Order fulfillment lead times
Flexibility	1. Supply chain response times 2. Production flexibility
Cost	1. Supply chain management cost 2. Cost of goods sold 3. Value-added productivity 4. Warranty cost or returns processing cost
Assets	1. Cash-to-cash cycle time 2. Inventory days of supply 3. Asset turns

Table 14.4	SCOR Level 2 Process Types and Categories	
SCOR Process Type	**Characteristics**	**Process Category**
Planning	Processes that align expected resources to meet expected demand requirements.	P1: Plan supply chain P2: Plan source P3: Plan make P4: Plan deliver P5: Plan return
Execution	Processes triggered by planned or actual demand that changes the state of material goods. These are source (S1-3), make (M1-3), deliver (D1-3), and return (R1-3) processes.	S1: Source stocked product D1: Deliver stocked product S2: Source MTO product D2: Deliver MTO product S3: Source ETO product D3: Deliver ETO product M1: Make-to-stock R1: Return defective product M2: Make-to-order R2: Return MRO product M3: Engineer-to-order R3: Return excess product
Enable	Processes that prepare, maintain, or manage information or relationships on which planning and execution processes rely.	EX1: Establish and manage rules EX2: Assess performance EX3: Manage data EX4: Manage inventory EX5: Manage capital assets EX6: Manage transportation EX7: Manage supply chain configuration EX8: Manage regulatory compliance EX9: Process specific elements (align SC/financials, supplier agreements) (*Note:* X = P,S,M,D,R)

Table 14.5	SCOR Level 3 Performance Categories and Measures
Process Element: Schedule Process Deliveries	
Performance Attribute Categories	**Measures**
Reliability	Percentage of schedules generated within supplier's lead time Percentage of schedules changed within supplier's lead time
Responsiveness	Average release cycle of changes
Flexibility	Average days per schedule change Average days per engineering change
Cost	Product management and planning costs as a percentage of product acquisitions costs
Assets	None identified

Thus, as can be seen by the information presented here, the SCOR model is used to describe, measure, and evaluate supply chain configurations. The model is designed to enable effective communication, performance measurement, and integration of processes between supply chain members. A standardized reference model helps management focus on management issues, serve internal and external customers, and instigate improvements along the supply chain. Using the SCOR software, virtually any supply chain can be configured, evaluated, and benchmarked against best practices, leading to continuous improvements and sustainable competitive advantage for the supply chain's participating members. At Nabisco, for instance, the SCOR model is used to link two separate foods divisions. Its U.S. Foods Division ships to warehouses, while its Biscuits Division ships direct to retail outlets. It also uses SCOR to see if its handling of returns is keeping up with the industry best practices.[23]

Summary

Measuring the performance of supply chains and their member firms is critical for identifying underlying supply chain problems and in keeping end customers satisfied in today's highly competitive, rapidly changing marketplace. Unfortunately, many firms have adopted performance measurement systems that measure the wrong things and are thus finding it difficult to achieve strategic goals and align their goals with those of the other supply chain members and the supply chain as a whole. Good performance measures drive performance and can turn a mediocre supply chain into a world-class supply chain that benefits all of its members.

Financial performance, while important to shareholders, is argued to provide too little information regarding the long-term effectiveness of the firm in satisfying customers. Thus, use of measures that say something about the firm's product quality, productivity, and customer service capabilities have begun to be used successfully in many organizations. World-class organizations realize how important it is to align strategies with the performance of their people and processes, and performance measurement systems give these firms a means for directing efforts and firm capabilities toward what the firm is trying to do over the long haul—meet strategic objectives and satisfy customers.

As was discussed throughout the chapter, performance measurement systems should be a mix of financial, nonfinancial, quantitative, qualitative, cost-oriented, process-oriented, and customer-oriented measures that effectively link the actions of the firm to the strategies defined by the firm's executive managers. Firms trying to manage their supply chains have an added layer of performance measure requirements—measures must be added that link the operations of member firms as well as linking the actions of the firms to the competitive strategies of the supply chain. Several performance measurement models were presented in the chapter that have been successfully used in supply chains to monitor and link performance—namely, the balanced scorecard and the supply chain operations reference models.

Key Terms

balanced scorecard (BSC), 444   **performance variance, 438**   **supply chain operations reference (SCOR), 446**

Discussion Questions

1. Explain what performance measurement has to do with a firm's competitiveness.
2. Are cost-based performance measures good to use? Explain.
3. What should be the primary objective of a good performance measurement system?
4. In building supply chain competencies, what are the trade-offs that must be considered?

5. List some of the traditional performance measures and describe their value in today's competitive climate.

6. Discuss the use of performance standards and performance variances. Do schools and universities use them? How can they be damaging to the organization?

7. What are functional silos?

8. What is the difference between a total productivity measure and a single factor productivity measure?

9. List some productivity measures for a restaurant, a quick-change oil garage, and an overnight delivery service.

10. **Discussion Problem:** Cindy Jo's Hair Salon is concerned about its rising costs of supplies, energy, and labor, so it is considering investing in better equipment, which hopefully will reduce the time required to perform most hair styles as well as resulting in better perceived quality by its customers. It predicts that the added investment will increase output levels as well as reduce energy costs, since some of the new equipment (hair dryers) uses less electricity. Using the following information, determine the current and expected single factor and total productivity measures. What other items should be considered before making this capital investment? Do you think the increase in output will overcome the capital costs?

Inputs and Outputs	Current (This Year)	Expected (Next Year)
Hairstyles per week	250	300
Labor costs per week	$960	$1,010
Energy costs per week	$400	$350
Material costs per week	$300	$325
Capital investment	$0	$12,000

11. What are the advantages and disadvantages of using labor utilization as a performance measure? Do these same arguments apply to machine utilization?

12. How could you increase labor productivity without increasing labor utilization?

13. What do you think a good labor utilization would be?

14. What makes a performance measurement system "world-class"?

15. Using the steps suggested for developing performance measures, create several world-class performance measures for a hotel's front-desk area; maintenance department; room service personnel.

16. How do supply chain performance measures differ from a single firm's performance measures?

17. What is perfect order fulfillment? Cash-to-cash cycle time?

18. Describe the four perspectives of the balanced scorecard.

19. What are the steps in developing a balanced scorecard?

20. What are the five process categories of the SCOR model and which one do you think is most important?

21. Describe what happens as firms progress through the three standardized levels of process detail in the SCOR model.

22. Which model do you think is best suited to measure supply chain performance—the balanced scorecard or the SCOR? Why?

Internet Questions

1. Starting in 2000, put together a time line of newsworthy company performance events regarding the Enron Corporation (http://www.enron.com).

2. Go to the U.S. Bureau of Labor Statistics on the Internet at http://www.bls.gov, and report on the labor and total productivity of the United States and of other countries listed. How does the United States stack up?

3. Go to http://www.economagic.com and look at utilization numbers for U.S. manufacturers. What is it now? What have the trends been for the past ten years?

4. Go to the Ritz-Carlton Web site (http://www.ritzcarlton.com) and see if you can find performance measures that are used in the company.

References

Evans, J. R., and W. M. Lindsay. *The Management and Control of Quality*. Mason, Ohio: South-Western, 2002.

Kaplan, R. S., and D. P. Norton. "Linking the Balanced Scorecard to Strategy." *California Management Review* 39, no. 1 (1996): 53–79.

Metters, R., K. King-Metters, and M. Pullman. *Successful Service Operations Management*. Mason, Ohio: South-Western, 2003.

Nichols, J. M. *Competitive Manufacturing Management*. New York: McGraw-Hill, 1998.

Wisner, J. D., and S. E. Fawcett. "Linking Firm Strategy to Operating Decisions Through Performance Measurement." *Production and Inventory Management Journal* 32, no. 3 (1991): 5–11.

Notes

1. D. Elmuti, "The Perceived Impact of Supply Chain Management on Organizational Effectiveness," *Journal of Supply Chain Management* 38, no. 3 (2002): 49–57.

2. Anonymous, "Solucient: 57,000 Lives, $9.5 Billion Could Be Saved If All Hospitals Performed as Well as Top 100," *Health Care Strategic Management* 21, no. 2 (2003): 6. Reprinted courtesy of Health Care Strategic Management/The Business Word, Inc.

3. B. L. Adams, "Performance Measures and Profitability Factors of Successful African-American Entrepreneurs: An Exploratory Study," *Journal of American Academy of Business* 2, no. 2 (2003): 418–24.

4. M. J. Ross, "Avoiding the Performance Trap: Measuring Your Achievements, Not Your Activity," *Annual Quality Congress Proceedings* (1988): 407.

5. Anonymous, "Study: CEO Involvement Key to Supply Chain Improvement," *Frozen Food Age,* 51, no. 12 (2003): 49. Reprinted with permission.

6. D. L. Anderson, F. F. Britt, and D. J. Favre, "The Seven Principles of Supply Chain Management," *Supply Chain Management Review* (Spring 1997): 31–43.

7. R. D. Blackwell and K. Blackwell, "The Century of the Consumer: Converting Supply Chains into Demand Chains," *Supply Chain Management Review* (Fall 1999): 22–32.

8. Adapted from D. L. Anderson, F. F. Britt, and D. J. Favre, "The Seven Principles of Supply Chain Management." Reprinted with permission of Supply Chain Management Review, Copyright 1997.

9. Adapted from J. M. Nicholas, *Competitive Manufacturing Management* (New York: McGraw-Hill, 1998); and J. D. Wisner and S. E. Fawcett, "Linking Firm Strategy to Operating Decisions Through Performance Measurement," *Production and Inventory Management Journal* 32, no. 3 (1991): 5–11.

10. S. Geary and J. P. Zonnenburg, "What It Means to Be Best in Class," *Supply Chain Management Review* (July 2000): 42–50.

11. Ibid., adapted.

12. "Buyers Are Hot on Internet, Wary about e-Procurement," *Purchasing Online* (15 June 2000).

13. Adapted from "Akamai and Gomez Align to Enhance Web Performance Measurement," *Business Wire* (4 March 2002); available from http://www.BusinessWire.com (© The Gale Group). Printed with permission.

14. S. Geary and J. P. Zonnenburg. (See Note 10.)

15. R. S. Kaplan and D. P. Norton, "The Balanced Scorecard—Measures That Drive Performance," *Harvard Business Review* 70, no. 1 (1992): 71–79.

16. S. Silk, "Automating the Balanced Scorecard," *Management Accounting* (May 1998): 38–44.

17. C. W. Chow, D. Ganulin, K. Haddad, and J. Williamson, "The Balanced Scorecard: A Potent Tool for Energizing and Focusing Healthcare Organization Management," *Journal of Healthcare Management* 43, no. 3 (1998): 263–80.

18. Adapted from P. Syfert, N. Elliott, and L. Schumacher, "Charlotte Adapts the 'Balanced Scorecard,'" *The American City & County* 113, no. 11 (1998): 32–33. Reprinted with permission.

19. P. C. Brewer and T. W. Speh, "Using the Balanced Scorecard to Measure Supply Chain Performance," *Journal of Business Logistics* 21, no. 1 (2000): 75–94.

20. Taken from the on-line proceedings of the Supply-Chain World—Latin America 2002 conference, Mexico City, Mexico http://www.supplychainworld.org.

21. Printed with permission from the Supply-Chain Council; available from http://www.supply-chain.org

22. C. Stedman, "Users Eye Standard for Supply Chain," *Computerworld News* (1 June 1998).

23. A. Saccomano, "Keeping SCOR," *Traffic World* 255, no. 13 (1998): 27–28.

Chapter 15:

LOOKING TO THE FUTURE OF SUPPLY CHAIN MANAGEMENT

Misconception: Wal-Mart is in the retail business. Mr. Jay Simmons, senior vice president and treasurer at Wal-Mart, says Wal-Mart is in the distribution business. Wal-Mart is more concerned with getting merchandise from the dock of Proctor & Gamble into the trunk of a customer's car in as little as seventy-two hours.[1]

In a 1962 issue of Traffic Management, a feature article told of Raytheon Corp.'s innovative use of punch cards to track airfreight shipments. The prospect of an Internet-enabled system that could track the movement of goods across the globe never entered the wildest imagination of anyone at Raytheon or anywhere else.[2]

Learning Objectives

After completing this chapter, you should be able to
- Discuss the current state and future challenges of supply chain management.
- Explain why supply chains are becoming more globally oriented.
- Describe how firms are expanding their supply chain management efforts to second- and third-tier members of their supply chains.
- Discuss why and how supply chains are making greater efforts to become more environmentally responsible.
- Explain how supply chains are becoming faster.
- Explain why some firms are outsourcing some or all supply chain management processes.
- Describe some of the ways supply chains are reducing total costs.

Chapter Outline

Expanding the Supply Chain
    Extending Progress Integration Throughout the Supply Chain
    The Global Expansion of Supply Chains

The Greening of Supply Chains

Increasing Supply Chain Responsiveness

Reducing Supply Chain Costs
    Reducing Purchasing Costs
    Outsourcing Supply Chain Management Functions
    Managing Inventories Along the Supply Chain

SUPPLY CHAIN MANAGEMENT IN ACTION   *Wal-Mart's Global Supply Chain*

The aisles are clean, the store is brightly lit, and "associates" in red polo shirts provide friendly service to customers who flock there for the low prices and the wide range of products offered. Throughout the store the image of a kindly old man appears in posters and photographs. His slogans and philosophy have been internalized by all employees, and they can tell you the story of his long march from humble rural roots to become a great leader. "And by the way, would you like us to skin that frog for you?"

Welcome to Wal-Mart in China, where the late Sam Walton has a new image: the Mao of retailing. There, as in Walton's home state of Arkansas, having the right merchandise is paramount. So the store in Shenzhen, just north of Hong Kong, is crowded with tanks of crabs, fish, frogs and shrimp, which can be taken home wiggling or be expertly gutted and cleaned on the spot.

Wal-Mart is mounting an audacious expansion that could double its sales within just five years, to $480 billion. Some of that growth will come in new markets abroad, where 1,200 stores in nine countries already account for about 16 percent of the chain's total sales. But even more growth will be won as the chain places itself in more U.S. neighborhoods and invades more product categories.

If you think Wal-Mart already sells just about everything, think again. Think PCs, ceiling fans, more fashionable clothing, gasoline, and even cars. "Their goal is to have a 30 percent share of every major business they are in," says Linda Kristiansen, a retail analyst for UBS Warburg Equity Research. The company plans to fatten profits by becoming more of a producer and even designer of its goods, especially clothing. It is making blouses in China and towels in India that it intends to sell everywhere from Berlin to Beijing and Boston. But fashion is a notoriously fickle business. And by diving deeper into the manufacturing of more of its products, Wal-Mart is braving a path that has brought grief to some of history's biggest retailers, such as A&P and Sears.

As it tries to leverage its size overseas, Wal-Mart may find it difficult to export one of its biggest advantages. Its expertise in managing high-volume inventory and supply networks does not work as well in Europe and Asia, where the highway systems are not as good and stores typically are smaller. So Wal-Mart has to become better at buying, reaching farther back into the supply chain to purchase at the factory such products as hardware and apparel that it now obtains from outside vendors and importers. "We realized that, as we continue to expand internationally, the need to leverage international and domestic buying power was key, and the only way to do it effectively is to do it ourselves," says Ken Eaton, who heads global procurement. The idea is to buy goods universally for all stores where feasible, so the twenty locations in Brazil can get the same price as the 3,400 Wal-Marts in the United States.

By becoming contractor, importer, and wholesaler, Wal-Mart expects not only to save money on the buy but also to cut down on inventory by speeding up the supply lines. Wal-Mart gets most of its towels from India, and today it reorders once a month. If one pattern gets hot and sells out early, sales are lost. In going direct, however, Wal-Mart will make the factories in India part of its Retail Link system. That allows vendors like Sara Lee (Hanes underwear, Bryan bacon) to dip into Wal-Mart's computers and track sales and replenish supplies constantly.

Global sourcing can provide the ammunition Wal-Mart will need to wage price wars against such powerful retailers as France's Carrefour, Holland's Royal Ahold and Germany's Makro. Each of these European companies got to foreign markets long before Wal-Mart did. At ASDA, the British chain Wal-Mart bought in mid-1999, the company was selling men's jeans for about $24 after paying $14 per yard for 50,000 yards of material to make them. Then the buy was moved to Bentonville, and the conversation went something like, "We'd like 6 million yards, please. Now what's your price?" Try $4.77 per yard. As a result, ASDA slashed its retail prices in half and upped its annual jeans sales to 1 million, from 174,000. ASDA is acquiring some 2,000 products from Wal-Mart's global network and has become Britain's leading seller of kids' clothes.

Wal-Mart's expansion has gone well in Mexico, where it is the country's largest retailer. And the company just completed a deal to crack the Japanese market by acquiring 34 percent of Seiyu, a well-positioned but struggling retailer. But Wal-Mart has stumbled badly in some countries, particularly Germany. "We could write a training manual about our experiences in Germany," Scott says. "We really did more things wrong than right." There, Wal-Mart faces tough competition from well-established chains, especially among grocers. The German managers Wal-Mart brought on board through two mergers resisted American help. "We've been trying to get the Germans culturalized; we bring them to Bentonville," says John Menzer, head of the international division. But Bentonville also had to learn a few things about Berlin. German shoppers found Wal-Mart's door greeters appalling, and they regarded the ever-helpful clerks as an intrusion on their private space.

From Wal-Mart's point of view, it is the Chinese who have turned out to be the best capitalists. At the store in Shenzhen, local managers hold Ping-Pong tourneys, stage fashion shows, and have clerks hawk products like paper towels in front of a large display. And that's just on Tuesday.[3]

Introduction

The past twenty-five years have been characterized by tremendous change in the areas of purchasing, transportation, manufacturing, warehousing, and information systems. These changes have brought about changes in the way new products are designed, produced, and distributed to customers and in the way companies and their relationships with suppliers and customers are managed. Companies have evolved from being strictly internally focused with adversarial supplier relationships and only a passive regard for customers to what we commonly see today—a significant effort placed on building long-term, mutually beneficial relationships with suppliers and customers; the sharing of ideas, plans, and information internally and externally; and listening to customers and end users with the goal of continually satisfying their needs. When done correctly, supply chains become formidable competitive entities, customers get what they want and continue to return, and all of the companies along the supply chain benefit.

A number of watershed events and technological changes have acted to bring about and hasten the practice of supply chain management. Transportation deregulation in the 1970s and 1980s allowed companies to think more about distribution strategies and logistics, without the constraints of regulatory laws. Marketing, purchasing, and production managers could work together to better manage the flow of products. During this same period, companies started investing in mainframe computers, which were just being introduced, to store and manage data. These computing systems were accompanied by software products to manage inventories such as material requirements planning (MRP) software; distribution requirements planning (DRP) software; manufacturing resource planning (MRP-II) software; and, eventually, today's enterprise resource planning (ERP) software systems. These and other systems, along with faster and smaller computers, allowed better overall planning and execution of plans to be done throughout the firm.

With the development and use of electronic data interchange (EDI) during the 1980s, companies were finally able to share information among departments and facilities within the firm, and among a few suppliers and customers in an automated, real-time environment. Finally, the Internet and its associated communication standards, along with the development and storage of hyperlinked information sources on the Internet known as the World Wide Web in the 1990s, allowed information retrieval and transmission across the globe and greatly facilitated the integration of processes among various firms. Today, **Extranets** are being formed to create supply chain Internets that restrict entry from outsiders, along with **Intranets,** which are companywide Internets for organizational members only.

Thus, as new technologies emerge in communication and information transfer, companies and their supply chains are finding new and better ways to satisfy customers, reduce costs, improve quality, and enhance competitive position. The important major trends occurring in supply chain management today are efforts to expand the supply chain, to integrate environmental standards among supply chains, to increase overall supply chain speed or responsiveness, and to reduce supply chain costs. These topics are discussed in detail in this final chapter of the textbook.

Expanding the Supply Chain

Efforts to expand the supply chain actually encompass two different issues. One is the effort to extend process integration to second- or third-tier members of the supply chain, or even farther. The second expansion issue is the creation of global supply chains. Let us discuss each of these issues separately.

Extending Process Integration Throughout the Supply Chain

As companies successfully integrate supply chain processes with immediate suppliers and customers, the desire to extend process integration with second- and third-tier supply chain members increases. Several surveys have shown this to be the case, and the practice appears to be gaining momentum.[4] The rapid advances in compatible communication software in recent years have added to this momentum by allowing better information visibility between supply chain partners.

New York–based BorgWarner Morse TEC, an automotive engine component supplier, uses a Web-based, real-time, collaborative supplier communication system called SupplyWorks MAX, designed by SupplyWorks, to provide its suppliers forecast and production schedules on-line. The system also automates supplier scheduling, inventory visibility, pull replenishment, supplier invoicing and payment, trend analyses, and supplier performance evaluation. Software implementation and user training took only about six months, and the cost to suppliers was minimal. The software also integrates with most ERP systems, and many of BorgWarner's suppliers are using the product to manage their suppliers as well.[5]

Web services present one of the newest opportunities for supply chain partners to connect over the Web.[6] The term *Web services* simply describes businesses that register with an Internet directory to advertise their services so firms can find each other and carry out transactions over the Web. Today, Web services are an attractive new model for flexible, quick, and efficient integration with customers and suppliers. It provides a way to link loosely coupled systems without binding them to any specific programming language or platform. Here's how it works:

- A firm provides an interface for software that can carry out a specified set of tasks.
- A service customer discovers and invokes the software service to provide a business solution. The customer commonly passes data to the provider and receives some result.
- A broker typically manages and publishes the service for the service provider.

XML, the family of Web communication standards, allows businesses to exchange data across the Web. One of the latest developments is **SOAP,** the protocol that has opened up the Web to program-to-program communication between firms; it is what allows customers and providers to exchange XML data. Thus, with SOAP, firms no longer need compatible ERP or CRM systems and servers. Firms now only need to think about what data to exchange, not how to get it from location to location. Mr. Toby Redshaw, vice president of IT strategy, architecture, and e-business at

Motorola, explains the advantages of Web services well: "When you map the supply chain today, starting with source material all the way to product repair, you'll find there are ten to twelve disconnected processes with big gaps and integration issues. Web services will help trading partners fill those gaps by providing better communication among the supply chain applications."[7]

Extending integration can also include reverse logistics, or integrating the process of product returns back up the supply chain. Competitive pressures, increased legislation, and the desire to better utilize resources are forcing many firms to design an effective reverse flow system and offer attractive product return policies. Thus, firms must deal with faulty, unwanted, worn out, damaged return products. Firms have a choice of either trying to sell these items at a discount, returning parts to their suppliers, refurbishing or remanufacturing the items, or disposing them in some way. Legislation extending manufacturers' obligations to take back and recover products has been enacted in Germany (packaging material), Taiwan (automobiles), and Japan (electronic equipment).

Today, there are a number of firms that buy returned merchandise at deep discounts and then resell it. Other firms, such as ReTurn, Inc., specialize in reverse logistics. They also offer a returns management software system to track returned products called DART (direct automated returns tracking). For Safeway in Great Britain, for instance, every two months all of the nongrocery returns from their U.K. stores are sent to a processing facility where pallets of items are scanned and sorted for disposal, either up the supply chain to suppliers or to a reseller.[8]

The Global Expansion of Supply Chains

A number of benefits, as well as potential costs and risks, are in store today for firms globally expanding their supply chains. As we read in the opening vignette about Wal-Mart's global expansion plans, many companies see global expansion of markets and use of foreign suppliers as strategies for enhanced profitability and competitiveness. Wal-Mart is profiting greatly from its use of global supply chains. Higher costs and risks, though, can be in the form of higher insurance costs, greater shipping costs, more tightly monitored and time-consuming customs clearing procedures, shortages and delays, political upheavals that can demolish foreign infrastructures, and foreign social problems that can cause a backlash of bad publicity. For example, VF Corp., the world's largest apparel company, has implemented NextLinx global trade management software to manage customs compliance in the countries they do business in. VF owns production facilities and has relationships with contract manufacturers in Mexico, the Caribbean Basin, and Asia. Material is cut in the United States, shipped out to Mexico and the Caribbean Basin to be sewn, and then shipped back to the United States to be sold. This operation alone creates the need for large numbers of documents.[9]

Understanding a supplier's financial condition is also important. Firms should get to know their suppliers' cost structures and financial health, particularly if they play a key role in a global supply chain. Suppliers on the financial edge can be driven to use many undesirable methods to remain profitable, potentially reducing the effectiveness of the entire supply chain.

Global expansion of the supply chain has also increased the need for capable third-party supply chain services providers. Due to the complexities and demands of global supply chains, a number of these services have partnered to provide international logistics expertise with domestic warehousing and distribution capabilities. For instance, UPS and the Fritz Companies, FedEx and Tower Group International, and AEI and DHL, as well as Deutsche Post and Danzas, have all combined to use existing infrastructures to create global "one-stop" supply chain service networks. UPS has acquired over twenty-five transportation and logistics companies in recent years to create a "global logistics footprint," said UPS Chairman Mike Eskew in a recent interview. At the same time, he said, UPS has been building up a technology infrastructure that is designed to help customers control global supply chains, including electric commerce capabilities. Some large global shippers are even turning to **lead logistics providers (LLPs)** for help. These firms are charged with overseeing their clients' third-party service providers.[10]

The Greening of Supply Chains

It was not too long ago that many firms viewed environmental issues as problems that politicians and consumers had to worry about. Today, firms are starting to realize that global supply chains are exposed to varying levels of environmental regulation and compliance issues. Thus, lax environmental performance in one country can be detrimental to the remainder of the supply chain, from an environmental responsibility perspective as well as an economic perspective. Supply chains and the way they are managed are increasingly seen as part of the environmental solution. Starbucks knows this very well and has made a point of encouraging foreign coffee suppliers to conform to its guidelines. Its coffee purchasing guidelines support its commitment to purchase coffee that has been grown and processed by suppliers who meet environmental, social, economic, and quality standards. Suppliers who meet and sustain these standards receive higher preference as well as compliance premiums when Starbucks purchases coffee.[11]

Customers are increasingly demanding to know where products come from, how they are made and distributed, and what impact future environmental legislation will have on the products they buy. Developing a **green supply chain** strategy involves collecting and analyzing environmental regulations and customer surveys from each of the supply chain firm locations; discussing the relevant environmental issues with the procurement, engineering, and quality control departments at each firm; developing green supply chain policies; communicating them to customers and suppliers along the supply chain; and then managing the program to assure compliance with the policies.

As discussed earlier in this chapter, an effective product lifecycle policy including take-back and recovery activities has become an important element in firms' overall environmental strategies. For instance, Kodak takes back and recycles over 85 percent of the parts in their single-use cameras. Xerox saves hundreds of millions of dollars each year by reusing and remanufacturing copy machine equipment and parts, while Ford is working on a goal to economically design and manufacture cars and trucks that come close to being totally recyclable.[12]

Increasing Supply Chain Responsiveness

As competition between supply chains heats up, firms must utilize more accurate information and better communication technologies to respond quickly to changing customer requirements, while maintaining low supply chain inventories. Data generated from sales to end customers, along with future plans that will impact demand, must result in timely forecasts that are communicated up the supply chain to manufacturers and their suppliers. This requires collaboration, use of accurate forecasting tools, and information visibility among all supply chain members.

During the investment-heavy 1990s, most large firms and many of their supply chain partners decentralized and invested in ERP systems. Now, these same firms must work toward integrating these many systems to achieve faster information retrieval and distribution, resulting in better overall supply chain information visibility and responsiveness. This type of **systems rollup** will be one of the major investments facing supply chain partners in the next few years. Integrating ERP and non-ERP systems throughout an enterprise must certainly be accomplished before a firm can have much hope of integrating processes with external supply chain partners. And the payoffs can be substantial. One such project at Celanese, a $4.5 billion chemical company, should be finished by the time you read this, costing Celanese somewhere in the neighborhood of $60 million and having taken three years to accomplish. Celanese thinks the systems rollup, termed OneSAP, will pay for itself in about two years. The e-Business Connection box describes some of the issues involved in the Celanese systems rollup.

At Celanese, rollup means integrating many SAP systems. Celanese's project, called OneSAP, began in summer 2001 and will last about 1,000 days. Celanese manages thirteen SAP systems scattered across five data centers that serve five business units. OneSAP, conceived by CIO Carl Wachs, will roll up the systems into one version of the enterprise software. After an eleven-month approval process that ended in June 2002, the board gave Wachs twenty-one months to pull it off.

One way to look at major ERP projects is as if they are railroad tracks. There are two rails to follow, a technical one and a cultural one, which are tied together. There is a sense at Celanese that the technical rail, the code, interfaces, and documentation is easy. Culturally, though, OneSAP is the hardest project in the world. That is because Celanese has traditionally operated as a holding company, letting its business units run themselves. Over time, they developed a fierce independence, which made it hard for Celanese corporate to make decisions for the whole company.

OneSAP is meant to change all of that, to get the business units sharing processes and systems while accepting that they are accountable to Celanese as a whole. "The real project is, we're trying to become one company, and this is how we're doing it," says OneSAP Integration Manager Russ Bockstedt. Culturally, that means Celanese must turn itself inside out. And to do that, Carlson says, "we're going to have to make people feel pain to an almost near-death experience. That's the only way to get to the ultimate goal."

If Wachs pulls it off, Celanese wins big. OneSAP means decommissioning fourteen major systems, both ERP and non-ERP, and the costs that go with them. Wachs has talked to peer CIOs who have realized operational savings in the 30 percent to 50 percent range by reducing the waste that comes from doing the same thing four different ways in four different business units.

"Rollups are not so much about replacing ERP as they are about redeploying what you have," says AMR Research Analyst Jim Shep-

herd. "Decentralized businesses are inefficient, and everyone needs to be more efficient now. They want centralized financing, for one, given they have to sign off on this stuff now. Customer requirements, like single invoicing, are driving them back to one system. And they're also realizing that a single view might give them opportunities to cross-sell and up-sell customers between business units."

If Wachs's soft-spoken exterior hides a tenaciousness, it also reveals a great deal of confidence. He says ERP "is not rocket science anymore. It's not easy, but it's mechanical." "I am not naive," he adds. "Proposing this to the board was the most difficult thing of my life." Wachs leans back in his chair. His feet are up, his hands clasped behind his head. "If this project goes bust, I will have serious issues."

Celanese uses training principles from the Project Management Institute and the six sigma philosophy of "total quality management." OneSAP gets money in predetermined chunks, when the team hits its milestones. Risks to the project are scored every month. And project leaders vouch for what they have accomplished in regular validation sessions. And, like Wachs, they fret more over cultural issues. They see two.

First, Celanese must fight its own consensus-building heritage. "We want adequate analysis but not paralysis," Bockstedt says at lunch. "We're seeking consensus only when it's appropriate," Carlson adds. "We are saying, 'What are the facts? Let's move on.' It hasn't always been like this."

The second cultural challenge is managing the massive pain Celanese will bring to its 12,000 employees. It is Carlson's job to manage that change. And as he sees it, there are three kinds of pain he will bring: "Jobs with new responsibilities. Jobs that change completely. And jobs that, yes, go away."

For the most part, a three-year project moves like one of those revolving rooftop restaurants. You do not feel the progress, but now and again when you look up, you are in a different place.[13]

In supply chains, communication is only as good as the information being communicated. When databases are not connected and infrequently updated, managers simply cannot obtain a realistic view of supply chain status, resulting in guesswork and inaccurate forecasts, ultimately leading to the bullwhip problems discussed in previous chapters. "Perhaps the biggest problem with forecasting accurately is **data cleansing**," says Katrina Roche, COO at Evant, a planning and replenishment software provider. Misspellings, typos, and missing information in databases can cause large errors in forecasts and other calculations. Many software providers such as Evant have developed software tools that can cleanse data by cross-referencing disparate data sets, synchronizing overlapping information, correcting inconsistencies, and removing outlier information.[14]

Poor visibility and poor communication ultimately result in higher inventory levels and longer customer order cycle times. Analysts at Forrester Research, for example, claim that up to half of most companies' inventories are safety stocks. Part of the problem is that managers do not reassess optimal stock levels frequently enough; and, without data visibility along the supply chain, updates occur even less frequently. ColorCon, a producer of pharmaceutical products, is using an Oracle application to help it reduce an order cycle time of eight to ten days down to five to seven days, because it can now provide suppliers with more accurate demand plans. Sun Microsystems uses a collaborative planning application from Manugistics. The centralized system allows management to share information about more than 100 products with its supply network. The system provides real-time notifications of unplanned events and helps managers anticipate shortages before they become a problem. Using the system has enabled Sun to reduce its order cycle time from several weeks to days.[15]

New technologies are being developed to help make information visibility and responsiveness along the supply chain a reality. One of these new technologies is the radio frequency identification (RFID) tag, first mentioned in Chapter 13. RFID gives companies the ability to encode product data and track merchandise more accurately. With RFID, each item or case can be uniquely identified, eliminating counting mistakes and shrinkage. RFID technology is shaping up to be the single biggest trend in warehousing and distribution.

Radio-frequency and other technological advances are making warehouses much more responsive to demand. For instance, Big Lots, the nation's largest broadline closeout retailer, replenishes about 350 of its 1,400 stores from one of only four strategically located distribution centers each week. Each distribution center has a conveyor system equipped with a bar-code reader that sorts merchandise by store and diverts it to the appropriate shipping lane and door. All activities are choreographed by a state-of-the-art **warehouse management system (WMS).** The system identifies incoming merchandise, noting overages, shortages, and substitutions. A bar-coded "license plate" is applied to every pallet and then scanned by a lift truck operator linked to the WMS via radio-frequency technology. The WMS tells the operator where to put the merchandise and later identifies pallets to be pulled so that shipping labels can be applied to the cartons. The WMS prints the product labels, the manufacturer's bill of lading, and the address labels.[16]

Manufacturing is another trend occurring in warehousing. New warehouse scheduling optimization technology is being developed to enable warehouses to manufacture items using due dates from tens of thousands of orders, while allowing the site to maximize throughput and resource utilization.

Reducing Supply Chain Costs

Over the past few years in the United States, the business mantra has been "reduce costs!" throughout most industries, and this trend is expected to continue. Particularly in economically depressed markets, cost reduction is often seen as the only remaining option for improving profits. Thus, for supply chains to stay competitive today, cost containment has to be an ongoing concern, along with the caveat that customers must still be satisfied with the products and services they are purchasing.

World-class companies are already developing and executing plans for reducing costs along their supply chains. "The best companies have supply chain costs that are half of their less efficient competitors," says Ian Smith, CEO of Consumer, Retail, and Healthcare at Excel, the world's largest third-party logistics provider. "If supply chain costs for the bad ones are 20 percent, and yours are 10 percent, that's a very significant competitive advantage."[17] These cost reduction plans typically involve reducing purchasing costs, outsourcing supply chain management functions, and reducing inventories along the supply chain. The importance of each of these elements in reducing supply chain costs is discussed next.

Reducing Purchasing Costs

It is no secret that saving purchasing dollars can increase pretax profits on a dollar-for-dollar basis. Particularly for low profit margin businesses, this can represent an attractive source of additional profits. But firms must be careful not to jeopardize existing long-term supplier partnerships when trying to reduce purchase costs, or to jeopardize long-term supply chain strategies. For example, during the 1990s, U.S. automobile manufacturers were focusing on obtaining price concessions from their supply bases as one means for reducing costs, while their Japanese counterparts instead focused on working collaboratively with their suppliers to identify where costs could be reduced. The results have been dramatic—domestic auto manufacturers and their suppliers were making little or no profits as of the early 2000s and seeing dwindling market share, while Toyota, Honda, and Nissan were experiencing growing market share and rising profits.

When downward price adjustments are demanded by the buyer, as in the preceding example, this can have a lasting detrimental impact on supplier relationships and performance. For instance, in December 2002, Tower Automotive announced it would not bid on the contract it had held to supply frames for the Ford Explorer because "the expected returns at (Ford's) targeted pricing levels did not meet our requirements," according to a statement from Tower. In fact, an annual survey of suppliers conducted by Planning Perspectives Inc. found that Ford was considered to be the most difficult of the six major automakers to work with. Since then, Ford has taken some major steps to repair supplier relations and has instituted a worldwide cost reduction program seen as more supplier friendly. Ford's Team Value Management program creates cross-functional commodity teams, with representatives from suppliers and Ford, to identify cost savings areas. Ford has already seen some significant cost savings with this program.[18]

Reverse auctions are seen by some as an additional tool for reducing purchase costs, and this practice is expanding rapidly among many firms who routinely purchase large volumes of commonly manufactured components. While many suppliers complain that reverse auctions are eroding profit margins, many nevertheless continue to participate to garner new business. At Sun Microsystems, the use of reverse auctions to purchase items like hard drives, memory, circuit boards, and cables has resulted in savings of at least 10 percent over traditional sourcing methods, according to Joe McGrath, director of procurement strategy for Sun.

On the other hand, Charles Crep, vice president of operations at Reptron Manufacturing Services in Tampa, Florida, argues that reverse auctions have the ability to damage and destroy buyer-supplier relationships. "Our company makes a great effort to set up a supply chain relationship," he says. "You don't have that opportunity on-line."[19] Thus, while the value of reverse auctions is questioned by many organizations, the practice appears here to stay and can potentially provide supply chain cost savings if used in the right situations.

Outsourcing Supply Chain Management Functions

A number of companies today are increasingly allowing logistics and supply chain management service companies to manage some or all of their supply chain processes. For large companies, these services can potentially generate tens of millions of dollars in cost savings per year. A number of commonly outsourced supply chain management functions include inbound and outbound transportation, warehousing, purchasing and inventory management, and systems management. As the complexity of global supply chains increases, companies tend to outsource functions that are not seen as core competencies. The demand is thus growing for third-party logistics and information technology providers, as well as for organizations with broad capabilities that can manage all of the third-party contractors. These lead logistics providers have been expanding rapidly to provide services to supply chains.

Bill Copacino, a managing partner at Accenture, a management and technology services company, has seen an increase in outsourcing key supply chain activities. "Outsourcing key supply chain activities involves major changes. When approaching these endeavors, we advise clients to view it as a merger rather than as outsourcing. Company leaders need the right mindset, and that includes moving beyond the status quo when outsourcing because they are building a new supply chain."[20]

For instance, UPS has recently been expanding its portfolio of supply chain management services. It offers freight services for all modes of transportation, international trade management, customs brokerage, total supply chain management consulting, financial services, and e-commerce solutions.[21] The Global Perspective box describes the supply chain services UPS provides to the National Semiconductor Corporation.

Schneider Logistics provides supply chain management services for General Motors and also acts as a lead logistics provider. It manages transportation and distribution of GM's aftermarket parts throughout North America. Additionally, it subcontracts out and manages portions of the operation that are not part of its core competencies.[23] In another example, Vastera began managing Ford's U.S.-global trade operations in September 2000. Following this success, Vastera took over Ford's Mexican-global trade operations in February 2001 and followed with Ford's Canadian-global trade operations a month later. Finally, in late 2002, Vastera assumed responsibility for Ford's global trade operations in Europe. By all accounts, the operations have been a success in reducing Ford's global supply chain costs.[24]

Managing Inventories Along the Supply Chain

One of the most significant opportunities for reducing costs as well as improving performance along the supply chain is the reduction of supply chain inventories. More and more, companies are utilizing contract manufacturers in low-cost operating environments such as Asia and Eastern Europe in an effort to reduce operating costs, and they are introducing new products more often as competitive pressures and customer tastes change. These trends have tended to extend the supply chain as well as make it more dynamic and complex. As a result, inventories tend to grow rapidly and product deliveries become uncoordinated and costly—common phenomena among global supply chains today. To counteract these trends, Home Depot is getting all members of its supply chains, including transportation providers and suppliers, involved in driving out costs by improving merchandising and inventory management; working with suppliers to improve stocking; and redesigning logistics, international distribution centers, transit facilities, and transportation routes.[25]

A recent survey of inventory best practices from the Institute of Management and Administration shows that the top three methods used for containing and reducing inventory costs are use of periodic inventory reviews, employing the ABC inventory classification method, and managing the entire supply chain. "We now manage the complete supply chain versus individual sites or nodes," says the manager of inventory logistics at a major pharmaceutical concern. He says inventory reduction will take place "primarily in safety stock but also will show us other areas for improvement opportunities."[26]

Systems that increase supply chain visibility are also making planning, purchasing, production, and distribution much easier and more efficient. Today, enterprise systems can look

Global Perspective

UPS AND NATIONAL SEMICONDUCTOR

National Semiconductor Corporation (NSC), a manufacturer of state-of-the-art digital technology based in Santa Clara, California, realizes substantial savings on its global supply chain costs by outsourcing its logistics activities. The company distributes semiconductor chips and related products to more than 3,800 customers worldwide. For a number of years, the company distributed directly from its manufacturing plants located primarily in Southeast Asia. As volumes grew and demands for faster delivery increased, NSC decided it needed the expertise of a 3PL provider to handle distribution and value-added inventory functions most effectively. In 2000, NSC chose UPS Logistics Group, based in Atlanta, as its 3PL provider, which opened a dedicated state-of-the-art distribution facility in Singapore in August 2000. The centralized distribution center receives shipments from NSC's manufacturing plants in Singapore, Malaysia, and the Philippines. UPS Logistics performs the basic functions of receiving and storing inventory; picking, packing, and shipping to customer specifications; outbound transportation; and a small amount of kitting.

"With UPS Logistics, we can gain access to tools without diverting from our core competencies. National's information technology systems were developed in-house and are coordinated with those of UPS Logistics, which include customs clearance, labeling, and trade compliance," says Larry Stroud, manager of global logistics at NSC. NSC has realized a savings of 50 percent in its global logistics costs since it began outsourcing its logistics. For National Semiconductor, outsourcing its international logistics needs has proven to be a cost-effective solution for supply chain management.

UPS Logistics uses a network of air carriers, freight forwarders, and the UPS package system to deliver each shipment within forty-eight hours on average. One of the chief benefits NSC realizes by using UPS Logistics for outbound finished goods is carrier flexibility. Says Mark Samoline, director of operations and technology at UPS Logistics Group in Singapore, "We are carrier-neutral; our job is to find the best mode of transportation at the best price." UPS Logistics divides the world into the Asian, European, and North American regions and consolidates individual shipments destined for each region into bulk shipments. This allows NSC to pay for one customs clearance charge instead of numerous ones. For example, upon landing at its first stop in the United States, UPS does an east-west split, which divides shipments into two sections, based on the region of the country. This system takes advantage of bulk shipment rates, which reduce transportation costs.

Another benefit is the crossdocking capability of the Singapore facility, which provides significant time savings. It saves processing time by offering greater cutoff flexibility and customer service. "Basically, by not putting the product away after it arrives, we can save as much as one day, and we are able to make an earlier flight cutoff time," Samoline says. The benefit of advanced information technology, carrier flexibility, and logistics expertise has made NSC's relationship with UPS Logistics one that will continue to grow and flourish.[22]

at a firm and its customers' and its suppliers' warehouses around the globe, analyze manufacturing and delivery schedules, and determine when inventories should be shipped and when they will be available. **Supply chain execution systems** such as warehouse, transportation, and logistics management software allow firms to get quick returns on their investments through more efficient use of transportation alternatives, lower system inventories, and better delivery performance. Using these supply chain systems, companies can connect to all of their supply chain partners; capture inventory data, location, and quality; develop accurate forecasts; and respond more quickly and effectively to market signals. With improved visibility, distributors can utilize crossdocking more effectively, they can plan and re-plan shipments while the goods are in transit, and they can notify customers of impending shipment arrivals. One World Logistics of America, a subsidiary of Honda Express, Inc., recently implemented a supply chain planning solution from SynQuest to reduce costs associated with delivering materials to vehicle assembly operations. One World now can quickly model complex inbound networks to balance transportation, plant and supplier inventories, and returnable container costs.[27]

Today, more and more companies are looking at implementing small solution systems they can deploy in short order that will yield quick results and short payback periods. For instance, Transcom, Inc., an international distributor of seals and bearings, uses HighJump's Warehouse Advantage software to manage inventory levels, order volume, and order status in a real-time Web environment. Within months of implementation, Transcom increased inventory accuracy to 99 percent and reduced the time it took to receive a container for shipment and move it through the system from four days to eight hours, cutting labor and line-picking costs. "We've eliminated 40 percent of customer service calls asking 'Where's my shipment?'" says Dennis Bollinger, Transcom's distribution/quality control manager.[28]

Summary

This final chapter of the text discussed the current trends and future outlook of supply chain management. A number of issues currently facing the practice of supply chain management are discussed, including the global expansion of supply chains; expanding the supply chain's influence to include second- and third-tier supply chain members; the greening of supply chains; increasing the responsiveness of supply chains; and reducing supply chain costs through purchase cost reductions, outsourcing supply chain functions, and managing supply chain inventories more efficiently. As competition among supply chains increases and the demand for varied products and services continues, supply chain members will need to become adept at improving the performance of their supply chains to maintain profitability. This has already become a continuous effort among leading supply chains and their members. A number of these companies were profiled in this chapter.

Key Terms

data cleansing, 461
Extranets, 456
green supply chain, 459
Intranets, 457

lead logistics providers
  (LLPs), 459
SOAP, 457
systems rollup, 459

warehouse management
  system (WMS), 461
Web services, 457
XML, 457

Discussion Questions

1. Explain what Web services are and how they aid supply chain management efforts.
2. Describe how reverse logistics impacts supply chain management.
3. Why are environmental compliance issues important in supply chain management?
4. What does information visibility have to do with supply chain responsiveness?
5. How does RFID technology increase responsiveness? Provide an example.
6. Describe several different ways that companies can reduce purchasing costs along their supply chains.
7. Describe how supply chain execution systems help to reduce costs along the supply chain.
8. What do you think the next trend in supply chain management will be? Why?

Internet Question

1. Search the Internet on the term *supply chain innovation* and report on several of your findings.

References

Chopra, S., and P. Meindl. *Supply Chain Management: Strategy, Planning, and Operation.* Upper Saddle River, N.J.: Prentice Hall, 2001.

Handfield, R. B., and E. L. Nichols. *Introduction to Supply Chain Management.* Upper Saddle River, N.J.: Prentice-Hall, 1999.

Notes

1. T. Lasanti, "Wal-Mart Continues to Redefine Retailing," *DSN Retailing Today* 42, no. 7 (2003): 9–10.
2. Anonymous, "Life Begins at 40," *Logistics Management* 41, no. 12 (2002): 14–16.
3. B. Saporito, "Can Wal-Mart Get Any Bigger? (Yes, a Lot Bigger . . . Here's How)," *Time,* no. 2 (2003) 38–43. © 2003 Time Inc. Reprinted by permission.
4. See, for instance, M. C. Mejza and J. D. Wisner, "The Scope and Span of Supply Chain Management," *The International Journal of Logistics Management* 12, no. 2 (2001): 37–55; and J. D. Wisner and K. C. Tan, "Supply Management and Its Impact on Purchasing," *The Journal of Supply Chain Management* 36, no. 4 (2000): 33–42.
5. G. Hasek, "BorgWarner's Improved Timing," *Frontline Solutions* 3, no. 12 (2002): 38–40.
6. F. P. Coyle, "Web Services, SImply Put," *Computerworld* 37, no. 20 (2003): 38–39.
7. B. Violino, "Waves of Change," *Computerworld* 37, no. 20 (2003): 28–33.
8. M. Wheatley, "Many Happy Returns," *Supply Management* 7, no. 25 (2002): 26–27.
9. K. Cottrill, "Made to Measure," *Traffic World* (5 May 2003): 1–3.
10. T. B. Gooley, "One-Stop Shopping," *Logistics Management* 41, no. 11 (2002): 45–50.
11. J. Bruss, "Starbucks Aims High," *Beverage Industry* 92, no. 12 (2001): 10–11.
12. Jayaraman, V., "Why Closed Loop Supply Chains?," working paper, University of Miami, 2003.
13. S. Berinato, "ERP Consolidation: A Day in the Life of Big ERP Rollup," *CIO* 16, no. 7 (2003): 54–63. Reprinted with permission from CIO. Copyright 2003, CXO Media Inc.
14. J. Caplan, "A Strong SCM System Is Essential to a Strong Bottom Line," *CFO.com* (21 May 2003): 1–6.
15. Ibid.
16. D. D. Graham, "Warehouse of the Future," *Frontline Solutions* 4, no. 4 (2003): 20–26.
17. P. Trunick, "4 Logistics Trends Driving and Driven by 3PLs," *Transportation and Distribution* (October 2002): 7–11.
18. D. Hannon, "The Automotive Buy—Suppliers: Friend or Foe?" *Purchasing* 132, no. 2 (2003): 25–29.
19. S. D. Chin, "Reverse Auctions Gain Momentum as Cost Toll—Chipmakers Grudgingly Join in Online Bids," *EBN* (3 March 2003): 1–4.
20. K. Krizner, "Supply Chain Outsourcing Becomes Popular in Tough Economic Times," *Frontline Solutions* 3, no. 5 (2002): 48–49.
21. K. Cottrill, "Running the Numbers," *Traffic World* (14 April 2003): 1–2.
22. A. Coia, "Leaving Logistics in Capable Hands," *World Trade* 15, no. 7 (2002): 26–30. Excerpt from World Trade Magazine, Copyright 2002, with permission.
23. P. Trunick, "4 Logistics Trends Driving and Driven by 3PLs."
24. "Outstanding Supply Chain Innovators," *World Trade* 16, no. 5 (2003): 14–15.
25. R. Handfield, "Reducing the Costs Across the Supply Chain," *Optimize* (December 2002): 54–60.
26. "Inventory Reduction," *The Controller's Report* (August 2002): 2–3.
27. R. Qureshi, "Inward Bound," *Works Management* 56, no. 1 (2003): 40–43.
28. E. Kay, "Where Should You Invest?" *Frontline Solutions* 4, no. 1 (2003): 16–20.

Case Study 14

Cisco Systems: The Supply Chain Story

A Company in Trouble

In August 2001, the San Jose, California-based, computer-networking company Cisco Systems Inc. surprised industry observers by announcing its first ever negative earnings in more than a decade. In the third quarter of fiscal 2001, the company's sales had decreased by 30 percent. Cisco had to write off inventory worth $2.2 billion and lay off 8,500 people. By the end of 2001, the market capitalization of the company was down to $154 billion and per-employee profit was $240,000 (down from $700,000 in 2000). This was in sharp contrast to the situation in early 2000, when Cisco was one of the most successful companies in the Internet world with a market capitalization of $579 billion.

Cisco—The Networked Supply Chain

Cisco was founded in 1984 by a group of computer scientists at Stanford. They designed an operating software called Internet Operating System (IOS) that could route streams of data from one computer to another. The software was loaded into a box containing microprocessors specially designed for routing. This was the router, a machine that made Cisco a hugely successful venture over the next two decades.

In 1985, the company started a customer support site through which customers could download software and also upgrade the downloaded software. It also provided technical support through e-mail to its customers. By 1991, Cisco's support center was receiving around 3,000 calls a month. This figure increased to 12,000 by 1992. In order to deal with the large volume of transactions, the company built a customer support system on its Web site. In 1993, Cisco installed an Internet-based system for its large multinational customers. The system allowed customers to post queries about their software problems.

Encouraged by the success of its customer support site, Cisco launched Cisco Information Online in 1994. This on-line service offered not only company and product information but also technical and customer support to Cisco's customers. By 1995, the company introduced applications for selling products or services on its Web site. The main idea behind this initiative was to transfer paper, fax, e-mail and CD-ROM distribution of technical documentation and training materials to the Web, thus saving time for employees, customers, and trading partners and broadening Cisco's market reach.

In 1996, the company introduced a new Internet initiative called the "Networked Strategy" to leverage its network for fostering interactive relationships with customers, partners, suppliers, and employees. Cisco wanted to ensure enhanced customer satisfaction through on-line order entry and configuration. Customers' order information flowed through the supply chain network, which consisted of Cisco employees, resellers, manufacturers, suppliers, customers, and distributors.

Orders from customers were stored in Cisco's enterprise resource planning database and sent to contract manufacturers over their Virtual Private Network VPN2. Cisco's suppliers could clearly see the order information as their own production schedule was connected to Cisco's ERP system. According to the requirements, the suppliers shipped the needed components to manufacturers and replenished their stocks. The business model aimed at en-

Source: © ICFAI Center for Management Research, India, http://www.icmrindia.org. Written by: A. Mukund, a Faculty Member at ICMR, India, and K. Subhadra, a Research Associate at ICMR, India. Reprinted with permission.

abling Cisco's contract manufacturers to start manufacturing build-to-order products within fifteen minutes of receiving an order.

Cisco gave top priority to order fulfillment and project management to achieve on-time delivery to customers. Third-party logistics providers were plugged into Cisco's database via the Internet. As a result, Cisco could, at any time, provide customers with information regarding the status of their order. Direct fulfillment led to a reduction in inventories, labor costs, and shipping expenses. Through direct fulfillment, Cisco saved $12 million annually.

Cisco's Internet-linked supply chain network enabled the automatic testing of products from any of its locations worldwide. While earlier prototyping used to take weeks, Cisco engineers were now able to do the same within a matter of days. This was because prototyping could take place at the manufacturer's site itself. After manufacturing, the product was connected to one of Cisco's 700 servers worldwide. Because of rapid sharing of demand information across the supply chain, customers could receive products faster. To sum up, this networked supply chain ensured

- shorter engineering-to-production cycle times;
- flexibility in designing, revamping, and retiring products in response to market demand;

and

- product quality, though major portions of the fulfillment process were outsourced.

Even though Cisco dealt with technically complex products like routers, it did not hesitate to hand over the manufacturing to a set of contract manufacturers. In order to ensure the quality of its products, Cisco relied on automatic testing. The company developed test cells on supplier lines and ensured that the test cells automatically configured test procedures when an order arrived. Cisco defined its core competence as product designing and delegated the rest—manufacturing, assembly, product configuration, and distribution—to its partners.

In August 1996, Cisco launched transactional facilities like product configuration and online order placement. These facilities were connected to its ERP systems. In the same year, Cisco upgraded its network infrastructure to better handle the increasing number of transactions. By the end of 2000, more than 75 percent of the orders for Cisco's products were being placed over the Internet. Aided by Cisco's Internet initiatives, the company's net sales grew at an impressive 78 percent annual growth rate, from $2 billion in 1995 to $9 billion in 1998. The company's fourth-quarter revenues in 2000 were $5.7 billion, up 61 percent from the same period in 1999. Operating profits also went up from $710 million in 1999 to $1.2 billion in 2000.

According to many analysts, the company's networking strategy had played a major role in its success over the years. Industry observers noted that ever since its inception, Cisco had demonstrated the power of networking and the benefits it could offer. Cisco owned just two of the forty facilities that manufactured its products. It did not own the distribution system that delivered the products to its customers; but through its network of suppliers, distributors, partners, and resellers and customers, it successfully coordinated all the activities necessary to provide products to its customers on time.

In spite of an efficient supply chain network, Cisco ran into some problems. Cisco's partners typically worked out their supply-and-demand forecasts from multiple points in the company's supply chain. Transactions between suppliers and contract manufacturers were not always smooth. There were time lags in delivery and payment and, thus, greater opportunity for error. As a result, suppliers were plagued by long order-to-payment cycles. In June

2000, Cisco discovered, to its alarm, that it was running short of some key components for some of its equipment.

Due to the shortage of components, shipments to customers were delayed by three to four weeks. Though demand for Cisco's products remained healthy, the revenues of customers who were used to delivery within two weeks were affected badly. The delivery performance was out of character for a company that prided itself on its relationships with customers and even compensated many of its executives on the basis of customer satisfaction.

The Cisco Connection Online and Integrated Commerce Solution Initiatives

In order to address the aforementioned problems, Cisco revamped its supply chain management system to reduce the long ordering cycles. The company launched Cisco Connection Online (CCO), which connected Cisco with all its suppliers and contract manufacturers on-line. As a result, when a customer placed an order, it was instantly communicated to all of Cisco's suppliers and manufacturers. In most cases, a third-party logistics company shipped the product to the customer.

CCO ensured increased coordination and connectivity between supply partners, thus reducing the operating costs of all constituents. Automated processes within the supply chain removed redundant steps and added efficiencies. For instance, changes in market demand were communicated automatically throughout the supply chain. This enabled the networked supply chain suppliers to respond appropriately.

CCO reduced payment cycles for suppliers and eliminated paper-based purchasing. As a result, suppliers agreed to charge lower product markups. Consequently, Cisco saved more than $24 million in material costs and $51 million in labor costs annually. CCO enabled Cisco's contract manufacturers to find out the exact position of demand and inventory at any given point of time. As a result, they could manage replenishment of inventory with ease. This resulted in a 45 percent reduction in inventory and a doubling of the inventory turnover. Cisco slashed the inventory holding of its suppliers and manufacturers and brought it down from 13,000 units (approx.) to 6,000 units within three months.

To get the most out of CCO, Cisco used Intranets and Extranets extensively. The Extranet was used for communicating with suppliers, manufacturers, customers, and resellers, while employees used the Intranet for communicating about the status of orders. Thus, through an on-line information and communication system, Cisco linked suppliers, manufacturers, customers, resellers, and employees seamlessly.

However, some of Cisco's large customers were not able to access CCO because it did not connect seamlessly to their back-end or electronic data interchange systems. These firms, typically telecom equipment distributors or network operators, lacked the time to visit the supplier Web sites to order the equipment they needed. So, Cisco introduced the Integrated Commerce Solution (ICS) for these customers. ICS provided a dedicated server fully integrated into the customers' or resellers' Intranet and back-end ERP systems. It facilitated information exchange between Cisco and them, besides speeding up transactions. It had all the e-commerce applications of CCO, with the additional capability of pulling order-related data directly from Cisco's back-end ERP systems on-line. At the same time, as the server was integrated into the customers' and resellers' back-end ERP systems, the end users needed to enter the order information only once; this order was simultaneously distributed to both resellers and Cisco's back-end systems, eliminating the need for double entry.

With these new Internet initiatives and sound financials for fiscal 2000, Cisco seemed all set to register even higher growth figures. However, in early 2001, the global IT business slowdown and the dotcom bust altered the situation. Reportedly, Cisco failed to foresee the changing trends in the industry and by mid-2001 had to cope with the problems of excess inventory. As a result, the company had to write off inventory worth $2.2 billion in May 2001. Cisco blamed the problems on the "plunge in technology spending," which Chambers called as unforeseeable as "a 100-year flood." Company sources said that if their forecasters had been able to see the downturn, the supply chain system would have worked perfectly.

The Problem and the Remedy

Analysts felt that the flaws in Cisco's systems had contributed significantly to the breakdown. During the late 1990s, Cisco had become famous for "being the hardware maker that did not make hardware." Its products were manufactured only by contract manufacturers, and the company shipped fully assembled machines directly from the factory to buyers. This arrangement led to major troubles later on.

According to analysts, Cisco's supply chain was structured like a pyramid, with the company at the central point. On the second tier, there were a handful of contract manufacturers who were responsible for final assembly. These manufacturers were dependent on large subtier companies for components such as processor chips and optical gear. Those companies in turn were dependent on an even larger base of commodity suppliers who were scattered all over the globe. The communication gaps between these tiers created problems for Cisco. In order to lock in supplies of scarce components during the boom period, Cisco ordered large quantities in advance on the basis of demand projections made by the company's sales force. To make sure that it got components when it needed them, Cisco entered into long-term commitments with its manufacturing partners and certain key component makers.

These arrangements led to an inventory pile-up since Cisco's forecasters had failed to notice that their projections were artificially inflated. Many of Cisco's customers had ordered similar equipment from Cisco's competitors, planning to eventually close the deal with the party that delivered the goods first. This resulted in double and triple ordering, which artificially inflated Cisco's demand forecasts. Cisco's supply chain management system failed to show the increase in demand, which represented overlapping orders. For instance, if three manufacturers competed to build 10,000 routers, to chipmakers it looked like a sudden demand for 30,000 machines. As Cisco was committed to honor its deals with its suppliers, it was caught in a vicious cycle of artificially inflated demand for key components, higher costs, and bad communication throughout the supply chain.

Cisco's inventory cycle reportedly rose from 53.9 days to around 88.3 days. According to analysts, Cisco's systems failed to model what would happen if one critical assumption— growth—was removed from their forecasts. They felt that if Cisco had tried to run modest declining demand models, then it might have seen the consequences of betting on more inventory. They felt that Cisco should not have assumed that there would be continuous growth. Having realized these problems, Cisco began taking steps to set things right. The company formed a group of executives and engineers to work on an "e-Hub" remedial program. Work on e-Hub began in late 2000. The project was intended to help eliminate bidding wars for scarce components. According to Cisco sources, e-Hub was expected to eliminate the need for human intervention and automate the flow of information between Cisco, its contract manufacturers, and its component suppliers. e-Hub used a technology called Partner Interface Process (PIP) that indicated whether a document required a response or not. For instance, a PIP purchase order could stipulate that the recipient's system must send a confirmation two hours after receipt and a confirmed acceptance within twenty-four hours. If the recipient's system failed to meet those deadlines, the purchase order would be considered null. This would help Cisco to find out the exact number of manufacturers who would be bidding for the order.

According to the e-Hub setup, Cisco's production cycle began when a demand forecast PIP was sent out showing cumulative orders. The forecast went not only to contract manufacturers but also to chipmakers like Philips semiconductors and Altera Corp. Thus, overlapping orders were avoided and chipmakers knew the exact demand figure. e-Hub searched for inventory shortfalls and production blackouts almost as fast as they occurred.

However, work on e-Hub fell behind schedule due to its complexity and the costs involved. According to Cisco sources, the company originally planned to connect 250 contractors and suppliers by the end of 2001, but it could link only sixty. It was reported that the number might rise to around 150 by mid-2002. Company sources said that e-Hub was just the first stage of its plans for automating the whole process of ordering and purchasing.

Meanwhile, the company's poor financial performance prompted analysts to comment that if the inputs were wrong, even the world's best supply chain could fail. They added that only the next boom phase in the IT business would prove the efficiency of e-Hub.

Questions for Discussion

1. Study the networked supply chain concept as implemented by Cisco. What are its strengths and weakness?

2. Analyze why Cisco landed in financial trouble in early 2001. Would you agree that Cisco's problems were largely caused by inherent defects in the company's systems? Or possibly was it just because they had failed to forecast a market downturn? Give reasons to justify your stand.

3. Aside from the information systems problems referred to, what other specific problems did you see in the case?

Case Study 15
Genexis and the Brazilian Pharmaceutical Industry

Hélcio Lima, vice president of strategic business at Genexis (http://www.genexis.com) contemplates the beautiful sunset through the large window of his São Paulo, Brazil, office. He had just come out of a meeting with the company's board of directors in which he received the OK to execute a project that could potentially launch Genexis into the world market in a new area and one of substantial added value for its clients. Genexis was going to become a value-added network (VAN) provider.

Instead of offering clients intermediary trade services, or what is now called a "marketplace," such as direct and reverse auctions and order automation, it would mean offering an information platform, management models, and business and telecommunication intelligence to its clients—distributors, drug manufacturers, and industry suppliers. These customers could then be guaranteed that the decisions taken within the various "links" of their supply chains would follow a proper and cohesive logic, giving their supply chains the maximum performance possible, without losing sight of each member's main business.

This point of view contrasts distinctly with the traditional management model, in which each firm's purpose is to maximize its individual performance even if this means harming the performance of other supply chain members and the chain as a whole, resulting in long-term damage for all the supply chain participants.

Hélcio felt that this was the exact moment for Genexis to place itself as the leader in this development for the pharmaceutical sector, which currently was undergoing substantial changes in Brazil, due to the release of "generic" drugs by the Brazilian government. With the release of the generics, logistics management within the pharmaceutical sector's supply chains became essential. Generics were causing a substantial reduction in the profit margins of drugs with proprietary brands, which in turn created substantial pressure to manage costs and supply chain logistics components.

It also made the "presence at the point of sale" and important aspect for the competitiveness of the drugs, from the manufacturing laboratories' points of view. Prior to generics, the sales effort for branded prescription drugs was directed toward the physicians who prescribed them. Today, servicing the drugstores held greater importance than ever before, since customers were provided information on both the branded drugs and the corresponding generics.

The market of pharmaceutical products in Brazil is very dispersed. There are approximately 55,000 drugstores in the country and 450 wholesalers/distributors, most of which are independent and non-exclusive, distributing drugs for approximately eighty to ninety medium- to large-sized laboratories.

The Origin of Genexis

The company that later became Genexis appeared in Brazil in 1994 as an answer to the need of the pharmaceutical industry for "sale maps," or the sales reports that each industry requested through its distribution channels. This information is highly strategic, since the

Source: © Profs. Henrique Corrêa (hcorrea@fgvsp.br) and Mauro Caon, Dept. of Production and Operations Mgt., Fundação Getulio Vargas Business School, São Paulo, Brazil, with the collaboration of Hélcio Lima of Genexis (http://www.genexis.com) as a basis for class discussion only. Used with permission.

industry allocates on average 25 percent of its revenues to promotional activities and sales force costs, with the goal of generating prescriptions to the patients from physicians, and demand for the product at the end of the chain, the consumer.

Up until 1994, the industry did not have an efficient and effective mechanism to measure the result of that substantial expense—whether the right physician was being visited at the right time and was prescribing the right product. This occurred because the companies performing these services at that time used a sampling method with results being shown to their clients only after some months when a possible corrective measure might already be too late.

In 1994, ITX was getting prepared to start rendering services to the local state-owned electrical energy supplier, gathering and processing data on the consumption of electric power, when, with the investiture of a recently elected governor, it had its contract terminated. Trying to take advantage of the existing infrastructure and the company's technical capacity, its founder and president Fernando Luiz Cabral, in informal talks with some people connected to the health area, identified the adaptability of the company's functions to gather, process, analyze, and make available in real time via EDI a large quantity of accurate pharmaceutical information.

Thus, in 1994, the first contract with the Bristol-Myers Squibb Laboratory was signed to develop a system to gather, format, and summarize drug sales information and register the clients of all the Bristol-Myers distributors on a daily instead of monthly basis. This allowed the laboratory to know the true demand per outlet throughout Brazil.

In 1995, with the experience gained by the development of the project for Bristol-Myers Squibb, the company, in consortium with Embratel (a Brazilian telecom company), won a public bid to apply the same methodology and technology to a much larger universe. In the beginning, there was the participation of twelve laboratories and approximately 100 wholesalers. By 1996, it offered services to twenty laboratories and 300 wholesalers. As a result of the growth both inside and outside the company, e-commerce activities were started and the first business management project for the Pfizer laboratory was developed.

1999 marked the beginning of negotiations between the company and the Pactual-Electro investment fund, which would culminate the following year with the creation of Internet Business Partners (IBP), resulting in the investment of approximately US$15.5 million for technology purchases and the hiring of human resources. At the same time, IBP acquired a share in the Healthlink portal, a start-up company that had the knowledge of the health-care market, through the development of corporate applications for hospitals. Finally the Genexis portal appeared, presently covering Genexis Farma and Genexis Healthcare.

Genexis Farma is an e-business portal for companies that make up the pharmaceutical segment (manufacturers, wholesalers, drugstores, hospitals, clinics), supplying real-time information on demand to support decisions and products that optimize critical management processes: demand, production, marketing, and sales.

Genexis Healthcare offers connectivity and services of added value for relationships between health operators, service companies, and professionals (authorization authentication and claims processing), possessing high synergy with the Farma group. Recently the company began its international expansion through the creation of Genexis Portugal.

Hélcio's Challenges

Hélcio understood there were great opportunities for profits and cost reductions in the pharmaceutical supply chain; if coordinated, cohesive management was possible. He also understood that some of the services already rendered successfully by Genexis for the last six years had made it develop some competencies that surely would be the "core" in this new business and, therefore, difficult to develop or imitate by potential competitors—for example, the daily gathering of information regarding the demand at the outlets.

The question now was how to best become technically and capably equipped to offer VAN services for the pharmaceutical sector and later for other industrial sectors. Which elements did Genexis already have and which still needed to be developed or purchased? How could the supply chain participants (many with conflicting interests and histories) be approached and convinced of the advantages that would result from a collaborative supply chain management? These were questions still with no answers, but Hélcio knew that he was looking at something that could alter completely the way companies would manage their supply chains in the future and the idea of leading these changes (with the inherent difficulties) made him sure that the next months would be extremely exciting and challenging.

Questions for Discussion

1. Put yourself in the position of the vice president of Genexis and structure the debate on how to approach the primary issue he is facing, namely, how they are going to get cooperation from all the supply chain participants?

2. Analyze the general supply chain management issue: do you think Genexis could manage to launch successful initiatives to perform in other market segments—such as the confectionery industry—that have a similar structure? What kinds of problems do you foresee with the broadening of their services in this way?

3. What major competencies should Genexis maintain and develop to grow in its current market? What strategic alliances, if any, should Genexis create to establish its VAN or service supply network?

Appendix I
Areas under the Normal Curve

This table gives the area under the curve to the left of x, for various Z scores, or number of standard deviations from the mean. For example, in the figure, if Z = 1.96, the value .97500 found in the body of the table is the total shaded area to the left of x.

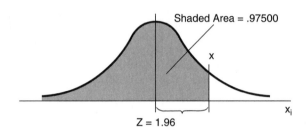

Z	00	.01	.02	.03	.04	.05	.06	.07	.08	.09
.0	.50000	.50399	.50798	.51197	.51595	.51994	.52392	.52790	.53188	.53586
.1	.53983	.54380	.54776	.55172	.55567	.55962	.56356	.56749	.57142	.57535
.2	.57926	.58317	.58706	.59095	.59483	.59871	.60257	.60642	.61026	.61409
.3	.61791	.62172	.62552	.62930	.63307	.63683	.64058	.64431	.64803	.65173
.4	.65542	.65910	.66276	.66640	.67003	.67364	.67724	.68082	.68439	.68793
.5	.69146	.69497	.69847	.70194	.70540	.70884	.71226	.71566	.71904	.72240
.6	.72575	.72907	.73237	.73536	.73891	.74215	.74537	.74857	.75175	.75490
.7	.75804	.76115	.76424	.76730	.77035	.77337	.77637	.77935	.78230	.78524
.8	.78814	.79103	.79389	.79673	.79955	.80234	.80511	.80785	.81057	.81327
.9	.81594	.81859	.82121	.82381	.82639	.82894	.83147	.83398	.83646	.83891
1.0	.84134	.84375	.84614	.84849	.85083	.85314	.85543	.85769	.85993	.86214
1.1	.86433	.86650	.86864	.87076	.87286	.87493	.87698	.87900	.88100	.88298
1.2	.88493	.88686	.88877	.89065	.89251	.89435	.89617	.89796	.89973	.90147
1.3	.90320	.90490	.90658	.90824	.90988	.91149	.91309	.91466	.91621	.91774
1.4	.91924	.92073	.92220	.92364	.92507	.92647	.92785	.92922	.93056	.93189
1.5	.93319	.93448	.93574	.93699	.93822	.93943	.94062	.94179	.94295	.94408
1.6	.94520	.94630	.94738	.94845	.94950	.95053	.95154	.95254	.95352	.95449
1.7	.95543	.95637	.95728	.95818	.95907	.95994	.96080	.96164	.96246	.96327
1.8	.96407	.96485	.96562	.96638	.96712	.96784	.96856	.96926	.96995	.97062
1.9	.97128	.97193	.97257	.97320	.97381	.97441	.97500	.97558	.97615	.97670
2.0	.97725	.97784	.97831	.97882	.97932	.97982	.98030	.98077	.98124	.98169
2.1	.98214	.98257	.98300	.98341	.98382	.98422	.98461	.98500	.98537	.98574
2.2	.98610	.98645	.98679	.98713	.98745	.98778	.98809	.98840	.98870	.98899
2.3	.98928	.98956	.98983	.99010	.99036	.99061	.99086	.99111	.99134	.99158
2.4	.99180	.99202	.99224	.99245	.99266	.99286	.99305	.99324	.99343	.99361
2.5	.99379	.99396	.99413	.99430	.99446	.99461	.99477	.99492	.99506	.99520
2.6	.99534	.99547	.99560	.99573	.99585	.99598	.99606	.99621	.99632	.99643
2.7	.99653	.99664	.99674	.99683	.99693	.99702	.99711	.99720	.99728	.99736
2.8	.99744	.99752	.99760	.99767	.99774	.99781	.99788	.99795	.99801	.99807
2.9	.99813	.99819	.99825	.99831	.99836	.99841	.99846	.99851	.99856	.99861
3.0	.99865	.99869	.99874	.99878	.99882	.99886	.99889	.99893	.99896	.99900
3.1	.99903	.99906	.99910	.99913	.99916	.99918	.99921	.99924	.99926	.99929
3.2	.99931	.99934	.99936	.99938	.99940	.99942	.99944	.99946	.99948	.99950
3.3	.99952	.99953	.99955	.99957	.99958	.99960	.99961	.99962	.99964	.99965
3.4	.99966	.99968	.99969	.99970	.99971	.99972	.99973	.99974	.99975	.99976
3.5	.99977	.99978	.99978	.99979	.99980	.99981	.99981	.99982	.99983	.99983
3.6	.99984	.99985	.99985	.99986	.99986	.99987	.99987	.99988	.99988	.99989
3.7	.99989	.99990	.99990	.99990	.99991	.99991	.99992	.99992	.99992	.99992
3.8	.99993	.99993	.99993	.99994	.99994	.99994	.99994	.99995	.99995	.99995
3.9	.99995	.99995	.99996	.99996	.99996	.99996	.99996	.99996	.99997	.99997

Appendix II
Answers to Selected End-of-Chapter Problems

Chapter 2
2. a. Breakeven quantity = 24,700 units; cost at breakeven point = $247,600
   b. Make = $210,000; Buy = $200,600
4. Total cost for Supplier 1 = $48.4 million; Supplier 2 = $47.1 million; Supplier 3 = $49.5 million.

Chapter 3
15. The weighted score is 89.

Chapter 5
2. a. $F_5 = 72,567$;
   b. $F_5 = 71,980$;
   c. $F_5 = 71,058$ (assuming that the forecast for period 1 = 68,000);
   d. $TAF_5 = 75,129$

Chapter 6
2. ATP = 30 (1), 10 (2), 10 (4), 20 (6), 20 (8).
4. Planned order release for Part F = 60 in period 2.
S2. a. EOQ = 1,000 units
    b. Annual holding cost = $7,500
    c. Annual ordering cost = $7,500
    d. Annual total cost = $15,000
S3. A items: 2,650, 6,840, 6,128
S4. $TAIC_{\$186}$ = $155,510; Stan and Laurie should take the discount.

Chapter 8
2. 2.5 hours
3. b. $\bar{\bar{X}} = 99.2$ and $\bar{R} = 8.4$
   c. $UCL_x = 105.3$, $LCL_x = 93.1$; $UCL_R = 19.2$, $LCL_R = 0$
5. a. 0.117 or 11.7%
   b. $\sigma_P = 0.102$
   c. UCL = 0.423; LCL = 0.
6. a. 0.73 complaints per day
   b. UCL = 3.3; LCL = 0
7. $C_{pk} = 0.82$

Chapter 9
10. $S_2 = 12,728$ units for all three warehouses.

Chapter 11
1. c. Location C has the lowest cost of $1,150,000.
3. X = 5.29, Y = 7.48.

Chapter 12
1. 5,545 feet. Put (1,8), (4,5), (4,6) closer together.
3. 2 full-time and 3 part-time workers
5. probability = 0.7
7. $\rho = 0.3$; $P_0 = 0.538$; $L_q = 0.059$

Chapter 14
10. Total factor productivity (old) = 0.15 hairstyles/$; total factor productivity (new) = 0.178 hairstyles/$.

Glossary

ABC inventory control system Prioritizes inventory items into Groups A, B, and C to determine which inventories should be counted more frequently and managed more closely.

acceptance sampling Inspecting a sample of goods produced or received, and then accepting or rejecting the entire batch based on the sample findings.

aggregate production plan (APP) A long-range materials plan to determine the quantity and timing of production for the future (usually 6 to 18 months).

air carriers Very fast, particularly for long distances, air carriers transport about 5 percent of the U.S. freight bill.

alliance development Refers to increasing a key or strategic supplier's capabilities.

application service providers (ASPs) Firms that design and maintain various programs for clients in an outsourcing role.

assignable variations Variations that are created by causes that can be identified and eliminated.

Association of Southeast Asian Nations (ASEAN) An association formed in 1967 to promote economic, social, and cultural development of the region through cooperative programs; today consists of ten countries.

associative forecasting Assumes that one or more factors (independent variables) are related to demand and, therefore, can be used to predict future demand; generally uses regression analysis to estimate future demand.

attribute data Data that indicate the presence of some attribute, such as color, satisfaction, workability, or beauty.

available-to-promise (ATP) quantity The uncommitted portion of the firm's planned production (or scheduled MPS).

backward integration Acquiring sources of supply.

balanced scorecard (BSC) A performance measurement model developed in 1992 by Kaplan and Norton (see Note 15, Chapter 14) to align an organization's performance measures with its strategic plan and goals.

balking Describes customers refusing to join a queue once they see how long it is.

barter The complete exchange of goods and/or services of equal value without the exchange of currency.

benchmarking Studying and copying what other firms do well.

best-of-breed solution Picks the best application or module for each individual function in the supply chain.

bill of materials (BOM) A record showing the components, their description, and the quantity of each required to make one unit of the product.

bill-back A "punishment" to a supplier in which the cost resulting from a late delivery or poor material quality is charged back to the supplier.

blank check purchase order Purchase order with signed blank check attached; clearly printed on the check that it is not valid over a certain amount.

blanket order release Used to release a specific quantity against a blanket purchase order.

blanket purchase order Covering a variety of items, negotiated for repeated supply over a fixed time period.

break-even analysis Computing the cost-effectiveness of make-or-buy sourcing decisions.

break-even model A useful location analysis technique when fixed and variable costs can be determined for each potential location.

bullwhip effect Magnification of safety stocks contained in forecasts and orders as one moves up the supply chain.

business clusters According to Michael Porter (see Chapter 11, Note 66), " . . . geographic concentrations of interconnected companies and institutions in a particular field. Clusters encompass an array of linked industries and other entities important to competition."

business cycle A cyclical variation such as recession or expansion.

business process reengineering (BPR) Radically rethinking and redesigning business processes to reduce waste and increase performance.

C_{pk} index Process capability index; measures the difference between the desired process variation and the actual process variation.

call centers Customer contact centers used in many organizations to improve customer service and supply chain performance.

capacity requirements planning (CRP) A short-range capacity planning technique that is used to check the feasibility of the material requirements plan.

capacity utilization The actual customers served or products produced per period divided by the capacity.

cash spin or free cash spin The potential benefits of reducing overall inventories or assets across a supply chain and re-deploying the freed cash or investing in alternate projects.

cause-and-effect diagrams Figures that illustrate potential groups of causes of problems for problem-cause analyses. Also called **fishbone or Ishikawa diagrams.**

C-chart Used to monitor the number of defects per unit of output.

center-of-gravity model A technique that involves mapping all of the market locations on an x,y-coordinate grid and then finding a central location that is closest to the markets with the highest demand.

centralized purchasing A purchasing department at a firm's corporate office makes all purchasing decisions. See **decentralized purchasing.**

channel equity Strategic buyer-supplier relationships that provide continuous and increasing value for all participants.

channel integration Extending strategic alliances to suppliers' suppliers and to customers' customers.

chase-demand strategy When the amount of capacity varies with demand.

chase production strategy A production strategy that matches its outputs to the demand pattern to avoid carrying inventory.

churn reduction Fewer customer defections to competitors.

Civil Aeronautics Act 1938 act that extended the Interstate Commerce Act to include regulation of air carriers.

clickstream The term used to describe how customers navigate a Web site.

closed-loop MRP An MRP-based manufacturing planning and control system that incorporates the aggregate production plan, the master production schedule, the material requirements plan, and the capacity requirements plan.

collaborative planning, forecasting, and replenishment (CPFR) As defined by the Educational Society for Resource Management (APICS), "a collaboration process whereby supply chain trading partners can jointly plan key supply chain activities from production and delivery of raw materials to production and delivery of final products to end customers. Collaboration encompasses business planning, sales forecasting, and all operations required to replenish raw materials and finished goods."

collaborative transportation management The sharing of forecasting, planning, and replenishment information among buyer, supplier, and transporter to increase efficiency and service.

common carriers Offer transportation services to all shippers at published rates between designated locations; they must charge the same rates for the same service to all customers.

Common Market of Eastern and Southern Africa (COMESA) Created in 1994 to foster economic growth in the region. The objective is to create a regional common market and eventually an economic community.

concurrent engineering Designing the production process as the product is being designed.

consolidation warehouses Used to collect large numbers of LTL shipments from nearby regional sources of supply, which are then transported in TL or CL quantities to a manufacturing or user-facility located some distance from the consolidation center.

consumer survey A questionnaire administered through telephone, mail, Internet, or personal interviews that seeks input from customers on important issues such as future buying habits, new product ideas, and opinions about existing products.

consumer's risk When a buyer accepts a shipment of poor-quality units because the sample did meet the acceptance standard; called a **type-II error.**

container-on-flatcar (COFC) service Service offered when standard containers are transported by rail; the same containers can also be transported by motor carrier, containerships, or airliners.

continuous improvement When both buyers and suppliers make ongoing efforts to better their capabilities in meeting customer requirements of cost, quality, delivery, and technology.

contract carriers For-hire carriers like common carriers; however, they are not bound to serve the general public.

Contracts for the International Sale of Goods (CISG) Governs international purchases and sales of goods, unless both parties elect to opt out.

contributor factory Plays a greater strategic role than a **server factory** by getting involved in product development and engineering, production planning, making critical procurement decisions, and developing suppliers.

control charts Created by firms to monitor process variabilities.

corporate purchasing cards See **procurement credit cards.**

cost-of-service pricing Used to establish prices that vary based on fixed and variable costs.

counterpurchase An arrangement whereby the original exporter either buys or finds a buyer to purchase a specified amount of unrelated goods and/or services from the original importer.

countertrade A type of transaction in global sourcing in which goods and/or services of domestic firms are exchanged for goods and/or services of equal value in combination with currency from foreign firms.

crossdocking Using warehouses not to store things but to receive, break down, repackage, and distribute components to a manufacturing location or finished products to customers.

cross-selling Occurs when customers are sold additional products as the result of an initial purchase.

customer contact centers Centers that integrate their Web site and their traditional call center to offer 24/7 support where customers and potential customers can contact the firm and each other using telephone, e-mail, chat rooms, and e-bulletin boards.

customer defection analysis The study of customers who have quit purchasing and why.

customer relationship management Includes strategies for meeting delivery due dates, resolving customer complaints, communicating with customers, and determining what distribution services are required.

customer relationship management process Provides the firm with the structure for developing and managing customer relationships.

customer service management process Provides information to customers while also providing ongoing management of any product and service agreements between the firm and its customers.

customs brokers Move international shipments through customs for companies, as well as handle the documentation required to accompany the shipments.

cycle counting An inventory management technique in which physical inventory is counted on a periodic basis to ensure that physical inventory matches current inventory records.

cyclical variations Wavelike movements that are longer than a year and influenced by macroeconomic and political factors.

data cleansing Finding misspellings, typos, and missing information in databases that can cause large errors in forecasts and other calculations, then removing them by cross-referencing disparate data sets, synchronizing overlapping information, correcting inconsistencies, and removing outlier information.

data warehouse One centralized database containing all customer information.

data warehouses Third-party services that store large amounts of data for their customers.

decentralized purchasing Individual, local purchasing departments, such as at the plant level, make their own purchasing decisions. See **centralized purchasing.**

Delphi method Qualitative forecasting in which a group of internal and external experts are surveyed during several rounds in terms of future events and long-term forecasts of demand; the group members do not physically meet.

demand forecast updating The process whereby a selling firm uses the information generated by a buying firm placing an order as a predictor of future demand.

demand management Using strategies or systems to match demand and available capacity.

demand management process Balances customer demand and the firm's output capabilities.

demand source Customer arrivals—can be infinite, such as customers arriving at a retail outlet, or finite, such as customers reserving seats for a concert at an arena.

demand time fence Also known as a *firmed segment,* stipulates that the production plan or master production schedule cannot be altered except with the authorization of senior management.

Department of Transportation Act 1966 act that created the Department of Transportation (DOT) to coordinate the executive functions of all government entities dealing with transportation-related matters.

dependent demand Term used to describe the internal or derived demand for parts based on the demand of the final product in which the parts are used.

design for manufacturability Simplification of parts, products, and processes to improve quality and reduce costs.

differentiation strategy Based on creating a product or service that is considered unique.

direct offset A type of countertrade that involves compensation in related goods and/or services. It usually involves some forms of coproduction or joint venture.

distribution center Name given to warehouse when it is actually used more for **crossdocking** than for storage.

distribution channels The ways products and services can be paid for or delivered to customers, such as store; home delivery; mail; and financial services such as ATMs and Internet.

distribution network System of global, regional, and/or local warehouses and transportation modes used to quickly deliver products to customers.

distribution requirements planning (DRP) Links production with distribution planning by providing aggregate time-phased net requirement information from warehouses to the master production schedule.

early supplier involvement When strategic supplier provides product and process technology and knowledge to support the buyer's operation.

eatertainment The combination of restaurant and entertainment elements.

economic order quantity (EOQ) The optimal order size to minimize total inventory costs.

edutainment Combines learning with entertainment to appeal to customers looking for substance along with play.

efficient consumer response (ECR) Developed by a grocery industry task force in the early 1990s in an effort to make grocery supply chains more competitive.

e-learning The electronic delivery of training materials and interactions with students over the Internet.

electronic data interchange (EDI) A standardized data transmission format for information systems communication between organizations.

electronic invoice presentment and payment (EIPP) Sending and receiving invoices and payments on-line.

electronic product codes (ePCs) Information placed on RFID tag that is then attached to a product to supply product, manufacturing, and supplier information to support product warranty programs.

enterprise resource planning (ERP) Software systems linked throughout an organization and its supply chain partners, providing real-time sales data, inventory, and production information to departments and supply chain participants.

entertailing Retail locations with entertainment elements.

European Union (EU) A European federation originally set up in 1950 and currently consisting of fifteen members; the EU is preparing to accept thirteen additional eastern and southern European countries.

event-based marketing Offering individual promotions tied to specific events.

everyday low prices (EDLP) When retailers adopt uniform wholesale prices without any sales or promotions to eliminate the problems of forward buying.

exempt carriers For-hire carriers like common carriers, but they are exempt from regulation of services and rates.

expediting A reactive approach used by purchasing personnel to speed up an overdue shipment.

exponential smoothing forecasting A sophisticated weighted moving average forecasting in which the forecast for the next period's demand is the current period's forecast adjusted by a fraction of the difference between the current period's actual demand and its forecast.

Extranets Supply chain Internets that restrict entry from outsiders.

facilitating products Supplies that must be managed that are consumed inside the firm and are not sold as part of the services, such as computers, furniture, and office supplies.

Federal Aviation Act of 1958 Replaced the Civil Aeronautics Administration with the Federal Aviation Administration (FAA) and gave the FAA authority to prescribe air traffic rule, make safety regulations, and plan the national airport system.

fishbone or Ishikawa diagrams See **cause-and-effect diagrams.**

FOB destination Pricing that is "free on board" to the buyer's location, which means the supplier provides the transportation and the buyer takes possession of the goods at their location.

FOB origination The buyer takes possession of the goods at the supplier's location and must provide their own transportation.

focus strategy Providing customized products and services to a narrow target market.

follow-up A proactive approach used by purchasing personnel to prevent late delivery.

forecast error The difference between actual quantity and the forecast.

foreign freight forwarders Move goods for companies from production origination to foreign customer destination using surface and air transportation.

foreign trade zones (FTZs) Secure sites within the United States under the supervision of the U.S. Customs Service. Foreign or domestic goods can enter without payment of duties or excise taxes. Final products can then be exported without paying these taxes.

forward buying When buyers stock up on supplies during special promotions, quantity discounts, or other special pricing discounts to take advantage of the low-price offers.

forward integration Acquiring customers' operations.

freight forwarders Consolidate small shipments to obtain truckload or carload prices.

functional products Commonly purchased items and supplies characterized by low profit margins, relatively stable demands, and high levels of competition.

functional silos Departments that are acting in their own best interests, without considering the impact these actions have on the firm, or other departments.

general freight carriers Based on the type of goods they carry, general freight carriers carry the majority of goods shipped and include common carriers.

global sourcing Using worldwide sources for core materials and supplies.

global supply chains Include foreign or overseas participants and/or markets.

granger laws Laws passed by midwestern states in the 1870s to establish maximum rates, prohibit discrimination, and forbid mergers for railroads.

green supply chain A supply chain that has collected and analyzed environmental regulations and customer surveys from each of the supply chain firm locations; discussed the relevant environmental issues with the procurement, engineering, and quality control departments at each firm; developed green supply chain policies; communicated them to customers and suppliers along the supply chain; and then managed the program to assure compliance with the policies.

group technology work cells Designed to process similar parts or components, saving duplication of equipment and labor, as well as concentrating the area where units of the same purchased part are delivered.

holding cost or carrying cost The cost incurred for holding inventory in storage.

hybrid purchasing organization Decentralized at the corporate level and centralized at the business unit level.

ICC Termination Act of 1995 Eliminated the Interstate Commerce Commission.

import broker or sales agent Purchasing and selling agent who performs transactions for a fee; does not take title to the goods.

import merchant Purchasing and selling agent who buys and takes title to goods, then resells them to buyers.

incoterms Uniform set of rules created by the International Chamber of Commerce to simplify international transactions of goods; International Commercial Terms.

indented bill of materials A multilevel bill of materials in which the materials are presented in outline form by levels.

independent demand The demand for final products or service parts; has a demand pattern affected by trends,

seasonal patterns, and general market conditions.

indirect offset Involves exchange of goods and/or services unrelated to the aerospace or defense sector.

industrial buyers Purchasers—typically manufacturers—who primarily purchase raw materials for conversion purposes.

information visibility The degree to which information is shared within the firm & to other supply chain members.

innovative products Products characterized by short product life cycles, volatile demand, high profit margins, and relatively less competition.

integrated logistics See **quick response** or **service response logistics.**

integrated logistics service providers Provide any and all logistics services to organizations for a fee.

intermediately positioned strategy Place warehouses midway between the sources of supply and the customers. Recommended when distribution service requirements are high and customers order product assortments from various locations.

intermodal marketing companies (IMCs) Companies that act as intermediaries between intermodal rail carriers and shippers.

intermodal transportation Combinations of the various transportation modes.

internal supply chain Functions within the company that share information and coordinate activities so as to maximize firm competitiveness.

Interstate Commerce Act of 1887 Created the Interstate Commerce Commission (ICC); required rail carriers to charge reasonable rates, to publish rates, to file them with the ICC, and to make these available to the public; and prohibited discriminatory practices.

Intranets Companywide Internets for organizational members only.

inventory visibility Sharing inventory information in real-time among supply chain participants.

ISO 14000 Introduced in 1996 by the International Organization for Standardization, a family of standards for environmental management.

ISO 9000 Developed in 1987 by the International Organization for Standardization, a series of management and quality assurance standards in design, development, production, installation, and service.

jury of executive opinion Qualitative forecasting in which a group of senior

management executives who are knowledgeable about the market, competitors, and the business environment collectively develop the forecast.

just-in-time production system An inventory management system that delays final assembly until a downstream customer order occurs; also called a **pull-type production system.**

kaizen The Japanese term used to describe the continuous efforts to reduce organizational problems.

kanban (Japanese for "card.") In JIT, a signal.

keiretsu relationships Cooperative coalitions between Japanese manufacturing firms and their suppliers.

key supply chain processes Sets of activities designed to produce a product or service for an internal or external customer. See Table 13.1.

knowledge management tool Contains information on contracts, client and competitor profiles, client sales histories, corporate policies, expense reimbursement forms, regulatory issues and laws, sales presentations, promotional materials, and previous client correspondence.

land bridge Transporting goods by water, land, and then water again, to a final destination.

lead factory A source of product and process innovation and competitive advantage for the entire organization; translates its knowledge of the market, competitors, and customers into new products.

lead logistics providers (LLPs) Firms charged with overseeing their clients' third-party service providers.

lead management tool Used by sales reps to follow prescribed sales tactics when dealing with sales prospects or opportunities to aid in closing the deal with a client.

legacy MRP system A broad label used to describe an older information system that usually works at an operational level to schedule production within an organization.

legacy systems Older information systems implemented as separate applications, with limited cross-communication capabilities.

less-than-truckload (LTL) carriers Move small packages or shipments that take up less than one truckload.

level-demand strategy When a firm utilizes a constant amount of capacity regardless of demand variations.

level production strategy A production strategy that relies on a constant output rate and capacity while varying inventory and backlog levels to handle the fluctuating demand pattern.

leveraging purchase volume Concentration of purchase volume to create, for example, quantity discounts or volume shipments.

linear trend forecasting Forecasting method in which the trend can be estimated using simple linear regression to fit a line to a time series of historical data.

line-haul rates The charges for moving goods to a nonlocal destination.

long-range planning horizon Usually covers a year or more, tends to be more general, and specifies resources and outputs in terms of aggregate hours and units.

make or buy The decision by a firm either to manufacture or to purchase materials or components.

make-to-order manufacturing firms Generally produce one-of-a-kind, specialty products based on customer specifications.

make-to-stock manufacturing firms Typically emphasize immediate delivery of off-the-shelf, standard goods at relatively low prices.

manufacturing flow management process Set of activities responsible for making the actual product, establishing the manufacturing flexibility required to adequately serve the markets, and designing the production system to meet cycle time requirements.

manufacturing resource planning (MRP-II) An outgrowth and extension of the **closed-loop MRP** system that incorporates the business and sales plans with the closed-loop MRP system and has simulation capabilities to answer "what-if" types of questions.

market dominance Position of a firm in which it is without market competition.

market-positioned strategy Located warehouses close to customers to maximize distribution service and to allow the firm to generate transportation economies by using TL and CL deliveries to each warehouse location; recommended when high levels of distribution flexibility and service were required and when there were few sources of supply.

master production schedule (MPS) A medium-range plan that is more detailed than the aggregate production plan and shows the quantity and timing of the end items or services that will be produced.

material requirements plan (MRP) A short-range materials plan that uses bill-of-material, inventory, sched-uled receipts, and a master production schedule to determine material requirements.

material requisition (MR) Issued by material user; first step in the purchasing process.

mean absolute deviation (MAD) A widely used forecast accuracy indicator that gives the evaluator a very simple way to compare various forecasting methods. A MAD of zero indicates that the forecast exactly predicted demand over the evaluation period; a positive value indicates that the forecast either over- or underestimated demand.

mean absolute percentage error (MAPE) The mean absolute percentage error has the advantage of providing the correct perspective of the true magnitude of the forecast error. The mean absolute percentage error is determined by dividing the absolute forecast error by actual demand and multiplying the outcome by one hundred to get the absolute percentage error, summing them, and then computing the average.

mean squared error (MSE) Mean squared error is a measure analogous to variance in statistics. The mean squared error is determined first by squaring the forecast errors and then averaging the sum of the squared errors. Both MAD and MSE are widely used measures of forecasting accuracy.

medium-range planning horizon Normally spans six to eighteen months and covers minor changes in capacity.

merchants Purchasers, including wholesalers and retailers, who primarily purchase for resale purposes.

micro-land-bridge traffic Transporting goods by water and then land, to a final inland destination.

mini-land-bridge traffic Transporting goods by water and then land, to an opposite coastal location.

mixed production strategy A production strategy that strives to maintain a stable core workforce while using other short-term means such as overtime, an additional shift, subcontracting, or the hiring of part-time and temporary workers to manage short-term high demand.

Motor Carrier Act of 1935 Brought motor carriers under ICC control.

motor carriers Trucks; the most flexible mode of transportation.

multiple-channel queuing system Multiple servers acting in parallel.

multiple-factor productivity In the formula for productivity, inputs are the sum of labor, material, energy, and capital costs. Compare to **single-factor productivity.**

multiple-phase queuing system Multiple servers acting in series.

multiple regression model When several explanatory variables are used to make the forecast.

natural variations Variations in process measurements caused by environmental factors that cannot be eliminated.

nontariff Import quota, licensing agreement, embargo, law, or other regulation imposed on imports or exports.

non-vessel-operating common carriers (NVOCCs) Operate very similarly to freight forwarders but normally use scheduled ocean liners.

North American Free Trade Agreement (NAFTA) Began on January 1, 1994, and removed (or will eventually remove) most barriers to trade and investment among the United States, Canada, and Mexico; many **tariffs** and quotas were eliminated immediately, and most others will be eliminated by 2008.

Ocean Shipping Reform Act of 1998 Ended the requirement for ocean carriers to file rates with the Federal Maritime Commission.

offset An exchange agreement for industrial goods and/or services as a condition of military-related export; also commonly used in the aerospace and defense sectors. See also **direct offset** and **indirect offset.**

offshore factory Imports or locally acquires parts and then exports all of the finished products.

open-end purchase order Like a blanket purchase order except that additional items and expiration dates can be renegotiated.

operating exposure In a global supply chain, the risk caused by fluctuating exchange rates affecting production, warehousing, and purchasing and selling prices.

option overplanning Increasing the proportion percentage of each component of the super bill of materials to cover uncertainty of options.

order batching An order of some magnitude placed with a supplier; this causes—until the next order is placed—no demand at all for the supplier's goods.

order cost The direct variable cost associated with placing an order with the supplier.

order-fulfillment process Set of activities that allows the firm to fill customer orders while providing the required levels of customer service at the lowest possible delivered cost.

outpost factory Set up in a location with an abundance of advanced suppliers, competitors, research facilities, and knowledge centers to get access to the most current information on materials, components, technologies, and products; since the facility normally produces something, its secondary role can be that of a **server** or an **offshore factory.**

outsourcing Giving noncore activities to suppliers so that a firm can focus on core activities.

P-chart Used to monitor the percent defective in each sample.

perfect order An order in which all of the "Seven Rs" are satisfied: the right product, the right quantity, the right condition, the right place, the right time, the right customer, and the right cost.

performance variance The difference between the standard and the actual performance.

petty cash Cash reserve maintained by clerk or midlevel manager in which reimbursement is supported by receipts.

piggyback service Refers to **trailer-on-flatcar (TOFC)** or **container-on-flatcar (COFC) service.**

pipeline carriers Hauls materials in a liquid or gaseous state.

place utility Created when customers get products delivered to the desired location.

planned order release The scheduled date for an order to be released.

planning factor The specific units of components required for making a higher-level part or assembly.

planning time fence Also known as a *tentative segment,* typically stretches from the end of the firmed segment to several weeks farther into the future.

point-of-sale information Typically refers to cash register sales information, regarding end-customer purchases.

Poisson distribution Customer arrivals in a random pattern; see formula in Chapter 12.

post-transaction costs Costs incurred after the goods are in the possession of the company, agents, or customers.

post-transaction elements Customer service elements that occur after the sale of the product or service: warranty repair capabilities, complaint resolution, product returns, and operating information.

pre-transaction costs Costs incurred prior to order and receipt of the purchased goods.

pre-transaction elements Customer service elements that precede the actual product or service: customer service policies, the mission statement, organizational structure, and system flexibility.

private carrier Not subject to economic regulation; typically transports goods for the company owning the carrier.

private warehouses Owned by the firm storing the goods.

process integration Coordinating efforts and sharing information to simplify processes and increase efficiency.

procurement credit cards or corporate purchasing cards Credit cards with a predetermined credit limit issued to authorized personnel of the buying organization.

producer's risk When a buyer rejects a shipment of good-quality units because the sample quality level did not meet the acceptance standard; called a **type-I error.**

product development and commercialization process Responsible for developing new products to meet changing customer requirements and then getting these products to market quickly and efficiently.

production kanban A light, flag, or sign used to trigger production of certain components.

product-positioned strategy Locating warehouses close to the sources of supply to enable the firm to collect various goods and then consolidate these into TL or CL quantities for shipment to customers; works well when there are many sources of supply, multiproduct factories, and assortments of goods ordered by customers.

public warehouses Owned by for-profit organizations that contract their services to other companies; can provide customized services for various shipments and goods.

pull-type production system See **just-in-time production system.**

purchase order (PO) A buyer's offer describing the purchased items; lists the terms and conditions of a purchase and becomes a legally binding contract when accepted by the supplier.

purchase requisition Procedural method or form by which departments request the purchase of goods and/or services.

pure services Services that offer few or no tangible products to customers. Examples are consultants, legal advisors, entertainers, and brokers.

push-type production system An inventory management system that generates an order at a preset order point from sales data, inventory, and production information. Associated with MRP systems.

qualitative forecasting methods Forecasting methods that are based on opinions and intuition.

quality circle A work group meeting regularly to solve quality problems in their work area.

quality of life From Jerry Mallot (see Chapter 11, Note 62), "a feeling of well-being, fulfillment, or satisfaction resulting from factors in the external environments." See also **quality-of-life factors.**

quality-of-life factors Per Jacksonville, Florida, Chamber of Commerce report (see Chapter 11, Note 63), a comprehensive set of factors, including education, economy, natural environment, social environment, culture/recreation, health, government/politics, mobility, and public safety. See also **quality of life.**

quantitative forecasting methods Methods that use mathematical models and relevant historical data to generate forecasts.

quantity discount model or price-break model Variation of EOQ model that relaxes the constant price assumption by allowing purchase quantity discounts.

queue discipline Describes the order in which customers are served.

queue management Tactics used to deal with excess customers.

quick response (QR) Developed by the textile industry in the mid-1980s as an offshoot of JIT; based on merchandisers and suppliers working together to respond more quickly to consumer needs.

quick response, service response logistics, or integrated logistics For wholesaling and retailing industries, when the supply chain management focus is on location, service, and capacity and issues more often than on manufacturing.

radio-frequency identification (RFID) tag Tiny microchip device attached to a product to relay information on the product's whereabouts as it moves through the supply chain.

rail carriers Compete most favorably when the distance is long and the shipments are heavy or bulky.

Railroad Revitalization and Regulatory Reform Act Commonly known as the *4-R Act,* 1976 act that made several regulatory changes to help the railroads.

Railway Passenger Service Act 1970 act that created Amtrak.

random variations Random peaks and valleys that are due to unexpected or unpredictable events such as natural disasters (hurricanes, tornadoes, fire), strikes, and wars.

rationing When demand exceeds a supplier's finished goods available, the process whereby suppliers allocate product in proportion to what buyers ordered.

R-chart Used to track sample ranges or the variation of the measurements within each sample.

Reed-Bulwinkle Act Gave groups of carriers the ability to form rate bureaus or conferences wherein they could propose rate changes to the ICC.

relationship marketing or permission marketing An extension of target marketing in which customers are allowed to select the type and time of communication with organizations.

reneging Describes customers leaving the line prior to completing the service.

reorder point When inventory levels become low enough that a predermined quantity of materials or supplies is automatically ordered to maintain a minimum inventory level.

request for proposal (RFP) Procedural method or form by which the buyer requests that potential suppliers propose solutions to meet the requirements of the job.

request for quotation (RFQ) Procedural method or form by which the buyer requests quotations for goods and/or services from potential supplier.

resource requirements planning (RRP) A long-range capacity planning module used to check whether aggregate resources are capable of satisfying the aggregate production plan.

returns management process Beneficial for supply chain management in terms of maintaining acceptable levels of customer servicer and identifying product improvement opportunities; includes activities such as environmental compliance with substance disposal and recycling, composing operating and repair instructions, troubleshooting and warranty repairs, developing disposition guidelines, designing an effective reverse logistics process, and collecting returns data.

reverse auctions An Internet activity in which qualified suppliers, at a predesignated time and date, enter a particular Web site and try to under-

bid competitors. Company identities are known only by the buyer; suppliers can monitor the bid prices until the session is over.

reverse logistics activities Managing product returns, warranty repairs, and product disposal.

reverse logistics services Disposition of returned products—including items being designated for repair, restocking, or redistribution—or auctioning of obsolete products.

right-to-work law From "Right-to-Work States" (see Chapter 11, Note 56), "secures the right of employees to decide for themselves whether or not to join or financially support a union."

risk pooling Also referred to as the *square-root rule* and the *portfolio effect;* describes the relationship between the number of warehouses, inventory, and customer service.

ROROs Roll-on-roll-off containerships that allow truck trailers and containers to be directly driven on and off the ship without the use of cranes.

rough-cut capacity plan (RCCP) Medium-range capacity plan that converts the master production schedule from production to capacity required, then compares it to capacity available during each production period.

running sum of forecast errors (RSFE) An indicator of bias in the forecasts; forecast bias measures the tendency of a forecast to be consistently higher or lower than the actual demand.

sales activity management tools Customized to each firm's sales policies and procedures; offers sales personnel a sequence of sales activities that guide them through the sales process with each customer.

sales force automation Term describing products that are used for documenting field activities, communicating with the home office, and retrieving sales history and other company-specific documents in the field.

sales force composite Qualitative forecast generated based on the sales force's knowledge of the market and estimates of customer needs.

sales order A supplier's offer; becomes a legally binding contract when accepted by the buyer.

sales territory management tool Allows sales managers to obtain current information and reporting capabilities regarding each salesperson's activities on each customer's account, total sales in general for each sales

rep, their sales territories, and any ongoing sales initiatives.

seasonal variations Peaks and valleys that repeat over a consistent interval such as hours, days, weeks, months, years, or seasons.

second-tier suppliers and customers The suppliers' suppliers and the customers' customers.

segment customers To group customers in a variety of ways to create more specialized communications about companies' products.

server factory Set up primarily to take advantage of government incentives, to minimize exchange risk, to avoid tariff barriers, and to reduce taxes and logistics costs to supply the regional market where the factory is located and is involved in making minor improvements in products and processes.

service capacity Usually defined as the number of customers per day the firm's service delivery systems *are designed to serve,* although it could also be some other period of time such as customers per hour or customers per shift.

service quality Occurs during the interaction between the customer and a service employee. Describes the ability of the service to satisfy customers.

service response logistics See **quick response.**

setup The process of setting up production equipment for the next production run.

shippers' associations From the American Institute for Shippers' Associations, "nonprofit membership cooperatives that make domestic or international arrangements for the movement of members' cargo."

Shipping Act of 1984 Marked the end of the initial push by Congress to deregulate transportation; allowed ocean carriers to pool or share shipments, assign ports, publish rates, and enter into contracts with shippers.

shortage gaming The process whereby buyers inflate their orders to satisfy their real needs when they determine that sellers are **rationing.**

short-range planning horizon Usually covers a few days to a few weeks depending on the size and type of the firm.

silo effect When departments act independently, with little motivation to understand how decisions impact other areas of the firm.

simple moving average forecasting Uses historical data to generate a forecast and works well when the demand is fairly stable over time.

simple regression model Associative forecasting in which there is only one explanatory variable.

simplification Reduction during production of the number of components, supplies, or standard materials used in a product or process.

single-factor productivity In the formula for productivity, the input is a single factor, such as labor hours, or labor, material, energy, or capital costs. Compare to **multiple-factor productivity.**

single integrator solution Picks all the desired applications from a single vendor for the ERP system.

single-sourcing Using a single source for core materials and supplies.

six sigma program A type of TQM program centered around statistical process control, popularized by Motorola, and referring to just over three data points outside the control limits for every million.

SOAP The Internet protocol that allows customers and providers to exchange **XML** data.

source factory Location dictated by low production cost, fairly developed infrastructure, and availability of skilled workers.

Southern Common Market (MERCOSUR) The agreement among Argentina, Brazil, Paraguay, and Uruguay formed in 1991 with the signing of the Treaty of Asuncion; created with the goal of forming a common market/customs union between the participating countries and based on economic cooperation between Argentina and Brazil that had been in place since 1986.

specialized carriers Transport liquid petroleum, household goods, agricultural commodities, building materials, and other specialized items.

square-root rule Estimates the effect of risk pooling; suggests that the system average inventory as the result of adding warehouses to the system is equal to the old system inventory times the ratio of the square root of the new number of warehouses to the square root of the old number of warehouses.

Staggers Rail Act of 1980 Permitted rail carriers to change rates within a zone of rate freedom, but the ceiling or market-dominance rate was established more definitively as 160 percent of variable costs and varied up to 180 percent depending on ICC cost formulas.

state utility Provided when services do something to things that are owned by the customer, such as transport and store supplies, repair machines, cut hair, and provide health care.

statistical process control The application of statistical techniques to monitor quality.

stockless buying or system contracting An extension of the blanket purchase order; requires the supplier to maintain a minimum inventory level to ensure availability to the buyer.

strategic alliance A strong relationship or partnership between customers and suppliers based on a strategic rather than a tactical perspective.

strategic partnerships Trading-partner relationships with top-performing suppliers and customers that enhance cost, quality, and delivery.

strategic sourcing Locating and developing good suppliers and integrating them into the firm's business processes and strategies in an effort to improve financial performance.

super bill of materials Presenting the bill of materials by using the percentage of each option used instead of the planning factor.

supplier base See **supply base.**

supplier certification An organization's process for evaluating the quality systems of key suppliers in an effort to eliminate incoming inspections.

supplier development Provision by a firm of needed technical and financial assistance to existing or new suppliers; used to increase pool of suitable suppliers.

supplier evaluation Assessing the performance of suppliers.

supplier management Getting a firm's suppliers to do what is desired of them.

supplier relationship management (SRM) Term that includes extended procurement processes, sourcing execution, procurement execution, payment and settlement, and supplier scorecarding and performance monitoring.

supplier relationship management process How the firm manages its relationships with suppliers.

supply base or supplier base The list of suppliers that a firm uses to acquire its materials, services, supplies, and equipment.

supply chain The series of companies that eventually make products and services available to consumers, including all the functions enabling the production, delivery, and recycling of materials, components, end products, and services.

supply chain execution systems Warehouse, transportation, and logistics management software that allows firms to get quick returns on their investments through more efficient use of transportation alternatives, lower system inventories, and better delivery performance.

supply chain integration When supply chain participants act together at all levels to maximize supply chain profits.

supply chain operations reference (SCOR) model A diagnostic, benchmarking, and process improvement tool developed in 1996 by the Supply Chain Council for integrating supply chains and measuring members' performance

supply chain performance measurement Used by firms actively managing their supply chains to determine whether or not strategies are working as expected.

supply chain visibility The ability of supply chain members to access the production schedule and demand information of upstream and downstream supply chain members.

system contracting See **stockless buying.**

system nervousness A situation in which a small change in the upper-level production plan causes a major change in the lower-level production plan.

systems rollup Integrating systems to achieve faster information retrieval and distribution, resulting in better overall supply chain information visibility and responsiveness.

target marketing efforts Efforts via e-mail or direct mail to target specific customer segments based on, for example, sales territory or region, preferred sales channel, profitability, products purchased, sales history, demographic information, desired product features, and service preferences.

tariff An official list or schedule of duties, taxes, or customs that are imposed by the host country on imports or exports.

tariffs Published import fees.

third-party logistics (3PL) All potentially outsourced supply chain management activities.

third-party service providers Shipping, warehousing, and logistics services that provide transportation, storage, documentation, and customs clearing services to many firms within a supply chain.

third-party transportation services Outside agents used by firms for the transportation function.

3PL providers Companies that are providing outsourced supply chain management activities.

threshold costs A firm's variable costs.

time series forecasting Based on the assumption that the future is an extension of the past and, thus, historical data can be used to predict future demand.

time utility Also called *time value;* created when customers get products delivered at precisely the right time, not earlier and not later.

total cost of ownership (TCO) From L. Ellram (see Chapter 3, Note 27), "all costs associated with the acquisition, use, and maintenance of a good or service."

total quality management (TQM) Strategy used especially by just-in-time production systems to ensure quality compliance among suppliers and with internal processes.

tracking signal A figure determined by dividing the RSFE by the MAD to determine if it is within preset acceptable control limits.

trading companies Put foreign buyers and sellers together and handle all of the export/import arrangements, documentation, and transportation for both goods and services.

trading company Carries a wide variety of goods for resale.

trailer-on-flatcar (TOFC) service Service offered when railroads purchase motor carriers that can be carried on flatcars to accomplish point-to-point pickup and delivery.

transaction costs Include the cost of the goods/services and cost associated with placing and receiving the order.

transaction elements Customer service elements that occur during the sale of the product or service: order lead time, order processing capabilities, and distribution system accuracy.

Transportation Act of 1920 Instructed the ICC to ensure that rates were high enough to provide a fair return for railroads each year, allowed the ICC to set minimum rates, allowed joint use of terminal facilities, allowed railroads to enter into pooling agreements, allowed rail company acquisi-

tions and consolidations, and prohibited railroads from issuing securities without ICC approval.

Transportation Act of 1940 Established ICC control over domestic water transportation.

Transportation Act of 1958 Established temporary loan guarantees to railroads, liberalized control over intrastate rail rates, amended the rule of rate making to ensure more intermodal competition, and clarified the differences between private and for-hire motor carriers.

transportation brokers Businesses that handle the transportation requirements of shippers and also find shipments for carriers for a fee.

transportation management Decisions involving cost and delivery methods, to optimize customer service.

traveling requisition Preprinted form used to request materials that are needed on a recurring basis.

trend-adjusted exponential smoothing forecasting A modification of the exponential smoothing forecasting method that includes a trend component when the time series show a systematic upward or downward trend in the data over time.

trend variations Either increasing or decreasing movements over many years that are due to factors such as population growth, population shifts, cultural changes, and income shifts.

truckload (TL) carriers Move shipments that take up an entire truckload.

type-I error See **producer's risk.**

type-II error See **consumer's risk.**

Uniform Commercial Code (UCC) Governs the purchase and sale of goods in the United States (except Louisiana)

value engineering Describes activities that help the firm to reduce cost, improve quality, and reduce new product development time.

value-of-service pricing Services are priced at competitive levels the market will bear.

variable data Continuous data such as weight, time, and length.

vendor-managed inventory (VMI) services Using a local supplier to manage a customer's inventory in the customer's storage and/or production areas.

vendor-managed inventory (VMI) When buyers allow suppliers to observe their demand, create a forecast, and determine their resupply schedules.

vertically integrated firm A firm whose business boundaries extend to include one-time suppliers and/or customers.

virtual inventory systems Allow supply chain participants to feed their inventory information into one shared database.

waiting time The time a customer waits for the delivery of a product; impacts the customer's view of service quality and the customer's satisfaction.

warehouse management system (WMS) Identifies incoming merchandise, noting overages, shortages, and substitutions.

water carriers Water transportation; very inexpensive but also very slow and inflexible.

Web services Describes businesses that register with an Internet directory to advertise their services so firms can find each other and carry out transactions over the Web.

weighted-factor rating model A method used to compare the attractiveness of several locations along a number of quantitative and qualitative dimensions.

weighted moving average forecasting Allows more emphasis to be placed on more recent data to reflect changes in demand patterns; weights also tend to be based on the experience of the forecaster.

withdrawal kanban A light, flag, or sign to indicate that a container of parts can be moved from one work cell to another.

World Trade Organization (WTO) The successor to the General Agreement on Tariffs and Trade (GATT); today, the only international organization dealing with the rules of trade between nations.

x̄-chart Used to track the central tendency of the sample means.

XML The family of Web communication standards; allows businesses to exchange data across the Web.

zone of rate freedom Used in several transportation acts. Allows carriers to charge fees over their variable costs, up to a set limit.

Author Index

Whipple, J.M., 83
Whitaker, Uncas Aeneus, 261
White, S.C., 106n.6, 106n.7
Whitfield, K., 335
Whitwam, David R., 268
Whybark, D.C., 186, 205
Wilder, C., 270, 430n.18
Williams, A., 59n.9
Williams, T., 395
Williamson, J., 453n.17
Wilson, Joshua, 119
Wilson, T., 85n.59, 154n.9
Wisner, J.D., 23n.10,17, 59, 106n.6,
    155n.20, 308n.37, 333n.19, 452,
    452n.9, 467n.4

Witwam, David R., 68
Wonacott, P., 360n.30
Wright, Terry, 323
Wylie, I., 307n.2

Y

Yam, R.C.M., 359
Yohn, E., 308n.40
Youssef, A., 361n.55

Z

Zacharia, Z.G., 22n.1
Zaino, J., 429n.3

Zasimovich, Tony, 289
Zeithaml, V.A., 395n.17
Zhou, X., 241n.18
Zieger, A., 23n.9
Zigas, R.P., 240n.2
Zigli, Ronald M., 261
Zimmerman, Jeff, 268, 269
Zonnenburg, J.P., 452n.10,11,14
Zotteri, G., 83
Zsidisin, G.A., 106n.15
Zygmont, J., 205n.6

Subject Index